JOHN D. MacDONALD

is known to millions of avid readers as the creator of the famed Travis McGee novels and as the bestselling author of such other books as *Condominium* and *One More Sunday*. As a novelist, MacDonald has few peers in the creation of characters, in observation and insight, and in terrific, exciting writing that keeps his fans turning the page for more.

NO DEADLY DRUG

shows us a different Macdonald as he not only shares the excitement of a controversial criminal case but attempts to broaden our understanding of the issues such cases raise.

"Does our system of criminal justice, particularly as it applies to cases given national publicity, need certain adjustments and changes?" MacDonald writes in his foreword. "We hope that the reader will not so lose himself in the compulsive game of weighing testimony and evidence that he will fail to see that this is our primary purpose."

NO
DEADLY
DRUG

John D. MacDonald

FAWCETT GOLD MEDAL • NEW YORK

A Fawcett Gold Medal Book
Published by Ballantine Books
Copyright © 1968 by John D. MacDonald

Library of Congress Catalog Card Number: 68-22622

ISBN 0-449-12809-1

This edition published by arrangement with Doubleday & Company, Inc.

Manufactured in the United States of America

First Ballantine Books Edition: June 1985

To All the Professionals

Author's Special Acknowledgment:

John Pete Schmidt suggested that we write this book. He worked with me every step of the way. It would not have been possible without him.

Contents

GUIDE TO KEY TESTIMONY

I will follow that method of treatment which, according to my ability and judgment, I consider for the benefit of my patients, and abstain from whatever is deleterious and mischievous. I will give no deadly drug to anyone if asked, nor suggest any such counsel.

HIPPOCRATES
460 B.C.–377 B.C.

Foreword

Each notorious trial in America creates a ready audience for books and magazine articles about the trial. Avid followers of the annals of contemporary crime, their appetites whetted by extensive newspaper, television and radio coverage, buy the books and the magazines in order to learn more about what happened, what the people were *really* like.

Yet, for the most part, such books are a disappointment as they contain very little more than did the newspapers, and they are limited in their scope and effect by the author's special pleading, as it is far easier to write about a trial from the presumption of guilt—or of innocence—than to write about it with the total objectivity which includes both presumptions.

Only from such an objective point of view can the adversary system of justice in the notorious trials of our times be properly examined. Were there not two sides, each worth presentation, there would be no trial, and no jury to sway with courtroom skills.

This book is intended to give the reader a seat in court during many many days of legal proceedings in the twin indictments for murder brought against Dr. Carl A. Coppolino by the State of New Jersey and the State of Florida. In this sense it is more an investigation of the apparatus of criminal justice in our times than it is a study of a specific trial.

All evidence and testimony from official sources has been kept in balance, so edited as to favor neither the defense nor the State. In the tactics and the strategies of both the defense and the State, where the jury is led into areas of plausibility and emotional logic, many devices are used to invert such argumentation and examine it from the point of view of both innocence and guilt, in much the same manner one might expect the individual juror to weigh and test the structures of evidence and testimony.

To this degree the reader may play the part of a juror, but a juror with the freedom to roam the courthouse corridors, talk with the reporters and the attorneys, mingle with the spectators, and visit the places where the incidents given in the trial testimony took place.

It is not the purpose of this book to solve mysteries, or provide clues. In the adversary procedure the question of actual guilt or innocence becomes, except to the lay observer, a purely secondary consideration of mild and passing interest. The name of the game is combat, endlessly subtle and intriguing. The thrusts and parries during combat confuse rather than illuminate.

Does our system of criminal justice, particularly as it applies to cases given national publicity, need certain adjustments and changes? We hope that the reader will not so lose himself in the compulsive game of weighing testimony and evidence that he will fail to see that this is our primary purpose.

THE PRELIMINARY HEARING

September 1966

≫≫≫

Chapter One

On the first day of September 1966, Dr. Carl A. Coppolino stood beside his chief counsel, F. Lee Bailey, in one of the new courtrooms in the Sarasota County Court House, in Florida, and, as a necessary part of the ceremony of arraignment, listened as State Attorney Frank Schaub read to him, in front of the bench where Circuit Judge Lynn Silvertooth presided, the indictment as handed down by the grand jury.

Dr. Coppolino's wife, Carmela, had been buried in the Musetto family plot in Boonton, New Jersey, in St. Mary's Cemetery exactly one year ago to the day.

Frank Schaub read the strangely clumsy and archaic document with no expression in his voice. His was a harsh and gravelly voice, and the words fell heavily, like stones.

"In the name and by the authority of the State of Florida: the grand jurors of the County of Sarasota charge that Carl Coppolino on the 28th day of August, 1965, in the County of Sarasota, State of Florida, did unlawfully and from a premeditated design to effect the death of Carmela Coppolino, make an assault on the said Carmela Coppolino, and in some way and manner and by some means, instruments and weapons to the grand jurors unknown, he, the said Carl Coppolino did then and there, unlawfully and from a premeditated design to effect the death of the said Carmela Coppolino, inflict on and create in the said Carmela Coppolino certain mortal injuries and a mortal sickness, a further description whereof is to the grand jurors unknown, of which

1

mortal injuries and sickness, to the grand jurors unknown, the said Carmela Coppolino then and there died and so the said Carl Coppolino did, in the manner and form aforesaid, unlawfully and from a premeditated design to effect the death of the said Carmela Coppolino, kill and murder the said Carmela Coppolino, contrary to the form of the statute in such cases made and provided and against the peace and dignity of the State of Florida.''

To those in the spectator section of the courtroom, looking at the backs of the defendant and his attorney, as this odd document— verbose, archaic, and clumsy of grammar—was read as part of the routine of the official arraignment, the two men, both in dark suits and white shirts, both dark of hair, made a strange contrast.

Carl, several inches taller than Bailey, stood in his habitual slouch. He was leaned down by his time in jail. His glossy hair was freshly trimmed. His shirt collar was loose around the pale and slender neck, and his suit jacket looked a half size too large for his dwindled frame. From the rear he looked like a youth of twenty.

F. Lee Bailey stood very erect. Even when motionless he exudes a flavor of beefy energy, of dramatic command. His skull is large under the dark and wavy hair. Head, shoulders, and upper torso are oversized for a man his height. He has the bull neck of the physical man, florid and rough textured.

From the rear they could have been the fifty-year-old dad standing beside his twenty-year-old son in time of trouble.

But after State Attorney Frank Schaub finished reading the indictment and the two men turned, their faces brought them back into chronological focus, the thirty-four-year-old defendant, the thirty-three-year-old attorney—Bailey with his theatrical face, heavy bones, blue eyes that slant downward at the outer corners as do the dark expressive brows, a small mouth, a general look of a slightly gamey handsomeness, so that one might cast him as the hard-drinking, womanizing private eye in a low budget television serial—Coppolino with a swarthy and narrow face, a great beak of Italianate nose, a quick, charming, and expressive smile for his wife sitting in the spectator section, lift of brows, shrug, elegant gesture of one arm, and grace in the way he takes his seat again.

On the morning of July 9, 1966, the *Herald-Tribune* of Sarasota, Florida, had carried on page one a story headed 2-STATE PROBE LAUNCHED IN DEATH OF SARASOTA DOCTOR.

This was the first mention of the Coppolino cases in the public press.

On July 15 a follow-up story quoted Sarasota County Sheriff Ross Boyer as saying that the investigation had begun in November of 1965. "I worked on the case by myself at first because it was so weird as to be unbelievable."

In the same story it was reported that William Strode, the Assistant State Attorney for Sarasota County, had called a grand jury to meet July 22 at 9 A.M. Mr. Strode said the law prevented him from making any comment on two previous grand jury sessions which had considered an indictment in the Coppolino case. Seven persons had testified at the first session. That grand jury's term had expired June 20, and a new jury had been empaneled on July 8.

On July 21, in Freehold, New Jersey, a Monmouth County Grand Jury returned an indictment of murder in the first degree in the death of Lieutenant Colonel William E. Farber on July 30, 1963, in Middletown, New Jersey. The grand jury returned this indictment after hearing the medical testimony regarding the eleven-hour autopsy performed the previous Saturday on the colonel's body by Dr. Milton Helpern, Medical Examiner for the City of New York. The New Jersey Prosecutor, Vincent P. Keuper, requested that the indictment be impounded by the Superior Court until the unnamed person indicted was taken into custody.

On Friday, July 22, the Sarasota County Grand Jury was in session all day and heard eight witnesses, then recessed until 9 A.M. the following Thursday, August 2.

During the day, while the grand jury was in session, County Judge John Graham issued a fugitive warrant for the arrest of Dr. Carl A. Coppolino, at the request of the State of New Jersey. Coppolino was arrested at his home at 3263 Pine Valley Drive that evening by sheriff's deputies. He was brought in wearing bermuda shorts and a sports shirt, and complained of feeling unwell. After he was booked and advised of his rights, he was examined by Dr. William Page and Dr. William Douglass who recommended hospitalization. He was taken to the Sarasota Memorial Hospital and placed under guard in a private room.

State Attorney Frank Schaub was phoned at his home by a newspaper reporter who suspected that Mr. Schaub might not have been advised in advance of the arrest by the Sheriff's Department. Mr. Schaub would make no comment.

On Monday morning, July 25, Frank Schaub called the Sarasota County Grand Jury back into session, and at twenty minutes past noon the foreman of the grand jury, Dallas Dort, returned to Judge Lynn N. Silvertooth an indictment accusing Coppolino of first degree murder in the death of his wife, Carmela, on August 28, 1965. On Monday afternoon Coppolino was served with the Florida warrant in his hospital room. At 9:30 P.M., after examination once again by Doctors Page and Douglass, Coppolino was brought back to the county jail from the hospital less than two miles away.

On that same Monday, in New Jersey, Vincent Keuper announced that Dr. Coppolino was the person indicted for the murder of Colonel Farber, said that the colonel had died of a double fracture of the cricoid cartilage in the throat, and that the State of New Jersey wished to try Coppolino first.

Coppolino, in the fall and winter of 1966, had an unusually boyish manner for a man in his early thirties. In repose his face was moody and masklike. But there was a quick effervescence about him, and an engaging social manner. His voice is pitched rather high and is light in texture. He speaks rapidly, and often wittily. In his fine-boned physical grace and his casual slouch, there was a flavor of elegance about him, an elegance frequently in contrast with that attentive, patronizing and slightly skeptical manner which is so typical of young physicians that one might almost begin to suspect it is taught as a required course in all medical schools.

When asked by the Court how he pled, the accused man stood mute at the advice of his attorney who contended that one could not enter a plea to such an indictment because of the improper wording of it. Judge Silvertooth then instructed the clerk of the court to enter a plea of not guilty on behalf of the defendant.

F. Lee Bailey had entered the case through a coincidence of friendship. He knew Dr. William Joseph Bryan of Los Angeles through having attended a seminar on the legal aspects of hypnosis given by Bryan, the president of the American Society of Hypnosis. Subsequently Bailey had brought Bryan to Boston to hypnotize his client, the Boston Strangler, in an attempt to find out the deep motivations behind Albert DiSalvo's acts. In November of 1965, accompanied by Mary, his bride of a month, Carl Coppolino had gone out to Las Vegas to sit in on a panel discussion of medical hypnosis at Bryan's invitation. In July of 1966, when Bryan read of Carl's simultaneous indictment for two murders in two states, he had phoned Mary Coppolino and spoken with her, and then had located F. Lee Bailey and asked him to consider taking over Coppolino's defense. Bailey was on a case at the time and when he had finished he flew to Sarasota, talked to Mary and Carl, and officially entered the case on August 8, Monday, after spending four hours with Dr. Coppolino on Sunday. At that time James "Red" McEwen of Tampa, then vacationing in Wyoming, was Coppolino's defense counsel. On the following Saturday, August 13, McEwen talked with Coppolino at the county jail, and then announced on Monday that Bailey would be the chief defense counsel in the case, and he would assist Bailey.

At about that same time James Russ, a prominent young defense attorney in the Orlando, Florida, area, was engaged to represent Mary Coppolino in the matter of her refusal to answer any questions put to her by the State Attorney, Frank Schaub, with the understanding that he too would assist F. Lee Bailey in the defense of Coppolino.

During the few weeks between Bailey's appearance on the scene and the preliminary hearing, there occurred the expected snowstorm of writs and motions and petitions, made more complex by the fact of two indictments, the New Jersey fugitive warrant, and the attempt to have Coppolino extradited to stand trial in New Jersey first. Usually these maneuverings are a sort of abstract warfare which do not involve the emotions of the laywers on either side. But it soon became evident to those who were following the action closely, and had a chance to talk to the lawyers, that a very genuine and very strong distaste for each other was shaping up between Frank Schaub and F. Lee Bailey, and could be expected to reach full flower during the preliminary hearing.

Frank Schaub, then forty-five, had been State Attorney for the Twelfth Judicial Circuit for six years. As a prosecutor, in addition to hundreds of lesser offenses each year, he had handled eighty-two homicide cases. He had asked for a first degree murder conviction nineteen times. Coppolino was his twentieth. Eleven times the jury returned a verdict of murder in the first degree. Five times, including Coppolino, they returned a verdict of second degree. Once the verdict was third degree, and once it was manslaughter. Appeals were pending at that time in the remaining two cases.

Twenty-nine times he had sought a conviction of murder in the second degree, getting it eighteen times, getting a manslaughter verdict nine times, and getting one verdict of not guilty. The remaining case resulted in the accused being adjudged incompetent to stand trial.

Thirty-four times he had sought manslaughter convictions and in thirty-two of those cases the jury returned a guilty verdict. The other two defendants were acquitted.

To handle this vast work load Schaub had six Assistant State Attorneys, one in each of the six major counties in the eight county circuit, and one investigator. His annual salary was fixed at $14,500. It is an elective office. He was elected to it in 1960 by a narrow margin, and won by a substantial plurality in 1964. Though he is entitled to maintain a private law practice, his sixty hour week on the job makes it impossible. He drives about 35,000 miles a year within the circuit.

Born in Mount Vernon, New York, he received his BS in Business Administration at the University of Idaho, after an interruption of four years in the Navy where he served as an instructor in athletics in the U.S. and overseas. He moved to Florida because of a severe sinus condition, enrolled in Stetson College of Law in DeLand, Florida, and got his law degree in 1948. He spent one year in a large Tampa law firm, moved down to Bradenton, Florida, in 1950, married a Tampa girl in 1951, ran for Justice of the Peace in 1952 on the Democratic ticket and held that elective post until 1960. One of his duties in that position was to act as judge of the small claims court.

This public prosecutor, this father of five young children, was as unlike F. Lee Bailey as a lawyer can be, in almost every respect but one. In his own way he was as forceful and determined and dominant a personality as Bailey. In a small group, when he was silent, you could feel the force of his presence, just as one could with Bailey.

But, unlike Bailey, there seemed to be little lightness or wit or flexibility in Frank Schaub. At the time of the preliminary hearing he was a strong-looking man with a beetling shelf of brow, dark brown hair, pale eyes, a solid jaw, and a rather narrow range of facial expression.

He could look gloweringly annoyed and impatient, or full of injured indignation, or warily suspicious, or full of bland satisfaction, and that was about the extent of it. His habitual expression was one of an unreadable impassivity. There was about him, to many observers, that very faint but perceptible flavor of kinetic violence, often an attribute of a man who has outgrown or has learned to control an explosive temper.

He favored dark brown suits, brown shoes, neckties which blended sedately with that basic color scheme. He had an air of restless impatience at times, which would not be unexpected in a man with dozens of other cases pending throughout the circuit.

In contrast to Bailey's elegant and articulate ability to select the exact word and the most telling phrase, Frank Schaub appeared to have a tendency to lose himself in the thickets of his own sentence structure, and then club his way out by brute force, letting the dangling phrases fall where they might. In contrast to Bailey's all-encompassing attention which seemingly could absorb, sort and file wildly diverse and simultaneous happenings and conversations, Frank Schaub appeared to be unaware of everything except that which he was focused on at that particular time. As a consequence it often appeared that he had failed to see or grasp an unexpected and momentary opening or advantage.

Whereas Bailey would alter strategy and tactics almost instantaneously to fit the changing pattern of the moment, Frank Schaub gave the impression many times of continuing to pound away at a target no longer available until at last he had finished that portion of the plan he had previously prepared. Bailey, using an exceptional memory, used no notes during direct and cross-examination, whereas Frank Schaub worked with yellow legal pad in hand, with most of his questions, particularly in direct examination appearing to have been carefully written out in advance.

Bailey would accept and immediately adjust to the unexpected revelation during examination which seemed to be at odds with his preconception of past events. Frank Schaub appeared to have a strong tendency to ignore the sudden and contradictory bit of testimony as long as he possibly could, apparently considering such surprises to be obstacles rather than opportunities.

It would not be fair nor accurate to term Frank Schaub a plodder. The work load is too heavy to permit him to work up each case in that exhausting detail which a plodding perfectionism would require. It would perhaps be a usefully descriptive analogy to compare his courtroom strategy and procedure to a bulldozer. He would appear to see and interpret the winding pattern of the trails ahead, aim himself at what appeared to him to be the logical termination point of the court action, would then lock the machinery in gear and lock the steering, and go grinding and rumbling off through the brush on a straight course toward his desired destination.

This was the man who opposed F. Lee Bailey in the adversary proceedings in Sarasota, and, the following April, in Naples, Florida, a stubborn and purposeful man, single-minded, giving the impression of being wary and suspicious of almost all those around him. He was irascible, and often quite abrupt. He was a biggish man with a heavy, soft, leaden voice, a tendency sometimes to mutter and mumble. He seemed to have a pressing desire, a compulsive urgency to get on with the job at hand and get to the next one with a minimum of flap and waste motion.

As the Coppolino case was in Sarasota County, Schaub was assisted by William C. Strode, who had been the Assistant State Attorney for three years. Unlike the post of State Attorney, the job of assistant leaves ample time for the private practice of law. Strode is a tall, relaxed, amiable man in his thirties, with a brush-cut and horn-rimmed glasses. He attended the Sarasota public schools, has an undergraduate degree from the University of Chicago, and also attended Stetson for his law training. Bill Strode appears younger than he is, has a gentle, engaging, self-deprecatory humor, and, as the Coppolino affair progressed, he gradually adapted himself to a curiously effective courtroom manner, a kind of sophisticated, ironic, "aw shucks" approach. As one reporter put it, "The thinking man's Huck Finn." Though he was to become totally and desperately involved in the prosecution of the case, he did not become emotionally involved in the personality clash between Bailey and Schaub.

The arena where the grand jury had met and voted to indict, where Carl Coppolino had been arraigned, and where, on the morning of Monday, September 12, 1966, the preliminary hearing was to begin, is the bastard offspring of the traditional dignity of courtrooms, and of contemporary motel and show biz architecture. There are no windows, and so the air is a constant fabricated chill, with a slight odor of chemistry and compressors. In the suspended ceiling of acoustic tile, a low ceiling which contains the conduits and ducts and p.a. system, are countersunk, behind frosted plastic, thirty-one large lighting fixtures, each filled with four yards of white harsh fluorescent tubing. In the spectator section, with its fifty-three gray, comfortable, upholstered, spring-up theater seats, and pale vinyl tile floor, the lighting enchances every wrinkle, mole, fingernail and texture with the merciless cruelty of motel bathroom lighting. In the unusually large arena of the court itself, beyond the dividing barrier of an ornamental rail of teak veneer and brushed aluminum, the lights glare down on wall-to-wall carpeting of a curiously unpleasant shade of red, a raw hue neither cherry nor tomato, and bounce off that color and illuminate the undersides of chins, of hands, of papers held in the hand, in strange pale pink.

The judge's bench is high, and sixty feet, perhaps, from the spectator section. To enter court, the judge climbs a small set of steps in his chambers, opens a door behind the high bench and directly behind his big black chair. The lower witness stand and the large jury box beyond are at the judge's left. The two very large tables for the prosecution and defense are aligned across the floor of the court, well back from the bench, with the defense table on the jury side. The bench and the walls are paneled in a medium wood, neither light nor dark. The chairs for the jury are in black nauga-hide, and so are the chairs for the attorneys. The attorney chairs swivel, and they roll on the red carpeting on brushed aluminum ball casters the size of tennis balls.

Though the architect certainly must have sought a look of permanence and dignity, somehow the courtroom has the flavor of a temporary theatrical solution, as though when the scene is done, the director satisfied, a crew will convert it to a ship's lounge or a hotel lobby. And because of the lack of windows, the constant temperature and illumination, when one leaves after the proceedings and goes down in the tiny little blue and white automatic elevators, as glaringly lighted as the courtroom, and out into the out-of-doors, there is the same sense of disorientation—and vague guilt—as in coming out of a motion picture to find that it is broad daylight.

This was Judge Silvertooth's first capital case. Among the several judges of the circuit, he stood next to the bottom rung in seniority. Cases in the circuit are assigned by lot. There is a small device into which balls of several colors are placed, each color representing a judge of the circuit. Lynn Silvertooth's color is black. When the Coppolino matter came up, and the lever on the machine was depressed, the black ball came rolling out.

This assignment system was devised to eliminate the traditional maneuvering of attorneys to have their cases assigned to specific judges, based upon how judges have dealt with similar cases in the past.

Names like Silvertooth, Silverthorn, Silverstaff are old Florida names, appearing frequently on the dusty rosters of the combat troops Florida sent northward into the Civil War. At age forty-three at the time fate assigned him the Coppolino matter, Lynn Silvertooth had been a practicing attorney in Sarasota. In March 1964 when population increases made an increase in the number of judges in the circuit necessary, Governor Farris Bryant appointed Silvertooth to the bench. Silvertooth ran for the office in November 1964, was elected, and was unopposed in the November 1966 election.

Lynn Silvertooth, well over two hundred pounds, gives no impression of softness. He is tall, massive, big-boned, huge in chest and shoulders. As Lynn Silvertooth had played football before attending the University of Florida, it is highly probable that had not marriage and the Marine Corps changed the timing,

9

and perhaps the motivations, he would have been most useful in a conference where durability is prized.

Lynn Silvertooth is a calm, amiable, ingratiating man. He has a long broad slope of bland forehead to a jutting ridge of bone over deep-set eyes. His cheekbones are high and solid, his dark hair straight, skin tone slightly swarthy. One standard question asked by people of the press corps coming down to cover their first Florida trial, and relating the man's name to his appearance, was, "Hey, is maybe the judge some kind of Indian?"

Judge Silvertooth is a man oriented to family, good friends, good cigars, fishing, cut-throat poker for small stakes. In social situations he manages to conceal those two factors which made him an ideal judge in the Coppolino matter in Florida. He has such a calm and absolute and total conviction of his competence to sit on the bench that he can relax while on the bench, allow some informal latitude, yet interpose the unmistakable iron of natural authority should anyone attempt to misuse the leeway he grants. Secondly, his mind is unexpectedly quick and subtle and complex, and there is very, very seldom any confusion or inattention on the bench, or any failure to relate the law to the events taking place.

A good example of his gentle and self-deprecatory wit took place in the judge's chambers in Naples while the jury was deliberating. Several reporters were there, talking to the judge, when his mother came in. He made introductions and explained that he had never let her come to court when he was presiding, but he had made an exception when she had asked if she could be present when he read his charge to the jury. As she is a personable and attractive woman, one of the reporters from the north said, "Mrs. Silvertooth, you are much too young a woman to have a son as old as the judge here."

Lynn Silvertooth said, "You should have seen me before I was assigned to this case."

In Sarasota, the preliminary hearing was conducted on the top floor of the new three-story addition to the original courthouse, which, prior to the exercise of tasteless practicality by several sets of County Commissioners in pasting pale, functional additions onto it, had been a noble and elegant structure, a distinguished adaptation of the best of the Spanish-Moorish flavor of the nineteen twenties.

It is a comment on contemporary architecture to note that one can walk from the second floor of the old courthouse directly onto the third-floor level of the addition.

10

The county jail is another appendage affixed to the original building. This hodgepodge occupies one city block on the southeast corner of Ringling Boulevard and Route 301. There, except for brief periods of hospitalization, Carl Coppolino had been held since his arrest on July 23, fifty-one days earlier. He was in an eight-prisoner complex on the third floor, a space thirty feet by twelve feet containing two small cells, each with two double bunks, a short hallway, and a day room. The day room contains a table with a bench on either side, a toilet, shower, and a washbasin. Each morning the bunk cells are unlocked and the prisoners can leave them and go into the day room for a breakfast of cereal, grits, and sausage. The cells each contain a toilet and washbasin.

Once in the day room the prisoners are not allowed to go back to their bunk cells during the day, or to sleep. They are given sandwiches at noon, and a hot meal in the evening. They can read magazines and books, play cards, talk, write letters during the day. Toiletry items must be in plastic rather than glass containers. They are allowed underwear, shoes and a razor, and provided with twill coveralls. They may have a personal radio. The county jail is not air conditioned. In the August heat felony prisoners can stand at the open windows and look out through the bars, hear the traffic sounds, hear the afternoon baseball and night baseball sounds from Payne Park, about two homeruns away, hear the clamor of the evening birds settling into the half-grown trees along that side of Ringling Boulevard. Coppolino's area had its windows on the south, and he could look across Ringling Boulevard at the Sarasota Terrace Hotel, at the stubby marquee over the side entrance to the cocktail lounge, and the old-fashioned lettering on the marquee spelling out MRS. O'LEARY'S and *SALOON*.

As he was in the maximum security section he was looking through steel bars of far greater cost to the county than the bars on the cells on the floor below. They are not solid steel. They are a hardened steel shell encasing an inner steel core set there in a permanent lubricant, so that in the event anyone should hacksaw into such a bar, the saw teeth, once they reached the inner core, merely revolve it back and forth in the lubricant, inaccessible and undamaged.

In a letter written from the cell on September 24, Carl Coppolino described it this way:

The mind cannot be imprisoned, that is true. But it can be bruised, twisted and sometimes permanently changed.

The loss of human dignity, personal degradation, lack of privacy, constant noise, poor food, filth—all these prey on the mind.

I have been in prison nine weeks with many weeks to live through.

Let me tell you a little bit about it. I won't go into the food and reading restrictions, you know all about that.

The cell block holds 4 racks and measures 6 feet by 3 feet. At night the door with bars slides shut with a swooshing noise. Facilities include a wash basin with only cold water & a toilet. It always smells. There are two cell blocks—total of 8 prisoners.

The day room has a metal table & two metal benches. There is a shower—only cold water—infested with roaches—and a wash basin.

The cell block is filthy. Roaches crawl over the bedding (a single sheet on a two inch mattress covering a metal rack. No pillow) and your body. Many times I awake and find roaches on my legs and stomach.

At 6 AM they open the cell bar door and you go into the dayroom. Here you are handed a metal pan similar to a pound cake pan with some warm grits and a dried salty sausage plus a cup of black coffee. Breakfast.

The temperature is usually in 100's. No breath of air. I, like the others, stay in my undershorts while the sweat pours down.

At 11 AM we get 2 peanut butter sandwiches. Nothing to drink. Lunch.

At 5:30 PM a hot meal in the same kind of pan used in the morning is served with coffee. It is so bad that I gag trying to eat it.

That is our diet. The only fruit is *4 prunes a week*. People here have signs of scurvy in their mouth and gums. It is usual for long term residents to have their teeth rot out.

At 9:30 PM we are locked up again in the cell block.

How about my physical condition? It needs proper diet, no emotional pressure, sunshine, fresh air, & exercise. Each attack makes my heart that much weaker.

I cannot accept absurdities. The height of absurdity to me right now is sitting in this jail. I consciously use ritualistic behavior to parcel out the time and block out the reality of the bars.

Just a week earlier, on September 17, four days after the preliminary hearing ended, he wrote the following letter:

Today is one of those screaming, falling sobbing days. My head has lost control to my primitive emotions.

I am beaten, just beaten.

I feel the whole world has seized my head in its enormous hands and squeezed out my brains. I can feel the sides of my head collapse. And I want to scream. I want to run and hide. To drop in my tracks, give up, or quietly cry myself to sleep.

I don't know how I could have been cushioned throughout life. But I must

12

have. Yet I have suffered every hardship that goes along with the product of a low income big city existence. I conquered all and became hard. But not tough.

I try to think about the goal—freedom. Reason says how many days, or weeks, or even months in jail is the small price to pay for ultimate exoneration and freedom—and years of peace and happiness with Mary.

But the waste, the utter waste of the precious time never to be recaptured. Lost forever. This poisons my spirit, makes me ill, drives me to tears.

And the FEAR. The numbness of the mind trapped in an unreasoning and unreasonable FEAR. The smell, the stench of FEAR on me who has never been afraid. Who has had the last rites twice, who has peered down that black abyss of unconsciousness seven times. Who has had such pain that survival seems impossible—all without fear.

Carl

Chapter Two

On Monday morning, September 12, Sheriff Ross Boyer took Coppolino down two flights and through into the newer addition and back up to the third floor to that same courtroom where the Sarasota County Grand Jury had met and heard witnesses and voted to indict.

The attorneys and newspaper people were already in the courtroom. Spectators were lined up waiting for the doors to be opened.

Schaub and Strode were familiar with the courtroom. For Bailey, Russ and McEwen it was new country, and during the hearing, particularly during the interrogation of witnesses by the state, they prowled it like cats in a strange barn. There are, it seems, effective and strategic places for attorneys to stand in relation to the judge, the jury, the witness on the stand. It is a kind of theatric triangulation, involving both presence and audibility. During the hearing they were adjusting to the geography of the empty jury box which, as seemed likely then, they would one day help fill with citizens who would then listen to these same witnesses. This gave the hearing, at times, the flavor of dress rehearsal, and gave an eerie look to the empty black chairs behind the heavy carved rail of the jury box, in perfect alignment, inanimate yet somehow attentive.

The preliminary hearing had been requested by the defense.

They had asked for it in the form of a petition, granted by Circuit Judge John D. Justice on August 29. (On that same Monday Coppolino was returned to the county jail after a second brief stay under guard in Sarasota Memorial Hospital, where he had been taken at the request of his personal physician, Dr. William L. Page, after he had complained of chest pains.) The accused has a statutory right to a preliminary hearing. It is a process whereby the public prosecutor is required to show in court that there is sufficient probable cause for holding the accused in connection with the indictment.

It is then up to the prosecutor to determine how much or how little of his case he will reveal in his obligation to provide the court with enough evidence for the court to rule that there is probable cause why the accused should be held to stand trial.

The local press had reported that there would be testimony by several witnesses. The representatives of the news media were in good attendance, many coming from far places. Sheriff Boyer had told Carl Coppolino to expect a concentration of attention from press and photographers who were stationed in the corridor outside the courtroom. When Coppolino was brought off the elevator, wearing a freshly pressed gray suit, white shirt, dark tie, and the strobes and bulbs began blinking, he smiled at the sheriff and said, "You were right!"

The breath of scandal, of infidelity, and the promise of revelation of much that has thus far only been hinted at in the news coverage had whetted a considerable appetite among a certain type of female spectator. Perhaps actually during the two days of the hearing, she was not present in the quantity she seemed to be. Perhaps it is only because this composite spectator made herself known, more visibly and audibly than the others who came to watch. She lined up well before the doors opened. She was over sixty, overweight, and clad in bright hot-weather cotton in large floral patterns. Knowing that standees would be ordered out before the session began, as soon as the double doors were unlocked she would come plunging in, huffing, avid for a seat and, with the tactics of an offensive lineman for the Rams, merciless about claiming one. She would settle into her seat with great satisfaction, and then, out of some conviction of utter righteousness, out of a sentimental identification with the young dead housewife, out of some inner warp or frustration, she would project almost tangible waves of indignant hatred at the back of the defendant's head some twenty feet beyond the rail. One can properly suspect that her comprehension of what was taking place in court was minimal. But believing herself to be in the midst of life, she would seize every opportunity which arose during the giving of evidence to make her little sounds and sniffs of pity, of shock, or outraged censure.

On the first morning of the hearing, when court convened, the spectator seats were occupied by forty-one women and twelve men. Of the men, six were of the working press. There were more women turned away than found seats.

The court was called to order at 9:30 A.M. A little group of witnesses for the state were brought in from the witness room and lined up in a row in front of the bench and given the oath simultaneously by the clerk of the court. They then marched back in single file into the witness room, and the first to take the stand was Dr. Juliette S. Karow, a general practitioner in Sarasota.

She looked to be approximately forty, a small, square-faced woman with a figure midway between trim and stocky. She had light brown hair touched with gray. She wore cultured pearls and eyeglasses with metal frames. There was about her a flavor of determination and controlled antagonism. Her speech was flat, precise, and so unemotional that, as she testified, she spoke in the manner of one who reads aloud from some professional text.

Frank Schaub handled the direct interrogation, establishing that her first contact with Carmela Coppolino in person had been in late April or early May of 1965, shortly after the Coppolinos had moved from New Jersey to Sarasota, when Carmela had stopped at her office to inquire about the feasibility of her practicing medicine in Sarasota. On the following Sunday, at her invitation, the Coppolino family went to her house and spent the afternoon and evening. Subsequent to that, her only other contact with Carmela had been two phone conversations.

She testified that shortly before six in the morning on August 28 of the previous year, Carl had phoned her, sounding upset, and asked her to come at once, without telling her what the trouble was. She said she arrived at about twenty minutes after six, at the new house on Bowsprit Lane in the development called Country Club Shores on Longboat Key. She testified that Carl met her at the door and said, "She is dead," and led her to the bedroom where Carmela was lying in bed.

"What was her condition at the time?"

"She was very obviously dead."

"Did you notice anything unusual?"

"Well, she was lying on her right side with her right arm under her. Her hands were clenched in fists. Both hands were of equal size and no discoloration. I felt that was unusual, that anyone lying in that position the hand would be swelled. Also,

15

the face was discolored on the right side. That was unusual because the pillow, being under her face, after death the blood would drain to the most dependent parts of the body.''

"How was the bedding?"

"It looked undisturbed."

"Did you form any opinion at that time as to whether the position of the body had been changed?"

"It looked to me as if she was in a very uncomfortable position. I wondered if she could have died in that position. It seemed likely that she did not."

". . . What did Carl have to say about his wife's death?"

". . . When I examined her I asked him if she had been ill. He said she had chest pains the day before. He suggested that she see a doctor but she refused."

"Was this the extent of the history that he gave you?"

"Yes."

"While you were there did anything else distract you?"

"Shortly after examining the body, Carl clutched his chest and acted as though he was in pain. He was taking little white pills. I was a bit concerned because he seemed to be taking quite a few. I asked him if he wouldn't like to go to the hospital. I was aware he had heart trouble before."

"Who told you that?"

"He had. He said no, he didn't want to. I said, 'Don't take too many pills.' He said, 'I know what I am doing.' "

She had then suggested to Carl that it would be best to get the small Coppolino daughters out of the house. He suggested Mr. and Mrs. Thomson, neighbors, and they came over at once, and took the children back to their house. This was the end of Mr. Schaub's direct examination, and he chose that time to introduce a certified document showing that there was at that time insurance on the life of the deceased and that the defendant was the beneficiary. F. Lee Bailey said that he did not see the relevancy of it but would not object, and so the court admitted it in evidence.

Bailey began his cross-examination by handing Dr. Karow a photo-copy of the death certificate and asking her to identify her signature. He then asked Judge Silvertooth to rule that her testimony about what happens to the blood after death is admissible only as when given by an expert witness. When the court so ruled, he asked Dr. Karow her qualifications. She said she was licensed to practice in Florida and Michigan, had graduated from medical school at the University of Michigan in 1951, interned at the Henry Ford Hospital for a year and in Detroit for a year. Under questioning she said that she had never been connected with any department of pathology, had never worked for a coroner or medical examiner, had observed dead bodies but "Not a whole lot." She said that the drainage of blood and the swelling of the hands is something a doctor would learn during his schooling.

Bailey then posed this question. "Are you giving us *all* of the conversation you had with Doctor Coppolino on the morning in question?"

"I cannot recall in detail every word that was said."

"Have you given us then all that you can recall?"

"Pertaining to the time of examining the body."

Here is a typical example of the subtle tactical game which must occur at any such hearing. In putting the witness on the stand, the prosecutor is intent on bringing out only those points pertinent to the purpose of the hearing. Later, with a jury present, he may well question the witness in those related areas which will bring out testimony more damaging to the defendant. He must take care not to open up any areas which, when developed on cross-examination, can have the effect of giving the defense a more complete discovery of what the testimony will be at the trial itself.

The defense wants to learn just how damaging the trial testimony may be, but they are restricted in cross-examination to those areas covered in the direct examination. Yet such is the informality at times in such proceedings that the witness ends up giving testimony far more inclusive and voluminous than anything which would be permitted at the trial. The discovery process works both ways, of course. In his cross-examination of a state witness, it is possible that the defense attorney can betray to the prosecution the direction of his private investigation of the witness, and the direction the defense will take.

Inasmuch as this was a public hearing, another factor was introduced. The press would give this testimony the page-one treatment, as the case had already attracted national attention. Eventually two juries had to be selected from among a public exposed to this coverage. Because a man will not be identified except on the basis of something which *seems* to be a significant indication of guilt, hearings such as this one in the case of Carl Coppolino cannot help but create a public assumption of guilt, thus vastly complicating the eventual chore of the selection of impartial and unbiased jurors.

Under Florida law, a circuit judge has sole authority to order whether such a hearing to show cause shall be open to press and public, or a closed proceeding in the judge's chamber or in the hearing room. There is nothing to prevent the defense from petitioning the court for a closed hearing, stating that the testimony might well create adverse public opinion for the accused, but there has been no precedent established through any ruling by the appellate court that the circuit court need heed such a petition as possible grounds for an eventual ruling of a mistrial if he does not.

Once the judge has determined that such a hearing will be in open court he has no control over the number of witnesses the state may wish to call, though he can elect to hear some of them in chambers if he chooses. In this case, though the hearing was ostensibly to show cause for holding the accused to face a charge of murder in the first degree, the state attorney had stipulated, prior to the hearing, that he would not oppose the posting of bond in this case.

Bailey went on to ask her, "Did you have further conversation with him later in the day?"

". . . Yes, we met at the funeral home. The director suggested I be present in case assistance would be necessary."

Then Bailey led her through her awareness of her responsibility in certifying the cause of death, and through her observations of the clenched hands, the uncomfortable position of the body, and asked her if she knew what a coronary occlusion was. The affirmative answer had an overlay of professional indignation.

"Did you also say her lip was bitten?"

"No."

"Did you examine her at the funeral home?"

"No."

"Did you ever examine as to whether her lip was bitten in one way or another?"

"I didn't examine in detail, but there was no evidence."

He then, through questioning, had her state that the only definite basis for her diagnosis was Carl's statement about the chest pain the day before.

"Did you point out that her hand was not swollen?"

"No."

"Why not?"

"It didn't seem relevant at the time."

"Did you point out to him that her face was discolored despite the fact that her face was on a pillow?"

"No."

"Did you tell anyone?"

"I talked to the funeral director about it."

One can imagine Bailey was not enchanted with that particular answer, and had perhaps hoped and believed that she had not brought up these matters with anyone until much later.

He changed direction at once. "Doctor Coppolino gave you no special instructions as to how to diagnose the cause of death of the decedent?"

"No."

"He gave no special instructions that the coroner be called?"

"No."

"As a matter of fact it was your responsibility to call the coroner if it was felt that there should be an investigation?"

"It was my responsibility in any sudden death without the attendance of a physician."

"Did you do that?"

"Yes."

"When?"

"After I examined the body I first called the Sheriff's Department. They said they would send an investigator. They also said they would send an escort to take the body for an autopsy. We waited for the escort. None appeared. After the first person from the Longboat Police came, he left. There was no escort who came. We called Dr. White [the county medical examiner] to find out how to proceed. He said he had not received a report from the sheriff's office as yet. He said the funeral director might as well take the body to the home and he would determine if an investigation should be made."

"You at that moment felt you had turned it over to him for any investigation that might be required?"

"Yes."

"Did you talk to anybody there at the funeral home?"

"Yes. I was there when Doctor White called and said it was okay to embalm the body."

"Doctor Coppolino at no time asked you to see that no examination was performed?"

"No."

"When were you next contacted by anyone relative to the death of Carmela?"

"Somebody up north, I believe the next day, somebody asked whether an autopsy had been performed and whether I felt she died from natural causes. I said I felt she had and no autopsy had been performed."

"And after that?"

"I think the next time was when Mrs. Farber came in the office . . ."

Here Frank Schaub objected that Bailey was going into matters not brought up on direct. Bailey explained to the Court, "The witness signed a death certificate in which it gives coronary occlusion. I am trying to determine whether that opinion still persists and if it has changed, why."

When the objection was overruled, Bailey asked Dr. Karow if on the day Mrs. Farber visited her she had the opinion that Carmela died of a coronary occlusion. Dr. Karow said she had certified it. She said that enough facts had come to her attention to cause her to question her own opinion at the time she examined the body. She said that in retrospect the condition of the face could be more important than it was at that time.

When she said that she would have to withdraw her original opinion of coronary occlusion, and could not have an opinion, and did not know what the cause of death might be, Bailey asked her what her opinion would be if the information Carl had given her were reliable.

Here Frank Schaub objected to the hypothetical question on the grounds that Bailey had laid no proper predicate for it, and that what Carl said was not in evidence. When the objection was sustained, Lee Bailey returned to some final questions about her examination of the body.

"I examined it as much as I would any dead body and to determine the cause of death and to assure that the body was dead."

"Did you remove the clothing?"

"I did not. Just the sheet. I did not remove the nightgown."

"Mrs. Coppolino was wearing curlers?"

"Right."

"And a nightgown?"

"Yes."

"Did you examine the skin?"

"I observed the skin."

"Did you see anything unusual about it?"

"No, I didn't."

"Were you looking for anything unusual?"

"No."

And that was the end of the cross-examination. Schaub's single question on redirect, before the witness was dismissed, merely established that no autopsy had been performed on the body in Sarasota County.

Schaub next called the father of the dead woman, Dr. Carmelo

Musetto, a portly balding man in his sixties who walked very slowly and took the stand with all the careful mannerisms of someone convalescent. He reached and adjusted the gooseneck microphone to the proper distance from his mouth, and during the questions which established his identity, address and relationship to the deceased, he kept two fingers resting on the flexible neck of the microphone stand, and looked steadily and implacably at the defendant rather than at his inquisitor. He wore a gold seal ring and a gold tie clip. His air toward Schaub was of an exhausted tolerance, and he appended "sir" to many of his answers in a sardonic and patronizing manner.

He claimed as his residence the house where his daughter had died. He had practiced medicine in New Jersey for over thirty years. He corresponded with his daughter and with Carl and had seen them frequently before they moved to Florida. It was his observation that his daughter had been in excellent health during the years preceding her death, and he said she had no history of a coronary condition.

"As a physician are you acquainted with the possibilities of a young woman still capable of having menstrual periods having a coronary attack? Is there a medical belief on that?"

Bailey's objection that the witness should be qualified as an expert before being asked for opinions was sustained. Under Schaub's questioning Musetto related that he had attended medical school at Long Island College Hospital, and before going into private practice had been on the staffs of St. Catherine's Hospital and Greenpoint Hospital in Brooklyn, and that during his fourth year of medical school he had been assigned to the Cardiology Clinic at The Brooklyn Hospital. He had then entered practice in Lumberton, New Jersey, and had been admitted to the staff of All Souls Hospital and Morristown Memorial Hospital in Morristown, New Jersey, St. Clare's in Denville and Riverside in Bloomfield. He had engaged in private practice from the 2nd of August, 1932, until the 26th or 28th of April 1960 when "I received my severe coronary disease."

He said that he was not a cardiologist, but added, "In our day, when we did not have cardiologists in the neighborhood, we had to treat our own cardiac patients. Therefore, I had tremendous experience in treating coronary patients before the specialists came along whom we could call upon."

Having qualified him as an expert, Schaub again asked him whether it was likely that his daughter had a coronary occlusion.

"My opinion is that in such a case it would be almost never-never."

21

Schaub next handed the doctor state exhibits 2, 3 and 4, and asked him to identify them. They were reports of physical examinations given Carmela at the Hoffman-LaRoche Laboratories in Nutley, New Jersey, where, at the time of her resignation to move to Florida, she had been Assistant Head of Professional Services at a salary of $15,000 a year. The reports were dated in 1959, 1963 and 1964.

It is logical to assume that at some point prior to the preliminary hearing Dr. Musetto had examined the reports. He had testified before the grand jury in New Jersey, and had testified before two grand juries in Sarasota County, in January 1966 and again in July of the same year. And one must assume that he had been interviewed at length by the state attorney.

Yet he sat in the witness box and slowly went through the exhibits, turning the sheets, reading, lips pursed in thoughtful concentration, expression betraying no emotion whatsoever. The long minutes passed. One could imagine him having done exactly the same thing hundreds upon hundreds of times, with the apprehensive patient sitting by the doctor's desk in his office, straining to see some clue as to his condition in the doctor's expression as he slowly read over the laboratory reports. At the termination of this ritual any patient would be certain that a very serious condition was being given very serious and sober attention. At last he sighed, nodded, stated what the documents were and handed them back, stating that they showed his daughter to have been in excellent physical condition at that time, and the reports were consistent with his own observations of her.

Next Frank Schaub had Dr. Musetto identify the signatures on state exhibits 5, 6 and 7, photostats of several insurance documents showing Carl to be the beneficiary on policies on Carmela's life, and that one policy had been increased just before her death.

Mr. Bailey said, "I am not going to object to any of these but I do not wish any lack of objection at this time to be construed as waiver of objection at the time of trial."

By further questioning of Musetto, Frank Schaub established that Carl Coppolino had been without gainful employment since December 10, 1962, and that in addition to Carmela's salary, Coppolino had a full disability income from health insurance, due to coronary disease. Schaub then asked the witness if he had ever had any discussion with Carl Coppolino about the insurance benefits he was receiving.

Dr. Musetto said that in August 1963 he had talked with Carl and Carmela in Middletown, New Jersey, about the death of Colonel William Farber.

"We were outside and I remember my daughter pointing over to the house and said, 'There is where a man died working over the weekend in his garden. He came down with a coronary.' I said, 'Who treated him?' Dr. Coppolino said, 'I treated him.' I said, 'You what!' "

Here Dr. Musetto displayed a heavy-handed histrionic talent, his voice and his facial expression registering shock and astonishment and consternation.

"You say Doctor Coppolino?"

"Yes. I said, 'You what?' He said, 'Yes, I treated him.' I said, 'What did you do for him?' He said, 'Well, his wife, Mrs. Farber, called me that her husband was sick. I went up there and rendered first aid.' 'And what did you find?' He said he found that the man had a coronary occlusion with a myocardial infarction. I said, 'Did you call a cardiologist?' He said, 'No.' I was *really* reprimanding him. I said, 'And you treated him, Carl? You didn't call a cardiologist? You know you are disabled. You know if the insurance company gets ahold of this they may cut your disability completely!' I also said, 'You realize treating at home went out with high button shoes . . .' "

F. Lee Bailey interrupted at this point from the defense table, saying, "Did you say high button shoes, Doctor?"

Dr. Musetto glowered at Bailey. "I said it went out with high button shoes."

"I thought you said high button shoes," said Bailey.

Dr. Musetto glowered at F. Lee Bailey. The elderly man's capacity for rage had been unmistakably established at the time of Carl's arraignment on September 1.

He had not cared to have his picture taken. He was being taken into an office in the courthouse complex. A wire service photographer stood in the corridor and tried to take the doctor's picture through the open office door. The doctor had seen him, whirled, picked a heavy glass ashtray from the desk and hurled it at the photographer with such force that he almost fell to his hands and knees with the effort. The photographer had ducked away and the ashtray had made a very impressive and lethal-looking scar on the corridor wall.

Bailey was consciously mocking the witness, needling him, quite aware of Dr. Musetto's low boiling point and, one can assume, angering him with the hope of making Musetto less able to deal with the upcoming cross-examination.

Musetto picked up the thread of his response to the question. " 'Treating at home,' I said to Carl, 'went out with high button shoes. You might put him in the hospital.' "

"Was Carmela present at this time?"

"She certainly was."

"Did you address any remarks to her in Carl's presence?"

"I said, 'Who signed the death certificate?' She said, 'I did.' I said, 'Did you treat him, Carmela?' She said, 'No.' 'Did you see him while he was alive with this condition?' She said, 'No.' 'Yet you signed this death certificate?' She said, 'Yes.' I said, 'Carmela, you will get yourself in a peck of trouble by doing that! You don't have an office here. You don't practice here in this community. Why did you do it for? What is the matter with you? I didn't bring you up that way!' She said, 'Well, I wanted to cover Carl because if Carl signed the death certificate the insurance company might find out. He might have his disability insurance discontinued.'"

Schaub then asked about the Coppolino income after they moved to Florida. Dr. Musetto said that when his daughter resigned from Hoffman-LaRoche, they had given her six months severance pay. Otherwise all they had was Carl's insurance benefits. He testified that Carl had told him that he did not intend to seek a Florida license to practice medicine, but that Carmela had taken the Florida examination in June 1965 and flunked the first part of it. He also testified that Carl claimed to be a hypnotist and had published a book titled *Practice of Hypnosis in Anesthesiology*.

"Directing your attention . . . to the 28th day of August, last year, when did you first hear of your daughter's death?"

"That evening at approximately six o'clock."

"Who advised you of this?"

"My daughter, Angela Imhof."

"Did you have occasion that day to talk to the defendant, Carl Coppolino?"

Musetto testified that he had two telephone conversations with Carl that day, and Schaub asked him to relate the first conversation.

"At first it was difficult to get any coherence from him. He said, 'Oh, Dad, I have lost my best friend. I have lost my right arm. Carm is dead. Oh, help me. Keep talking to me.' In between this asking me to help him and crying over the telephone he told me. I said, 'How did she die?' 'She died of a heart attack, a coronary occlusion, a massive myocardial infarction.'"

"Did he tell you the source of this information? Let me ask you, did he say whether or not there had been an autopsy?"

"Well, that took two phone conversations to get that answered completely."

"What was said with reference to an autopsy by Carl Coppolino on the first conversation?"

"I asked him if the medical examiner had examined the body. He said, 'Yes, yes, yes, I know Doctor White has done an autopsy.' 'Where are the results?' 'I haven't got them yet.' "

"Were there further discussions concerning the autopsy in the second conversation?"

"I called him later that evening and while we were talking he said, 'Oh, by the way, Dad, Doc White has just got through talking to me. He called me.' 'What did he say?' 'He said that he found a massive coronary occlusion, myocardial infarction at autopsy.' "

"What was Carl's comment as to that finding? Did he have anything to say?"

"He was speechless, sir."

"Did he tell you what Carmela's condition had been on the day before this?"

"Yes. He said that late that afternoon she had been suffering with what appeared to be indigestion and that she had taken some pills for antidigestion. He mentioned names. I don't recall what he said she had taken, and after that she sort of felt better."

"Did he say what he had done that evening, what they had done?"

"They had been home, that he had played cards with her, and that about eleven o'clock they had a drink. I asked what was the drink. He said it was a Bloody Mary, so I said, 'What is a Bloody Mary?' He said, 'You know, vodka and tomato juice, and then she felt better. We went to bed about midnight.' "

"I will ask you what your daughter Carmela Coppolino's religion was."

"Roman Catholic."

"She was a practicing Roman Catholic?"

"Yes."

"Were you acquainted with her views concerning divorce?"

"Absolutely against divorce!"

As Frank Schaub relinquished the witness to cross-examination and walked back to the state table with his notes, Dr. Carmelo Musetto stared fixedly at Coppolino. There was an apparent and unmistakable balefulness about that long and direct gaze. And one could reasonably expect, and read into that stare a certain flavor of grim satisfaction. The beloved daughter was dead. The father had taken the stand to testify against the ex-son-in-law. He would not and could not have done so had he not believed that the man he stared at had slain his daughter. The only conceivable byproduct of that circumstance had to be hatred.

Lee Bailey got up slowly and strolled in unhurried fashion toward the witness, wearing a mocking half-smile.

His first question was put in a mild and casual fashion.

"Do you know whether or not anyone ever asked her to get a divorce?"

"I have heard."

"No. Of your own knowledge, from talking to her, do you know if a divorce was ever requested?"

"No."

"Who did you hear it from?"

"From the neighbors."

"When did you first hear it?"

Schaub objected on grounds of materiality, and was overruled by Judge Silvertooth who said, "You asked the question. He has the right to cross-examine on it."

"Neighbors have names. Would you give us a name?"

"Mr. and Mrs. Norcross and the Thomsons."

Musetto said that he had heard of this in February, right after he and his wife had come down to the Sarasota house on the 24th or 25th of January. He said the Norcrosses had told him that Carl had left Carmela for three days in August, just before their wedding anniversary and had returned on their wedding anniversary and asked Carmela for a divorce. But Norcross had not told Musetto who had told him all this. Nor could Musetto say from whom the Thomsons had heard it.

"From your knowledge, your daughter and son-in-law got along harmoniously?"

"To the best of my knowledge."

Bailey then switched abruptly to Musetto's competence to give expert opinions in the field of cardiology. "Was it this *extensive* experience that enabled you to form an opinion that the death of your daughter by a heart attack was extremely unlikely?"

"Yes sir."

"I believe your exact words were never-never?"

Musetto with a patronizing smile said, "No . . . *sir*."

This was so much less than fencing it could accurately be called quibbling.

"*Almost* never-never?"

"Yessssss," said Musetto, with a congratulatory smirk.

"Converting that into some syntax of reasonable certainty, do you say that it is extremely rare for a thirty-two-year-old woman to die of a heart attack?"

"Yessssss."

"You do?"

"Yessssss."

"How many people have you treated or been familiar with who in their early or middle thirties have died of a heart attack?"

"None."

Registering astonishment, Bailey had Musetto repeat how many years he had been seeing patients, and then asked him when he had last treated his daughter as a physician. After more quibbling, using the device of failing to understand the question, Dr. Musetto said that he never treated members of his own family. Asked the name of the last doctor Camela had consulted about the state of her health, Musetto said that it would have been so long ago he could not begin to answer the question.

"You mean you are able to tell us under oath that she has not consulted any doctor for say five or ten years?"

"The only ones I know are the routine physicals she had at LaRoche laboratories and whatever physical they may have given her when she attended school."

"Didn't you tell us you knew that Carmela Coppolino had not complained of any symptom related to heart trouble at any time prior to her death?"

"Right."

"Do you know that as a fact?"

"I do."

Bailey leaned against the rail of the jury box and hesitated for a few moments, studying the witness. The next question would perhaps have been to ask him how he could know it as a fact. But Musetto looked a little too anxious to be asked the question. It seems likely that Musetto tended to use Carl as his authority for the fact. He decided to approach the question from a different angle. So he began with the day before the death. He led Musetto through the reported complaint of indigestion, with continued quibblings as exemplified by this exchange.

BAILEY: *(in reference to August 27)* Where was Dr. Carl Coppolino?

MUSETTO: *(smilingly sardonic)* I don't know where he was.

BAILEY: *(irritably)* Your information is that he was in Sarasota, right?

MUSETTO: *(with triumphant satisfaction)* That is what I am *told!*

These seeming trivialities are important when one thinks of

them in terms of analogy to other contests. This sparring in a preliminary hearing can be compared to a pre-season exhibition game in professional football. The shape of the contest is the same as it will be during the regular season. But the more proficient team will not exploit to any great extent the defensive weaknesses they uncover, nor will they reveal all the aspects of their own offense. It is a time for experimentation, to find out what might work well during the regular season, and what sequences might best be discarded and removed from the play book.

Establishing Musetto's knowledge of Carl's report of Carmela's complaint, Bailey then said, "So in fact Carmela *did* complain to a doctor about some discomfort on the day of her death?"

"I don't get the full meaning of your question."

And, later along, "Would you like to change your original statement and tell us that you don't know whether or not she consulted any physician?"

"No, I do not."

And, a few minutes later, during the extended exchange, "I will put it to you a third time. Do you know of your own knowledge what doctor last examined your daughter Carmela Coppolino prior to her death?"

"No."

"So that your earlier testimony you know that she had not seen a doctor or made any complaints was incorrect?"

"No, I will not say that."

"Now, I think you have said with a high degree of certainty that the likelihood that your daughter would have died of a heart attack with no history or warning is extremely remote in your experience as a doctor?"

"Are you quoting my words?"

"I am asking your opinion once again."

"I said rarely, never-never "

"I think you said almost never."

"Almost never-never, rarely never-never—all mean the same to me."

"Transposing that into our language, does it mean that it is rare?"

"Yes. I would say very rare . . . If I *may*."

Bailey then asked him if it was his opinion that his daughter did not die of a coronary occlusion. Schaub's objection that there had been nothing on direct examination about the cause of death was overruled.

"Doctor, did you have this opinion on August 28th, 1965?"

"I had the feeling that my daughter did not die of a coronary."

"Was it an opinion?"

"Yes. It was an opinion."

"What did you do about it?"

"I thought."

"You were told there was an autopsy?"

"Yes."

"You are able to read and understand an autopsy report, aren't you?"

"Yes."

"You are able to discuss with another physician the findings of an autopsy and understand them as a medical man?"

"Yes."

"Did you call Doctor White and find out what he found?"

"No. Because I believed Carl explicitly."

"You were satisfied that because Carl told you that there was a myocardial infarct, that that was a fact?"

"Definitely."

"At some point did you have cause to believe that that was *not* a fact?"

"Yes."

"When did that first occur?"

"It was a slow, progressive, evolutionary thought in my mind. It was no set time that here at two minutes after ten P.M. on date number X that Carmela did not have a coronary. This evolved slowly in my mind over a period of months. The thoughts of it analyzed in my mind."

"As to a time when you finally made a decision, when did you first tell somebody in your opinion that she had not died of a coronary?"

"I told that to my wife."

"When?"

"It was in November of 1965."

"When was the first time you told anyone in authority—and I refer to any public official or law enforcement officer—that you believe the cause of death was misstated on the death certificate?"

"My attorney in Morristown, New Jersey."

"When?"

"Now, I may be wrong on the date. If I had a calendar I could tell you the date. It was in December 1965."

"Of course your attorney is not a public official. Who was the first public official that you told about your suspicions?"

"The State Attorney of Florida."

"When?"

"It was December 1965."

"Prior to that time you had never checked with Doctor White to determine whether or not Carl's statement of the autopsy was accurate?"

"No."

"When did you first learn that no autopsy had been performed?"

Mr. Schaub objected to a "fishing expedition" outside the scope of the direct examination, and was overruled.

The question was repeated and Musetto said, "Well, I must place the date exactly. Carmela died on the 28th of August, and her body was shipped to Boonton the 29th of August, Sunday. Monday night Mr. Tom Lewis, funeral director of Boonton, New Jersey, who handled the remains of my daughter, called me to his office. Do you want me to give you the whole story?"

"He told you from an examination of the autopsy . . ."

And again Mr. Schaub stood up, his tone of voice expressing a heavy and somewhat petulant indignation. "Your Honor, these are matters completely outside the scope of the direct. This witness was not asked whether or not an autopsy was performed. He was asked if there was a telephone conversation with the defendant and what the defendant said. If he has knowledge or doesn't whether an autopsy was performed, it was not brought out on direct, and I move therefore that this line of questioning be overruled and stricken. I feel that it has no place in this proceeding at this time."

Judge Silvertooth said, "The objection is overruled. Just answer the question. Don't go into a long detail."

And so Bailey again asked Dr. Musetto the date when he first learned that there had been no autopsy.

"Monday, August 30, 1965."

"Within two days of death!" Bailey exclaimed, and such is the art of the accomplished cross-examiner that one cannot know whether he had known this fact before he began the examination, or whether it was indeed a surprise to him. One can risk surprises when no jury is present.

"That is right."

"So you learned that Carl's statement to you on the telephone was not accurate?"

"Right."

"Having that fact, and that you as a physician with some experience in heart cases felt it extremely unlikely that Carmela died from a coronary, why didn't you then go to the authorities?"

Musetto hesitated, shifting on the stand, looking very uneasy and uncomfortable. And this, of course, is where the elusive logic of emotional reaction runs counter to the imposed logical pattern of the courtroom, where all events, being seen in retrospect, seem to demand specific responses at the time they happened. It is the marvel and mystery of the human animal that we so often act in ways that do not yield to logical analysis. There is no adult alive who cannot look into his own past and identify many points where decisions were made, or not made, and say—I should have done this—or—I should not have done that. And, because of the intervening exercise of logic and appraisal, once the results of the act or the failure to act are made evident, we are often at a loss to reconstruct whatever reasons we thought valid at that time.

Dr. Carmelo Musetto was handicapped on the stand by his own reluctance to admit that there had ever been any prior inconsistency in his pattern of behavior. The more proud, stubborn, volatile, and competitive a man may be, and the more accustomed he is to dignity and standing and public respect, the more difficult it is for such a man to make any admission of oversight or of impulsive and contradictory acts. Perhaps it is because such an admission would be at odds with the image the man has of himself, the image of careful appraisal and flawless wisdom.

"I have no reason to give you," he said. "I was lost. I was a lost man."

"Despite the fact that you were lost?"

"I was an aggrieved and a lost man."

"Despite the fact that you were lost, you did not go. *Did you!?*"

"The answer is yes. I did not go."

Bailey merely stared at him for a few moments, as though to underline how incomprehensible such behavior appeared, then said abruptly, "Where do you live now?"

"At the present time I am living at 591 Bowsprit Lane, Longboat Key, Sarasota, Florida."

"Who did you buy the house from?"

Frank Schaub was sustained when he objected to the question as improper. Bailey said, "Your Honor, I believe it goes to the bias of the witness. It was bought from the defendant." Schaub stated that it would not establish bias, and the court again sustained Schaub's objection.

Bailey then moved on to the area of Musetto's alleged unwillingness to cooperate with the defendant and provide his representatives with the same information he was providing the state attorney, with Bailey saying in response to Schaub's frequent

31

objections, "I am trying to show that this man is swinging with the state and severely biased to the defendant."

Of course, here again the law affronts human emotions. One must be certain that were Dr. Musetto not convinced his daughter had been slain by her husband, he would certainly not have entered such an alien and uncomfortable arena. To expect such an emotionally involved witness to cooperate as willingly with the defense as with the state is to require an objectivity no parent of a dead child could ever achieve.

Finally, after various maneuverings and misunderstandings, Lee Bailey was permitted to ask: "Have you been asked to discuss the matter [the case] by representatives of the defendant?"

"No. I have not been asked."

"Did you make an appointment to talk with me in your home in August of this year?"

"No *sirrrrr!* I did not make that appointment. I was asked to make the appointment."

"Did you agree?"

"Yesssss!"

"And then you went off and stayed out until seven o'clock in the morning and didn't keep the appointment?"

"Right!"

Schaub objected to the line of questioning as improper cross-examination, and was sustained, but Dr. Musetto was trying to be heard while Mr. Schaub was voicing his objection. "The witness wants to say something," Judge Silvertooth said. "What do you want to say?"

"An appointment by Mrs. Coppolino had been made for Mr. Bailey to come to my house, but it was not to discuss this case. It was for some other matter."

"What other matter?" Bailey asked.

"Mrs. Coppolino told me that since you were going to accept the $22,000 that I owe Carl as down payment for your fee in this case it would be nice if I would meet the man to whom I would make future payments, period."

"Then why did you go out and stay out until seven o'clock?"

"After Mrs. Coppolino left the house I thought it was better if I did not meet you at this time."

"Did you talk to Mr. Schaub in the interim?"

"Yes. I went to Mr. Schaub's office."

"He told you to get out of your house?"

"He did not!"

"Who told you to get out?"

"My attorney. Mr. Renfrew."

32

"The purpose of getting out of the house was to avoid meeting me?"

"Absolutely!"

"You have been carrying on a correspondence with Carl during the time you have been conferring with the state authorities?"

When Mr. Schaub objected, the court asked the purpose of the question. Bailey withdrew the question and handed Dr. Musetto a typewritten letter. Musetto testified that he had dictated it the previous March 16, and signed it, and that was his signature.

"On March 16th you told Carl Coppolino that he is a man of fairness, honesty and integrity beyond reproach. . . ."

Here there occurred a great deal of legal squabbling, Schaub saying that if it was to be submitted in evidence there was a proper time for it, Bailey saying that the credibility of the witness was at issue. Dr. Musetto wanted to read the whole letter aloud. Schaub objected to that and was sustained, but the court ruled that Bailey could question Dr. Musetto about that portion of the letter he had already quoted.

"As of March 16th did you honestly feel that Carl's fairness, honesty and integrity were beyond reproach when you said so?"

"I had a reason to say that."

"You wanted him to drop the amount of mortgage?"

"No. It was not money. I felt that he had not played fair with me."

"You had signed a mortgage for a certain amount?"

"After that I felt that he did not play fair with me. With that letter I was hoping I could move him to play fair with me."

"That is why you alluded to his honesty and integrity?"

"That is right."

"That is why you signed 'Father of Carmela who misses her very much'?"

"I do miss her."

"But this was about money?"

"It wasn't about money."

"What was it about?"

"It was a letter in reference to the fact that Carl had not been honest with me."

"You are asking to reduce the mortgage?"

"I was asking for his honesty."

"You said he was *very* honest."

"I said that, yes."

"Do you know where the Key Pharmacy is?"

"Yes."

"Do you have some photographs with you that belonged to Carl Coppolino?"

When Frank Schaub objected again on the grounds of it being improper cross-exmination, Bailey said that he would call Musetto again as a defense witness if necessary.

At this point a Bradenton, Florida, attorney, Warren Goodrich, came to his feet from a chair against the side wall of the courtroom. He was representing both Dr. Musetto and Mrs. Farber at the preliminary hearing insofar as their civil rights were concerned. Goodrich is a tall, bland, heavy, white-haired man, carefully barbered and tailored, who looks as if he could be cast as the U. S. Ambassador to a small friendly country.

He said, "Doctor Musetto has been subpoenaed *ad testificandum*. We are prepared to produce the papers called for in a subpoena *duces tecum* at the time he is called as a witness, and not in cross-examination."

At this cabalistic pronouncement, Bailey deferred further cross-examination, informing Schaub that he was finished with his cross, but had Dr. Musetto under subpoena as a witness for the defense.

The hearing was recessed for the lunchtime break.

Much had been revealed beyond what had been printed about the case against Carl Coppolino before the hearing. Press, spectators and attorneys rode down to the ground floor in the little blue and white candybox elevators, and walked out into the bright humid glare of the subtropic September noon. The handiest exit from the new courthouse wing is almost directly across from the side entrance to the Sarasota Terrace Hotel.

It dates back to the same period as the original courthouse, but its ten stories are of a style which might be termed Office Moorish. After having changed hands a bewildering number of times—at one point being advertised, despairingly, as "the tallest motel in the world"—it has, one might say, fallen upon good times in the past couple of years, having been purchased by Arthur Allyn, the owner of the Chicago White Sox baseball team. The Sox train at Payne Park, about three hundred yards east and slightly south of the hotel, and live at the hotel during spring training. An adjacent convention center has been built. The bar lounge, which had been called the Driftwood Lounge and the Tenth Inning under previous ownerships has become, in key with Chicago mythology, Mrs. O'Leary's—she of the arsonist bovine—and there are curious similarities between that redecorated bar lounge and the courtroom across the street. The big armchairs in the bar lounge are of the same black nauga-hide.

The walls are a shade of red very close to the carpeting of the arena of the courtroom. Daylight is suppressed. The air has the same chilly taint of a manufactured commodity.

The defense team had made the hotel its headquarters during the various legal maneuverings leading up to the hearing. And so at breakfast before court, and at lunch, and at the cocktail hour after court, the press and attorneys and county officials brought the continuing dialogues across the four lanes of Ringling Boulevard, from the formal arena to the informal one. It could be likened to an intricate game of three-dimensional chess after the first dozen moves had been made. Had any advantage been obtained on this level, or that? Could some strategic weakness be observed, or was it too early to tell? Can one see the shape of the game plan as yet? Why had one adversary made this particular move? Would it develop into a trap play? Was it merely an ill-advised move, a mistake which might later prove critical? Is what has already been revealed of any significance in predicting the eventual outcome of the game?

For the impartial and objective observer this initial period is characterized by one continuing and insoluble problem. The partisans seem to demand that one choose sides. Mr. Bailey's habit is to divide the press corps into two groups, calling them, "the guys in the white hats (defense oriented) and the guys in the black hats (prosecution oriented)." It is the creed of all intense combat: If you are not for me, you are against me.

As the adversary system demands the use of all possible weapons both in and out of court, the news media become valuable as areas of leverage whereby public opinion can be swayed. Thus the working newsman with access to the public becomes the target of a special kind of seduction. All contemporary criminal lawyers of national reputation—Bailey, Belli, Edward Bennett Williams, Percy Foreman—are men of impressive personal charm. Charm can perhaps be described as the ability to relate totally and instantly to someone, to listen to what he says with an intensity that makes him feel unique and special, to give that someone the feeling that he or she alone has been singled out to share the thoughts and emotions of the charmer, because of all the people on the scene, he or she is the most perceptive and understanding one.

It is an exercise in the pragmatics of instant intimacy, and when it is brought into full focus upon someone of that naïveté resulting from inexperience or tender years, it can turn a supposedly impartial observer into a hot partisan: Partisanship will color what he or she writes or broadcasts about the contest, and writes or broadcasts about the skills and talents of the defense attorney. If the newsperson so seduced should happen to be highly competent in digging up facts useful to the defense, when there is no legal requirement for full disclosure, then the new convert is of considerable tactical use also.

In this regard it is interesting to note that the victim of the seduction is of maximum utility to the defense if, through the charm and persuasion of the defense attorney, he or she can become totally convinced of the innocence of the defendant. There is a certain irony in observing that the matter of guilt or innocence is of rather less moment to the average defense attorney in a capital case than it is to the partisans he gathers around him. His concern is with the evidence, and whether or not the State can prove its case beyond a reasonable doubt. Under our system a verdict of not guilty is not a verdict of innocence. It merely means not proven beyond a reasonable doubt.

Once a newsperson has been converted to a defense partisanship, this condition is obvious to the prosecution, and thus all flow of information aside from actual testimony is cut off.

For the impartial observer who can and does remain impartial, a certan amount of Machiavellian corruption is imperative if he is to keep the pipelines open and maintain the flow of tactical and strategic information from both the defense and the prosecution. It is not enough, unfortunately, to constantly affirm and prove one's impartiality and ability to keep one's mouth shut, not if there is the desire and the intent to observe and report a great deal more than the superficial and self-evident. One must appear to be defense-oriented in order to have access to the behind-the-scenes flavor of the preparation of the defense, and at the same time manage to convince the prosecution that one's apparent alliance with the defense team is a necessary gambit in pursuit of the goal of an eventual job of reportage in depth of a celebrity trial.

Yet because of the either-for-me-or-against-me flavor, any freedom to move between the two armed camps must be based upon being able to prove to each a certain usefulness, or there can be no dialogues of any intimacy whatsoever. The proof of loyalty is in talebearing, a grubby activity at best. One does not wish to assist either side, as objectivity cannot be achieved when one has become a part of the apparatus. The most acceptable procedure is to impart only those nuggets of information which one has discovered are already known to the adversaries. And it is well to be wary of any revelation from either side which might easily be false information which you are expected to take to the opposing team. Corruption is a suitable word because it becomes at last an exhausting exercise in guile, equivalent perhaps to the feats of memory, timing and deception necessary for a man to maintain two separate wives and families across town from each other.

Eventually one adversary will win and one will lose, and if the game of deception has been played out properly, the loser will come to believe you betrayed him, and the winner will believe he won in spite of your efforts to betray him. In such notorious trials the opponents lose all grasp on professional impartiality. Were they not highly competitive, they would be in some other line of work. Too often both reputation and future rest on the verdict. Intensity warps and distorts. The accused fades into the woodwork. And such is the compounding of suspicion of duplicity, that toward the end of such contests perhaps one would have to go back to the dinner parties given by the Borgias to find the same flavor.

This is not to be considered a critique of the operating methods of criminal lawyers or prosecuting attorneys under our present system of handling capital cases. You need only imagine yourself—regardless of your guilt or innocence—hiring a Bailey, a Belli, a Foreman to fight for your life. Would you wish him to use every weapon that comes to hand, from charm to deception to television appearances, to help save your life? Would you want a gladiator so motivated by his own pride and ego and hotly competitive spirit that the idea of loss becomes unthinkable? Or would you settle for a routine, sedate, unimaginative nine to five fellow who never becomes personally involved, and who, should the jury convict, would pick up his papers and say it was tough luck and walk away?

On the question of guilt and innocence, F. Lee Bailey told a story one morning at breakfast at the Sarasota Terrace Hotel. He said that there was a very moral and upstanding attorney in the Southwest who had a policy of never defending a guilty man. He was told that an Indian named Joe had been arrested and wanted to see him. He went to the jail and learned that Joe was charged with drunk and disorderly, assault, resisting arrest, and had done hundreds of dollars of damage to a local saloon. So he went to the cell block and interrogated Joe.

"Did you do all that, Joe?"

"No."

"Were you drunk?"

"No."

"How many drinks did you have?"

"One!"

"How big a drink was that, Joe?"

Joe held his hand up and measured a space between thumb and finger of about an inch and a half and said, "One drink! One!"

"Look me in the eyes, Joe. Do you *swear* you had just one drink?"

"Swear! One! One drink!"

So he took the case and put his client on the stand and after direct interrogation the district attorney took over.

"How many drinks did you have, Joe?"

"One!"

"How big a drink was it, Joe?"

Again the Indian held thumb and forefinger apart. "One drink!"

"Okay, Joe. What did you drink that drink *out* of?"

The Indian made a gesture with his arms like embracing a bear, and said, "Drum!"

Chapter Three

Mr. Schaub's first witness of the afternoon was the neighbor, Mr. George Thomson, and the direct examination was taken over by Mr. William Strode. Mr. Thomson was a construction superintendent involved in large-scale tract housing in the north before retiring to Florida. He was a florid big-boned man in his sixties who thought over each question before answering in a heavy, slow, well-articulated manner.

He said the Coppolinos had moved into their home right across the street a week or ten days after the Thomsons had moved in, and that they were quite friendly with them, and had visited back and forth a few times. Over one four-week period he said that Carl would come over alone three or four times a week just prior to the dinner hour and they would have a cocktail together.

On the morning of August 28, 1965, they had received a phone call from a Dr. Karow sometime between 6:15 and 6:45, informing them that Mrs. Coppolino had died, and would they come over. Knowing that Carl had had a series of heart attacks, Mr. Thomson asked Dr. Karow if she didn't mean Mr. Coppolino, and she said that it was Mrs. Coppolino who had passed away.

Thomson and his wife dressed quickly and went over.

"Doctor Carl Coppolino was sitting at a bullnose counter in the kitchen with his head in his hands."

"Who else was there?"

"Doctor Karow."

"At that time did you have any discussion with the defendant?"

"He said to me, 'Carm is dead. Carm is dead.' And that she had a massive coronary occlusion."

"Did he relate how he found her?"

"Yes, he said he had gotten up about five o'clock to go to the bathroom and found his wife dead."

"Did he relate any of the events of the preceding evening?"

"He said that he had gotten home about eleven o'clock that evening. He and Carmela had a nice talk. She said she would enjoy or would like a drink and he said he had made her a Black Russian."

Thomson explained that he had introduced Carmela to that drink on one occasion when they had been over at the Thomson home, and said that it was composed of vodka and coffee cordial or liqueur. Carl had said that after he had made Carmela the Black Russian they had a nice conversation and went to bed. Strode asked what had happened next.

"We spoke to Doctor Karow about the children and asked if the children knew. She said no, so my wife went in to tell the children that their mother had passed away, and we made arrangements then to take the children over to our house. They got their little bags packed and came over to our house."

(During the testimony in the hearings and the trials in the Coppolino matter there were rare times when a phrase or a sentence would suddenly seem to leap out from the labored give and take of examination, and create an extraordinarily vivid and lasting image. This was just such a moment, when that big elderly man with the sun-reddened face, protruding blue eyes, big hands of the ex-laborer, said without any sentimental emphasis whatsoever: "They got their little bags packed and came over to our house." At such times communication seems to find a new and more resonant level.)

Thomson testified that the original plan was for the children to stay with them for a while, but later that morning Carl said he thought it would be best to get the children out of the area and that somebody would be over to pick them up. He said the Thomsons had thought that a good idea at the time also. Mary Gibson picked them up.

"About what time in the morning did Mary Gibson pick the children up?"

"I would judge it to be around ten-thirty in the morning, or somewhere in there."

"Did the children seem to be acquainted with Mary Gibson?"

"Yes. They did. They called her by her first name and seemed happy to see her."

"Did Carl Coppolino thereafter spend any time in your house after the death?"

"Yes, he stayed at our house that Saturday night."

"Did you have any discussion with him that day concerning the funeral arrangements or anything of that nature?"

"Yes. He said that all funeral arrangements had been made and anticipated that burial would be the following Monday." He said he did not know what cemetery, but that it was to be a local burial.

"Was there any discussion about Carmela's family?"

"Yes, we had quite considerable discussion about whether her family knew about it, and he said no and he didn't want to tell them."

"Did this seem normal?"

(Here is a very apt example of the latitude which is permitted at a hearing where no jury is present. Had a jury been present it is not probable that Strode would have asked that question. And, if he had asked it, there would have been immediate outraged objection on the part of the defense, as the question calls for an opinion on the part of the witness, for a subjective evaluation of what is normal and what is not normal behavior. Of course, such objection could have been made at the hearing also, and would have certainly been sustained, but possibly the defense was interested in Thomson's attitudes and opinions as a possible guide to how best to handle him should he be a State witness in the Florida trial.)

"Not to me. We had discussion about them being very nervous and high strung and that sort of thing, so in the conversation it developed that there was a sister-in-law, Carmela's sister, and I asked if she was a pretty stable individual. He said she was. I suggested then that he get in touch with her and let her relate the information to the rest of the family."

"Were you and your wife both discussing this with him at the same time?"

"There were separate discussions and also discussions together. This discussion I just spoke about was between Doctor Carl Coppolino and myself. There were further discussions in our

40

home at the kitchen table, and he indicated that he didn't want to tell Carmela's family. Of course, my wife couldn't understand that at all." He said that both he and his wife—his wife particularly—urged Carl on that Saturday to tell Carmela's family of her death. Also, later on that same day, Thomson had driven Carl to Shannon's Funeral Home.

"When we got to the home Doctor Karow was there, and after the undertaker and Carl got through discussing the regular questions about background and Carmela's maiden name and that sort of thing, they went into another room. I would suppose they went in to select a casket. I asked Dr. Karow if there had been an autopsy. She said no, there had not been. Then after Carl Coppolino got through his discussions with the undertaker, going back to the car, crossing the parking lot I asked Carl if there had been an autopsy, and he said, 'Yes, it was a massive coronary.' "

"Did he say who did the autopsy?"

"No. I didn't pursue it any further."

"Do you know how Carmela's body happened to be shipped to New Jersey instead of the plans to have her buried here carried out?"

"Yes. Carl Coppolino told me there had been numerous phone calls with his in-laws in Jersey. They tried to prevail upon him to let them have the body up there and take care of funeral arrangements at that end. He said he was reluctant to fight with them on it, that he just couldn't take all that excitement."

"Did he attend the funeral after she was shipped north?"

"No."

"Did he stay here in Sarasota?"

"Yes."

"Did he ever go up north?"

"Several days later. I wouldn't be sure of the exact date, but it was several days later that he went up north."

"How do you know that he went up north?"

"He borrowed my bag for the trip."

Thomson then testified that on the evening of Sunday, August 29, a next-door neighbor named Norcross who had some business dealings with Carl came and asked Thomson if he knew where Carl was. Thomson said that he did not. Norcross used the telephone at the Thomson house and located Carl at Mary Gibson's house.

"During this first day or two after the death, did the defendant ever discuss remarriage in your presence?"

"Yes. He said that he thought it best that he get married right away."

Thomson said that he believed Carl had made that statement on Sunday morning, August 29. Asked about his observations of how much time Coppolino spent with his family, Thomson said that he knew Carl had been playing a lot of bridge afternoons and evenings at the Maxwell Bridge Studio because Carl had told him so. He said he did not know who Carl played with or against, and noticed nothing unusual in his attitude toward his wife and children except that he didn't seem to spend much time with them. Asked if he was gone a good part of the time or most of the time, Thomson answered, "A good part of the time. I wouldn't know about most of the time."

James "Red" McEwen took the cross-examination of George Thomson for the defense. Earlier in his career he had been the State Attorney for that Judicial Circuit which includes Tampa. He is a partner in the large Tampa law firm of Gibbons, Tucker, McEwen, Smith and Cofer. Of late years he has appeared more often as counsel for the plaintiff in civil suits for damages resulting from accidents than in other types of court cases. He has the reputation of being able to secure some unexpectedly sizable verdicts for his clients. Just into his sixties at the time of the Coppolino problem, the once carroty hair has turned to white, with just a trace of rust. He is a relaxed, amiable, soft-spoken man, with the sallow complexion and pale blue eyes of the red-head. He gives the impression of being more slender than he is. A Florida native, he can adjust the degree of "cracker" in his accent to fit his appraisal of the aggregate background of the jury. He has an ugly-likable face, an engaging grin, a considerable store of worldly wisdom about the foibles of the human creature, and tolerance to match the wisdom. He can, during examination, switch unexpectedly to the castigating severity and disapproval of the trained prosecutor. He is addicted to wearing in court various suits and sports jackets and slacks of astonishing contrast to the usual dark and subdued tailoring of the profession. Behind the soft voice, the accent, the leisurely manner in which he drifts across the courtroom—behind the gentle blue eyes and the warm smile there hides an exceptionally tough-minded and determined and proud man.

Under the unstressed and casual cross-examination George Thomson stated that Carmela had never discussed her health with him on any occasion, nor had Carl mentioned his own heart condition. He guessed that Carl had been playing bridge three or four months at the time of Carmela's death. The last time he had seen Carmela alive was on Friday morning, the morning before her death, when they had gone out to get their respective mail from the curbside mailboxes. Carmela had waved to him from across the street and he had waved back.

"Was Doctor Karow standing or sitting near you when you spoke to Doctor Coppolino and he told you that his wife had died from a massive coronary?"

"Doctor Karow was sitting on one side of the bullnose counter in the kitchen and Carl Coppolino was on the other side, and I was at the end of the bullnose."

"Did she take issue with that statement, that his wife died of a massive coronary?"

"No."

"Did she say anything either way?"

"No."

"Did you ask her?"

"I asked her at one point if there had been a history of heart trouble, and I believe she said that she understood that quite some time ago Carmela did have an attack."

He said that Carl had been there while he had that conversation with Dr. Karow on the morning of the death before they had taken the Coppolino children across the street to their home.

McEwen took Thomson back through the conversation with Karow in the funeral home, and with Carl while crossing the parking lot.

"Do you recall specifically whether he said one [an autopsy] had been performed, or thought one had been performed?"

"I recall specifically that he said one had been performed."

"Do you know whether he actually had been told that?"

"I don't know that."

"While you were talking to Doctor Karow at the funeral home, did she seem to be disturbed about the need for an autopsy?"

"No."

Here Frank Schaub objected on the grounds that McEwen was asking the witness to speculate as to the condition of the mind of Dr. Karow, but the objection was overruled.

Questioned further Thomson recalled that the body was shipped north either on the day of death, or on Sunday, the following day, and that Carl had gone north on the following Thursday or Friday. When Mr. McEwen asked if Carl was going to the home of Carmela's parents, Thomson said, "No. I don't think he was going to his [Dr. Musetto's] home. He told me he was going up north and intended to stay at a hotel or motel and he was going to call Doctor Musetto to let him know that he was there and have Doctor Musetto come over to see him, and that he was only going to stay one night."

Thomson was then asked how the subject of Carl's remarriage had come up when Thomson and his wife had been talking to Carl.

"He was asking what he should do, what he was going to do. My wife suggested that he just stay where he was for a while and possibly get a housekeeper to come in and take care of the children temporarily until he decided what his future plans would be."

Monica, said Thomson, was eight years old, and Lisa was two and a half or three. He said he had said nothing when Carl spoke of remarriage, and could not remember what his wife had said.

"When he was talking about the possibility of remarriage, did he say he might remarry to have someone to take care of the children?"

"Yes, he mentioned that."

Thomson had not heard any discussion of the possibility of a divorce, and knew of no difficulty between Carl and Carmela. When McEwen tried to ask him if any third person had attempted to tell him there was difficulty between the husband and wife, Schaub's objection was sustained. When McEwen tried to ask Thomson if he had ever discussed with Dr. Musetto any difficulty between the Coppolinos which might lead to a divorce, another objection on the grounds that it asked for hearsay was sustained.

Red McEwen finished by asking, "Within a period of a very few minutes you had two discussions about whether an autopsy had been performed. You mentioned it to Doctor Karow. She told you that none had been performed, and that was the first of the two statements. Then as you were leaving with Doctor Carl Coppolino, and Doctor Karow was not there, he told you that one had been performed. Did you take issue with him and say that you heard to the contrary?"

"No sir."

"Did you ever discuss that phase of it again?"

"No sir."

William Strode used a brief redirect only to elicit from George Thomson his opinion that when he and Carmela Coppolino had waved to each other while getting their mail from the curbside mailboxes, she had seemed to him to be in good spirits. He then called Shirley Thomson, George Thomson's wife, and in his direct examination of her brought out certain additions to her husband's testimony. Mrs. Thomson, mother of three daughters, and five times a grandmother, took the stand and sat primly there in white gloves and a starched white collar. Her face was narrow and sensitive, and she had the look of a person in rather poor health, an appearance later confirmed by her testimony, which accounted for her nervous manner and the appearance of the insomniac. As she awaited Strode's first question she seemed to be bracing herself for the performance of an unpleasant chore which, nonetheless, was a civic obligation and hence inescapable.

"Did you have a clear view of the Coppolino house from your home?"

"Oh yes."

"Did you ever have occasion at night or in fact late in the evening to observe the Coppolino home?"

"Yes I did."

"Did you ever notice anything unusual?"

"I noticed that the lights were on many a night until quite late because I was a very bad sleeper and I am up walking the floor a few times at night. I noticed the lights were on until early in the morning."

When she said she'd had occasion to observe the defendant in relationship to his family, Strode asked her if she had noticed anything unusual in his relationship or actions toward his family.

"I always felt he was detached from them. He didn't seem to care whether they were there or not. That was the feeling I got."

She said she could not say whether he spent a great deal of time away from his family as she did not watch his comings and goings. She said that it seemed to her that he was playing bridge every day and sometimes twice a day.

"How about the evenings? Did he play at night?"

"Yes, he was supposed to have been bridge-playing. I don't know."

"Are these some of the nights that you noticed the lights on late?"

"Yes . . . one-thirty and sometimes two o'clock. [The lights] On the garage and over the door and the porch lights were on outside."

When she would get up again and the house would be dark, she would presume he had returned home.

Strode took her through the events of the morning, repetitious of her husband's testimony up until she repeated how Carl had said he had gotten up at 5:00 to go to the bathroom and found Carmela was dead. He asked her if Carl was sleeping in the same bed with Carmela, and she said, "I imagine so." She said she was familiar with the bedroom and had entered the bedroom later on Saturday morning after Carmela's body had been removed.

"I went in and tidied up and changed the sheets and picked up the dirty towels. Not dirty but damp towels. And we put away Carmela's pocketbook and little things that we thought would be a reminder of her. We just sort of straightened up in general, although everything was in A-1 shape. Everything was immaculate."

She said that it was a double bed, and the sheets were clean, not soiled in any way, and she had not observed whether they were wrinkled or not. She said she had found the damp towels in the bathroom and put fresh ones up on the towel racks.

She confirmed her husband's testimony that Carl had stayed at their home just that one night, Saturday night, and said that after that she did not know where he stayed. He then asked her about the conversation about remarriage.

"At breakfast Sunday morning when I was giving him his breakfast he was saying what he should do. I suggested him getting a housekeeper. I suggested trying to get some Amish people. I thought they might be good, or some middle-aged woman that would come in and be glad to have a home. He said he couldn't go that way. He would just have to get married again."

"Did this seem unusual to you?"

"To say the least!" she said, snapping out the phrase with considerable emphasis. The Court sustained Bailey's request that the question and answer be deleted.

Establishing that she had not gone to the funeral home, Strode then asked her of Carl's attitude about notifying Carmela's family of the death.

"He just didn't want to. He wasn't going to tell anybody up north. He wasn't going to tell her parents or his parents—they would get too excitable and he wasn't going to go through with it. I told him he had to. How do you not tell a girl's parents that she is dead?"

She said she believed he planned to have a Mass said for her on Monday and bury her on Monday.

"Did you hear any of the discussions about whether Carl was going to attend her funeral up north?"

"He wasn't going to attend it. He said he had contacted his doctor up north and his doctor said it would be suicide—he just wasn't well enough." He did not mention the name of the doctor in the north, she said.

She said that when he did go up north just after the funeral and flew back the next day, "We volunteered to meet him at the airport. He said it was all taken care of. That was all I knew about that."

"Have you ever seen Carl Coppolino prior to the time he moved into your neighborhood in April of 1965?"

"Yes. I saw him when he was down buying the lot when we were also buying a lot."

"Who was with him?"

"Mrs. Farber."

"Who else?"

"No one. Just he and Mrs. Farber in the car."

"What were they doing?"

"Just sitting in the car. In fact, they were riding through laughing and talking and having a time."

"What was your impression?"

"Mr. Norcross had been trying to sell us the idea of buying the lot, of course, and he said, 'You are going to have two doctors living across the street with you, and by the way, this will be your new neighbor if you buy this lot.' This was Doctor Coppolino coming in the car. Seeing they were all laughing I said, 'That is nice. They look like a nice couple.' Norcross said, 'That isn't his wife. That is his next-door neighbor.' I thought that was kind of a swinging thing, and let it go."

She had hesitated for a moment, looking for the right phrase, and had half-smiled and then said, ". . . kind of a swinging thing . . ." The manner in which she said it brought immediate laughter from the spectators. There had been no trace of any malicious satisfaction or condemnation in her manner. Had there been, one could doubt that the laughter would have been as spontaneous. She had said it with a kind of rueful awe which underscored the incongruity of that phrase upon her lips. Judge Silvertooth, as soon as he could control his own smile, addressed the spectators, saying, "Ladies and gentlemen, as members of the public you are permitted to sit in the courtroom but not demonstrate by laughing concerning anything you hear during the case."

Red McEwen was unable to do very much with her on cross-examination. Only a few of her responses provided any information not already covered.

"But even with this staying out at the hours you have talked about, you know of no trouble between Carmela and Doctor Coppolino?"

47

"No. He never discussed any problems or ideas with us at all. She was a very reserved girl and we weren't that close."

"When he told you that he was not going to the funeral and also told you that the doctor had suggested that he not go, did this cause you to have any harsh feelings toward him?"

"No, I don't think so. I thought it was a little strange, but I also told him that his place was with the children. If he felt he should stay with the children I think they needed his care."

"These two people, Mrs. Farber and the doctor, didn't make any effort to conceal themselves from you?"

"No."

"When the doctor told you that he was not going to call the relatives, did he mention the fact that Carmela's father was suffering from a rather serious heart condition?"

"No, I don't remember that he did. I know he said that they were very excitable and he just dreaded telling them."

It was on Strode's redirect of but three questions that further information was developed.

"You said in response to Mr. McEwen's questioning that you didn't know of anything wrong between the Coppolinos. Did you feel everything was all right?"

"The only thing after that, I knew he went away for the weekend and left her with the children. We invited them into the pool at the Norcross home. We were taking care of their pool. She looked lonesome and had the kids. I said, 'Come in with us.' We suggested that she call Carl so we could all go for a swim. She said he was away. We wondered where he was—in fact, asked. She said she didn't know. 'He went away to think, so I let him go.' "

"Did you consider that normal?"

"Well, I think she should know where he was going."

"But she didn't know where he went?"

"She said she didn't know."

Mr. McEwen handled a deft recross in five questions:

"Do you know whether as a matter of fact that on the very same weekend Mrs. Coppolino actually went to where he was and saw him?"

"No. I didn't know that."

"Did you know that Doctor Coppolino did some writing?"

"Yes."

"And whether he was busy on one of his books at the present time or not you don't know?"

"I don't know anything about it."

"Do you know anything about how authors do act, whether they have to get away from others for a while?"

"I don't know anything about authors."

"You mean you got upset because he was gone on a weekend?"

"I didn't get upset. I thought it was a little bit strange that he left his wife and children and she didn't know where he was. For a man that has two years to live and has a heart condition and just goes off and doesn't let his wife know, I thought it strange. It didn't upset me."

The next state witness, also examined by Mr. Strode, was the pretty young blonde daughter of Mr. and Mrs. Earl M. Norcross, Pat Galenez. Pale burnished blonde hair cropped short, modeled to the shape of her head, with bangs to just above the level of dark brows. Quite lovely eyes, wide-set. A rather small, pinched and severe mouth.

She said she was now living in Miami, but at the time of Carmela's death she was with her parents at 527 Bowsprit Lane, next door to the Thomsons and almost across the street from the Coppolino home.

"Prior to August 28th, 1965, did you see Carmela Coppolino very often?"

"Yes. Practically every night."

"How about Carl Coppolino?"

"Not too often."

"Did you visit with Carmela in her home?"

"Yes. I used to have coffee with her."

"On these occasions was Carl Coppolino there?"

"Seldom. If so, just for a few minutes."

"In other words, those evenings that you had coffee and visited with Carmela every evening, Carl was gone every evening?"

"An hour a day I visited with her. Five-thirty to six-thirty."

"And did you say Carl was usually not there?"

"Usually not there."

"Did she say where he was?"

"I didn't ask."

"Were the children there?"

"Yes."

"Directing your attention to August 27th, 1965, did you see Carmela that day or that evening?"

"Yes."

"About what time did you see her?"

"I went over about six o'clock and stayed until nine-fifteen or nine o'clock." He asked her why she had stayed longer than usual. "We were watching television and she was finishing dinner with the children."

She testified that Carmela had not complained of any illness, had not complained of chest pains, that she seemed in very good spirits, and appeared to be in good health.

James Russ, the attorney from Orlando and also a former prosecutor, took the cross-examination of Miss Galenez. He appeared to be in his late thirties, medium stature, trim and fit, with a black brush-cut, good shoulders, a tanned, toughly handsome face. One might have expected him to have much the same style of interrogation as F. Lee Bailey, intimate, flexible, with a wide range of expression in both voice and face. But his was quite a different style. He spoke very loudly. He asked his questions in a great strong flat unemotional and unaccented voice which seemed to have the effect of obviating any possible personal contact between him and the witness. As he did not change expression, or alter the cadence of his voice, the questions seemed to have a substance of their own, as if they became a third entity, something projected into space by a device programed to place them there. The courtroom manner and habit of the successful attorney must always be the adjustment, through long experimentation, of ability to effectiveness. Everyone is well acquainted with how disconcerting it is to be at a social gathering and try to converse with someone who addresses you at close range in a voice you could hear distinctly in the next room. Such a technique must certainly give a courtroom attorney an advantage the witness cannot anticipate. The impact of the huge, flat, honking delivery, with each word given equal weight, spacing and perfect enunciation has the effect of decreasing rather than enhancing the witness's comprehension of what is being asked. It is as if one were to attempt to read a book with print so gigantic that each page would contain only one word. One can also assume that such delivery is a delight to the court reporter, as it approximates the speed of delivery on the phonograph records used by learners.

After establishing that she was teaching school in the Miami area, Russ asked, "MISS GALENEZ, WOULD YOU TELL US THE TIME PERIOD WHEN YOU FIRST BECAME ACQUAINTED WITH MRS. COPPOLINO UP TO THE TIME OF HER PASSING AWAY IN AUGUST OF NINETEEN SIXTY FIVE?"

"I can give just a summation. I arrived here August 22nd, and I think maybe once or twice before I met Doctor and Mrs. Coppolino when I was home from college on the weekend. After I got down here on the 22nd I talked to her several times and had coffee with her in the late afternoon and early evening."

"So then actually the greater part of your contact with Mrs. Coppolino took place between the 22nd of August and the 28th of August 1965. Is that correct?"

"Yes."

"Were you at her house *every* afternoon between five-thirty and six-thirty P.M. during this span of five days?"

"I could not say every day. Quite often."

"Can you tell us what your best estimate is as to the number of times you were at her home in this late afternoon visit between the 22nd and the 27th of August of 1965?"

"I couldn't give an estimation. Quite a few times especially during the last two weeks. I was over there practically every night."

Miss Pat seemed to be growing increasingly uneasy, her previous certainty and assurance becoming increasingly frail.

"Did I understand you to stay initially that you came home on the 22nd of August, 1965?"

"Twenty-first of August."

"From the 21st to the 27th of August does your arithmetic give you about six afternoons?"

"Yes."

"I would like to know if you would tell us out of these six afternoons your best estimate as to the number of these . . ."

"Five or six times. An estimate."

Russ then established through her testimony that during these five or six visits she and Carmela had not discussed the state of Carmela's health, that on no occasion did she take her evening meal with the family, but they ate three or four times when she was present. She related that on the evening of Friday the 27th she had arrived as they were finishing dinner, and she thought it was hamburger steak, but she said she could not really remember. When she left at nine-fifteen, Carmela was just putting the children to bed and she walked Pat Galenez to the door. No one else had been there but she and Carmela and the children.

Russ said he had no further questions but said that the defense had subpoenaed her and wished her to stay as a witness. The Court asked her to remain in the witness room.

It is not improper at this time to make some conjectures about

51

the testimony of Pat Galenez, conjectures which have no bearing upon the portion of her testimony of value to the prosecution, the portion which concerns the behavior and demeanor of Carmela Coppolino on the evening before her death. It could not be considered significant to the state's case how often the girl had visited the Coppolino home, but only that she knew Carmela well enough to have gone there and spent approximately three hours with her on the eve of her death.

Quite obviously the sudden and unexpected death of Carmela Coppolino came as a horrid shock to the young college girl who lived just down the street. It is equally obvious that close and enduring friendships require more than five or six brief visits over the span of six days to bring to full flower.

Pat Galenez (guh-LAY-ness) identified with Carmela Coppolino in the same way that countless young girls have identified with young married women in their neighborhoods. It is a kind of "trying on" of life, to visit and see more clearly than one can see in their own home the actual shape and dimension of the words married and children and wife and homemaker.

"We were close friends. I was over there all the time."

This is part of the process of identification. It is the way the young test their own emotional capacities and visions.

There is no harm in it, nor intent to harm. Sudden death could dramatize and, in retrospect, enhance the identification. And to Pat it was a very real and very lasting thing. Death stamped it more deeply on mind, memory, and emotion.

Of course she had no possible way of knowing that many months later this identification and affirmation would involve her in the official investigation into the death of Carmela Coppolino. Nor could she have guessed that the death could have been anything other than what it seemed—a sudden, tragic heart attack.

And that, of course, was the advantage which James Russ sought and took in his cross-examination of the girl.

Though her words implied a closeness and a friendship between Pat and Carmela, Russ caught her between the cruel strictures of the calendar, and established the total relationship as having occurred during those very few days between Pat's return from school and the last evening of Carmela's life.

By focusing upon the brevity of the relationship he was thus able to give it the flavor of brief and casual acquaintanceship, as distinct from the long, warm, intimate friendship which shadowed Pat's testimony.

This, of course, is one of the harsh and necessary facets of the art of cross-examination, to so pin happenings down to the actual specifics of them that whatever coloration inadvertently enters the testimony being given is carefully peeled away until, finally, the relationship appears far more trivial and meaningless than even the actual testimony avows.

Cross-examination will always deal bluntly with even the hint of subjective evaluations.

The strategy is quite apparent, of course. If by cross-examination a witness can be brought to the point of abandoning all subjective evaluations, then there is created the false impression that the actual testimony has changed during cross-examination, even though it does in truth remain the same.

The *impression* of change, of retreat from an established position, of dwindling the weight of a relationship can, in turn, serve the adversary purpose of casting a small cloud of doubt across the total weight of the factual testimony given, testimony which remained unchanged during direct and cross-examination.

And another aspect of this technique is just as apparent. It is usually quite distressing to a witness to be restricted to an ever narrowing factual area and deprived of the chance to include those emotional tones which to the witness, and to almost everyone, have more of the flavor of truth than do the actual facts at issue.

Frank Schaub conducted the direct examination of the next witness for the state, Dr. Edmund Leslie Webb, who stated that he was an anesthesiologist licensed to practice medicine and was associate director of the E. R. Squibb & Sons laboratories. Webb was in his middle thirties, a slender, small-boned man of medium height with a slender, sensitive, intelligent face, careful barbering and tailoring, an air of watchful self-possession on the stand, considerable precision of speech in an accent typical of the Briton who has been educated in the United States.

Mr. Schaub moved swiftly to the testimony most significant to the state's case. After establishing that Webb was acquainted with Carl Coppolino, he asked, "Have you ever furnished him with any medicines or drugs?"

"Yes, I have."

"What drugs?"

"Pronestyl, vitamins and succinylcholine." (SUCK-sin'l-KO-lean)

"When did you send him succinylcholine?"

"On two occasions. One was early in 1963, and the second one was July 21st, 1965."

"At whose request were they sent to him?"

"He wrote a letter stating his interest in doing some research."

"Did he state the nature of the research?"

"He wished to work with succinylcholine to see if it could be detected in the body of a cat."

"How much of this did you send him on July 22nd of 1965?"

"There were six bottles. Twenty-eight hundred milligrams."

"Would you please describe to us what succinycholine is?"

"It is a muscle relaxant drug. It is used in anesthesiology for the purpose of making the surgical field more convenient for the surgeon. It is sometimes used in the practice of psychiatry."

"Were you acquainted with Carmela Coppolino?" He testified that he was, and that he had met them both at the same time when they had come to intern at the Methodist Hospital in Brooklyn when Dr. Webb had been in his first year of residency at the hospital. Asked if he saw a great deal of them, Webb replied, "Oh yes. We lived together, shall I say, for almost a year . . . Carmela left the hospital in 1959 but Carl stayed on for some years and I saw him frequently." He said he had visited their home on several occasions and they his, that they had talked of medicine, and he had never heard any comment about Carmela's having any heart condition. Mr. Schaub then relinquished the witness to Mr. Bailey for cross-examination.

Lee Bailey asked Dr. Edmund Webb one hundred and forty-four questions during his cross-examination. In both the New Jersey and the Florida trials there is a considerable amount of testimony regarding the use and properties of succinylcholine chloride, and much of it is a repetition of the testimony given in this cross-examination. This confrontation between Bailey and Webb is used as the definitive description of the drug and what it does, with this cross-examination condensed wherever it has proved possible to do so without warping the essential balance of the testimony.

Bailey conducted the cross-examination without notes. He asked his questions swiftly and Webb made immediate reply. In swiftness, control, and as an example of how thoroughly the trial attorney must absorb disciplines alien to his training, it is a classic example of a cross-examination of an expert witness in a highly technical area.

Webb stated that part of his duties at the Squibb laboratories was to review the literature that accompanies the drugs to physicians, that the Squibb brand name for succinylcholine is Sucostrin, and that it is produced by other pharmaceutical houses under other trade names, one being Anectine. Bailey asked him to explain what happens when an injection of succinylcholine is made intravenously into the human body.

"First of all a weakness develops. This weakness usually starts at the head and shoulders, the arms and legs, and this is closely followed by a complete relaxation if the dose is sufficient."

"Is it possible for a person who has just received an intravenous injection to walk or move?"

"It would depend on what you mean by just received. I would estimate there would be a period of 15 or 20 seconds where you would be fully capable of walking."

"An intramuscular injection is absorbed and takes effect much more slowly?"

"Correct."

"By the way, this is called a depolarizing drug?"

"Yes."

"When this is taken [injected] into the bloodstream what happens to it?"

"It is hydrolyzed. It is destroyed rather rapidly. The effect, providing the dose is not excessive, is very brief."

"What is an excessive dose?"

"Any dose more than recommended."

"What dosage is recommended by Squibb as the maximum?"

"Intermittent injection of 30 to 90 milligrams. This may be repeated."

"Succinylcholine will cause a block at the myoneural junction?"

"Yes."

"Is this drug used in chest surgery to keep the patient from bucking?"

"Yes."

"Succinylcholine is not used as a substitute for anesthesia?"

"No."

"Something else must be used in order to prevent the sensation of pain?"

"That is right."

"Now, is it not so that one who has been injected with succinylcholine is not able to breathe because of paralysis of the mechanism which operates the lungs?"

"If sufficient is given, yes."

"And it is common practice for anesthesiologists to breathe for the patient while the drug is taking effect and until that effect dissipates?"

"Yes."

"If the physician or anesthesiologist does not breathe for the patient the patient will suffocate?"

"The respiration would cease, yes."

"Death would eventually follow?"

"That would depend on the period of no breathing."

"Would succinylcholine chloride alone cause unconsciousness prior to the time that the brain lost consciousness for lack of oxygen?"

"No."

"In other words, although an injection were received the person would remain conscious after the time that it took effect and the lungs were paralyzed, or at least as long as you could hold your breath. Is that correct?"

"That has been shown to be true."

"The sensation felt by one injected and thus paralyzed by succinylcholine would be one of suffocating, unable to get air. Isn't that correct?"

"I don't think I have ever spoken to one who has been under those circumstances."

"I understand. But physically the lungs are unable to take oxygen or to exhale?"

"Yes."

"So the reaction would be similar to that of a man who has a great weight on his chest and he can't operate his lungs? In other words, a reactive gasping for oxygen in a conscious patient?"

"Sounds very logical. He would not be able to gasp."

"There is very little research on succinylcholine on its effect on people except under controlled situations in hospitals during surgery?"

"That is right."

"Have you done some experimentation yourself in this area with animals?"

"No."

Bailey then asked what amount is necessary for a given period of paralysis, and Webb said that it is very difficult to determine that exactly. The weight of the patient would be a factor. In giving intramuscular injections to children the recommended dosage is one and a half milligrams per pound. Bailey asked him how quickly the drug hydrolized, meaning how quickly it would break down in the bloodstream into its separate chemical components.

"Very rapidly. It is destroyed in two processes. First succinylcholine (succinyl-di-choline) is changed to succinyl-mono-choline fairly rapidly and to succinic acid, which is a longer process."

[At this point some oversimplified chemistry is helpful to understand Webb's answer. The drug before injection is a com-

56

plex molecular linkage which contains two molecules of choline and one molecule of succinic acid. They are combined to form the more complex molecule of succinyl—di (meaning two) —choline. To hydrolyze means to break down into the simpler molecular forms which were originally combined in the laboratory to make the basic drug. He said that fairly rapidly the drug would lose one molecule of choline, and thus become succinyl—mono (meaning one)—choline. And then, over a longer period, this new compound would separate into one molecule of choline and one molecule of succinic acid.]

"Eventually all that will be found in the bloodstream of the person will be succinic acid and choline?"

"I don't know that."

"Have you read the book by Doctor Foldes on muscle relaxants?"

"I know much of his work. I don't believe I have read a book on it."

"Have you ever heard as a doctor that succinylcholine does break down into succinic acid and choline?"

"Yes. I have heard that succinic acid is a natural body chemical."

"And the same for choline?"

"Yes."

"Do you know any chemical compound which may be found in a body that has received an injection of succinylcholine chloride that would not be found in the normal body?"

"That takes me beyond my research or knowledge. I know of none."

"Do you say that a large overdose of this drug would cause some remnants to show that might be determined by a pathologist or toxicologist?"

"I understand from the literature a certain proportion is excreted under changes in the urine. If this would be found in the urine this would be prima facie evidence that the drug had been given."

"Following intravenous injection will any of the components of the drug be absorbed in tissue so that in a body that has been embalmed it still will be found?"

"I don't know the answer . . . We have never researched it. I know that certain studies indicate that under radioactivity succinylcholine may be found in the tissue."

"Now—with respect to intramuscular [injection], do you know whether or not any recognizable and strange chemical—and I

57

mean by strange, not in the normal body—is found in the tissue or muscle following death?"

"I don't know."

"Is it fair to say that, as a doctor employed as you are, there is no answer to this question?"

"We have never deliberately killed animals to find out."

Bailey switched then to the two occasions when Webb had delivered succinylcholine to Dr. Coppolino. Webb said he had a record on the second shipment, but that the first was delivered by hand by Dr. Webb in the early part of 1963 and he could not remember the month. Webb said that he was aware at that time that Coppolino was not working because of a heart condition. He said he had given Coppolino one thousand milligrams of Anectine, a dry powder form of succinylcholine, which when mixed with water would form one thousand cubic centimeters to be given by injection. Webb testified that regarding the 1965 shipment Dr. Coppolino said that he wanted to kill a cat. He said that the request came in a personal letter which he had put aside and had been unable to find, but to the best of his recollection he had gotten the letter in June of 1965, toward the beginning of the month. He had ordered the succinylcholine to be sent on July first, and it had actually been shipped on July 23.

Bailey asked him what the shipment consisted of.

"Four bottles of Sucostrin [sue-KOSS-trin], two hundred milligrams each, and two bottles, a thousand milligrams each."

Each bottle, he said, had contained the same amount of fluid, ten cc's, so that four of the bottles had a strength of twenty milligrams per cc, and two had a strength of a hundred milligrams per cc.

"The twenty milligram strength is intended for intravenous injection. The hundred milligram strength is intended to add to dextrose or saline for intramuscular injection."

Webb explained that the intramuscular injection would act the same as the intravenous injection, but more slowly.

"What would you say would be the time from the actual discharge of the needle into the muscle that breathing would stop?"

"Between seventy-five seconds and three minutes. There may be a few more moments before respiration is depressed."

"How long does it take a dose of succinylcholine, just one shot received intravenously, to cause paralysis of the lungs?"

"Paralysis of the lungs is very difficult to answer. It really does depend on the dose. We say it is brief. It may be from one minute to five minutes."

"When it is necessary to paralyze the lungs or muscles in that area for surgical purposes, is it not common practice to give an intravenous drip?"

"Yes."

"And that is because the initial injection given tends to break down too rapidly until the surgery is complete? Is that right?"

"That is right."

"In order to cause death, are you able to say what size injection it would take, how many cc's in, say, a healthy 32-year-old woman of 120 pounds, intravenously?"

"I can tell you what an approximate dose would be to cause a cessation of respiration. I don't know whether it would cause death."

"What would cause loss of respiration?"

"Intravenously, 90 milligrams."

"How long will the sensation last?"

"Probably a minute to two minutes."

"And during this time, and as a matter of fact, from the very moment it was taken into the bloodstream, it would begin to hydrolyze?"

"That is so."

"As it hydrolyzes it loses the ability to block the junction?"

"Yes."

"No matter how much is injected at one time it all hydrolyzes (breaks down into succinic acid and choline) at the same rate?"

"I don't know that. I would not suspect it to be true."

"You mean the more of the drug received within a given bloodstream the longer it takes for the system to hydrolyze it?"

"I would say it is in proportion to the amount given."

"In order to cause paralysis for, say, ten minutes, would you say a very large injection would be necessary?"

"It would have to be I would say by infusion or by intramuscular. I don't think you could do it [otherwise]."

Identifying infusion as a slow, intravenous drip directly into the blood vessel, Bailey said, "In other words, no matter how much of this drug was administered in one shot into the bloodstream, paralysis for as long as ten minutes would not occur because of the hydrolyzation of the drug?"

In 1959 at Yellowstone National Park the Craighead brothers began a series of scientific studies of grizzly bears that continued for several seasons.

The problem was to immobilize the bears so that they could be measured, weighed, marked, then fitted with collars containing small radio transmitters which gave off a constant signal so that, by triangulation their patterns of movement around Yellowstone could be traced.

The early solution was the use of a gas-operated rifle shooting a projectile syringe of Sucostrin.

Speaking of one of the early ones thus immobilized, Dr. Frank Craighead said, "The bear was constantly growling and moving spasmodically. It was like working over dynamite with a damp fuse."

While the bears were immobilized, the ears were slit and colored tags were fastened through the slits so that the bears could be identified at a distance. The date and identifying number of the animal was tattooed under the front leg.

Later, after the immobilization by Sucostrin, the bears were then given a second injection of another drug to render them unconscious while this work was done.

"Probably not."

"What quantity of the drug [intramuscularly] would it take to paralyze the lungs for ten minutes?"

"I don't think I would have any way of knowing that."

"These injections, in good medical practice, are not given intramuscularly?"

"It is preferred intravenously because you can predict the action."

Going then back to the shipment to Carl Coppolino in July of 1965, in response to Bailey's questions Webb said that Carl had explained that he wanted to do some research on cats, to find out whether there was evidence that succinylcholine was (could be) detected in the bodies of cats after death.

"Did he tell you anything about the effort to determine the amount of succinylcholine that should be given to a given weight of body in order to find the length of paralysis?"

"No, he did not."

"Well, as a doctor, are you aware that there is a problem among anesthesiologists as to the correct dosage of a drug of this sort?"

"Yes."

"In order to have enough paralysis, but not be stuck with it long after the operation with a patient not breathing?"

"That is true."

"Is it not true that despite the literature there is a vagueness for the precise formula for the amount of drug for a given situation?"

"That depends upon experience and discretion."

"And whether or not there has been, to your knowledge, no complaint or concern by anesthesiologists who are unnecessarily held in an operating room while waiting for a patient to come around from an overinjection?''

"It does happen."

Bailey again reverted to the shipment to Dr. Coppolino. Webb said he had seen Carl and Carmela in March, just before they had moved to Florida. Through a series of questions Bailey established that Coppolino had requested the drug openly, had made no attempt to have Webb conceal his request in any way, or refrain from mentioning it. Webb said the drug was available generally to doctors and hospitals, used frequently in various kinds of surgery, was not rare, was not a narcotic, and thus sales of it did not have to be reported to any special agency. He established that an anesthesiologist could walk into a drug supply firm and pick it up without making a record.

Webb related what contact he had had with Carl Coppolino after sending the drug. He said he'd had two or three letters from Carl, with no reference to the drug in them. Carl had called Webb's office the day after Carmela's death to tell Webb of her death, but Webb had not been in and the secretary had taken the message. Webb had tried to call him back that night but had not been able to get in touch with him, and did not think he had spoken to Coppolino since. Nor, since the death of Carmela, had Coppolino gotten in touch with him in any way for the purpose of asking him to forget about the succinylcholine transaction.

Dr. Webb had copies of the shipping orders of all shipments made from Squibb to Coppolino in the folder he had taken with him to the witness stand. He stated that he had been approached by law enforcement authorities and questioned about the drug transaction, the effects of the drug and its traceability, but had not been approached by anyone representing the defendant.

He testified that since he had first been questioned about this matter, he had not conducted any tests on the drug, nor had he been requested to. But he had had conversation with the medical authorities conducting such tests—Dr. Helpern and Dr. Umberger—and he had furnished them with Squibb's Sucostrin for their tests.

Frank Schaub took Dr. Webb again for redirect. Mr. Bailey objected to the first question and was overruled. The question was, "Would it have done any good for Doctor Coppolino to hide the shipments that you sent him if you were put under oath?''

When Mr. Schaub rephrased it, it was still not clear to Dr. Webb what he meant. He tried a third time. "In other words, if the defense counsel alluded to a failure of the defendant to ask you to keep secret the fact that the shipments . . . In other words, you told him that you had received no request to keep it secret. If such a request had been made it would have had no effect on you?"

"They would not have been shipped."

Schaub then asked about any precautionary measures in the use of the drug appearing in the brochures.

Webb said there were two main precautions. "One is the respiration may be depressed, and unless respiration is supported there is a danger of the drug having a bad effect. The second is that depending on physical conditions it may prolong the action of this drug."

Schaub then ran into difficulty when he used the expression "toxic dose." Webb said it was the purpose of the drug to render a person immobile.

"Will that [an overly large dose] have an effect, intramuscular or intravenous, of taking approximately the same length of time to cause death as would be caused in that same person due to a lack of oxygen?"

"I have no way of knowing that. . . . The larger the dose which is given, either intravenously or intramuscularly, one may expect a larger effect. Nevertheless, the length of cessation of respiration is not proportional to the dose. It depends on how healthy the person would be. It depends on physical conditions. I wouldn't know when to say that death would result. I can only say when the maximum muscular relaxation would occur."

Schaub reverified the amount of the drug shipped, and finished his redirect. On recross Lee Bailey again asked what Carl Coppolino had said he intended to use the drug for.

"He wanted to see if it could be detected in the bodies of cats."

"Didn't he say, in fact, that he wanted to run experiments on various animals to determine the quantity present in certain muscles when the patient was under anesthesia?"

"No." And then Bailey ascertained that Webb recalled being interviewed on August 16 by a man from Bailey's office named Andrew Tuney, but could not recall precisely what was said. Bailey handed him what was most probably Tuney's report on the interview. Webb examined the pages and said, "This last portion was never mentioned in my presence."

"That is not your recollection," Bailey corrected. "Now, would you examine the last page?"

Webb did so and said, "It states that I experiment with

animals. I do not personally experiment. We have biologists and Ph.D.'s who do the animal work."

"And the promulgation of information is your responsibility in the final analysis?"

"Yes."

"So the experiments, I take it, are performed to your satisfaction?"

"Yes."

"You say you don't have the letter Carl wrote you requesting the drug?"

"I do not."

"It was discarded?"

"I would rather say I put it somewhere."

"Misplaced?"

"Misplaced, not discarded."

"Do you think you might find it in the future?"

"Yes. I feel one day it will turn up."

"I hope it is in time. No further questions."

Chapter Four

The state's final witness for that first day of the preliminary hearing was Dr. Milton Helpern, Chief Medical Examiner of the City of New York, that white-haired veteran of dozens of capital cases, businesslike as he took the stand, totally at ease, an affable grandfather-image superimposed upon a great professional dignity.

Frank Schaub took him through a lengthy routine of qualification which, as there was no jury present—or even if there had been—F. Lee Bailey could have terminated at any moment by rising to stipulate that the defense would accept Dr. Helpern as an expert in pathology and forensic medicine. But this was the first time Lee Bailey had ever seen Dr. Helpern. He sat at the defense table and watched and listened to the elderly doctor in much the same manner that a clean-up hitter might watch a new pitcher throw his warmup pitches.

Cornell Medical College, Bellevue Hospital, Assistant Medical Examiner, Deputy Medical Examiner, then Chief since 1954. Professor and Chairman of Forensic Medicine at the New York

University School of Medicine. Certified by the American Board of Pathologists. Member and past president of the New York Pathological Society. Fellow of the College of American Pathologists. Fellow and past president of the American Academy of Forensic Medicine.

And at last Mr. Bailey said, with a little nod and smile at the doctor, "Being from the northeast, I seem to have heard of Doctor Helpern. I think we can stipulate to his expertise in pathology."

Under Schaub's examination Dr. Helpern stated that his office had begun a post-mortem investigation, under his supervision and control, into the cause of death of Carmela Coppolino on December 17, 1965, and that the conclusion concerning the cause of death was finally determined in June of 1966. The post-mortem examination had disclosed no natural disease in the body. The heart was found to be completely normal. There had been no prior autopsy on the body, and no indication of prior surgery. An autopsy and toxicological examination were made.

When Schaub asked for Dr. Helpern's conclusion, Bailey said emphatically, "Objection! I don't think there is a foundation sufficient for that at this time unless we are told what was done and whether this man did it."

Judge Silvertooth said, to the witness, "You stated that you performed this autopsy yourself?"

"Yes, Your Honor."

"Overruled."

Bailey said, "I don't think he performed the toxicology. I would like to know if he is relying on his own observations or what was told him."

Frank Schaub said to the Court, "It was done under his direct supervision and he performed the autopsy."

"Overruled," said the Court, and Dr. Helpern stated his conclusion.

"After the completion of the autopsy and the study of all the organs and tissues, which included a microscopic study as well as a naked-eye examination, and after a consideration of the complete toxicological examination which was carried out in a toxicological division of our agency . . ."

"May I interrupt?" Frank Schaub said. "Was this toxicological examination conducted by professional chemists or medical doctors?"

When Helpern said that they were not physicians, but trained chemists, Schaub again asked for his conclusion as to the cause of death.

"I concluded that the cause of death was an injection of succinylcholine."

Dr. Helpern said he had formed the opinion that she did not die of coronary occlusion. He said the findings that he had given as the cause of death were consistent with the determinations of the autopsy.

"And were they consistent with the toxicological findings?"

"Well, the conclusion was based on the autospy and the toxicological findings."

He said that she was capable, at the time of death of having menstrual periods, and the reproductive system was normal.

"The autopsy was carried out in the usual manner, and it was a complete autopsy in which all parts of the body were explored and examined. This included the systematic examination of all the body organs, the neck organs, the skull and brain, and all of the body cavities, the extremities, the back as well as the front of the body. And as a result of the autopsy it was determined that the organs were all in normal condition. The only abnormal finding in the autopsy was a puncture wound, a needle puncture in the left buttock that extended into the subcutaneous fat. This was the only abnormality."

"Directing your attention to that abnormality, could this puncture wound have been consistent with an injection by a hypodermic needle?"

"Yes."

"I will ask you, in consideration of the size of this puncture wound and the location of it, in your opinion would this have been the result of a hypodermic needle self-inflicted?"

"That is a difficult question to answer. I would say that from the direction of the track, from the location of the wound, that it would not be the site of a self-inflicted puncture."

Schaub then asked about the toxicological examination.

"A complete toxicological examination was carried out. All the organs were submitted to the chemist, including the brain and liver, and I would say most of the organs were submitted to the routine analysis for ordinary toxic substances, such as sleeping pills, narcotics, metals, the various substances that one routinely looks for. This portion of the analysis was carried out very extensively, and nothing was found. And ordinarily this would have been the completion of the toxicological examination. However, on the basis of information that we received, further examinations were made, particularly for succinylcholine, and after a very tedious analysis I received a report from the chemist that this substance was found, or that the component portions of this substance were found.''

"Was anything disclosed by either your autopsy or this lengthy toxicological examination that indicated a cause of death other than one resulting from the administration of succinylcholine?''

"No. No other cause of death was found.''

Consider, then, the dimension of the problem faced by F. Lee Bailey as he arose to question Dr. Milton Helpern. Attorneys who were not connected with the case and were interviewed subsequent to the hearing stated that Frank Schaub could have shown sufficient probable cause by putting only Karow, Musetto, Webb and Helpern on the stand—all doctors, incidentally. After such testimony, Bailey's attention certainly was directed toward the shape and strategy of the defense in the anticipated Florida trial, and his purposes could best be served through achieving the maximum of discovery in his cross-examination and through eliciting, both by chance and by design, statements from any and all state witnesses which might later be of value if they differed in any significant degree from the testimony these same persons might give before a jury when far less latitude would be permitted by either side.

As with all previous witnesses, as soon as the state had released them for cross-examination, Frank Schaub moved to his habitual place, about fifteen feet in front of the bench, and about fifteen feet from that end of the jury box nearest the witness stand. He would stand there facing each witness, along the diagonal of a triangle formed by the witness, the usual position of the defense attorney near the jury rail, and Schaub's observation point. He would stand with his hands behind him, left hand clamped on his right wrist, chin lowered so that he looked out from under the projecting bony ridge of brow. It was his habit to rock slightly back and forth, heel to toe, and any tension he felt was betrayed by the way he worked the fingers of his right hand, constantly extending the fingers and clenching them again into a fist.

From that vantage point, when Lee Bailey would interrupt his examination to go to the defense table and return with a document for the witness to examine, Frank Schaub would move forward too, a half step behind him, and to Bailey's left, craning his neck to see and identify what document it might be which, after identification, Bailey might offer in evidence.

As Lee Bailey did not use notes during cross-examination, it was plausible that when he did have a sheet of paper in his hand, he was going to show it to the witness. Aware of Schaub's habit, Lee Bailey, while questioning Dr. Edmund Webb had gone to the defense table and picked up some random piece of paper and, studying it, had walked toward the witness stand. Frank Schaub had fallen in step with him and followed him, trying to see down over Bailey's shoulder. But, a foot or two from the witness stand, Bailey stopped and moved back toward the jury box railing, so quickly that it left Frank Schaub standing near Webb, looking startled.

Bailey with a look of great astonishment, brows raised, stared at Schaub and said, "You wanted something?"

Frank Schaub, his ears red, shook his head and moved back to his customary post. It was a deft little trick, designed to irritate Frank Schaub and make him look foolish. And one might suppose that, entirely aside from the increasing antagonism the two attorneys felt toward each other, such a tactic might have some cumulative value, as the adrenalin of anger does not improve any man's intellectual ability.

So F. Lee Bailey walked across the red carpeting under the constant harshness of the fluorescent panels, a tidy thoughtful lion in a den of Daniels, perhaps realizing that the testimony of Milton Helpern—plus the fact that it *was* the fabled Milton Helpern giving it—constituted the biggest obstacle to a successful defense of his client. Frank Schaub positioned himself. Milton Helpern looked expectantly, and perhaps warily, benign.

"Are you a chemist?" asked Lee Bailey.

"No."

"Then I take it that the conclusion that you gave this court is in fact a conclusion of your chemist, Doctor Umberger?"

"May I explain? The chemist reported what he found, and his report, being positive as it was, is not necessarily conclusive of the cause of death. The responsibility for concluding about the cause of death is that of the pathologist who does the post-mortem examination. I might explain that toxicological examinations are only part of a post-mortem examination."

"Then apart from the report that you got from your chemist, what did you find as evidence of the remnants of succinylcholine?"

"I found a normal body, a puncture wound and a track in the buttock and nothing else."

"Then from your own findings you can't say what went in the pucture wound?"

"That is correct, as far as naked-eye examination of the tissues. As far as microscopic examination of the tissues, I could not conclude what had been injected or introduced into this body. That was determined by the chemist, and on the basis of his determination I made my own conclusion."

Establishing that the chemist was Joseph Umberger, and that he had not accompanied Dr. Helpern to Sarasota, Bailey asked if he might see Helpern's report.

"I might say that his report was made to me orally. I was following this case very closely, and although I have a copy of this report, it is not the report in writing that has led me to this conclusion. I have been in consultation with him on many occasions concerning the findings in this case. In other words, this is (not) just a routine type of procedure where you see a report and you include it in the findings."

[In many instances in direct quotations from the official transcript of the hearing, words inadvertently altered or omitted are shown in parentheses. This is one of the few instances where a key word—(not)—was omitted, thus changing the entire intention of the statement by the witness.]

Dr. Helpern had opened his bulging briefcase on his lap and put on his half-lens granny glasses and dug out a document of two sheets stapled together and handed it to Mr. Bailey, along with another document. Bailey remarked that the second sheet on one document was torn. Helpern said it was not torn, that there had been nothing on the bottom of the sheet. "Why was it removed?" asked Bailey.

The question had a clear imputation of some kind of deception or subterfuge. It implied that the noted Milton Helpern would indulge in hanky-panky. Stung, Helpern said with indignant petulance, "For the reason it got creased and really fell off that report, and all that it has on it is the same that you have on the other report there. I think this is the same one. It is a copy of a portion of this one."

Bailey, looking at the three reports, asked what it was in those reports that justified the conclusion of an evidence of the drug in the body. He stood by the witness stand holding the reports so that Helpern could point out portions of them and they could both read them.

"In this report with this listing, and I might say that these are the work sheets that were prepared by Doctor Umberger and prepared in front of me at the time the report was completed. You will see that the succinic acid is marked positive. It comes out in this particular fraction of ratio, and also the choline that is marked positive. This . . . plus this . . . was interpreted as evidence of succinylcholine in the body. You will notice that all of the other analyses are essentially negative except for the fact that certain substances were found which are constituents of the embalming fluid and that is about all. Everything else was negative."

"I notice that the report has been altered apparently more than once."

"Not altered," said Helpern, obviously annoyed at the use of that particular word.

"Typing scratched out and something else written in."

"Corrected. That is right, and that is the original report."

Following is the text of the typed report (Lab #C5415/65) as originally prepared and submitted to Dr. Milton Helpern by Charles Joseph Umberger, Ph.D., Chief of the Toxicological Section:

> Liver and brain tissue removed at autopsy from Dr. Carmela Coppolino showed chemical findings for both choline and succinic acid. Control cases examined by the same procedure failed to show either substance.
>
> The positive chemical findings indicate quantities in excess of normal or medicinal levels in the organs of Dr. Coppolino. It is possible that the choline and the succinic acid were derived from the drug succinylcholine which is rapidly broken down into choline and succinic acid following absorption by the tissues.
>
> Examinations for chemical compounds other than those normally found in tissues yielded negative findings.

According to the testimony given at both the hearing and seven months later at the Florida trial, Dr. Umberger and Dr. Helpern conferred on this matter and the inked changes in Dr. Helpern's handwriting resulted in this final form of the same report:

> Liver and brain tissue showed positive chemical findings for both choline and succinic acid.
>
> Control cases examined by the same analytical procedure did not show either compound to be present.
>
> The positive chemical findings by the method employed indicated significant quantities of these substances which when present in normal or medicinal amounts are not detectable. Succinylcholine is rapidly broken down into choline and succinic acid following absorption.
>
> Systematic analyses of liver, brain, kidney, for toxic compounds other than those found in the embalming fluid, or as a result of decomposition were negative.

Bailey then asked, in reference to Dr. Umberger, "You rely on his opinions, do you not?"

"I rely on his findings."

"But not being a chemist, there are times when you must rely upon his expertise?"

"As far as the detection of these substances I rely upon him entirely. As far as the interpretation of these findings, then I have to interpret them in the light of the entire autopsy."

Bailey then went back to the puncture wound, confirming that Helpern could not find a demonstrable cause of death, that this was not the first body with which Helpern could not come up with a demonstrable cause of death, and then asking, "The reason was not apparent?"

Helpern, in a testy and forcible tone, said, "Are you telling me something or asking me something? Let me answer the questions. I will be *glad* to do it. There are cases, rare cases, in which it is not possible to demonstrate a cause of death, an anatomical cause of death. And there are cases of poisoning where it is not possible to detect the poison for the reason that the poison is not looked for. No toxicological examination routinely determines *all* poisons. The more you know about a case the more apt you are to find the offending substance. Now in this particular case this substance would not have been found if it had not been especially looked for. It does not show up in the routine-type analysis which is done in the chemical laboratory."

"Succinic acid is present in every body, isn't it?"

"Not so that it comes out this way."

"Is it present? Did you understand the question?"

"There are some forms of succinic acid present, yes."

"It is a natural body chemical?"

"Well . . . yes."

"And choline is present in the human body at the time of death in the average case, is it not?"

"It may be present. Yes."

"What do you mean—it *may* be?"

"What I wanted to point out is that with the ordinary methods of analysis we do not detect succinic acid and we do not detect the choline and when we look for it and find as we do now, then it is present there in excess, and the combination does not come out such as it did in this case."

"Are you saying that choline is not normally present? Or is not normally present in the quantity in which you found it?"

"It is not normally present to appear in a routine examination such as this one."

"You say this was a routine chemical examination?"

"Not routine in the sense that succinylcholine was looked for, but routine in the sense of toxicological examinations peculiarly showing excessive amounts of this substance rather than the normal amounts."

"Doctor Umberger reported to you that it was possible that the choline and succinic acid were derived from the drug succinylcholine?"

"He reported to me more than that."

"This was his initial report?"

"This is why the report has been written as it is."

"I see he scratched that out."

"Yes."

"But this was his initial finding?"

"He was being conservative there."

"Did he say that?"

Bailey was pressing the doctor with such vigor that Schaub objected that the doctor was not being given a chance to answer. Bailey replied that he did not want a lecture. Judge Silvertooth said, "The doctor is capable of answering the questions. You, by redirect, can qualify things not spelled out."

Bailey then asked when the Umberger report using the word "possible" was first given to him. Helpern said that it was at the end of June or sometime in July, and after discussion they had corrected the report.

"In other words, as I understand it, Doctor Umberger prepared a written report and gave it to you. Then you had a conference and you had him alter it?"

"No! I didn't have him alter it."

"Why did he alter it?"

"Because the original report does not explain what the corrections explain. Why don't you read both copies? I will be glad to read the first portion in the second part."

Lee Bailey then read aloud the original report with the inked changes, and Dr. Helpern read aloud the amended report. It is interesting to note that in the amended report, as read by Dr. Helpern, that sentence which appears in paragraph two of the Umberger original, and paragraph three of the amended report remained unchanged, and read, "It is possible that the choline and succinic acid were derived from the drug succinylcholine which is rapidly broken down into choline and succinic acid following absorption by the tissues."

Yet evidently there was a subsequent amendment, as the four-paragraph version on page 69 is the one submitted in evidence at the Naples trial the following April.

When Helpern said the two reports were the same, after he had finished reading aloud the amended one, saying that the second report more clearly states the case, Bailey said, "Doctor Umberger said it was possible?"

"Don't take one phrase that he said. Take the whole report."

"I have the whole report. The strongest word I see is 'possible.' "

Helpern read aloud for the second time the third paragraph, beginning, "The positive chemical findings indicates . . ."

When he finished reading the paragraph, he said, "That may sound like a mild statement to you, but to me it is a very definite statement, because the report does not indicate any other possible source and very clearly excludes any other possible source of these compounds."

"Wait a minute! You say it excludes other possible sources of compounds which you agree are always found in the body?"

"But by this method of analysis they never show up."

"You are talking about the quantity not the type?"

"In other words, under normal conditions these substances are not detected in the chemical analysis."

"Why not?"

"I am sorry. I am not a chemist and I cannot tell you. As far as this chemical examination, these findings are Doctor Umberger's and the people who work with him in the lab."

"The interpretation is yours?"

"No. The interpretation of the report is Doctor Umberger's. The opinion as to the cause of death is mine."

"Now is it fair to say that your opinion is based upon what you consider to be findings of an excessive amount of two chemicals which are always present in the body?"

Helpern rephrased it. "My opinion is based on the chemical examination which revealed both choline and succinic acid which ordinarily, when in ordinary amounts or medicinal amounts, do not appear in the findings of a chemical examination."

Bailey asked the succinic acid level of a body interred for four months. Helpern said he did not know, but that it would not be revealed by the type of analysis done in this case. Bailey asked when they had last tested for succinic acid. Helpern said that Umberger had tested for it in unembalmed bodies which had presumably died during operations in which succinylcholine had been administered, and had found none. He did not know of any other exhumed case where such a search was made.

"Is this the first time that you have testified in your life that succinylcholine was present in a corpse that was exhumed after four months?" Helpern said it was. "Of course, in a capital case, you don't give your medical opinion on possibilities, do you?'' Helpern said no. Bailey asked him, ''Can you tell this court any reason, other than the excess of or the concentration of these two chemicals, that leads you to this conclusion that you have given us?''

''I would say that the autopsy did not disclose any cause of death other than the positive findings that these substances were found when the chemist analyzed it, and that is the basis for my conclusion in this case—an entirely negative autopsy, plus an injection site in the buttock, and chemical findings.''

''How many cases do you know where a person was killed with succinylcholine?''

''I don't know of any.''

''This is number one, if any?'' Helpern answered that it was the first case he had ever encountered.

''So that you would say that your experience in arriving at conclusions in cases of homicide involving succinylcholine is rather new?'' Helpern said it was. Bailey said, ''How much succinic acid, if you can tell us, is present in my body right now?'' Helpern did not know. ''How much would have been present in Carmela Coppolino without an injection?'' Helpern said that he did not know, but that if you test for it in the way that was used, you would not pick up ''this particular radical of succinic acid.''

''You would not pick up more? Or any?''

''You won't pick up any.''

''If it is present in the body why can't you?''

When Helpern said there were a lot of things in the body that are not detectable, Bailey asked how he knew they were there.

''Well, you know they are there. You can test for various compounds in bodies by special types of analysis, but in a routine examination conducted by the toxicologist, even with the special examinations made here, the routine toxicological examination does not pick up these substances. That does not mean the substance is not detectable by a toxicologist working in a laboratory or by a chemist, but we are using analytical procedures here which are not scaled to detect normal or medicinal amounts. These procedures are devised to detect excessive amounts, and from a practical point of view this is extremely important to be able to have a threshold of discovery which brings out the abnormal and not the normal.''

Under questioning Dr. Helpbern said he did not know how the tests were performed, and knew the properties of succinylcholine in only a general way, but from the standpoint of interpreting an overdose in the absence of any cause of death, he felt sufficiently familiar with it to deal with it in a homicide case.

"You mean to say that your opinion is caused principally because you can't come up with any other cause of death?"

"To a certain extent, yes."

"Were there cases of heart failure where there is no organic reason?"

"I wouldn't say there were cases of heart failure. That is a meaningless remark in trying to describe the cause of death. The heart stops in everybody, but that is not the same as heart failure."

Asked about the possible effect of succinylcholine on the heart, Helpern said it did not act directly on the heart. Bailey queried him about lethal dosage, and Helpern said so much depends upon how it is administered, and how rapidly, and body weight that he would not want to offer an opinion as to how much would kill a person.

"You have given an opinion in a capital case that succinylcholine was the cause of death. Can't you help us a little with that [the dosage]?"

"I would say a large amount."

"What is a large amount? Gallons? Or quarts?"

When he was irritated, Helpern's voice became louder and more harsh, and he screwed his face into a pugnacious scowl that was strangely reminiscent of how he must have looked as a small boy in one of the survival-oriented playgrounds of Manhattan where he had grown up.

"You *know* the stuff is given in milligrams! So don't talk about gallons!"

"Do *you* know it is given in milligrams?"

"Yes."

"Tell us."

Dr. Helpern, explaining that he did not want to get into the field of anesthesiology, said that for the ordinary patient, thirty to sixty milligrams during the course of an ordinary operation, and much more could be given if the operation lasted a long time. The effect depended on how much would be given at any one time. He said that for a woman of Carmela's age, the relaxant dose would be thirty to sixty milligrams, "but to cause death a considerable amount in excess of that would have to be given, but don't ask me for the amounts because I have had no experience with fatal cases other than this one."

"A case of first impression," said Lee Bailey. "How much did Carmela weigh? Do you know?"

"Yes. At the time of the autopsy, 140 pounds."

"Do you know how much she weighed at the time of death?"

"I would say more because the body loses weight after death."

As this testimony about the weight of the dead woman had no particular significance during the hearing or the eventual trial, it can be used here to illustrate the type of minor inconsistency which can plague anyone trying to achieve accuracy in writing up the account of a complex trial. Snapshots of Carmela and her children taken in front of her home shortly before her death certainly did not suggest a woman of that heft. She had been five feet six inches tall. People interviewed who had seen her shortly before her death guessed her weight in an average range of 120. One guessed 110. One guessed 130.

Marjorie Farber can be assumed to be a reasonably accurate source, as she had not seen Carmela from the time the Coppolinos left New Jersey in April of 1965 until Marjorie arrived in Sarasota the week before Carmela's death. Had she put on weight, certainly Marjorie would have noticed it, particularly wearing the sun clothes typical of August in Florida. In August of 1967 Marjorie Farber said, "Carm, at 5 feet 6 could not possibly have weighed over 125 pounds, and probably weighed less. Actually, she was built very much like Mary Coppolino, except with smaller bones and narrower shoulders. She had to fight the good fight to keep her weight down in her hips and thighs. That's where she had a tendency to put it on. But she still wore size ten shorts, and even if she'd weighed 130, she'd have been too big for that size. No, they've got it all wrong somehow."

Though in retrospect it seems quite trivial, when such glaring inconsistencies arise during the course of hearings and trials, and one has no way of ascertaining what will become important and what will not, at last there is a kind of compulsive need to eliminate all such inexplicable contradictions. Certainly all bodies coming into Helpern's building for autopsy are carefully weighed and measured. And if he had any doubt as to body weight, he had his autopsy report there to consult to refresh his memory. This discrepancy has never been resolved.

"Of course, if you don't know what quantity of succinylcholine would be necessary to kill that body, I assume you have tried to find out from experts."

"Only to a certain extent. Actually that absolute amount is not important to me. It is based on this report which tells me that this amount is far in excess of what would be found if a medicinal dose had been given. In medicinal doses one does not find any succinylcholine, and this has been tested out in cases during the six-month period that elapsed when this case was studied. Prior to that time this was not a case that confronted us. The exact amount that might have been given here, I don't know."

"How *much* succinic acid did Doctor Umberger find in the organs in Carmela Coppolino?"

"He found enough to recognize but not to quantitate."

"You can tell us in milligrams?"

"No."

"You don't have any idea?"

"No."

"How much choline?"

"I can't tell you the exact amount. All I can say is he found the choline and he found the succinic acid."

"I want to know if you have any estimation?"

"I am sorry. There was no quantitation carried out. They had all they could do to come up with the qualitative. It was a great deal of work to analyze for this substance."

"You mean the men were *instructed* to come up with the findings?" Bailey's tone was one of incredulity and indignation.

Milton Helpern was shocked, affronted and furious. "Counselor, that is not fair! You *know* I didn't say that. I *resent* that!"

"I am sorry. You don't know?"

"Don't argue with the witness," said Judge Silvertooth.

"You *know* I didn't say or mean that!" Helpern complained angrily.

"Did you say they had all they could do to come up with that?" Bailey asked.

"Yes I did! Because this was a difficult and long analysis. It was not a routine analysis to be done in a few minutes. This analysis was a protracted one over a long period of time and long effort to be gone over and over and checking over this material. This is a very difficult analysis. That is what I mean when I said they had all they could do."

"They were looking for evidence of succinylcholine?"

"They certainly were! If we hadn't know about that, we wouldn't have looked."

"No question about it?"

"No question."

"When you say, 'all they could do to come up with it,' you mean 'just barely found it'?"

"No. They had a very difficult analysis. That is what I meant."

Then there were repetitious questions about succinic acid, and about its detectability in "normal" quantities in the body, then

Bailey moved to the question of the intramuscular injection. Helpern testified he had found but one needle puncture which he could not trace into any artery or vein.

"How big a needle was used?"

Helpern dug into his briefcase again. "Would you like to see it?" He took out a photograph and Bailey moved in beside the witness to see it as the doctor pointed to it. "I can't tell you how big the needle was. You are looking at the left buttock. This is the crease between the buttocks. The skin is somewhat flattened, but the puncture is there. I have a closeup of that too. This is the waistband of the panty that was on the body, and there is the puncture right there, and there is the track leading down from it which is clearly discernible. You can see the hemorrhage."

"How deep is it?"

". . . Just lateral to the needle puncture already described reveals a needle track with evidence of hemorrhage a distance of a half inch. That is the measurable portion of the track. The fat tissue is not as well preserved."

"Is that all you have on the puncture?" Helpern said it was. He had described it, sectioned it and photographed it. Asked what kind of sharp instrument had made it, he said that in his opinion it was a needle puncture. "It could have been a sewing needle?" Bailey asked.

"Any needle could make a puncture like that, if you want to assume a needle was used. As a doctor, and finding a puncture where I found it, I assumed it was a hypodermic needle. That is a reasonable conclusion for me to come to."

Helpern could say nothing about the gauge of the needle, except that it had probably been of fairly good size because, "it made quite a track." But he couldn't be sure of that. Bailey next approached the question of the rate of absorption of an intramuscular injection. Helpern said it could be rapid or slow because the muscle varies. If the injection is into an area quite vascular, it would be rapid.

"The injection we are talking about didn't go in the muscle at all?"

"I could only trace it into the fat."

"As far as you could tell, anything that was injected went into the fat?"

"No. I could only trace the portion that went into the fat, but I have no right to say that it didn't go into the muscle."

"And you have no right to say it did?"

"I can't say, except I saw a track directed toward the muscle."

Helpern would not speculate on how long a person might

remain ambulatory, but said that if a person were conscious he would feel an injection of the kind described.

"It would smart, wouldn't it, a good-sized needle in the buttock?"

"Not necessarily. A needle in the buttock, aside from the penetration of the needle, the pain may be very momentary, and there would be times when an individual would be unaware of the passage of it. A puncture in the buttock, which is not a very sensitive area, might very well go unnoticed."

"Do you think a person might not wake up?"

"Might, or might not."

Hazarding a guess about how soon a person might be immobilized, Helpern said that depending on the size of the dose, a large dose injected into the buttock might immobilize a person fairly rapidly, within a matter of minutes, or possibly less. He said that whether or not the person got up might depend on whether or not they were aware that an injection was being given, because the only pain would be that of the needle going through the skin. Were this done at a time when the person was not very sensitive, then that person might not even be aware of it being done. He said that he was not aware of the rate at which the drug hydrolyzes in the bloodstream.

He said that he had conferred with Webb and others about succinylcholine and its properties. "But only in a general sort of way. I did find out that this drug can be lethal so that actually the dosage of that [drug which] would have a lethal effect, you might say, *is* a quantity, and whatever that quantity is, I don't have to know. All I have to know is that this drug is lethal. . . . I am concluding that it was lethal in this case."

"I know you are. So the quantity that might have been injected is pertinent to your conclusion?"

"I would say that enough was injected to be lethal without being able to give you a figure. I am sorry. I cannot give you the figure."

Bailey was bedeviling the man, and Helpern was becoming visibly more impatient and irritable. "You don't even know how much a lethal dose is?" Bailey asked in sad wonderment.

"I don't *have* to know! I have to know that this drug is lethal if given in excess. I don't have to carry the lethal value around in my head!"

"Do you have to try to bother to find it out before you give us your opinion?"

"I wouldn't give my opinion if I didn't have a chance to look it up. I would have to look it up."

78

"*Did* you look it up?"

"No!"

"Do you have *any* idea how much she might have been given?"

"I know the drug is lethal in excess and that is sufficient. Now, the absolute value in that is just like knowing how much of this substance or that substance can cause death. The important thing is to know that something is lethal. For example, I know that a large amount of salt injected would not be lethal. It might cause irritation. I am not interested in the value. I am interested in the effect of it. I don't have to carry these figures around in my head to say it is lethal. You don't disagree, do you?"

"Of course I do! This is not a carrying-around-in-your head. You are testifying in a capital case."

That response made Helpern so angry he came dangerously close to incoherence. "I *can* testify in this case! Capital or not, it doesn't change the meaning at all. The opinion is the same whether capital or any kind of case!"

"Don't you require some reasonable medical certainty before you give the opinion?"

"I *am* giving opinion with a reasonable medical certainty. I am not trying to be frivolous. I am not trying to speculate."

With surprising speed Milton Helpern was visibly and obviously getting himself back under control.

"Alcohol is lethal in sufficient amounts, is it not?"

"Frequently."

"Whereas comparatively small amounts are not even dangerous." Helpern agreed. "So that you and I can take a drink and we are still alive?" Helpern's smile was affable and charming as he agreed.

"But the fact that alcohol is lethal doesn't tell you that it will kill unless you know how much he had!"

Schaub objected on the grounds that the question was repetitious. Bailey said it was a relevant source of inquiry. Schaub again termed it repetitious.

Lee Bailey said, addressing the bench, "Your Honor, I think it is relevant because this man's opinion is obviously the fulcrum of the case, and while disclaiming any knowledge of the elements, he sticks to his own conclusion. I am entitled to explore it. It is an unprecedented case given by a man who expresses ignorance of the drug."

Judge Silvertooth said, "We are getting somewhat into repetition because of the fact that the doctor has answered the same question several times. I will allow this particular question but I may cut it off."

"I have no desire to be redundant, Your Honor," Lee Bailey said. "Getting an answer from the doctor is not the easiest thing." He turned back toward the witness. "Do you leave it with this court that it is irrelevant as to how much was—or how much may have been—injected into, for instance, this victim?"

(Persons attending capital case hearings and trials for the first time are often puzzled and disconcerted by the apparent assumption on the part of the defense counsel, when cross-examining witnesses for the prosecution, that murder has been done, exemplified by Bailey's reference here to Carmela as "this victim." However the process of logic will show that in order to question the steps by which someone has arrived at a conclusion, it is necessary to accept the conclusion for the time being, otherwise there could be no communication regarding the steps taken to arrive at the conclusion. And because verbal communication is often short-circuited by what the semanticists call trigger words, if the cross-examiner insists on qualifying the term every time, saying, for example, "the alleged victim" he merely keeps the witness more completely on guard by constantly reminding him that his testimony is not acceptable to the defense.)

Again Helpern insisted that the actual amount would be meaningless to him, that varying amounts could be lethal. "We found a large amount as evidenced by the fact that it came out at all. The amounts which are ordinarily used in anesthesia cases do not show up in chemical examination. And even if they did show up, if a large amount were given over a prolonged period of time, it wouldn't disprove what I said."

Helpbern said he understood that in operations they could give up to 500 milligrams by drip over a long period. He said he had learned from Dr. Webb, and from another man who uses the material, that it would take a massive intramuscular dose to be lethal, and that this was the first case Helpern had encountered.

"So you are not relying on any experience with this drug in forming your opinion except what you have gathered in the course of this case?"

"I am relying on experience in performing autopsies and trying to determine the cause of death. And the fact that there has not been a case before does not make it impossible for me to render an opinion in this case. I don't see any reason why the fact that this is the first case I have encountered makes it impossible for me to conclude that a drug which is known to be lethal if given in excess, when found in this body, why it is wrong to conclude, or in error for me to conclude that this person died from an overdose.''

"Can you point to one single word in the medical literature where it is authoritatively stated that the presence of succinylcholine can be detected from succinic acid and choline?''

"No.''

"Can you tell me the name of one qualified pathologist who will say that is a medically accepted fact?''

"No. I think this is the first case of this type.''

"So you have an experiment involving just one case?''

Helpern objected testily to the use of that word, saying that he made a post-mortem examination, and was not experimenting. Bailey then asked him what other drugs broke down into succinic acid and choline. Helpern said he did not know of any others. He testified that he did not know the source of succinic acid in the body. Asked if Carmela's body could not have produced this succinic acid, Helpern again mentioned the control bodies, saying no such results were obtained from them, and that he did not have to understand or elaborate upon the biochemistry of succinic acid in the normal body, in that by the method of analysis used one does not detect succinic acid or choline even when medicinal amounts of succinylcholine had been administered directly before death.

Asked about the number of autopsies he had performed, Helpern said he had personally done from sixteen thousand to eighteen thousand, and had supervised three or four times that many. Bailey asked if in all those autopsies, and all those toxicological reports, was it true that never before had they found succinic acid. And once more Helpern testified that Dr. Umberger's tests do not pick up succinic acid in the way that he had found it this time.

"Doctor Umberger said that the possible explanation of the presence of this drug was the injection?''

Irritably, Helpern said he was not going to quibble about the word possible, "a word he uses in a certain sense as a chemist and try to interpret the whole report on that one word.''

Lee Bailey then queried him about the oral reports and conferences with Umberger. Helpern said Umberger had reported that the two substances he found were derived from succinylcholine.

"He did?''

"He did.''

"Do you know whether or not he was aware that succinic acid and choline are found in the body anywhere?''

"Doctor Umberger is a very fine chemist and very rare in his field. I don't know what else he knows or learns, but he did tell me that in this case he felt the succinic acid and choline were derived from the succinylcholine."

"But he did not put that in his report?"

"I think he did."

"If you had found another cause of death, would you nonetheless say that succinylcholine was injected into this body?"

"If I found another cause of death I would still say that succinylcholine was injected into the body, but if I found another cause of death that could compete with this for consideration, then I would have to say that I would not know which of the substances was the lethal agent. If I found, for example, a degree of heart disease that was incompatible with life, like a ruptured infarct of the heart, then regardless of succinylcholine, the cause of death would be the rupture of the heart. It (the autopsy) was to find what was wrong with this body. It was done very carefully. After a careful and painstaking search that took many hours, because the importance of this case was considered, nothing was found other than a puncture and an indication to go ahead and look for something. Frankly, if we didn't have the information that suggested this as a possibility [the succinylcholine], this might not have been discovered, you see. There is nothing automatic about a chemical analysis."

Bailey then questioned Helpern about the control bodies used, asking, "In order to conclude on a first-time basis that the presence of succinic acid was abnormal, you would have to examine quite a number of bodies for the same thing?"

Helpern did not know how many bodies, saying merely, "There were several cases that were examined. Other examinations were made in which this particular finding—I think it was done by chromatography—this particular 'spot' as the chemists call it, was not found. So that because they were looking for this preparation, and carrying out this analysis very exhaustively, they *did* find something which led them to go back and work on this thing in the way they came up with this answer. I don't know (about) that. I am not a chemist. I am not trying to evade the question, but I don't want to talk about something I am not personally skilled in doing. I would leave that entirely to the chemist. If I thought that you wanted Umberger here to ask questions of, and you had asked me to bring him, I would have been very glad to bring him."

"You mean you had no idea we would want to talk to Umberger?"

"No, I really didn't."

82

"It was really *his* opinion?"

"No. It is *not* his opinion. It is his findings."

Bailey asked why it had taken from December to June to arrive at the opinion. Helpern said that the load of routine work in the lab made these special tests go slowly. He said he did not form his opinion until sometime in June, and reported orally he was satisfied the findings represented succinylcholine. Thereafter he continued working on the tests. On July 1, when Frank Schaub had gone to New York and had a conference with Helpern and Umberger, "then it was more or less finalized."

Under questioning, Dr. Helpern said he had talked with Dr. Millard White (the Sarasota County medical examiner) during the later part of July. Dr. White had called him, and Helpern had "transmitted to him in essence what I have told you here. The autopsy findings, the negative findings, the puncture mark and the chemical findings."

Asked if he had arrived at his opinion as to the cause of death at the time of the conversation with White, Hepbern replied, "Yes, or before that."

Schaub objected when Bailey asked if any written reports had been filed by Helpern's office since the time of the conversation with White and the formation of his opinion. Schaub said, "Objection to written reports. The man is here."

Bailey said, "I am entitled to impeach on his reports if I can find any."

"It is repetitious and immaterial," said Schaub.

Dr. Helpern said, "I have a report but I haven't filed it with Mr. Schaub, and you are welcome to go over it. . . . It is the unedited transcript of the original data, of the original dictation which was dictated at the time of the autopsy."

Mr. Schaub said, "I would like to ask the doctor if he relied on it in the course of his testimony. If he didn't, it has no materiality."

Bailey stated that Helpern had read from it. Schaub did not think so, so the Court asked the witness if he had relied upon it.

"No. I have a very good recollection of this case. While everything I testified to is in that report, the only time I really referred to it was to give a precise measurement as to the depth of the needle puncture in the left buttock."

Schaub repeated his objection, saying Helpern had not had to refresh his memory. Lee Bailey said, "This is a report of autopsy that this man carried into the courtroom and placed on this counter. He says he didn't rely on it or refer to it. This is the only autopsy. I think the defense is entitled to know what is in it.''

"There is not entitlement to it," said Frank Schaub. "These are his notes. I don't see the materiality."

One might reasonably suspect that with the defense so determinedly attacking the opinion as to the cause of death, the importance of the detailed autopsy report would be to see if, therein, there was some finding which the state pathologist thought of no importance, but which a defense pathologist might consider significant as possibly pointing toward some alternative cause of death.

Judge Silvertooth sustained the state attorney's objection, and Lee Bailey shrugged and said, "We can get it from oral testimony." He walked all the way back to the corner of the jury box farthest from the witness stand and said, "Tell us about the autopsy. First, how did you start?"

Of course it was evident that if Dr. Milton Helpern did then examine his report during the recital, the Court would doubtless have honored the defense request to have access to the written report. But one can assume Dr. Helpern had not been placed in any mood of cooperation toward Bailey during the cross-examination thus far.

Helpern explained that the autopsy request had come from Dr. A. Malcolm B. Gilman, the County Physician of Monmouth County, and that the body—after prior identification by Dr. Musetto, father of the deceased—was autopsied on December 17, 1965, after three and a half months of interment in the family plot in Boonton, New Jersey. The autopsy started at about eleven o'clock that Friday morning, with a number of people present.

"At that time I took photographs of the head, of the body, and I also took photographs of the buttock to show the puncture which I already described. Actually, I think I photographed the buttock before I photographed the face, because as the body was being placed on the table it was in a prone position, and I took the opportunity there of washing the skin and removing some of the macerated portion of the skin, and I found this very clearly evident puncture in the left buttock and photographed that. The other buttock showed a few small bruises in the skin, and a careful search did not reveal any punctures. That was confirmed by incisions in the skin.

"I incised the puncture to establish it was a needle track. I did this to my satisfaction.

"Then I photographed the face. There was a considerable

84

amount of mold that had appeared—that had developed during the post-mortem period, as is often the case.''

(There were small sounds and uneasy shiftings and changes of facial expression among the spectator females indicating, perhaps, that this was not the type of revelation they had hoped for. Had Milton Helpern gone into some of the peripheral details as reported in the complete autopsy entered in evidence in Naples, Florida, the following April, it might have pleased them more. They might have relished knowing she had been buried in a pale blue cotton dress, double-breasted, with a belt, which at the time of the autopsy had faded to white, that she wore a slip, white panties with a lavender trim, tan nylon hose, that her white bra was in place, that she wore a rosary and crucifix with pale blue beads, and that on the inside of the wedding ring Dr. Helpern took from the appropriate finger was engraved *C.A.C. to C.A.M. 3–18–56.* Yet had he gone into all the detail of the autopsy report, there were other matters therein which would have distressed them far more than the mention of the mold. He would have spoken of the trocar wound, the place where the undertaker had inserted the long, thin, sharp, metal tube used to suction out the body fluids, spoken of how that wound in the left upper quadrant of the abdomen was sealed with a screw button. And it is entirely possible that some of them might have attempted to leave in great haste regardless of the rule against leaving except when court recessed, had Dr. Helpern repeated a rather unfortunate simile he used in the report describing some of the partially decomposed tissues as being of the consistency of apple butter.)

''The body was in an excellent state of preservation as a result of the embalming. The autopsy was carried out in the usual way. The incision was made into the body cavities. The body organs were systematically examined and removed. Particularly the heart was very carefully looked over for the reason I had been informed it had been certified the body had died of coronary heart disease. There was no coronary heart disease at all. I went through every millimeter of the heart. It took me quite a long time to do this. This was not a casual examination of the heart. I had a purpose in making the examination as thorough as I did. I examined the valves of the heart and muscles of the heart, and the heart was in an excellent state of preservation as a result of the embalming.

''Then I examined the lungs. They were essentially normal. The liver was well-preserved and normal. Kidneys, adrenals—all of the organs were in that state. The uterus was normal except the endometrium was in a sort of premenstrual phase. This is one of the phases that the endometrium undergoes.

"The skeleton was normal. The brain was entirely normal. I examined the base of the skull and extended the incision into the neck. I examined the throat organs and there was no evidence of trauma, and I looked very carefully for any evidence of disease and for any cause of death which you might call structural or anatomical, of an obvious or not-so-obvious nature.

"I found the body of a healthy woman, and then because of the puncture and because of the absence of the cause of death, I then removed the organs and sent them and personally gave them to Doctor Umberger for his study."

"What organs?"

"I removed the liver and the brain and the stomach and the blood clots, the kidneys . . . practically everything that was available. I also removed the subcutaneous fat around the needle puncture and from both buttocks and gave them to him."

Bailey then picked him up on the difference in wording as between Helpern saying he had heard she had been certified as dying of coronary artery disease, and the certificate itself which says coronary occlusion.

"That would be the same thing. . . . I designated it as coronary artery disease. You have it designated as coronary occlusion. In other words, coronary occlusion is another way of saying that the coronary arteries and that the lumen is blocked. The word coronary occlusion is used when the process is considered an acute one, you see. Something fresh."

"You mean that no occlusion can occur unless the disease is present?"

"An occlusion of the coronary arteries does not occur in the absence of the disease in a coronary except when an embolism from some other part of the body carries a thrombus there. But I would say that the coronary arteries showed no disease and that there was no evidence of coronary occlusion, disease or no disease. There was no occlusion and there was no disease, so that your question really can be answered no disease, no occlusion, and this issue as to whether you can have an occlusion without disease does not pertain. The heart was well-preserved and permitted valid observation. It was normal in size and normal in every respect."

Establishing that Dr. Helpern had been given facts about the case prior to the autopsy, Bailey asked him if he was looking in partiuclar to determine coronary trouble, and whether or not there was evidence of succinylcholine.

"I was trying to determine the cause of death, and in view of the fact that the death had been certified resulting from coronary occlusion, I looked particularly to see if there was any disease in the heart and there was none.

"Now, I was also given some information of succinylcholine having been a possibility in this case. In other words, whenever you do an autopsy on exhumed cases it isn't like working on a fresh body. You have the advantage of certain information about the circumstances, you see. Possibly if I had done this autopsy in a fresh case, I might not have even found that puncture, because it is a funny thing that in a case you don't look for the fine points without being advised about the possibility. It is very easy to overlook a puncture wound in the buttock. I dare say that in some autopsies I have overlooked punctures, not having been advised of the fact that this may have been an issue in the case. Having been told that this possibility might have existed, I looked the body over completely for any site of puncture wounds. I found it quickly because I happened to be looking at the back of the body before the front as it was placed on the table, and really to my surprise I was somewhat amazed at how evident this puncture was."

Establishing that there were no other puncture wounds, Bailey asked him if he had any idea how long prior to the death of Carmela the puncture had been made.

"It looked fresh."

"As much as a day before?"

"Well, it looked younger than that. It looked more recent than that. The day before, the puncture would not look so intact as a puncture. In other words, if you look at it in the photograph it looks like a crater. A puncture that is a day old would be covered with a crust and show some reaction. Microscopically there would be no reaction at all in this tissue, so it was very fresh. I think it is reasonable to conclude it was a fresh puncture. If you ask whether in seconds, minutes, or ten minutes, I can't say."

Bailey asked him if he thought it was unlikely to have been self-inflicted because of the angle of the track. Helpern said he thought it unlikely for the reason people do not inject themselves in the buttock. When asked, he indicated that the angle of introduction of the needle was almost a right angle, coming in almost from the side, entering four and a half inches from the midline of the buttocks.

Under further questioning Helpern said that it was an obvious mark, easily found, yet if a pathologist or medical examiner were not looking for a needle site, he would not be too critical if they did not find it. Bailey asked, "Are you able to tell us with any degree of certainty that the puncture wound was not made after death?"

Helpern explained his affirmative answer by saying, "There was rather a conspicuous hemorrhage along the track, and a puncture made after death through the subcutaneous fat would not show hemorrhagic extravasation. I would say this was a puncture made before death, and if you pin me down and say, Could it have been made a second before or a second after, I can't say. This is a possibility. I determined (this as an ante-mortem puncture) from my experience in examining punctures both ante-mortem and post-mortem."

Queried about the process of embalming, Helpern answered, "When a body is embalmed a form of embalming fluid is injected into the vessels of the body and also into the body cavities, and the formalin fixes the tissues depending upon how effectively it is carried out. Now in this case the embalming was very satisfactory. The only changes that were evident of a post-mortem nature was this slight maceration of the skin, slight discoloration of the skin and there was a growth of mold on the face which was rather conspicuous. This mold actually dries out the tissues and acts as a preservative, so that I would say that the embalming fixed the tissues just like a pathologist puts it in a bottle of formalin."

In his manual on courtroom medicine, Volume Three, entitled *Death*, Marshall Houts gives a more detailed appraisal of the effects of embalming than appears in the testimony at either trial:

"Embalming is one of those luxuries practiced almost exclusively by those who subscribe to 'The American Way of Death.' No other country in the world routinely embalms its dead. While this custom is a great financial boon to funeral directors and undertakers, it often presents a serious medico-legal impediment to the investigation of the cause and manner of death.

"To clearly appreciate the problems involved, it is necessary to understand the embalming technique.

"The basic procedure for embalming is to remove the blood from the circulatory system and the other fluids which are found in the gastrointestinal tract, the bladder and body cavities, and to replace them with embalming fluid.

"This is accomplished by inserting a large, hollow needle called a trocar into strategic locations. The trocar is attached to a vacuum or suction apparatus, and the fluid is aspirated from the various body cavities. Cannulas (hollow tubes) are placed in different blood vessels and the blood is withdrawn from one cannula while embalming fluid is introduced through the other in order to infuse embalming fluid throughout the vascular system.

"An abdominal trocar puncture may be made in the epigastrium. The trocar is then pointed in all directions to penetrate the organs and structures in the chest and abdomen so they may receive the embalming fluid.

"The embalmer may make surgical incisions over the large blood vessels in the neck, armpits and groins to expose the vessels for draining out the blood and injecting the embalming fluid.

"The principal ingredient of embalming fluid is formaldehyde; and the exact formula is fixed by law in many states.

"The formaldehyde causes the protein in the various parts and organs of the body to coagulate. This causes the tissues, muscles and organs to harden, shrink, stiffen and bleach. If the embalming process is thorough and complete, these drastic changes extend throughout the entire body.

"The embalming process is designed to produce changes in the dead body, not to preserve evidence as to the cause and manner of death. We must immediately recognize that these changes make the task of the autopsy surgeon extremely difficult in many types of cases, impossible in others. They, in turn, magnify the problems of the attorney with a death case.

"It must be recognized from the outset that embalming obscures and confuses certain pathological entities. An inexperienced autopsy examiner may draw totally erroneous conclusions if he does not differentiate between the ante-mortem conditions and the post-embalming changes. Some of the most common grounds of error are:

(a) Subcutaneous hemorrhages which produce the characteristic black and blue marks of ecchymosis may be 'ironed out' and diminished so that the extent of the bruising cannot be accurately determined.

(b) Penetrating wounds, stab wounds, bullet wounds and injuries by blunt forces may be identified after embalming. It is not unusual however, to have an inexperienced autopsy examiner confuse an ante-mortem wound with an incision made during the embalming process. Any doubt should be resolved through histologic (microscopic) tissue examination. In some instances the reckless insertion and manipulation of the trocar by the embalmer makes it impossible to trace the exact course of the wound through the body or to measure accurately its penetration into an organ.

(c) Massive hemorrhages into the chest and abdominal cavity are sucked out by the trocar. This makes it impossible to measure the amount of internal bleeding which preceded death.

(d) Changes in the size, weight, color, consistency and gross appearance of the body organs are often indicative of various disease processes. Since the embalming fluid causes the muscles and organs to harden, shrink, stiffen and bleach, accurate determination of these changes for diagnostic purposes may be seriously impeded.

(e) The embalming fluid may create discrete and hardened areas in the lungs which simulate ante-mortem thrombi (plugs in the blood vessels). These hardened areas may also simulate pneumonia. The embalming process prevents the discovery of air embolism (a bubble of air obstructing a blood vessel). These artifacts may be differentiated by histological tissue examination.

(f) Embalming may preclude the qualitative detection of many poisons such as alcohol, carbon dioxide, paraldehyde, chloral hydrate, ether, chloroform and the cyanides. Therefore, the failure to find evidence of these poisons at the autopsy of an embalmed body does not mean they were not present prior to death. Certain other poisons such as carbon monoxide, strychnine, the barbiturates, and the heavy metals may still be detected even though the body has been embalmed.

Even assuming that the poison is detected qualitatively, the embalming makes a reliable quantitative analysis almost impossible.

(g) Death by drowning, strangulation and smothering, which are often missed routinely by the inexperienced autopsy examiner may be completely obscured by embalming.''

Bailey asked about the chemical contents of embalming fluid and Helpern said that it was formaldehyde and water, with a variety of coloring matter and other chemical ingredients according to the particular brand, and the contents is listed on the label. Asked if he had checked to see what embalming fluid had been used, Helpern said that Dr. Umberger had done so, and had discovered that in addition to the formaldehyde, there was ethylene alcohol, benzoic acid, and some salicylates in the fluid used.

When asked if any of the control bodies had been embalmed, Helpern replied, ''I do not recall whether controls were done on this. All I know is we have had many embalmed bodies to examine and we have done general examinations on cases that have been embalmed. I mean, these systematic studies have been made, and in none of the other cases had Doctor Umberger ever found any of the substances which were found here, namely the succinic acid and the choline.''

Bailey in his questions pointed out in such other non-control cases, Umberger would not have been looking for succinic acid and choline, and that Helpern had previously stated that if they had not been looking for these compounds in this case, they would not have found them. Asked again about control cases, Helpern said, ''Apparently this was done. There were several embalmed cases that were autopsied, not so long dead as this person, that were included in the controls. I am quite certain that there were some embalmed cases that were done. Every once in a while a body comes in that is embalmed before the death is reported, and we have to work with an embalmed case, so that I would say that when he talks about controls, he is talking about embalmed controls."

Dr. Helpern said that they had done no animal experimentation, that he was aware from having read something in the newspapers that Dr. Gilman had done some experimenting, but that, "Our report is entirely independent of anything that Doctor Gilman may or may not have been doing his own way. None of our opinion is based on his findings."

In one of his more abrupt transitions Lee Bailey wanted to know if a blood clot could cause death. Helpern asked where. Bailey said in the heart. Helpern told him he did not mean a blood clot, but a thrombus. A clot forms after death, a thrombus during life. Bailey asked if the embalmer might not pump out a thrombus in a coronary artery.

"No. Absolutely not. There is one thing about the heart and embalming. Embalming does an excellent job in preserving the heart, so that I would say one gets the most desirable results from the study of an embalmed heart. What the embalming does is not wash out a clot but sometimes it clots the blood with this fluid in the vessels and makes it look like a thrombus. Mistakes have been made the other way. On microscopic examination of the blood we found nothing formed by the formalin. If there was a thrombus there, that would be the best thing for it, and there would be no possibility of overlooking it."

"When an incision is made to put in the formalin, how large is it?"

"Several inches. It goes into the jugular or carotid. As I recall, it went into the base of the neck. Sometimes in the femoral region, to draw out some of the blood, but any clot which is present in the vessels is fixed. Any thrombus is fixed by embalming. If you don't embalm a body where there has been a clot, sometimes a clot will liquify. But embalming preserves the heart. In this case the heart was very well-preserved, and I am positive that there was no thrombus in any of the vessels of the heart."

Asked how soon after death a thrombus could dissolve, Helpern estimated it would remain in the heart up to forty-eight hours, unless the body decomposed, but he found no evidence of decomposition prior to embalming, had there been one, he would have found it in the heart. He added that you do not see thrombus with normal coronary arteries, and in this case there was no basis for any embolism.

"Do you believe that your ability to determine the presence or absence of coronary trouble in the body is in any way diminished by the fact that it is embalmed and interred for a period of time?"

"No. As a matter of fact, I would say the ability to evaluate it is enhanced by embalming."

"What percent of autopsies that you have conducted have resulted in no ascertainable cause of death?"

". . . the ordinary chemical examination, the ordinary microscopic examination and the autopsy do not provide an answer in perhaps five percent of the cases. To be fair about this, the cause of death is a very difficult thing to determine. Most people have an idea that when you do an autopsy it is like opening a box, or an inventory, sort of taking inventory. It doesn't work that way. It is a very complicated problem and it can be overlooked even when you try . . . because you look for certain information and you may not be able to arrive at the cause of death. The information may come from strange sources that really makes an autopsy a simple case. But I would say that autopsies in their initial stage are not (often) solved. I would say in five percent or maybe even a little more, we don't find the cause of death in the autopsy."

"Did you ever hear of the head-drop test?" Helpern hadn't. Bailey asked, "In connection with the ascertainment of the presence of succinylcholine?" Another negative response. "Have you had a full discussion with Doctor Umberger about the method he used?"

Helpern said he did not go into the finer details of the analysis carried out in this case. Bailey said, "You don't know whether he tried what is known as the head-drop test?"

"No. I don't know. I would like to know."

Bailey closed with a few questions as to where Dr. Umberger might be, and his availability to come down.

It was then five-thirty. It had been a very long day, and seemed even longer than could be accounted for by the actual hours of testimony. The two hours of the cross-examination of Milton Helpern seemed the longest and most exhausting part of the day.

Just as court was recessed, Carl Coppolino turned and located Jerry Crady, the jailer, in sheriff's deputy uniform, standing by the far wall near the railing between the floor of the court and the spectator section. Carl snapped his fingers loudly and pointed at Crady, who gave a start and came quickly to Carl, taking out of his pocket a small metal pill box as he came. Mary Coppolino went through the gate to sit beside Carl, a hand on his shoulder, as Carl took some small white pills. The attorneys milled around, collecting their books and papers and briefcases. The spectators left slowly, with backward stares at the accused and his wife. The press photographers in the corridors took shots of the witnesses as they left.

Outside it was hot and bright, and the sun was high. The out-of-town contingent moved across to the Saloon. F. Lee Bailey, as alert and fresh as when the day had begun, white shirt unwilted, gold watch chain looped across the tailored vest, pussycat grin in place, radiated a total confidence.

He told of a phone conversation he'd had long distance with Carl Coppolino a few days previously. He had phoned the jail and then Carl had phoned him back as soon as he was brought down. After they had discussed certain matters Lee Bailey had said, "Carl, I've got a surgeon from Cleveland here in my office who'd like to say hello."

He then turned the phone over to Dr. Sam Sheppard, then awaiting retrial. Dr. Sheppard's opening line to Coppolino was, "I know how it feels, buddy."

Chapter Five

As on the previous day, the spectator line in the corridor was long. When the doors were opened they came in at that curious gait of people who yearn to run and do not quite dare. They pounced, scrambled, darted for seats.

As on the previous day there were over two score who did not land in one of the fifty-three seats. And as on the previous day the tall, elderly baliff, Tony Monella—looking somewhat like a guard in an art museum—announced that when the court was called to order, the standees would have to leave. His voice was loud, his meaning clear. Yet they stood there, clotted inside the double doors, staring at the accused seated at the defense table with a kind of mass emptiness of face and expression. They stood in that staring silence of small crowds who stand and gape at the scene of an accident. They stood there for a full thirty minutes. When the court was called to order they were reluctant to leave, and were finally herded out by the bailiff and two sheriff's deputies, who also dislodged one elderly man who was crouched on the floor close to the seats, trying to look invisible, and one small old lady who was trying to share a seat with a friend.

When Frank Schaub said he would like to call Mary Coppolino as a court witness, Jim Russ asked that any presentation of the witness be taken up in chambers first. The judge, the attorneys, and the court reporter recessed to the judge's hearing room.

Schaub explained his position by saying, "The witness that we seek to call is a witness that the state has subpoenaed who we feel has particular knowledge concerning matters in this cause. It is testimony that the state cannot vouch for. If called as a witness by the state, she may prove to be a hostile witness against the State of Florida. I, as state attorney, do not wish to assume the responsibility of jeopardizing the state's case by calling her as a witness for the state and thereby vouching for the truthfulness or candor of her testimony. I do not believe the state should be bound by her testimony, having good reason to believe that this witness has a personal interest in seeing that the defendant is not convicted, and may attempt to conceal material facts bearing upon the question of guilt of the defendant on this charge, and to the detriment of the state. Therefore, and for the reasons so stated, I now ask that Mary Coppolino be called as a witness by the Court, and examined and cross-examined by the prosecution and the defense, but not as a witness for either the state or the defendant, all in accordance with the law of the state. We would show to the court that the record will disclose that the state has caused this witness to be placed under subpoena several times, and in each instance she has refused to be examined."

"What do you intend to show by the witness?" the judge asked.

"Number one, that she had an affair going with the defendant at the time the crime occurred. That she was a woman of some means. That she had an inheritance protection. We wish to find out whether or not one of the motives was financial gain. She can relate those matters to the court. We can show to the court further that less than one month after the death of the deceased she and the defendant applied for a marriage license at the culmination of this affair. We also intend to show by her that she was with the defendant the night before the death, contrary to what the defendant has related to us, and other various matters."

Lee Bailey, in response, said, "Mr. Schaub has made an offer of proof to the court that is serious. I am willing to put her on as to matters before the death which could be relevant to motive to see if he can show motive, or if he is blowing smoke. I would like to call that. [In the sense, one must assume, of calling a bluff.] If he wants to probe around as to why she married the defendant after his wife's death or anything that happened after Carmela's death, I don't think that is relevant to the motive."

When Mr. Schaub said he would go into those events prior to the marriage, Judge Silvertooth said that at this stage he would allow it for anything prior to the death, saying, "That doesn't mean I won't allow it after death at the trial."

James Russ then said it was his contention that Mary Coppolino had a privilege arising out of the marital relationship which would permit her to decline to answer any questions about the marriage or the premarital relationship. He was, of course, speaking as Mary's personal attorney. The judge stated that the only thing in issue in the cause, and the only thing he had to look to, was the rights of the defendant, not an individual witness. Bailey said that he had stated his position in the matter, but he couldn't very well waive the rights of Mary Coppolino. The judge then ruled that they would proceed on the basis of sticking strictly to events prior to the death.

William Strode, Schaub's assistant, then asked about the three children who had been subpoenaed and had not been produced the previous day. Russ said, for the record, that he represented them. The judge asked their ages, and Schaub said the youngest was nine or ten, the oldest nineteen, and said he did not believe the state would call the fourteen-year-old one. The judge asked him what he intended to prove by the children.

Schaub said, "The nine- or ten-year-old has been adopted. [This was certainly not a revelation of any new fact insofar as Judge Silvertooth was concerned. On the ninth day of the previous June, weeks before the indictment and arrest of Carl Coppolino, Judge Lynn Silvertooth had heard the Adoption Petition of Mary Williams Coppolino, and had signed the two decrees, Number 19,883 and 19,884, making Monica Ann and Lisa Marie Coppolino the lawful children of Mary Coppolino.] She is the child of the defendant. She has therefore been in the care and custody of both of them at various times since this death occurred. Because Mary Gibson has resisted subpoena so much, we have not endeavored to subpoena the child before. On the other hand, this child was present and it has been shown she was in the house when this death occurred and could very well have observed something.

She was physically present that night, that morning, and therefore we feel that we should have the right to ask her. I think the court should first determine if she is an intelligent girl."

"What would she know that the nineteen-year-old wouldn't?" the judge asked.

"The nineteen-year-old is the daughter of Mary Gibson. She has had ample opportunity to observe the affair. She has had ample opportunity to know what happened at her household the night before and the night of this murder."

After hearing more argument, the judge ruled, "On a preliminary hearing the Court can call Court witnesses. It doesn't mean anything at the trial. What happens in the preliminary hearing will have a great bearing on whether I would allow you to call them at the trial. Frankly, it doesn't bother either one of you at this stage. When the witness is called, there will be no statements or comments made that this witness is called as a Court—or adverse—witness. I am allowing this as a Court witness at this stage, which is in the record, but there will be no comment in front of the reporters. That could have an adverse effect, because I could rule contrary."

Mr. Russ again asked that the restriction placed on the questioning be defined, and Judge Silvertooth said that the questions could cover up to the death, and the date of death, through the 28th of August.

And so the preliminary hearing was resumed, and Mary Coppolino was called to the witness stand.

She was a trim and attractive woman, nearing forty, wearing a long-sleeved beige silk suit with a short jacket trimmed in white, a white blouse. Her dark chestnut brown hair was worn in a bouffant boyish cut, with bangs and sideburns. She carried a large leather purse and white gloves.

She was born and raised in the small community of Faunsdale, Alabama. Mary Williams, the only child of the town pharmacist and drugstore owner, fourth generation of the Williams family in that town. One can imagine that the rigid codes and stratifications of the culture of the small towns and cities of the South provide much in security and satisfaction to the girl children. She was an only child, pert and pretty. Everyone knew who she was, and she would grow up knowing all the involuted relationships, all the old scandals and adventures.

Her daddy had picked up tracts of timber land over the years. (He died in October 1966, a month after the preliminary hearing, and two months before the New Jersey trial.) Her mother, very active in club work and charity work, was a member of the D.A.R. and of the Daughters of the Confederacy.

She was a student at the University of Alabama for a short time and married Gordon Gibson on October 6, 1945. He was on the military staff of the United States Embassy in Mexico City, and he took his Alabama bride back to Mexico with him for the few months remaining before he was returned to civilian life.

Gordon Gibson, and his first cousin, Lloyd Gibson, were of French Canadian descent. Gordon's father was a retired civil service worker. Lloyd's father was a successful dairy farmer. There were five boys in the family and they formed a basketball team that toured the South playing exhibition games with organized teams and consistently winning. Lloyd's father had purchased a considerable tract of Florida Panhandle land fronting on the Gulf of Mexico, about midway between Panama City, Florida, and Mobile, Alabama. Gordon and Mary Gibson went back to that area, later incorporated as Fort Walton Beach, and Gordon began that kind of tourist-oriented, real-estate-oriented scrambling which can pay off very well if the area is growing. Gordon went into many ventures on his own, beginning with a motel, and into others with Lloyd Gibson, such as a golf course and real estate subdivision in North Carolina.

At the time of their divorce in May 1963, Gordon was a fairly tall, slender man with dark wavy graying hair, a prominent and aggressive-looking jaw at odds with a quiet and reserved manner. He could call himself a self-made man. He had been a mayor of Cinco Bayou for several years. He owned various pieces of property, rental buildings, pieces of shopping centers. Mary—more commonly known during her years in Fort Walton Beach by her nickname "Pony"—had done her share, working behind the motel desk during the first tough years.

Though Gordon had done well, Lloyd Gibson had done perhaps twice as well.

Gordon Gibson had formed a closely held family corporation under which he conducted his business affairs, called Gib-Nett, Inc.

The final decree was granted in Okaloosa County on the 21st day of May, 1963. Mary was granted custody of their two daughters, Harriet Williams Gibson, then age sixteen, nicknamed Heidi, and Claire Sterling Gibson, then twelve. She was given child support money in the amount of $200 per month per child until they should reach the age of twenty-one, plus $700 tuition for Heidi for the coming school year, and a sum to be agreed upon for the subsequent years.

In addition, Mary Gibson was awarded 6579 shares of common stock of Gib-Nett, Inc., plus a $20,000 note from the corporation, a residential dwelling and five acres of land in Faunsdale, Alabama, the family homestead and residential dwelling and its contents in Cinco Bayou, three rental houses in Cinco Bayou, and six building lots in Cinco Bayou, and one vacant lot adjacent to the Fort Walton Beach Municipal Golf Course, with the provision that Gordon would pay off the indebtedness thereon.

Lloyd Gibson and his wife were also divorced at about the same time. Mrs. Mary Gibson moved to Sarasota, Florida, with her daughters and, after renting a house for a time, purchased a new home in October 1964 in a development called Forest Lakes, southeast of the city. Eight or nine months later she met Dr. Coppolino, and became his bridge partner.

This was the background of the doctor's wife, the woman who took the stand September 13. A merry, talkative, lively, well-grooomed woman with the distinctive accent of the small-town South. A saucy and challenging and sometimes overly girlish woman who seemed to be half-appalled and half-enthralled by the danger and drama of the situation in which she had found herself. One can imagine that the most disconcerting aspect of the situation to her was to find herself suddenly without status or public support. She had grown up with the sure knowledge of who she was. Right after the war, during the early years in Fort Walton Beach what status she had was the residue of Faunsdale, but over the years Gordon Gibson had made enough of a success of his affairs to give her new status as his wife. Though it is questionable to ever generalize about any certain class of person, the upper middle-class woman from the small town in the deep South seems to have certain identifiable characteristics. An awareness of and dependence upon small social protocol—such as knowing exactly when and where one should wear gloves. An awareness of "face" in the Chinese sense—an iron pride which keeps one from ever letting down, of ever showing faults and weaknesses. A well-honed sense of status—one can imagine that in the pharmacist's household, a medical doctor was always mentioned with considerable respect. A considerable shrewdness about property and money—but kept well-hidden, as that is one of the areas which southern ladies are required to be unable to comprehend. A shrewdness in the quick appraisal of the stranger, because social survival in the small cities of the South where population is fairly static requires as much guile, dissimulation and careful maneuvering as does Arabian politics. A strong and mannered nest-building instinct, the drive to create the securities

98

of the home place through children, interior décor as in the service magazines, a proper ceremony of cooking, eating, drinking, entertaining. And, finally, an obligation to try to always put people at their ease, to be vivacious, semi-flirtatious, lively, full of an undemanding chatter and a variety of ways of flattering and pleasing the listener.

This was the woman who, gloves and purse in hand, walked resolutely to the stand to face the questions Frank Schaub would put to her. For weeks Schaub had been trying to force a chance to take a statement from her, but James Russ had managed to block every subpoena through legal maneuvering.

After establishing name, address, and relationship to the accused, Schaub asked her if she had known Carl Coppolino in August of 1965. Yes sir. July of 1965? Yes sir. June of 1965? No sir.

"When and where did you first meet him?"

"I do not know the exact date that I met Doctor Coppolino. I first saw him at the Maxwell Studio. I would say this would be approximately the middle of July. I took a bridge lesson there and he was in the class. This was on a Friday, but the date I don't really know. I am sure you could check their records."

"Are you quite certain you never met him before July of 1965?"

"I never saw Carl Coppolino before in my life until I walked in for a bridge lesson at the Maxwell Studio. I had been taking lessons for better than a month, and he was sitting at the bridge table."

"After you met him on this day, when did you next see him?"

"The next time I saw him was at the Maxwell Studio of Bridge."

"Was this the following day?"

"It could possibly have been the following day. The next time I played bridge with Doctor Coppolino, Mrs. Maxwell asked me if I would play in the afternoon with Doctor Coppolino, and I didn't remember who Doctor Coppolino was, but I said yes, I would be glad to have a partner for the afternoon game. It is hard to remember just what date this was because it wasn't important."

He asked her when she had next seen him. "It must have been sometime the following week. I don't know whether I played bridge with him again or I next had a lesson with him again. You see, I didn't control the lessons. Mrs. Maxwell set up the lessons. They were 'playing' lessons. The group varied. It depended on who was scheduled on what day. Routinely, I took a lesson on Wednesday or Friday. Usually it was Friday. It was at Mrs. Maxwell's convenience, and I don't have records."

"You say you met him on one occasion and then saw him the following week? That was the next time you saw him? Is that correct?"

"Yes."

"Did you see him the day after that second meeting?"

"You know, you are asking me questions about trivia, and it was a year ago, and to remember dates . . . Today anything that I can tell you that would help you, I am very glad to do it, but I can't be specific because it wasn't important at the time. Do *you* remember who *you* saw on what day last year?"

Her manner was snippy, combative, and, as was evident to the press, spectators, and the officers of the court, would certainly have made an unfortunate impression on a jury had one been present. It is possible to suggest that her attitude could have resulted from two factors: First, quite possibly as a tactical device, her attorneys had led her to believe that, because they had been able to block all his attempts to subpoena her and take a statement from her, Frank Schaub could not cause her any particular difficulties once she took the stand, with her attorneys present, and submitted to his questioning. Additionally, she could not be blamed for feeling a considerable hostility toward Frank Schaub, as she believed that he was personally rather than professionally involved in what, to her, was a misguided campaign against her young husband. She believed that Frank Schaub alone was responsible for the weeks Carl had spent in the Sarasota County Jail, swiftly shedding that weight she had managed to put on his spare frame by taking extra pains to prepare dishes which would tempt his appetite. As it would be only human for her to assume that others would feel as she did about these matters, one can suspect that she believed that she was "handling" Frank Schaub successfully.

"After the second meeting," Schaub asked in his heavy, plodding and methodical voice, "when was the next time you saw him?"

"I don't *know* when the next time I saw him was! I possibly— the rest of that month—saw him two or three times a week playing bridge."

"Are you speaking of the month of July?"

"Yes."

"Would it be possible that you saw him every day for the remainder of that month?"

"No sir." Schaub asked her then how often she saw him in

August. "Pretty much on the same routine. I would see him at a bridge lesson, and as I got to know him better, we would make our own arrangements, because all people that play duplicate keep a calendar. Of course, Doctor Coppolino played with other people. I was not always his partner. I played with him I would say in a game possibly from two to four times a week, and I saw him then."

"Would you carry him to the bridge games, or would he carry you?"

"That would be a silly thing to do. I have my car and live on one side of town and he on the other."

"That doesn't answer the question."

"No sir. I went to the studio myself."

"He went by himself?"

"I don't know how he got there."

"Did you and he leave together?"

"I may have walked downstairs and out with him."

"We are speaking of August," Schaub reminded her.

"But he didn't offer me transportation to and from the Maxwell Studio to my knowledge. I don't remember him picking me up from my home to go to Maxwell Studio of Bridge."

"Did he ever pick you up during the month of August at your home and take you anywhere else?"

"In the month of August?" she said with thoughtful frown. "You know, once Carl played with me at Forest Lakes [Country Club]. I don't know what the month was, whether it was July or August, and at that time I did ride from my house to the country club in his car."

"Is it your statement that you have only ridden with him one time to the bridge club?"

"This wasn't to a bridge club. This was to a private game held at Forest Lakes."

"Is it your statement that he only escorted you out only one time during the month of August?"

"I don't think that Doctor Coppolino *escorted* me." To fill in here the flavor of her testimony, it might be useful to give a phonetic spelling of the way she pronounced that word. Es-COE-ted. She speaks rapidly, but drags out the word she wishes to emphasize. She was correcting Schaub in the sense of social usage of the word, and did so with a small, assured and reprimanding smile.

"The question is: Did he come to your house and you went with him?"

"To my knowledge, he picked me up and we went to Forest

Lakes and played. I am not sure. Possibly we could have played at Forest Lakes twice. If you will check the records you can get the information. I am aware of one time that he picked me up at the house."

"But you say positively that he didn't pick you up at your home more than two times?" Russ objected on grounds of harassment. Schaub explained to the Court the witness was being evasive. The objection was sustained.

"It is so hard to remember," the witness said.

"How many times did he pick you up at your home during the months of July and August of last year?"

"Mr. Schaub, I think one time I am positive I rode from my house, which is approximately three blocks to the club, in Carl's car and returned the same way. I have no knowledge of him picking me up and taking me anywhere else."

"Did he ever pick you up and take you swimming?"

"Pick me up at my house and take me swimming? No. I have been to the beach twice with Doctor Coppolino but he didn't pick me up at my house." Under questioning she described the two occasions. "Shortly after I met him he said that his family would like to go to the beach. I said, 'Fine. Let's all go and meet each other.' He said fine, we would get together in some manner. It worked out that they couldn't go, and when I met Doctor Coppolino at the beach his family was not there. I talked to him briefly. This was at Point of Rocks. I walked down and showed him the rocks and left. Later Carmela called me and asked me for lunch and this is the way all of us met. I don't call this an appointment or being escorted. We went down with the children to Venice one day, and this was possibly in July or August because summer school was in session. We didn't stay long. He wanted to know the area where he could get shark's teeth. He rode down with the children and I. Claire was in summer school. I came back to school to pick up Claire [the younger daughter of her first marriage]. I don't know where I picked up Doctor Coppolino. Maybe at the school, because Heidi and I left the house together. I don't remember where we met him."

When Schaub asked if she had gone to the beach with Coppolino more than twice, she said that she had a recollection of just the two times. Under questioning she said that she had never had dinner with him during those two months, but had lunch with him many times at the bridge school with the other students, the sandwich and cola drink traditionally served.

"Did he have lunch at your house during this time?"

"Let's see . . . You know, it is so hard. When you have lived with someone so long, it is hard to remember how many times they ate at your house. I never invited Doctor Coppolino to my house as a luncheon guest. I can think of one time in particular that he came by. I had been out all morning. He had been trying to call me to see if I wanted to play bridge. When I came in from school with the children—they were in summer school—he came by because the phone was out of order. We were having lunch. I am sure he had a sandwich with us that day, but I never invited him as a luncheon guest.''

"Is your answer 'one occasion'?''

"My answer is, to my recollection Doctor Coppolino came by the house one time in particular and we were eating and he had a sandwich with us. If there were other times, I do not remember inviting Doctor Coppolino to my house as a luncheon guest, if this helps you in any way.''

"Directing your attention to the month of August, how frequently did Doctor Coppolino come by your house that month?''

"I have no idea how often Doctor Coppolino came by my house. There was no reason for him to come to my house by appointment nor by invitation. I don't know. I am sure he dropped in at times, but I don't know.''

"Would it be correct to say almost every day during August?''

"This would be very *incorrect*, to say every day in August!''

"I said *almost* every day.''

"What *is* almost every day?''

"Five days out of the week.''

"You have done a lot of investigating. You have a lot of information at your fingertips . . .''

Mr. Schaub interrupted to ask the Court to instruct the witness to answer the question. He then rephrased it.

"Isn't it true that he visited your home once a day for at least five days a week during the month of August?''

"I wouldn't think so.''

"Do you know?''

"I don't know anything, Mr. Schaub. I told you that I couldn't give you anything specific. I wish I could. How can you take last summer's trivia and turn it into today's specific—something you did, something unimportant last year?''

Judge Silvertooth said to her, "I realize people *do* get upset, but . . .''

"I am *not* upset!'' she said.

"All you can do,'' said the judge, "is answer the questions. Don't elaborate.''

"If it isn't there,'' she said, "I can't get it out.''

When once again Schaub rephrased the question, she replied, "I am not in the position to give you an answer. I do not know."

Frank Schaub then elicited an immediate and energetic objection from Lee Bailey when he asked Mary Coppolino what Carl had to say on August 27, 1965, about a letter Mary had gotten from her ex-husband, Gordon Gibson ". . . stating that if you did not tell Carmela Coppolino about you and Carl . . ."

Bailey objected that the question assumed a fact not in evidence and asked if he could see the letter. Frank Schaub announced that the witness (Gordon Gibson) was in Nicaragua. The objection was sustained, but after further argument and a discussion at the bench, Schaub was permitted to ask, "During the month of August of last year did you receive a letter from Gordon Gibson?"

"I don't have knowledge of receiving a letter from Gordon Gibson in the month of August of last year. I was home with my family and out of town for a couple of weeks. Gordon was down for a week in August, and to my knowledge I don't think Gordon and I did any amount of corresponding. I spoke to him on the telephone. I have no knowledge whatsoever of any mail received from Mr. Gibson in the month of August. I don't know of any letter in my possession from Mr. Gibson written in the month of August. I have one written yesterday."

F. Lee Bailey stood up and said, "The question has been answered. The answer is no."

"She has not said no," Frank Schaub repled.

"She said no letter in the month of August," Bailey replied.

Mary Coppolino said, "I did not receive to my knowledge any letter through the mails of the continental United States of America from Gordon Gibson in the month of August. I was with him very much in the month of August and spoke—"

"*Please*, Mrs. Coppolino!" said Lee Bailey. "The question has been *answered*. Don't elaborate."

Schaub then asked her if she had a phone conversation with Gordon Gibson in the latter part of August concerning any letter. Mary said no. Bailey objected. The Court sustained the objection. Schaub asked if during July and August she and Gordon Gibson had been discussing a possible remarriage. Mary said, "No. The month of June."

"I will ask you whether or not during July or August of last year you were riding in an automobile with Gordon Gibson in Sarasota, and the defendant, Carl Coppolino, followed you about in another automobile?"

The dictionary definition of ''to bridle'' says, ''To draw up the head and draw in the chin as in disdain or resentment.'' It describes Mary Coppolino's reaction to the question.

''Now, by following about,'' she said, ''whom was following whom?''

''That Carl Coppolino was following you and Gordon Gibson around Sarasota and that you were not able to shake him?''

''Never am I aware of an incident in which it was impossible to shake Doctor Coppolino from following Gordon Gibson and myself. I am aware of the incident to which you have reference to, and would be very glad to go into it with you.''

''If you will do that, please.''

''I think that the incident that Mr. Gibson has in mind—in fact I know, because I discussed it with him when he was here last month—that Mr. Gibson and I had dinner on St. Armand's Key. We were walking around looking in the store windows, which is a lady-folk's pastime. As we left going down to the beach to get an after-dinner drink, we passed the road going into Lido there, and there was a loud horn-blowing, and Doctor Coppolino pulled up beside the car and said, 'Hi! Where are you all going?' He had met Gordon previously—I think the same day. What day this was I don't remember. I said, 'We are going to get a drink.' He said, 'May I join you?' By that time Mr. Gibson was upset at being joined by another male. He said, 'I have changed my mind. I wouldn't like a drink.' I said, 'Sorry, Carl. We are not going to get a drink. I guess I am going to go home.' He said, 'Fine.' He turned around and to my knowledge, Doctor Coppolino was in front of my car which Mr. Gibson was driving. He had flown down here. We went back to St. Armand's, and Doctor Coppolino turned left and blew his horn and waved like he was going home, and we continued on across the causeway slowly. When we got to the traffic light, I don't know how in the world it happened, but Doctor Coppolino was sitting in front of us at the traffic light with his hands behind his head. Gibson said, 'That looks like Doctor Coppolino.' I said, 'Yes, I believe it is.' Mr. Gibson turned and went down the trail [Route 41, the Tamiami Trail] and said, 'He will probably follow us.' I said, 'What in the world for. You told him you didn't want to drink with him.' Mr. Gibson drives very fast. I wish the Sarasota police would have talked to him because I do not like to drive fast. He became lost off Orange Avenue and had stopped at a dead end street. I said, 'This is enough! What in the world do you think we are doing? I would like to live a little bit longer than this.' If Doctor Coppolino was following us you would have to ask Doctor Coppolino. To my knowledge he wasn't, except that one short period of time our car was behind Doctor Coppolino's car. Does this help you?''

"Prior to your marriage or during this period of time we are speaking of, did Doctor Coppolino ever discuss any hypnotic ability with you?''

"I don't remember any discussion of hypnosis per se, because I didn't know anything about it and wouldn't have gotten into it either.''

"Then your answer is that he did not?''

"Not to my knowledge or recollection. I knew he was a physician and anesthesiologist.''

Lee Bailey rose again and said, "Please, Mrs. Coppolino! There is no question before the court.''

She gave him a flustered smile and said, "I am a bad witness.''

"Just answer the questions,'' said Lee Bailey and sat down.

Schaub then asked her if she had seen Carl on August 15. She thought for a moment and said she believed that on that day she was returning from a trip home (Faunsdale, Alabama) and was driving most of that day. She testified she had not seen him on August 16.

"Did you see him on the 18th?''

"No sir. Not to my knowledge. I came back here—''

Bailey said sharply, "The question has been answered! It is no! Just answer the question!''

"I am too cooperative,'' Mary said to Bailey. She turned to Schaub. "I am really sorry, but you see I am perfectly willing to tell you.''

"I will ask you what the names and addresses of your parents are.''

Frowningly indignant, Mary Coppolino turned in the witness stand and looked up at Judge Lynn Silvertooth and said, "Is this relevant?''

The judge struggled for a moment to conceal his startled amusement. Bailey was on his feet at once, to say, "Objection! Please, Mrs. Coppolino. Let *me* be the attorney. I object because it is irrelevant.''

"Sustained,'' said Judge Silvertooth.

"Are you the only child of your parents?''

"The only one I know anything about,'' she said. It was that kind of saucy impudence which, acceptable and unremarkable in social situations, is as jarring in a courtroom as would be a snare drum in church.

"Are they people of some means?''

"No sir." And when Schaub tried to pursue it, asking about timber interests, Bailey objected and was sustained, though Schaub said it was relevant as part of the motive. He then moved on to the day before the death, August 27, 1965, a Friday, and asked when she first saw Carl that day. She said she had a bridge lesson in the afternoon at the Maxwell Studio and Carl was in that class. She said she went to it by herself, and did not leave with him when she went home in her own car. She said that on Friday evening there was a bridge game, rather than a lesson, at the studio, and she met Carl there and played bridge with him.

"Did you return with him to Bowsprit Lane?"

"No sir."

"Did you and he leave the bridge game together that evening?"

"My child was with me."

"That wasn't the question."

She looked up at the judge and said, "What does he want?"

Schaub said, "Did you leave the game with him?"

"I walked out with him. Yes."

"Did you then proceed to leave with him in the same car?"

"If you will let me tell you . . ."

"I think that warrants a yes or no," Schaub said. "Either you left in the same car or you didn't." Mr. Russ said the witness could explain the answer. The judge said she could answer yes or no and add her explanation. Mary testified that she had left in the same car with Coppolino, and thought that it was at about 10:30, when the games were usually over. She could not remember what time it was. Schaub asked if it could have been 11:30. She did not think so. Twice more he asked her if she had gone to Coppolino's home that night.

"The only time in the month of August that I was ever in Doctor Coppolino's home prior to Carmela's death . . ." She paused for thought, and corrected herself. "I wasn't ever there in August. I was there in July for lunch one day. That was the only time for me to be in that house."

He asked her if she had been there the 28th of August. She said she had not been in the house that day, that she had picked the children up at the Thomsons' across the street. She testified she had heard from Carl at about 9 A.M. that day, and had been asleep when he had telephoned her. He moved back to the evening of the 27th, to establish once again that she had been with Coppolino at the Maxwell Bridge Studio in the afternoon and again in the evening. She was obviously anxious to expand on the events of that evening, but Schaub gave her no opening, and terminated his direct examination at that point.

F. Lee Bailey's thirteen questions in cross-examination are worth covering completely as an example of how much can be done in a very brief span.

"On the night of the 27th you said your child was with you?"

"Yes sir."

"Which child?"

"Harriet."

"Were you separated from her at any time during that evening?"

"No sir."

"Did you bring your own car to Maxwell's?"

"Yes."

"Did you drive it home?"

"Yes sir."

"You were not at Doctor Coppolino's house at any time?"

"No sir."

"Did you ever, prior to the death of Carmela, have any discussion with Doctor Coppolino about marriage?"

"No sir."

"You say in June you were considering remarriage to Gibson?"

"Yes sir."

"And you decided against that course of action?"

"Yes sir."

"Did Doctor Coppolino have anything to do with your decision?"

"I didn't even know him."

"Was the decision made and given to Gibson prior to your first meeting with Doctor Coppolino?"

"I don't know as it was given to him any specific date. We were just discussing the possibility of getting our differences ironed out. It was never a discussion that we were going to get married again on X date."

"Mrs. Coppolino, is there any doubt in your mind that you never met Doctor Coppolino before the middle of July 1965?"

"None whatsoever!"

"Never laid eyes on him?"

"Didn't even know he existed."

The next witness for the state was Patricia Edwards Adomat, housewife, a slender, slow-moving, slow-speaking southern woman with an air of total, unruffled composure. Her southern accent was, though quite distinct, far more leisurely than Mary Coppolino's. For example, on Mrs. Adomat's lips "Yes" became a two syllable word which might be phonetically spelled Yea—yuss. And Mary became May-Ree.

William Strode took the direct examination, establishing that Pat Adomat had lived at 3267 Pine Valley Drive for twenty months, right next door to Mary Coppolino, and had known Mary during that period, having met her while their houses were being simultaneously constructed. She said her house was immediately next door to Mary's, and that she had a clear view of it, and knew Carl Coppolino, having met him around the last of June or the first of July of 1965.

"Where did you meet him?"

"I met him at Mary Gibson's house."

"Do you recall what he was doing there at that occasion?"

"They had been to the beach that morning."

"How often did you see him at Mary's house?"

"Well, almost every day for quite a while."

"Starting when?"

"Well, the car was there and I saw him there in June, but I didn't meet him in June, or the early part of June. I met him either in late June or the first of July."

"Did you become acquainted with his car?"

"Yes."

"What kind of car?"

"A 1965 Oldsmobile. It is green."

"And you say you saw it there in June?"

"Yes."

"Did you see him there in June?"

"Yes sir."

"How many times?"

"Well, almost every day for a while there."

"That was in June?"

"It was in June."

"How about July? How many times did you see him there in July?"

"Well [pronounced Way-yull], he was there every day unless Mary was out of town. Mary took some trips that summer. I don't remember just when she took the trips. Of course, he wasn't there then."

"Were you a friend of Mary?"

"Yes."

"Never had any disagreements with her?"

"No."

"How about in the first part of August, how often was Carl Coppolino at Mary's home then?"

"Well, daily unless she was out of town."

"What time of day would you see him there?"

"He would come in the mornings and he would go away in the afternoon. He would be back in the evening."

"He was there every evening?"

"Just about."

"How long would he be gone in the afternoon?"

"Oh, a few hours. Say two, three, or four hours. Something like that."

"Then he would be back in the evening?"

"Yes."

"Would they go out together in the same car?"

"Yes."

"In the evenings?"

"In the evenings."

"From the early part of June on?"

"Yea-yuss."

"Were they dating?"

"I guess you could call it dating. I don't know."

"What did you observe of their relationship?"

Here James Russ stood up and said, "Let's get down to a specific date instead of running all over the summer of 1965." The judge sustained the objection and requested Strode to ask more specific questions.

Through questions, Strode established that the witness had seen them go into Mary's house together in June, but had no way of knowing whether they were there alone, or one or both of the children were there. She said she had been in the house with them in July.

"How did they appear?"

"Very happy, gay and joking. You know."

"When did you find out that Carl Coppolino was married?"

"Well, Mary told me when she introduced me to him."

"Did this surprise you?"

"Yes. I was shocked."

Whereupon Bailey and Russ both leaped to their feet, stung by this almost classic example of an improper question on examination. In a voice half-pained, half-angry, F. Lee Bailey said, "What in the world did my brother ask that question for, knowing it is incompetent and irrelevant and immaterial? What do we care what this witness thinks?"

"If counsel has an objection," said Strode, "he can argue to the Court."

"We move that it be stricken from the record," Russ said.

The Court sustained it, and Russ added, "Further direct counsel not to ask that type of question again."

110

"Proceed, Counsel," said Judge Silvertooth.

After again establishing the morning and evening routine of visits during August as observed by Mrs. Adomat, Mr. Strode directed her attention to the 27th of August, the day before Carmela's death, and asked her if she had seen Carl on that day.

"I remember seeing him in the evening on that day. . . . He and Mary were going out in his car about seven o'clock in the evening, and they waved to me and I waved back. I was emptying my garbage."

He asked if there were any children with them, and she said they were alone in the car. She did not know what time they returned, or see the car again that evening.

James "Red" McEwen took over the cross-examination. He stated in gentle tones that he wanted to be certain how many times she had seen Carl at Mary's house in August. He started with the 27th. "Let's work it backwards." She said she distinctly remembered seeing him that evening, that it was still daylight, and there was no child in the car with them.

When she could not be specific about the other days in that same week, saying, "There were days missed, and days Mrs. Coppolino was out of town," McEwen handed her a little wallet calendar card to follow. She thought she had seen Dr. Coppolino there on the evening of the 28th.

"Was he there on the 27th after you saw them leave?"

"Not that I know."

"Was he there during the afternoon?"

"No, he wasn't. I had his children. This was a Saturday."

"I am talking about the 27th, *before* his wife's death."

She did not remember. Nor, when McEwen asked, could she remember whether or not she saw him on Thursday, or on Wednesday.

She said she remembered the specific date, remembered seeing him that Friday evening because of what happened that night. She asked if she could explain.

"My child went over to Mary's. I have a little girl nine years old, and she came home and told me that Mrs. Coppolino had died and that Mary had the two Coppolino children at her house and could she stay over there and play with them. I said yes, and I went over there to see if there was anything I could do to help. Later in the day I took the two little children and Harriet to the swimming pool. . . . That is when I [heard], the night before, that I knew he had been there the night before."

McEwen then took the week beginning Sunday, August 22, and then the week beginning August 15, but she could not be specific about any given day of the week, and repeated her earlier statement: "I said it was almost every morning and almost every night."

In response to his questions she testified that she did not say anything to Mary Gibson about the situation, and that she and Mary continued to visit back and forth. She had not seen the Coppolino children over there at any time during that period, nor their mother.

He finished with August and said, "How about the month of July? I am not quite sure yet what date you said that you met Doctor Coppolino. Could you help me by looking at the calendar?"

"I can't give you the specific date."

"Before or after July 4th?"

"I think it was after July 4th."

"It could have been as much as a week?"

"Yes."

"So July 4, 1965, fell on a Sunday and it could have been as long as the following Sunday or after that. Would that be a fair statement?"

She said that it would. He asked her if it had been on a Sunday and she said it was a week day, that she had gone over to borrow something. "They are friendly. We borrow things back and forth. Mary asked me to stay to lunch. I had lunch with them. The three of us had lunch."

She said that Mary had mentioned that she and Carl were playing bridge at the Maxwell Studio. And she testified that on the other occasions when she saw him there, the children were there quite often.

"Can you be a little more helpful as to how long before you were actually introduced to him that you saw him?"

"It must have been close to a month."

"From the time you first saw him, did the visits increase in number or about the same rate from the beginning?"

"About the same rate from the beginning."

She again affirmed that the almost constant visits went on throughout the month of June.

"Was there ever any effort on the doctor's part to conceal himself from your view?"

"No."

"Why was it that you were paying so close attention to these visits?"

"The way my house is built the open part or working part of my house is toward Mary's house. My garage is on that side. When I drive in my garage I can see her house. My garbage cans

112

are on that side. If I throw out the garbage I can see. My utility room and cleaning supplies are on that side. If I cook out I see into her yard. My patio is on that side. I never see anything that goes on in my other neighbor's yards, but that is the way my house is built.''

He asked her if she knew Gordon Gibson, and when she said she did, asked her if she had seen Gibson at Mary's house during June. She thought she had seen him there once or twice in the daytime, in the early part of June, prior to the fifteenth of the month. She said she did not see any other men there that she could not identify during the month of June, but said she had seen Lloyd Gibson there in May.

"When did it first become important to start remembering that there was some man there all the time?"

"It is not important to me."

"You kept no record of it?"

She looked at him with a bland astonishment. "Why, no!"

"Were the visits in the early part of June as frequent as they were in August?"

"Yes. Why, I thought May-ree had a houseguest—because the car was always there."

In a series of unrelated questions, McEwen took her back over ground previously covered, then asked, "Was your husband ever with you on any of the occasions that you say you saw these two people together during the month of July 1965?"

"I don't know."

"Was he ever with you during the month of June that you say you saw the doctor and Mary Gibson together?"

"You would have to ask my husband. I really couldn't tell you. He is subpoenaed and he is here."

He asked the same question about August, and she did not know. He asked when her husband had met Dr. Coppolino, and she said not until after Mary and Carl were married.

Mr. McEwen walked slowly to the defense table and whispered for a few moments to Jim Russ and F. Lee Bailey. He went back and lounged against the jury rail, facing the witness and said, "One point we were about to overlook. Did you and your husband ever talk about the fact that you had seen Doctor Coppolino there at Mary Gibson's house as often as you said you did?"

She said she had told him about it, had mentioned it in passing, and nothing more, and that it had happened after she had met Coppolino.

"You told your husband that you had been seeing him over there a great deal?"

"Yes."

"But you don't know when you told him that?"

"No. Not exactly."

After a very brief redirect by Mr. Strode to establish that she had no personal knowledge of Mary Gibson's movements aside from what Mary Gibson told her, Pat Adomat was excused, and mid-day recess began.

It is of importance to note that in this preliminary hearing, as in both trials "the rule" had been invoked, meaning that no witness could remain in the courtroom and hear the testimony given by the other witnesses. Thus Mrs. Adomat had no idea of what her neighbor, Mary Coppolino, said on the witness stand. But Mary Coppolino was, as a Court witness and by agreement of opposing counsel, permitted to remain in the spectator section during the examination of other witnesses.

During the recess one newsman queried F. Lee Bailey about the quite obvious lack of instruction and advice given Mrs. Coppolino as to how to comport herself under examination. Lee Bailey said, "This isn't a trial. We let her go on cold to see how she does. You have to understand that sixty percent of the testimony given in a hearing will never be permitted in front of a jury. By letting her go on cold, we can tell what we should warn her about if it ever comes to her having to testify before a jury, which doesn't look very likely right now. Mostly it will just be a problem of getting her to restrict herself to answering the questions instead of trying to carry on a conversation."

Chapter Six

It was at 1 P.M. that second day of the hearing that the two children were examined in the judge's chambers—Monica, age nine, elder daughter of Carl and Carmela, and Harriet, nicknamed Heidi, elder daughter of Mary and Gordon Gibson, age nineteen.

It is an ugliness, at nine or nineteen, to be caught up in the austere and deadly formalities of justice. Perhaps in this case the ugliness was compounded by that growing personal antagonism

114

between Schaub and Bailey which had turned the usual mock-combat of courtroom adversaries into a real involvement of the emotions.

Judge Lynn Silvertooth, when they took the little girl first, showed a special warmth and empathy when he said to her, "You have to tell the truth, the whole truth and nothing but the truth, just like in Perry Mason."

Bill Strode conducted the direct examination of the child. "Monica, we are here on something today I am sure you would rather not talk about. Quite often in our business we have to talk to children about unpleasant things, and we are not picking on you or not trying to do anything to embarrass you or make you feel bad. You understand that?"

"Yes."

"The judge is doing his job, the court reporter and Mr. McEwen and Mr. Russ and Mr. Schaub. We are not trying to embarrass you, or don't want to hurt you or hurt anybody. It is necessary that we talk to you about the time that your mother died. I know this is something not easy for you to talk about. You understand this. We are trying to find out exactly what happened. Everybody is trying to find out what happened the night and day before she died. First, I am going to ask you if you remember the day before she died. Do you recall that?"

"No."

"Do you remember the day she died?"

"Yes."

"When did you first wake up in the morning?"

"I think it was about eight o'clock."

"Who woke you up?"

"Mrs. Thomson from across the street."

Mrs. Thomson had come into her room and awakened her. She had not gotten up during the night. She could not remember what time she had gone to bed. Strode reminded her that it had been a Friday night and asked her if she stayed up late on Friday nights.

"Usually until about eleven on Friday."

"What TV programs do you see on Friday nights?"

"Well, I see *Gomer Pyle* and *Hogan's Heroes.*"

She said she had watched television that Friday night and remembered seeing some of those programs, and thought she had stayed up until about eleven.

"Had your daddy come home before you went to bed? Or was he still out?"

"I think he was still out. I am not sure."

115

"But he had been out all evening the day before your mother died?"

"I think so. I think playing bridge or something."

She said that they usually had supper at five, that her mother had fixed it. She did not remember what they had, and she thought her mother had eaten with her and her little sister.

"Did she say anything about feeling sick at any time during that day?"

"No, she was perfectly cheerful. I remember that day I was playing and I tried to talk to her. She kept telling me to leave her alone because she was studying on some exam she had to take."

She said her mother had stayed home all evening and there had been no visitors.

"How about Pat Galenez?"

"No."

"You don't remember seeing her?"

"No."

"You don't know what time your father came home that evening?"

"No."

"You do know who Pat Galenez is?"

"No."

"A blonde lady? The young lady that lives with Mr. Norcross?"

"Oh yes. I remember her."

"Maybe she was there that evening, or do you remember? Do you think she was there that evening?"

"No. She wasn't there that evening."

"Was she there that afternoon do you think?"

"I don't remember."

"How about the time you were eating supper, did she come in while you were eating supper?"

"I don't remember."

She did not remember what time her father had gone out that evening to play bridge. She said he might have had supper with them, but couldn't remember if he did or didn't. Strode asked her if he went out to play bridge often during that period.

"Yes. Every morning before lunch he always used to go out and play bridge."

"And in the evenings usually?"

"Some of the time in the evenings."

She had heard no unusual noises that night, and nobody else came in, unless they came in while she was sleeping. He asked her when her parents' anniversary was, but she could not remember even the month.

116

"Do you remember that your father went away for a few days just before the middle of August and was gone for two or three days?"

"I don't remember that."

She did remember swimming in the Norcross pool with the Thomsons, and thought that the day before her mother died, she had swum there, but could not remember if her mother had gone swimming also. She had no recollection of hearing her mother and the Thomsons talking about her father being gone for a few days.

"Do you recall that when he came home that he brought her some flowers? Do you remember her having some yellow roses?"

"Yes."

"Hadn't he been away for a few days when he brought those?"

"I don't know that he brought them, but I saw some yellow roses on the dining-room table."

"That was shortly before your mother died?"

"Yes sir."

"Can you think of anything else that the judge should know about the situation at the house or anything else that has occurred to you that you thought was unusual?"

"No."

Strode indicated that he had finished. Judge Silvertooth said to the defense attorneys, "You may cross-examine if you want to. But I will rule that I won't allow her to testify in that courtroom."

There was no cross-examination.

It is one theory about memory that it is a function of our sum total of experience, and that our sense of time is also related to that cumulative total. A year had passed, and one year is over ten percent of the lifetime of a nine-year-old child. Thus the summers of childhood have the feeling of a golden endlessness. According to this theory, the memory of a nine-year-old as to the specifics of her life when she was only eight, would be akin to a forty-year-old being asked to recall specific things that happened when he was thirty-five. Thus time sense is related to sensory accumulation, a child doubling its input of information in the years from five to ten, whereas for the forty-year-old, it has taken twenty years to double the input.

Monica's eighth year was part of a misty past. To the adults who interrogated her, last year was yesterday.

Frank Schaub conducted the direct examination of Harriet Williams Gibson, establishing name, address, age, then asking her when she had met Carl Coppolino. She thought it was sometime after July 1st of 1965. She could not remember where she had first seen him, either at the bridge studio or at her home. She said he had come over to her home once or twice but could not remember which month.

Shaub asked her when she had first seen Carl Coppolino on the day Carmela died.

"They called my mother and asked—I don't remember what time it was. I remember the children came over real soon because he was real nervous and everything. He was upset about his wife dying. He wanted somebody to take care of the children. I believe that is what it was. Mother was the only one he could turn to for something like that."

"Did he speak to you when he got there?"

"I didn't really see him that much. I was taking care of the children, mostly."

"What did he do?"

"I can't remember what he did. I think he went back home and left the children over there. I didn't really talk to him. I didn't know him personally to talk to him. I wasn't close to him at all."

"You had never been in his company before, along with your mother?"

"Just with my mother . . . But I don't remember when it was."

He asked her if she had seen Carl the evening before Carmela died. "Over at Maxwell's," she replied. "Mother played bridge. He went in his car and Mother went in hers. They met over there."

"Did they leave together?"

"No. He had his own car and he left. Wait a minute. I am getting confused. It was late and Mother said that she was thirsty. Carl said he was thirsty and said, 'Why don't we get something before going home?' The only place open was McDonald's and we got something to drink. He got in his car. I think he went in his car. So we all went to McDonald's and he went home."

"Did you take him back to his car, then?"

"Yes."

"What time was that?"

"It was late. I don't remember."

"After midnight or before?"

"Real late to me. I'm a sleepy head."

Schaub directed her attention to the day Carmela died. "I ask you whether or not Carl Coppolino that day came to your home and appeared excited, happy, and danced with you in the yard or anything of that nature?''

"Before she died?"

"No. Right after."

"He wasn't thrilled about it. He was upset."

"Did he say anything to the effect, 'It is finally over'?"

"No."

Strode interposed a question. "Did he pick you up in his arms and whirl you around?"

Lee Bailey said in a tone of incredulity, "This is the day Carmela died?!"

Heidi said, "I hardly saw him at all that day because I was taking care of the children while he was making arrangements and calling the family." Schaub asked if he had talked to her directly. She said, "He didn't *say* he was sad. He *acted* sad. He didn't cry or anything like that or say, 'My wife is dead.' ''

As Frank Schaub finished, Judge Silvertooth said, "I stated before, you can cross-examine if you want to. But I will rule at this time, subject to your right of cross-examination, that this witness does not have to testify on the preliminary hearing."

Lee Bailey said, with smiling irony, "I believe Mr. Schaub would not want to call her. Because of the inferences, and because we have a stenographer, I would like to establish something."

The judge gave permission. First Bailey established, through his questions, that Heidi had never seen him before today, and had never talked with him before, and in testifying about Carl was relying wholly on her memory, not on anyone's suggestions.

"The next door neighbor, Mrs. Adomat, said Carl Coppolino was over there every day, morning and evening, all during the months of June, July and August. Is that true?"

"No sir."

"How many times to you think he was at your house before his wife died?"

"Three times at the most."

"Afternoon or evening."

"I believe it was the afternoon."

"How many times do you believe your mother played bridge during July and August."

"Once or twice."

"A week?"

"A week."

Schaub took over on redirect, and established that she had gone to summer school, but had come home each day at noon.

"If he had come any time from noon on during this time or in the evening . . ."

"I would remember it."

"You would have seen him?"

"Yes."

F. Lee Bailey said, addressing himself to Judge Silvertooth, "I asked Mr. Schaub to state whether or not he intended, between now and the time of trial—if he intends to subpoena this girl for private investigation. I suggest he do it right now."

Frank Schaub said, "She is a nineteen-year-old person, a high school graduate, and perfectly capable of answering to a subpoena. I don't think the suggestion by Mr. Bailey is well taken."

Bailey said, "I would like the record to reflect that Mr. Schaub is afforded the opportunity to put questions to this witness that are relevent. And he declines to ask further questions. I will raise that fact at any time that any subpoenas are issued."

"Any investigations done by the state," said Frank Schaub, "will be done by our office and not by Mr. Bailey."

Lynn Silvertooth said, "Frankly, I will probably have to rule on that at the time motions are filed. I am not sure whether I have the authority to restrict the subpoena powers."

"I am not either," Lee Bailey commented. "With the state of the record as it is, Mr. Schaub can only wish to question this witness in private to harass her. If he has an honest question to ask, he can do so in the presence of all of us."

Judge Silvertooth terminated the proceedings at that point, and soon the open-court hearing was resumed.

The exchange between Bailey and Schaub in chambers is an illuminating example of the cat-and-mouse game of discovery, as it is played in a preliminary hearing. It was obvious to Bailey that Schaub hoped to make some use of the girl in the state's case other than what had been brought out in his direct examination of her. The defense wanted to know what that might be, so that during the trial they would be—through their own pretrial investigation—prepared to counter in such a way as to diminish or destroy testimony damaging to the accused. Bailey's gambit was to attempt to force Schaub to reveal what other use she might be to the state's case, on the basis that if he did not reveal it now, he could not interrogate her further prior to trial.

The tenet of full pre-trial discovery, that supposedly admirable condition which would exist when the state would be required to expose to the defense every facet of the state's case, would—according to some philosophers of the law—substitute a new evil for an existing one.

120

When one comprehends that partial discovery gives the unscrupulous prosecutor, the man more interested in his own batting average than in fairness and justice—the chance to misuse the element of courtroom surprise by springing surprises which can impress a jury, but which could be logically proven to be of no value in assessing guilt had the defense been given the opportunity to learn of it in advance, full discovery seems an admirable advance in jurispurdence.

To invent an example, a prosecutor could, toward the end of the state's presentation of its case, swear a surprise eyewitness to an act of murder, one who claims to be able to identify the accused. Forewarned, the defense might have been able to come up with testimony to the effect that the supposed eyewitness has defective vision, was drunk the night of the crime, and has been one of those compulsive "witnesses" who, in the past, have claimed to have witnessed crimes they could not possibly have seen.

Yet when one assumes a diligent and scrupulous prosecutor, one who has checked and rechecked all aspects of his investigation and is convinced of the guilt of the accused beyond a reasonable doubt, when such a man is opposed by a diligent, brilliant, well-financed defense team, complete pre-trial discovery provides the defense the opportunity to "blow smoke," to prepare in advance to bring forward witnesses who will so cloud peripheral aspects of the testimony of key witnesses that the flavor of a reasonable doubt will pervade the essential aspects of such testimony. After all, while it is the task of the state to obtain a verdict of guilty, it is not the task of the defense to secure a verdit of innocent. The defense must work toward a verdict of not guilty, based upon not proven beyond a reasonable doubt.

To take the invented eyewitness situation again for a moment, it is true that there can be no genuine "surprise witness" in that the state must furnish the defense with the listed names and addresses of all persons subpoenaed or to be subpoenaed, and who might reasonably be called as state witnesses. Such persons are informed by the prosecutor that he cannot order them not to speak to defense counsel. They have the right to make their own choice, to answer or to refuse to answer defense questions. Were such a list supplied to the defense to contain scores of names, it is possible that through the pressure of time and sheer numbers, a damaging key witness could be overlooked during the defense investigation of the list.

Under the adversary system, if the state is required to expose all its evidence to the defense, without any obligation on the part of the defense to a similar disclosure, it becomes evident that in those capital cases defended by celebrity attorneys at high cost, convictions will be more difficult to achieve, regardless of the ethical position of the prosecutor.

However, we should all bear in mind how very few of these celebrated criminal lawyers are in practice on a national scale at any given time, and how rare are those capital cases which attract national attention.

In the July/August 1967 edition of the magazine *Trans-Action*, Abraham S. Blumberg, Associate Professor of Law and Sociology at John Jay College of the City University of New York, gives some appropriate statistics in an article entitled *Lawyers with Convictions*. Mr. Blumberg had eighteen years experience in criminal law as defender and prosecutor.

He writes, "Between 1950 and 1964 in the court I studied, from 75 to 90% of all adversary trials ended in conviction. In all years less than 5 percent of all indictments ended in adversary trials. . . . The Gideon, Miranda and Escobedo decisions were greeted with such lively delight or anguished dismay that outsiders must have thought that the Supreme Court had wrought some magnificent transformation in the defense lawyer. Actually, the court in these cases was perpetuating the Perry Mason myth of an adversary trial, while in the lesser courts of the nation the dreary succession of 90 percent negotiated pleas continued.

"These decisions have not changed the nature of the court bureacracy and, if anything, the pressure for guilty pleas and the drive for efficient production may grow even stronger, and the position of the defendant as a bureaucratic client further hampered by race, poverty and class, may become weaker and weaker.

"Courts, like many other large modern organizations, possess a monstrous appetite not only for individuals, but for entire professions. Almost all those coming under an organizational authority find their definitions, perceptions and values have been refurbished in terms largely favorable to the particular organization and its goals.

"Thus, the Supreme Court decisions extending the right to counsel may have an effect which is radically different from that intended or anticipated. The libertarian rules will tend to augment the existing organizational arrangements, enriching court organizations with more personnel and elaborate structure, and making them an even more sophisticated apparatus for processing defendants toward a guilty finding."

When the courtroom was called to order again, Mr. Strode announced that the state had finished its portion of the preliminary hearing, and moved that the Court find that probable cause had been established, and to bind the defendant over and continue him in custody for trial on the issues by a jury. He seemed to be basing his motion on the fact that the defense had been able to indulge in extensive cross-examination. Looking astonished, the judge said, "You are moving before the defense puts on its case?"

Legal argument began, but Judge Silvertooth interrupted. "I will save a lot of time. The motion is denied."

The defense called Mr. E. A. Adomat, and Lee Bailey made the direct examination, establishing that Mr. Adomat was the area division manager of Florida Power and Light, and worked eight to five on weekdays, and frequently during the evening. He said that he knew Mary Gibson, and that she had moved in when her house had been completed about a month before the Adomat house. He said there was a normal friendly neighborly relationship between them and Mary Gibson, and he saw her about once a week, in the Adomat home or in Mary's back yard. He said he had introduced himself to Carl Coppolino after Carl's marriage to Mary, and thought he had seen Carl once previously, perhaps several months before he met him.

"Did you know anything about Doctor Carl Coppolino from your wife or word of mouth at the time you first saw him?"

"No sir. I tried not to pry in her business."

"Prior to the death of Mrs. Carmela Coppolino had you heard any rumors?"

"No sir."

"It had never been brought to your attention that Doctor Coppolino was a house guest of your neighbor prior to August of 1965?"

"No sir."

Mr. Adomat said he knew he had seen Carl once at Mary's house prior to meeting him, but could not say whether that had been in June, July, August, or September, and was not aware at the time he had seen Carl whether Carmela was alive or dead. He said it had come to his attention, through the newspaper, that Mrs. Coppolino had died, but he had not discussed it with his wife. He knew about Mary taking the Coppolino children to care for, and said they had been in his house

"Did your wife ever complain to you or remark to you that

123

Doctor Coppolino was a daily and evening visitor of Mary Gibson?"

"I don't think so. If she did, I didn't pay any attention to it."

Under questioning, he said he had met Gordon Gibson a month previously, and could have met him before.

"I think I had been introduced to him. We cook in the back yard and sometimes Mary would bring some of her friends over and introduce them. I think I may have met Gordon Gibson then."

"Do you think you ever met Lloyd Gibson?"

"I think so. But it was just a thing . . . like I remember you." Adomat paused and evidently decided that it had not been a very apt simile. He looked quizzically at Lee Bailey and said, "I will probably *remember* you!"

It was a compliment, and Bailey acknowledged it in the same tough-minded appraising way it had been given by saying, "I will try to make sure you do." He then went back over ground previously covered, the one time Adomat had seen Carl, and the testimony that Adomat had not met Carl until after they were married.

"Does Mrs. Adomat drink a great deal?"

Mr. Adomat seemed slightly startled but not angered by the question. "I don't think so. I am not home all day, but I don't believe she does. I buy the whiskey."

"How rapidly does it disappear?"

"I buy a bottle every two weeks. And I drink some of that."

"Does Mrs. Adomat take any drugs of any kind?"

"I think she does, but I don't know what they are."

He said he knew who her doctor was, said calmly that she had a past history of epilepsy, and took Dilantin Sodium capsules.

"How about Stelazine?"

"I don't know. She takes two or three pills, and I take pills as a matter of fact."

Questioned about the relationship with Mary, Adomat said that the relationship had been pleasant, with no arguments or hostility that he knew of. Bailey then asked him if the sheriff had asked him to keep an eye on the house next door and see what he could report. Adomat could not remember the sheriff's exact words, just that he had been asked if he would help if he could. Schaub objected on the grounds of materiality, and when the Court sustained the objection, Bailey relinquished the witness for cross-examination by the state.

This was the first time that Frank Schaub had a chance at cross-examination of a defense witness. As he began, F. Lee

Bailey walked over and positioned himself in the same spot Frank Schaub had occupied while Bailey had cross-examined the state witnesses. Lee Bailey tucked his chin in and stared at the witness under frowning brow. He teetered back and forth from heel to toe. He clasped his right wrist behind himself in his left hand, and clenched and stretched and worked the fingers of his right hand. It was a deft and mocking imitation, and when the state attorney noticed it, he was not amused. His ears reddened. Bailey kept it up for a few moments and then went, smiling, back to the defense table.

In the cross-examination Schaub established that Adomat was in an executive capacity with Florida Power and Light, and consequently was involved in civic activities which frequently kept him away from his home in the evenings. He guessed that it would average out at one evening a week. He then asked Adomat what Carl was doing at the time he first saw him.

"Well, he was coming around the back of the house and he looked in the back window and the back porch door, which is a screened porch. I saw him because I was sitting on my little patio outside of my back door cooking a steak on a barbecue grill. . . . I talked to the man and asked if I might help him because I knew Mary was out of town. He said no thank you, and went back around the house."

He could not remember what month it was, only that Mary was out of town at the time. And that was the end of the cross-examination.

There was a rustle and whispering and stir from the spectators when Marjorie Farber was called as the next witness. She wore a navy blue suit with a white rolled collar, pearls, a gold crucifix on a gold chain. She looked crisp, composed, but with a hint of inner tension in the compression of her lips.

This was the first of the three confrontations between Marjorie Cullen Farber and F. Lee Bailey. It began in low key, and in a focus of total attention from everyone in the courtroom. He established that she lived at 581 Bowsprit Lane, next door to the home once owned by Carl Coppolino. She testified she had known Carl since 1962, when she had been living with her late husband, Colonel William E. Farber, at 50 Wallace Road, Middletown, New Jersey. Carl and Carmela Coppolino had previously moved from Wallace Road to Florida. She testified that she and Carmela were very good friends. She had visited many times with Carl and Carmela at their home, and when Bailey asked her to describe the husband and wife relationship, she

125

said, "I would say a very compatible young couple." She knew of no quarrels.

"How often would you see Carl Coppolino from December of 1962 until he left New Jersey?"

"Quite often." Asked to be more specific, she said, "Well, every day practically."

"How was that?"

"I got to know Carl and Carmela quite well because he had been ill and he had asked me to drive him to the library and different places, and that is how the relationship more or less started."

She said he was at home because of his illness. He was interested in doing some writing. She would drive him to the library. He was writing a book about the use of hypnosis in anesthesiology, a book which had since been published.

"What was your relationship to Doctor Coppolino?"

"He was a *very* good friend."

"Anything more than that?"

"In a sense."

"What sense?"

She hesitated for just a moment, lifted her chin slightly and said, again with stress on the qualifying word, "We were *very* intimate."

Under Bailey's rapid and persistent questioning she testified that they had become intimate in February of 1963, and that the relationship had continued thereafter in New Jersey, and on trips they had taken together to Puerto Rico and Sarasota. She had come down to Sarasota with Carl on one trip, and they had each bought property on Bowsprit Lane.

"Where were you on the night of August 27th, 1965?"

That classic question, strangely trite, yet ever-powerful, came as a sudden and shocking transition. She said she was at home with her children.

"Did you leave the house?"

"No sir."

"Were you familiar with the floor plan of the Coppolino house?"

"Yes."

"Did you know where Mrs. Coppolino slept?"

"I know where her bedroom was."

"Did you know how to get into the house?"

"I stayed there as a guest when we first arrived in Sarasota."

"You were familiar with it?"

"In a sense."

"All of the doors?"

"I went in the front door and out of the front door."

"Do you know where Carl slept?"

"They slept together in their own bedroom."

"How do you know that?"

"Because that is the way it was."

"Could you tell us that of your own knowledge?"

"Well, they had their bedroom and there was a double bed in their bedroom. There was another room which was a guest room, and Monica and Lisa had their own bedroom, twin beds. The night I stayed there with my children Carmela and Carl stayed in their own bedroom and my one daughter stayed with their daughter, and I stayed in the guest room with Lisa."

He asked her who had seen her in her home on the 27th of August, in the evening, and she said her children had. She said she had retired about midnight.

"Did you leave the house that night?"

"I left the house earlier in the evening, before midnight. Yes."

"Did you leave it after midnight?"

"No sir."

"Can you tell us if anyone else saw you besides your children in your home?"

"No sir."

"Other than your children, can you tell us of anyone who knows that you were asleep that night until five in the morning?"

"I was in my apartment with two children."

"Is there anyone else that can tell us that you were there?"

"I don't know."

"Your house is fifty feet from the Coppolino home?"

"I was not living in the current residence."

"Your present residence is fifty feet away?"

"Approximately."

"At that time you were staying in an apartment house called the Dorset?"

"That is right."

"Do you know of a drug called succinylcholine?"

"I have read about it, yes."

"Did you know it by that name prior to August 28th, 1965?"

"Not by name."

"Did you know of a muscle relaxant that was a fluid?"

"I had been told about a drug by the defendant."

"Had you ever seen any such drug?"

"Yes."

"Have you ever used any such drug?"

Mrs. Farber's civil attorney, Warren Goodrich, stood up and addressed the Court, saying, hand raised, "Just a minute . . ."

Bailey spun angrily and snapped, "It's too late for her to take the Fifth!"

Judge Silvertooth recessed the court for a conference in chambers, leaving the witness on the stand.

In the chambers Warren Goodrich explained his position, saying that he was acting soley and completely on behalf of his client, and was advising her to respectfully decline to answer any question which might tend to incriminate her. He said he had been retained by Mrs. Farber late the previous Friday afternoon, and, "I do not know whether Mrs. Farber has immunity from prosecution for the alleged crime or complicity therein in the State of New Jersey."

After both sides had presented legal argument, Judge Silvertooth said, "This is a preliminary hearing, and I am always in a position to find out between now and the time of trial whether or not this witness can be forced to go on the witness stand and testify. In other words, I can order the state attorney to get that information available for the Court immediately so I can ascertain this information. Let it be noted by the Court at this time that the state attorney's office shall obtain from the state attorney's office in New Jersey the exact facts as to whether or not there is or is not immunity. And I want something in writing." He agreed to advise the defense of what was learned from the New Jersey officials, and to tell the defense how he might rule on it at the Florida trial.

It made a long awkward time for the witness to remain in the witness stand, with Carl Coppolino sitting at the defense table, facing her across some twenty feet of the cherry-colored carpeting, and with the press and spectators watching her for small signs of tension and discomfort as the long minutes ticked by. She maintained the illusion of complete composure at, one might suspect, considerable cost.

Court was called to order. The court reporter read the last question asked, "Had you ever used any such drugs?"

Warren Goodrich said, "The witness respectfully declines to answer on the grounds that the answer might tend to incriminate her."

"Were you friendly with the Coppolinos when you visited Sarasota?"

She said that she was. She said she had arrived in town on the 22nd of August, the Sunday before Carmela's death, and saw them frequently that week. He then asked her if she had seen Mary Gibson prior to Carmela's death. "I met her in Sarasota on St. Armand's Circle with Carl Coppolino." They had been sitting in an automobile. Carl had introduced them. She said she had later called Carmela by phone.

"As a result of this encounter with Mary Gibson and Carl?"

"No. To tell her that Carl would be over to pick up Monica, his daughter, and take her home." He asked her how many times she saw the Coppolinos that week.

"The 22nd was Sunday, and Monday was the 23rd. Carmela and I went out looking for an apartment. We found an apartment, the Lido Beach Apartments, and my children and I had dinner with the Coppolinos and their children at their home on Longboat Key. We moved into the apartment that evening after dinner, and the next day I was out there with my children and visited with Carm in the afternoon [Tuesday]. Wednesday evening Carm invited me to come out after dinner, which I did, and I visited with Carm. Thursday I don't really remember whether or not I saw either of them on that day or had any communication. I do remember that either on Tuesday or Wednesday Carl came over to visit me and brought me two little coffee cups as sort of a welcome type thing. And then, to get back to Thursday, I am not clear on that day. Friday I saw Carl and, as it turned out to be, Mary Gibson. I saw him sitting in his car and went over, and he introduced me to this lady who turned out to be Mary Gibson. I didn't get her last name at the time. Then, as I say, I went home and called Carm to tell her Carl would be by my apartment to pick up Monica, and she thanked me for calling. Later on that evening Carl did call me back around a little after dinnertime."

"What was said?"

"He told me that I was spying on him and he did not appreciate my Gestapo methods."

"That was because you had called Carmela and said, 'Your husband is fooling around with Mary Gibson'?"

Schaub objected that Bailey was doing the testifying, and was sustained.

"Had you made any complaint to Carm about Mary Gibson?"

"I had no reason."

"Did you do it! Not, whether you had reason."

"No!"

"But you say Carl accused you of spying?"

"That's what he said."

"Did he specify what the acts of espionage were?" There was

considerable sarcasm in Bailey's tone at this portion of the questioning.

"No. I was completely amazed at his attitude. After all, he called me and accused me of spying on him. I couldn't understand."

"Before you had left New Jersey you were close friends?"

"Yes."

"As a matter of fact, you were intimate?"

"Yes sir."

"Were you in love with him?"

"No."

When Schaub objected that the question was immaterial, the judge pointed out that she had already answered it.

"Was it in order to be with Carl that you came to Florida?"

"No."

"Did you come down to Florida in order to get him to marry you?"

"No!"

"On the date Carmela died were you asked to take the children?"

"No."

"Did you complain to anyone on that day that you should have been asked to take the children?"

"I didn't complain. I may have made a comment about it."

"Did you go to the funeral home where Carmela's body reposed on the day of her death?"

"Yes."

"Did you have a conversation with someone there?"

"Yes. Mr. Shannon."

"Did you tell Mr. Shannon that it should have been you who took the children?"

"I don't remember. I was in a complete state of shock."

"Did you accuse Carl on that day, before Mr. Shannon, of having caused Mrs. Coppolino's death?"

"No."

"Are you sure of that?"

"Absolutely!"

"Did you tell Carl's mother that you expected to be the next Mrs. Coppolino? Did you say that?"

"I did not!"

"Did you set out, on or about the day of Carmela Coppolino's death, to cause her husband to be accused of that death?"

Strode objected to Bailey leading the witness, and was sustained.

Bailey said, "Under the circumstances, Your Honor, I think I could justifiably ask that the witness be declared hostile, but I will rephrase the question. Did you go to anyone after Mrs. Coppolino's death to discuss the subject of her death?'' Strode again objected, but was overruled, the Court judging that the question was not leading.

"Yes. . . . The first person I talked to about Carm's death was Doctor Karow.'' She had talked to her on October 28, two months after Carmela's death. After she had talked to some FBI agents, and then to Sheriff Boyer of Sarasota County, and his investigators. He asked her if she had made an accusation of murder. When she said she did not believe she had made a direct accusation, he asked her if she had suggested that she believed Carl had killed his wife.

"I was highly suspicious. I could not accept so many conflicting things that I had been told by Carl and by his mother, and I just—I was in a terrible state of indecision about this whole situation because this is not the type of procedure one goes through, as far as I am concerned.''

"I asked whether or not you suggested to anyone that Carl had killed his wife. That calls for a yes or no.''

Strode objected again, saying, "To this question I am going to object. There is no materiality as to what this witness discussed with anybody or what her suspicions or accusations, in rebutting the state's case. The only competent evidence that defense can put on is rebuttal.''

Lee Bailey said to Strode, "If you are asking for an offer of proof I will say she knows more about the death.''

"He is cross-examining his own witness,'' said Strode in an aggrieved tone.

Lee Bailey said firmly and with obvious confidence in his position, "I am entitled to show that someone else *did* kill his wife if he did not.''

The objection was overruled. The next question was ruled out as being too leading. Finally Bailey boiled it down to, "What did you say to the sheriff?''

Whereupon Mr. Goodrich arose and took the Fifth for his client, on the grounds that the form of the question was too general.

Bailey with a moment of hesitation and a shrug of his shoulders, turned to another matter. "Mrs. Farber, did you, after Carmela's death, do anything with reference to Doctor Coppolino's professional standing?''

"Not that I know of.''

"Did you take steps to prevent him from getting a license?''

"I have no authority in that area."

"Did you make an effort with somebody who does have the authority to prevent him from getting a license?" When Mr. Strode objected, saying, "The materiality is impossible to perceive," Lee Bailey said to the Court, "The pattern of this woman's conduct is highly important to this case. We are entitled to get it out. She has refused to talk to representatives of the defendant. We are entitled to find out whether any of these things are so." The objection was overruled.

"Did you request any individual to use his influence to see that Carl Coppolino never got a Florida license?"

"Possibly. I remember vaguely something in a letter."

When Bailey asked her why she had done it, Strode objected, saying that Bailey was not trying to impeach anything the state had presented. He said that if Bailey had anything in rebuttal, he should put it on. The state had not called Mrs Farber. The state did not go into the the defendant's professional standing, and Mr. Bailey was going into the pattern of conduct of a witness the state had not called.

Bailey said that the witness had tried to prevent Dr. Coppolino from being licensed, and he wanted to know why.

Strode repeated that Bailey was trying to establish a pattern of conduct detrimental to his client, and that it had nothing to do with the state's presentation to show probable cause.

"I intend to incriminate Mrs. Farber," said Bailey, and the Court overruled the state's objection.

Again he asked her why she had tried to do that to Dr. Coppolino.

"Because I don't trust him."

"Did you attempt to cancel any lectures he was giving in Las Vegas in the fall of 1965?"

"Through suggestion, yes."

"Why did you suggest that he be scratched off the panel of a medical program in the fall of 1965 in Las Vegas?"

"Because I didn't trust him."

"Did you ever ask Doctor Coppolino to marry you?"

"Never!"

Bailey was overruled on his next three questions on grounds of materiality—what was the difference in their ages, had she talked to Mr. Schaub about the case, had she appeared before any grand juries, but was permitted to ask if she had gone to the FBI and to Sheriff Boyer of her own volition, and she said she had.

"Why did you seek out these men in order to give them your story?"

"Because I was very concerned about Carm's death."

"Were you concerned about the fact that Carl had not married you?"

"I was very concerned about Carm's death."

"Concerned in what way?"

"I couldn't accept it."

"Did you wish to prosecute the doctor or have him accused?"

"I wished to find out why or how her death happened."

"You wished to cause an investigation?"

"Yes."

"Did you wish to do that badly enough so that you yourself admitted to serious criminal conduct?"

Predictably, Warren Goodrich hopped up again, waving the Fifth. Bailey said that it was a matter of record that the witness had testified before the Sarasota County Grand Jury.

Goodrich said, "On behalf of this witness, this matter has been thoroughly gone into with the Court in chambers, and any attempt to go into it now, and further volunteering of information by counsel, since all the proceedings in chambers are on the record, can only be an attempt to communicate to others and not to the Court."

With the objection sustained, Bailey asked, "Did you, Mrs. Farber, in your effort to cause an investigation, give certain information to these people about something that happened before Carm's death?"

Goodrich came up with the Fifth again, and said of Bailey's question, "It violates the limits which have already been prescribed by His Honor in chambers. This was the type of proceeding assured by the Court we would not be engaged in—the continued rapidity of asking a question, the answer to which he knows must exceed the limitation placed upon him in chambers."

Bailey replied, "There is no way in which the answer could possibly incriminate this witness. I ask that her claim of privilege be stricken. I asked about an event which occurred prior to Carm's death. It was just whether or not it was in furtherance of a plan to involve the doctor. I do not inquire as to what that is, because of Your Honor's ruling."

"Counsel well knows," Goodrich replied, "that the invariable rule of law on this question is that it is the right of the witness to determine whether the question will lead to or tend to incriminate the witness. And we have gone into this in chambers. It was clearly agreed that the repeated asking of a question designed to continue to force us to invoke privilege was not as to the matter under discussion, but as to any other matter, that it would not be engaged in by counsel. We have not objected when he inquired into the events concerning the prosecution immediately before the Court."

Bailey withdrew his question, and asked her how long she had known Dr. Musetto. She said she had been on a friendly basis with him since meeting him in New Jersey. She admitted to having had frequent discussion with him about this case.

"As a matter of fact, you are both represented by the same attorney, Mr. Goodrich?"

And to this Goodrich objected with genuine indignation and dismay. "This is not material! I was not retained by this witness for anything in connection with the other witness. I am retained in each case by one lawyer from St. Petersburg and one lawyer from a northern state. It is entirely a coincidence, and the purpose of asking this question is not only to embarrass the witness but to embarrass counsel. This is not a proper question, and to which we object."

"Sustained," said the judge.

With a small bow and quick bright smile, Bailey said, "My purpose is never to embarrass Mr. Goodrich."

"I am sure that is ture," said Mr. Goodrich with a trace of acid.

Bailey turned to the witness. "How frequently do you see the doctor?"

"Not too often."

"Do you know a woman named Mrs. Plaut?"

Mrs. Farber looked puzzled. "No, I don't think so."

"Did you have a conversation with Mrs. Plaut several weeks ago?"

"Objection," said Mr. Strode. "This is immaterial. She has not been called as a state witness."

"Strike the question," said Mr. Bailey, with mock show of resignation. "With the rulings made by the Court as to this witness's ability to take the Fifth Amendment, we must conclude at this point."

The state had no questions. Marjorie Farber looked startled that it had ended so quickly and inconclusively with odd questions about some woman she could not place by name. She had no way of knowing that Bailey was referring to Teri Plaut, the tall, slender, striking brunette, the distaff half of his crack investigation team.

Chapter Seven

The next witness for the defense was Dr. Millard B. White, who had been the Sarasota County Medical Examiner for fifteen years. James McEwen conducted the direct examination of the doctor.

The pertinent testimony elicited during the direct examination was that to the best of the witness's recollection, Dr. Karow had told him over the phone from the Coppolino home that she felt that the death was from natural causes, and that a law enforcement agency was there at the time investigating the case. He later learned that it was a representative of the Longboat Key Police Department. He had not ordered an autopsy, had not seen the deceased, living or dead, had not gone to the funeral home.

Later, in July of 1966, on the 22nd, less than two months before, he had talked to Dr. Milton Helpern in New York by long distance, and after the call had come directly to the courthouse and testified before the grand jury. He said he had known Dr. Helpern for a number of years, having met him while attending conventions. He had then reported to the grand jury what Dr. Helpern had told him over the phone.

There was a long period of sustained legal quibbling and squabbling about whether or not Dr. White should be permitted to relate what Dr. Helpern told him over the phone to report to the grand jury. Most of it succeeded in thoroughly confusing Dr. White who, at times, completely lost the thread of what he was being asked.

At last he was permitted to relate the conversation. "The conversation—may I use the points?—was that the autopsy showed the individual was healthy and that there was no natural cause of death. Two, that in one of the buttocks, and I don't recall which one, there was a penetrating wound in the skin which had been interpreted to be a needle track. Three, that the individual did not die of coronary occlusion. Four, in the body I think he found evidence of a drug similar to choline or di-choline. . . . Succinyldicholine or monocholine. This is the total information."

"No quantities of this drug? Whether he made the test or someone else made that test he didn't say?"

"He said he had his toxicology department working on these problems."

"Did you ask him specifically to state to you, or did he offer to state to you, the opinion that this person came to her death as a result of succinylcholine?"

"No sir."

Frank Schaub in cross-examination tried to find out if Dr. White thought or believed that Dr. Karow had been the attending physician before the patient had died rather than afterward, but as he was asking for a mental process, Russ's objections were sustained.

Several years ago a law was passed in Sarasota County which makes an autopsy mandatory in all cases—other than obvious accidental death—where the deceased has not been attended prior to death by the physician signing the death certificate, and where the deceased has not been attended by that physician at the time of death.

The rather gaudy episode which precipitated the passing of this law was when the death of an obese woman was certified as coronary occlusion by the physician who examined the body after death. Later, due to certain rumors and suspicions, the body was given a more careful examination, one which discovered the tiny puncture wound in the crease of the flesh under the left breast, made by the ice pick which had caused the coronary problem.

It is a fair assumption that Dr. Juliette Karow was unaware of the law, and unaware of the fact that never having attended Carmela in life, as a physician, she was not entitled to certify the cause of death and sign the certificate. Yet she was aware of her obligation to report the unattended death to the authorities. Had the Coppolino residence been in the county jurisdiction, autopsy would have been automatic, as the Sheriff's Department, having been instrumental in getting the autopsy law passed, would not be other than scrupulous in adhering to it. Had the death occurred in the city of Sarasota, the investigator would have recognized the legal necessity for autopsy. Insofar as Dr. Millard White's function is concerned, as County Medical Examiner he does not decide the need for autopsy on his own cognizance. He awaits the autopsy request from the investigating authority.

Informed that Longboat Key was not in county jurisdiction, Dr. Karow had phoned Chief Corsi of the Police Department of the Town of Longboat Key. Evidently he had arrived between seven and eight and, according to his best recollection as related to Sheriff Boyer months later, he arrived at the home on Bowsprit Lane just as the people from the Shannon Funeral Home were trundling the body out to the hearse, in the usual transport wrappings and metal basket, completely covered. He said that he asked to see Carl Coppolino, but was told by Dr. Karow that Carl's heart condition was aggravated by grief and that he was having severe chest pains, and she could tell him whatever it was he wished to know. And though Chief Corsi was aware of the mandatory law, and doubtless, through his questioning, aware that this situation was one which came under that law, thus requiring him to make the official request of Dr. White, and to advise Shannon to hold the body for autopsy and not begin the embalming process, for some reason he did not apply the law to this situation. It is plausible to assume that had Dr. Karow been aware of the restriction the law placed upon her, the lack of the certification of death would have forced Corsi into the mandatory routine, wherein Dr. White would have been the certifying physician. One might assume Chief Corsi was "doctored" out of the required routine. One physician was being carried away when he arrived. Another was having a heart attack. The third had certified the cause of death. Here was professional knowledge, status, plus an inversion of logic: doctors *do* autopsies rather than have autopsies done on them. And there is always the inference that all doctors know each other, all have access to mystery unfathomable to the layman, and all move in patterns acceptable to all their fellows. So one humbly gathers the minimal information required, apologizes for having to be a nuisance at a time like this, and leaves quickly.

Sarasota County Sheriff Ross Boyer was called as the next witness for the defense. A tall man, balding, with heavy and rather fleshy features. He had been dieting for many months and the weight loss was more apparent in his body than in his face. His habit of movement was still that of a heavier man, unaccustomed to the leanness of his body so suddenly acquired.

He had been at that time the Sheriff of Sarasota County for many years, after serving originally with the Florida State Highway Patrol. The system of partisan elections for law officers creates a situation wherein the man who can successfully hold office for many terms must be adept politically as well as being a competent officer of the law. It is interesting to note that a few years previously when the new Republican strength in Sarasota County manifested itself, the broom swept almost clean. Ross Boyer was one of only three Democrats in office who survived that surprising election

In these days of increasing dependence upon technology in investigation work, and on the social sciences in such interrelated areas as crime prevention and riot control, the election of men to executive and administrative posts in law enforcement is a practice of dubious merit. One need only imagine what the result of the prior election would have been if, during the month preceding the balloting, there had been several serious crimes in the area which had not been solved by Election Day. Law enforcement would seem to be an expensive area in which to practice on-the-job training of a new incumbent.

The glasses which Ross Boyer wore had the effect of softening his face, of giving him a more scholarly and thoughtful look. When he took them off to rub his eyes, his face looked far more blunt and powerful. The upper lids are fleshy, the eyes hooded. Even in the most casual conversation, he has one of the tricks of the long-time officer of the law, a habit of listening with chin tilted up, face absolutely expressionless and immobile, eyes riveted on the speaker. The impression is one of absolute attention, plus considerable skepticism. It is disconcerting.

On the stand Ross Boyer had the habits of the experienced police witness. He paused long enough after each question to give the state ample time to enter an objection. He spoke loudly, clearly, factually, and volunteered no subjective opinion.

He testified that the first time he had seen Marjorie Farber it had been at his request, and that she had been accompanied by counsel, and that the second time he had seen her she had been without counsel.

He stated that he had spoken with Dr. Milton Helpern twice in person, the first time in Helpern's office in New York on December 17, 1965, and three or four times by telephone.

When F. Lee Bailey asked Boyer the substance of his January 1966 telephone conversation with Dr. Helpern about the investigation into the cause of death of Carmela Coppolino, Bill Strode immediately objected on the grounds that the question asked for hearsay.

Bailey explained, "Your Honor, Doctor Helpern testified and we seek to impeach him on prior inconsistent statements." When Strode repeated his objection, Bailey said, "It is a recognized exception to the hearsay rule." Strode argued that Helpern had not been asked for that conversation during the defense cross-examination, which would have laid a predicate for Bailey's line of questioning of the sheriff.

When the Court asked for Bailey's basis for an exception to the hearsay rule, Bailey said, "Evidence of a prior inconsistent statement. I am not concerned with the truth of the matter declared but the fact that the statement was made, as bearing on the weight of Doctor Helpern's testimony. . . . I must point out that this man, being the Sheriff of Sarasota County, I wouldn't embarrass by asking questions prior to the proceeding. I think this witness is important and he can give it. I think that these are relevant conversations as to whether or not Doctor Helpern really has in his own mind a cause of death.''

The judge sustained Strode's objection, and so Bailey then asked the more specific and acceptable question as to whether, in January, Dr. Helpern had said he had a cause of death. No. In February? No. In March? No. And in none of those conversations had Doctor Helpern said how much longer it would take to complete the tests.

Boyer testified that he had seen Helpern in April in person in the Medical Examiner's New York office.

"I went there for the purpose of finding out if there had been any final findings. He brought in Doctor Umberger, Doctor Devlin, and Doctor Gohy—I think that is his name. The four doctors and I sat there an hour and forty-five minutes. He tried to explain to me the different examinations and tests that were being made, and that they had not at that time found the cause of death.''

"Did he tell you that he expected to find it shortly?''

"No, he did not.''

Prevented from asking if Helpern had told Boyer how much longer experimentation would be necessary in order to find a cause of death, Bailey asked, "Did he tell you what the findings were as of that date?''

"He had no conclusive answers at that time.''

In cross-examination, Strode's only question, affirmatively answered, was, "Right up to the last time you talked to Doctor Helpern [in April], did he indicate tests were still going on?''

The defense called James Foy, the investigator for the state attorney's office, who had been employed by Frank Schaub on July 1, 1965. (Prior to his employment, there had been no investigator assigned to the state attorney.)

Of all the witnesses who appeared for both sides in all trials and hearings in the Coppolino matter, James Foy is the one most difficult to describe. Medium height, medium build, dark hair, regular features, probably in his thirties, very little expression in his face. Though it was not permitted later at either trial, artists were permitted in court in the spectator section, and allowed to sketch the participants. A very competent artist said after the hearing that after four separate attempts to sketch Mr. Foy, he had given up in despair, as there seemed to be no distinctive characteristic he could give subtle exaggeration so as to create a recognizable likeness. Foy seemed uniquely suited in appearance to an investigative role, as it would seem likely that one could see him twenty times in the course of a day and never actually notice him.

Bailey asked Foy if he had made certain recordings of the voice of Carl Coppolino. Foy said no, and that he did not cause them to be made, and he had not installed any equipment in the home of Marjorie Farber. Asked if he was aware of any recordings having been made, Foy said, "Yes." Over Schaub's objections, Bailey was permitted to ask Foy if he knew who had made the recordings. Yes. "Jim Moore of the Florida Sheriff's Bureau."

"But you yourself did not wiretap?"

"I participated in it in that I was there at the time. However, I did not install the equipment nor did I control it." He said he had watched it being installed and he had heard Carl Coppolino's voice come over the wire on either one or two occasions during a twenty-four-hour period. He had no idea whether or not the tapes had been preserved.

"Have you done any other wire-tapping in this case?"

"No."

The defense rested their case. Mr. Schaub said, "We ask that Your Honor bind the defendant over for trial. We submit to the Court the evidence has shown probable cause to believe that Carl Coppolino murdered Carmela Coppolino as alleged in the indictment."

"The case is set for trial in November," ruled Judge Silvertooth.

"As it was before this hearing was started," Bailey commented.

With the proceeding to show reasonable cause thus terminated, the Court immediately began the second scheduled matter, the question of habeas corpus, and whether the defendant should be released on bond.

Because of two sovereign states being involved, it became a series of legal thickets not only incomprehensible to the layman but, one might suspicion, formidably complicated to the legal minds as well.

Though it is probably unfair and inaccurate to attempt to simplify such a jungle, and might even be thought an impertinence, here is a report of the sequence of prior events in shortened format:

1. Coppolino had been arrested on the basis of a fugitive warrant issued by New Jersey, for the murder of Colonel Farber.
2. After he was in custody, the Florida indictment was read to him and he was charged with the Florida murder of his wife.
3. New Jersey demanded extradition, and Florida refused.
4. Prior to the preliminary hearing, the state had waived its right to insist that the defendant proceed with meeting the burden of proof in a bond hearing and had agreed that the bond hearing could be dispensed with, saying however that it was not because the presumption of guilt was not great or the proof was not evident, but because it was not the defendant's proper remedy because of the outstanding fugitive warrant. The defense had refused to accept the waiver. [In the hearing on this motion of September 8, the Thursday prior to the preliminary hearing, Judge Silvertooth said, "I think all you gentlemen know, and it so appears to the Court, that the state probably is more or less consenting to bail to avoid the defendant through his counsel obtaining certain testimony prior to the trial."]
5. County Judge John Graham accepted a defense motion to quash the fugitive warrant on the basis that there was no logic in having such a warrant outstanding if Florida would not extradite.
6. Frank Schaub went to his superior in Tallahassee, Governor Haydon Burns, and secured from him a Governor's Rendition Warrant. This, in effect, when turned over to Sheriff Boyer, ordered him to seize Carl Coppolino and request the New Jersey authorities to come and get him. It meant that were Coppolino freed on bail, he would still remain in custody to be turned over to a New Jersey law officer and transported to Monmouth County to answer the original indictment against him.
7. Bailey argued vehemently that Frank Schaub by quietly securing the rendition warrant was conspiring to deprive Carl Coppolino of his civil rights. Boyer, Judge Graham, a secretary from the governor's office, and Frank Schaub himself were all placed on the witness stand.
8. The Court set bail at $15,000.
9. Boyer served the rendition warrant on Coppolino in open court.
10. As a delaying tactic, the defense did not post bond, and thus Carl Coppolino remained in the County Jail, technically under custody on the Florida charge.

Though it was intended that all this would take place during the same session, there was an unanticipated interruption.

After the preliminary hearing had ended, and the complex and involved legal argumentation had been going on for some time, Carl Coppolino signaled to Sheriff's Department Detective John Townsend, on duty in the courtroom to bring him a pill.

Coppolino's color was not good. Fifteen minutes later he asked for another, and Townsend hurried to him, taking the metal pill box out of his uniform pocket. Coppolino had begun to perspire heavily in the cool courtroom. He was the color of wet cement, and the overhead fluorescence made his face look, with its sharp highlights, as if it had been oiled.

Almost fifteen minutes later, at 5:40 P.M., Judge Silvertooth called a brief recess. Mary Coppolino went through the gate to sit beside Carl. He began to hunch over with pain and have visible spasms. Dr. Page, Carl's physician was summoned, and Page's partner, Dr. Robert Windom, responded. Minutes later two ambulance attendants appeared, briskly wheeling a stretcher along. As they lifted Carl Coppolino onto the stretcher, Mary hurried out to the corridor and commandeered one of the self-service elevators and stood holding the doors open.

When they came wheeling Carl toward the elevators, supine, with a sheet up to his chin, his lips were pulled back in a grimace and his chest was heaving convulsively. He appeared semiconscious. The attendants wheeled him right by the waiting elevator and on down the corridor. An Associated Press photographer caught that particular moment, caught the look of blank surprise on Mary's face.

"Where are they going with him?" she demanded, and was told that the elevators in the new wing are too small to hold a standard stretcher, and they had to take him through and down in the old part of the building where dimensions were more generous.

The balance of the habeas corpus proceeding was postponed until seven in the evening of the following day, on the assumption Carl Coppolino would be able to appear. The sheriff and his chief deputy, Jack Royal, picked Carl up at the hospital, clad in a navy blazer, dark slacks, white shirt and tie, and took him directly to the court. Dr. Coppolino gave the impression of being physically weak and shaky in contrast to the previous two days in court. After the proceedings he was returned to his jail cell.

During the hearing, F. Lee Bailey had stood mute on the Governor's Rendition Warrant, indicating to the informed observers that Coppolino would stand trial in New Jersy first.

That Wednesday evening, in the shadowy darkness of Mrs. O'Leary's Saloon across from the courthouse, the defense team seemed both dismayed and depressed. Ideally they had hoped to have Dr. Coppolino released on bail and then tried first in Florida on the date already set of November 7, less than two months hence.

It appeared to them that the Florida case was the weaker of the

142

two, and, as one of the Coppolino attorneys expressed it, "The thing to do is go up to New Jersey with a Florida victory under our belt."

During the next several days it was not at all clear what would actually happen. New Jersey did not send anyone down to pick up the prisoner. Bond was not posted.

Contradictory statements appeared in the press. On Thursday morning, September 15, Frank Schaub denied knowing of the warrant signed by Governor Burns and said he had not asked for it. On the same day when contacted by the press, Governor Burns said, "I want it understood that I issued the warrant at the request of the state attorney."

On Friday, September 16, the defense attorneys announced that they would not fight the extradition proceedings. On the same day the Sarasota *Herald-Tribune* reported as follows: "The Governor did say that the rendition warrant was requested by Schaub last month when the State Attorney feared that bail might be set and the doctor might leave the area. Schaub has always freely admitted that he had discussed a rendition warrant with the Governor and explained that he was fearful last month that a preliminary hearing to show cause would be held before he could contact one of the State's key witnesses, Dr. Milton C. Helpern. He said he discussed the warrant in an attempt to protect the State of New Jersey in the event Coppolino was freed before the key witness arrived back in the United States from an extended lecture tour in Europe."

It is useless to speculate on whether the Florida trial would have occurred first had Frank Schaub not secured the rendition warrant. One thing is clear. The rendition warrant was more fuel for the fire of antagonism between Schaub and Bailey. The Thursday, September 15, newspapers quoted F. Lee Bailey as saying that Frank Schaub "is not telling the truth" about his role in the rendition warrant affair.

In response to that, Frank Schaub prepared a statement which he released to the press, and was printed in the Sarasota *Herald-Tribune* on Friday, September 16. It reads as follows:

I sincerely regret that Lee Bailey has felt it necessary to make a personal attack upon me in the press. My own feelings toward him tend more toward pity than resentment. I accordingly told the reporter Mr. Bailey had delivered his statements to that I did not choose to conduct a running argument with him in the press. I advised the reporter that not only would I not comment upon his statements but in addition do not care to hear them.

However, having had my own share of disappointments in the practice

143

of law, I feel that some comment is needed and I certainly hope Mr. Bailey will accept it for the reasons it is given.

I have great concern for any young attorney who, as Mr. Bailey has done, advises the court that he doesn't have to read law because he makes the law. I readily appreciate the desperation he presently feels, and I recognize that his inexperience has not enabled him to cope with the frustration he obviously feels he has encountered here.

Quite frankly I was very impressed at the beginning of the preliminary hearing Monday with the potential Mr. Bailey demonstrated. I felt his comportment, demeanor and fine delivery were the equal of those demonstrated by Bill Strode and many of the other better Sarasota trial lawyers when they also were relying upon a background limited to six years of legal experience.

I, therefore, was very disappointed to find that, unlike so many of Sarasota's better trial lawyers, Mr. Bailey has not learned to "roll with the punch."

While in his inexperienced exasperation he may have thought a personal attack on me to be based on sound trial tactics, I want to assure him that I do not subscribe to such practices. I really believe Mr. Bailey is motivated by what he believes to be the best interests of his client rather than in accumulating personal publicity.

I, therefore, anticipate that after he has been thoroughly indoctrinated into the intricacies of trial practice by such an experienced prosecutor as Vincent Keuper in New Jersey, he will be a much wiser young man when he returns here for trial on Nov. 7.

I am confident he will be taught in New Jersey to argue his case in the courtroom rather than in the press.

And nothing happened. Carl Coppolino stayed in jail. Newspapers tried to make headlines out of nothing happening. On Monday, September 26, two weeks after the public hearing had begun, the Clerk of the Sarasota County Circuit Court received a motion mailed from Orlando, Florida, by James Russ asking that the Court forbid all members and employees of the state attorney's office, Sheriff's Department, and other officials to discuss the Coppolino case with any newspaper, television, or radio newsmen with news coverage in Sarasota County.

In the motion Russ alleged that, there had occurred, "extensive, pervasive and reoccurring publicity prejudicial to the defendant's constitutional right to a fair trial, circulated among the public through the news communication media. This prejudicial pre-trial publicity has apparently been assisted and nourished by the cooperation and comments to representatives of the media from both police and prosecution officials since both groups have been repeatedly identified as the sources from which the prejudicial, pre-trial publicity emanated."

Mr. Frank Schaub's response was immediate, and surprising.

He did not make any public statement. Instead he filed, in response to Russ's motion, his own "motion for clarification." Motions thus filed become a part of the public record.

He stated in his motion for clarification that most of the publicity had emanated from the defense. He said he had no objection to the restrictions Russ requested, provided they were made applicable to the defense as well. He attached page one clippings about Dr. Coppolino's various hospitalizations and alleged, in his motion, "The prosecution has good reason to believe that such claims of coronary attacks were without medical foundation and were simulated in an effort by the defendant to obtain publicity which would create public sympathy for the defendant." He went on to request the Court to, "clarify the question of the medical condition of the defendant by directing that he submit to a physical examination by qualified medical experts who also be directed to inquire into the question of whether or not the defendant has now or at any time in the past ever suffered from a coronary condition necessitating medical treatment and hospitalization."

When this was brought to F. Lee Bailey's attention, he made a statement to the press that he "had never seen anything like" Frank Schaub's motion. "The use of motions to disseminate opinions that would be clearly improper if stated to the press is not my idea of ethical conduct, and I don't intend to let it pass. I have never encountered this kind of conduct in any other area of the country in which I have practiced." Bailey said that he did not "plan to battle Mr. Schaub in the press," but that he would "deal with Mr. Schaub in other ways."

Also on that same Monday that Russ's motion was received, Carl Coppolino's civil attorney, Johnson Savary of Sarasota, filed suit in Circuit Court against the Educators Mutual Life Insurance Company, in Dr. Coppolino's behalf, stating that the company ceased paying Carl his disability insurance of $150 a week in August 1965, and requesting that the company pay the back disability installments for 55 weeks, totaling $8350 plus court costs and legal fees, and also reinstitute the regular weekly payments until 260 weeks had elapsed from the time of receipt of the first total disability payment. An exhibit affixed to the policy filed with the complaint showed July 30, 1962, as the date the policy had been taken out.

At last, on October 3, the man from New Jersey came to take Carl Coppolino back to New Jersey for trial.

THE BAIL HEARING

October 1966

<<<<<<<<<<<<<<<<<<<<<<<<<<<<<<<<<<<<<<<<<<<<<<<<<<<<<<<<<<<<<<<<<<<<<<<<<<<<<<<<<<<<

Chapter Eight

Dr. Carl Coppolino had arrived in New Jersey on the evening of October 4, in the custody of John M. Gawler, Chief of the Monmouth County Prosecutor's detective staff. Gawler had flown to Florida and, in compliance with Governor Haydon Burns' rendition warrant, Sheriff Ross Boyer had turned his prisoner over to Gawler.

Though he had been granted the right to post bond in the amount of $15,000 after the preliminary hearing in Sarasota on September 12 and 13, and though he certainly had the means to post bond, he had, on the advice of his attorneys, chosen to remain in the Sarasota County Jail in an effort to force trial in Florida first, as his attorneys believed the case in Florida to be the weaker case and, if he could stand trial in New Jersey after being acquitted of the murder of his wife in Florida, his chance of a New Jersey acquittal would be enhanced. F. Lee Bailey had discussed the situation informally with defense lawyers of national reputation, and had been told that if Coppolino were tried first in New Jersey for the Farber murder, Bailey's chance of winning acquittal was probably a hundred to one.

But all motions by the defense had been denied and New Jersey had the first turn at bat. The New Jersey indictment by the grand jury on July 21, 1966, came four days prior to the Florida indictment.

Gawler had planned to take Coppolino up on Eastern Airlines, but a half hour before leaving leaving the Sarasota County Court House, a representative from Eastern phoned and said it was

147

against airline policy to transport a prisoner in custody. So instead of the mid-day direct flight to Kennedy, the pair boarded a late-afternoon National Airlines flight at Orlando, Florida, which made five stops on the way north and landed in Newark after nine in the evening.

Sheriff Ross Boyer was quoted as saying, regarding the Eastern Airlines refusal: "They told me that due to the notoriety connected with the case they didn't want to add to the anxiety of their other passengers, so they refused to honor the tickets."

On October 5, Carl Coppolino had been arraigned before Superior Court Judge Elvin R. Simmill. Represented by F. Lee Bailey, Coppolino had pleaded innocent to the murder of William Farber, and when Bailey requested a bail hearing Judge Simmill set a date of Thursday, October 20, at 9:30 A.M. when he would hear arguments on that motion and any other motions the defense cared to present. Because both Bailey and Prosecutor Vincent Keuper were committed to other cases, no date was set for the New Jersey trial at that time.

And so for two weeks Coppolino was kept in the maximum security section of the Monmouth County Jail, in a private cell in that section reserved for homicide defendants and troublemakers, under 24-hour supervision by the desk officers. And on a brisk, bright, windy October morning he was handcuffed and placed in the police wagon in the alley beside the Hall of Records, and driven up the hill to the courthouse.

The small city, long ago, bore the name of Monmouth County Court House. "Freehold" also had a flavor of the law—meaning the form of tenure by which an estate is held. The old courthouse once stood where the County Hall of Records is now—that remarkably undistinguished public structure which contains the county jail.

The "new" courthouse is far handsomer, an impressive stone structure atop a knoll where the Battle of Monmouth was fought in 1778, and where young Molly Pitcher hustled water to the Revolutionaries.

(Later, during the trial itself, O'Shea's December 11 lead in the Boston *Herald-Transcript* was to be: "Two hundred years ago Molly Pitcher put Monmouth County on the map; today Marjorie Farber is keeping it there.")

The courthouse faces the long slope of a spacious open park. The houses that face the park are genuinely old, stately, well-cared-for. The wind was drifting the bright leaves of autumn that morning, scurrying them across the park, past the towering marble and bronze statue of Liberty Triumphant. The spectators who walked up the hill from town that morning hunched their shoulders against the wind, and tucked their chins into their topcoats.

Coppolino was placed in the small detention cell in the basement of the new courthouse until Judge Simmill disposed of the small bits of routine business before the court. His is the task of assigning cases to the judges of the Superior Court. Attorneys were present, a score of them, awaiting his decisions, and awaiting chances to ask for postponements.

It was easy to see that they did not relish making any presentation which might irritate Elvin R. Simmill. Simmill has the manner of one accustomed to authority. He was at one time Speaker of the State Assembly of New Jersey. He is a man of some intellectual force. He has an elegance of phrase, a quick and rather bitter wit, and a reputation for harshness while wearing the robe which is in total contrast to a warmth and easy charm in social surroundings.

One young attorney, as Simmill was making quick assignments of the cases on the docket, explained hesitantly that a co-counsel on the case being assigned had not come up from Atlantic City as he had not wanted to make the trip without being certain the case would be heard that day.

Simmill gave him a frosty smile and said, "Inform your colleague that we are not running a valet service here, and that the case of X verses Y will be heard by Judge So-and-So in Room 304 exactly . . . thirty-five minutes from now."

Simmill had assigned the Coppolino case to himself, not for the sake of the pursuit of notoriety. The chance of publicity in such matters is, for a judge, a far lesser consideration than the chance of mistrial or reversible error. In murder trials a judge can never become a hero. He can very easily become a bum. Judge Simmill could have assigned the case to one of the less senior judges of the court. His colleagues would have thought it a chicken-like act.

He would handle the Coppolino trial in his own courtroom, 308. Oak bench, oak furniture on the floor of the court, oak panelling from the gray, marbelized, asphalt tile flooring up for the first three feet, then plaster painted apple green—or courthouse green—on up to the acoustic-tile ceiling with its inevitable countersunk fluorescence. Aluminum rail separating the spectator section. Aluminum rail across the front of the tiered jury box, with maroon velvet hung from it. Five big windows, three along the side wall, two behind the spectators, all with narrow metal venetian blinds customarily kept closed. A clock. A calendar.

149

Flags. And that slightly dusty and dispirited flavor of all those public rooms where, over a period of time, people have been ground exceedingly small. Forgotten emotions leave a state patina.

A small courtroom. Fifty spectator chairs, twenty-five on each side. But later there would be thirty-two on each side, and when the verdict was announced, over eighty people were in the small spectator space and by some miracle of accommodation and tolerance, all were seated.

After the case list had been distributed and the laywers had left the court, some dozen remained—taking this chance to see the fabled F. Lee Bailey on stage for the first time in New Jersey.

Also seeing him for the first time was young Joseph Afflitto, assisting in the defense of Carl Coppolino. Afflitto, twenty-six years old, dark, tall, slender, an amiable and diligent attorney from Wayne, New Jersey, at the other end of the state, had been suggested to Lee Bailey by Bailey's faculty contacts at the Boston University Law School. Afflitto had been in practice only a few months when F. Lee Bailey asked him to help in the Coppolino defense.

There were less than twenty members of the press crops at the bail hearing, and the spectators who came and went numbered no more than a dozen at any one time.

Coppolino, in dark suit, white shirt, striped tie, was brought in and sat for several minutes in one of the end chairs in the jury box, directed there by the bailiff, until other matters were taken care of. He then moved down to the defense table, with F. Lee Bailey and Joe Afflitto.

The first matter under consideration was the application for bail, and the first witness called was Dr. Paul K. Bornstein, an internist and cardiologist from nearby Asbury Park, a specialist in diagnostics who had been in practice for thirty-three years. He had been summoned to the Monmouth County Jail by Warden Earl Smith and, as an impartial and independent physician, had given Carl Coppolino a two-hour physical examination which had begun at 5 P.M. on the previous Monday, October 17.

In his testimony Dr. Bornstein stated, without any qualifying phrases or fuzzy terminology that, as a result of his examination of the defendant, he diagnosed Coppolino's ailment as coronary artery disease with anginal syndrome.

A lay explanation of this disease is appropriate at this point in the account of the hearings and trials. The principal coronary artery—in cross-section like a piece of garden hose—supplies blood to the heart muscle wall. When this large and essential

150

supply of blood which nourishes the muscle cells is reduced for any reason, there are sharp pains in the chest. The heart beats erratically and less efficiently. Less blood and hence less oxygen is carried to the brain and to the extremities. The patient becomes faint, pale, sweaty and apprehensive. Should the reduced supply continue, muscle cells of the heart wall will die due to the lack of nourishment and, if he recovers, there will be scarring which can be identified through interpretation of an electrocardiogram.

Coronary artery disease is a catch-all term which includes the restriction of the blood supply through arteriosclerosis which, through deposits on the interior wall of the artery, permanently restricts the supply of blood through the artery, but which takes place over so long a time that with patients who are reasonably active there is a compensating improvement in the nourishment of the muscle cells through the increasing size and efficiency of smaller blood vessels in the area. Most medications for the pain of angina expand these blood vessels and thus improve the blood supply. The catch-all term also includes clots which diminish or completely block the blood supply, and instances where the fatty deposit on the interior wall tears and forms a flap which results in partial or complete blockage, termed a coronary occlusion rather than, in the case of the clotting, a coronary thrombosis.

Another condition, about which less is known, and which is applicable to Carl Coppolino is a constriction of the coronary artery which is caused by an involuntary contraction of the muscle sheath of the artery itself, an interwoven layer of muscle fiber between the smooth inner and outer walls of the artery. The condition where this muscle layer contracts is generally called a "heart spasm." It reduces the effective size of the artery and its capacity to carry blood to the heart. This condition may exist with or without the typical hardening and inner wall deposits typical of the atherosclerotic condition.

The physiological reason for the muscle fiber in the arterial wall is to permit, throughout the range of demand, from the deepest sleep to the most violent exercise, a regulation of the flow of the blood to the heart, a control device which is supplementary to the rate at which the heart beats. The malfunction—the spasm which reduces supply below the demand of the heart muscle—is believed by some cardiologists to be related to emotional tension, though—as in the case of classic chronic migraine which rhythmically constricts the blood vessels of the brain—only a partial correlation of tension and attack can be established. Hereditary correlations are also obscure.

151

This particular kind of coronary artery disease is most likely to be misunderstood by the layman, because one expects that an "attack" must result in a lengthy period of hospitalization. This is because the attacks which accompany other forms of coronary artery disease cause damage to the heart muscle, danage which must be allowed to heal and scar.

But in the case of the muscular spasm, when it is severe enough and lasts long enough, the patient faints, and as soon as he loses consciousness, the muscular constriction usually ends and full blood supply is apparently restored. Thus actual heart damage from this form of coronary artery disease, a damage that would show up on the electrocardiogram, is rare.

It is possible, experimentally, to induce the symptoms of this form of coronary artery disease by pharmacological means. Sufficient quantities of digitalis taken by a person with a healthy heart will create a condition of digitalis toxicity which will simulate heart spasm.

Also procainamide hydrochloride U.S.P., marketed by E. R. Squibb & Sons under the trade name of Pronestyl, can create the same symptomology, at least to the extent of the observable symptoms of heart spasm, one of which is the rapid and irregular beat of the heart as it attempts to perform without sufficient nourishment of the muscle.

In the Squibb literature on Pronestyl, one portion reads: "In the absence of any a-rhythmia, the heart rate may occasionally be accelerated by conventional doses, suggesting that the drug possesses anticholenergic properties. Larger doses can induce atrioventricular block and ventricular extrasystoles which may proceed to ventricular fibrillation. These effects on the myocardium are reflected in the electrocardiogram: a widening of the QRS complex occurs most consistently; less regularly, the P-R and Q-T intervals are prolonged, and the QRS and T waves show some decrease in voltage."

The literature also says, "Digitalis-induced ventricular extrasystoles and tachycardia may at times be suppressed by careful and judicious administration of the drug."

In all fairness, in view of the conflicting medical views of the condition of Carl Coppolino's health, it should be pointed out that the "attack" which accompanies heart spasm duplicates in every way the symptoms which would result from a partial blockage of the coronary artery caused by a clot or occlusion. Weakness, extreme sweaty pallor, sharp chest pains, a trembling of the hands, rapid, irregular and shallow beating of the heart, a feeling of being far away—of sinking, of emotional fear and depression, dryness of the mouth, coldness and numbness of the extremities . . . all these are typical of reduced nourishment of the heart muscle regardless of cause. The fact that the patient who suffers such an attack as a result of this spasm-tendency can resume his normal activities within twenty-four hours should not be construed as placing the validity of this particular form of coronary artery disease in question.

Under questioning by F. Lee Bailey and then by Vincent Keuper, Dr. Bornstein affirmed his diagnosis *[On October 4, the evening Coppolino was admitted to Department J, Dr. Frank Niemtzow, the jail physician examined him and pronounced him fit, and then told a local reporter that he had found no hint of any heart weakness.]* and went on to say, "In my opinion he does not *have* to be removed from the jail. . . . It would not change the progression of his coronary artery disease. . . . Whether he is in jail or out, the emotional component will still be there."

Questioned as to whether a man who had suffered a weight loss from 160 pounds to 130 pounds since arrest and incarceration should be left in jail, Bornstein said that the weight loss was precisely what he would recommend to his patients with the same problem.

F. Lee Bailey then called Dr. Charles W. Kelly to the stand. Kelly, an internist and cardiologist, had been in practice fifteen years, and had been Carl Coppolino's doctor when the Coppolinos had lived in New Jersey. Dr. Kelly appeared to be about forty. He had the saturnine look and swarthy skin-tones of the dark-haired Irish. His manner was lethargic, as if wearied by overwork, and there was a detached, semi-involved flavor about his testimony, as though he could not help thinking, while on the stand, of all those other patients in need of his attention.

When Kelly recounted his background in order to be qualified as an expert witness, the account of his educational history ended with his saying he had spent two years at Boston City Hospital as resident and chief resident.

Whereupon F. Lee Bailey, in a whimsical mockery of regional chauvinism, said elegantly, "I suggest, Your Honor, that the latter experience alone would qualify him." The judge was amused.

In testimony, referring to his notes and his office file on Carl Coppolino, Kelly testified that he had first seen Coppolino as a patient on February 12, 1962. Coppolino stated that since the previous August—1961—he had been having chest pains as a result of exertion or stress, and that he had taken nitroglycerin and received rather prompt relief.

153

The time sequence here is interesting. The affair with Marjorie Farber began one year later. At the time of Kelly's examination and diagnosis, Carl Coppolino had not yet gone into partnership practice with the two other anesthesiologists, nor begun practicing at the Riverview Hospital in Red Bank. Carl and Carmela were living in Nutley, where Carm worked at Hoffmann-LaRoche. She was to become pregnant the month after Carl visited Kelly's office in Red Bank.

On examination Carl's pulse proved to be irregular. Kelly diagnosed his condition as coronary artery disease and, because he was so young for this condition, referred him to Dr. William Dock, under whom both Kelly and Coppolino had studied, but because any report of Dock's findings would have been hearsay, Kelly was prevented from recounting them.

Kelly testified treating Coppolino from February 1962 until March 1965, hospitalizing him on two occasions. More recently he had examined Coppolino just one week previously, four days before Bornstein had examined him. He said that the patient complained of heart pain of greater intensity requiring greater amounts of nitroglycerin, that pain awakened him in the night, that he was eating poorly, and had a numbness of his feet and lower legs. Kelly said he noted a severe weight loss, a diffuse acne eruption on the face, and, in examining the eyes, a condition called arteriovenous nicking, which is merely an early sign of some arterial stiffening. Heart sounds were of good quality, the rate regular, and the electrocardiogram within normal limits. However he had taken a ballistocardiogram and judged the result abnormal. The procedure, as he explained it to the court, was to place the patient on a flat surface, face up, and attach instrumentation which charts the headward and footward movement of the body with each ejection pumping of the heart.

Under Bailey's questioning, Kelly revealed that he had the records of the several times Coppolino had been hospitalized in Florida, and felt they confirmed his diagnosis. He said that Coppolino's medication at that time was nitroglycerin, and that for a person with his condition he would prescribe a marked restriction of activity and the avoidance of as much stress and strain as possible.

F. Lee Bailey was, of course, attempting to show that his client's health was impaired by being confined in jail. So he began to try to get Kelly to say that the extreme smallness of the cell in which Carl was confined would have an adverse effect on a person with his condition. But as Bailey was trying to develop that point, over the objections of Keuper, Carl signaled to Bailey

154

and motioned him back to the defense table and whispered to him for a few moments. Bailey withdrew his question and went on to other matters. After the hearing Bailey said that when he had seen the cell he had thought Carl was confined to that cramped space at all times, but Carl had interrupted him to tell him that during daylight hours he had the run of the day room onto which the cell door opened.

He had elicited from Kelly the fact that Carl had moved to Florida for health reasons, and he went into the matter of the weight loss. Kelly had been in the courtroom during Bornstein's testimony. He agreed with Bornstein that the weight loss was good for the patient.

Bailey then turned the witness over to Vincent Keuper who could very well have refrained from asking any questions at all. Perhaps had all this been in front of a jury, Keuper would not have engaged in any cross-examination. But by doing so, he demonstrated the way any fishing expedition can backfire.

Keuper tried to get Kelly to agree that by being in a cell, Coppolino was having a "marked reduction of activity" and thus the incarceration was beneficial, only to discover that Kelly had previously prescribed a certain regulated form of exercise. To recover lost ground, Keuper asked if Kelly had prescribed that when he had seen Coppolino the week before. Kelly said he had not, because his purpose in seeing Coppolino was to make a diagnosis at the request of Florida lawyers representing an insurance company, not treat the disease. Keuper tried next to recoup by asking if coronary artery disease could be cured.

Kelly's answer was, "If the symptoms of coronary disease disappeared and the cardiograms taken were normal, and this were to continue indefinitely and the patient were to die of cancer, then one might be able to assume that he had a cure, yes."

The only small brownie point he made was to have Kelly testify that one of the factors in his diagnosis of coronary artery disease had been the history given him by the patient.

When Keuper tried to explore the point that it was Dr. Sheehan, not Dr. Kelly, who had admitted Coppolino to Riverview Hospital and that, in fact, Kelly had not seen Coppolino in the throes of an attack, Kelly testified that he had seen Carl within twenty-four hours of his admission to the hospital each time, and had found him suffering from acute coronary insufficiency.

Kelly testified he had seen Coppolino once or twice a month during the three-year period he had treated him, and that to go into all the medications he had tried would take a further twenty minutes of testimony.

By then Mr. Keuper was trying to find some graceful way to finish the cross-examination. He brought it back to the examination in the jail, and to Kelly's testimony that Carl had said there was an intensification of the anginal pain.

"Because of the fact he was under indictment for murder?"

"I'm not examining—I'm not involved with this murder."

"I *know* you are not involved with this murder. I am asking a question whether the fact that he is under a murder indictment would have any effect upon his condition."

"I would say so."

"Is that what you were talking about? The stress of confinement?"

"I think they are separate. I'm talking about the emotional problem of a murder indictment and you're talking about the problem of confinement to a jail. Now I think there is a difference between them."

"Isn't there a relation between the two?"

"Oh, I would say so."

"You would say so?"

"Yes."

"That's all, Doctor."

And so the frail point was made that granting bail would not change the factor of emotional stress, but as this had been self-evident from the beginning, Keuper gained nothing. The slight loss he suffered was in demonstrating to F. Lee Bailey that when confronted with an unexpected answer, Vincent Keuper found it difficult to turn that answer to his own benefit and, in fact, tended to increase rather than diminish his own difficulties in such situations.

When Kelly was excused, Judge Simmill asked Bailey if he had any other medical evidence to present. When Bailey said no, the judge asked Mr. Keuper if he had medical evidence to present, and with a certain heartfelt sincerity, Mr. Keuper said, "No. No medical evidence. No *sir*."

Mr. Keuper thereupon presented various affidavits and cited, as an argument against the granting of bail, a New Jersey case where the Court had commented that when a person is under an indictment for murder there is a tendency to abscond. He said that he believed that with two indictments, the urge to abscond had been increased.

F. Lee Bailey then proceeded with the second portion of his application for bail—the constitutional right of a defendant to

156

seek and be granted bail—and called as his next witness Dorothy Jeffress, the young Negro housekeeper who had been a live-in domestic with the Coppolino family from January 1963 when Carmela had come home from the hospital with the new baby, Lisa Marie, until December 1964, some four months before the Coppolino family had sold their house and moved to Florida.

Miss Jeffress was a very lean, sharp-featured, coppery-dark girl in her middle to late twenties. She wore a bright, new, and quite attractive suit, dark green with a small pattern. Her hair appeared to be freshly coiffed. She walked briskly to the witness stand and took her seat, her manner one of jaunty confidence. She answered Bailey's time-and-place questions swiftly, and with a great economy of words. But her responses were puzzling because, to the spectators, she would hesitate and spar with Mr. Bailey at the most unexpected times.

"Can you tell us whether or not anything unusual was brought to your attention on that day?" (July 30, 1963)

She paused, tilted her head. "Unusual like what?"

"Did something happen that sticks in your memory?"

Another pause. "Oh. I think it was the date of the death of the Colonel."

Obviously she was not attempting to be uncooperative. But she seemed to be expecting Mr. Bailey to trick her in some devious and unexpected way. Also, she appeared to be taking great pains to sit in a graceful and attractive fashion, even to the position of her hands.

Quite suddenly a possible reason for her manner and her responses became clear. Like so many other millions of Americans, she had been exposed to many years of cinematic courtroom drama and to untold hundreds of Mr. Perry Mason's clever victories in the television courtrooms. It was this exposure which had prepared her for her moments on stage, and her grooming, manner and responses were an amalgam of all the women who had been interrogated by Perry Mason. It is a common phenomenon in our day to superimpose the unreality of fictional drama upon the more angular and rude materials of reality. Though she was responsive to the questions asked, she was wary of a trickery long advertised by the scriptwriters, and she had prepared herself to be, in a sense, "on camera."

She testified that Dr. Coppolino came downstairs that morning between 9:30 and 10:00 as was his habit, and had coffee only, as usual. He generally did not go out of the house until about noon, but she recalled that on that particular day he had left the house between 10:00 and 10:30. She was less certain of when he had

157

returned. She thought it was between 1:00 and 3:00 in the afternoon.

She could recall no mention during the day of the illness of Colonel Farber, nor had there been any conversation in the morning about the doctor having gone out in the middle of the night to treat the colonel.

"When the doctor did return to the home, he did not return alone. Mrs. Farber came with him."

"Did you notice anything unusual about them?"

"When they arrived they both went into the kitchen, into the dinette area and there they sat and had a drink of—I don't know—something."

"What was it?"

"At that time there was a bottle of gin on the table and they had a drink of gin."

"Then what happened?"

"Well, the doors got closed on me. I don't know. They closed the doors in between the den and the kitchen. The dinette area."

She said she had not heard any of their conversation and that Mrs. Farber had left after a half hour to forty-five minutes later, and she estimated it was between 4:30 and 5:00 when she left.

She testified that it was Mrs. Farber's practice to come to the house every day, but that was the only time she had ever seen her have a drink there. She remembered seeing Colonel Farber in the house but once, possibly in February or March, when the two couples had gone out together for the evening.

She testified that Carl had remained in the house the rest of that day. She said she had seen Mrs. Coppolino when she had returned from work, and then became irritated at Bailey for no apparent reason when he asked her if she had seen Carmela before she left for work that morning.

"Of course I did!"

"Did you have some conversation with her?"

"I always say good morning."

"Did you have some conversation with her that day?"

"No. I don't conversate. No, we don't conversate. What do you mean, conversation?"

"Talk! Did you talk to her that morning before she went to work?"

"If I say good morning, I'm talking."

Bailey turned away to keep her from seeing the smile that would certainly have infuriated her. Then he asked her about the time when Carmela returned from work. The maid testified that Carmela always came home between six and five after six.

Considering the long drive from Nutley down the Garden State Parkway in all kinds of weather and traffic, this was an almost eerie consistency.

Miss Jeffress had answered the phone when Marjorie Farber had called at 6:30 and asked for Carmela. She did not hear Carmela's words to Mrs. Farber, but remembered hearing Carmela say, after she hung up, that Colonel Farber, "had died, or passed. Those were her words to me." They were said, the maid testified, in a normal tone of voice.

"What happened after the telephone call was received?"

"I choked on a hamburger."

"You choked on a hamburger?"

"Yes."

"When you recovered from that trauma, what did you do next?"

"Well, I got myself together."

Dorothy Jeffress said that "Mrs. C." had gone upstairs and gotten her stethoscope and gone out and returned in approximately thirty minutes.

"When Mrs. C. came back she only made one statement to me and that was that the Colonel was all blue on one side."

"Did she elaborate at all on the fact that he was all blue on one side?"

"No. She said he was—had been dead some time and he was quite blue on one side.

That phrase was perhaps, for her, the most memorable of her testimony at the bail hearing

Bailey established that when she had left the employ of the Coppolinos in December 1964, there had been—at least in Miss Jeffress' interpretation of the word—no disagreement with them.

"No," she said. "I was told to leave."

Bailey looked relieved as he turned her over to Vincent Keuper for cross-examination. It had been a calculated risk to subpoena a state witness. He knew that Dorothy Jeffress had testified before the grand jury which had returned the indictment, and that she had talked to Mr. Muzzi, one of the investigators from Keuper's office, and that she had refused to talk to Andrew Tuney, one of Bailey's investigators.

F. Lee Bailey had no way of knowing what the girl had, or what she thought she had. The bail hearing provided him with a chance to question her under oath, size her up, try to detect whatever degree of hostility toward his client that she might have. It was his chance to find out just how damaging she might be when she testified at the trial itself, and thus he was using the bail hearing as a vehicle for pre-trial discovery. He could not reasonably assume that her testimony would be beneficial to the defense case. Her testifying before the grand jury made of her a state witness who would be called, very probably, to testify for the state at the trial.

But because he'd not had access to her, or to her testimony, he could not know whether it was merely supportive of the state's case, or if it was key testimony which could be hugely damaging. He had to take his calculated risk in front of the newspaper people. At that time he could not anticipate just how he would plan the structure of the defense. As far as he was able to tell, when he subpoenaed her as a defense witness at the bail hearing, she might turn out to be an eyewitness of some significant and damaging act on the part of the defendant, or even an eyewitness to murder, or one who claimed to be an eyewitness. The possible malice of any witness has to enter the defense attorney's calculations. He knew that Miss Jeffress had worked for the Coppolinos and that she had not remained in their employ during their last four months in New Jersey.

If there was indeed malice enough toward her previous employer for the young woman to distort facts under oath, then the time to find out about it would be at the bail hearing rather than during the trial itself. *Had* there been malice, and of course this is only conjecture which had to go on in Bailey's mind before she ever took the stand, then it would be his responsibility to separate fact from malice and impeach the witness. But, of course, no malice was apparent in the examination of the witness. Imagine, however, what Bailey's task would have been had the girl testified to some incident which could be made to appear very damaging to Coppolino. Countering such testimony would then become essential to his winning the case, and the testimony would have altered the whole shape of the defense case, and would have caused additional pre-trial investigative efforts. Additionally, the revelation of additional damaging testimony, regardless of its validity, would have resulted in more newspaper coverage so slanted as to greatly complicate the already considerable chore of finding an objective and unbiased jury in New Jersey.

To those in the small audience who were aware of the risk Bailey was taking, and of his reasons for taking it, it was curious that Bailey stopped his examination right at that point where Miss Jeffress testified as to Carmela's return to her home after pronouncing Colonel Farber dead. It seemed at the time that it would have been equally plausible and useful to him to have taken her through the events of the next few days as well, to see if her usefulness to the state depended upon something she had seen or heard subsequent to the day of the colonel's death.

(F. Lee Bailey said that same day, after the hearing, with a mixture of glee and satisfaction: "She has nothing. Absolutely nothing, She can't help their case at all.")

Vincent Keuper than cross-examined Dorothy Jeffress. In a series of fifty-seven questions, most of which took her over the same ground as covered by Bailey, he established the following additional points: Miss Jeffress had not been instructed by the state not to talk to defense investigators; she could see the Farber home from inside the Coppolino home, and saw Carl go there on the morning of the 30th; Carmela went to work at 7:30 the morning of the 30th and did not return home at all until between 6:00 and 6:05 that evening. She had been sent on a two-week vacation beginning August 12, and from July 30 to August 12, she did not hear Carl or Carmela mention the colonel's death to her or each other; Mrs. Farber continued to visit the Coppolino home daily, having lunch with Carl and remaining two or three hours, and the children were fed separately by Dorothy Jeffress; sometimes Mrs. Farber would come over when Carmela was there, but usually she was there when Carmela was at work.

When Keuper finished, Lee Bailey came back on redirect to explore more thoroughly a point he had merely touched on before. In a brief series of nine questions, he established that when Marjorie had come back from the Farber home with Carl that afternoon, they had remained in the dinette area with the door closed the entire time

"And at no time did they go out into the back yard then?"

"Not that I know of."

Bailey then called Dr. C. Malcolm B. Gilman, the County Physician of Monmouth County, a title equivalent to that of coroner or medical examiner. Dr. Gilman, an elderly man, wore a dark brown suit, a faun-colored waistcoat and carried a walking stick. He had graduated from Cornell Medical School, done two years of post-graduate work in pathology and surgery at Johns Hopkins, had taught anatomy at Cornell and had directed the Cornell Research Station under the General Education Board of the Rockefeller Foundation

Under questioning, Gilman stated that, as a pathologist, he would estimate that in from 5 to 10 percent of all autopsies performed, no cause of death is determined.

He stated that just prior to December 10, 1965, ten months previously, he had received information about the death of Colonel Farber which led him to believe that he might have to make an investigation. Yet—and Bailey leaned heavily upon this point—the body had not been exhumed at Arlington National Cemetery until July 1966, three months previously. Asked what information he had received about the death of the colonel, Gilman produced a copy of the December 6, 1965 interview between Marjorie Farber and State Attorney Frank Schaub, held in Schaub's office in Florida.

Bailey asked for a recess so that he might read the Farber interview, but Vincent Keuper said that it should be determined whether Dr. Gilman relied on the Farber statement in determining the cause of death, or whether he relied on the autopsy. Judge Simmill asked Bailey to develop that point before taking the recess.

Bailey then had Gilman confirm that in the course of the autopsy he had found a fractured cricoid cartilage, and demonstrated by pointing to his own neck where that cartilage is located—just below the Adam's apple.

"Doctor, you have an affidavit in which you have given an opinion of strangulation as the cause of death. If you had found just a fractured cricoid cartilage and had no facts from an eyewitness, you would not necessarily have come to that conclusion, would you?"

"Not necessarily."

"Isn't your opinion of strangulation predicated to some degree upon the statement—which you believe—by Marjorie Farber that she saw the man suffocated with a pillow?"

"To a minor degree, as part of the picture, as part of the medical substance. Any medical condition goes by history and by examination."

"The only information you have as to any pressure being placed on the throat of Colonel Farber by a human being is through the statement that has come to your attention, is it not?"

"No. By the autopsy."

"The autopsy disclosed a fractured cartilage. Did it disclose the means by which it was fractured, in the autopsy itself?"

"No."

"Is some part of your medical opinion that strangulation—manual strangulation by a human being—is the cause of death drawn from the history [Marjorie Farber's statement] you have gotten?"

"A very small portion of it."

162

"But some part of it is?"

"Well—a fractional part of it—yes."

"Yes. And all of that history of events came from Marjorie Farber, didn't it?"

"All of that particular history. Yes."

Thus was foreshadowed the shape of the defense—that the cause of death was related to the Farber statement, and if the Farber eyewitness account could be discredited, perhaps so could the autopsy affidavit saying the colonel had been manually strangled. In any criminal defense it must be remembered that to discredit does not necessarily mean to utterly destroy, but only to discredit to the point where a thoughtful man, considering all the evidence presented in court, would have a reasonable doubt as to the guilt of the accused.

Vincent Keuper saw immediately the potential weakness in the state's case which Gilman's response had created, and asked permission to interrogate Gilman briefly. Here are his key questions and responses:

"Did you arrive at your conclusion as to the cause of death without the use of that statement?"

"I did."

"During the course of your autopsy did you know what the cause of death was, before you started it?"

"No indeed!"

"And it was only as the result of the autopsy performed by you and Dr. Helpern that you determined the cause of death?"

"That is correct."

Keuper had hastily patched the damage. The court granted Bailey's request to examine further. Bailey established that Mr. Muzzi, a detective in the prosecutor's office, had given the statement to Dr. Gilman. Amid a wrangle of attorneys over the legal point of whether or not the authenticity of the statement had been established, Judge Simmill took over the interrogation of the witness. This procedure, in the informal arena of a hearing, is permissible when the Court wishes to equate a contradiction in testimony. It would constitute error to pursue this same end during a trial with the jury in the box.

Judge Simmill, with an impressive clarity and exercise of logic, asked Dr. Gilman; "The question, Doctor, is: You say in your affidavit that death was due to strangulation from pressure on the cricoid area of the throat with fracture of the cricoid cartilage."

"That is correct."

"Now, did you arrive at that conclusion solely from the autopsy?"

"I did."

"Did you rely upon the statement you have to determine that it was strangulation?"

"No, no."

Simmill pointed at the railing in front of the jury box. "Well, fracture of the cricoid cartilage can take place if the man fell down and caught his neck on that rail, couldn't it?"

"That would be most unusual. Very, very unusual."

"Well, where did you get the opinion that death was due to strangulation?"

"Because when the cricoid cartilage is fractured it bends in just like a ping-pong ball and it stays in. It doesn't pop back out."

Simmill hesitated. The answer was not responsive to the question, at least not without further development. Simmill looked bemused. Dr. Gilman was evidently not attempting to be obtuse. His conviction that he had answered the question was evident. His thought processes merely did not work within the patterns of logic required by the law. Judge Simmill turned the problem back to Bailey.

Bailey led him step by careful step through the way he had acquired Marjorie's statement, his belief that it was genuine, the fact that he had read it before the body was exhumed. But then when F. Lee Bailey asked if it was not true that there would have been no exhumation without Marjorie's statement, Gilman startled and possibly alarmed him by saying there would have been an exhumation anyway.

"Did you have information from another source that aided your opinion of homicide?"

"From the exhumation of Doctor Carmela Coppolino," Gilman said, thus dissipating any alarm Bailey might have felt.

"Is it fair to say, Doctor, that you didn't have a cause of death of Carmela Coppolino until this summer, 1966?"

"Is it fair to what?" And here was demonstrated how F. Lee Bailey combines a sensitivity to the nuances of voice and expression with a great flexibility of approach, so that at the slightest clue he can, without hesitation, take advantage of something which has been only hinted. Gilman had seemed a little too baffled by the question. One might suspect that in his moment of brief hesitation before rewording, and totally changing, the question, Bailey was wondering if it could indeed be possible that Gilman had never been told the cause of death in the case of

Carmela, and, if so, what bearing that might have on the strategy of the Florida case, should it ever come to trial.

"Is it fair to say that nobody ever gave you an opinion as to the cause of death of Carmela Coppolino?"

"That's correct."

"Now was it for that reason that you exhumed the colonel?" Bailey asked, and worked his way back to the Farber statement, to the pillow over the face, to the anticipation that the exhumation would show suffocation. "Might show," said Gilman. "Or might not."

"When a person is suffocated there is a phenomenon which leaves little spots called petechiae. Is that right?"

"Yes."

"Would you spell it for the court?" Bailey asked Gilman.

Judge Simmill said, "P-e-t-e-c-h-i-a-l. Petechial hemorrhages."

"Thank you, Your Honor," said Bailey with smile and half-bow of appreciation of the range of the Court's knowledge. And with a small and amused nod, Simmill acknowledged the thanks. In these small ways a relationship was developing between these two men, both totally professional, both afflicted with a mocking wit, both intensely curious and with flexible and sophisticated minds. Judge Simmill's unconcealed enjoyment in following Bailey's examination of the witnesses stimulated Bailey to a degree of adroitness he perhaps could not have sustained before a judge less secure in the exercise of authority, less subtle of mind—the kind of man who, whether he be judge or broker or salesman, is so lacking in quickness and cleverness that not only can he not follow it, but believes it superficial and objectionable in comparison with the stolid and rigid thought patterns of sound and solemn fellows like himself

Bailey led Gilman back full circle finally with: "Don't you in every case in determining cause of death take into account the facts given by eyewitnesses as to what they saw at the time the death occurred?"

"Take into consideration, yes."

"And did you in this case?"

"I did."

But Gilman testified he had not expected to find a fractured cricoid cartilage.

In a long series of questions, Bailey elicited answers about the other kind of physical damage Gilman would expect to find after a case of manual strangulation. He got Gilman to say that the colonel's body indicated a man in good physical shape for age fifty-two, that the cricoid is a fairly tough piece of cartilage, that to dent it would take a high concentration of pressure, and that nothing in Marjorie's statement indicated that Colonel Farber's windpipe had been the subject of great pressure during the murder.

"It could if one hand was at the lower end of the pillow and pushed in. Extreme pressure on the pillow."

"You are conjecturing, are you not?"

"Well . . . perhaps, sir."

After establishing that no petechial hemorrhages had been found, Bailey asked, "Was there anything remarkable about this entire autopsy except for the dented cartilage?"

"Yes. This was a man in excellent health for his age."

"This body was interred for three years. . . . Had it decomposed to any extent?"

"Yes, the features of the face were gone. The skin and musculature of the hands were entirely gone, but other than that the general body was in a remarkable state of preservation. . . . The skin had turned to what we call adiposier. The surface skin had become a part, chemically, of the subcutaneous fat."

Bailey asked if pressure that could break the cricoid would not bruise the skin. When Gilman said not if done through a pillow, Bailey asked, "Doctor, do you have an opinion as to whether or not through the ordinary household feathered or plastic pillow such pressure could be transmitted by a human finger or thumb to cause this damage? Right through the pillow?"

"I don't believe it was the finger or thumb. . . . I believe it was the heel of the hand."

When Bailey asked the same question in another form, Gilman said he believed it possible, said that he had heard of cases, that they were in the literature, that he could find the references, and that similar damage to the cricoid was caused.

Gilman further testified that the method used would not be likely to leave bruises that Carmela or the funeral home personnel could have seen, that the autopsy disclosed no evidence of bruising. The autopsy, he said, had disclosed possible needle marks under the skin or in the adiposier, but not to a reasonable medical certainty and, "His heart was in remarkably good condition for a man of his height and weight. There was a slight amount of atherosclerosis which occurs at fifty-two, but the lumen—that is, the lining of the vessels was in excellent condition and patent—that is to say, wide open."

Bailey then asked Gilman to list the causes of death that would no longer be detectable in a body after three years in the ground. Gilman listed slow heart failure with pulmonary edema, liver failure, kidney failure. Queried by Bailey he agreed that ventricular fibrillation could be another such cause. Asked again about petechial hemorrhages, Gilman said that they were not found, and that he would not expect to be able to detect suffocation by a pillow after three years.

Next Mr. Bailey moved along to the fact, admitted by Gilman, that they had looked for some evidence of succinylcholine chloride having been injected into the colonel, and led Gilman swiftly through the practiced litany of hydrolyzation into succinic acid and choline, which are normal chemical components in small amounts in any body alive or dead.

"Now, did you have the organs of Colonel Farber tested, for instance, by Joe Umberger up in Doctor Helpern's lab?"

"I did."

It is always possible, of course, to detect subtleties where none exist. But let us imagine for a moment that Bailey suspected that Dr. Gilman might be reluctant to relate just what had been done insofar as chemical tests on the colonel's body tissues were concerned. The knowing folksiness in the phrasing of the question indicates an intimacy which may or may not have existed. Intimacy carries a flavor of prior knowledge. Consider the impact of the question had it been asked in this manner: "Where any tests on the organs of the deceased conducted by Doctor Joseph Umberger, the Chief of Toxicology in the Office of the Medical Examiner of the City of New York?"

Also a certain reluctance to impart any more information than that which is specifically asked for is symptomatic of the adversary system insofar as the testimony of expert witnesses in pre-trial hearings is concerned. As the defense can be expected to wheel its own platoon of experts into position at the trial to refute the testimony of the state experts, the less revealed of the actual details of the expert investigation, the less direct and on target will be the refutation.

Thus the expert witness at a hearing defends the sum total of the state's knowledge by restricting his answers to exactly what was asked, and no more. And it is up to the defense attorney to use his skill in examination to learn as much as possible.

It is then possible to "hedge" when answering questions, and it is an honorable device, and up to the defense attorney to detect it and reword his questions to elicit what might otherwise never be revealed.

Had Bailey asked the question in the second form shown above, in its more formal structure, the witness might realize that as he had no knowledge of whether or not Umberger had actually performed the tests himself, or merely directed them to be performed, he might answer, "I do not know."

It would then be up to the defense attorney to follow up with the question, perhaps, "Were any tests performed by anyone under Doctor Umberger's or Doctor Helpern's direction on the organs of the deceased?"

But surely "Joe Umberger up in Doctor Helpern's lab" must have talked to good old Lee, so why try to hedge on something that is already known? Yet, was it already known, or merely suspected?

"And what did Joe report to you?"

"Well, as a matter of fact I haven't gotten the final report. I have been trying to get the final report but I think that—well, I don't know. I don't know what they have found out because I haven't been able to get a report."

Bailey then, through questions, drove home the point that during the autopsy on the colonel there would have been no search for needle marks had not Marjorie Farber's statement contained references to injections. At this point Judge Simmill commented that quite obviously Mr. Bailey'd had an opportunity to read Marjorie's statement. He was making wry reference to the earlier request for a recess to give Bailey a chance to read it.

"I have, Your Honor, to the extent necessary for this examination."

Bailey then asked Gilman exactly what had been done in the autopsy. Dr. Gilman was so anxious to explain what he had been doing to assist in the succinylcholine research during the six month interval before they had exhumed the colonel that he seemed to genuinely hear a different question than the one being asked him. At last, with an air of disappointment and frustration, Dr. Gilman was diverted from relating his experimentations and proceeded to answer the question:

"The head was opened, the chest was opened, the abdomen was opened, and all of these organs were examined and sections of tissue taken of all the organs. The preserved parts of the body were stripped about a quarter of an inch wide and down to the muscle. The areas of the arms were stripped into these long narrow pieces—then the thighs, the lower legs, the back—and then these pieces were cross-sectioned, the idea being to look for needle marks, the minute straight line hemorrhage which follows a direct injection. . . . The organs, the gross organs remaining, were then sent to the chemical laboratory [Umberger] for study."

"Now, Doctor, in the course of your investigation of this

death did you interview the people who handled the body after the death in the course of embalming it and burying it?''

"Well, as I say, the findings to me were suspicious that there were injections.'' The total irrelevance of answer as related to question was as if the communication were taking place over a bad phone connection with a great deal of random noise on the line. The random noise was, of course, the doctor's own thought processes refusing to accept or even notice Lee Bailey's abrupt transition to another line of questioning. Should anyone think such inattention unusual, it is suggested that he arrange to tape a casual half hour conversation with friends, then play it back and discover how much of it he is actually hearing for the first time—an illuminating and humbling experiment.

Bailey accepted Gilman's unresponsive answer and pursued the matter of injections further, and asked the doctor if he had conducted some experiments. Gilman answered happily that he had.

"Was the description which was in *Time* magazine accurate?''

"No!'' said the doctor with a sudden and surprising irritability. "Hell, no! Or anything else!''

Bailey then asked to approach the bench and Judge Simmill ordered a ten-minute recess, during which counsel could confer with him in chambers if they so desired.

Gilman's ire was stirred by the following passage from a full page story in *Time* magazine for August 5, 1966:

An informer suggested that Sarasota County Sheriff Ross Boyer look into "something odd" about Carmela's death. According to Boyer, the tipster was Marge Farber. Suspicion focused on succinylcholine chloride, a muscle relaxant commonly used by anesthesiologists. The drug is injected into patients to depress breathing temporarily during some operations, but an overdose can kill within ten minutes—and traces of the compound disappear from the body almost immediately.

Thus for Dr. Malcolm Gilman, chief medical examiner of New Jersey's Monmouth County, where Carmela formerly lived, began seven months of painstaking detective work. Gilman imported six rabbits to his farm, injected them with lethal doses of succinylcholine chloride, buried them (one with embalming fluid) and a month later disinterred the bodies. Sure enough, he reported, autopsies revealed telltale traces of the drug's components, though not of the compound itself. As a result, Gilman had Carmela's body exhumed and a four-month analysis performed on vital

169

organs. Said Gilman, "What we found was enough to make us exhume Colonel Farber's body."

It was in that same article that *Time* called Coppolino "Dr. Strangelove," and labeled the colonel's lady "Good Neighbor Marge."

The wrath of Dr. Gilman would seem to be justified if the thirteen demonstrable errors in fact in the balance of the article carried over in the same ratio to the *Time* report of the doctor's experimentations.

The piece ended: *As the onetime winter home of the Ringling Bros. troupe, Sarasota is accustomed to circuses. Not so Fox Run, where one resident last week repeated in horrified tones the oldest caveat of modern living: "You never know who your neighbors are."*

Chapter Nine

After the recess, Bailey continued his redirect of Dr. Gilman. Evidently, if he was not furthering his expressed motive, to convince the court that Coppolino should be free on bail, he was learning things useful to his strategy and tactics in the trial to come. It is in just such instances that the layman becomes confused by the indirections and misdirections of court procedure. If Keuper had relinquished his right to cross-examine, would that have put an end to the Gilman testimony at the hearing? Or would Bailey have had the right to continue his direct examination after reading the Marge Farber statement? Additionally, how much of Bailey's direct was involved with pre-trial discovery, and how much of it was aimed at shaping the direction and flavor of the national news coverage of the hearing?

Again Bailey went to the bruises, the pillow and the ping-pong cave-in, reaching new ground finally when Gilman testified that the two small bones near the cricoid which are occasionally broken in manual strangulation were intact, as was the whole of the thyroid cartilage, the ala wing, the voice box and the larynx. Everything was intact except for the one dent, which Gilman testified as being a quarter of an inch deep. Bailey used coins from his pocket to have Gilman demonstrate the relative sizes involved. In so doing he dropped a coin, made a quick joke about it, missed at his first stab at picking it up, got it on the second try. Though he kept smiling, one could assume his flush was of irritation. The court is theater. Any bungling which occurs should be by careful plan for some tactical purpose. An authentic clumsiness flaws the performance, corrupts the control and the elegance.

Gilman testified that the lumen, the interior wall of the cricoid cartilage was approximately the size of a twenty-five-cent piece, but more elliptical than round, and that the dented area was roughly one third of the area of the coin, an irregular area much like the crumpled denting of a ping-pong ball, reaching from the edge over to the center of the elliptical area.

Bailey then returned to the question of who had handled the dead body, and learned that Gilman had talked to the funeral directors in Red Bank to satisfy himself that the neck damage had not occurred during the preparation of the body for burial.

He reapproached the question of why Gilman had hesitated six or seven months before exhuming the body. Gilman had the authority to exhume, didn't he? And he had the Farber statement? So?

The questions were rapid and Gilman, slightly rattled, said, "We don't do these things on hearsay."

"Do you want to tell me that you didn't believe her story and that's why you didn't do it?"

It was transparent what Gilman wanted to explain, but he could not find any organized way of answering which did not wander into unresponsiveness. He was aching to say that from the Farber statement of injections and smothering, and the knowledge that the colonel had been buried almost two and a half years by the time they got the statement, the odds against finding proof of suffocation or injection marks was so remote as to not justify exhumation. And, as to the question of finding proof of injections of succinylcholine through chemical analysis, if they could not find a lethal dose in a far fresher corpse, there was little expectation of proving a non-lethal dose in the colonel's body.

Any two or three stage line of reasoning will always be impossible to explain in testimony unless the interrogator cares to permit it, and asks those questions which will permit it. Yet Gilman had been qualified as an expert, entitled to give subjective evaluations, and thus it is safe to assume that had Vincent Keuper asked that the witness be given a chance to give a full and complete answer, the Court would have so ordered. Also, in the absence of this assistance from Mr. Keuper, the witness himself could have appealed to the Court to be given an opportunity to answer completely. Possibly his difficulty was more a certain fuzziness in expressing himself, an inability to articulate what he so clearly wished to explain.

Bailey then asked an old question in a brand new and, to press and spectators, a most startling way: "Now, your position in December was, despite the fact that this woman says, 'I tried to kill my husband and then Carl Coppolino came in and did kill him while I watched,' that this wasn't enough information to exhume the body. That was your position?"

The reporters sat hunched, scribbling like the wind, catching the exact words before the imprint on memory faded. This is always the clue to the lead, unless, of course, something even more shock-laden is revealed. It did not seem likely that this could be topped.

Some local attorneys, interviewed that evening, seemed astonished and puzzled by Bailey's tactics, saying that they thought he had weakened his case. But here, as in most other demanding professions, it would seem that an insistence on traditional methods diminishes effectiveness. That apparent "risk" seen in restrospect, was an almost obligatory piece of strategy. Yet few attorneys would have seen it in that way at that time.

Bailey knew that Marjorie Farber was the cornerstone of the state's case. He knew that she would not recant her statement. He suspected that she had gone so far, she would appear in court and testify. Thus, that information would ultimately be revealed. And it would be his task in defense of his client to destroy the effect of that testimony by destroying the witness. In that moment he began the process of destruction, because he made people wonder why he had dared to bring it up. So, they thought, if Bailey brings it up, then it isn't all that important, is it? If he couldn't prove it didn't happen that way, why would he spill it?

Also, by being the one to release that information in public for the first time, he took the play away from the state, took away the state's chance of effective dramatics. He released it on his own terms, so that it would be old hat by the time of the trial and, either inadvertently or by intent, demonstrated once again that no courtroom appearance by F. Lee Bailey could ever be termed dull.

* * *

The New York *Daily News* used the following lead on Friday, October 21:

Seven months before Dr. Coppolino was indicted in New Jersey for the murder of his onetime friend and neighbor, retired Lt. Col. William E. Farber, the colonel's widow made a statement to authorities in which she was quoted as saying:

"I tried to kill my husband, but Coppolino came in and did kill him and I watched."

This was disclosed yesterday by the defense attorney himself, F. Lee Bailey, during questioning of a witness at a bail hearing for Coppolino in the Monmouth County Court House, Freehold, N.J.

And the subliminally significant word therein is "himself."

Again Bailey kept digging for the reason for the delay, getting Gilman to admit that suffocation might leave petechial hemorrhages, and the longer the body stayed in the ground, the less likelihood of finding any. Gilman said he had no reason to doubt Mrs. Farber's story, but then said that he had no corroboration whatsoever of Mrs. Farber's claim. And he kept trying to testify that they were working intensively on the Carmela Coppolino case.

He testified that the colonel had been exhumed in July because they were not satisfied with the cause of death of Carmela, and did not know what it was at that time.

This response, which tied the two cases together, made it more possible to proceed with other details about Carmela with less risk of a sustained objection by Keuper. Such was Gilman's tendency to drift away from the point at hand, not out of evasiveness but out of a kind of compulsion to follow a subjective thought pattern rather than the pattern of the questions, that at times it was as though Bailey were the farm boy with the switch, slowly herding toward the barn an amiable steer who kept spotting tufts of appetizing forage well off the path.

Here are the key questions and responses in sequence, with Dr. Gilman's digressions deleted:

"What date, if you ever have, did you learn of an opinion by some competent authority as to the actual cause of Carmela's death. You didn't have it by the time you disinterred the colonel?"

"No."

"Have you gotten it since? Has anyone ever told you that he has an opinion as to the cause of death?"

"No, I do not believe I have ever gotten a direct opinion, only by hearsay."

"I take it during the course of these two running investigations you and Doctor Helpern maintained contact with one another?"

"Oh, we maintained a very close liaison."

"You would, I assume, be talking with him from time to time to find out if he had come up with anything?"

"That's right."

"And after Carl was indicted in both places you continued to have contact with Doctor Helpern?"

"That's right."

"From Doctor Helpern personally you never heard that he has come up with the cause of death, true?"

"That's correct."

"There was no particular development of any significance that by itself caused you to give the order [to exhume the colonel]. Is that true?"

"That's correct."

"All right. That's all, Doctor. Thank you *very* much."

And the boy with the switch rolled the big barn door shut and walked away, smiling.

F. Lee Bailey then asked if the two statements he had examined during the recess could be marked for identification. One was the Farber statement, and the other was a statement by Dr. Juliette Karow. Keuper objected to the Karow statement on the grounds that it was not material to the issue.

"No," said Bailey. "I'm sorry. It is very germane. I think it is germane."

"It has nothing to do with this case," Keuper said.

"I don't think you can separate the two."

Judge Simmill said, "Well, I haven't seen the contents."

They were given to the judge. The Farber statement was marked D-2. As the judge scanned the other one, Bailey said, "Juliette Karow is a witness to whom Mrs. Farber talked before going to the authorities. In other words, her statement which we will attempt to authenticate in Florida by affidavit or by bringing her here would be a prior inconsistent statement of Marjorie Farber."

The judge, frowning, said that there was nothing in Karow's brief affidavit inconsistent with the Farber statement.

"I expect," said Lee Bailey, "some of the impeaching evidence to be much more highly detailed than the affidavit."

"How does that help you?" asked the judge.

"I told you about reading it," Bailey explained, "I know

something about it. We had Doctor Karow in Florida [at the preliminary hearing] but the conversation always involved both cases. [She implies:] 'I know this is a homicide because that is a homicide.' The two are inextricably tied together. It is one package deal. Doctor Karow is a witness, and a witness for the state down in Florida. The statement would be helpful to us in putting together a statement to bring up to Your Honor.''

Judge Simmill sustained Keuper's objection and the Karow affidavit was not admitted. Bailey asked for a week to either present new affidavits or come back with new applications for out-of-state subpoenas. The judge ordered a continuation of the hearing to whatever time would be convenient to Mr. Bailey. (Bailey was to start the Sam Sheppard trial in Cleveland the following Monday, October 24.)

The judge then went through the other motions submitted by Mr. Bailey, various discovery motions, requests for data in the hands of the prosecutor, the autopsy report, details of the indictment, and similar items. All were granted and, at a few minutes past one in the afternoon the court went into recess and the bail hearing was continued without a new date set. Carl was returned to his cell at the Hall of Records. Bailey remained behind to talk to Keuper, the judge, and others. Mary Coppolino, Joseph Afflitto, and several of the reporters went down to the American Hotel where Bailey would join them.

It should be noted that this was in no way intended to be a violation of Judge Simmill's order to both prosecution and defense as well as law-enforcement officers, to make no statement to the press about the pending trial, and to grant no interviews. There is a valid working understanding in such situations. It is perfectly obvious that there will be friendships between members of the defense team and the working press dating back to other trials in other places. Strangers in a strange town, they will talk and drink and eat and laugh together, because both are in gypsy professions. It is obvious that recognition of the code has to be implicit and complete, because one cannot be expected to continue indefinitely the off-the-record warning. And it is equally obvious that any violation of this understanding would make the overeager reporter as welcome in the future as a Syrian at a bar mitzvah. So the talk was of the Sheppard case, the Boston Strangler, and the hearing that had just ended. Not that there was any total disclosure. Every law school would appear to give required courses in Deception and Misdirection.

But somebody asked Joe Afflitto what he thought of Lee Bailey after working with him for the first time, and Joe said,

"He wasn't anything like I expected. I don't know exactly what I *did* expect, but he seemed a lot quieter, sort of more casual and relaxed and . . . I guess you could say *proper*."

It could have been a little side-bar item, if anyone was foolish enough to use it. However, somebody was fool enough to use something else. Mary Coppolino was understandably worried about her husband, about his weight loss, and the rash, and his complaints about chest pain. There was no "interview." Mary sat at the table in the hotel dining room and, in front of the group, she complained loudly and long.

A reporter for a metropolitan paper made a story out of it, constructing quotes from memory, and writing the story in such a way that it appeared as if Carl Coppolino's lawyers, by their presence at the "interview" were condoning this sort of publicity, and using Mary as a vehicle for the release—because they fell under the judge's directive and the accused's wife did not.

The story had her saying, "They are already treating Carl as though he is a convicted murderer. I know he'll be proven innocent and this kind of treatment is sad. I'll really despair if they don't permit him out on bail. I just know they'll kill him before he can prove his innocence."

After the story came out, Warden Earl A. Smith made a public statement that Coppolino was getting the same treatment and consideration as all other inmates. "There is no prejudice against him and no special favors for him. She has never indicated any discontent to us, and the doctor has made no complaints."

And this public statement drew an immediate rebuke from Judge Simmill, who wrote a memorandum to Sheriff Paul Kiernan advising him that the warden had violated his directive that all court personnel refrain from public discussion of the case, and calling upon him to instruct Smith to make no further statements.

As the situation endangered the amiable relationship Bailey had begun to establish with the Court, and as the story left an entirely false impression, Bailey flew to Freehold from Cleveland during the first weekend recess in the Sheppard trial, late on Friday, September 30, and risked rebuke by Judge Simmill by issuing a clarifying statement, saying that he did not believe his remarks would be in violation, and saying he had written to the judge to inform him directly of the truth of the situation.

"Any statements critical of the jail and of those in charge, attributed to Mrs. Coppolino are absolutely false," Bailey said. "I was there and I have read the article. I am incensed over the impression that was given. Carl is getting very, very good treatment. The warden has been mindful of his condition and has given him every consideration to which he has been entitled.

"Mrs. Coppolino is naturally hopeful that he can be released on bail. But her remarks reflect more frustration that he is in jail, any jail, rather than any comment on this jail."

Thus was the situation cleaned up. But with one final touch. Rumor has it that something unfortunate happened to that reporter's credentials at the second Sheppard trial, and it became necessary to get up very very early and line up with the spectators in order to get into the courtroom to be able to fulfill the requirements of the assignment. Also, the other press people immediately became very guarded in conversation and around that particular reporter, for fear that something they had picked up on the understanding that it would be held confidential might find its way into another "interview."

The incident and its resolution show how very important it is for a defense attorney to make and maintain good relationships with any judge he must appear before, and how seriously any potential rifts are taken. The defense attorney is not trying to curry favor, or butter up the judge. He knows that he will have to ask certain favors and dispensations. On one of the trial days he may wish to ask for an earlier than usual recess in order to have time to prepare to meet some unexpected development. He must beg the Court's indulgence in many small matters of convenience which, though not directly related to either law or evidence, facilitate his task. One cannot easily ask nor receive such indulgences from a judge with a memory of lack of pretrial cooperation with the wishes of the Court. When both sides are cooperative with the Court, before and during a trial, it is far easier for the Court to maintain an amiable impartiality.

Mary Gibson Coppolino was, of course, expressing her deep resentment of one of the curious inequities of our system of law. She could not understand it, and does not to this day, because it is a matter of convenient administration rather than of justice.

During the selection of the jury, during a trial, and during the charge to the jury much is made of the presumption of innocence, of the cloak of innocence which supposedly enfolds the person accused of a capital crime. In a county jail there will be three classes of prisoners: those who have been sentenced and are serving short terms, those who are awaiting trial and could be out on bond, but who cannot afford it, and those rare and occasional ones who can afford bail but who, by reason of a charge of murder in the first degree, have not been given the privilege of putting up bond. Those not yet brought to trial are innocent in the eyes of the law. They have, in the legal sense, committed no crime. They have not been judged. Yet they suffer the same deprivations as those who have been convicted: restricted visiting hours, jail food, strict supervision, compulsory obedience to command, regimented hours, jailhouse uniforms, supervised and limited amusements.

So the wife cries, "They are *punishing* him and he is innocent!"

She means innocent in the ultimate sense, but the law says that he is indeed considered innocent until proven guilty beyond a reasonable doubt. At first superficial appraisal one can feel that the man who is not entitled by law to put up bond should be incarcerated in some special way, in better surroundings, with—in fact—every comfort and convenience he can afford, giving up only his liberty.

But on further analysis one realizes that the only difference between the man not entitled to bail and the man who has not the resources to post it is a difference of economic status. They are both innocent until judged guilty, and what should apply to one should apply to the other, because if it is not made applicable to both, it would mean that that particular form of justice was for sale.

Ideally, the legally innocent and the legally guilty should not be incarcerated in the same place under the same conditions. And, ideally, all jails, institutions, charity hospitals, homes for the aged, should have trained dieticians, occupational therapists, psychologists, useful libraries and recreational facilities, substantial operating budgets, and highly trained administrative personnel.

Until utopia arrives, the detention of those awaiting trial will be based upon the pragmatics of economics, not the ultimate equities. The Coppolino, the John Doe, the felon, will all be housed alike, fed alike and treated alike, because that is all the tax structure can provide, and the only available response is to rationalize or apologize, always the cheapest assault on all inequities.

And so the advance units of the media and the defense team scattered, and would return again with reinforcements in forty-six days to begin the selection of the people who would sit in judgment upon the pallid and ailing doctor.

Freehold had, for the newcomers, a curious flavor of remoteness. It is so far from Manhattan that only a small portion of the 9000 population endure that deadly daily journey by the express buses which are scheduled to make it in one hour and five minutes and too often take an hour and a half. Perhaps the remoteness is due to the curious highway situation. Though huge highways, multi-lane, divided, fast, arrow across the state in all likely and unlikely directions, they all carefully avoid Freehold by at least twenty minutes driving time on narrow old roads, which seem to be marked to increase the traveler's sense of confusion and disorientation rather than diminish it. During the trial, venturing out of Freehold by automobile meant spending a good deal of time trying to find it again.

There are small industries in the area. Electrical testing equipment, corrugated boxes, precision parts, plastic molding, ladies coats, baby blankets, glass containers, electrical fittings, sportswear, kitchen cabinets, outdoor furniture pads, extruded plastic tubing, a branch plant of Nestlé, making various chocolate products, bed springs, paper converters, and diagnostic reagents. But when one asks about the local economics, the usual answer is, ''Things have never been the same since the carpet mill folded.'' The town reportedly perks up from early August to mid-October when they have sixty days of harness racing at the Freehold Raceway, a new and handsome plant. But there is an elusively shabby flavor about the small city, even though it is the county seat. Twenty-five churches and one movie house. One weekly newspaper with a circulation in the Freehold area of 3640. The County Airport has one runway, 4000 feet long. Two railroads service the Freehold area—but only for freight. No passengers. There is no radio station. The nearest hospital is in Neptune, eleven miles away. (The Riverview Hospital in Red Bank is fourteen miles away.) There are no smart exclusive shops. The nearest golf course is a twenty-minute drive, for a fast driver.

During the trial, when the skimpy and stale-looking Christmas decorations were strung across the streets in the shopping area, a local businessman stood at the bar at the American Hotel at lunchtime and shook his head and said to several newspaper people, ''Don't get me wrong now, but why couldn't you people have cooked this all up for maybe March, when we could have used it? Sure, it's a lot of new business for everybody, having a trial here, but just a couple of weeks before Christmas? Who needs it this time of year?''

There was some shabbiness, and the carpet mill had folded long ago, and to get a train ride you had to be a crate of something, and the trial brought some strange ones into the jammed corridors, and there are probably cleaner and tidier bus stations in Syria and Nigeria, but the people of the town were kind, interested, considerate, and somewhat wistful that we had all come at the wrong time and would all be gone so soon.

THE JURY SELECTION

December 1966

≈≈

Chapter Ten

On Sunday afternoon and evening the men and women who would report the Coppolino trial had been arriving in Freehold from distant places, taking rooms at the downtown American Hotel for the most part, a few settling in at outlying motels. They came from Florida, Cleveland, New York City, London, Philadelphia, Boston, Chicago . . .

They moved in like a platoon of infantry veterans assembling in an occupied village. They dug up the essential survival information, and traded it with each other. What's going to be the phone setup? How about the telex? How late is Western Union going to stay open? What's the bit on getting laundry done? How about the food around here? Who else is coming in? Who's been assigned? I didn't get credentials, so who do I see? What are the judge's rules about interviews? Is Theo here yet? Anybody seen Doc Quigg? Who's covering for the *Times*? Where do you do your drinking? What's the transportation to New York like? Bailey in yet? Any chance of a last-minute change of venue? What's the general attitude around here about Coppolino? How much are you paying for your room? Can you buy out-of-town papers around here? What's this Judge Simmill like? How long are they guessing for picking a jury? When do they get started tomorrow? Now until two in the afternoon!? Why? O'Shea said Bailey has a hearing in Boston tomorrow morning, and he'll fly down after it's over. Anybody know where Keuper has Marge Farber stashed? What are the odds on Bailey winning this one? Is Mary Coppolino giving any interviews? Look, should I rent some wheels, or can I make out without them?

The members of the opposing teams were assembling. State Attorney Frank Schaub flew up from Florida to observe the case for whatever benefit it might give him when and if it became his turn to prosecute Carl Coppolino in Florida on the charge of having murdered his wife. Warren Goodrich, Mrs. Farber's civil attorney in Florida, had come up with her to represent her civil interests, along with the necessary local attorney, George Chamlin.

Bailey had acquired the services of a Monmouth County attorney in addition to Joseph Afflitto, from distant Wayne, New Jersey. The new man was Joseph Mattice (muh-TICE), a balding man in his middle years who could bring many years of local practice and acquaintanceship to bear on the special problem of jury selection. One can assume that Bailey's team of investigators, Andy Tuney, the ex-lieutenant of the Massachusetts State Police who had headed up the detail assigned to finding the Boston Strangler, and Mrs. Teri Plaut, that high-style hawk-slender multi-talented paragon, had done some active homework on the list of prospective jurors.

The final Bailey weapon in the vital combat of jury selection was very large and very improbable—a vast sandy overweight doctor of medicine, lawyer, and hypnotist named William J. Bryan, who claimed to be a blood descendant of William Jennings Bryan. Bryan's avowed specialty on the Bailey team—one that he had exercised to some advantage in the second Sheppard trial, apparently—was to watch every little quirk and twitch and physical mannerism of every prospective juror and, with knowledge of the defense case Bailey was planning to present, recommend acceptance or rejection of each juror on whether the mannerisms he exhibited fitted or did not fit the psychological pattern necessary for acceptance of the defense thesis.

Bryan was accompanied on his flight from his Sunset Strip headquarters by a case of dried meat, a staple of his diet, and by a breath-catchingly lovely secretary, so fantastically uncommunicative that when asked her name, she would smile and say, "No comment."

On that Sunday night before the jury selection began, an area television station broadcast a syndicated Joe Pyne show which had orginated weeks earlier in California, and on which Bill Bryan had been a guest, or more accurately, a victim.

The Joe Pyne Show is a painful public forum for the nut, the masochist, and for those whose hunger for public exposure is stronger than their judgment. Bryan detected some sort of crafty conspiracy in the rebroadcast in the area of the trial the night before it began. "I was on Joe's program twice before, and we got along just fine," he said. "But this last time he tried to cut me up. Why did they fly that tape here just at this time? *Very* peculiar. *Very, very* peculiar."

The group that became known as the Bailey team stayed at a Congress Inn, a motel at the edge of town. Bailey, Afflitto, Mary Coppolino, Bryan, Mrs. Susan James (someone eventually wheedled a name from the pretty secretary), Teri Plaut, Andy Tuney, Paul Holmes—the veteran reporter who had recently resigned after years on the Chicago *Tribune* and who had done two Sheppard trial books and was doing a book on Coppolino from Carl's viewpoint—Ed Linn, the author and journalist who had done a *Saturday Evening Post* feature on F. Lee Bailey and was gathering material for a book on Bailey—and later some of the defense witnesses, and also Wicki Bailey, the little cupcake second wife of the man who, as the week began, was headlined in one metropolitan daily as "The Flying Mouthpiece."

On Sunday afternoon the more painstaking of the newsmen were up at the Monmouth County Court House, inspecting, measuring, taking notes about the courtroom and the immediate surroundings. As is true in all fields of human endeavor, these very few who took that trouble were the true professionals, the veterans, the most successful.

On Monday afternoon the courtroom was called to order forty-one minutes past the scheduled 2 P.M., due to Mr. Bailey's delayed arrival from Boston. Spectator attendance was light, due to the popular belief that the selection of the jury is a long, tedious, boring affair.

It is long. Portions of it are tedious. But it is anything but boring to the defense attorney and the prosecutor, or to any spectator who takes the trouble to learn the rules and watch and listen carefully.

Carl Coppolino looked far more fit than at the bail hearing in October. He had gained back at least ten of the thirty pounds he had lost, and was up to a hundred and forty or more. Mary had taken the suit he was wearing to the warden's office that morning. It was an iridescent grayish green gabardine. His dark hair was neatly trimmed.

While waiting at the defense table he chatted with Joseph Afflitto, and leafed through the legal-sized files Afflitto had brought with him and placed on the table. Mary Coppolino, trim in a gray tailored suit and black kid gloves, hair freshly styled, smiling and confident, sat just inside the rail in front of the press section.

And at last it began.

Lee Bailey opened with a motion for a continuation of the trial to a later date, and a change of venue, arguing that area newspapers were carrying accounts of the case prejudicial to his client, and that on the following morning he would submit to the Court a bundle of clippings supporting his contention.

Judge Simmill ruled that he would hold the motion in abeyance until Bailey had the chance to observe the coverage of the first day of the trial, and until he had submitted the clippings he spoke of.

Next Bailey moved that the Court not exclude from the jury any prospective juror who admitted religious or conscientious scruples against the death penalty. He argued that the basis of customary selection was prejudicial to the defendant because it resulted in the selection of a group of people of "a more cruel bent" than the average cross-section of the Monmouth County population. This motion, as Bailey anticipated, was denied. Finally, not in the form of a motion, but as an information to the Court, Bailey said that a court order commanding Dr. Milton Helpern to permit the defense pathologist, Dr. Ford, to examine the throat organs of the late Colonel Farber had not been complied with.

Judge Simmill looked inquiringly at Prosecutor Vincent Keuper who arose and explained that two appointments had been made. The first was not kept by Mr. Bailey's pathologist. The second could not be kept because Dr. Helpern had been hospitalized. A third appointment could now be arranged. This was acceptable to Mr. Bailey.

While waiting the newsmen had a chance to study the copies of the printed list of two hundred and fifty prospective jurors on the panel. The list gave names, addresses, occupations. It was noted that on the panel there was one Italian barber, one mortician, two chemists, forty-four housewives, and twenty-four people of apparent Italian heritage.

During this first day of jury selection, Dr. Bryan sat over on one of the chairs at the side of the courtroom, facing toward the jury box. Later he was to move to the defense table, so that there were five of them there: Bailey and Bryan, Afflitto, Coppolino and Mattice. . . . And, all alone, at a table of the same size placed directly behind the defense table, sat Vincent Keuper.

This was the procedure. The prospective jurors were held in a room on a lower floor. The judge had met with them earlier and instructed them in their responsibilities, including not discussing the case at all among themselves.

Names were drawn by lot by a court attendant who turned the crank on a small drum, reached in and selected a name. Each prospective juror would be brought in one at a time and either selected and sent into the jury room, or dismissed and told to return home.

One can imagine each juror unprepared for the impact of such a concentrated attention from so many people when he or she came in, and was asked to raise their right hand and be sworn. A further confusion was caused by a part of the New Jersey formula for swearing a prospective juror which asks the juror to "look upon the accused" and then be seated in the witness stand.

The uniformed bailiff at the front of the courtroom was a large gray-haired man, professionally wary, with the cold blue eye of the reliable policeman. From the moment the cuffs were taken from Coppolino's wrists each day just outside the corridor doorway at the forward area of the courtroom, directly to the left of any witness in the stand, the accused was the immediate responsibility of Callahan.

During recess when he would go into the corridor and retrieve the semi-smoked length of narrow cigar which he kept atop the outside ledge of the doorframe, a place useful only to a man so tall, he stood near the open door in such a way that Coppolino was always in the corner of his vision. Over the years he had been assigned to Elvin Simmill's courtroom, number 308, the cigar had burned out so many countless times upon the oak frame, ember end extending, that it had umbered a peach-sized area of the tan plaster corridor wall.

He would hold the Bible for the swearings, and the thin elderly clerk of the court, standing by his table beyond the judge's bench, would call out the words of the swearing across the twenty feet of arena. With almost every one, when asked to look upon the accused, they would look in confusion at the defense table so close to them, the five men there all looking up in inquisitive appraisal.

"I whisper to them which one is Coppolino," said the big bailiff during a recess. "A lot of them want to think it's Bailey they're supposed to look at."

The bailiff would, oath completed, direct them into the witness stand. Judge Simmill would then, in a patient and measured tone, leaning toward the prospective juror, say, "We are here endeavoring to select a jury in the case of the State of New

185

Jersey versus Carl Coppolino. The accused has been charged with murder in the first degree. . . ."

He would explain what the alleged crime was, and then ask those questions which would eliminate the prospective juror for obvious cause with the least waste of time.

Do you have any religious or conscientious scruples which would make it impossible for you to return a verdict of guilty, knowing that the penalty is death?

Do you have any scruples about sentencing a person to life imprisonment?

Have you read or heard anything about this case? And, if so have you formed an opinion?

Are you personally acquainted with any of the principals or any of the attorneys on either side?

Has there been any crime of violence in your immediate family?

Are you or any of your immediate family connected with law enforcement in any way?

Do you know of any other reason at all why you could not serve as a juror in this case?

It was interesting to note that though Judge Simmill had to go through this same routine over and over again, he did not ever let it degenerate into a repetitious flatness, into a bureaucratic indifference. His approach was personal. He varied the form of the questions. He was convincingly interested in each and every person who took the stand.

After his portion of the *voir dire,* the examination as to qualification, bias, and prejudice, those who passed that hurdle were turned over to the opposing attorneys for further examination.

The defense and prosecution took turns as to who would examine first. If the defense did not uncover any reason during its turn as to why the prospective juror should be removed for cause—in the form of a motion sustained by the Court—then Vincent Keuper could question if he chose, and would be first to question the next prospect.

Once a prospective juror had passed all three hurdles, then there remained only the final hurdle of the peremptory challenge, that right of the defense and of the state to refuse to accept a certain limited number of veniremen without giving any reason.

Under New Jersey law, and in line with our philosophy of law which gives the defendant the most advantage, Coppolino's attorney had twenty peremptory challenges at his disposal, and the state had twelve.

The adversaries take turns in giving their final decision on each venireman found qualified to serve. And this is where it becomes a cat-and-mouse game.

For example, imagine a situation where only a few more jurors must be selected to fill the box. Assume that both sides have only a few "perempts" remaining. The defense attorney is examining Mr. Jones. He knows that it is his turn to speak first, either accepting the juror or using up another of the challenges he has been so zealously hoarding. He is not quite sure he wants Mr. Jones on the jury. If he were quite sure, he would take no chances. He would use a perempt and get rid of him. But this is in the nature of a hunch. And so, continuing the *voir dire* (pronounced variously by attorneys and judges as vwar dare, vwor dear, vwar dyer) he can choose to phrase his questions and adjust his manner in such a way that he seems to be establishing a chummy and marvelous rapport with the juror. Then he can say happily that he accepts Mr. Jones, taking the calculated risk that the prosecutor, conned into thinking that here is a defense-minded juror, will eliminate him on a precious peremptory.

Now imagine that it is his turn and he wants Mr. Jones on the jury. He will make every attempt to conceal this eagerness. He will go back often to the defense table for whispered consultations with his co-counsel and perhaps the defendant. He will phrase questions which indicate a state of doubt. Finally, after much hesitation, and with an air of reluctance, he will accept Mr. Jones, hoping to con the state into also accepting him.

Depending on the acuity of the opposition, the defense attorney can invert this procedure if necessary, giving the warm welcome to a venireman he really wants, and acting dubious about the one he is suspicious of, hoping the prosecutor will read it as a con act and react accordingly.

The situation is less risky, of course, when it is the turn of the state to announce their decision first. Then, even with those jurors on which the defense knows it will have to use a peremptory challenge if necessary, it is possible to try to gull the prosecutor into being a cat's paw and using a state perempt in the interest of the defense. All the same games can be played with far less risk.

In all cases each side will have whatever leverage in decision-making which results from prior investigation of members of the jury. The use of this must, of course, stop short of any violation of ethics, such as hiding a personal friendship which the juror, during the judge's portion of the examination decided, for some reason, not to admit. To oversimplify, a man who had been discharged from his job for suspicion of theft, and later cleared and rehired would be, all other factors being equal, an excellent defense juror, as he would be painfully aware of how pure coincidence can put a man in a helpless situation.

Privy to such information, the defense attorney during *voir dire* would take pains not to ask any questions which might reveal this past incident to the prosecutor.

Because of a rather unusual procedure under New Jersey law, called by some "New Jersey Roulette," all fourteen jurors had to be selected with equal care. In New Jersey, at the conclusion of a case, and after the judge's charge to the jury, the fourteen names are put in the squirrel cage and tumbled. The first one drawn out is automatically the foreman of the jury. The next eleven are the jurors who will deliberate. The remaining two are the alternates, who are then sequestered until a verdict is returned, so that they may take the place of any juror who falls ill during deliberations.

Throughout a trial each juror knows that the chances are six out of seven that he will serve on the jury, so each will pay the closest possible attention, in contrast to those states where at the time of selection the alternates know they are alternates, and know they will serve only in the relatively unlikely event of a juror falling ill. This would seem to dilute their feeling of direct responsibility.

The New Jersey system of examination of the veniremen one by one is perfectly suited to F. Lee Bailey's exceptional ability to relate in a direct and personal way to each individual, to adjust by instinct to that image most likely to disarm the prospect, to charm him, to make him speak freely and readily. One might call it a capacity for instant friendship. It is the gift of relating with such a warmth and directness to the individual that he feels important and appreciated, and possibly the most interesting person Bailey has faced that day. It is difficult to think of a more useful tool in jury selection than simple likability. And to enhance it, Bailey adjusts his vocabulary, attitudes, manner to that level which, without flavor of being patronizing, best strikes a responsive chord. Certainly these relationships established during the examination result in a jury which at least feels amiable toward Mr. Bailey.

Because of the nature of the case, and the defense plan, one could say that the ideal defense jury would have been made up of youthful and emotionally flexible people of good intelligence, of some direct or indirect relationship with the professions, arts, sciences, people of wit and tolerance.

An ideal prosecutor's jury would be composed of middle-aged

people of a severe and inflexible morality, suspicious of professional and intellectual attainments, conscious of living in a world where evil exists, and feeling a responsibility not only to society but to their own safety and self-esteem to stamp it out.

In either case, eleven of one and one of the other could result in a hung jury and a retrial, provided the loner was sufficiently stubborn.

Keuper sat alone.

F. Lee Bailey had his table of cohorts, and though he frequently solicited opinions from all of them, including the defendant (pronounced by Judge Simmill as de-fen-DANT—rhyming with "slant") Bailey operated like a board chairman who owns 51 percent of the corporate stock. (Opinions are welcome, but the decision is mine.)

The first prospect did not get past the judge's examination. He said he had formed an opinion as to the guilt or innocence of the defendant. It is safe to assume he thought the defendant guilty.

The next man, a structural engineer, survived the judge's examination. It was Keuper's turn to examine first. He at once established the pattern he would follow throughout the entire selection procedure, with a few very rare and brief exceptions. "No questions," said Keuper.

Bailey stood up and walked over and greeted the man by name, and established one of the patterns he would follow. In a chatty and friendly way he asked Mr. Hunter what newspapers he had read regularly, and how closely he had followed the Coppolino coverage.

"Do you think it's possible that he did it?"

The question startled Hunter. "That's a hot one."

It became increasingly obvious that the man had some prejudice against the defendant, and so Bailey then began to use questions that led the man further and further toward some specific expression of this heretofore concealed conviction of guilt.

The question that did it was, "Would it influence you if the Florida case was never touched upon in this court?"

The man said it would, and Bailey moved that the man be excused for cause. Simmill so ruled.

The third prospect was all too eager to serve on the jury. This alerts the suspicions of any defense lawyer. A sort of half-hearted willingness to perform this time-consuming civic duty is far more reassuring. When Bailey could not find any way to cloud the man's avowals of complete impartiality, he used his first peremptory challenge to get rid of him.

A woman was next and was excused by the judge when she said, with a certain flavor of righteousness, that she had formed an opinion about the case. It was evidently an unfavorable opinion of Coppolino's innocence. After she left, Lee Bailey asked the judge if it would be permissible to ask such rejecteees, for the record, if their opinion was favorable or unfavorable to the defendant. Here one can assume that Bailey was warehousing ammunition in the event of a conviction, where such data could be used to show the appeals court that the community was prejudiced against the defendant by the publicity Bailey had brought up in his opening motions. The Court accepted the suggestion.

The next two were excused by the judge, one for too much financial hardship involved in serving, another for an unfavorable opinion.

The seventh prospect to be sworn, James E. Jerram, Jr. of Matawan, a young, dark-haired, pleasant-looking man, became the first juror accepted. Keuper, taking a first turn, asked but one question. "Are you married?" "Yes sir."

Bailey questioned him for a long time, delving for evidences of any conviction of guilt, appraising the man. As he was the only one selected that day, he was the lead in the newspaper stories. He apparently was the owner of one of those concession arrangements whereby he leased or owned equipment which makes ice cream bars which are then distributed to area retail stores and to route men. So in the newspapers he was termed everything from Ice Cream Manufacturer to Good Humor Man. The implications of the latter seemed more popular with the news desks.

There was time for but one more name and number. A banker from a branch of the Manufacturers Trust in Raritan got past only the first three questions put to him by Judge Simmill. When he said he had read about the case, the judge said, "And have you formed an opinion about the guilt or innocence of the defen-DANT?" He had.

"Is it favorable or unfavorable to the defenDANT?"

"Unfavorable, Your Honor."

"Thank you for your candor. You are excused, sir."

Eight prospects. Five unfavorable opinions. One juror. One defense peremptory challenge of the twenty permitted.

During the examinations Lee Bailey had conducted, as well as during his earlier arguments on motions, another facet of over-all

190

defense strategy became clear. Bailey was revealing, in the presence of the press corps, newsworthy attitudes regarding the Florida indictment, hints as to the structure of the case for the defendant, and clues as to his oppinion of the state's case and the state's witnesses. No reporter who was expected to file at any length on a day of jury selection could help but feel grateful to F. Lee Bailey for adding that verbal spice to the proceedings.

When he argued about publicity, he sought to bar from jury duty anyone who had read of the Florida arrest and indictment of Carl Coppolino, saying, "Jurors could be unfairly influenced by the double-feature, Your Honor. It could lead them to believe that lightning doesn't strike twice, or, he did it again."

The judge agreed that if one were to believe what had been printed in the papers, Coppolino "has already been convicted in Florida." But he said if a juror admitted having read about the Florida case, but testified to an open mind, and had not formed a conviction from what he had read, he should be eligible to serve.

Bailey argued that there was really no way that a juror could reveal to the court whatever subconscious conclusions he may have drawn from the Florida case, and because the Freehold trial would be limited to something which had happened two years earlier, there would be nothing in the Freehold trial to counteract that subconscious conclusion. He pointed out that, unfortunately for the defendant, the newspapers had given the impression the Florida case against Coppolino was the stronger one. "As a matter of fact," Bailey said, "the Florida case is very weak."

A few moments later, when asking about the delay in having Dr. Ford examine the throat tissues of the deceased colonel, and finding that the second delay was because of Dr. Helpern being hospitalized, Bailey hinted what his attitude toward Helpern would be by asking acidly, "Does he own them?" This was a gratuitous hint because Bailey would, of course, realize that the tissues were in the personal custody of Helpern in order to safeguard the "chain of possession," so that during the trial the defense could not establish any reasonable doubt as to the exhibit being the actual portions removed from the body during the autopsy.

During his often lengthy *voir dire* of the veniremen, Bailey frequently asked, "And how would you feel if you learned that no murder had been committed?" At another point he spoke with a certain contempt about how Florida had "shuffled the doctor up here for trial." And he began to lay the groundwork for that guessing game which seems endemic in all capital cases, by saying to several prospective jurors that it might be possible that Coppolino would not take the stand, then asking if that would prejudice the juror against the defendant.

This, of course, is a ticklish strategic consideration. For hundreds of years, under the heritage of English law, in a capital case the defendant could not take the stand and testify in his own defense. The presumption was that he would lie. It is vain to attempt to guess whether the defense will put the accused on the witness stand until the state has finished its case. The texture, detail, and persuasiveness of the state's case will determine whether the risk should be taken. Whether the accused is innocent or guilty, there is always a risk of a particularly damaging cross-examination, or of rebuttal witnesses called by the state who will contradict testimony given by the accused, thus more than canceling out whatever favorable impression he might make on the jury through his own recital of events, and his manner and persuasiveness in telling his own side.

During that first day, Judge Simmill controlled the proceedings in a manner which was sufficiently relaxed as to invite, during the swearing of the first juror selected to serve, a lapse in courtroom decorum.

Possibly one exchange with a juror had misled the press corps. One man, during the judge's interrogation, said that he had never read anything about the Coppolino case anywhere.

"I am sure," said the judge, "that all of the newspapers represented in this courtroom must be frustrated."

After a few more questions had established that the prospective juror *had* seen one paper, but claimed that all he could remember from it was a photograph of F. Lee Bailey, the judge inquired politely, "And does his picture do him justice?"

The man looked warily at Bailey and nodded and said, "Yes sir."

This kind of relaxed amiability is possible only when the judge is confident of his own ability to control his courtroom.

When James E. Jerram was being sworn as the first empaneled juror there were rustlings and whisperings from the press section as the reporters were verifying the spelling of the man's name with each other, and his occupation.

Elvin Simmill, interrupted the swearing and said, loudly, firmly, and most impressively, "Don't you realize out there that this man is taking an oath before God?"

Mr. Jerram was then sworn in a perfect silence, and when the court was recessed for the day, big Paul Callahan took custody of him, to go with him and pick up his clothing at his home, leave his car, check him into the Hitching Post Motel on Route 9, and take him to dinner in a private dining room at the American Hotel.

F. Lee Bailey and several members of the Bailey team went down the hill and into the bar lounge at the American Hotel, where Bailey took over, for the duration of the trial, a big round table in an isolated corner between the end of an L-shaped bar and the jut of a two-doored entrance alcove from the sidewalk. At least fifty reporters and photographers jammed into the open space in front of the table. All knew the stipulation of the Court, that there would be no discussion of the case by any attorneys for either side, by any principals in the case, by any witnesses, by any county personnel.

Bailey chatted briskly and amusingly about the Sheppard victory, about some maintenance problems involving the landing gear of his aircraft. He was drinking vodka and tonic, an unlikely drink during the Christmas season in New Jersey, and so were a lot of the others. Somebody who had followed the team in Cleveland said to some other reporters who hadn't, "So now we got an in-drink for this one. In Cleveland he drank Bloody Marys. So everybody drank Bloody Marys. Here, you watch. Everybody on vodka and tonic."

A few reporters were rash enough to risk questions about the trial of Coppolino. If they were leading questions, Bailey ducked them very deftly. When they were direct, he would stare at the questioner with such a vivid, contemptuous hostility, mixed with a mocking amusement that the offender usually eased back into the throng, out of range.

Then one reporter edged toward the corner where Bailey sat and whispered something to him. Lee Bailey's face darkened immediately, and he raised his voice to a pitch which silenced everyone.

"Gentleman, I have just been informed that one of your number has just been good enough to inform Judge Simmill that I an conducting a press conference here. I want it clearly understood this is not a press conference. We came for a drink and to relax. I do not recall inviting anyone. Nor do I recall being rude to anyone. If we have to hide ourselves that is what we will do. If that be the case, please don't anyone speak to me, mention my name, take my picture."

Thus was the status of the evening assembly spelled out, and

193

so it would remain until the entire jury was selected and sequestered, when the Court's order could and would be relaxed.

It was at 6:00 P.M. that evening, quietly, privately and off-the-record that F. Lee Bailey said to two newsmen he could trust: "If I can't win this one, I'll pull down my shingle."

Chapter Eleven

The slow process of jury selection resumed at 9:30 A.M. There was no mention of the promised motion for continuance and change of venue due to the "prejudicial publicity" Bailey had mentioned on Monday.

Had Judge Simmill believed that the coverage by those newspapers commonly read in Monmouth County had significantly reduced the accused's chance of a fair trial, he could and would have exercised his option under New Jersey law to bring in a "foreign" jury panel from another county, ideally one as far from Monmouth County as geographically possible. This procedure is less cumbersome, expensive and time-consuming than actually moving the entire trial out of the area.

F. Lee Bailey had not arrived in court when the jury panel parade began. A Mrs. Michaels, an office clerk from Asbury Park, was excused when she hesitated, and with a wary glance toward the defendant, said she had formed an unfavorable opinion of his possible innocence. Joseph Mattice examined the next prospect.

But Mr. Mattice could not quite manage to elicit an admission strong enough for removal for cause, and used the second of the defense peremptory challenges. Bailey arrived in time to quiz the third prospective juror of the day, quite obviously did not want her, struggled to lead her into grounds for cause, gave up and used up the third defense peremptory. Next came a bright and personable young TWA flight engineer who got along so famously with Mr. Bailey that Vincent Keuper expended his first challenge and separated these brand-new friends for all time.

Then came a Mr. Reitzel from Asbury Park, seating himself and expressing an unfavorable opinion toward the defendant, and getting up with that mildly startled look of those who did not know that the opinion made them unsuited to jury service, and

194

being shown the way out by Callahan. A housewife took his place, a Mrs. Phelan who said she knew absolutely nothing about the case, and thus gave Bailey nothing to use to find cause, so he used the fourth defense challenge. Three challenges in five prospects was a bad batting average. She was replaced by a Mr. Gerald Bench, who was a merchant from Matawan expressing a conviction of guilt. The next was yet another Long Branch housewife, this one a widow, and, from her responses, aching and burning to serve on the jury. She did everything but say please. When she said she had not read about the case, Bailey then asked her if anyone had ever discussed the case in her presence. "Oh no," she said blandly.

Under further questioning she said she had read "a little bit" about the New Jersey case, but didn't know a thing about any Florida case.

Bailey said, "Maybe it will be decided that Carl Coppolino will not take the stand. Wouldn't it seem unusual to you that an innocent man wouldn't get up and say, 'I didn't do it!'?"

"No. It wouldn't seem unusual."

When he could do nothing with her, and it was quite obvious he did not want her, Bailey tried to have her removed for cause, giving as his cause a "lack of candor," because there was no news story on Coppolino which did not mention both indictments. He was overruled. He used the fifth peremptory challenge for the defense. On the previous seven names called, the defense had used up four challenges!

The seventeenth name called thus far in the empaneling was the first to be excused for not believing in capital punishment. He was a Mr. Brown, retired, from Shrewsbury. It had been forty-five years since anyone had been put to death as the result of a Monmouth County trial.

Number eighteen was a civil service clerk-stenographer. She lived in Middletown and worked at the airbase. She was Mrs. Marjorie H. McFadden. She wore a plaid suit in two shades of green, she was slim, medium tall, blonde, and possibly in her forties. During Judge Simmill's questioning she said that there had been a crime of violence in her immediate family. Bailey took over. She seemed bright, introspective, thoughtful, and there was a flavor of sincerity to the responses she gave. After searching carefully for prejudice, and after several whispered consultations with the others at the defense table, Bailey accepted her. So did Keuper, and she was sworn as a juror and sent off to join Jerram in the jury room.

The next called was a retired police officer who had spent

forty-four years on the Long Branch Police Force, and had been the chief of police for the final eighteen years. He said he had not read about the case and had not been interested in reading about it because, "I had seen so much of it."

A lawman is poison to the defense in any capital case. Yet the fact of having been an officer of the law does not make a man unacceptable for jury duty. Chief Ed Boyko survived the judge's examination. Bailey had to make him admit prejudice, or else use up yet another perempt.

Bailey moved affably and directly toward that key question which, properly done, will result in removal for cause. After he was certain he had established a friendly rapport with the man, he got around to Boyko's familiarity with the machinery of the law. In essence his line of questioning went: Now wouldn't it be pretty difficult for you to realize that this man had to be indicted by a grand jury after a police investigation, and he had to be arrested and charged and arraigned, and brought to trial, and he had all the usual safeguards along the way . . . wouldn't it be difficult for you to assume that all the law officers were wrong and all the evidence was wrong, and that somehow all the machinery you are familiar with had misfired and brought an innocent man into court to be tried for murder? Wouldn't that be a pretty remarkable exception to the way these things work, in your experience? Wouldn't you have a certain amount of difficulty in really making yourself believe the accused is innocent until you hear something that might make you think otherwise?

And Boyko was taught that he could not really make an honest presumption of innocence, and admitted it, and was excused for cause.

The next prospect, and the third person acceptable to both sides—to the astonishment of many in the press section—was the Reverend Earl C. Snyder, a Methodist clergyman who admitted that it was a bad time of the year for him to have to be away from his duties to his flock, but that they would understand that he also had a duty as a citizen. He was thirty-three years old, dark-haired, presentable, an articulate man of a sufficiently nimble mind to seem to enjoy fencing with F. Lee Bailey during the long *voir dire*. Some felt he was a little too emphatically in favor of the death penalty. Ministers on a jury are believed to be a bad defense risk, though this could be more superstition than a result of logical appraisal. Bailey, with the bright brisk manner of one who is joyously flaunting tradition, at last accepted him.

Keuper asked but one question: "Is there anything in your

religion that would prevent you from voting for a verdict of murder in the first degree?''

''No sir,'' said the Reverend.

When one realizes that Bailey had begun to indicate another aspect of his case, by asking prospective jurors if it would unduly prejudice them should they learn that the defendant had been playing around, the amount of risk in accepting the Reverend Snyder is increased. An acquittal would let a sinner go free.

The prosecutor used his second of his twelve peremptory challenges on the next one, a housewife and ex-legal secretary. Among other questions Bailey asked her if she would become prejudiced against the defense were she to see on the stand, ''. . . a woman your contemporary whom the defense will attack with vigor.'' He also, for no other reason perhaps than to call attention to the man's presence in the courtroom as an observer, asked her if she had ever heard of Frank Schaub.

The next venireman, Robert W. Lingenfelter, became the fourth juror. He was about thirty years old, dark, slight, sallow—a laboratory technician with Western Electric. During his examination, Judge Simmill said with a caustic irony, ''Western Electric wrote me they were going out of business if you were selected for jury duty.'' The mild and perceptibly nervous young man did not confirm this appraisal of his importance to his company.

In his examination of Lingenfelter, Bailey once again made it quite clear that the defense would hotly contest charges that any murder had taken place, and that he would accept only those jurors who could keep a clear distinction in their minds as between adultery and murder.

After the young technician was sworn and sent to the jury room, Bailey during his examination of the next prospective juror provided a suitable lead for any reporter who cared to use it. While questioning the man about what he had read about the case, ostensibly to detect any area of prejudice, Bailey asked, ''And have you read anything about the collapsed coffin theory on Colonel Farber?''

(During the lunch break which followed Keuper's using the state's third challenge on that venireman, the working press busily interviewed each other to find out if anyone had ever read or heard of any collapsed coffin theory up to that point, and no one had. That does not mean of course that it was *not* printed somewhere. It can mean only that if it was, it did not attract much attention.)

Presumably Bailey was telegraphing the defense explanation of the broken cricoid cartilage. It is impossible to determine what

Bailey thought to gain, or actually gained, by introducing that factor at that particular point. One result became evident during subsequent testimony by state witnesses. Warned of Bailey's possible ploy, the expert testimony was tightened to attempt to refute that possibility prior to its being brought up.

In another question a few moments later to the same man, Bailey said, "Suppose it comes out that the defendant had not been a 'good boy,' that he had been fooling around with a woman at the time of the colonel's death?"

The tabloid Philadelphia *Daily News* combined both inferences into a single bold black page one head the next day, December 7:

PLAYBOY DOCTOR'S
MACABRE DEFENSE:
COFFIN CAVE-IN

When court reconvened after the lunch recess, F. Lee Bailey once again brought up the matter of Dr. Ford being given a chance to examine the throat organs and tissues of the deceased, saying that the defense might have to consult as many as ten pathologists. Keuper told the Court that it could be arranged at Dr. Ford's earliest convenience.

The first afternoon prospect distinguished himself by being excused for a cause which no one else shared during the entire jury selection. He had no objection to the death penalty, but he had a conscientious objection to life imprisonment!

The two women who followed him were quickly excused as each of them, during the judge's examination, said they were not in favor of the death penalty and could not vote for it.

The third woman of the afternoon proved acceptable to both sides and became the fifth juror sworn. She was Mrs. Arline L. Salisbury, a registered nurse who had received her training in Vermont, the wife of a bank clerk. She was blonde-gray, with delicate features, a worn and sensitive face. She wore a double-breasted red sweater-jacket, a red skirt.

As he was establishing a friendly rapport with Mrs. Salisbury, Bailey asked her how things were down in the jury panel room.

"Oh, they'll be glad when it's over in that jury room," she said. "Everyone was saying they just hated to come up and have to face this."

"I hope word isn't getting back that they're being worked over up here."

She sighed and smiled and shook her head. "Nobody ever gets back down," she said. "When somebody is called, everybody just waves goodby." And she lifted her arm in a token wave. She was relaxed, amusing, and obviously intelligent.

When he asked her if it would affect her ability to presume the defendant innocent if he never took the stand in his own defense, she pondered for a few seconds and then said, "I would *hope* he would be able to speak for himself." Perhaps no other prospective juror answered so aptly.

Bailey's wording in questioning her about prejudice and infidelity was if it would bother her to learn that "at or about the time of the death, the defendant was carrying on a little extramarital fooling around." He also wanted to know if it would turn her against the defense, "If you saw Mrs. Farber in some degree of discomfort."

Bailey spent a long time on the next prospect, a man who seemed to have a certain amount of prejudice against the accused, but who would never word it in such a way he could be removed for cause.

"Do you attach any significance at all to the fact that this man had been indicted for *two* murders?"

"Well . . . it runs through your mind."

"Sort of a passing thought, eh?" Bailey said sourly, and finally he used the sixth of his twenty defense preempts on the man.

The twenty-ninth name selected from the panel, Edward S. Samsel, became the sixth juror. He was in his middle thirties, sizable and sturdy, a lineman with the power company, with a weathered outdoor face, a hard square jaw, small eyes, and—unlike most of the others who had sat in that same chair—almost utterly immobile, devoid of any nervous habits or mannerisms.

After the usual series of questions, searching for prejudice, Bailey worked around to the question he had asked several of the other men he had found acceptable. "Would you want a man like yourself serving on this jury if you were the accused?" There was a hesitation, a small smile that came and went quickly, and he answered that he would.

The judge recessed the court for the mid-afternoon break, and in the corridor one of the members of the Bailey entourage said that, as was the opinion of the press section, he had been fairly certain Lee Bailey would not accept Samsel. But at the end, when he had seen Samsel smile, he suddenly knew that Bailey would accept him.

Bailey was detained and was not in court when the next panelist was called, a lady employed as a florist. She survived

Simmill's queries, and Joseph Afflitto took over the defense *voir dire*. He had a notebook in his hand.

It was obvious that she might well be hiding a prejudice against the accused. And the suspicion was well enough warranted to require a peremptory challenge if Joe Afflitto could not elicit some response which would have the judge excuse her for cause.

Quite obviously Joe had written down the general line of questioning Bailey had followed in such cases. But he did not have Bailey's intuitive ability to structure the line of questioning to the individual on the stand. Afflitto kept finding himself with no follow-up question to ask, and so he would have to pause, think, look at the notes, and try another direction.

But he persisted, and finally he got what he was looking for when he asked her, "Do you suppose that an entirely innocent man could be indicted at about the same time for two different murders in two different states? What did you think when you read that?"

"Well . . . there must be something in it," she said, and Afflitto's motion that she be excused for cause was promptly granted.

The next prospect was excused when Keuper used the state's fourth challenge.

The thirty-second member of the panel, and the last one called on Tuesday, was a Mrs. Marian DePagnier, a young, sturdy, dark, quite attractive machine operator—a factory worker. Keuper asked her if she felt that if she were selected, she could listen to the evidence and render a fair and impartial verdict.

"I will try," she said in a small voice.

Keuper accepted her.

Bailey smiled at her for a moment and then said, with a flavor of courtliness and gallantry, with a flourish as though he had doffed a plumed cap, "The defense will accept this lady's promise that she will try."

No questions at all!

The precision of F. Lee Bailey's instinct can best be illustrated by the observed fact that throughout the trial itself, Marian DePagnier's dark, thoughtful, brooding gaze was fixed upon the chief counsel for the defense.

Court recessed until the following morning. And, bit by bit, the team and the corps reassembled at the hotel. It was agreed that Joe Afflitto had done well in his single turn at bat. He could not be expected to come within a league of Bailey's eerie skill in relating immediately to people, in improvising a structure of inquiry which would lead them, step by step, to exactly where he wanted them. Joe had done what he had wanted to do, and what he had been expected to do, so he was batting one for one.

At the hotel various statistical theories were argued out between the newsmen.

". . . Bailey'll use all his challenges, the whole twenty. Know why? Suppose there's a conviction. He appeals it on the basis of publicity. So the appellate court wants to know why, if these people were all so prejudiced, he didn't have to use all his challenges."

"Look here. We've got seven keepers out of thirty-two. So that's fourteen out of sixty-four, right? So we used up nineteen names today. So we get a jury sometime on Thursday. Right?"

". . . Let me add this up. Seven keepers. Eight prejudiced against the defendant. Three against the death penalty. And . . . ten challenges, six by Bailey and four by Keuper. That's only twenty-eight! What's wrong?"

"Nine prejudiced, not eight. And the police chief who couldn't presume innocence makes thirty. Oh, and one hardship case excused yesterday, remember? But who the hell was . . ."

"The guy who had scruples against life imprisonment!"

"Thirty-two. Check."

"Say, you notice something else? On three of Keuper's perempts, he used them after Bailey had asked the person if they wanted to serve on this jury, and they answered yes."

"Say, what was that bit about Simmill congratulating Big Bill Bryan today? I missed it?"

"Oh, the Executive Director of the American Institute of Hypnosis just got word he's passed the California bar examination, and Bailey told the judge. So all of a sudden there's four lawyers sitting with Carl."

"And didn't the captive anesthesiologist look natty today in that light gray suit?"

"It's kind of strange, you know. Other big trials I've covered, the defendant sits like a lump while all this is going on. But there's Coppolino up there, staring, studying, whispering, writing notes, voting yes or no on the people from the panel. He turns around and beams at Mary. She throws him a kiss. Know what it makes me think of? Like an actor lands a bit part and he's trying to fatten it up during rehearsal."

The morning session started off with a venireman who stated his unfavorable opinion most forcibly. "Thank you for your candor," said Judge Simmill, excusing him.

Carl was in the same light gray suit he had worn on Tuesday. On the previous evening Mary Coppolino had arranged to have a different suit pressed, a black mohair suit, for Carl to wear on this day. She had spoken of it to some of the reporters in the bar at the hotel, saying in answer to a question, "Now I don't know *how* many suits Carl has, but I can tell you he likes having nice clothes."

But when she took the black suit to the jail the next morning, she was told that she had arrived too late. During a recess she announced with a certain irritation that she had arrived in plenty of time, but that Warden Smith was "feuding" with her, ostensibly because of the remarks she had made about how they were treating him, remarks unfortunately printed in a New York newspaper at the time of the bail hearing in October.

Thus Carl was condemned to wear the same suit two days in a row, and Mary remarked that it depressed him.

Local attorneys and the press corps were in good attendance. The public attendance was still light. Bailey had not yet arrived.

The second man passed the judge's interrogation. To observers he seemed a little bit too emphatic about having no opinion. He was, in addition, far older than those which Bailey had found acceptable. Joseph Mattice in the defense *voir dire* tried to root out a sufficient basis for removal for cause, but could not manage it, and the defense used its seventh peremptory challenge.

Then, in rapid order, three were excused because they were against capital punishment: a machinist, a doctor's secretary wearing a yard of pearls, the wife of a post office employee. It had become evident that those opposed to the death penalty fell into two classifications, those who genuinely felt that it is barbarous, distasteful, and degrading to society to put a human being to death—and those who did not really care much one way or the other, but knew that this was the easiest way to avoid jury duty, and had a lot of Christmas shopping to do. It is impossible to pick any individual and say that their avowed conscientious objection was fraudulent. The uneasy truth and the convincing lie cause too much overlap. But it was obvious that Simmill was becoming restive, and that the percentage of those opposed to capital punishment was climbing too abruptly.

The thirty-eighth panelist called was the first Negro to appear on the stand, a mortician of seven years' experience, and with a banker's dignity. F. Lee Bailey had arrived a few minutes earlier, and took over the defense examination. In asking what newspapers he read, Bailey found that here was yet another of the constant readers of the New York *Daily News*. He turned and gave a wry glance toward the press section, and said, "Despite the wide circulation and manifest integrity of the *Daily News*, can you delete from your mind all that you have read, and make your judgment solely on the evidence and testimony to be presented in this court?"

In the prolonged examination, Bailey grew increasingly cordial, speaking of, "the twelve jurors of which you may well be one."

"Would you feel under community pressure to convict Carl Coppolino?" he asked. In another question he leaned with a subtle weight upon the word "minority" in relation to Carl's ethnic background.

Finally, rather than the usual abrupt acceptance, Bailey made of it such a warm and effusive welcome to the "new juror" that he in effect guaranteed the exercise of the fifth peremptory challenge by Keuper.

Came next a man who was excused because of being a friend for many years of both Judge Simmill and Joseph Mattice, and then an aquatic biologist excused for reasons of business hardship, and then a neatly dressed gentleman in his middle years employed by IBM as a trainer of business machine operators.

When asked to look upon the defendant, he stared anxiously and nervously up and down the table of five men, trying to identify Coppolino. Callahan made the whispered identification, and the man focused upon Dr. Coppolino, smiled, bobbed his head and was seen to say something. Despite this cordiality, during Simmill's examination he revealed that he believed Coppolino was probably guilty, and so was excused.

(During the mid-morning break a reporter approached Callahan as the big man was relighting his door-top cigar and asked him what the IBM man had said to Coppolino. "He said 'How do you do?'," replied Callahan. He shook his head in wonderment. "There's always something new. All the years I've been doing this, that's the very first guy who ever acted like it was an introduction.")

The next four names drawn were all women, three housewives and a bank employee, three of them with convictions of Coppolino's guilt, and one of them opposed to death. The court recessed for the mid-morning break.

The first panelist when the court was called back to order was a telephone company engineer who seemed to be the sort of individual Bailey was prone to accept. It was natural that the press corps would try to guess Bailey's decision during the prolonged examinations.

This man was professional, intelligent, and articulate. When

203

Bailey asked him how things were going down in the panel room, the man said there was no apprehension, "just nervous excitement."

Bailey learned the man had read the *New York Times Magazine* supplement feature on Milton Helpern, and asked, "Do you have a built-in admiration for Doctor Helpern based on what you read?"

"Well . . . he has certainly reached some remarkable conclusions."

Bailey examined very carefully and, at times, almost hesitantly, returning to the defense table to check and recheck the opinions of the others. When asked if he had any reluctance about serving, the man said that he did not want to miss Christmas with his family.

"I think we can reasonably assure you we are not going to be tied up here for Christmas," Bailey replied.

After a whispered consultation at the table, Bailey used the eighth defense peremptory challenge.

Next there was called in order a man who thought Coppolino guilty and two women opposed to capital punishment, and all those in the courtroom were increasingly aware of having run through seventeen names without finding the eighth juror.

The fiftieth person to take the stand became that eighth juror. He was Herbert M. Pleshko, an accountant, a rather saturnine man of about forty with an almost oriental cast of feature, a swarthy complexion.

Bailey's examination seemed to consist of questions styled to remove him for cause rather than to retain him. For example, instead of asking, "Has anyone discussed this case in your presence?" Bailey would ask, "How many people have discussed this case in your presence?" There seemed to many to be a detectable eagerness on the part of Pleshko to serve on the jury. But the adversaries found him acceptable.

Three more women were called, one a chemist, one a young and handsome Negro housewife, the third a housewife married to a CPA. All were opposed to the death penalty. Judge Simmill, in a slight display of testiness, said to the third as he excused her, "I have to respect your opinion . . . though I may disagree with it."

The next was a young housewife who seemed to many to be a splendid prospect for the defense. With her, Bailey phrased his infidelity question differently. "Suppose that the evidence was that he *did* do a little swinging?" Evidently Keuper too felt she was defense oriented. He used his sixth challenge on her.

When the next man, a shipping clerk, was called and said that he did not believe in capital punishment, the judge's obvious irritation led him to further questioning on that point.

"You mean to say that you cannot imagine a crime so heinous you would vote for the death penalty?"

The man said, apologetically, "I couldn't stand it."

"In other words, Herman Goering should still be alive?"

The man humbly bobbed his head and the judge excused him.

When the next prospect, a woman employed as a technical editor said that she too did not believe in capital punishment, Judge Simmill asked, "You cannot imagine a crime so heinous that you would approve of a sentence of death?"

"I don't think anything is bad enough for that."

"And that includes Mussolini?" Simmill asked.

F. Lee Bailey came to his feet immediately, and said, "Let's stay with the Germans this morning, please, Your Honor."

It broke up the courtroom and it broke up the judge, because it was incredibly quick and deft and perfectly timed.

Number fifty-seven, the last name drawn before the lunch break, became the ninth juror. He was about forty, a Ukrainian mining engineer working for Anaconda. His name was George Phillips. He had the accent of his Slavic derivation. He had a square face, a thoughtful manner. When the judge asked him if there was any reason why he could not serve, he said that he'd had a heart attack, but was now in good health.

One can well wonder what the effect would have been on George Phillips had there been any specific testimony about Carl Coppolino's heart condition, if Phillips would have comprehended on both an intellectual level and an emotional level, the difference between coronary artery disease which creates an insufficiency but does not cause actual muscle destruction, so that the patient can be up and about the day after an attack, and a coronary occlusion which even if only suspected and not entirely verified from the readings of the electrocardiogram requires two weeks in hospital, and in the mildest form permitting a positive diagnosis usually requires three weeks.

In the give and take of Bailey's long, searching examination Mr. Phillips was completely at ease, entirely under control, and gave the impression of actually enjoying the exchange. He came through as a man with a quick, bright, analytical mind, but the predominating characteristic he showed was strength, certainty, the habit of command.

But toward the end of Bailey's *voir dire*, he displayed certain human qualities, or frailties. Bailey was asking if Mr. Phillips would be prejudiced against the accused if it was shown that he had "stepped out of line."

"We are all human beings, and I step off the line myself."

"I trust that is only a suspicion, and not a statement of fact," Bailey said. "You don't look the type."

Deadpan, Phillips said, "You *do* look the type."

Flushing and grinning, Bailey said, "I'll have to take the Fifth on that. The juror's acceptable."

During the lunch recess Lee Bailey was heard to remark, regarding Phillips, "There's my foreman!"

It is fair to assume that Bailey had not yet learned at that time, or had momentarily forgotten, that curious aspect of the New Jersey Numbers Game whereby the first name drawn from the completed panel of jurors becomes the foreman.

At the hotel men's room that day at lunchtime, a reporter conducted an impromptu and unusable interview with one of the prospective jurors who, during the Tuesday morning session, had been excused because of objection to the death penalty. He was a sizable, ebullient, outgoing fellow in a checked sports jacket, with a loud voice and a New Jersey accent.

"What are they saying about it down there in the panel room?" the reporter asked the excused juror.

"Well, they were saying they were pretty sure he did it, all right. Say, I just saw the jury coming out of the dining room there and I see they took that minister, and they took a guy with a bad heart! He's had one heart attack already. Geez, that's pretty rough, you know, that kind of thing for a guy with a bad heart."

"The Ukrainian?"

"Huh? Yeh, that's the one. An engineer. George something. You know, I called my wife and told her I saw George with the jury and they'd called him, bad heart and all. I told her about the kind of people on the panel and you know, they get interested in who they take."

"What do they pay you?"

"A lousy five bucks and I lose two days off work and when I went up I said to the judge about not believing in the death sentence and . . . off I go! I don't know what I got so all nervous about."

The first prospect after lunch was a housewife on which Bailey used his ninth challenge, perhaps thinking that in age, background, and attitudes she might identify too closely with Marjorie Farber.

The fifty-ninth panelist, William H. Ellis, an engineer with

ABC television, Channel 7, became the tenth juror. He was in his forties, slightly overweight, with curly silvery hair carefully barbered, and a handsomely tailored suit. It became reasonable during Bailey's examination to conclude that Bailey wanted him. He filled the requirements of professional standing and intelligence, and in addition he was employed behind the scenes in an industry where one can assume that the transient affair is not a matter of as great moment as it might be in more sedate professions with no show business additive.

Bailey again found a way of diminishing the possible effect of the double indictment by inquiring, as he was determining how much Mr. Ellis had read about the case, "And you read of where they got cold feet in Florida and sent him up here for trial?"

Mr. Ellis was accepted and was sent to join the other nine jurors.

The next two prospects, two men, a tolls supervisor and a civil engineer, had previously formed convictions of Coppolino's guilt.

F. Lee Bailey used the tenth defense challenge on the next man, an operations engineer, who—though he had no discernible prejudice against Coppolino, and indeed seemed to know very little about the case—gave the impression of being a rather rigid and unyielding person.

Next came a grower of flowers who stated he opposed the death penalty on religious grounds, prompting the judge to ask him what religion negates the death penalty, and then quote the eye for an eye, tooth for a tooth passage in the Old Testament.

Keuper used his seventh challenge on the next man, a chemical engineer who had once served on the grand jury, and seemed to have the best knowledge of the law of any panelist yet called.

Bailey used his eleventh challenge on a man listed on the jury list as a machine operator.

The next man said that he knew Vincent Keuper. The judge, determining the extent of the relationship, did not find sufficient cause to excuse him. Bailey asked but one question. "Knowing Mr. Keuper as you do, do you really think he would prosecute an innocent man?"

Judge Simmill said, "Let the record show that he shrugs his shoulder and raises one eyebrow quizzically. Excused for cause."

The next man opposed the death penalty, and the man after that, the sixty-eighth vireman to be examined, the last prospect of the day, became the target of the twelfth defense peremptory challenge.

It had been a long day. The adversaries had gone through thirty-six panelists to find Pleshko, Phillips, and Ellis.

Late that evening there was a grotesque little distraction, a long range intrusion by Dr. Sam Sheppard. He appeared on the Johnny Carson show on NBC and while chatting with Carson he happened to mention that when he came into the Cleveland courtroom to hear the jury render its verdict, he had brought along a .45-caliber automatic tucked into his jock strap. New York news desks got hold of their people in Freehold with the request to get a comment on this intimate revelation.

Later, when he appeared on another program, the David Susskind Show, again for the purpose of plugging the sales of his book, Sheppard went into more detail, telling Susskind that the automatic pistol had not been loaded, and that the courtroom was staffed with some large, armed, nervous lawmen, and if the jury had brought in a verdict of guilty, he planned to stand up and point the gun at somebody, knowing there could be no quicker way to commit suicide.

Chapter Twelve

In his book, *Trial by Jury*, published in 1965 by Chilton, a Washington attorney named Samuel W. McCart has this to say about the myths and methods of jury selection:

Lawyers evaluate veniremen on the information about them which has been acquired from pretrial investigation, from observing them about the courthouse and in previous trials, and from observing them during the voir dire. *During the* voir dire *the veniremen may be required to identify themselves, perhaps by standing, and they are required to speak in answer to questions. The wise use of the information so gathered may mean the difference between a case won and a case lost.*

In everyday life, when we meet a stranger we evaluate him; we size him up. We get an impression that we will like him, be neutral, or be lacking in harmony with him. Our future relations are affected by this evaluation. The evaluation is much more important in litigation.

A lawyer may rely on his natural ability to size up people, taking an interest in items of appearance which are beyond what he regards as normal. Or a lawyer may make a study of physiognomy or phrenology. These pursuits are not accepted as sciences by all people, but the fact that one book on the subject (How to Measure Your Power by H. H. Belkin) sold over 600,000 copies is evidence of general interest. The author does not pose as an authority on these subjects and will go no further than to briefly summarize some of the characteristics, which, according to Belkin's book, are indicated by certain physical features. Some of these are: Eyebrows meet and eyes are close together—narrowmindedness. Narrowly closed eyes—deceit. Upper lid covering more than a third of iris—secretiveness. Round, wide eyes—credulousness. Large, round eyes—perception. Small eyes—short on emotion. Downcast eyes—timidity and over-caution. Pointed ears with no lobes—dishonesty. Flat-topped ears—tight with money. Short upper lip—sensitiveness, fears criticism, loves praise and flattery, responds to charm. Long upper lip—individualistic, impervious to flattery, responds to logic. Drooping corners of mouth—pessimism. Upturned corners of mouth—optimism. Wide mouth—generosity. Full lips—emotional.

Another applicable study is antropometry, which is based on the physical aspects of the human body. This study divides people into three classifications. Endomorphs are round and soft of body, have wide faces, short necks and tend to be obese. They have bland faces, are deliberate of speech, even-tempered and relaxed. They are amiable. These qualities make them more generous to criminal defendants and civil plaintiffs. Mesomorphs have square, athletic-type bodies, strong voices and seem to be older than their age. They give particular attention to facts. They are, therefore, for the side which has a strong factual basis. Ectomorphs are lean, underweight, and have fragile features. They have weak voices and an appearance of intentness and strain. They are least amiable and generous. These qualities make them less generous to criminal defendants and civil plaintiffs.

When we speak of securing favorable jurors, it is commonly understood that choice is mainly based on possible bias. That is true very often, but it is advantageous to go deeper and learn what sort of man the venireman really is. We have no dispute that men of repulsive ugliness, men obviously deformed, and men extremely tall or short tend to develop resentments. We can accept the fact that these men acquire peculiar mental attitudes, because we can see a cause. We associate a type of mind with what we see. Is it then not reasonable to suppose that physical characteristics reflect type of mentality as well as types of emotional response? Those lawyers who accept these physical factors as valid will use them to get jurors of the type of mind most

209

desired in the light of the facts expected to be proved in the particular case at trial.

Veniremen who have not been selected for the jury have no reason to feel hurt, slighted, or rejected. The reason may have been that they appeared undesirably intelligent, unduly wise in human nature, or too smart to be beguiled. The fact is that a venireman seldom has any basis for knowing why he was not selected to sit. We have followed custom in speaking of selecting a jury, when, in fact, we do the opposite. We reject veniremen, and those who are not rejected form the jury.

The first prospect on Thursday morning was acceptable to both sides. He was Alfred Philibert, a retired machine-shop manager, the oldest juror chosen thus far. He was in his sixties, a heavy man, seemingly mild, rather vague, and quite amiable.

With him, as with many of the previous veniremen, Bailey, early in his examination, asked, "Do you think Colonel Farber is dead?" It seemed to shock and puzzle them, and it is fair to assume that was his purpose in asking it. He knew they would appear all braced and primed for the questions they imagined he would ask. This was certainly not one of them. It gave Bailey and the others seated at the defense table a chance to observe how the prospective juror reacted to what appeared to be some kind of a trick.

Then, in rapid order six were dropped based upon Judge Simmill's examination. Two women, both housewives, and two men—one a television repairman and the other a labor supervisor—thought Coppolino had probably committed the crime of which he was accused. A woman supervisor opposed the death penalty. A man had personal knowledge of the case.

Bailey spent a long time on the next one, a shipping clerk born in Ireland, a young man of charm, of a total and pleasing candor, who seemed able to better guess the direction of Bailey's questions than many of higher station and more education who had preceded him on the stand.

With his chameleon-like adaptability, F. Lee Bailey actually began to structure his sentences in a way which matched the brogue of the pleasant young man. For example: "And now evidence may creep into this trial that the defendant occupied his time with a lady not his wife."

They got along in fine fashion, seemingly enjoying each other, and the prosecutor used his eighth peremptory challenge on the young man. In the compulsive guessing game during the lunch break later on, there were some who said that Bailey had made the mistake of revealing to Keuper how much he wanted the young man on the jury, and there were others who said that Bailey had been worried about the effect on an Irish Catholic of the testimony of Irish Catholic Marjorie, with her gold cross and Bible, and had faked-out Keuper into using a perempt.

Next there were three men excused, a builder with a conviction of guilt, a dairy manager who opposed the death penalty, and then a warehouseman and volunteer fireman who, during examination by Bailey, gave answers which were so unresponsive to the questions Bailey asked, even when the man was obviously trying to be responsive, that Bailey and Keuper agreed by mutual stipulation that he should be excused.

After a housewife who opposed capital punishment, the eighty-first person examined, Robert A. Loosch, a civil engineer in his thirties, proved acceptable to both sides and became the eleventh juror. Mr. Loosch was so intent on answering all questions with all the necessary qualifications to his answers that he gave the impression of being evasive.

Judge Simmill said to him at one point, "You talk like a lawyer. Lawyers never give a direct answer either. Engineers have to be exact, don't they?"

Loosch was reluctant to serve on the jury, yet did not give those answers which would have gotten him off, though he must have been aware of how easy that would have been.

Bailey told him he would be "locked up for a week or ten days at the most."

He said to Mr. Loosch, "We're not here, you know, to find out if he did it, but if it will be proved that he did it."

As one of his final questions, Bailey said, "You know we can challenge and get you off the hook. Would you resent us for not so doing?"

As F. Lee Bailey was finishing his examination of Robert Loosch, Joseph Mattice attracted Bailey's attention. Carl was slightly hunched, his face pale and sweaty. It was 12:23. Judge Simmill called a recess, as he had promised to do at any time Coppolino felt unwell.

It was stuffy in the courtroom and attendants opened some windows. There was a little flurry of activity and concern at the defense table. Bailey had asked for water and a bailiff had brought a paper cup of water. He handed it to Bailey. Bailey handed it to Dr. Bill Bryan for Bryan to give it to Carl, to take with his pills. William J. Bryan, doctor, lawyer, and hypnotist, in distracted agitation, drank the water. Lee Bailey stood and stared at the giant multi-professional, with his head cocked to one side, forehead corrugated in pained query, while somebody hustled more water. Mary Coppolino had come forward from the chairs aligned against the railing, and sat by her husband.

In about five minutes Carl Coppolino felt better. Court was resumed. Loosch was accepted as a juror. Bailey, questioned in the corridor by the press, said, "Carl's fine. They called the recess to give him a pill because he was generally tightening up. He's okay."

With Loosch the original list was within one name of being exhausted and they went to the reserve list for another supply of prospective jurors. The court was recessed for the mid-day break.

When proceedings began once more, and as the swearing of the venireman began, Lee Bailey got to his feet and interrupted the swearing, saying, "Your Honor, before we continue may we have the defendant?"

Judge Simmill was startled to look down and see that Carl Coppolino was not at the defense table, that he had not been brought back in by the bailiff. This was vivid evidence of how, after the initial curiosity, the accused seems to be dwindled by the protocols and ceremonies, so that at last he is a two-dimensional image awaiting whatever label those ceremonies will affix to him.

The next prospect, an organic chemist, created a curious incident. He was personable and intelligent, with a precise, pragmatic mind. Bailey spent a long, careful time with him. He was found acceptable. But after he was approved by Keuper and by Bailey, the man asked the judge if he could say something, and the judge looked both incredulous and irritated as the man explained that he did not see how he could possibly serve, as due to his wife working nights, he was the only one in the house in the evening with three children aged six, ten, and twelve, and he could not find anyone to take care of them. So after the judge asked acidly why he had not thought to save the time of the court by so stating when in the very beginning he had been asked if there was any reason why he could not serve, he was excused on the grounds of hardship by consent of the attorneys. Bailey's annoyance at losing the man made it quite clear that he had considered the chemist a first-rate defense juror.

As all were awaiting the arrival of the next person who had been called, Lee Bailey chose this moment to tell Judge Simmill that he had served a subpoena on Frank Schaub, the Florida prosecutor, sitting there in the "audience of lawyers" in the double row of chairs inside the rail against the wall opposite the

212

jury box, but that Mr. Schaub had resisted service of the subpoena, claiming that this court did not have jurisdiction over him.

Judge Simmill beckoned to Frank Schaub to rise and explain what he meant, saying that Mr. Schaub must be aware of the fact that he would have to honor a defense subpoena.

Mr. Schaub said in a heavy and aggrieved tone that Mr. Bailey had not stated the situation correctly. He said that he had airline reservations to go back to Florida this weekend, and at this time of the year such reservations were hard to get. He would make himself available later, but he was present only as an observer, and he wondered if his transportation would be paid back from Florida, and how he could get another reservation back at this time of year.

Judge Elvin Simmill listened and hitched and gathered himself for that type of response which has, over the years, removed at least a hundred square yards of hide from local members of the bar, while Bailey stood bemusedly off to the side of the line of fire, wearing about one half of his pussycat smile. It is possible that F. Lee Bailey believed that some useful purpose might be served in putting Frank Schaub on the stand as a defense witness, possibly in relation to Marjorie Farber's statement about how the colonel met his death. It is equally possible that F. Lee Bailey had no intention of using Frank Schaub, but was taking this opportunity to so deepen and widen Schaub's already evident dislike of Bailey that the chance of Schaub's making mistakes during the Florida trial, if one took place, would be enhanced.

"Mr. Schaub," said the judge, "I will advise you that you are under the jurisdiction of this court when subpoenaed. I will remind you that your official position places you in the role of *amicus curiae* [friend of the court]. I will inform you that we are not operating a travel agency here. Nor are we concerned about the travel expenses of persons not subpoenaed by the State of New Jersey. I wish you luck in your travel arrangements and the reimbursement of the expense thereof. But I will tell you that the subpoena is binding upon you. We expect you here when needed, Mr. Schaub."

"Yes, Your Honor," said Frank Schaub and backed away and sat down. The judge asked the bailiff to bring in the next venireman.

During that short wait, a reporter saw Lee Bailey write something on a corner of a sheet of a yellow legal pad, tear it off and reach back and put the note on Keuper's table. He saw Mr. Keuper read it and put it into a pocket. At his first opportunity the reporter accosted Mr. Keuper in the corridor and said, "Can you tell me what was on that note Lee Bailey handed back to you?''

Mr. Keuper was wary. He glanced in both directions and said, ''Not for a newspaper story, you understand.''

''Of course.''

F. Lee Bailey had writeen, ''I will pay your expenses to Florida and give you half my fee if you will let Frank Schaub try your case.''

Keuper grinned and said, ''I asked him and he promised me he'd sign his name to it after the trial is over.''

After the next two men were quickly excused, one opposed to the death penalty, and the other with an unfavorable opinion already formed, Bailey used his thirteenth peremptory challenge on a man who seemed to have some sort of unfavorable chemical reaction to Bailey himself, accusing him at one point of ''I think you're trying to put words in my mouth.''

The next three, one physicist and a pair of housewives, were quickly disposed of. The physicist was excused by consent on grounds of hardship, and one housewife for her view of the death penalty and the other for her opinion of Coppolino.

The eighty-ninth prospective juror became the thirteenth juror. She was Mrs. Lillian F. Schwartz, the wife of a music teacher, a woman in her middle years, bespectacled and earnest. With only two more seats to fill, and seven challenges left, those newsmen who thought they had a clear picture of Bailey's selection strategy began to wonder why he was spending so much time upon her. Mrs. Schwartz was nervous about being sequestered beyond December 22. She had two boys in the Army. They would be coming home on leave. Bailey told her that unless the jury was in actual deliberation, a meeting could be arranged.

And he finally confounded those who thought they could read him by accepting Mrs. Schwartz.

And then there was a housewife with a primly unfavorable opinion of the accused, and a banker and another man disapproving of capital punishment. Keuper used his ninth challenge on a woman who owned an apartment house and seemed quite taken with the defense attorney. A lady and a gentleman came out against death. Bailey used his fourteenth challenge on an articulate and marginally contentious accountant.

Number 97. Male, a machine operator. Against capital punishment. Yes, Your Honor, even if we'd caught up with Hitler.

Number 98. Male. Electrical engineer. Yes, Your Honor, I

have formed an opinion. Is it favorable or unfavorable to the defendant? Unfavorable, sir.

Number 99. A Negro physicist. And when he said firmly that he could not serve on a jury where the state was demanding a sentence of death by electrocution, there was an almost inaudible murmur of dismay in the press section. That would have wrapped it up with a nice lead. The ninety-ninth prospect, the fourteenth juror, was a Negro physicist.

Number 100. Male. Auto assembler. Against the death penalty.

Number 101. Gloria Izbiki. Against the death penalty.

Number 102. A housewife. The judge asked, "Is there any reason why you cannot serve on this jury?"

"Well . . . it's going to interfere with my Christmas shopping."

The judge said, "Your husband might be glad to hear that."

She became Keuper's tenth peremptory challenge.

Number 103. Albert Treger. Foreman. Bailey examined him. He managed to throw Lee Bailey off stride when Bailey asked him if his name was pronounced Tree-ger or Tray-ger.

"Either one, sir," said Treger, which is surely a degree of personal indifference unlikely to be surpassed in that or any other jury selection.

When he said that he would not like to be locked up over Christmas, Bailey said, "If we're not through here by December 24th, I'll plead my client guilty."

Treger had dark blond hair, a high forehead, a hard and competent-looking face. His smile was quick, his manner pleasant.

"Accept this juror," said Lee Bailey.

"Accept," said Keuper.

"Bailiff, bring the rest of the jury back in here," said Judge Simmill, "and they will be sworn as a whole."

They stood and were sworn. It was 4:06 P.M. on Thursday, December 8, at about the normal time for adjournment.

Ten men. Four women.

Seven of the fourteen were admittedly regular readers of the New York *Daily News*.

There was a civil engineer

        a mining engineer

        a television engineer.

There was a clergyman, and an accountant, and a nurse.

There was a lineman for a power company.

There was a foreman, and a female factory worker, and a housewife.

There was a young ice cream concessionaire, and a young corporate junior-executive type.

There was a retired manager of a machine shop.

And a clerk-stenographer.

The ages averaged out to thirty-eight, just four years older than the defendant. Six could legitimately call themselves of the professional class, as could the defendant. On balance it was considerably more intelligent than the average jury.

The consensus that night at the hotel, among the newsmen, was that it was a defendant's jury—provided, of course, that state did not present a case so locked up and reinforced and impregnable no jury could acquit. But in that event, should this one convict, it would be with a recommendation for mercy.

THE TRIAL

December 1966

Chapter Thirteen

Before the court was called to order at 9:30 that cold gray morning, the more experienced reporters in the press section knew the structure of the state's case.

They knew that Prosecutor Vincent Keuper would open with his key witness, Marjorie Farber. Otherwise she would not have come into court accompanied by her civil attorneys and taken a seat inside the rail, with Warren Goodrich from Florida at her left, George Chamlin of New Jersey at her right.

They sat in the first row of two rows of chairs placed at the left wall of the arena, facing the defense table, the prosecutor's table behind it, and the jury box beyond.

There she was, in a wool suit in a dark shade of royal blue, with an underblouse of white with a small shawl collar. Leather pumps and purse in navy blue. Little white gloves, scalloped at the wrists. It would be difficult to guess what goes through a woman's mind when she dresses for court, dresses to be stared at, questioned and, if within the capacities of F. Lee Bailey, publicly shamed.

She looked tired. Her eyes were slightly red. Her face looked more eroded than at the preliminary hearing three months ago in Sarasota. Yet she had that same look of pert and competitive assurance. Some of that assurance could certainly come from her own awareness of being an exceptionally attractive woman—attractive if it could be proven she was but thirty-four—remarkable indeed for her admitted fifty-two.

Those who were seeing her for the first time—reporters,

217

spectators, employees of the Monmouth County court—looked with that special avidity which seeks to answer a basically sexual question: What was this between the colonel's lady and the barber's son, eighteen years her junior?

They could sense a heartiness about her, a lusty heft of trim and solid haunch, a quizzical and skeptical brightness of eye, the look of a vital woman who has lived deeply, laughed loudly, told the joke, drawn to the inside straight, danced all night, driven too fast, hammed it up in amateur theatricals, and then had horrid reality intrude on her wry fantasies.

Some of the area reporters who had attended the bail hearing in the same courtroom in October had seen Carl in person at that time, and had seen only newspaper pictures of Marge. At the bail hearing they had wondered what the young doctor had seen in a woman biologically capable of being his mother. Now, a dozen feet from the vital reality of Marge, they could wonder what she had seen in the sallow young anesthesiologist.

Frank Schaub, the Florida prosecutor who would later seek a conviction in the Florida trial, sat at Chamlin's right. In the additional chairs just inside the rail, lined up in front of the press section, and facing the bench, four people sat in a row. Paul Holmes, the elderly Chicago *Tribune* reporter who had done the two books on the Sheppard trials, with Mary Coppolino on his left, and, in the two chairs to Mary's left, the Bailey investigation team—Andy Tuney and Mrs. Teri Plaut.

The jail-pale defendant had been brought in to sit at the defense table without, for the first time, the huge and implausible bulk of Dr. Bill Bryan seated nearby. The jury selection was over. Bryan's task of jurymandering, as one local attorney had termed it, was over, and he had gone back to the Sunset Strip. Carl sat with his attorneys, young Joseph Afflitto, and old Joseph Mattice, and young burly-dapper F. Lee Bailey, their four tailored backs to the table a few feet away where sat Vincent Keuper in his imperturbable patience, completely alone.

There were almost too many strong personalities present for an arena so small. A reporter leaned over the rail and asked Mary Coppolino a whispered question. "How far away would you say Marge is from you? Six feet?"

Mary measured with narrowed eye and turned her head half-way around and said with a sour smile, "Four feet . . . toe to toe."

Judge Simmill entered swiftly, black robe swinging, and the court was called to order. F. Lee Bailey moved for a change of venue, basing his motion on the fact that of the one hundred and

218

three prospective jurors questioned, twenty-five had been excused because they already believed Coppolino guilty, and basing it also on the concept that the knowledge that Coppolino was under indictment in Florida was prejudicial to a fair trial in Freehold.

Judge Simmill, articulate, thoughtful, intellectual, could have merely denied the motion, but chose to explain why he was denying it.

"I have noted the candor and the integrity of the responses you have received from the members of the jury. No matter where you went in New Jersey, you would find the publicity was there before you. And you could not find a more impartial jury if you went to Timbuktu. No one seems to be *after* Carl Coppolino. This community is certainly not inflamed over this matter. Motion denied."

Bailey then asked if the judge would instruct the jury to ignore the Florida case, and the judge said that he would do exactly that . . . at the proper time.

"Call the jury."

They came in and took their seats in the two-level jury box behind the low draping of dusty maroon velvet which had the look of mortuaries and shopworn stage sets.

The jury had achieved that odd unity typical of all juries, that group obligation to attempt to conceal any reaction.

Once the jury had been completed and sworn, a network reporter had said that the names sounded like a roll call for a platoon in one of those war movies full of stock characters: Jerram, McFadden, Snyder, Lingenfelter, Salisbury, Samsel, DePagnier, Pleshko, Phillips, Ellis, Philibert, Loosch, Schwartz, and Treger. All present, sir.

Vincent Keuper began his opening statement. He moved and spoke in measured pace, with towering dignity. One of his postures, the one most often used, was to stand dead center, facing the jury, fingertips of the right hand on the jury rail, left hand in the side pocket of his suit coat, looking solemnly from face to face.

He opened very effectively, turning the wit and charm of F. Lee Bailey during the *voir dire* of the jurors to the state's advantage by saying that at this time we would leave all the banter and levity behind us, because we were now concerned with a most serious business.

Was there a slight tremor in the biblical voice? Did the hands shake somewhat? After all, had he not made an opening statement in over thirty other capital cases prior to this one? Had not many of them been in this same familiar courtroom? But now every seat was filled in both press and spectator sections. All the extra seats inside the rail were occupied by participants and by local attorneys who had come to watch F. Lee Bailey for the defense. The overflow of spectators stood in the corridor. The press would file their stories to New York, Boston, Philadelphia, Florida, Cleveland. Even for a man of sixty-four years, solidly and amiably entrenched in the political and social and legal structures of his home place, this was a kind of exposure which, perhaps, made him remember his very first appearance in court as a prosecutor.

Thrice he told the jury that he was asking them to bring in a verdict of guilty of murder in the first degree, with no recommendation of mercy.

The old testament flavor of his statement was enhanced when he said that he demanded the electric chair for a man who had broken the commandment, "Thou shalt not covet thy neighbor's wife, but also, thou shalt not covet thy neighbor's life."

He told the jurors that he alone had made the judgment that death should be sought for Coppolino. "This defendant did plan the murder of William E. Farber, and he executed that plan, and he did kill William E. Farber."

He returned to his indirect attack on Bailey's deportment during the four days of *voir dire* by reminding the jury that Bailey had spoken of the affair between Carl and Marge as a "swinging" affair, and that Coppolino had merely been "stepping out of line, philandering."

"But, ladies and gentlemen, I know the society of Monmouth County respects a marriage vow. Coppolino not only took the wife of William E. Farber, but took the life of William E. Farber."

He seemed at his most effective in these areas. However, in his brief opening statement—and all who had been in court for the first four days of the week had come to expect brevity from Mr. Keuper—he touched upon the factors of hypnotic influence, of the "love plan" conceived while the adulterous couple were on a motor trip to Florida, of how as a result of this plan Marjorie and the colonel slept in separate bedrooms thereafter. He spoke of an undetectable drug, of Carl's telling Marge many times that it could not be detected, of Marge being a witness to the delivery of the drug to Coppolino . . . and in these areas Keuper seemed far less effective.

There is one possible and evident reason. It is the same inhibition which prevents many people from being able to tell a naughty joke effectively no matter how badly they wish to make their audience laugh. It was as if Keuper could not quite believe the tawdry bits he was relating, yet of course this was not the case because, had he not achieved belief months before, he would not have pursued the prosecution of the case.

Rather he spoke of incidents, relationships, influences so far outside his comfortable and customary world that he was ill at ease in the chore of booming them out at the listening jurors. One wondered then if the jurors might not have the same flaw in achieving any belief that such things can happen in the world, that such relationships do exist, that lust can warp reality as readily as can narcotic addiction.

As he spoke Marjorie Farber swallowed visibly at regular intervals. A few times she closed her eyes for several seconds, then would open them quickly and lift her chin. She sat with white gloved hands folded in her lap, legs crossed, right over left.

Keuper was indeed brief, and ended upon a dramatic and oratorical note which would have been more effective had a few moments of silence followed it rather than the immediate and imperative voice of F. Lee Bailey. It was another of those essential tricks of flexibility and awareness which so closely relate the courtroom to the stage. Bailey moved instinctively and swiftly to step on Keuper's closing line, and then began in a very intimate, informal, conversational, reasonable style, sitting with one haunch on the mahogany corner of the defense table, right hand in the trouser pocket, using one method of checking the degree of attention he receives by dropping his voice to such a level that even the nearest jurors must lean, strain, tilt the head to hear his words.

Bailey was as brief as Keuper had been. He took just seven minutes, ranging from end to end of the jury box, returning a few times to perch on the corner of the defense table for several moments.

Bailey, as is true of the top rank of criminal defense lawyers in all times and places, has the rare gift of being able to extemporize with force, elegance, organization and the spice of the felicitous phrase.

He said that the story of the murder of the colonel was "a cruel hoax. William Farber was not murdered, and therefore Carl Coppolino could not have done it. The hoax was created by a fifty-two-year-old woman who was cast aside and initiated a plot to destroy Coppolino."

He said that the State of New Jersey was resting its entire case

221

on the testimony of this one witness, and then, in an unexpected reference to the Florida case, he said that from the day Carl's first wife died and Carl didn't turn to Marge, she began to talk to anyone who would listen, casting suspicion on Coppolino.

Explaining that he was going to be severe in his cross-examination of Marjorie Farber, Bailey said, "This woman drips with venom on the inside and I hope before we are through you will see it drip on the outside.

"She wants this man so badly she would sit on his lap in the electric chair while somebody pulled the switch, just to make sure he dies.

"This is monumental, shameful, and demonstrable proof of the fact that hell hath no fury like a woman scorned."

With these two comments he ended it. And while delivering them he had leaned close to the jury, turned, and gestured across the courtroom at Marjorie, who, chin up, stared back at him without expression.

In the long history of the adversary system in criminal law, one tactic has been proven a thousand times and more. In cross-examination of a woman, a child, an old person, a handicapped person, if the attempt is made to destroy then destruction must be complete, as partial success, in that it creates jury sympathy for the witness, is worse than no success at all.

And so, at ten o'clock that morning, Marjorie Farber was called by the state. Before she was sworn, Judge Simmill called her closer to the bench to give her a special warning. She stood flanked by her two civil attorneys, both sizable men, and she looked very small there, standing erect, looking up at the judge.

He told her that he had read her statement taken by the Florida authorities just one year previously. "I have seen your statement and it seems to incriminate you. I must warn you that it is not necessary for you to testify. Consequences may flow from your testimony which may incriminate you. Do you understand this?"

"I do."

"And you will testify with the understanding that you cannot be forced to, and of the possible results?"

"Yes, Your Honor."

"Swear the witness."

She moved slowly as she took the stand, and it is not customary for her to move in that controlled and measured way which is one of the most common signs of an intense emotional strain.

Vincent Keuper began his direct examination by establishing that she had first met the defendant in the fall of 1962, when Carl and Carmela had been walking up Wallace Road in

222

Middletown, the residential street where the Farbers and the Coppolinos both lived.

Keuper did not ally himself with his witness. There was about him no flavor of attempting to either aid her or obstruct her. He stood for most of the time near the state table, questioning her over the heads of the four men at the defense table, the defendant and his three attorneys. Teri Plaut, seated just inside the rail in front of the press section, had the bulky defense "book" open on her lap, and followed the testimony, relating it to the defense copy of the detailed statement Marjorie had made to Frank Schaub in December 1965.

Carl, slumped and motionless, kept his eyes on Marjorie.

She had met them again at a Christmas party at another home on Wallace Road. She had heard Carl telling someone about the heart attack he'd had earlier that month. In January she had gone to the Coppolino home with a gift for the new baby, Lisa Marie, the Coppolinos' second child, second daughter, born the sixteenth of December.

Marge related how she had told the Coppolinos that she'd stopped at the hospital at Fort Monmouth when she'd gone to buy the gift as she was having a series of checkups because of a very bad cough. She said that both Carl and Carmela, being physicians, had asked her questions about how she was being treated. She said that to the best of her recollection it was Carm who had suggested she stop smoking, and when Marge said it was impossible, Carm suggested that perhaps Carl could help her through hypnosis . . . "which I thought was interesting, but I didn't make any . . ."

"I object! I move to strike!" said F. Lee Bailey.

Marjorie looked baffled. "Don't tell us what was interesting," Judge Simmill directed.

"Oh, I'm sorry."

"Just tell us the conversation," the judge explained.

Mr. Keuper added his instruction. "Mrs. Farber, just tell us what was said by you, what was said by the defendant or what was said by someone else in the defendant's presence."

It was at that point that F. Lee Bailey began to use that perfectly acceptable procedure to rattle and upset the witness. Only a witness who has been qualified as an expert is entitled, of course, to testify as to his thoughts, impressions, reactions, and valuations. The trained lay witness, such as a police officer, is accustomed to relating just his objective observations, without comment about them.

But for the untrained lay witness, particularly when testimony

223

impinges on emotional areas, it is an almost impossible feat to eradicate all subjective phrases and attitudes from any report of what happened.

". . . which I thought was interesting . . ." is not a responsive answer. The special discipline was particularly difficult for a woman like Marjorie Farber. Articulate, outgoing, shrewdly intelligent, intensely feminine and emotionally oriented, she could not restrict herself totally to objective and responsive answers. And so F. Lee Bailey took advantage of this limitation by objecting to even the most fleeting subjective nuance imbedded in otherwise responsive answers.

". . . much to my amazement . . ." Object!

". . . and my reaction . . ." Object!

". . . I had finally decided . . ." Object!

". . . I was very surprised . . ." Object!

". . . It's not easy to remember . . ." Object!

". . . I'm trying to put this in a . . ." Object!

After about fifteen minutes of the direct examination, the harassment at last imperiled Marjorie's careful control, and she glared at Bailey in open anger and irritation, at which he arched his brows and smiled at her in whimsical, knowing disdain.

As with most of the tactical weapons of the law, this too is selective. At one point when explaining the hypnotic indoctrinations when she said, "I felt silly," no objection was made, and one could imagine the failure to object was hardly an oversight on Bailey's part.

It was established that the next time she had seen Carl was when he came to her home in the middle of the morning of February 4, 1963.

From a Theo Wilson interview with Marjorie Farber as printed in the New York Sunday News *on May 14, 1967: "I still remember exactly how Carl looked when he came to my house that first day. He was white-faced—he had parked his car and walked up the hill—and he was wearing a turquoise shirt, which was all right, I guess, but he was clammy-handed, and, oh, I don't know, like an oyster. Anyway, I wasn't thinking about him particularly as attractive or exciting."*

On the stand, Mrs. Farber testified that Carl had explained the therapeutic values of hypnosis to her that morning when the two of them were alone in her house, and then, with little interruption, and to the obvious fascination of the jury, explained the tests Carl had given her when she had agreed to have him try hypnosis.

224

"The first test was to stand up. I had to stand up in the middle of the room and imagine that I had to—I had my arms out and to imagine that I had, that I was holding two pails, and he told me that I would, that the left pail would get heavier and heavier and he said I should only listen to the sound of his voice, which I did, and he started to tell me that the left pail was getting heavier and heavier and that the bricks, he was putting bricks in the pail, and much to my amazement it actually happened."

"I move 'to my amazement' go out, Your Honor," Bailey said.

Judge Simmill said, "Yes. 'Much to her amazement' will be stricken and the jury will disregard whether or not she was amazed."

"What happened?" asked Mr. Keuper.

"Well the left imaginary pail did go down, my arm did go down. And he told me I was an excellent subject. So, then, the next—I, of course, asked him what do we do now? And he told me to find a comfortable chair in the living room, the most comfortable chair, and if there was a figurine or anything in particular that I liked for something to concentrate on, to look at and so I picked out a little—there happened to be a little soldier figurine and he put it on the coffee table. He told me to sit back in the chair and to relax and not to listen to anything but the sound of his voice. If the phone rang, not to pay any attention to it. If the dog barked—any outside noises, not to listen to anything but the sound of his voice, and so then, he started to talk and he told me that I was going to relax. That I was going to become very comfortable and that my eyes would close and that I would be getting sleepier and sleepier, and this, this happened, my eyes closed and I, I, I just couldn't keep my eyes open and I was—and he kept talking and talking and I could, I could tell where he was in the room by the sound of his voice. I could hear the car, cars going by. I could hear these other sounds but his voice—I just listened entirely all the time to the sound of his voice and he told me to imagine that I had a balloon tied to my left wrist, and I did imagine that, and he said that my left arm, my left arm would start, would start going up, and it did, it started to go up, and all this was not of my doing . . ."

Marjorie actually appeared to have achieved through the explanation a semi-hypnotic state. Her arm lifted slowly, and she sat with her eyes closed, neck muscles slack, head drooping. Her voice had the uninflected and slightly slurred sound of the hypnotic subject. It would not be totally implausible to imagine she had achieved semi-trance. The good, suggestible subject is intent on pleasing the hypnotist through obedience to suggestion. Here she was determined to let the jury know how it was, and in her attempt to please them through demonstration, she moved perhaps into a borderline state.

F. Lee Bailey took immediate and hilarious advantage of this rather eerie situation.

Mr. Keuper, in a very abused tone of voice, said, "If Your Honor please, I object to Mr. Bailey snapping his fingers while the witness is reciting her testimony."

Judge Simmill, eyes on the witness, had not seen Bailey lean forward with an anxious expression and, holding his hand low, snap his fingers several times as though to bring Marjorie out of her trance. But the jury had seen it, and thus certainly any persuasiveness in the testimony was thereby diminished.

The judge said, eyebrows arched, "I didn't know that he was."

"Well, he snapped them twice now and I wish Your Honor would tell him to stop it."

"Will you desist, Mr. Bailey?"

Bailey said, "May the witness be instructed to keep her eyes open instead of putting on a show?"

"The witness will not be instructed to keep her eyes open. She will be instructed not to put on a show, but the Court doesn't see how she is putting on any show."

She explained the rest of the first session, and how Carl had implanted through repetition the suggestion she stop smoking, and had told her that it might take over thirty sessions to make her stop smoking, yet she told the court she did not smoke again after that very first session.

With the demonstration portion of her testimony over, she reverted immediately to the air of cautious and somewhat pugnacious alertness with which she had taken the witness stand. Hers is a husky voice, her speech patterns colloquial, using often that wry Connecticut drawl which, as a social asset, tends to make the amusing remark more amusing, the bitter comment a little more tart.

There had been a second hypnosis session on Tuesday, the next morning, February 5, and none scheduled for Wednesday. But she had seen him on Wednesday afternoon when she had come back from shopping at the commissary at Fort Monmouth.

"Where?"

"Out in his—in the driveway, he had a folding chair; he was sitting in the sun."

"With relation to your home at 50 Wallace Road in Middletown Township, where did the defendant live?"

"I had to go past his house to get to my house . . . I mean there were several houses and his house was here, and then you go up there. My house was up on the hill."

Middletown, New Jersey, exists merely because the Garden State Parkway is nearby. It was spawned by land developer out of Exit 114, a profitable mating in the rolling woodsy land of horse and apple. The old place names in that area have precisely the homely cadence a shrewd developer appreciates. Bamm Hollow. Fox Run.

It is a spurious community, a contrived place without focus or center or any survival relationships between those who live there. There is too much newness and no shared memories.

The velvety asphalt curves through the rolling contours, centerlines drawn in a sharp orange-yellow. Windows sparkle. Maids wear uniforms. The steeper the hillsides, the more elaborate the homes and plantings. Sports cars, station wagons, poodles, redwood, pastel delivery trucks, yard men, songbirds . . .

And it grows as more roads are paved, as more houses sprout on the raw mud of the building sites.

Wallace Road was unpaved in early 1962 when Marjorie Cullen Farber first saw it. She parked her car down on Bamm Hollow Road and trudged up the hill, up the muddy ruts and selected a building site on a natural knoll halfway up the hill. Soon the road was paved and the elaborate house was begun, patterned after a pillared formal style Marge had admired when she and the colonel had lived in Virginia.

Several months after the Farbers had moved into their home at Number 50, Carl and Carmela Coppolino moved into Number 35. It is on the left as you turn into Wallace Road, several houses from the corner. It is a shingled split-level, obviously chosen from a builder-developer plan book. It backs into a stand of young and slender trees, with a shallow ravine behind it, and an upslope beyond the ravine. The contour of the land across Wallace Road is knolled, so there is little view from the home where once lived the young Coppolino family. The hill is steep enough so that the highest part of the roof of number 35 is at a lower level than the foundations of the far more impressive home at number 50, across the street and perhaps a hundred yards further up the Wallace Road hill.

The visitor can easily become lost driving the curving streets, past the blind sparkle of the windows, past the silent and lovely homes. There is a sense of apartness, of alienation, as though luxurious apartment houses in the heart of the city had been dismantled, brought to these hills, scattered in effective arrangement. There is a quality of make-believe in the contrived community, a sense of no one being concerned or involved in anything which might happen next door, across the street or up the hill. Nothing can ever matter too much. Life becomes restless, unreal and dissassociative.

"Your house was across the street?"

"Yes sir."

"Go on."

"This Wednesday I did my shopping, and I had this terrific, overwhelming feeling that I just had to get back to Wallace Road, and I couldn't understand what it was, and the whole thing was based on the fact that I wanted to get back to see this Carl. And, when I drove home, when I went past his house, he was sitting out there in the driveway in a folding chair, and I got out of the car, and my whole feeling was of this tremendous overwhelming—I couldn't understand it, but that is the way I felt. I just had to be with this man. I didn't know him, but I just wanted to be with him. He got me a chair and I sat down next to him, and I had to touch him."

Here Keuper digressed to introduce in evidence a series of photographs of the Farber home and a floor plan of the home. As is true in the introduction of many exhibits in criminal cases, it is often difficult to guess the reasons why they are introduced. It is possible that by showing the exterior photographs of the house Mr. Keuper wished to establish the status and station of this woman on the stand.

Perhaps he wished to establish the reality of the house. He knew he was getting into areas which would seem like fantasy to the jurors. If they could see the pictures perhaps they could more readily accept the reality of events, having the image of where they took place.

After a brief recess, Vincent Keuper continued his difficult task at 10:38, taking the witness into the events on the morning of Thursday the 7th and Friday the 8th.

As there were frequent objections from Bailey as to the witness describing her state of mind instead of actual happenings, and because it follows closely the statement taken by Frank Schaub on the sixth of the previous December, perhaps the direct quote from the interview is more useful than the actual trial transcript.

*   *   *

Thursday he came back up to the house—in the morning—about 9:30 something like that—kids were in school. And I sat down in a chair and he sat down in a chair—where he'd sat when he was giving me these sessions, as they were called. And we were talking and I said well, when are you going to, you know, start the hypnosis. And I don't remember what he said, but I finally said to him, I said you know when, well, I said I feel very peculiar—I don't know if these were my exact words or not, but this will give you the general idea. I said do all of your patients react to you this way? And he said, what do you mean? And I know now he was just making me say what I had to say. It had to come out. I said, I just have such a strong feeling toward you, and, ah, he was sitting there looking at me with that sort of look that—the way he would look at me and could make me fall asleep. . . . So, this irresistible urge to touch you, and I said I just want to know if this is sort of like a dream sequence. Next thing, we were in each other's arms and were kissing each other like long-lost lovers. Now this is Monday, Tuesday, Wednesday, Thursday. Well, Thursday we were in each other's arms. He never did put me in a so-called trance where I had my eyes closed. He tried to get me down the hall to my bedroom, and I remember saying something to him—well, what about your heart condition, and he said, and I have often wondered just what he meant by this: Well, I guess I could pretend we did. And that was that. We went out into the kitchen and had some coffee and I suppose we kissed each other again. And there were phone calls that afternoon. Friday he came back to my house, and we fell into each other's arms and that is the day that we went to bed as lovers. This is a pretty fast falling in love situation, I would say. I have never experienced this sort of situation. I mean this complete overwhelming, overpowering urge to be with this man. I mean just—well it's uncomprehendible as far as I was concerned, but that's the way it was. And it continued.

F. Lee Bailey, through his frequent objections when she covered this portion of the history of the affair in court—objections almost invariably sustained—was accomplishing his purpose with Marjorie and another purpose with the jury. It began to seem to the spectators, as it must have to the jurors, that she could certainly have disciplined her responses in such a way as to cause less interruption to the narrative all were eager to hear. The blame for interruption fell upon her rather than upon Bailey, and she began to seem both stubborn and uncomprehending.

"When next after that did you see him?"

"I saw him constantly from that time on."

"Was there anyone at home on any of those occaions when he visited you at your home?"

"No sir. My children were in school, my husband would go to business in New York."

"Where would you engage in these intimacies with him?"

"At my home."

"Was your husband and his name ever discussed?"

'Not at that time, no, sir. Everything was very nice."

"When for the first time was your husband's name discussed?"

"We took a trip to Miami Beach."

"Who did?"

"Carl Coppolino and I. We went to Miami Beach in March, while . . ."

"At whose suggestion was the trip made?"

"Carl made the suggestion."

"Can you tell us about the conversation that brought about this trip to Miami Beach?"

"He invited my husband and me to his home with his wife, Carmela, and that is when he broached the subject of my going to Miami Beach with him because of the weather conditions up here in New Jersey; it was too cold, because of his health."

"Mrs. Farber, do you recall when that was, the approximate date?"

"About the middle of March, I believe."

"All right. Now, continue. What took place, what was the conversation when you were all assembled?"

"Well, Carl suggested, or he asked my husband point-blank if he would mind if I went to Florida with him and my husband was quite surprised at this."

No more surprised, perhaps, than the jurors, the spectators and the assembled press. Even though Carl later made public admission of the affair and the trips, it is difficult to comprehend an assignation so brazen, or an attitude so permissive on the part of the colonel and Carmela. Adultery is traditionally a sneaky operational problem of lies and tricks and cover stories. It is the boldness and the simplicity of the approach which astonishes, and its success which astounds.

She then testified that she and the colonel went home and had an argument about it, and that the colonel did not like the idea. F. Lee Bailey objected then to this statement as it was not made in the presence of the defendant. Again, from the December 1965 interview:

230

* * *

So we went to Florida and of course I was registered in my own name and he in his name and had separate rooms. That was the Cadillac Motel in Miami Beach.

—Let me ask you this. Did your sexual relationship continue while you were in Miami Beach at this Cadillac Motel?

Oh yes. Oh yes. That fact was the point behind the whole thing, I guess. But just the idea so that we could be alone together someplace and he took off his wedding ring while we were down there which actually may not sound very significant to other people, but to him it was important. And he took it off and then he told me all about his—from the day he was born practically—everything that ever happened to him. And the agreement between us was this relationship—he said we have to live two lives, he said; after all you know he had his wife and I had my husband, and we had to learn to live two lives actually. And we had awful battles because he was, I don't know, he was very strange, very peculiar, very domineering. Everything has to be his way. And he is a great twister of words. And I found myself apologizing many times for things I suppose it wasn't necessary for, but I—we would get into these awful arguments that I would actually start because I was jealous at that time . . .

Stayed at the Cadillac Motel for about a week. Left in March, '63. Came back and it was Easter weekend when we came back, and my husband and my two girls were—my husband acted very strange—of course Bill and I were really champing at the bit at that point. We weren't arguing or fighting, or anything, but we just weren't getting along, because I was all wrapped up in Carl. Whether or not Bill had any idea, I don't know.

And another angle of view from Theo Wilson's interview with Marge as printed in the New York *Sunday News* of May 14, 1967:

I was never normally motivated in that affair. I never changed my story. I told them (the authorities) from the first about the hypnosis, that I was unable to stay away from him from the time he hypnotized me.

No matter what anybody said, it was not just an extra-curricular suburban housewife affair. If I were that type I'd never have become involved with Carl, and I'll tell you why:

First, I was his wife's friend. Second, he was supposed to be a sick young man, dying on the vine, with only five years to live.

231

Oh, yes, that's what he told me, that's what he told everybody, all of the time. The classic case of the brave, dying hero.

I'm not trying to be nasty, but he has a terrible ego, obviously.

Now, to return to Vincent Keuper's direct examination:

"While you were in Miami Beach was your husband discussed at all?"

"Yes. That is when Carl wrote out what he called a love plan. He had written down things that I was supposed to do when I got home."

"Do you recall what was written down by the defendant, Carl Coppolino?"

". . . Yes, there were several suggestions. That my husband and I should not sleep in the same bedroom. That we should live as brother and sister and that I should try to either get an annulment or a divorce."

". . . At that time were you and your husband occupying the same bedroom?"

"Yes sir."

"Twin beds, single bed, or what?"

"Well, twin beds on a single headboard."

"What if anything was done in furtherance of the love plan?"

"Well, we went back to Middletown and I did as I was told about trying to make my husband move out of my bedroom, our bedroom, I should say, at the time and he objected to it very strenuously."

"Object!" said Mr. Bailey forcefully, and when the Court sustained it, he asked once again that the judge instruct the witness.

Judge Simmill, with a kindly and wearied patience said to Marjorie, "*Don't* tell us of your own mental functioning. Tell us the words, what was said, and don't tell us, for instance, 'your husband didn't like the idea.' Do you see what I mean?" When she said she did, the judge said, "The jury will disregard the fact that her husband objected strenuously."

Under the same line of interrogation, Keuper established that in about a month Marge had managed to establish the separate bedroom plan, and marital relations between Bill Farber and his wife had ended.

Had not all of the testimony up until that point been preliminary to an eyewitness account of murder, and had not everyone in the court been aware of that ultimate target of the interrogation, it would have been more obvious that here we had much the same farcical situation which has made Italian marital comedies so successful at the box office. Much of the bitter humor depends upon how very seriously the participants take their grotesque predicaments.

These particular actors were curiously assorted: A fifty-two-year-old colonel, recently retired after twenty years of service, making the long and deadly commute each day to an insurance office in Manhattan; his Irish wife age forty-nine, in the seventeenth year of her second marriage, an AA and a lapsed Catholic; an unemployed anesthesiologist-hypnotist of Sicilian descent, who would be thirty-one years old on May 13 of that year; his wife, a year younger, of Italian descent, who had been his classmate in medical school, who had interned with him in the same hospital, and who was driving each working day back and forth along forty miles of the Garden State Parkway to Nutley, New Jersey, while a live-in Negro maid took care of the Coppolino children.

Any flavor of comedy and farce ceases, of course, when one adds the children to the mix. At the time of the Miami Beach adventure, young Bill Farber—the only child of Marge's first marriage—was nineteen and a Marine. Colonel Farber had legally adopted him. The two daughters of Marge and the colonel, Victoria and Elizabeth, were fourteen and nine. The two daughters of Carl and Carm, Monica Ann and Lisa Marie, were age six and age three months.

So it had begun in February, when there were only a very few houses on brand new Wallace Road in brand new Middletown, begun on weekday mornings in the wintry season, when there were but four souls in the two homes—Carl and Marge in the Farber home, the maid and the infant Lisa in the Coppolino home.

One can successfully speculate that the essentially outrageous suggestion of the colonel's lady becoming a traveling companion for the ailing young doctor could neither have been made nor ultimately arranged in a more rooted and structured society. Had the two couples had even three or four other couples as mutual friends, frequently seen, one doubts that convention could have been so totally flouted.

—Where did you say Marge went, Charlie?

—Oh, she and Carl went down to Miami Beach for a week, Grace.

—Really!?

Perhaps it would not have stayed the eager lovers, because sexual hunger can add false substance to the most frail and

233

obvious rationalizations. But one can reasonably assume that had they been members of some integrated social group, the fear of being thought overly gullible by their friends would have put some iron in the objections of the colonel and the lady doctor.

There was, in addition, a flavor of bawdy comedy in the concept of the young doctor who, while drawing total disability from health insurance policies because of a heart ailment which made the practice of anesthesiology too strenuous, eagerly embarked—ostensibly for the sake of his health—on a tropic journey which judging from the look and manner of the witness on the stand, would require an impressive reserve of energy.

All such murky speculation on the part of press and spectators was forgotten as Vincent Keuper took her from dalliance to death.

"Was your husband discussed at all at any time after you returned from Florida?"

"Yes, sir. During the course of one of these conversations, or he was doing the talking, he told me about a drug that was not traceable. We had a dog that had gotten quite undisciplined. . . . Well, Carl told me about a drug that could be used to—that was not traceable, that caused instantaneous death and he told me that it might be a good idea to use it on the dog we had and then he told me that he had contacted Dr. Edmund Webb, who delivered this drug to the Coppolino home. That's when I first met Dr. Webb."

Through questions, Keuper established that the day after Webb had delivered the drug, Carl had spoken to Marge about Bill Farber.

"He, Carl said that . . . 'That man has got to go.' "

"What else was said? What did you do? What was your reaction?"

"Well, I didn't know what he was talking about at first and then he said, 'That man has got to go,' and I was very upset and shocked by this suggestion of Carl's. I told him he must have been crazy or out of his mind to even think of such a thing . . . Carl set a date. He said, 'The first of July, he's got to go.' I said, 'No,' and it continued over and over and over like a—''

Marjorie Farber was in tears at that point, and her voice had become despairing and dramatic. Bailey objected to the dramatics, and the witness was cautioned to compose herself. She had a rapt and absolute attention from everyone in the courtroom.

It is curious to note that as he took her closer and closer to the climax of her testimony, Vincent Keuper became ever more

234

antagonistic toward her. He was giving her no help. He was, it could be suspected, creating antagonism in the minds of others too. One wondered if he could not control his moral distaste, or if he was merely unaware, or if this could have been by design.

Certainly he was far from being a novice. Presuming design, he was taking a subtle risk. By obvious antagonism he was divorcing the state, and himself, from any implied approval of her morals or actions. He knew what Bailey hoped and intended to do with her. Had he taken an attitude of gentle concern, of assistance and understanding to make it easier for her, perhaps she would have been less prepared for the assault by F. Lee Bailey. It is even possible that by establishing her as the victim of both himself and Bailey, he was hoping to engender sympathy for her and, if she could survive the Bailey attack—which would have to surpass any antagonism Keuper had shown—the sympathy might carry the day.

The issue was vividly clear. If the jury believed this witness, they would convict. If they could not believe her, they would acquit. Belief or disbelief had to be engendered within the carefully circumscribed limits of the rules of the game. There is a curious artificiality about one of the rules which pertained to the examination of Marjorie Farber.

Both the defense and the state had copies of the statement she had made in Florida a year earlier, covering these same events. There were certain portions of that statement which the state would try to introduce and the defense would block. There were other portions which the state would obstruct if the defense tried to bring them up. Other parts of the statement would be mutually ignored, as though by some previous consent. The emphasis by each side was in the interest of using the testimony on the stand, guided by the previous text, to establish the strongest case for either guilt or innocence. This is a selectivity process wherein the adversary system places more weight upon impact than upon completeness.

Alternating between periods of agitation and an enforced calm, Marjorie told, hesitantly, of how on Saturday, the 27th of July, she had taken the drug Carl had given her, in a little vial with a screw top, along with, in the same envelope, a disposable syringe with hypodermic needle, and had mixed it that night in water in a bathroom glass and filled the syringe according to his instructions. She testified that he had told her to inject it into her husband where it wouldn't show, preferably a leg area, where there might be veins or scratches or bruises.

". . . I filled the syringe with this solution and I threw out the syringe full. I put it . . . I got rid of it. I didn't want . . . I just . . . I . . . I . . . this was all very objectionable. I just couldn't do this thing. So I threw it out."

"When did you see Carl Coppolino again after that?"

"I saw him the next day, Sunday."

"Where?"

"We went to the movies in the afternoon."

"Did you discuss with him any of the events that happened the night before?"

"I don't remember. I can't recall."

"Did he ask you any questions about what happened the night before?"

"I don't remember."

She testified that she had seen him again on Monday the 29th, but she was not sure where.

"Do you recall whether or not there was any conversation had between the two of you?"

"No, I don't really recall any specific conversation."

"Do you recall any conversation you had with him after the incident of Saturday night?"

"No sir."

And in this again, the flavor of farce, of the grotesque. Lovers side by side in the iced darkness of the Red Bank movie palace on a summer Sunday afternoon, the reflected images from the big screen touching their faces with cinemacolor pastels, whispering as lovers do. Motion pictures are our morality plays, full of retributions, and we sit in a commercial darkness and, as we have been taught to do, we identify with the good guys in the white hats, and we suffer with them while greedily anticipating the downfall of the guys in the black hats. In a few days the affair would have lasted half a year.

But her responses had caused puzzlement. Each person in any court thinks himself a capable judge of the truth, to be able to identify it when he hears it. Has anyone ever called himself a poor judge of human nature? Keuper had demanded that the woman be believed. Bailey has proclaimed her story a cruel hoax. We are all lied to, all our lives, for little reasons and big reasons. The ability to sense it is a survival mechanism, and so, subconsciously we make a judgment of each statement which affects our lives.

There are familiar little check points and guidelines. What will the liar gain? What is his track record in the past? Does his story contradict something we know to be fact? Is there some physical quirk or mannerism that makes his story suspect? Does his statement violate *emotional* logic?

This inability of the witness to come up with any memory of anything said on Sunday or Monday seemed to violate the tenets of commonplace emotional logic. Wouldn't it be the sort of thing one would almost be compelled to remember?

Yet the rules of emotional logic apply also to the carefully calculated lie. Thus it could be inverted. *If* she were perpetrating a cruel hoax, and if none of this had happened, would it not be an almost compulsory part of the lie for her to say, "I told him I couldn't bring myself to do it. I told him I threw the stuff out. He was very angry with me. He said I had to do it, I had to make myself do it."

Yet to go one step further, and assume an extraordinary craftiness, could she have declared an inability to remember merely because it lent more of a flavor of veracity than that anticipated conversation which would have been so easy to devise?

There seemed no emotional logic in either interpretation, that of truth or of falsehood, and hence a troubled frown on several foreheads in the jury box, and some sidelong glances, raised eyebrows, quick shrugs among the members of the press.

During the Florida interview she had related:

And so he gave me this hypodermic needle and this powder, it looked like white powder in a little tube about that big, and he said to mix it with water and he had a lot of disposable needles because he gave himself injections and medicine to keep his blood count down. And he gave it to me in an envelope with an elastic tied around it—the needle and this thing—the poison or whatever it was. All I know is what he said it was supposed to be. I don't know what the name of it was. It didn't have a name on it. And the Sunday—the 28th, wait a minute the 30th of July, well Sunday was a very, very hot day and Bill was working out in the yard and Carl's family were visiting him. His mother and father and sister, and Carl didn't want to be with his family and, well he and I went to the movies. It was so hot he had to go somewhere where it was air-conditioned. There were all these excuses and reasons he could always get away with it because his family, you know, he was the lord and master in everything. So, that may sound sarcastic, but that's the way it was. And, well that was on Sunday and I was supposed to do this thing that night. He had even suggested I knock Bill out with a baseball bat, and wrap a towel around it—good God.

*   *   *

I was supposed to do it Sunday night and I couldn't do it. I mixed up some of it, no I didn't even mix it up, I just got it out and looked at it. And I didn't do it. And then Monday Bill went to work and I can't remember what conversation I had with Carl, but probably he said that I would do it that night.

Before the fascinated eyes of the fourteen jurors, Keuper drew Marge into the events of Monday night, after Bill Farber had gone to bed in the downstairs room where he had been sleeping alone for three and a half months. He had Marge step out of the witness stand and indicate that room on the floor plan of the Farber home, affixed to an easel and admitted previously in evidence.

"Monday night I mixed the solution. I had some of this powder left and I mixed up another solution, filled the syringe and I had a terrible struggle. I paced the floors. I went downstairs and upstairs and downstairs. I don't know how to describe this feeling. I was doing this thing. I couldn't stop myself. It was absolutely over and beyond my own free will."

After several sustained objections by Bailey at the way she was attempting to describe her emotional state, and after another lecture from the judge, she testified, "I went into my husband's room and he was asleep. He was lying on his side and his, he was—this is just like a picture. (*objection sustained*) He was lying on his side and his legs were exposed and I bent over him with this syringe in my hand and I, I started to put it in his leg and I started to push the plunger down and I couldn't, I froze, I couldn't do it and then my husband jumped up and he said he had a charleyhorse. (*objection sustained*) He jumped up and I helped him into the bathroom and he sat on the toilet and said he felt—(*objection sustained*) Well, he was ill. He had a form of diarrhea. He was gasping. He fell off the toilet and he fell on the floor. I tried to help him and I couldn't lift him because he was too heavy so I called up Carl to 'come up, please help Bill.' "

After it was established that she did not know what time Carl arrived, but that it was sometime in the middle of the night, and that Bill was then in bed and conscious when he arrived, though she had no recollection of how he had gotten back to bed, she testified about what Carl had done.

"He had his medical bag with him and he filled a syringe with a sedative, which he gave to my husband, and he told Bill this would make him relax and sleep.

"He was in bed and he was conscious. Then Carl told me to

238

get a plastic bag. I didn't know what he wanted it for, but I got one.'' (*objection sustained*)

''Well, I got the plastic bag. It happened to be one of these dry cleaner type things and I gave it to him and he put it over Bill's head and started to suffocate Bill and Bill was nauseated and I told him to stop it, *leave him alone*, and he did. I wanted to change the pillowcase because it was soiled and he said all right, I could do that but not to wash the pillowcase. Then we left Bill. He was resting and I guess we went into the, the other room, the TV room and I was so glad to see that Bill was all right.'' (*objection sustained*)

Mrs. Teri Plaut, the Bailey investigator, was following the account of the same happenings in the defense copy of the Florida interview with Mrs. Farber:

And Bill came home from work. He had been very upset with his boss and I remember he was agitated about that . . .

. . . Bill was pacing around, and I had some Librium Tranquilizers—a form of tranquilizer Carm had given to me. It's one of the products of the Hoffman-LaRoche Company. It's ten milligrams—you know, just to calm you down. Well, I said to Bill, why don't you take one of these. That was over a period of time and he kept telling me to leave him alone. And I said, well I want to help you. Well, he took a pill in his hand but he didn't actually take it, and well, it wasn't harmful or anything. I had taken them once in awhile. But, well, he finally, I guess dozed off. I was upstairs and I mixed up some of this white powder with water and filled the needle. I don't know how many—you know, how much it would hold, and I remember going downstairs and trying to work up the, whatever it was that it took to do it, and finally I did stick the needle into Bill's leg. And he jumped and he got up and he said he had a charleyhorse in his leg—cramps in his leg.

I don't know what caused it, why he jumped up, and I'm very thankful that it didn't take effect, that I didn't give him the whole thing. Because he just got a little bit, and he got up and went into the bathroom, and it apparently had some sort of relaxing effect on him, because he had diarrhea, as I remember correctly, and he felt nauseated. Now whether or not he threw up—I don't know. No, he didn't do that. He fell on the floor and he was choking. It almost did it, but I am so glad it didn't.

And, well, I walked over to him, lying on the floor. I just walked over to him and watched him, and it just didn't mean a thing to me. It was, I can't explain it to you, but I am telling the truth. And so I called Carl and I think, I don't know, sometime in the middle of the night, it was maybe 3:00, and Carl came up and, and he had his medicine bag—you know, the bag that the doctors carry, and I don't remember how Bill got in bed. This part is still vague to me, I don't know whether he walked in by himself, or if Carl and I helped or if just I helped him. But anyhow, he got into bed somehow and Carl gave him something, an injection which was to calm him down and make him sleep. That's what he told Bill. In the meantime, he asked me for some plastic—you know, like, I think it was from a dry cleaning bag, and he put it around Bill's face, over his head, and he was trying to suffocate him, and I told him to stop it—to leave him alone and he did, he stopped. That's what I can't understand, why I would do what I did and then tell him to stop what he was doing, and, maybe the real me was coming through this other thing. And so, then Carl went out, and I know Bill was nauseated from this something, smothering business. And I wanted to take the pillowcase and change the pillowcases and Carl says Well change the pillowcase but don't wash it. And I said why not, and he says I want to show the bastard, or something like that—show it to him. Really, he hated Bill, why I don't know, Bill never did anything to him. And, so that was Monday in the wee hours, and Tuesday morning I had an appointment at the dentist.

. . . And I remember saying this was a good place for me to be—to the receptionist—because I was up half the night with my husband because he was sick. Of course I was so darned relieved that he was sick and not anything else. Because, I really was relieved. I was so glad that nothing had actually happened.

Just as Keuper established that Marjorie had seen Carl later that day, after he had left the Farber home at five or six in the morning, Judge Simmill pointed out that it was eleven-twenty.

"Before we get to this phase of it, gentlemen, it's time for a mid-morning recess and I think that we all need a respite."

Chapter Fourteen

Vincent Keuper resumed his direct examination of Marjorie Farber after the brief recess. Marjorie said she thought she had stopped by and seen Carl at his home on her way home from the dental appointment. She knew she had seen him at ten or eleven on that Tuesday morning, but was not certain of where, and had no recollection of what was said.

She was able to testify in more detail about what was said and what was done when Carl came to her house around noon or 1 P.M. that same day. She said Carl asked how Bill was, and then the two of them went into the downstairs room where Bill Farber was in bed.

"Carl told Bill he was going to give him another sedative, and he fell asleep."

"Did he call it a sedative?"

"I don't really know what he called it, but he gave him an injection of some sort to make Bill relax; and the sedative was taking effect on Bill and Bill and Carl got into a discussion; and Bill was quite groggy, and he said something to the effect that he wanted Carl to leave him alone, get out of here; and that is when Carl picked up the pillowcase that he told me not to wash during the night, and he showed it to Bill, and he shook it in his face, and he said, 'You ungrateful bastard, I saved your life last night'; and then he threw this pillowcase at me and I went out of the room and went into the laundry room."

From the laundry room she said she could hear voices, and Bailey objected to her saying they were angry voices, but the judge permitted her to testify that Carl and Bill were arguing.

"Did you then return to the room where your husband was lying in bed?"

"Yes."

"Was the defendant still there?"

"I was out—I didn't go into the room at that time. I was out in the TV room, and that is when Carl came out from where my husband was, and he was furious, he was absolutely—"

"What did he say?"

241

"He said, 'That bastard's got to go.' He said, 'That man has got to go,' and he took out the—he had the same syringe—"

"What did he say and what did he do?"

"He said, 'That bastard has to go. He has threatened me and my family. Nobody is going to talk about me like that, and he has got to go.' And his eyes were popping out of his head practically."

"Did you say anything in response to what he said?"

"I begged him, leave us alone, leave Bill alone!"

Marjorie, with those two phrases—Leave us alone!—Leave Bill alone!—spoke very loudly. She almost cried the words out, in imitation of the way she could have said them to Carl. It was plea and command, with overtones of utter emotional exhaustion and a disgust for the concept of helplessness being attacked. It seemed then, and in retrospect, the most effective moment during the direct examination, because it had a tingle of reality about it, yet a few minutes later she gave a far different impression . . .

". . . And while I was telling him this, he was filling the syringe with more of whatever he was taking out of a bottle. And he went into my . . . husband's room and I just stood there in the TV room, like I was frozen to the spot."

She then went into the bedroom, where Carl had finished giving Farber the injection, apparently.

"What did he say or do, Mrs. Farber?"

"He said, 'He is a hard one to kill. He is taking a long time to die'; and then he pulled this pillow out from underneath my husband's head, and he put it over his—just put it over him, and he leaned full weight right down on him like this, and I just stood there and looked at him."

She gave that line a slow reading, spacing the words out, underlining her confession of having stood by and not done a thing to prevent murder. And she began to cry and was given smelling salts by a court attendant. Somehow the reading of the line and the collapse had a dubious sound and look.

The jurors try to exercise logic and life-experience to sift truth and lie—and as in the standard charge given to juries, credibility must be measured against what the witness may gain or lose by so testifying. Here was a woman of considerable vitality, articulate, dramatic, who, from the moment she had begun to talk about the death of her husband—thirteen months before, and thirteen hundred miles away—had been moving inevitably toward these public revelations. And freshness or spontaneity is inevitably leached out of the oft-told tale, yet when it is dramatic the teller

242

must certainly feel the obligation to tell it in a dramatic way, because it would be grotesque to relate such events with an air of indifference. To this extent it must become a set piece, and inevitably have a taint of artificiality about it.

The woman had the additional handicap of "little theater" experience, but only to the extent of the plays mounted and staged and performed by officers and their wives in that curious village culture of the peacetime army in overseas assignment.

Taking the stand could not have been as she had expected it to be, because she had become accustomed to the awe and fascination and belief of those outside the structure of the law, and, one must assume, to a certain satisfaction on the part of the prosecutors of two states.

Rationally she would know that there would be the inevitable confrontation with F. Lee Bailey, and she would be curious about it, nervous, planning responses to imaginary tricks and devices.

Whether her story was truth or fabrication, one can assume she had expected a setting more like the staging of cinema and television, and perhaps a prosecutor who would lead her through the torment of revelation with a fatherly understanding and concern.

But Keuper stood remote, well over six feet tall, armored by all those habits and attitudes of a conservative life which put a Marge Farber outside the range of his comprehension, and certainly outside any possible reach of his most grudging approval. Though in New Jersey the county prosecutors are appointed— with the advice and consent of the Assembly—rather than elected, a man who is in his third term, as was Keuper, must be a reasonably skilled political animal. His having been Democratic County Chairman in Republican Monmouth County is evidence of this essential flexibility. He towered and asked his questions in a hard, heavy, expressionless voice, and any emotional response whether it be real or improvised, is difficult under such attentions.

Further, it seems as if all our dramatic responses to crises borrow so heavily from the climactic scenes of tired scenarios that the genuine becomes smothered by a kind of compulsory triteness. Housewives, facing the sudden heartbreak of betrayal, emote old fragments of *Peyton Place* and *The Edge of Night*. So what seems most faked is often bitterly real, and what seems most genuine is often but imitation. It seems to depend upon the quality of the lines we borrow. One might even assume quite plausibly that the line which rang true—Leave us alone! Leave

Bill alone!—was the spurious one, and the collapse which seemed so contrived was genuine.

What the jurors were thinking could not be guessed. But the focus of their attention was unmistakably intense.

"Will you try to tell the jury and the Court where his hands were placed?"

"He put the pillow over my husband's head, and face, and chest. . . . He was standing at the head of the bed. The bed was like—this is where my husband's head was. I was standing over there at the door. And he pulled the pillow out, and my husband's head sort of turned over that way. He was completely relaxed. My husband was unconscious at that point from this drug. He was—"

"I object!"

The judge sustained Bailey's objection by instructing the witness: "You may say that he wasn't conscious, but whether or not he was unconscious from the drug is inadmissible."

Keuper asked her again where the defendant had placed the pillow. Without Keuper's instruction, and without objection from Bailey or admonishment from the Court, Marge Farber came quickly out of the witness stand to a small table set directly below the judge's bench. She snatched an imaginary pillow from under an imaginary head, saying, "He put it over like this. He pulled it out from under him and he put it over his face and chest, and he just leaned down like this . . ."

She placed the heel of her right hand against the table top, and placed her left hand atop her right hand, and stiffened both arms and leaned with all her weight in that fashion.

". . . and he just leaned down like this, and he just looked at me and I looked at him, just like that . . ."

Again, in silence, there was that elusive aroma of reality, and she went quickly back into the stand and sat as before.

"What did the defendant say?"

"He told me to wipe some blood off my husband's hand."

"What else did he say. . . . Do you recall what the words were that he used?"

" 'I want to turn him over so he'll look like he died in his sleep.' "

"Was he dead?"

"Before he turned him over, he opened my husband's eye, and he said, 'He is dead.' "

"What did you do then?"

"He told me to write a note to my children and say, 'Daddy is sleeping. Don't disturb him.' And that is what I did. . . . I pinned it on the door.''

She testified that she and Carl walked down the hill to Carl's house, and that the maid, Dorothy Jeffress, was there. For the first time during her testimony Judge Simmill had to ask her to speak more loudly. Marjorie could not remember whether or not she saw the Negro maid, or whether or not she was inside the house at all. But she remembered sitting out in the back yard and talking with Carl, and saying, "What are we going to do? What am I—what are we going to do? . . . or something like that. I don't know the exact words.''

As there had been confusion about how to testify as to conversations which had taken place three and a half years earlier, and as Marjorie seemed unwilling or unable to invent a conversation which would have the substance of what was said, and kept inciting Bailey's objections by trying to tell about the conversation instead of creating a reasonable facsimile, Judge Simmill said to her with patient instruction, "Mrs. Farber, I don't remember the exact words I used five minutes ago. All the prosecutor is asking is for your best recollection. Nobody expects you to say verbatim what was said three and a half years ago. Do you understand?''

She did, and testified as to Carl's response: "He said that there was nothing to worry about, everything was all right; and he told me at that time when Carm got home from work, that I should call her and have her come up and take a look at Bill . . . I was to call Carmela when she got home, but not to call until after they had dinner, which would be around 6:30.''

She could not recall any other part of the talk she'd had with Carl at his home that Tuesday afternoon. She thought she probably went home about four or five o'clock. She called Carmela as instructed between 6:30 and 6:45. Carmela examined the body while Marge waited out in the hall. Arrangements were made, and Robert Worden of the Worden Funeral Parlor came that evening and removed the body. Keuper established that there was no viewing of the body in New Jersey, no funeral services at all in New Jersey. The only services had been at Arlington National Cemetery. Carl had not gone. Carmela had driven down, however, with Marge.

Keuper finished at 11:37. The total time for his direct examination was one hour and fifty-one minutes. There was a feeling of shock in the courtroom at the sudden termination. Each area of questioning of any key witness seems to create additional questions which so obviously—to the lay mind—require asking, that one is deluded into believing that the interrogator will swing back to that area and cover those portions which he seemed to miss the first time around. And, perhaps, we have become all too accustomed to the requirements of dramatic presentation that any production end on a high and significant key. Too often these things merely dwindle away, and what seems to be a dead spot in the ritual of question and answer suddenly turns out to have been the end of it. Marge too seemed surprised at how abruptly it had ended. One cannot presume to guess at the strategy of prosecution and defense. Cross-examination cannot go into areas not covered in direct examination. Nor can redirect explore areas other than what was covered in cross-examination. Before opening any door, the trial attorney must be reasonably certain there is nothing beyond that door which, in the hands of the opposition, can damage his position.

Marge may have wanted the chance to make more explanation of her actions, more justification for the public record. Her Florida statement would seem to indicate as much:

Carl came up to see Bill, to see how he was. This was around noon. And I remember asking Bill if he wanted anything to eat, and he said, "No, leave me alone. I want to rest."

I had called Bill's office to tell them he wouldn't be in because he was sick. And Carl gave Bill something, some sort of injection of some sort. I don't know what it was. And, oh, I remember he showed Bill the pillowcase, and he was arguing with Bill about—the fact that "You don't appreciate that I saved your life last night"—and I guess I took the pillowcase and put it in the washing machine, which was on the same floor.

. . . Bill had been nauseated. He didn't remember any of this stuff. Of course he doesn't know why he was nauseated. So I was in the laundry area which is off the recreation area, away from where Bill was with Carl, and I heard them arguing about something. Of course, Bill was very groggy at that point from whatever Carl had given him. I don't know—it could have been morphine for all I know, cause Carl took morphine himself for pain. And 'cause I didn't look in his bag I have no knowledge of what was in that bag. But I was in the recreation room where the laundry was, and Carl came out—his bag was lying on the coffee table there, and he took out one of those big hypodermic needles, and he filled it up and he said, "You—" he said. "That bastard's got to go. It's either—you make your choice—if I walk out of here you'll never see me again." I said . . . I don't remember what I said. It seems that he said, "He can't say what he said

about my family to me," he said, "He's got to go." And he was in a rage. He wasn't raving, but I mean he looked like he was very angry. And, of course, this was all very quiet. And, what I said to him about his walking out—I don't remember what I said. But he did go in and he gave Bill another of this needle full of whatever it was, and he—this was just a matter of a few minutes. And I just stood there watching—in the doorway—just watching. Bill's bed was this way. And he told me to wipe the blood off Bill's hand—off his right hand.

. . . Bill had very difficult veins to get, and apparently he must have given him an injection in his hand someplace. I don't know—I don't remember.

. . . And then he had the pillow over Bill's face and he—he was just leaning on him with all his might and I just stood there and watched him—just like a zombie. Just—it didn't mean anything. And he suffocated Bill with the pillow. And then he said—during the—this is all vague to me—"He's a hard one to kill," or, "It is taking him a long time." —what the exact words were—but that's the gist of the thing. And I wiped the blood off Bill's hand and we turned him over. He said, "Help me roll him over," and he said, "Put him on his right side." So he looked, you know, like he was in a sleeping position. And we went down to his house and I pinned a note on the—outside the door for my daughter—for my children, and said, "Please do not disturb Daddy because he wants to sleep." And he went down to his house and sat outside and drank lemonade or something or other, and I do not remember what the conversation was about, but I know I was very agitated. He told me to wait until Carm got home that night from the office. To call and she would come up and check Bill. Because, apparently, Carl couldn't do it because he wasn't supposed to be doing any kind of practice because of his heart condition or he would lose his insurance, disability or whatever he gets. So that's how it happened. And she . . .

. . . Well I went home and—this was not my plan. I was just doing what I was told. I believe it firmly. The only reason I can tell you this is because I don't feel guilt in relation to what I have told you, which probably doesn't make sense to you, but that's the way I feel. Because I . . . I know that I'm not this kind of a person. I wouldn't do this sort of thing if I had my own free will. I believe that I wasn't capable of—and I'm not just trying to say this to let myself off the hook.

I went home then and my daughter Victoria is the one who went in. She got in just before I did and she went in and she said, "Daddy looks awful funny." I said, "Well, come on, leave him alone. I'll take care of him after." She had a date to go to the movies with one of her friends—and I, of course, I knew what the situation was. And I cannot understand, I can't understand how I did this—well, anyway, I'm rambling on. But she left and then Carm got home, and—well between 5:30 and 6:00. Well I called and asked her to come up and she—to see Bill because I thought there was something wrong. And she came up and she examined him with her stethoscope and she said he was dead. And I—my reaction was—not for anybody's benefit—I mean, just, well, I couldn't react. I reacted like—I can't explain to you how. I knew it was so, but it was hard for me to relate to it. And so, then after that—then Carl came up and you would never know that he had anything to do with this thing at all from the attitude—lack of anything that—you know, it's too bad or something like that. I didn't know how I was acting, I was—

Q Did Carmela sign the death certificate on your husband's death?

A Oh, yes, she—

Q What did she show as being the cause of death?

A I think it said coronary thrombosis.

Q Do you know how she happened to arrive at that conclusion?

A Just from—

Q From what you told her or what Carl told her?

A Well, from what I told her and of course Carl had been up there the night before, she knew that. And, then he had seen Bill during the next day. But of course she didn't know about anything else.

Q Was there an autopsy performed upon Bill?

A No, there wasn't. As a matter of fact my sister asked me why an autopsy wasn't done, and I said well, I didn't know. I mean, what are you going to say? I think I did say—I did say to her—that it didn't seem to be necessary. Bill died July 30th, 1963. He was buried in Arlington National Cemetery on August 7th. And we got back from the funeral, to New Jersey, and Carl and I went to Atlantic City for the weekend. Not registered as Dr. and Mrs. Coppolino at that time. In October we went to San Juan and registered as Dr. and Mrs. Carl Coppolino with Carmela's consent. The reason behind that being the fact that it would be cheaper. The following spring we went to San Juan—in May, and the first time we stayed at the American Hotel and the second time we stayed at the—I can't remember the name for the place, but I could find out. And then we came to Florida as Dr. and Mrs. Coppolino, and I drove the car and we stopped—you

248

know we had to stay at motels—and we came down in January 1964 and the idea for that trip was for me to find a place to live down here. Which I did—I bought property on Longboat Key. And Carl bought the lot right next door. And then we went back to New Jersey from here after buying our lots—January 1964—and then we went to San Juan in May of 1964—is that right? —Yeh. And I in the meantime had decided that—Then in the last of 1964 our physical relationship ended as far as I can remember, I would say—end of '64 or early '65. In reference to Carl's heart condition, I had often wondered how he could be as strong as he appeared to be, because we had intercourse at least once a day, and while we were on these trips—went away on these trips together—it was at least three times a day. I don't know how he did it. But, anyway, they started their house down here and they moved down here in April of 1965. When they came down here Carl called me many times, and he was very upset and missed me, and as a matter of fact he cried over the telephone because he couldn't stand being alone, and I wrote him that I was doing a lot of thinking about this relationship and I told him if and when I ever get down there—my house was on the market for sale—and it just wasn't being sold—and I said that if my daughters and I ever got down here that I was going to have to make my own life and I couldn't be at his beck and call—I didn't say that, but that's what I meant.

F. Lee Bailey began his cross-examination immediately. He had given his total attention to the direct examination, of course. He had studied the December 6, 1965, interview. He had discussed all the matters therein with Carl Coppolino. He had the written reports of his investigative team. It requires a special organization of the mind to stay within the areas of the direct examination when so much other material has been made available, yet for the defending attorney any mental lapse from this discipline is not critical. The prosecutor must always be more cautious, as such a slip can set up an appeal for a new trial.

Bailey began by standing behind the defendant, his hands on Carl's shoulders, and speaking quietly from there to the witness.

"Mrs. Farber, will you look at the defendant, please? Is it fair to say that you hate the defendant?"

"No."

"Do you like him?" (*objection on materiality overruled*)

"I don't have any feelings one way or the other about him."

"You have no feelings about the defendant at the present time?" [flavor of amusement and incredulity]

"That's right!"

"Do you appear here as a witness under subpoena?"

"No sir."

"Do you appear voluntarily?"

"Yes sir."

"Have you come at your own expense?"

"Yes, I have."

"How many people have you talked with prior to telling the story that you have just told to this jury?"

"Quite a few."

"Twenty?"

"Oh, no."

"Ten?"

"My attorneys?"

"Your attorneys?"

"Yes."

"Yes. Mr. Chamlin, Mr. . . . ."

"Where is Mr. Chamlin from?"

"Pardon me?"

"Where is Mr. Chamlin from?"

"He's from New Jersey."

"Is he sitting over there?"

"Yes sir."

"And you have another attorney in the courtroom?"

"Yes sir, certainly."

"And that's Mr. Goodrich from Bradenton, Florida?"

"Yes sir. Yes."

"These are your personal attorneys?"

"Yes sir."

"And you have hired them to represent you in connection with this case? Is that right?"

F. Lee Bailey has moved around to a position near the rail of the jury box and quite close to the witness. He used no notes. The questions came very quickly.

"Yes."

"You are paying counsel, aren't you, to represent you?"

"Oh yes."

"To be here in court?"

"Yes sir."

"Did you direct Mr. Chamlin to appear here and observe the jury being empaneled?"

"No sir."

"So that you say if he came and attended court while the jury was being empaneled that was not in serving you. Is that correct?"

[affirmative nod]

"You didn't know anything about that?"

"That's right."

"Have you had many conversations with the attorneys about your appearance here today?" (*objection—materiality—overruled*)

"Well, not many, not really."

"Have you gone over your testimony with them?"

"Yes."

"And have you discussed the manner in which you would testify?"

"Well, I was told to tell the truth."

"I asked you if you had discussed the manner in which you would testify."

"No."

"Did you discuss the matter of cross-examination?"

"No. I don't—I can't answer that with a yes. No, I didn't. No, we did not."

"You did not. Now, I take it that on the day of your husband's death you did not call the police?"

"No."

"But you say you went back and helped to cover it up according to a plan, is that right?"

"Yes."

"You went back and covered up the murder of your husband. Is that right?"

"Yes. I don't quite understand that question. What do you mean 'cover up'?"

"So that nobody would know he had been murdered. Calling Carmela over and all that business?"

"Oh. Yes. Yes."

"Yes. To hide the murder?"

"Yes."

"Now I take it at the time Carl killed your husband with the pillow he wasn't acting at your insistence?"

"No, he was not."

"You didn't want him to die, did you?"

"No. I didn't."

"How soon after he died did you decide to assist the defendant in covering up the murder?"

"Apparently right then and there."

"Right at the time he was killed you decided to help hide the fact that he was killed, is that true?"

"Well, I had no choice in the matter, Mr. Bailey."

251

"All right. I'm not asking you whether you had a choice. I'm saying, did you make the decision *then?*"

"I made the decision through Carl's guidance, yes."

"Did you yourself conscientiously decide to aid and abet the murder of your husband immediately after he was dead?"

"I guess the only honest answer is yes."

"Well, it's an honest answer that we'd like to have and you say the honest answer is 'yes,' is that right?"

"Well you won't let me say anything else. I had no choice in this matter!"

"Will you just answer the question, please?"

"Pardon me?"

"The honest answer as it stands and the way you want to leave it with the jury is, 'Yes, immediately upon your husband's death you decided to assist his killer.' Is that true or isn't it?"

"Yes."

"All right. Were you in love with Carl at the time?"

"At the time I thought I was. Yes."

"How old are you, Mrs. Farber?"

"I'm now fifty-two."

"And how old is the defendant?"

"I think he's thirty-four."

"Did you tell him immediately after your husband died that you would help him because you were in love with him?"

"No."

"When was the last time prior to the murder of your husband that you told the defendant you loved him?"

"I don't remember."

"Were you in love with your husband, Mrs. Farber?"

"Yes. I was in love with him."

"And when you saw him being killed, did you feel sorry for him?"

"I don't have the words to tell you how I felt."

"Just answer the question."

"Yes, I felt very sorry."

"You felt very sorry?"

"Yes, I did."

"Did you do anything to interfere with his demise?"

"No, I did not."

"Why not?"

"I couldn't."

"You couldn't? Why?"

"Because of the hypnosis. I had no free will."

"Are you representing to this jury that while your husband

was murdered you were unable to interfere because you were under hypnosis?''

''Yes sir.''

''Tell us at what time on July 30th Carl put you under hypnosis.''

''It wasn't necessary constantly to be putting me in a so-called trance because his influence was such that it wasn't necessary.''

''Were you under hypnosis at all times with Carl Coppolino?''

''As far as I'm concerned I was.''

F. Lee Bailey had begun by feinting and sparring very lightly and delicately, beginning in that always-safe area of the motive for testifying, implications about the cost of the trip and kindred matters. He watched her, and moved about, and varied the tone and cadence of his questions. He had confronted her three months before in another courtroom, involving a different indictment, a different death. But at the Sarasota preliminary hearing in September, not only had there been no jury, but he had been restrained by Marjorie's Florida attorney, Warren Goodrich, from edging too close to the circumstances surrounding the death of Colonel Farber, on the basis that she need not respond to any question where her answer might tend to incriminate her.

Such a hearing, with press and public present, but without jury or verdict, is strangely like a *tienta* as compared with the actual bullfight. At a *tienta* held usually at the small private bull ring at a breeding ranch, the guests and the matadors who have been invited work the calves and heifers with the capes, checking the bravery of the blood line, the trueness of the charge. The matadors learn a little about the habits of that particular stock, their eyesight and their quickness. But there is no death, and little blood. The formalities of the contest are loosely observed, and there are jokes and laughter.

So it is with a preliminary hearing. The seriousness is there, of course, because it is indeed preliminary to the trial itself, but there are the small legal jokes. Bailey certainly had some ideas of how Marge would be on the stand when a jury watched and listened. He had some thought of what his best avenues of approach might be. But now it was real, and the life of the young ex-lover was the stake in the game. F. Lee Bailey could not risk testing immediately what he had learned in the preliminary hearing, could only advance with a certain caution, completely sensitive to her every reaction, movement, intonation, change of expression.

[At intervals during the three days preceding her appearance on the stand, Vincent Keuper had two men taking turns at mock

253

cross-examination, making it as rough for her as possible, just to prepare her for Bailey. But the best training presupposes sparring partners who are well acquainted with the style of the actual challenger. They could not guess at Bailey's style because he is flexible enough to adjust his pace and purpose to the responses he gets.]

He had after ten minutes begun to find his line, begun to find the best way to work her and run her. Her story had a flavor of the grotesque, the ugly, the absurd. He had to so force these elements that he could turn it all into an unbelievable silliness.

And so he began speaking of the "murder" and the "killer," and questioning her closely about the homely little events of a home killing. In so doing he progressed from a mild and polite interest to an increasingly contemptuous sarcasm, a nimble irony, larded with weary shrugs and such sardonic glances at the jury that the scenes as she redescribed them began to have a flavor of fantasy. When he inquired politely if she had done anything "to interfere with his demise," there was a caustive elegance about the phrase, and an overt air of disbelief which stung her visibly.

He took her through how much she might have known about how much Carl knew of hypnosis, making the point that before she had ever told anyone about hypnosis, she knew that Carl was the author of a medical text on hypnosis. He moved closer to the defense table and perched on the corner of it, arms folded, and asked her about the suggestions she had described to the jury, asked her why she had kept her eyes closed when describing the sessions to the jury. When asked, she said she could not remember Carl ever suggesting to her, under hypnosis, that she kill her husband.

"But when he put you in a hypnotic trance at any time, you knew when he was placing you under hypnosis, didn't you?"

"Yes."

"All right. He would sit down and relax you?"

"Not always. No. Because after the first few sessions it wasn't necessary. He's an expert in this field and I happen to be a very good subject."

"By the way, when you were going through the motions and describing what happened, were you using a little autohypnosis?"

"I'm not aware of having any knowledge that way."

"But you are highly suggestible, you say?"

"Apparently."

"You don't say that Carl ever placed you in a trance, told you to relax and went through the usual preliminary steps and then said, 'Marjorie, I want you to kill Bill.' He didn't do that, did he?''

"If he did, I don't remember it."

"And you do remember the incident where the pail was getting heavy and you recall what he was saying all the time under hypnosis?"

"That's right."

"And, as a matter of fact, on each occasion when he used hypnosis to cure your smoking problem you remember the conversation, don't you?"

"Yes."

"Now when did you first feel a compulsion to get rid of Bill Farber?"

"It wasn't my idea."

"When did you first feel a compulsion to kill your husband?"

That question bothered her. It had an unexpected baldness about it. Yet were there no induced compulsion, then she was a rather commonplace accessory to murder.

"After the series of suggestions that Carl was giving me about 'That man has to go.' ''

"Is that all you say Carl ever said about killing your husband?"

He had moved close again. "Yes."

"When you had the needle in your hand, Mrs. Farber, was it your purpose to kill him with it?"

"I guess that was the idea."

"What do you mean, you *guess* it was the idea? Were you going to kill your husband or weren't you?"

"That was the purpose of the situation. Yes."

"There is no guessing about that, is there?"

"I'm sorry I used the wrong words."

"Yes. This wasn't a casual event in your life, was it?"

"Not at all."

"How much time did you give to thinking about it before you decided to stick the needle in him, Mrs. Farber?"

"As I said earlier, Saturday, the 27th, I couldn't do this thing."

"Well, if you couldn't do it on the 27th when did you decide you could do it?"

"I don't believe that I decided anything."

"When were you first aware, *first* aware of a thought in your mind that you were going to kill Bill Farber?"

"Sometime during July as it was processed through my mind through Carl."

"After the 27th when were you first aware that you intended to kill your husband?"

"After I filled the syringe on the 29th."

"At the time you filled the syringe it was for the purpose, you say, of killing your husband?"

"Yes."

"Do you represent that you were in a trance at that time?"

"Yes. I am convinced that is—"

"How long prior to that date do you last recall being hypnotized by Carl overtly?"

Over eleven questions and eleven responses, Bailey tried to get her to name a specific date, blocking each time her efforts to attempt to testify that she was in a "constant waking trance."

"Well, it would have to be the morning of July 30th," she said at last.

Here Bailey began to drive harder. He would bend forward abruptly from the waist as he asked the short hard questions, a curious and thrusting bow, face flushed, head cocked to the side. It was an unusual habit, and one likely to disconcert most hostile witnesses.

"Did he sit you down and give you instructions?"

"It wasn't necessary to do that."

"No. Please don't tell us what was necessary."

"He did not do that."

"All right."

"No."

"All right. Now I'm asking you and I would like you to tell this jury when was the last time prior to the date that you decided to kill your husband when Carl Coppolino sat you down and gave you suggestions which you knew were hypnotic suggestions."

"I don't remember."

"You don't remember?"

"That's right."

"So the hypnotic trance in which you find yourself as you decided to destroy your husband had been going on for a time and you can't tell us how long, is that correct?"

"That's right."

"If you were under the compulsion of this trance how was it that on the 27th you were unable to kill your husband? Did something happen after the 27th?"

"I don't know how to answer that question."

"Well?"

"I can't answer."

"I'm going to ask you to answer."

256

"I can't answer."

"Give us your best answer. Do you know of any reason why on the 27th you couldn't kill him?"

"Because I didn't really want to. I didn't *want* to."

"But the trance had you and you were compelled to do it, isn't that what you have told us?"

"Yes."

"Well, why didn't it work on the 27th? Do you know?"

"It didn't work on the 27th."

"I said *why* didn't it work, what was different about that day when you couldn't do it? Were you feeling more charitable on that day?" This last was said with a vicious irony.

"I don't know."

"You don't know?"

"I don't know."

"But on the 30th I take it you were overwhelmed by the trance and reluctantly and against your will you set about the business of poisoning your husband."

"Yes."

"You gave him a shot in the leg?"

"Yes sir."

"He jumped up and said he had a charleyhorse, is that right?"

"Yes sir."

"And he went to the john and his bowels were incontinent?"

"Yes sir."

"Had he any diarrhea prior to your injection of this drug that you were aware of?"

"No."

"And this followed immediately after the injection?"

"Yes."

"How much of the drug did you get into him before he jumped up?"

"I have no idea."

"Some of it?"

"Well, I would assume some or he wouldn't have been ill."

"How far was the needle in?"

"I don't know. It was a very small syringe."

"What was the drug?"

"I can't pronounce it properly."

"Would you recognize the name if I gave it to you?"

"Yes, I would."

"Does succinylcholine chloride help you?"

"Yes. Thank you. Yes."

"Did you know at the time that you had this drug that it was succinylcholine chloride?"

"No. I didn't know the name of it."

"You never asked, 'What's in this syringe? What's going in there?'"

"No."

"Did you ask him?"

"No. Yes."

"Were you interested in what the drug was?"

"I knew what it was, not as far as the name was concerned, the trade name, but all I knew it was supposed to cause instantaneous death."

"Had Carl told you that succinylcholine chloride couldn't be traced?"

"Pardon me?"

"Had Carl told you that succinylcholine chloride would cause instant death? . . . Did he tell you the drug by name at the time?"

"I don't recall."

"When is the first time you recall hearing the name succinylcholine chloride?"

"I believe it was in Florida."

"This was long after your husband's death?"

"Yes."

"So that all the time you were living in New Jersey you didn't know the name of the drug?"

"That's right."

"Did you not kill your husband because you decided not to or because he jumped up?"

This abrupt transition is a typical Bailey device, and he uses it often and well in cross-examination. He drives at one point for question after question, and then with no pause, no change in manner or intonation, shifts to a different area completely.

"I could not do it."

"Well, he jumped up. Did that interfere with your attempt or had you already decided to cease and desist your attempted murder?"

"I could not do it and I stopped."

"How long before he jumped up did you stop?"

"I had taken the needle out and then he grabbed his leg and said he had a charleyhorse. I don't know how many minutes or seconds."

"How long?"

"I don't know exactly how long."

258

"Don't you have any recollection?"

"It was not a matter of his jumping up and interfering, no. I did not want—"

"Mrs. Farber! Please. Do you have any recollection of how much time elapsed between the time you withdrew the needle and the time he jumped and said, 'I've got a charleyhorse'?"

"It was very quick."

"Very quick?"

"Shortly afterwards."

"Was it a matter of seconds?"

"I would say I really don't know. I didn't have a stop watch on. I couldn't—"

"All right."

"I wasn't timing it!"

Here, as before and as would happen many times, Bailey would drive her very well and in his intended direction until he pushed her a little bit too far. Then she would flare up, and blaze back at him. Usually when this happens any witness becomes less convincing. But to many in the court that Friday, Marge became more convincing when she was angered.

"Was it less than an hour? Was it less than an hour?"

"It was very short. I would say maybe thirty seconds."

"Thirty seconds?"

"Thirty seconds, sixty seconds. I don't know. I can't give you an evaluation of the actual time lapse."

"Did he grab for the spot where you injected him?"

"Yes sir."

"And so it was apparent to you that the pain he thought was a charleyhorse was really the needle injection?"

"I would assume that. Yes."

"Had you any experience with giving injections, Mrs. Farber?"

"No."

"You had never been a nurse, had you?"

"No sir."

"Have you ever given an injection to anyone?"

"Yes."

"You have? For Carl's benefit or for some other purpose?"

"Years ago I gave my grandmother insulin for diabetes."

"Now, when Carl gave you the poison and told you to help Bill Farber along his way with it, did he tell you where to put the needle?"

"Yes."

"Where did he tell you to put it?"

"In the leg area where there were more likely to be veins, scratches or bruises."

"Did he tell you to look for a vein so you could put it right in the bloodstream?"

"No, no."

"He didn't tell you that?"

"No."

"What part of the leg area did he specify? Did he point out any part on his own body?"

"I just said what he said."

"Did he point out any part on his own body and say, 'Put it in here'? Did you ask him whether or not you should look for a vein?"

"He told me what to do."

"Did you ask him whether you should look for a vein? Just 'yes' or 'no.' "

"No, no, I didn't."

"And outside of the general instruction to put it in the leg, did you get anything more specific as to how to accomplish this injection?"

In the subtle art of the cross-examination certain rhythmic patterns appear. One could plausibly suspect that Bailey had taken her into a specific area which, during the presentation of the case for the defense, he might hope to prove unlikely and illogical. The object of the cross-examination is not only to elicit information, but to direct the weight and the balance of it, so that something which the jury does not yet comprehend will be implanted so unforgettably that later, when the missing piece of information is supplied by witnesses for the defense, the jury will say, "Ah! *Now* I see!"

This insistence upon asking the same question in several forms and variations also can exasperate the witness. We are all accustomed to answer questions, and we are used to being understood. When a witness cannot understand why a certain question is being asked over and over, he cannot only become irritated, he can also begin to feel that little twinge of alarm we get when we begin to think there was something we missed, or forgot, or never knew . . . especially when repetition gives it a weight of importance we cannot comprehend.

"Now, how big was this hypodermic syringe that you *say* you filled with this poison?"

Here for the first time, F. Lee Bailey began to use the device of imbedding the seeds of skepticism in the structure of the questions instead of using merely the nuances of his tone of voice.

"Well, it was a small one. It was—I'm no expert."

"How long in inches, please?"

After eight questions, and some assistance from the Court, the judge, at Bailey's request, handing him a pencil for size comparisons, Marjorie Farber testified that the part which contained fluid was about an inch and a half long, of a total length including the needle of two inches, and that she had no idea how many cubic centimeters of fluid it held.

It is necessary to mention at this point that the witness was getting very little help from the state. Keuper had objected four times in the very beginning of the cross-examination, each time on materiality of the question, and had been overruled three times.

Vincent Keuper did not object to the questions being repetitive, even though there was a possibility of his being sustained by the Court. Nor did he enter other objections at that time even though the odds were that he would be overruled. Either interjection might have given the state's key witness some elbow room, some breathing space, some time to gather herself for the next sustained assault by Mr. Bailey.

"Were you told how much to use?" [How many cc's]

"I can't remember."

"You can't *remember!* [*sardonic incredulity*] In other words, as you were getting these instructions on how to kill your husband from the defendant, you are unable to remember how much poison you were told to use?"

"That's right."

"Did you ever ask Carl how much poison it's going to take to kill him?"

"I do not ever remember asking him anything. He told me what to do."

"I asked you, Mrs. Farber, if you asked him how much poison it would take to kill your husband and the answer is 'yes' or 'no.' "

"I don't know."

"You don't recall?"

"That's right."

"Did you make any inquiries as to whether or not the death that your husband would experience would be painful?"

"No."

"Did you care?"

"That's very difficult to answer."

261

"Yes. I'm sure it is. Will you answer it, please?"

"Did I care?"

"Did you care whether or not he died a painful death, Mrs. Farber?"

"As I recall, I don't remember thinking anything."

"You don't remember caring. Is that right?"

"No. I didn't say that."

"All right. Well, despite this compulsive trance in which you found yourself, did you have any thoughts about what a nasty thing it was to kill Bill Farber? . . . Do you have difficulty answering that question?"

"Yes, because . . ."

"Is it because, Mrs. Farber, you never thought about killing your husband?"

"That's true. I didn't want my husband dead."

"You never thought about it at all?"

"No."

"Until Carl Coppolino brushed you aside and then for the first time you thought about the death of your husband as a killing. Isn't that true?"

"No, it is *not* true!" Once again, by trapping her in that manner, he had made her lose control and, as before, her anger made her seem more plausible.

Also there were many in the courtroom who were puzzled about the way she seemed to create problems for herself. Certainly, having heard the opening statement by F. Lee Bailey, she knew what the defense would be. She knew that Carl would either directly deny the whole thing on the stand, or the defense would prove how it could not have happened that way with or without the testimony of the defendant.

Under those circumstances it seemed odd that she should not have taken the easy way and said, in answer to Bailey's questions, "Yes, I didn't want Bill to be in pain and I asked Carl if he would be, and he said that it would be instantaneous and he wouldn't feel a thing."

It even seemed likely that if her account of murder was true, that she very well might have asked such a question of Carl and gotten such a response. Her stubborn insistence on taking the hard road made her a considerable enigma.

Having angered her, Bailey quickly took another line, saying, "All right. It would appear, Mrs. Farber, that you didn't tell the authorities about this case for some time. Is that correct?"

"That's right."

"Now, did the trance in which you found yourself ever diminish or evaporate? Are you under Dr. Coppolino's trance today?"

"No."

"Any question about that in your mind?"

"No."

"You mean he has lost control of you?"

"Yes."

"When was the first time you felt that the compulsion had diminished to the point where you could act on your own judgment?"

"Any time I got far enough away from him."

During the interview with Theo Wilson of the New York Daily News *in May of 1967, Marge said, apropos of the hypnotic compulsion, "Who wants to be a middle-aged Trilby?"*

It was now ten past noon, and Bailey was gaining strength by heightening the flavor of absurdity with each series of questions.

"When was the first time after you attempted to kill your husband, Mrs. Farber, that you were aware of a return of control of yourself?"

"I would say when he and his wife and family moved to Florida."

"Then he lost control of you?"

"Yes."

"Did he sit down and give you some suggestions that you not tell anybody about this whole deal?"

"No."

"He never did that, but he told you to keep your mouth shut?"

"As a matter of fact—"

"Did he tell you that?"

"He threatened me."

"Did he tell you to keep your mouth shut?"

"Yes."

"Was it under hypnosis that he said this?"

"I was still under his influence at that time."

"Were you under hypnosis?"

"Yes."

"Where did the hypnosis take place in which you were given this suggestion?"

"I don't know."

263

"Then, how do you know you were under hypnosis? Do you have a recollection of the event when the suggestion was given?"

"It could have been in his house or it could have been in my house."

"You are telling this jury that you went through a session with Carl Coppolino where you were told or threatened under hypnosis not to reveal to the authorities the nature of the death?"

"Yes."

"But you are unable to picture the event in your memory as to where it took place?"

"That's right. He did threaten me."

"He threatened you?"

"Yes."

"He told you he was going to kill you if you told anyone? Is that right?"

"No."

"He was going to do something else?"

"Oh, yes."

One would reasonably expect that Bailey's next question would be, "What was he going to do?" But one of the basic rules of cross-examination is never to "go fishing." In both direct and cross, never ask questions when you are not reasonably sure of the answer, and sure that it will help your side. Fishing expeditions too often present the attorney with an ugly and saddening surprise. Tactically speaking it might have been better had Bailey stopped that line of questioning one question sooner.

But he switched then and asked: "Did you ever discuss with him the fact that you were parties to a murder, after the death?"

"Yes, I did."

"You had some talk with him about it?"

"Yes."

"Did you have any talk before Carmela came over with him, about the possibility that somebody might do an autopsy on the body?"

"I was not aware of the technicalities of a sudden death."

"I am going to ask you the question again. Did you have some talk with Dr. Carl Coppolino after the murder about the possibility that an autopsy might be done?"

"Yes."

"Was this the first time you have ever told anybody that you talked about an autopsy?"

"Yes!"

"Is this the first time since July 30, 1963, that you are able to recall that there was talk about an autopsy with Carl?"

"Yes!"

"You never mentioned it before?"

"No!"

During the lunch break a local attorney with years of court-room experience pointed to this particular exchange as the point where the witness began to "go bad," saying, "When you can get them to suddenly 'remember' something that the jury can figure the normal person wouldn't be likely to forget, then you put the wedge in that crack and see how wide you can open it. Understand, I'm not saying she didn't suddenly legitimately remember about that autopsy bit. Things like that can happen. But you've got those fourteen people sitting there hanging on every word and each one saying to himself that by God *he* wouldn't forget something like that if he'd helped knock some-body off. You noticed she got sore then? The Irish temper? Let me tell you one thing about this Bailey kid. Most run-of-the-mill defense attorneys in the criminal area have two or at the most three strings to the bow on cross. This Bailey's got more than you can count. He's six different people and every one of them is saying in forty different ways she's unbelievable. Hell, it's the heart of the case, and he has to clobber her good, or they fry his man. There's an old joke about how you define a man who is good at cross. They say he could put Diogenes on the stand and make a jury believe he stole the lantern."

"What did he tell you about the autopsy, now that you are able to remember?" [with a venomous sarcasm]

"He told me not to worry about it. I said, 'What if they do an autopsy?' He said, 'Don't worry about it.' "

"He said, 'Don't worry about it'? Was that the end of the conversation?"

"Yes, that's all."

"He didn't say anything further than, 'Don't worry about it'?"

"No."

"Did he tell you that you would be the one that would have to authorize an autopsy if one was to be done?"

"I knew nothing about—"

"Did he tell you that?"

"No."

"Did he tell you that if an autopsy were done on a suffocated person that petechial hemorrhages would show and give away the fact of murder?"

"No."

Here was another example of that ploy of putting new defense information into a question, which F. Lee Bailey had used so extensively during the *voir dire* of the jury panel, feeding the press—who would feed the public—little advertisements about coming events, to whet the appetite.

Also worth noting is that useful gambit of the trial lawyer, the deliberate use of the technical jargon of other trades and professions. One is inevitably reminded of Melvin Belli, defending Jack Ruby on the basis of Ruby's "psychomotor epilepsy," and "fugue" state.

Overused, this ancient device can alienate jurors by seeming to patronize them. Used to the proper tactical extent, it gives the attorney, in the eyes of the jury, a suitable sheen of knowledge, preparation, and secrets eventually to be revealed.

Inevitably it sends the press people up and down the corridors during the next break, trying to find somebody who knows how to spell the word.

Petechial—pronounced peh-teék-ee-ul—means pin-point. The question would have been far less impressive had Bailey substituted pin-point for the medical word.

He went on to ask with wide mock astonishment: "He never mentioned that to you?"

"No."

"Didn't order you *not* to give an autopsy?"

"No."

"Did he give you any instruction as to how to handle the funeral director when he arrived to take the body?"

"No. He and his wife discussed—"

"I asked if he gave *you* any, Mrs. Farber. You say that he did not?"

"No. He didn't."

"Now I take it you threw the rest of the poison away somewhere?"

"I don't know what I did— Yes, I did, I destroyed it. I don't know what happened to it."

"As I understand it, your first answer was that you didn't recall what you had done with it?"

"Yes. It disappeared; I don't know where it went."

"Carl didn't tell you what to do with it, did he?"

"No."

"In other words, after the killing was accomplished, not as planned, but with a pillow, he never told you, 'Get that poison out of here' or what to do with it?"

"No."

266

"Just walked out of there and left the poison, whatever it was, sitting in the house? Is that right?"

"I don't recall what happened to it."

He pressed the same point for eleven more questions, getting her to say that she thought she had given it back to Carl during the night, and then bringing her back to her original statement that it had disappeared. On this note, rather than returning with a new angle of approach so abruptly as to try to keep her off balance, Bailey paused, and with shrug and sigh, he let the jury see the quizzical, mocking, savagely amused disbelief on his face. It is an actor's face, the eyebrows particularly mobile. He had taken her in a little circle of inadvertent contradiction. The pause underlined it, and it had the flavor of the bull ring flourish where, after a series of passes, the confused animal ends up fixed in its tracks.

He returned with the question: "Did I understand in your earlier testimony you to say that when you called Carl to come over, that he did what he could to help Colonel Farber?"

"Yes."

"Did he say at the time that the murder was incomplete and we better finish him off? Anything like that?"

"I don't recall any conversation."

"So that the sequence is that, pursuant to an instruction, and in the hypnotic trance, you attempted to inject your husband with a poison?"

"Yes."

"He reacted by having diarrhea?"

"Yes."

"You called Carl Coppolino and reported your husband wasn't well?"

"Yes."

"And he came over and tried to help you?"

"Yes."

"Did you tell Carl when he arrived that you just tried to kill your husband?"

"I don't know what I said."

"Did you tell him you mixed up the drug?"

"I don't remember if I told him anything or not."

Again there was the puzzlement in the courtroom, here and there in the press and spectator sections the furrowed brow, shrug, shake of the head. It is entirely possible that the preparation given her through the mock cross-examinations preceding her actual ordeal had actually resulted in her making a worse impression than she would have if the state had let her go on cold, particularly if one were to assume that in the essential elements of her eyewitness story she was telling what had actually happened. If she was telling those important truths, she was, either deliberately or unconsciously, telling only a kind of selective truth in other areas. Truth as an absolute, capable of proof and demonstration, exists largely in the physical world of two plus two, and the apple falling from the tree. Subjective truth is always filtered through the emotions, and must inevitably undergo whatever change the emotions demand. When asked why we have acted in a certain way, or failed to act in a certain way, we will always give that answer which conforms to our own inner image of ourselves, and is consistent with that self-identification.

The answer will then be our personal truth. And because the web of all motivation is so tangled and subjective and personal, there can be no way for anyone to genuinely refute what we perceive to be our own inner truth. The only viable test of these personal truths is the acceptance of them by those who know us well, as they alone can determine whether truths are consistent with whatever image and behavior pattern we have revealed to them in the past.

But courts of law deal with the pragmatics of a situation. The law asks when, where, how, who and what. When the law asks ''why,'' when it deals with deepest motivations and the strongest emotions, then our explanations are judged by strangers who hold them up to their own inner mirrors, and then make a decision on a basis of conjecture.

At the first trial of Dr. Coppolino, the testimony given on the stand by Marjorie Farber was the pivotal point of the case. And thus it becomes necessary to guess at those alternative judgments which must have passed through the minds of the jurors.

Quite obviously the jury did not believe her. Had she been believed, the accused would have been convicted. It was just as obvious that she expected to be believed, for otherwise she would not have testified against her ex-lover knowing she had no guarantee of immunity.

It would be a grotesque oversimplification to say that the jury considered only two alternatives—that either she was being as totally honest as memory would permit, and all happened just as she described it, and she spent all those months in a trance state, subject to Coppolino's will, or that she was, as Bailey tried to paint her, a woman spurned who, out of a desire for vengeance had concocted a story of murder in an attempt to have her ex-lover convicted of murder in the first degree.

No, there was a third area of conjecture, and it must have been just as compelling an area of speculation to the jurors as it was to the press and spectators.

Obviously she had experienced a very long and traumatic episode involving certain elements of hypnosis. Admittedly she was a good hypnotic subject. There was the additional element of a physical affair, which induces an emotional state, a condition of vulnerability well known to alter anyone's perceptions of objective reality. There were the additional elements contributing to her vulnerability, elements deriving from the factors of age, geography, emotional needs, texture of imagination, marital status, personal emotional history. Certainly it was a justifiable speculation to wonder if, during her convalescence from this experience, she had unified all of these random contributive elements into that kind of consistent, cohesive, subjective truth which she could thoroughly believe because it was consistent with her own image of herself and consistent with that image which her friends, relatives and children valued and believed.

The jury, listening to the direct examination and the cross-examination, had to use the common human talent for appraising the emotional logic of the situation in deciding whether or not to believe her.

We all find a total consistency more believable than a story imbedded with those inconsistencies which are the product of an inner conflict.

"I started to perform a certain act and, before I could complete it, I learned that I could not go through with it."

Such statements indicate conflict on a subjective level. As we are often caught up in the same dilemma in our own lives, on usually more trivial matters, these confessions of conflict make us uneasy, and were we to be asked why we began, and why we stopped, we would find it awkward to respond.

F. Lee Bailey directed much of his attack at these subjective hesitations, and as her response used the trance state as a reason for the conflict, it afforded him endless opportunities to ridicule her and to make her account sound unbelievable.

It is possible that when he tried to develop areas of absurdity by dwelling upon the mechanical details of her story, his task was made easier by the customary instructions she would have been given before ever taking the stand.

"If you do not know, and do not remember, *say* so. Don't try to fill in with what you think might have probably happened because you might come up with something that could not have happened. And Mr. Bailey will make the most of any inconsistency he can find."

It is fair comment to say that imposing such a restriction upon Marjorie Cullen Farber could have diminished her believability. A conversational caution is alien to her manner and outlook. She might have said, "I do not know," or "I do not remember," to a more pedestrian attorney and sustained little damage.

But Bailey, time and again, would say, "What!!? You don't *remember!!?*" Each time he said it with that broad burlesque of astonishment which underscored and drove home the phrase he did not utter aloud: "How could anyone *possibly* forget!"

"Mrs. Farber, is Carl Coppolino the first person you laid eyes on after you tried to kill your husband?"

"Yes."

"And you still had a memory of trying to kill him with poison, didn't you?"

"If you can believe I was in such a state of shock—"

" 'Believe' is for the jury, Mrs. Farber. Did you at the time Carl arrived still remember that moments before you had tried to kill your husband? Just yes or no."

"Yes, and I was glad that Bill was alive."

"But you *did* remember trying to kill him?"

"Yes."

"Now, when did the affection that you had for your husband dissipate to the point where you could bring yourself to put the needle in?"

"When did my what?"

"You had some affection for your husband. You didn't want him to die, you said."

"I didn't want him to die. That's right."

"But at some point you were overcome, and you took this needle and injected it into his leg for the purpose of killing him, an attempt to murder?"

"That's right."

"And, how long before you did this act did you have a change of heart so that you could do it?"

"As I told you earlier, it was during the evening of Monday on the 29th that I knew that this thing that I had to do had to be done."

"And the thing that you had to do was kill your husband?"

"I was supposed to inject this drug into my husband. I don't know if I had the thought of kill in my mind."

"I see."

"But I do know that what I was supposed to do was to put that injection in him."

"You say that you were told the drug would cause instantaneous death, is that right?"

"Yes."

"That was before you mixed up the potion and filled the syringe?"

"That's right."

"And you say that you went to inject your husband with it?"

"Yes."

"But it wasn't with the purpose to kill him, is that right?"

"That's right."

"What was your purpose in injecting your husband with a poison that caused instantaneous death, if it wasn't to kill him?"

"I wasn't operating at my own free will."

"Yes, I know, but what was your purpose in injecting him?"

"I can't answer that honestly."

"Were you aware of any purpose?"

"I can't answer that question."

"You say you can't answer it honestly?"

"That's right."

"Why can't you be honest, Mrs. Farber?"

"Because if I try to answer it the way I would like to answer it, you won't let me answer it."

"You care not to follow our rules? The question I am going to put once more, and then I want your honest answer: What was your purpose in sticking into your husband's leg a deadly and instantaneous poison?"

"I was doing something that I was told to do. *That* was my purpose."

"At the time you inserted the needle?"

"Yes."

"Did you feel a desire not to put it in?"

"That's right. I couldn't do it. I couldn't do it."

"But something moved your hand and the needle kept going closer and closer. Is that right? Against your will?"

"That is what I said I did. Yes."

Bailey was herding her back into an almost impossible corner, taking a maximum advantage of her desperate need to believe beyond any doubt that she had functioned under the influence of Coppolino's control of her, the habit of hypnosis, the suggestibility.

"Is that what you did, Mrs. Farber?"

"Against my will! Against my will!"

"Did the needle get in under the skin by compulsion, and against your will?"

"Yes sir."

"Did you push the plunger under compulsion?"

"I started to push the plunger."

"Did you get some of the fluid into him?"

"Apparently."

"But it didn't kill him?"

"That's right. It didn't."

"When Carl came over did you say, 'Look, Carl. What *about* this poison? I gave him a little bit and it didn't kill him?' Did you have a conversation about why it didn't work?"

His abrupt shift into black parody startled her. She shook her head and she smiled and said, "No." The smile was startlingly inappropriate. It can perhaps best be explained by something Marjorie said that evening sitting at a table in the bar lounge of the American Hotel, when asked what she thought of Lee Bailey. She cocked her head and with a quizzical look, said, "You know, maybe this sounds crazy, but in some funny kind of way I *like* the guy, and I kept wishing on the stand I could really talk to him, could really tell him the whole thing."

So perhaps her smile had been the rueful recognition of his swiftness, and damaging change of pace—the smile of the fighter who, after contending with a damaging left jab, is suddenly smacked with a right-hand lead. Many sensed an odd similarity between Bailey and Mrs. Farber. They are both combative, nervy, articulate, dark-haired people of shorter than average stature, and both far handsomer than average. Both have that hearty and intensely personal flavor of strong sexual magnetism. Both have a talent for that black and bitter humor which so readily offends the sanctimonious. They are mercurial people, sensitive to the impact they have on others, both of the breed which in this era is called the swingers, and both very concerned and conscious of the image they present, in manner, dress, habits. One can suspect that as a team they would be formidable. As opponents they seemed to take an almost perceptible relish in each other, and in the game they were playing. On the surface it was deadly conflict. They were each aware of the size of the stakes. But on some secondary level they took pleasure in the tricks, in the wit, in the exchange, and this was not hampered by their individual belief that they were each winning. Marge was absolutely confident her testimony would convict Carl. Bailey was increasingly confident he could destroy Marjorie in the eyes of the jury. And that's what counts.

"Why did you smile?" asked Lee Bailey, swift to take every advantage. "Is there something funny about this case?"

"I think it is very serious. I am sorry I smiled."

"You won't smile again, I hope. Did you ever discuss with Carl about why the poison didn't work?'

"No."

"Did you care?''

"*Yes*, I cared. I said that earlier that I was so glad my husband wasn't dead.''

"I know you *said* that, Mrs. Farber. When Carl came in did you tell him how glad you were that your husband hadn't died?''

"That's right; I did.''

"He treated and helped your husband as a doctor?''

"Yes. He did.''

"Did you say, 'Carl, I'm glad that you are able to help'?''

"He had given Bill a sedative injection.''

"What kind of a sedative was it? Did he tell you?''

"No. He didn't.''

"Well, did you tell him that you had gotten some of this poison into your husband?''

"I don't recall.''

"You don't recall him asking?''

"I don't recall telling him anything about the injection.''

"I thought this was done under his direction?''

"Yes, it was.''

"At his suggestion?''

"But I don't recall discussing it afterwards.''

"You mean when he came over you kept from him the fact you just tried to kill your husband?''

"I don't recall any discussion whatsoever.''

"Are you conscious of having deliberately withheld the information from Carl Coppolino?''

"I don't have any recall of any sort of conversation pro or con on this.''

"You tell us [incredulity] Doctor Coppolino appeared at the door and walked in and without saying a word gave your husband a shot of something—made no inquiry as to how your husband was?''

"He found him, my husband was on the floor in the bathroom—''

"Did Doctor Coppolino walk into your home without saying a word, no conversation passing between you, and go about the business of treating your husband? Did he do that or didn't he?''

"I asked him to help Bill.''

"So you had some conversation with him! Your request was that he help Bill?''

"Yes.''

"You did not say, 'I just gave him a shot of that stuff you gave me'?"

"I don't recall that."

"You don't recall whether you told him?"

"I don't remember if I said anything about it or not. I really don't."

"When you said 'Carl, I want you to help Bill' did you really mean it? Did you want Bill to be helped?"

"Yes."

"How did you think he was going to help him if he didn't know what was wrong with him?"

"I don't know."

"You don't know?"

"I can't answer that question. I don't know what I said to him." She looked frowningly thoughtful as she replied, and this change of expression and slight hesitancy clued Bailey's next question.

"Did you ever think of that before? That you had failed to tell Carl how to help the man you just tried to poison?"

"I don't recall."

"Is this the first time anybody ever asked you that question, Mrs. Farber?"

"It is the first time you have ever asked me the question. Yes."

"Is it the first time *anyone* has ever asked you the question?"

"To my knowledge, yes."

"You have had no chance prior to today to think about any answer to that question. Is that correct?"

"I would say so. Yes."

"Without an opportunity to think about the answer, you don't have an answer. Is that correct?"

Vincent Keuper made his sixth objection at this point, bringing his score up to three sustained and three overruled.

"Was there any indication, anything Carl did or said to indicate his murderous intent when he came over to treat and assist as a physician William Farber early in the morning of the 30th day of July?"

"That is when he asked me to get a cellophane or plastic bag, I should say."

"So first he tried to help him and then with the bag tried to kill him?"

"I asked him to help him."

"And he did. Isn't that right?"

"Yes. I don't remember how my husband got into bed. I can't

274

remember that, from the time he was in the bathroom. And I called Carl, and when Carl came up, I don't know how Bill got into bed. I don't know whether Carl helped him—"

"I didn't ask you that. *Please* don't ramble on. You last saw your husband in the bathroom, you *say*. Is that right?"

"On the floor. Yes."

"And then you went to the door to let Carl in?"

"He came in by himself."

"When you got back he was in bed?"

"Yes."

"Any other adults in the house that might have carried him into bed?"

"No."

"Did you carry him into bed?"

"No."

"Did Carl carry him into bed?"

"No. He was too heavy."

"Did the children get up and carry him into bed?"

Could not Keuper have stood up at this point and said, "Your Honor, the witness has testified that she does not remember how her husband got back into bed."?

"How many children were in the house at the time?"

"My two daughters."

"How far were they from the room?"

"Upstairs."

"A different floor?"

"Yes."

"I assume that when you got back to the bedroom you drew the inference that he had walked to the bed, or crawled, or got there under his own movements?"

"Yes."

"You told Carl he was on the floor of the bathroom and he had diarrhea?"

"Yes."

"You gave him the information about the diarrhea for the purpose of enabling Carl to help Colonel Farber, didn't you? Isn't that why you told him?"

"I said I don't recall that I said to Carl about Bill's illness one way or the other. I do not *remember* that."

"Mrs. Farber, please. A moment ago I asked you if you told him about the diarrhea, and you said yes. Now, was that statement true or wasn't it?"

"I don't remember."

"You don't *remember?!*"

"I don't remember ever saying that I told you."

When, as in this instance, F. Lee Bailey was able to increase the speed and tempo of his questioning, and bring her along in equal speed and pace, he was often able to develop an advantage due to the ever more limited time she had to consider her replies. The brain can sustain total alertness and an undivided attention for only so long. Question and answer achieve such a rhythm that at last the questioner, as in a rapid volley on the tennis court, can put a little twist on the ball that goes unnoticed. Any objection by the state in such instances serves, of course, to interrupt the rhythm and destroy the tempo of the cross-examination for a few moments, regardless of whether the objection is sustained or overruled.

The intensity and speed of the questioning can be judged by realizing that at this point Bailey's cross-examination had lasted only forty-six or -seven minutes.

"So despite your desire that Carl help your husband, you told him nothing about what you had observed, and the symptoms, and the experience about the deadly poison? You told him nothing about that, is that right, that you can recall?"

"That's right."

"If you had told him, do you think you would remember?"

"I probably would. Yes."

"Did you fail to tell him because you didn't really want Carl to save your husband?"

"If I don't have any recall, how do I know whether I failed or succeeded or anything else? *I don't know!*"

Again, with the flash of anger, she recouped a little, but between these little incidents of plausibility, she was losing each time more than she gained. He kept her skillfully in her most disadvantaged areas of testimony.

"No memory whatsoever?"

"Pardon me?"

"Have you found this to happen in other instances? Gaps in your memory between events?"

"I think this is a human failing, don't you?"

"Have you ever had this experience before?"

"I don't remember every single thing I have ever done. Yes."

"Was this an unusual event in the course of your life? To try to kill someone?"

"This was *extremely* unusual."

"Does it stand out pretty clearly in your mind what happened that night?"

"Yes. What I can remember stands out. Yes."

"To the best of your recollection, Carl walked in, and with no information from you proceeded to treat the colonel?"

"Yes."

"And do you represent that Carl didn't ask you what was wrong?"

"I do not remember what was said."

"If he did ask you, you don't recall?"

"That is true."

"Now, following your abortive attempt to inject the poison, your feelings toward your husband were of affection, I take it?"

"Uh . . . If I were to say that I had no feelings about anything at that particular time, that would be an honest answer."

"Then the answer that you had before, when you said that you were glad he was still alive, I take it is not correct?"

"Yes. That *is* correct!"

"When you were glad, is that a feeling?"

"I'm not a semantic artist, so I'll do the best I can."

"But you *are* a human being. You know that being glad is a feeling."

"I was *very* glad."

"You were glad. So you *did* have feelings?"

"Certainly."

"When Carl came in at your request, treated your husband? And during this time you felt glad and not homicidal? Is that right?"

"I was relieved."

"You were relieved that he was alive and going to be all right?"

"Certainly!"

"When Carl tried to suffocate him with a plastic bag, did you say yes? How did you feel about that?"

"I told him to stop it."

"You told him to stop it?"

"Yes. I did."

"Did you run over and grab the bag, or rip it up, or interfere with what he was doing?"

"I don't recall, but I told him in no uncertain terms to stop it."

"And you meant it when you said stop it, didn't you?"

"Yes."

"I understood that you were under Carl's hypnotic trance. You remember saying those words that night?"

"I'm really telling you what I said to the man!"

"Were you under his hypnotic trance and at his direction and control at the time you said, 'Stop it, Carl!'? Was that compulsion?"

"I would like to think that the real me was coming through."

One can guess that Bailey was trying to get her to say, in one way or another, that she had emerged from the trance state. He could not have had her say it in a manner more useful to his taste for withering sarcasm.

"That the real you was coming through! Was the 'real you' the homicidal you, or the non-homicidal you, Mrs. Farber?" Here Keuper's seventh objection was overruled.

"I am not a homicide," she said.

"You are not a homicide?"

"No! I am *not!*"

"You never participated in any killing, did you?"

"Never!"

"Never!" Bailey moved even closer, and again he hammered at her, with that sharp forward inclination of his torso, face flushed, voice harsh. "This whole story is a cock and bull story, isn't it? (*objection sustained*) Didn't you make this all up, Mrs. Farber? (*objection sustained*) Did you fabricate this story?" (*objection sustained*)

"What did you *mean* when you said that you never participated in a murder? *Did* you or *didn't* you participate in the murder of your husband?"

He had rattled her. His unexpected anger had startled her, as had the objections by Vincent Keuper at that point. She seemed to have wanted to answer the accusation she had made it all up. She hesitated and defended herself by a kind of cool sarcasm which made a rather questionable impression at that particular juncture.

"You want a yes or no answer on that, I presume?"

"Is there any question in your mind as to whether or not you were a participant in the murder of your husband?"

"If I had seen . . ."

"Is there any confusion in your mind as to whether or not you were a participant?"

"It isn't a real situation as far as I am concerned."

"It isn't a real situation?"

"I did not relate it to something that I actually saw with my two eyes. I cannot relate to it although it happened. I saw it."

"How do you know you didn't dream it if you can't relate to it? You said it isn't real. Was this all a bad dream?"

"Oh, no!"

"But you can't say it was real?"

"I cannot believe that I, me, took place . . . took part in this story that has just been told here. I cannot—"

"But you ask the jury to believe that you took part in this story?"

"I was not acting of my own free will, Mr. Bailey."

"You were under a trance?"

"Yes."

"And you were under the same trance when you interrupted the attempted murder of your husband with a plastic bag and ordered your controller to stop?"

"Yes."

"All right. Now did Carl say, 'Marge, when I begin to kill this guy, you stop me.' Did he say that?"

She shook her head rather than saying no. It was not from any inability to speak. It was as though a verbal response would have to her way of thinking merely dignified a ridiculous question.

"Did you feel it was his compulsion to have him stop, or was it your own free will?"

"I don't know! I don't *know!*" (exasperation, torment, despair)

"But you *do* know you stopped him?"

"Yes."

"Did you feel at the time you stopped him you were compelled to do it?"

Mr. Keuper stood up and said, "*If* Your Honor please, I object to this because we have been over it time and time again. Now it's beginning to become repetitive."

"I haven't got an answer yet," said Mr. Bailey, and the Court overruled the objection.

"Did you a moment ago say that you caused Carl to stop because the real you was coming through?"

"I did say that. Yes."

"All right. Did you mean by that that your act in stopping Carl was an act of your own free will as Marjorie Farber? Is that what you meant?"

"I don't know. I guess that's what I mean. I don't know. It's very difficult, Mr. Bailey."

"*I'll* say!"

"This is not a usual situation. I have never been in—"

"You have never been in it?"

"Under hypnosis."

"Did you say you were never in it?"

"I have never been in a situation like this in my life."

And with that response, and the way she said it, once more she regained some lost ground. One can suspect that from time to time she managed to disconcert F. Lee Bailey with her refusal to break and run, with her resilience and fighter's ability to regroup and fight some more.

"Well, did you stop him?"

"Yes."

"At the time you stopped him you wanted your husband not to die?"

"That's right."

"So your will and the act that you did coincided. Right?"

"That's what I said. I told him that I wanted him to stop."

"When you said stop, Mrs. Farber, you were expressing your own will?"

Again Keuper objected, and Bailey made a very slight change in his angle of approach, asking, "Is it fair to say that for that brief moment, you weren't under a trance?"

"It might be a fair question."

"Is that your best recollection?"

"I don't know. I don't recall."

"You don't know. (Said wearily, with shrug, meaningful glance at the jury, as if to say, "Well, we have to give up on that one because she just won't answer.") Well, how long did Carl sit around before he went home?"

"I don't remember how long he stayed at the house after that. I believe he left about five or six o'clock in the morning. I don't really remember exactly."

"And you called him again to come over? Or did he come over?"

"You mean the next day? I saw him—"

"At your home?"

"I saw him when I was on my way either to or from going to the dentist in the morning. I had an appointment that morning."

"Was he dropping in to look in on the patient?"

"I saw him when I was in my car, and he was in the car."

"Did you see him in your home, Mrs. Farber?"

"Oh yes. He came up to the house that afternoon."

"Did he come over to check on the patient?"

"Yes. Yes, he did."

"All right. Did he give another sedative?"

"Yes."

"When he walked in the door did he say anything then about killing your husband."

"No."

"How long was he there before he got the pillow and killed him?"

"About an hour, I would say."

"Now, Mrs. Farber, going back just a little bit when Carl said about your husband, 'He's got to go,' did you inquire as to why he had to go?"

"I didn't ask him anything. He told me."

"All right. He told you, 'Bill has got to go.' Now was there any clear reason in your mind at the time you heard that statement *why* your husband had to die?"

"He told me that Bill had threatened him and—I don't like to use this kind of language, but he said: 'That bastard threatened my family and threatened me and he's got to go.' "

"All right. Now, the first time, many days before the killing, the first time that he said, 'Bill has got to go,' did he mention threats at that time?"

"No."

"No. It was sometime later that he talked about the threats, wasn't it?" She nodded her head yes. "Did you testify on direct examination the first time threats were mentioned was at the time of the killing?"

"That's right."

"All right. So when he first said, 'He's got to go—' "

"Yes?"

"—you understood that to mean the man must die?"

"Yes. . . . I didn't believe he actually meant what he was talking about. That he was referring to my husband."

"You understood that he was saying, 'Bill Farber's got to die'?"

"That he was out of his mind."

"All right. Did you say, 'Carl, I think you're out of your mind?' or argue with him, or did you remain silent?"

"I didn't want— How do you react to something like this? I was completely shocked."

"Well, you could react by saying, 'I'd rather you didn't knock Bill off.' That's one of the things you could do."

This is a weapon Bailey uses effectively, to couch a phrase in such a colloquial way that it demeans the person in whose mouth he puts the words. It has an effect of outrage, shock and bitter humor.

"Well, I don't casually talk like that."

"Well, you could object in more profuse language if you thought it appropriate. Did you ever say, 'Please don't kill him, Carl. He's my husband'?"

"I didn't want anything to do with this."

"Did you want him to die when you first heard, 'He's got to go'?"

"No."

"Did you react at all to the suggestion that your husband be executed?"

"I didn't want any part of it."

"Well. You didn't want to be involved, or you didn't want him to be killed?"

"I did not want him killed."

"You did not. All right. Was that because of some positive feeling for your husband over all these years?"

"I don't believe in— One just doesn't go around taking other people's lives."

"One doesn't?" (mock astonishment)

"No! One doesn't."

"No? But in the face of this opportunity or offer to put your husband to death you said nothing?"

"I said I was shocked."

"Did you tell Carl that you were shocked?"

"That's who I was talking to. Yes."

"All right. Now who did you report this to? That someone had threatened your husband's life?"

"I didn't report it to anybody."

Here he achieved a useful jury-effect. He knew, of course, that she had not made any such report. He was using the question to remind the jury of what happens in the orderly world outside the courtroom, and at the same time he was building toward his next question which would serve to stunt any sympathy she might be receiving.

"Well, were you good enough to tip Bill off that somebody might be out to get him?"

"Well, the whole idea was so completely unrealistic, I mean, that it was just ridiculous. I just— Well, I just couldn't believe it."

"I'm sorry. I understood you to say a few moments ago you thought Carl meant he was going to kill, or, 'I'm going to kill him,' when he said, 'He's got to go'?"

"Yes."

"Did you take that to mean . . ."

"I asked him what he was talking about."

"Oh. He *did* speak back?"

"I did ask him what he was talking about and then he explained it to me, that my husband had to go."

"Had to go?"

" 'That man has got to go.' "

"Did you and Carl at that time have a plan to run off together?"

"No."

"Was he in love with you?"

"He said so."

"And you were in love with him?"

"I thought I was."

"Did you understand that the killing of the husband was to facilitate your intimacies?"

". . . I don't know. I don't know what the point of the whole thing was."

"You don't know what the point of it was. Was it to get the insurance?"

"No."

"How much insurance did you get? Fifty thousand?"

"About that."

"And of course all his property went to you, I take it."

"Yes."

To many of the observers, Bailey's strategy here was obscure. After trying to establish in the jury mind the point that inasmuch as Coppolino had access to Mrs. Farber at any time, it seemed quite pointless to slay a husband who was not obstructing the affair, he immediately suggested another motive. One might suspect that a very suggestible hypnotic subject with control over $50,000 and a handsome home might seem enticing to an unemployed anesthesiologist.

Appraising it from an assumption of Carl's innocence, and from the assumption, previously stated by Bailey, that the Colonel had died of natural causes, the insurance and inheritance seemed to have little bearing on the defense case at that point, aside from seeming to weaken it.

It was only much later, when testimony was presented regarding whether or not the Colonel should be hospitalized, that Bailey's purpose became understandable. All trial attorneys learn very quickly that the mention of a nice round sum of money, like $50,000, makes a permanent mark on the collective memory of the jurors.

"Well, you say that to the best of your knowledge he wasn't

283

killed because he was standing in the way of your love affair. Is that right? Is that true? Is it true, Mrs. Farber, that the purpose for killing your husband was not because of your romance with Carl?''

''. . . I think he said— He told me about I'd be better off without him.''

''Did you say anything that he'd be better off, or the two of you would be better off without him? Didn't you say that?''

''Except to be a manipulation of my life and my husband.''

''All right. I see. Now, when he suggested that your husband be killed you were shocked because you didn't want him killed. Right?''

''Right.''

''And when the purpose was explained it turned out that the killing was for your benefit. You'd be better off without him.''

''That's what he said.''

''Well, did you tell Carl at that time that, 'Well, no, as a matter of fact don't do it for my sake'?''

''I don't recall what I said to him.''

''Mrs. Farber, isn't this the only man you ever talked with about committing a homicide? You never got involved in anything like this before or since, have you?''

''No.''

''No. A rather unusual event in your life, this conversation about murder.''

''Very!''

''Now when he said, 'He's got to go,' and you understood that to mean he's got to die, did you believe that he'd go through with it?''

''No.''

''You yourself never had any desire to kill your husband at any time, did you? Just the compulsion?''

''Well, no. I didn't ever want to kill my husband.''

''Had you been having a little trouble with Bill Farber in the spring of '63?''

''Yes. Due to the fact—''

''You had been to some lawyers about domestic problems, hadn't you?''

''Yes.''

''And you had been to see a marriage counselor at some point?''

''Yes.''

''You had arguments with him?''

''With my husband. Yes.''

"Yes. Did Carl take sides in these arguments?"

"Oh yes."

"Between you and your husband!? He would sit there and go for one or the other?" (fascinated incredulity)

"No, no!"

"Did he ever sit down with Bill Farber and argue with him?"

"I understand there was an argument between Bill and Carl, but I wasn't there."

"Not what you 'understand.' Did you ever see one?"

"No."

"Can you name a witness who ever saw Carl threaten or argue with Bill Farber? Besides yourself, of course. You can't?"

"Well, if I'd been a witness I would have seen the other witness, wouldn't I?"

"No. Do you know of anyone, can you identify a person through any source of information that can tell us that Carl and Bill had an argument or that Bill was threatened or that there was some overt hostility?"

"I think so."

"Would you give me the name please?"

"I'm not really sure."

"Well, give us the name and we'll check it out."

"Because I'd hate to involve somebody in something that wasn't true."

"This is a man on trial for his life and you are required to give me his name, so please do."

"I think it was Ben Harris."

"Ben Harris?"

"I think. I'm not sure."

Bailey turned and spoke across the floor of the courtroom to his investigative staff. "Please make a note of it." He turned back to Marjorie and said, "All right. Your recollection is that Ben will be able to come in and tell us of some hostility between them?"

"I don't even know if they still live here. I have been away from this area."

"Never mind that. We'll find him. Where did they live when you knew them?"

"Right across the road."

"Now your recollection is that Ben Harris would have some information about threats or arguments?"

"This is very vague, Mr. Bailey."

"Very vague?"

"I'm not absolutely sure. But that is to the best of my

285

knowledge. I think he is the one who was told about— I don't know. I'm not quite sure on this thing."

"You say that you never saw Carl do it yourself?"

"No."

"Now, prior to the time that it was decided to exterminate your husband because you'd be better off without him, did Carl ever ask you, 'Marge, would he ever give you a divorce'?"

"Carl suggested that I try to get a divorce."

"I understand that. But before deciding to kill him did he inquire as to whether or not you could get one peaceably? A divorce?"

"Well, I did go to see some friend and discussed it with him."

"I think my question—"

"Informally."

"My question, Mrs. Farber, was whether or not Carl sought to learn from you before resorting to murder whether divorce was out of the question. Did he ask you?"

"Yes. Carl and I discussed divorce."

"Now did you tell him that you couldn't get one? Or that you could get one?"

"I didn't tell him anything until I found out from someone else that I could not."

"You could not get a divorce?"

"That's right."

"You learned that Bill wouldn't give you one?"

"I learned that I had no grounds. From an attorney. A personal friend. Informally."

"I see. You communicated that to Carl, that you didn't believe you could get one because you didn't have any grounds?"

"After I talked with this friend of mine, who happens to be an attorney."

"What was the date of this communication?"

"I don't remember."

"Was it a month or two months or six months before your husband's death?"

"It was before my husband's death."

"How long before your husband's death?"

"It would have to be between February and July, I would assume. I would assume it would be June, May, April, something like that."

"Did Carl's first statement about your husband, 'He's got to go!' immediately follow your telling Carl you couldn't get a divorce?"

286

"I don't recall."

"Do you remember ever at any time prior to the death of your husband asking Carl, 'By the way, why are we killing him?' Did you ever discuss it with him?"

"Well I did say earlier that he had said to me, Carl had said to me the fact that I'd be better off without Bill. Everybody would be better off without Bill."

"And you told us you were opposed to it right up to the time it happened?"

"That's right."

"I now ask you, Mrs. Farber, whether or not you ever inquired of Carl as to why it was necessary to kill him since you didn't feel you would be better off without him?"

"I can't give you cut and dried answers on these things."

Bailey is so adept at the parry and the thrust, that a response of this kind can almost guarantee a wicked edge on the succeeding question. "Can you give me just a little one on this? Just a little answer? Why didn't you determine why your husband had to be killed? Weren't you interested?"

"Well, the only answer I can give you, Mr. Bailey, is the fact that I just did not have free will. I was brainwashed, in my vocabulary, by this man and apparently he had a vicious hate for my husband. I didn't have this terrible animosity."

"Well, Mrs. Farber, will you try and help the jury determine whether or not there was any possible motive for your husband to be killed by Carl Coppolino? Now, did something happen? What was it? Was it hate? What did it come from? Do you know? He wasn't having any difficulty getting along with you because of intrusion by your husband, was he? Prior to the time he threatened death?"

"No."

"One time your husband did make a little objection to your running around the country together— Isn't that true?—taking trips."

"Yes."

"And of course you went right on doing that right up until the time he died. Is that right?"

"I took one trip with Carl to Miami Beach before my husband died."

"All right. Prior to the time Carl first threatened to kill your husband or said, 'He's got to go,' did anything happen to your knowledge that might have provoked a murderous attack?"

"Yes."

"What happened?"

"The day that my husband actually died—"

"No! Mrs. Farber!"

"—Carl had an argument with my husband—"

"*PLEASE, PLEASE*, Mrs. Farber! *PLEASE!* My question was—prior to the first time, many days before your husband died, that Carl Coppolino said, 'He's got to go,' which you believe to be a statement that he intended to murder, prior to that time, what happened between them? What was the cause?"

"Well, the only thing I can possibly give for a cause was the fact that Carl is so egotistical he doesn't want anyone interfering with what he wants to do."

"Oh, Mrs. Farber, do you mean that his love for you was so deep he couldn't stand the thought of your husband being with you and that's why he killed? Was that his purpose?"

"That's the insinuation, I presume."

"Is that what you meant to say? Was his love for you that complete?"

"I mean to say that Carl, as I know him, or knew him, unless he's had a complete change of—"

"No! Please! Please! Please! (with an imitation of an almost tearful exasperation) Do you know of any act or transaction—"

At this point Judge Simmill told Bailey that Mrs. Farber was trying to answer him, and that he should let her answer. Bailey said that his question had not gone to her opinion of the defendant's character. "Don't interrupt her," said Judge Simmill. "You asked her why and she is telling you why." And, of course, that sort of question—the "why" question—is best avoided in any cross-examination. Any witness is entitled to answer fully and completely any question asked. The Court will protect the witness's right to answer completely. The "why" question can open the flood gates by eliciting a full response which goes to all the subjective evaluations and judgments of the witness. But due to inexperience, Marge Farber fumbled her opportunity, answering merely, "Well, the only reason I could possibly give you is that Carl was jealous."

"Of Bill!?"

"Yes."

"Of course Carl could have you pretty much any time he wanted, didn't he?"

"Yes."

"Did he tell you, 'I'm jealous of Bill and I'm going to get rid of him'?"

"He told me at one time he had asked his wife, Carmela for a divorce."

288

"No. Did *he* tell *you*, Mrs. Farber? Please don't volunteer. Did he tell you that he was jealous of your husband and therefore he wanted to kill him?"

"I do not recall."

"Mrs. Farber, am I the first person that ever inquired of you as to why Carl killed your husband?" Marge shook her head no.

"Who was the first person who ever inquired why . . ."

Keuper entered his thirteenth objection, this time on the grounds of materiality and was overruled, and Marge said that the question had been asked when she had first talked to the authorities a year previously. Bailey went to the defense table and came back with a copy of the interview between Mrs. Farber and Frank Schaub, on July 6, 1965, in the state attorney's office in Bradenton, Florida. As he leafed through it he asked her if she had given the authorities a reason for the killing. His reference source seemed to make her uneasy.

"Well, I can't remember what's in that. I haven't had the pleasure of reading that."

Judge Simmill said to her, "Regardless of what's in that, ma'am, did you or did you not give them a reason for the killing?"

"My reason was based on the fact that I was hypnotized and I couldn't stop him."

Mr. Bailey said, "No. Did you give them a reason why *Carl* wanted to do it? Not why you did it, but why Carl wanted to kill him?"

"I can't remember."

And yet once more F. Lee Bailey went after the same point, and after seven insistent questions varying but slightly in form, Keuper stood tall and said in an aggrieved tone, "Now, if Your Honor please, the witness has already answered that question before."

"Several times," said Simmill dryly. "Is there an objection?"

"Yes, there is."

"Sustained," said the Court.

Bailey glanced at the courtroom clock. It was twelve minutes before one. The court-wise ones always adjust the dramatics of interrogation to the inevitable interruption, knowing that if they can end on a particularly damaging note, the entire session will, in retrospect, seem to have been more damaging than, perhaps, it was, just as the ring-wise fighter ends each round with a flurry of punches.

"You say you put a note on the door?"

"Yes."

"So that your children wouldn't disturb the colonel?" (with a hint of cool distaste)

"That's right."

"And that only indicated that he was sleeping, recovering from his illness?"

"Yes."

"Who discovered the body, Mrs. Farber?"

"My daughter, Victoria, had come in the house just before I had and she walked in the room. She came out and she said to me, 'Daddy looks funny,' and I told her that—she had a date to go out with one of her friends to a movie, and I knew why Daddy looked funny and I told her that—I diverted her because—"

"I didn't ask for the conversation, Mrs. Farber. You say your daughter discovered the body?"

"Yes."

"Okay. Was it right after that—"

"And she wasn't aware of what the situation was."

"What?" (angrily, as if to say "Can't you stop babbling?")

"Pardon me."

"What time was the discovery made?"

"Well, it was while I was on my way home from the Coppolino house."

"What time of day, please?"

"Pardon me. In the afternoon. Around five."

"You left Carl around that time that afternoon?"

"I said earlier I think between four and five, but I think it was later than that because—it had to be around five, between five and five-thirty because of Victoria's coming into the house when she did."

"You have a clear recollection of having left the (Coppolinos') house between five and five-thirty?"

"As close as I can remember, yes."

"You went in and your daughter discovered the body and came out to you and said that Daddy is dead and you agreed he was dead?"

"There was no discussion about that."

"He didn't look right, you said. You already knew he was dead?"

"Yes."

"Then you picked up the phone and called Carmela?"

"At six-thirty. Yes."

"How long did you have to sit around with this cadaver before you made the phone call?"

"I went upstairs with my daughter, Victoria, and cooked her dinner."

Mr. Bailey gave it the dramatic pause. He boggled at her, and then said with horror and pained disgust. "With a dead body lying in the bedroom, you cooked *dinner!!??*"

"I cooked her a hamburg."

"All *right!*"

Marjorie, looking both embarrassed and indignant, said, "If you'd like to know about my state of mind—"

Judge Simmill said, "Nobody asked you that."

"Excuse me."

"Don't volunteer, ma'am," said the judge.

Bailey asked her, "Did you do any other odds and ends before you called Carmela?"

"No. That's all I remember."

"When you called Carmela, did you tell her that your husband was dead?"

"No, I did not tell her that."

"How long a period of time did you sit around and wait?"

"I *didn't* sit around and wait! All I recall is coming in the house right after Victoria and her saying what she said, going upstairs—the house was a bi-level so you had to go upstairs to the kitchen, and cooked her hamburger and by that time it was six-thirty and I called Carm."

"So that you arrived at home, you feel, around five-thirty?"

"I would hazard a guess, yes."

"And it was upon your arrival that your daughter said something about your husband?"

"She came in the house just before that."

"So you waited an hour before calling any doctor?"

"That's what I was told to do. I was told to call Carmela at six-thirty and that's what I did."

"After your husband had been killed, how much time did you spend talking with Carl?"

"Oh, it would have to be two or three hours."

"Did all the conversation take place in one location?"

"As I recall we were out in the back yard."

"Were you sitting in the back yard for two or three hours?"

"That's the only place I remember being."

"Were you sitting in the back yard for two or three hours?"

"I don't know."

"What time did you arrive in the back yard?"

"Oh, I guess around two—two-thirty."

"What time did you leave the back yard?"

"I don't remember."

"During this period of time did you have a lengthy conversation?"

"Yes."

"Now, Mrs. Farber. Amongst the people that you have talked with is a man named Frank Schaub. Is that right?"

"Yes."

"Did you have a long conversation with him last fall?"

"Yes."

"And did you describe this affair to Frank Schaub?"

"Yes."

"And he is the prosecutor of Sarasota County in Florida?"

"Yes sir."

"Is the statement that you gave to Mr. Schaub an accurate statement?"

"To the best of my knowledge it's accurate."

"Did you tell Mr. Schaub that after Carl's suggestion that you do away with your husband, did you say this: (reading from interview) 'Well, yes. The idea was—as a matter of fact, I remember saying that I would do it because I didn't want him to have any responsibility for this.' "

Keuper's fifteenth objection was that the authenticity of the statement had not been established. But the judge ruled the question was proper. Bailey read the excerpt again, and when she did not recall saying it, he let her examine the document to refresh her memory. He went around to stand close to her left shoulder and hold the document in front of her. Such is his vitality that he emits an almost tangible force at close range, and he seems to be aware of it and to use it as part of his arsenal. She then admitted saying it, when her memory was refreshed. She was uncomfortable in the trap, and he moved back to stand in front of her, and in nine questions he carefully closed his trap, ending with; "Mrs. Farber, as between what you have told the jury about wanting nothing to do with it and what you told Mr. Schaub about wanting to assume the responsibility for murder, could you tell us now what the fact was?"

"Well. Let's see."

"Yes?"

"I see that you have a document here that says that I said that I would do this."

"No! Please answer my question. I want you to now decide and tell this jury whether you adopt the statement that you made earlier today that you wanted nothing to do with this or whether you would like to adopt the statement you made to Mr. Schaub a year ago that you intended to do it and assume the responsibility. Which of those statements is true?''

''Both of them.''

''They're *both* true!?!''

''That's right.''

''You now say you wanted to do the killing to protect Carl?''

''Yes.''

. . . ''So that anything you might have said about not wanting to do the killing then would be in error. Is that right?''

''No. It would not be.''

''You did want and you didn't want to? Both at the same time?''

''That's right. A conflict.'' And in finding exactly that right word, that understandable fragment of parlor psychiatry, she undid a perceptible amount of the damage the Schaub statement had done.

He asked her if she had mentioned the conflict to Mr. Schaub, and she said that though she didn't see it in that paragraph, she felt that she must have said something to that effect. And she said, ''I believe it (the interview) says I was so enamored of the man I would have done anything that he told me to do.''

''Are you telling this jury that you were willing to kill your husband for Carl Coppolino because of your love for Carl Coppolino? . . . Was that your motivation in killing your husband? To please Carl because you were in love with him?''

''I don't recall having any motivation whatsoever except the fact that he told me to do this thing.''

''Why did you insist on assuming the responsibility?''

''I can't give you an honest answer.''

''You can't give me an honest answer?''

''I can't answer that question.''

''You can't answer that question?''

''I was not under my own free will, Mr. Bailey. I cannot—''

And F. Lee Bailey turned to the bench and suggested that it might be a convenient time to adjourn, if the Court please. It was one minute before one o'clock and the court was recessed until two.

Chapter Fifteen

When the recess came, the reporters who had to file by telephone eeled their way through the congestion, heading for the basement press room. There was a curious attitude of exhausted bemusement among all the media representatives.

A twenty-five-year veteran of an untold number of notorious trials said wonderingly, "I have seen them all, and I have never seen a morning like this in any court anywhere. Good God, where do you start? What do you use for a lead? I never took so many notes. My hand is about to fall off, and I've got how many leads I could use? Ten? Thirty?"

The density of the flow of information, the tightly organized factual flood was to a large measure due to the final preparation for the cross-examination which F. Lee Bailey had made the night before.

He had dinner Thursday evening with Mary Coppolino and the investigation team of Andy Tuney and Mrs. Teri Plaut. Though they spent a long time at table, Bailey had only a shrimp cocktail. After dinner he sat in a brooding and thoughtful and lonely silence at a horseshoe bar in Asbury Park, scotch in hand, often with head lowered and eyes closed. Had he attempted the same kind of isolation at the bar at the American Hotel, he would have been badgered by the press and the celebrity seekers. After an hour he stirred as though coming out of sleep and said flatly that he had completed his examination of Marge Farber. The next step was to play back that examination against the pooled information of the group. The trial run began at midnight in Bailey's room at the motel on the outskirts of Freehold, the motel where the "team" was staying.

Present were Mary, Andy and Teri, young Joseph Afflitto the defense attorney from Wayne, New Jersey, a journalist who was doing research for a biography of F. Lee Bailey, and a reporter from Florida who had been covering the indictments since the time of Coppolino's arrest five months previously.

Mr. Bailey positioned himself atop a mirrored bureau, shoes and suit coat off, tie undone, feet planted on a chair, a newly opened bottle of Cutty Sark on the bureau close at hand.

Andy Tuney had the defense file of affidavits and letters and investigation reports. Teri had the transcript of the preliminary hearing in Sarasota in September. Joe Afflitto had the transcript of the bail hearing in Freehold in October. Mary Coppolino and the Florida reporter had their accumulated memories, knowledge and opinions.

For over two hours, F. Lee Bailey, without notes, covered the facts, conflicts, contradictions of the case, anticipating what Mrs. Farber's testimony would be under Keuper's direct examination.

He would pause and point a finger at one person or another for confirmation or contradiction. While they spoke, he would take a small nip from the fifth of scotch. The journalist kept his tape recorder going, taping the entire session. Bailey did not permit any digression from the matter at hand, nor any talk between the members of the team. When any such interruption threatened, he would drop his voice to a lower key, level a cold stare, and say, "Would you let the defense finish its examination of the witness, please?"

At last, after all the facts were recited, corrected, edited, and digested by those in the motel room, an informal session of conjecture and theory began. At one point the Florida reporter found himself with his head hanging over the foot of a bed, with Bailey pressing a pillow down on his face, throat and chest and theorizing that it would be impossible to inflict a double fracture of the cricoid cartilage in this manner. The practice session broke up at about three in the morning, less than seven hours before F. Lee Bailey began his opening statement to the jury. The scotch stood low in the bottle. Bailey was still fresh and alert, showing neither tiredness nor the effect of drink.

On the evening of October 19, 1966, a Wednesday evening, the day before the bail hearing in the Monmouth County Court House, F. Lee Bailey explained one of the reasons for his success . . .

"By the time I am called onto a case, I'm way behind. The prosecution has had months to put their case together, conduct investigations, take affidavits from witnesses.

"They keep working and I start working. But they work the kind of day they're used to. Say they work a forty-hour week at their trade. How much of that is actual work? Three hours a day? Four? So I am working a twenty-hour day and I am driving my people to their maximum effort.

"By the time we get up to the point of a hearing, I am still behind but by not as much. I have closed some of the gap. Then

somewhere between the hearing and the trial, I pass them, and I then know more about the facts of the case and the law than they do. And I keep working at the same pressure, widening the lead.

"Then we come into court, and instead of their handing me a lot of ugly surprises, I have a few for them. They find out they should have asked a few more questions of their witnesses. They find there are some precedents under the law they didn't happen to locate. This business isn't a lot of spellbinding. The biggest part of it is hard work. And the only thing that counts is the evidence, and the defense lawyer had better know it cold before he walks in, or he isn't going to do a job for his client."

During the lunch recess that first Friday of the first trial, Lee Bailey went over the jottings Andy and Teri had made of real and fancied contradictions in the testimony as given on the stand by Marge Farber, and listened to the comments and suggestions and appraisals of Afflitto and Mattice, the New Jersey attorneys for the defense, and checked with Carl Coppolino to see if Carl had caught anything in Marjorie's testimony which could be turned to advantage.

Potential spectators, galvanized by radio and television news coverage of the pungent testimony, headed for the already over-crowded courthouse area.

And the newspaper leads began to take shape:

The New York *Daily News:* "Swearing she was hypnotically entranced, under a strange magnetic spell that drove her into the arms of Dr. Carl Coppolino, a weeping Marjorie Farber twice today stood up in the witness chair to show Carl's jurors how, she said, her husband was strangled to death by her 'jealous' onetime lover as she stood by and watched."

The New York *Times:* "Mrs. Marjorie C. Farber told the jury here today that she had watched Dr. Carl A. Coppolino smother her drugged and unconscious husband."

The Philadelphia *Inquirer:* "Mrs. Marjorie Farber, a smash-ingly attractive blue-eyed brunet, told Friday how a hypnotic, illicit love affair led her to twice attempt to murder her husband and finally to stand by as her lover finished the job, then put a note on the bedroom door to inform her children: 'Daddy is sleeping.' "

There were discussion groups down at the foot of the hill at the American Hotel, formed by those journalists who would not file until the day in court was over. Arguments were settled by flipping notebook pages and locating the quote in dispute.

Waitresses and bartenders hovered nearby, learning what had happened from the fragments of confused argumentation.

How was Lee Bailey doing with her so far?

Five people would give five different answers. It was as if a championship fight had been recessed for an hour after the third round. It was a majority opinion that, in view of the materials she was working with, Mrs. Farber was doing as well as anyone could expect, and possibly better than Bailey had anticipated.

Is she making it all up, or did it happen?

In one discussion group the opinion seemed to be on the side of it being all an invention, by a discarded woman out to nail the doctor, until one man who had been a police beat reporter for many years said, "Now hold it a minute, you guys. Look at it this way. Her story makes it a real sloppy killing. They kept sticking needles in the poor son of a bitch. But it takes a pillow to do it. He has diarrhea and a charleyhorse and he falls off the john, and she doesn't know how he got back in bed, then there's the bit about the cleaner bag and all that does is make him throw up, and then there's that nutty thing about saving the pillowcase he threw up on. Listen, I've covered a lot of killings. And so many times the guy they are trying to knock off, or the woman, is so much tougher than anybody figured. And it keeps turning into some kind of a sick joke, where they kill him and he gets up and runs around and they kill him again and so on until they finally make it. Now I have listened to a lot of frame-ups too. And they are very neat and tidy. And the person trying to lay it on somebody else makes themselves look like an angel. Okay. Play this little game for a while. Bailey is setting it up to prove the old boy died of heart or something. Assume he did. Assume Marge wants to nail the doc. Is it logical she'd come up with diarrhea, laundry bags, wiping blood off his hands, and all those gaps and empty places in her memory? Or would she make it real neat, like maybe Carl sneaking in to give the colonel a shot and her coming home unexpectedly and catching him in the act, and having him confess and having her agree to cover for him when he says that if she doesn't, he'll confess that they planned it all together. Listen, the real ones are pretty often very badly managed. Real sloppy. And in any frameup she wouldn't be making herself look so lousy, like with that sign for the kids. Wow!"

And so that concept was argued back and forth, achieving partisanship from some, derision from others. Reporters searched their notes and brought up bits of testimony which seemed to "prove" one point of view and refute another. There was much discussion of how Bailey would proceed with the balance of his cross-examination, and how well Marge Farber might stand up to it. The adversary system is combat, with a winner and a loser, and somehow it depersonalizes both the defendant and the witnesses. They become gambits to be used or misused by the adversaries. It became much like a press box at half-time, with sports reporters conjecturing as to whether Unitas was being given enough time to get set to throw the long one, and whether in the second half Bart Starr would stay on the ground and protect the Packer lead.

But always the conjecture kept coming back to the basics of motivation, as expressed by the reporter who asked, "So if it *did* happen exactly the way she says it happened, will somebody please explain to me why she's up here in New Jersey with no guarantee of immunity, spilling the whole thing?"

And so it hung in the balance, as it would for the long, hard, driving days, and only the jurors knew what they were believing and what they could not believe.

It was time to go back up the hill. Back to the third floor, Room 308, Judge Elvin R. Simmill presiding, to find that more than two hundred potential spectators were jammed into the corridor, each one hoping to be able to grab one of the less than forty spectator seats available. There was no line, no crowd control. They were tightly compressed, shoving and elbowing each other. They were almost all women, but there were some local attorneys wedged into the throng, trying to look as though they were really no part of it.

The Bill of Rights speaks of an accused man's right to a public trial. Yet it could be argued that insofar as notorious trials are concerned, it is such a special breed of overly avid persons, clawing and cawing for a seat, eager for some soiled quiver of participation that they cannot properly be considered to be the "public." Almost without exception they are the warped ones, functional on a day by day basis, but with a sickness in them.

Among the working press in Freehold, they became known as "Harpies' Bazaar."

The bailiff on the rear door of the courtroom, pipe-smoking Jack Lang was managing to keep a small area around the doorway cleared, and as the press was struggling through the pack, Jack kept instructing the reporters to hold on high their credential letter from Judge Simmill. As is typical of all groups, a few of the press people were too dense or too self-involved to realize that Jack was concerned with having the waiting herd realize he was admitting only those with authorizations. They, the very few, felt that as Jack had come to recognize them and let them in without showing The Letter during the latter part of the jury selection, his sudden insistence on The Letter was some kind of exercise of petty authority.

There was one very savage little old lady in the front rank of the waiting populace, furled umbrella in hand, possibly sharpened, or would have been had she thought of it. She loudly and bitterly resented members of the press being admitted to the reserved press section before the public could get in. She squalled that she was going to write to all the editors, protesting such favoritism. She was a taxpayer. She had a right. Her taxes had helped pay for the courthouse and for the very chairs that were being reserved for these out-of-town parasites. And she made the interesting promise that if she had to kill someone to get into the murder trial, she would do so. A cool, weary and overworked young man from a metropolitan daily paused on his way by this seething and noisy little woman and looked down at her and said, "Lady, I *have* to be here. What's your excuse?"

Somehow the savage old lady seemed to be an almost inevitable counterpoint to the teenage girls who watched Coppolino being hustled into the police wagon to be transported from the jail up the hill to the courthouse and squealed, "Hey! He's pretty cute. I wooden mine hoppin' ina that truck with *him!*" And the old lady was in perfect harmony with the woman in one of the spectator seats—having waited in line since five A.M. that wintry morning—who was overheard saying to her friend, "Gee, I hope Ed got Donny off to school okay."

"I saw it with my very own eyes," is good for many long winter evenings of conversation. But one wonders, considering the hostile avidity of those who made it to a seat, how what they saw and heard compares to what they *think* they saw and heard. When the most objective members of the press corps, and even the attorneys themselves are in dispute over a complex chain of events, it is reasonable to suspect that for each lay spectator, reality was filtered through such an intricate mesh of ignorance, prejudice, and conceit they would be unable—if given the complete trial transcript—to identify that portion they experienced.

Chapter Sixteen

As Marjorie Farber took the stand it seemed reasonable to predict that F. Lee Bailey would not pick up the questioning at that narrative point where it had ended at the lunch break. Marjorie would have had time to play the game of "I should have said . . ." and good tactics would imply denying her the chance to answer once again the same question last asked.

So in his first cluster of eight questions, Bailey established that she had lunched with her attorneys and had talked about the case and her testimony and had been given advice on how to testify. Then he moved to the area of the warning given her by Judge Simmill when she had first been sworn. Keuper objected on the basis that it had taken place before the jury had been brought in, and after a conference at the bench between the two attorneys, Bailey positioned himself once again in front of Marge Farber and asked: "You were advised by the Court that your testimony here today may incriminate you for the crime of murder, or for a crime?"

"Yes."

"Are you aware of that as you sit here and testify?"

"Yes sir."

"You have had the advice of counsel now for some months, have you not?"

"Yes."

"Counsel have also advised you that by giving testimony against Doctor Coppolino, you yourself are incriminated of the charge of murder?"

(state objection overruled)

"Yes."

"And despite this advice you have elected to testify voluntarily against the defendant?"

"Yes."

"Have any promises been made to you that you will not be prosecuted?"

"No."

"When did you first tell anyone, any authorities in New Jersey about this whole affair?"

300

"In June (of this year)."

"Where did that conversation take place, or where did you make any statements about the death of your husband?"

"In Mr. Keuper's office, and in front of the grand jury."

"Have you had any conversation with any representative of the State of New Jersey about whether or not you will be arrested in this matter?"

"No."

In four more brief questions he established that arrest had not been mentioned to her, that she had not asked her counsel to look into the matter, that she was not under arrest, and that nobody had made any move to arrest her since she made the disclosures.

And, properly leaving the curiosity of the jurors unsatisfied in this area, Bailey switched suddenly to questions re-establishing certain points made in the morning testimony regarding the hypnotic power of Carl Coppolino over Marjorie Farber—that it had continued until about the time he had moved from Middletown to Sarasota, and that she had been relieved to be out from under the spell. He then moved to new ground by asking her if she had become aware of having participated in a murder only after the spell had worn off.

"Prior to that time had you had any real awareness of your participation in this murder?"

"I knew what had happened but I could not relate to it as it relates to me sitting right here."

"Well, is it fair to say that you viewed the whole affair like a TV program?"

"Yes. It was like something I had observed. I was like another person observing this whole scene."

"Did you, in your interrogation in Sarasota, which we described this morning, describe the murder of your husband as being like a TV program?"

"Yes, because it is very difficult for me to still relate to everything that I have told you so far today."

"Is it difficult for you to accept the fact that it is real?"

"I accept the fact that it is real, but I cannot—the whole problem is the fact that I was completely—all I can say, I was in a trancelike state when I was with this man, and the relationship was broken off—the hypnosis, and this terrible conflict within me that was me and this other person that was dominated by Carl."

"Where is the other person now, by the way?"

"I'm referring to myself."

"I understand that, but that other person within yourself that Carl used to dominate, what happened to it? Is it still around?"

"It is gone."

"When was the last time you were aware of the other person's presence?"

"When I was with Carl, when I had this constant—"

"No, Mrs. Farber. What is the date that you were last aware of your other half?"

"I can't recall that."

"Was it a year after the death of your husband? Or more? Or less?" After two more questions in which he insisted on her naming a date, she said that it would have been October 1964.

"As of October 1964, and since that time, have you had any confrontation with the other person, the one that Carl would dominate?"

"No."

"So, since October 1964, you have been acting of your own free will?"

"I could say that."

"When you were in the trancelike state, Mrs. Farber, were you able to carry about your normal household chores?"

"Oh, yes."

"Were you able to drive an automobile?"

"Yes."

"And did you visit with friends?"

"Oh yes."

"Can you describe to the jury any of the differences in your conduct that you were aware of, your motions and actions and speech when you were in the trancelike state, as against your normal manner?"

"My interpretation would be that I thought I was behaving normally, but I realize I wasn't."

"Now Mrs. Farber, I want you to answer my question, please. Can you describe anything unusual about your conduct or speech that occurred only when you were in a trance?"

"My conduct with Carl wasn't what I would normally have done."

"I'll try and rephrase that."

"But that is my conduct!"

"Did you walk any differently? Did you walk like a zombie when you were in a trance?"

"No."

"Did you have glassy-eyed stares? Was there *anything* that

somebody would notice about you, or could notice, showing the trance?"

"Well . . . friends would comment about the fact that I seemed different."

"Did they comment about the fact that you seemed to be in a trance, or acting like an automaton?"

". . . It was noticed that there was a definite change in the way I behaved; my attitude was different."

"Your *attitude* was different. Was the attitude the only manifestation of which you were aware of the trancelike state of Carl's influence?"

"As it was told to me by my friends."

"Did Carl use you as an instrumentality for any other crimes after your husband's death?"

"No."

"Did he ever try to get you to kill any other people?"

"No sir."

"He never did? Did he make any plea to you that the two of you run off together?"

"No."

"You said you went to the Cadillac Motel in Miami with Carl?"

"Yes."

"And that fact was known to both your husband and his wife?"

"Yes."

"And approved by them. Right? And you didn't register as Doctor and Mrs. Coppolino down there, did you?"

"No sir."

"And you stayed in separate rooms, didn't you?"

"Yes."

"Now, Mrs. Farber, you said that you were relieved when you finally realized that Carl's hypnotic power had dissipated, and you were your own self again in October of 1964. Where were you living then?"

"Fifty Wallace Road."

"I take it it was your desire not to fall back under the spell of Doctor Coppolino?"

"That is what I would have preferred. Yes."

"By the way, didn't you once tell Mr. Schaub in describing Doctor Coppolino that he seemed to have the powers of a witch?"

"That sounds like something I would say."

"Do you believe in witches?"

"No."

"Will you tell the jury why in the face of your desire to avoid getting into Doctor Coppolino's trancelike spells once again, you went down to Florida to live? Why did you do *that?*"

"Because I had bought property in Florida, and I wanted to go down and live on my property. I am a free agent."

"Which just *happened* to be right next door to the property in which Doctor Carl Coppolino resided?"

"That is true."

"When was the first time after Carl Coppolino left Middletown that you were aware of a desire to go down there and live?"

"I had the desire from the time I bought the property in 1964—January. I returned immediately to here, this area. Carl was with— We went to Florida together."

"You went down and looked at property and both bought lots next door to each other?"

"Yes. And we returned and I put my house immediately on the market to be sold. And the only reason I didn't get down there any sooner is because the house didn't get sold."

"Will you tell me please, in answer to the question that I put to you, when was the first time after Carl left Middletown that you were aware of a desire to go down there and live? Was it immediately when he left Middletown?"

"Regardless of where he had gone, I had—I wanted to go to Florida."

"Had you always had the desire ever since you bought the property?"

"Yes. That was the idea."

"After October 1964—when you popped out of the trance, you hadn't bought any house down there, had you?" This is typical of Bailey's saturnine ability to select exactly the right words to make testimony sound ludicrous and inane.

"No sir."

"Did you make any effort to exchange the property you had bought for some property that wouldn't be right next door to the man who had made you a killer?"

"No. I didn't."

"Weren't you terrified of him, Mrs. Farber?"

"I wasn't interested in him one way or the other."

"My question was: Weren't you terrified of him in view of what he had made you do?"

"Well . . . I can honestly say that I had a fear of him. Yes."

"If you had the fear, why did you go down and build a house

on the lot next to his house, so that you would be living right under his elbow? Was that because of fear that you did that?''

"Do you want me to answer the first question or the second one?''

"Tell me why you built the house there after you realized what he had done?''

"I built the house in Florida after the death of Carmela, because he had told me he was going to remarry. And I could see no reason why I shouldn't build there, because he wasn't going to be next door, and also I had the offer of a job.''

"When did you contract for the building of the house on the lot next to Carl Coppolino? When did you sign the papers?''

"I believe it was October or November of 1965.''

"Prior to that time had you any plan to build there?''

"Ah . . . that had always been my idea, but when I went down to Florida—''

"Had you any plan, definite (house) plan to build there?''

"I had a plan. I had an idea I was going to build there, but I wasn't quite sure.''

"When you arrived in Florida in August 1965 . . . did you look up Carl Coppolino?''

"My daughters and I stayed overnight in their house.''

"You were his *house* guest!?!''

"Well . . . he also had a wife. I was *their* guest.''

"Were you his house guest when you first arrived in Sarasota in August 1965?''

"Yes sir.''

"Did you let him know you were coming?''

"I talked to his wife and she asked us to come and stay overnight.''

"In view of your fear of Doctor Coppolino and his hypnotic powers which caused you to become a murderess, why did you accept the invitation?''

When Keuper objected to the unfair form of the question, Judge Simmill directed Bailey to rephrase it.

"You did tell us that when you injected your husband with a needle and syringe it was because of the hypnotic trance, didn't you?''

"Yes.''

"And that when you went over and made false statements to Carmela in order to make it look like a natural death, that was part of a hypnotic trance. Right?''

"Yes.''

"And that in October of 1964 you found that you were no

305

longer in a trance, and you realized what a bad man Carl was. Is that right? Did you tell us that?''

"I didn't say he was bad, but I was—"

"You realized what you had done?"

"Yes."

"And in your judgment that was a bad thing to do, wasn't it?''

"Uh-huh."

"Now why did you accept Carmela's invitation to go to the very house where the man who had done this to you was?''

"Because she was my friend! And I liked her and she liked me!"

"Did you have any fear that Carl might grab you again and put you back under the trance? Did you think of that? Did you learn from someone he no longer practiced hypnosis, or lost his powers?''

"I didn't know what he was doing!"

"Why weren't you afraid that Carl would put you back under the trance, Mrs. Farber?"

"I just didn't think about it."

He asked again, made her repeat her answer and said, "All right. That's your answer. (and you're stuck with it, lady) Is it fair to say that by the time you got down and received this invitation and accepted it, you had forgotten all about this killing of your husband?''

"I have always been aware of it."

"Were you aware of it, did you remember it the night you walked into Carl Coppolino's house as a guest?"

"No. I wasn't thinking about that."

"You mean you weren't thinking about it, or you had forgotten it?''

"I had been forced to bury it within myself."

"So at that time it was buried within yourself?"

"Yes."

There had been a strangely effective dignity about the manner in which she had spoken of burying it within herself, but F. Lee Bailey with that flexibility and actor's intuition, stepped firmly upon her line by repeating it in an ironic tone which turned it into pure corn.

"And it had been from, you said, July 30th, 1963, until August of '65 buried within yourself?''

"That's right."

"And it had stayed there all the time?"

"Yes."

"Now during this time you had made no move to ask the authorities to prosecute Carl for what you knew to have been murder. Is that right?"

"That is right. I did not."

"You understand that this killing—as you have described it—was murder, didn't you?"

"Yes."

"And you knew what murder was, didn't you?"

"Yes."

"But you didn't dig it up from within yourself and go to the authorities and make your confession back then, did you?"

"No. I didn't."

"Did you still have a romantic interest in Carl Coppolino in August of 1965?"

"No, I didn't."

"Would you say that you felt indifferent toward him?"

"No. I looked on him as a friend."

"You weren't in love with him, were you?"

"No."

"Did you try to take up once again your illicit relationship?"

"No."

"So that after Carl left Middletown, you never slept with him again. Is that right?"

"That is correct."

"Did you ask Carl to take you out or to show you some attention?"

"I didn't see him enough to ask him anything."

"Did you make that request?"

"No."

"That he show you some attention?"

"No."

"Were you interested in somebody else at the time?"

"No, I wasn't."

"How many times did you visit with Carmela and Carl after you arrived and before her death?"

"We arrived on the 23rd of August, which was a Sunday. We being my two daughters, Victoria and Elizabeth, and we stayed overnight and on Monday Carm and I went out to find a place for me to live."

"You say Carm was your friend?"

"Yes."

"Did you ever make an effort to warn her that her husband was a killer?"

"Never."

307

"I see . . . *(This sort of gratuitous comment which serves as a response to the previous answer of the witness and a preface to the next question would be, with many interrogators, merely a conversational tic, an habitual bridge. Bailey, because of his flexibility of voice and nuances of tone and expressive face, can use these bridge-phrases to underline in a memorable way the answers he wishes a jury to note. What did he see? That it is odd not to warn a friend of a danger? Or was there no warning because no danger actually existed?)* . . . Now, Mrs. Farber, just prior to the death of Carmela Coppolino did you encounter the defendant with a woman named Mary Gibson in front of a drugstore, talking?"

"I saw him, Carl, sitting in a car."

Bailey turned and looked toward the row of chairs just inside the rail on the press side of the small spectator section. He asked Mary Coppolino to stand up. She stood until Marjorie identified her as the woman she had seen with Carl, and until the judge told her she could sit down again.

Bailey then went back to the Carl-Marge relationship, establishing that the two little Coppolino daughters played with Marge's children, called her Auntie Marge, and that Marjorie was on friendly terms with Carl that day she encountered Carl and Mary Gibson.

"And you never had gone up to Carl and said 'Carl, that was a terrible thing you made me do in that hypnotic trance'?"

"Of course not."

"Now, on or about the 28th day of August it came to your attention that Carmela Coppolino had died, did it not?"

"Yes."

"On that day you paid a little visit to the Shannon Funeral Home, did you not?"

"I went to see Carm, yes, that night."

"When you went to the funeral home you already knew that Carl had asked somebody other than you to take the children?"

"Yes."

"Didn't you complain about it rather bitterly to Mr. Shannon at the funeral home?"

"I don't recall any of the conversation that Mr. Shannon and I had at that time."

"You went down to see the body?"

"Yes."

"And you told Mr. Shannon that you were upset with Carl because he had let somebody else take the children other than you, didn't you?"

"I don't remember any of the conversation."

"Do you deny making that statement?"

"I did not deny anything. I do not remember any of the conversation."

"So if Mr. Shannon says that is true, you certainly wouldn't dispute it, I take it?"

This can be a most damaging device, as it carries with it the implication that the statement was actually made. Yet the very phrasing of the question "if Mr. Shannon says" makes of it a hypothetical question and entirely proper in cross. Also, it pits the investigation and research of one side against the other. Suppose Keuper had interviewed Shannon and taken an affidavit, and was certain that Marjorie had made no such statement to Shannon. Then he could stand up and object to the question and ask if the defense intends to produce Mr. Shannon. If the defense then says that it will produce Mr. Shannon, the question will be permitted. Should the defense then fail to put Mr. Shannon on the stand, the judge, in his charge to the jury, should point out this failure. In each case where a line of questioning is permitted on the grounds of either side promising to "tie it in" to the chain of evidence, either by producing a witness or a document or promising to ask subsequent questions which will make the relationship clear, it is the responsibility of the judge to make a notation of each such promise by either side and check them off the list as the promises are fulfilled.

Had Keuper sufficient confidence in his witness to be quite certain she had not made that remark to Shannon, he could have risked objecting at that point. But when one is not quite certain, the semi-hypothetical question can be an effective trap, because the objection merely underlines it in the collective memory and attention of the jury, and sworn testimony by Shannon that she *had* made that statement would then have been doubly damaging.

It should be realized that Bailey was in a very significant area here insofar as damaging Marjorie Farber's credibility in the eyes of the jury is concerned. One cannot make it appear that a witness is lying on the stand merely by exaggerating the grotesqueries and inconsistencies within the alleged falsehood. Such an attack must be reinforced by setting up a plausible motive for the lie.

Keuper did not object. She answered Bailey's question by saying, "I certainly don't remember saying anything like that. I would have no reason to." He asked her if she was angry because somebody else had gotten the Coppolino children.

"The only anger I had was the fact that Carl . . . had not gone to see Carm laid out. . . . In her coffin."

This unexpected response was what was called, in the corridors of the courthouse, a brownie point for Marge. She had what was—to Lee Bailey—a disconcerting talent for bouncing back from a low point with sudden information that Bailey did not need or want at that stage, and which came too quickly for him to stop it, and which blurred the jury-effect he was trying to achieve at that point. He had to risk letting her give answers which were to some degree unresponsive, because so many of them contained matters he could put to use. But now and again she would put an unexpected curve on the ball.

"You were angry about that, so you went to see her?" It is possible that Bailey was slightly off balance when he asked this question. It is possible that after he asked it he thought of several others he might have asked to better effect, such as: *What time was it when you left the funeral home? Were they closing up shop, drawing the blinds, turning out the lights? No? Then what made you so certain that Doctor Coppolino would not view his wife's body?*

"I went to see her because I loved that girl!"

"I see. Had you loved her back when you were running around with her husband?"

"That again has to do with this relationship that was forced on me by Carl and the hypnosis. I had a normal friendly relationship with Carl."

Bailey then barked at her, his tone contemptuous. "Did you love her back when you were running around with Carl? Yes or no!"

"I loved her like a sister," Marge said, suddenly tearful.

"All right. When you were down in the funeral home did you criticize the fact that Carl hadn't bought the most expensive coffin? In front of Mr. Shannon?"

"I did make that remark."

"You asked him the price range and whether it was the best they had, didn't you? *Didn't* you?"

"I think I said, 'I'll bet that's the cheapest coffin in the place.' Only because that's what was said when my husband's coffin was bought."

He repeated her statement in the form of a question, then went on to ask: "I take it at that point you were feeling a little hostility toward Carl Coppolino."

310

"I was feeling a *great* deal of hostility at that time."

"And only a few days before, you had felt none?"

"Only because Carm died very suddenly. That's all I was concerned about. Any hostility I had was—"

"Was your hostility increased over the last time you had seen Carl prior to her death? Just yes or no."

"Yes."

"Did you say to Mr. Shannon, 'I'll bet he killed her,' or words to that effect? Did you accuse him then and there?"

Whereupon Mr. Keuper *did* object on the grounds of having the defense represent that they would produce Shannon, and Mr. Bailey promised he would. The judge told Marjorie she could answer. She answered by saying she did not know, whereupon Bailey pressed hard to turn that protective device into a plus for the defense.

"Did you make the accusation? Yes or no."

"As I say, I don't know. I don't know!"

"You don't know!!" Lee Bailey paused, having used his flexible voice and actor's face to indicate astonishment that she would not know whether or not she had made such an accusation at that time. "So you want it left that on the day Mrs. Coppolino died you went down to the mortician and accused Carl of killing her and you don't remember one way or the other? Is that the way you want it left with this jury, Mrs. Farber?"

"I don't believe that I said that."

"But you don't deny saying it."

"I can't imagine why I would say something like that."

Judge Simmill said to her, "The answer is— You don't know. Is that right, ma'am?"

"I don't know."

"All right," said Mr. Bailey.

"Sorry," said Marge.

"Shortly thereafter did you go see somebody and complain that you thought maybe Carl had disposed of Carmela?" At Keuper's objection the Court ruled she could answer yes or no.

"Yes."

Having established that it was Dr. Juliette Karow in Sarasota that she went to, the physician who had signed the death certificate on Carmela, Bailey asked Mrs. Farber if she had told Dr. Karow of her suspicions.

"I told her my story," Marjorie said. One of the most forlorn games any spectator can play in the courtroom is to detect what strikes him as an unfortunate nuance, and then assume that it had the same subtle effect upon the jury. She had lifted her chin and

311

said with a certain rather practiced smugness—I told her My Story—and the way she seemed to add caps gave it a resonance of the slick paper magazines for the housewife market, and the daytime agonies of dramatic television. Were her story completely true, completely fabricated, or composed of varying quantam of truth and invention, the subtle emphasis upon My Story is understandable. By ugly accident or calculated design she had been lifted out of her customary contexts and translated into untold tons of newsprint and gallons of ink. Few can handle a notoriety which has been sought over a period of years and work. How unlikely then, for anyone to suffer instant and rather murky notoriety and retain objectivity about their own social, cultural and psychological dimensions.

Under questioning she stated that on or about October 28 she had told Dr. Karow about New Jersey and the colonel.

"Within a day or two after Carmela Coppolino's death did you say to someone, 'I may be the next Mrs. Coppolino'?"

"Never!"

"Did you say that to Carl's mother?"

"No!"

"You *remember* that you didn't say *that!?*" Bailey used an air of surprise and an ironic emphasis to underline for the jury the fact that after she had said so many times, "I don't know," and "I don't remember," here was one question which elicited a very direct and firm answer, emphatically delivered.

"That is true!"

In twenty-one short, rapid-fire questions Bailey established that Marge Farber had unburdened herself first to Dr. Karow, and then to Dr. Karow's priest. She tried to tell him that she had gone back to Mr. Shannon before going to Dr. Karow, but he blocked her from telling why she had gone to see Shannon again, letting her testify merely that she had not told Shannon her story. She admitted that she knew at that time that Carl's children were being cared for by Mary Gibson, but said the fact did not irritate her. She admitted that she knew in talking to Dr. Karow she was making admissions of a serious crime, knew she was taking a risk in talking to someone she had never seen before and did not know, and gone to her merely because she was the attending physician. But again, on the twenty-first question, Marge irritated Bailey by bringing up that point which perhaps he had kept her from testifying when he blocked her from saying why she had gone back to Mr. Shannon.

"You were convinced of that (that Carmela's death was not a

312

natural death) so you went and tried to get the doctor who signed the death certificate to believe that you were right. Right?''

"I asked her if an autopsy had been performed.''

"Please! I'm talking about your purpose, not your conversation!''

"It was my purpose to find out if an autopsy had been performed.''

"All right. *After* you found that out, what was your purpose in telling her the story about the death of William Farber in Middletown?''

"Because Carl had killed my husband and I was convinced he had killed his wife.''

"So you told Doctor Karow—being the first person in over two years—you told Doctor Karow about this murder story in Middletown in order to persuade her there was grounds to your suspicion about Carmela?''

"I told her the story. Now whether or not it persuaded her—''

"Was that your purpose? Yes or no! Was that your purpose in making this disclosure for the first time?''

"That was the basis on which my suspicions were—''

"No! You told her to persuade her, didn't you?''

"No. I merely told her the story.''

"You only told her? But it was not for the purpose of persuading her that this was not a natural death—meaning Carmela's? You say this was *not* your purpose, do you?''

"The only way I could . . .''

"No, Mrs. Farber. Do you say that that was not your purpose, to persuade her of the validity of your suspicion?''

"I don't know whether I was trying to persuade her or not. I just had to tell her the story.''

"And you don't know now—today—what your purpose was in making this serious disclosure to a perfect stranger?''

"Yes, I know what the purpose was. It was because of Carm's sudden death.''

"And you wanted to convince her? Doctor Karow?''

"Whether I convinced her or not, I wanted to tell the story.''

"You wanted to convince her! Right? You wanted to convince her?''

"If I wanted to convince her I wouldn't have to do anything.''

"Did you *want* to convince her? Will you answer that? Will you give this jury a direct answer?''

"Yes.''

And here Mr. Bailey had performed that useful feat of the skilled questioner, of turning nothing into an impression of something. Witnesses get weary. Having been trapped time and again, sometimes they sense a trap where none exists. Possibly she saw some semantic flavor about the word "persuade" which made her wary. At any rate, she had become wary and careful for no perceptible reason. It was totally obvious to anyone in the court that there could have been no other possible reason for Marge's having told Dr. Karow the New Jersey story other than to cause Dr. Karow to look upon the circumstances of the death of Carmela with some increment of skepticism. The more Bailey insisted, the more stubborn and wary Marge became. Yet because any denial violated common logic, the ultimate "yes" was inevitable. Bailey insisted because her stubborn refusal to admit the obvious made her look as if she was hoping to conceal something, and as if she would be equally devious in all things. Here a certain tirelessness is of vast benefit to the interrogator, if he knows *when* to belabor the obvious.

In a further series of brief questions she stated that she had talked the matter over with counsel, and then gone to see Ross Boyer, the sheriff of Sarasota County where, after the counsel had kept her from incriminating herself, she had discharged him and gone back alone and told the same story to the sheriff. Subsequently she talked with representatives of the Florida prosecution, and told them her story and of her suspicions. She said she had not spoken to anyone from any insurance company, nor had she told her story to Mr. Shannon. She admitted she had been aware of the risk involved to herself, and had assumed the risk in order to encourage investigation into the death of Carmela Coppolino. She further admitted that she had been advised by both Mr. Goodrich and Mr. Chamlin, her attorneys, that there was no way to provide her with immunity in the case.

"Do you have any idea, Mrs. Farber, when you leave this courthouse or when you finish your testimony whether or not you are going to be prosecuted for murder?"

"No. I have no idea."

Lowering his voice, Lee Bailey leaned close to her and with what one of the female reporters called his pussycat smile, he asked her, "Well, did you bother to ask anyone?" For the second time in a few minutes Keuper informed Bailey that he couldn't hear him. Bailey asked the question again, and she said she hadn't asked anyone. He pursued the point, wording it in such a way that the jury might think it odd that she had not asked about what might happen to her. He asked her if she expected to be brought to trial, and she said she didn't know, before Keuper could get his objection in. The objection was sustained.

Bailey shifted quickly to the circumstances of Carl's marriage

314

to Mary Gibson. Marjorie said she wasn't angry or upset about it, that Carl had told her he was going to marry Mary. By questions he underlined the date of Carl's marriage as October 7, and the date Marjorie had gone to Dr. Karow as October 28, three weeks later.

"Is it fair to say that the marriage provoked your efforts to get Carl in trouble?"

"No. It's not fair to say that at all!"

"Oh? Had you been doing quite a bit of thinking about this whole matter before you went ahead and disclosed it to Doctor Karow?"

"Yes. I had."

"But something caused you to wait from August 28th when you first had the suspicion, you say, until October 28th. Why didn't you go to Doctor Karow the first day?"

"Because I was in a terrible state of shock."

"Not too bad a state of shock to suggest that the casket picked out by Carl was a cheap one. You weren't too shocked for that, were you?"

"I'm inclined to be a little bit sarcastic at times. It was a bitter remark. Yes."

Then F. Lee Bailey, because it was a key point in the defense case, took the calculated risk of asking another "why" question:

"Now, Mrs. Farber, will you explain to the jury why you have come, not knowing what the consequences are that may await you, to tesitfy against Carl Coppolino? Why you were willing to take this risk to testify against this man on trial for his life, voluntarily and without promise of leniency? Tell them, please. Tell the jury."

"Because, based on my suspicions of Carmela's death, the knowledge of my own husband's death, I felt that this man might possibly kill his present wife. And I wanted to stop him. That is the whole reason and nothing more."

"So, you are here today to protect the present Mary Coppolino? Is that right?"

"Maybe myself. I don't know."

"Carl never made any move against you even after he found out you were making these accusations, did he? Did he?"

"No."

"Never threatened you? Or came over and told you to shut up, or anything else, did he?"

"I don't know whether or not he was aware of what was going on."

"You set up a phone call with the authorities tapped on the line where you accused Carl of murder, did you not?"

"I didn't accuse him of murder."

"Didn't you say in December of 1965, 'Carl, I think you killed your wife,' on the telephone where it was being tape recorded?"

"I don't recall if I said those words."

"Didn't you say, 'Carl, what will we do if they dig up Bill's body?' "

"That sounds familiar."

"It was taped by the authorities. You made a prior arrangement to trap Carl, didn't you?"

"Yes."

"Your purpose was to get him to say something."

"That's right."

"You had no talk with him about this from the date of Carmela's death or, in fact, at any time prior to the time you made your call without warning. Isn't that true?"

"That's right."

"You did in that conversation, which was taped, accuse him of murdering his wife, didn't you?"

"I don't recall making an accusation."

"Did you suggest it? Did you suggest it?"

"I think what I said was I wonder if they would find out about Bill."

" 'What will we do if they dig up Bill?' "

"I don't remember if I said dig up, but it had something to do with Bill."

"His response to you was, 'What do I care if they dig up Bill?' And that is on the tape?"

"If you say so."

"He didn't say anything indicating he really gave a damn about Bill, did he? He didn't indicate that would worry him in any way, did he?"

. . . "I said, 'We have a common bond in Bill,' or words to that effect, and he said that he agreed."

"*What* did he say? (incredulity) You are representing *this* is the conversation you had that was taped by the authorities?"

"As close as I can remember."

"What did he say about the fact that you feared the exhumation of Bill's body? Didn't he say it couldn't matter at all to him? That he didn't care if they dug up the body?"

"I don't honestly remember."

316

"You don't deny that he said that? But you can't remember?"

"It is possible that he said it."

"Your purpose in cooperating with these authorities was to assist them in getting a case against Carl, wasn't it? Because you wanted him prosecuted, didn't you?"

"I would like to see justice done, whatever it is."

"You want to see *justice* done?"

"Whatever it is."

"Is *that* your purpose in coming here today to tell the truth to this jury? For the purpose of justice? Is *that* why you are here?"

"I am here to tell the truth."

"Yes, I understand that. (poisonously sarcastic) Is it for justice that you are here, Mrs. Farber?"

"—Yes."

"Why do you hesitate?"

"Yes!"

"Then it isn't to protect Mary Coppolino primarily, but for justice as a citizen that you come here today with your story? Is that right?"

"Both."

"Both?!? When did your sense of justice first begin to cause you to want to disclose the crime in which you had participated?"

(objection sustained, with request to rephrase)

"When you broke out of the trance in October 1964 and realized that you had been used by Carl to commit a murder, did you feel that you wanted justice to be done then, even if you had to admit to it?"

"He had threatened me if I ever—"

"Please, Mrs. Farber! Did you have a feeling that you wanted justice to be done in October when you regained your own free will?"

"I would have liked to have had it done, but I didn't know what to do."

"It didn't occur to you to go down to the police—"

"I didn't know what to do."

"Do you know where the police station was in Middletown?"

"When a man has threatened you, what do you do?"

"Did you know where the police station was, Mrs. Farber?"

"Offhand I couldn't tell you. I could find it if I wanted to, I am sure."

"You didn't try to find it, did you?"

"No."

Bailey then established that Marge's relationship with Carl had been friendly in October 1964, and on up to the time when the Coppolinos had moved to Florida in April, and that it was Carl's habit to phone her once a week from Florida.

"The man threatened you and you continued to socialize with him?"

"If you'd let me say what he said to me!"

"You have told us that he threatened you, but I understand you continued to have friendly conversations and socialize. Is that true?"

"Yes."

Sometimes, as with the next question, Bailey would ask his question in a gentle, troubled, questing manner, as though genuinely concerned about the witness and her problems. "Why did you feel any friendly inclinations to a man who had caused you to participate in a heinous crime, and then threatened you? Why did you do that?"

"Fear."

"Fear? Okay. The same fear that failed to inhibit you from staying in his house the first night you got to Florida? Is that right?" And having asked a question that defied any answer, he hurried on to ask: "Mrs. Farber, did you, other than going to Doctor Karow and the priest and the authorities to cause an investigation into this murder, did you make some effort to influence people to interfere in Carl's life, not connected with the investigation?"

"I don't know how you mean that."

He had glanced at the clock before swerving to a new direction It was seven minutes before three, the usual recess time.

"I'll make it more specific. You knew Carl was a doctor licensed to practice in New Jersey, and inactive because of a heart condition, didn't you?"

"Yes."

"You knew that he intended to take the medical exam down in Florida, didn't you?"

"I had heard about it."

"You wrote a letter to a man named Richard Del Torto and said, 'See if you can use your influence to prevent him from getting a license down here'?"

(objection overruled)

"Yes, I did."

The typewritten letter is reproduced at this point to illustrate how Bailey used it in cross-examination:

* * *

318

Dear Dick, et al:

Your letter was so well put, and I know how you felt, trying to write in answer to the information I had given you. Now, I am going to really tell you my innermost thoughts re Carl and how to assist in the possible defeating of him right now. He is slated to go to Las Vegas in November to be on a panel, in his capacity as an "expert" in the field of Hypnosis, relating to Anesthesiology. If you have any *pull* with the powers that be, in your Co. I'd do everything to see that he's asked *NOT* to Come, not needed, a replacement has been made. Also, he is planning to take the Florida State Med. exam in Nov. also, to be able to practice here. I understand that *politics* play quite a part in who gets the ticket and who does NOT. I do not have to spell it any clearer, do I? It would be such a blow to that terrible *Ego* of his, first, rejection by the panel, and then the Medical Board here. He plans to practice Hypnosis. I think that it would be the most dangerous weapon ever allowed if he is turned loose on an innocent public. He has no scruples whatsoever, about hurting, harming or steamrolling anyone, including his own parents, as well as his wife, in the past. As for friends, do you know you are the only one, but perhaps Tom Daniels (and that nothing to speak of) and an occasional visit from Doctor Ed Webb, (he worked with Carl in Brooklyn on the team under Doctor Wallace) that I know of. He just does not have any friends, and his attitude toward me makes me realize that he is a most peculiar person. Even the neighbors here in Florida have no respect for him now. All this I've gotten through casual chats. Talk about being 'hoist by one's petard' he has done it.

If he can pull a snow job on the people here, I will be muchly surprised. He cannot live in a vacuum too long, and his bride will begin to be aware of the collosel (sp) error she has made. He feels that his intellect is so far above anyone else's he cannot tolerate the average "stupid" person. It pleased him to have me a slave to practically his every whim. I realize how much time and effort I had given to him in N.J. So, when they moved, I naturally, was lonesome, but I also felt relieved, that I could live my OWN life, for a change. In my letters to him, I told him so, in no uncertain terms, but that if and when I ever got to Florida I had to live my own life. The reaction was first of awful sorrow, then of indifference; this is friendship? Plus a letter saying he was losing his mind, and needed help. He also wrote the same to his sister, his mother told me so when she was here. Well, you know how I feel about it, I think he has really flipped, if his actions of the past re: Carm, his marriage so soon, means anything. He can operate at a certain level, but the moral sense is gone. There are one or two things he said to me that indicate he was not himself, although one would think so, if you didn't know him well. And the inability to tell me that he was going to be married the date, and so forth (I had to quiz him) indicates a strong sense of guilt. He hadn't even made a change of address, when he moved into Mary's house, unless the P.O. made an error. A Special Delivery came to the so-called good friend across the street Earl Norcross who called me to ask if I knew where Carl could be located. The Special is the copy of his new book, The Billion Dollar Hangover, which Carm practically did for him with the help of

319

Hoffman and LaRoche's library, secretaries, mimeograph machines and so forth paper postage. . . .

I told him he was not a writer, he was a brain picker, at one time. He took a lot from me, for some reason, even here. I asked him some very pointed questions and also told him to his face he needed help. He agreed with me, too. I also told him to make haste slowly, we know what he did about that. Carm's father and mother wanted to come down to help out, instead of going on their world's cruise, Carl told them to go. Then he said that her father was not interested in coming here. I know this only because he Dr. Musetto wrote to me, answering my letter of sympathy. He Carl also said her father had suggested some ladies he Carl might be interested in meeting later on. Her father is so grief stricken, I know that Carl had to be lying about that. I don't believe that Doctor Musetto, from the words he used, to me, could possibly say what Carl indicated. If the doctor and his wife had come here, instead of going to Europe, Carl would certainly have to curtail the quick marriage plan, wouldn't he?

"Divorce, Italian style" is the thinking I have had. Not a wholesome form of thought, I agree. But what would you think when all of his actions before, during and since Carm's death indicate almost a plan? So, now you understand why I have been so upset and full of anger. If I had any power to stop him, as the director of your Co. might have, plus the whispering campaign that goes over the country via medical circles, I would be right in there pitching, and you know it. I know the reason they had any friends at all was because of Carm. He didn't want anyone to come to their home most of the time, and he made it very difficult for her. You were the exception, the balance was the family, and then Carm had to almost plead with him to get his permission. He was always the magnanimous husband, allowing Carm to have people in. She was more than a dutiful wife, I must say. Plus knocking herself out to make him comfortable, her tolerance and understanding were more than I have seen anywhere, and will never see again. I wonder how Mary will measure up when the glow has worn off this flash-in-the-pan romance? Carl had said to me that perhaps he will walk out on her some day, or maybe something will come of it. This was said, I think, for me to think that he was only doing this for the sake of the children. He has forgotten to whom he spoke. He has yet to do anything that was not for his OWN benefit, and I know it. He wants Mary and he has got her. I wonder what the fates will do next.

I hope you will think about what I have said, and in the area of defeat: re Carl, give it serious thought, or do you feel that it is not for us to decide these things? I am thinking of the apathy that goes on in our cities when someone is raped, murdered, or harmed in some way, and people answer, when asked why they didn't do something, "I didn't want to get involved." Well, this is one time I get involved up to my ears, if I thought it would stop a madman on the loose. And I have to think of not only myself, but my children, and the families included. There are many ripples in the pond, when the stone is dropped. Does anyone care enough to do something?

I feel as you do, Carl doesn't exist, but Carm did, and now is gone. I want to know *why* she is not here. I have a deep conviction that my feelings in this matter are right. I do not believe she was supposed to die when she did, it was not her true destiny, it was interfered with by a destructive force. I won't say more.

> Well? (handwritten in red ink)
> Love MARGE

". . . When did you write this letter? Do you recall?"

"Shortly after Carmela's death."

"You tell us still that you didn't have great feelings of hostility toward Carl at this point?" (objection, repetitious, overruled) "You hadn't made your statement to Doctor Karow at this time, had you?"

"No."

"But you did want Mr. Del Torto to ruin Carl's chances for becoming a doctor, and you wrote him making that request, didn't you?"

"Yes, I did."

Bailey turned to Judge Simmill and asked if he might have the letter, inasmuch as it was part of the court's file. It is probable that Bailey knew the letter would be in the office of the Clerk of the Court rather than in the judge's possession at the bench, and asked for it merely as a device to further rattle Marjorie Farber. When Judge Simmill said he did not have it with him, Bailey said he did not need it at that moment.

"At some time you found out that Carl was invited to lecture at the American Institute of Hypnosis in Las Vegas in October, didn't you?"

"Yes. I knew that."

"You learned of the impending marriage and his intent to take a honeymoon in Las Vegas when he was there to give his lecture? Did you know about that?"

"No, I didn't. I knew he was going to get married, but I didn't know where he was going."

"You knew the convention in October was to take place very shortly after his marriage, didn't you?"

"I didn't jump to any conclusions about what he was going to do."

"Did you write a letter to Mr. Del Torto asking him to see if he could find out who was running this seminar and get Carl's invitation revoked?"

"Yes, I did."

"Why did you do that, Mrs. Farber?"

Again it was a "why" question, and once again she turned it back upon him by saying, "The same answer I gave you in Florida."

The semanticists speak of "trigger words" and "trigger phrases" as being those components of conversation which tend to stifle communication by shunting the attention of the listener off into some divergent path, into some subjective imagery triggered by the word or phrase. In that same sense, her reply was inadvertently a trigger which could have, and probably did, blur jury attention. Until that point the jurors had not the slightest clue that Bailey and Marjorie Farber had ever been in confrontation before. So perhaps they wondered how it had happened, how it had come out, what was said. Did these two know each other better than it appeared?

"I am asking you why."

"I didn't trust him. I don't trust him."

"You learned that he was an invited speaker. You took it upon yourself to write and get Mr. Del Torto to prevent him from speaking to a bunch of doctors because you didn't trust Carl. Is that your answer?"

"Yes. It had to do more with his getting a license than the speech."

"But you say you did this because you didn't trust Carl?"

"Yes, that is very true."

"Do you tell this jury that you did not do it because you wanted to get him in any way you could? Was that your purpose?"

"I didn't trust him."

"Did you want to hurt him professionally?"

(objection, repetitious, overruled)

"Yes."

"You *did* want to hurt him professionally?"

"I didn't want to see him get his license because I didn't trust him as a physician."

"You didn't want to see him speak to a group of physicians because you didn't trust him?"

"Yes."

"You were worried about what he might do to the physicians?"

"Not necessarily. The first point is the most important one. About getting his license."

"The second one I am questioning you about. And the jury will decide what is most important. Now, tell me who you were protecting with your mistrust when you tried to cancel the speech to the doctors in Las Vegas?"

(objection, immaterial, overruled)

"No. I just said it in the letter. I don't . . . But it had to do with not trusting him in any area. I had no idea about his—"

"When you said it in the letter, did you want Mr. Del Torto to act on it and take steps to cancel that speaking appearance?"

"Yes."

"Because of mistrust?"

"Yes."

It was three o'clock.

Mr. Bailey asked of the judge, "Is it appropriate to recess now?"

"If it won't interrupt your train of thought, it is *very* appropriate."

In his dry emphasis on "very," Judge Simmill was most probably paying a weary tribute to the density of the cross-examination, the huge quantity of question and answer covered in so short a time. It did not seem possible that she had been under cross-examination for only two hours and thirteen minutes thus far. One hundred and thirty-three minutes which, in the official transcription, require one hundred and twenty-two type-written pages.

Cross-examinations as intensive are very rare, as under the adversary system there is usually a consistent effort on the part of the other side to keep breaking the tempo to protect the witness. This is done through objections, through raising points of law, through requesting conferences at the bench.

For all those in the court required to follow it, it was an emotionally debilitating experience. How much more wearing it must have been to be a participant.

In the corridor one reporter, unfamiliar with the strategies of examination, said irritably, "Why does he keep hopping around so? When he gets onto one thing, why doesn't he finish it? I tell you, he's driving me nuts."

Any complete answer to that question would probably have to have several parts. For one, Bailey had to be absolutely confident that, in those matters to which he intended to return, his memory would be superior to hers. Regarding a single episode, the witness is not likely to contradict herself while the questions are directed at that single segment of the past. But if a hundred questions on other matters are answered before the cross-examination returns to pick up that episode, her chance of remembering precisely what she had said was less than his, as his was the advantage of knowing just what he was after.

Other matters were dropped because he sensed that by pursuing them further he could gain no advantage. He would not return to those. Others were dropped when he took the chain of events to precisely that point where he could harvest the maximum advantage, and where by leaving them, never to return, before giving her a chance for the explanations she felt she should be entitled to make, he made her feel frustrated and angry.

By hopping back and forth in time and space he prevented her from ever bracing herself for the next area of inquiry.

By dropping certain lines of questioning, he gave her cause to worry about how much he did know and how much he didn't know.

And, finally, it would be puerile to think of the cross-examination as a search for truth. It is the function of the cross-examination to destroy the credibility of a witness for the other side. This is very rarely accomplished by the pursuit of fact, but is a process of using all the tricks and persuasions to achieve certain emotional effects. Demonstrably, we all tend to come up with an emotional reaction, and then build a structure of logic to support our decision, so that we can tell ourselves we are sober, thoughtful, intelligent, unbiased people. And when we sit upon a jury, we do not suddenly become what we want to believe ourselves to be.

Chapter Seventeen

F. L. Bailey began the very short, but appropriately explosive final segment of the day's cross-examination, by introducing and having Marjorie Farber identify Defense Exhibits 1, 2, and 3.

D.E. 1 was her letter to Del Torto dated October 9, 1965. It was four typewritten sheets. D.E. 2 was another letter from her to Del Torto dated October 17, 1965. D.E. 3 was a handwritten letter dated August 31, 1965, on two yellow sheets, from Marge to a person not immediately identified.

He then began questioning her about the morning of Carmela's death, establishing that she had gone over there, had been on friendly terms with Carl, and had even picked out the clothing in which Carmela was to be buried. She denied that Carl had told her he didn't want to see her any more, or to stay away from him.

"That never was said?"

"No."

"He never said to you, 'Marge, don't bother me'?"

"Not that I remember. No."

"Do you know Louise Dennis?"

"Oh yes."

"Did you write her a letter a couple of days after Carmela died?" (Exhibit D-3)

"Yes, I did."

"Did you write to Louise Dennis in that letter that Carl had said to you, 'Don't bother me'?"

Marge looked both uncomfortable and annoyed. "If it is in the letter I must have said it. He must have said it to me."

"A moment ago I believe you said that wasn't said."

"I didn't recall his saying it."

"Did that refresh your recollection when I reminded you of the letter to Louise Dennis?"

"Yes, if that is what he said to me. If I wrote it, it has to be true."

"You say you don't remember at this time whether you wrote it?"

"I don't remember right this minute. That's right."

"I wonder if you would read through that and see if that refreshes your recollection."

"Just this page?"

"I just want you to read it to yourself to refresh your recollection. You read it as rapidly as you see fit."

He again moved in close to her and behind her, behind her left shoulder, adding the tangible persuasion of his physical presence at close range to the effect he hoped to get from the potentially damaging statement in the letter.

Soon he said, "Have you read enough to remember the letter that you wrote now? Does it come back to you that you wrote Louise Dennis a letter on August 31st, 1965?"

"This is quite obvious that I wrote a letter, but I cannot remember everything that is in this letter unless I read the whole thing." She handled it with more calm and poise than one might expect.

"You *do* recognize it?"

"Oh yes."

Keuper stood up and said, "If Your Honor please, he asked the witness to read it, and I think she should be able to read it."

Bailey explained to the Court, "For the purpose of determining if it is her letter, and refreshing her recollection as to the writing of the letter."

Judge Simmill said, "And as to a statement made in the letter."

"Yes," said Mr. Bailey, and still close to Marge said, "Look at the top of the third page of that letter and reading down six lines, I ask you whether or not you wrote Louise Dennis, 'He asked me not to bother him,' underlining the word 'bother'?"

"That's right."

He took the letter from her and moved back to face her once more at close range. There is a possibility that Keuper might have been successful in forcing the entire letter to be read aloud to the jury. But at the time the letter was introduced, Mr. Keuper, sitting at the state table had read it carefully and thoroughly.

Doubtless, as he read it, he was attempting to estimate what the effect of the whole letter might be on the jury. Bailey had had it marked for identification, but not introduced as evidence. Much later, after all the testimony was in, Bailey had it introduced as evidence, but Keuper had no way of knowing at that time whether he would or not.

One might guess that he was afraid the reference in the letter to Alcoholics Anonymous might have a bad effect.

Here is the entire letter which the jury took into the jury room with the other items of evidence:

Tuesday Aug 31, 1965

Dear Louise [Dennis]

I hate to have to write to you with such awful news. Perhaps you know already, but Carm died in her sleep sometime Saturday a.m.

I cannot believe it. She seemed okay. We stayed with them on Sunday a week ago and although she was rather tired looking, she certainly didn't seem about ready to go but who are we to know anything.

The one thing that has me very disturbed is Carl's attitude. You'd never know that we'd been such close friends— His health most certainly seems better— He took up duplicate bridge recently & the week we've been here since last Saturday night (We got there on Sunday) he had been out until twelve, one & two o'clock *every* night & gone most of each day.

According to Carm, when I commented on it, she said he seemed to thrive on it, & if it made him happy, so what! So—I minded my own business.

Even knowing we were arriving on Sunday didn't keep him home—he got at home at 2 am he said when I saw him Monday at breakfast— Anyway, he was most friendly and cordial but left for his bridge lesson & we saw him at dinner— In the meantime Carm and I went looking for a completely furnished apartment where we have been since Monday night.

It is very pleasant—faces the Gulf of Mexico & there is a pool in

326

back— I've been so upset first with the attitude of Carl and then her death— Coronary occlusion was diagnosed by two m.d.'s— Carl asked for an autopsy, but doctor didn't seem to think it necessary, that I am really fighting by the hour not to go to pieces.

He has children at some ladyfriend's home (a divorcee) for the time being— I could have stayed at his house, during day, but I guess he wanted them out of house. So that is that— She and I have met once and she is an Alabama gal—has two girls 17 and 14—and lives miles from this area—ten or twelve—so-so in appearance—only saw her in her car—

Monica and Elizabeth were so glad to see each other and now I don't know what Carl is going to do about everything— He suggested I buy his house, as he could move to a smaller place— I said all he needed was another Dorothy (maid) and to stay put—why move—such a mess etc . . . and their place is so nicely arranged. He said he had no morbid feeling about it so I suggested the above. He wants to stay in this area anyway? I think he is very mixed up in many areas and I hope he will snap out of it.

No one but the girls and I went to see Carm laid out— She looked lovely, if one can use such a term— She was sent to her home Boonton, N.J. after her father INSISTED— Carl wanted her buried here and *NO* families—but she is where she should be— He did NOT go to see her laid out, nor is he going to funeral.

I found out about Carm by calling up there Saturday a.m.— He hadn't called me and I wonder if he would have? Louise, you'd not know Carl in his *attitude* toward me— I had to beg him to let me come out there on last Saturday morning. I realize he realized he was thoroughly confused as he finally said please come—

I picked out the things she wore—and then left after a few hours— He is staying at a neighbors across the street and that is the last time I've seen him. He did call me re: his house though—he asked me not to *bother* him.

Well, I certainly am not, but I feel there is something radically wrong with him (mentally). Shock, I suppose—but he had his wedding ring off— Guess he figured the marriage was ended—but I am surprised he thought to do it! He always wore it in N.J. and had it off a few days before all this happened. I made a remark about it— He had come to get Monica who was here with Elizabeth for the day last Friday & he said "It interferred with playing cards"??? I just don't get it and probably will never understand.

In spite of all this tragic situation I feel I will get into the swing of things soon—an awful lot has happened in one week week. It was enough to make me want to throw everything into the car and get out of here fast, to N.J. or some sane place. It all seems crazy at this point. But I must continue to fight my own battle with my own strength—after all—I don't have to leave here just because of him— He is just one, or another pebble on the beach.

I think his mother's coming down after the funeral but he was very vague about that too.

Thank God for A.A. It is very good here and
I've gone to three meetings.

But I tell you I am very curious to see what will transpire within the next few months, or years! With those two little girls he'll no doubt find himself a wife to help out! I'm wondering about this divorcee? He just met her through playing duplicate bridge and what info I can get out of her is that she doesn't really know him very well— BUT that is where the two children are— He told his neighbors he didn't ask me as I didn't have enough room—which is certainly true enough— and I guess he felt it would be better for girls to be away for awhile— So that makes sense, I guess.

Please write and tell me your doings— I hope yours is a nice, placid, normal, quiet life— Brother, if I ever say again my life is dull, I'll be coo-coo!

I have an interview tomorrow with the head of ARVIDA, a thirteen million dollar real estate outfit— And if I am sponsored by him for the exam I'll feel more secure. I can't take exam for six months, to be legal resident— Then I want to get a house to rent! This is a one bedroom and twin beds— Girls are in there & I sleep on what they call a Bahama bed—very comfortable and smart looking, in living room.— Everything is furnished even to soap and toiler paper— Nice little kit. and we eat at table in din room— Which looks over the Gulf of Mexico— Sunsets are gorgeous and the water so ever-changing—

I was up early today & in pool at seven a.m.—and across in Gulf later— I fell asleep on the beach and the old Col. in next apartment came over and woke me up— He took me out to dinner last night (a well-preserved seventy I think) and he helped me a great deal and he told me a great deal and he told me about his coming marriage— Apparently there are men available here but I am taking one thing at a time.

Love & do write,
MARGE

It is equally obvious that had there been anything in the letter to Louise Dennis which would be specifically useful to the prosecution, Bailey would never have used it to drive home the point that Carl had, indeed, told Marge not to bother him. He made certain the point was not missed.

"Did Carl tell you not to bother him, Mrs. Farber?"

"The answer is yes, because it is in the letter."

"You mean, if it weren't in the letter, you would say no?"

"No. I wouldn't have remembered it until you showed it to me."

"But you now remember it?"

"Yes."

"You wrote that because he had said in fact to you within forty-eight hours of his wife's death, 'Don't bother me.' Had you been bothering him?"

"I don't remember bothering him, but apparently I was or he wouldn't have said it."

"A great deal of that letter, of course, is about Carl, isn't it? Do you remember that?"

"And Carmela's death."

"Yes. And your concern and so forth?"

"Yes."

"You said that Carl had been unpleasant? Or acting strange?"

"Yes, he was."

"And you felt that he was because he was in shock over the death of his wife. Didn't you write that?"

"I didn't read that far."

When he asked her again if she wrote that in the letter, Keuper again submitted to the Court that she should be allowed to read the letter. Judge Simmill ruled that if she could not remember without reading the letter, she could read it, and if she could remember without it, then she need not.

Without handing her the letter, Bailey questioned her again, and she admitted writing to Louise Dennis that she had thought Carl was acting strangely because he was in shock over the death of his wife, and then he switched abruptly to ask her the date of her marriage to William Farber. She replied February 1, 1947, without hesitation. He asked if prior to that time she had been of the Catholic faith. She said she had been, as Keuper objected on the grounds of materiality. Bailey asked to approach the bench and make an offer of proof. The conference at the bench did not last thirty seconds. The judge permitted that line of questioning, and over two objections by Keuper on grounds of materiality, both overruled, Bailey established that she had not been a practicing Catholic during her marriage, that after the colonel's death she had discussed going back into the faith with Carl, and that he had encouraged her to do so, and together they had gone by car to New York City in the spring of 1964, to the church of St. Francis of Assisi, where they both went to confession. She admitted that her reason for going to the confessional was to be readmitted to the Church.

Then Bailey came to the point which doubtless had caused the judge to rule that he could pursue that line of questioning.

"Did you do anything about making Carl the godfather of your children?"

(objection on materiality overruled)

"Yes."

And Carmela had become the godmother, of the two Farber daughters age sixteen and ten at that time. Then Bailey asked her if she had been sincere, or had she gone through the process because Carl had suggested it.

(objection on materiality sustained)

"At the time you asked Carl to become the godfather of your

children, and he accepted and did become the godfather, did you still remember the killing of your husband by Carl Coppolino?" (objection—immaterial—overruled)

"No. I did not think about it."

"I asked you if you had forgotten how you *say* your husband died, when you asked him to become godfather, and made him the godfather of your children."

"I have never forgotten how my husband died."

"You knew it at that time?"

"I knew it at that time."

"And, notwithstanding the fact that you *say* he killed your husband, you made him the godfather of your children?"

"I was still under his influence."

It seemed at that moment that F. Lee Bailey would have been better off to have stopped that line of questioning just short of his last question. He had exposed an emotional inconsistency which one could assume the jurors would have difficulty equating. The nightmare scene of injections, blood, laundry bag, vomit and smothering did not seem to fit a couple who, eight months later, were in the hushed sacramental world of incense and obligation, candles and confessional, the sign of the cross, the murmured sins, and the symbolic and emotional entrusting of one's children to the fellow assassin and the betrayed wife. We require bad to remain bad, good to remain good, the black hats forever in place, the white hats denoting an unchanging virtue.

It seemed for a moment that had he left it sooner, the woman would have been forever damned as liar through such an inconsistency the jurors could have balanced the two images in no other way. But Bailey was in pursuit of another kind of inconsistency, and it is impossible to say whether it was more or less effective than the one already achieved.

"Was this because of the trance that you did this, Mrs. Farber?"

"Yes sir."

"Well, since you escaped this trance later that year, I believe it was October, did you take any steps to change your status with respect to the Church, after the influence was gone?"

"I have continued to be a Roman Catholic."

"And is it fair to say that the re-entry by you into the Catholic faith wasn't part of the trance activity? Wasn't that of your own free will?"

"I went back to the Church of my own free will. I had thought about it before I had ever met Carl Coppolino."

"This was something you wanted to do?"

"This was something I wanted to do."

"And, causing him to become the godfather of your children was, I take it, from the hypnotic powers of Carl Coppolino?"

"Yes."

"Well, can you tell us how it was that you were able to make decisions on one matter, and then were compelled to make decisions by Carl on another? Did this free will come and go every now and then?"

He would not, of course, accept her insistence that she had prayed for guidance, and said, "Mrs. Farber, I am not interested in your prayers."

"That is the only way I can answer it."

"My question is this, and I ask you to answer it: You have told this jury that you were in a trance for more than a year and you couldn't control what you did, and you were under Carl's influence. Now I want you to determine whether or not from time to time during the trance period you would find yourself in control of your own faculties and be able to make decisions of your own."

Keuper objected on the grounds that there was no testimony presented that she had been under a trance as to everything she did, and was overruled.

"I was able to make decisions, yes."

"What percentage of the time, let's say in the summer of 1963, were you able to make decisions on your own, and what percentage of the time were you in a trance subject to Carl's mystic powers?"

"I suppose picking up groceries or something like that. I mean, this is—"

"Tell the jury the kind of things you could do of your own free will and make decisions about, and the kind of things Carl influenced."

"Just normal everyday living as far as being a housewife— which I was."

"I know two things you have told us. One: The murder of the colonel and getting Carmela to cover up your story. And the other accepting Carl as godfather to your children. Did he raise the idea that he be godfather and ask or did you suggest it first?"

"Both Carl and Carmela were the godparents of my children who were converted to Catholicism."

"Was that at their request or at yours?"

"I believe I asked them."

"But you say you asked them because of Carl's trancelike powers?"

"I am since sorry that Carl's name is on the certificate."

"Yes. (total ironic agreement) I daresay. I am asking you whether or not that decision to ask Carl was induced by his trancelike mystic hypnotic power?" (description of the power becoming more derisive)

"I don't believe so."

"Didn't you tell us a little while ago that the only reason you made the man you say killed your husband, the godfather of your children was because you were compelled to do so because of the trance? Didn't you just tell the jury that?"

"If I said it, I certainly didn't mean it the way that you have interpreted it."

"You say now that the decision was made of your own free will?"

"At this point I don't know. All I know is that they were godparents of my children."

"And you are unable to tell us now whether you deliberately made them godparents of your own free will or whether Carl caused it by making you request it through his mystic power. Is that right? Is that the way you want to leave it?"

"That's right."

"You don't really know what the reason was that you made it?"

"That's right. They were the only Catholics I knew."

Her statement seemed shockingly out of context, seeming for a moment to be patronizing, as if it had not been her habit to associate with Catholics. But then it seemed revelatory of that strange and unnatural isolation of newcomers in a suddenly improvised community, that rootless boredom which had made an affair between such a disparate pair possible. Had it been an old and settled street, had the Farbers been there several years before the Coppolinos moved in, had the Farbers been integrated into the neighborhood and community, one can reasonably doubt that she would have accepted him as a lover, or that he would have had the temerity to suggest it.

Bailey veered abruptly again, asking her, "Was Bill sick at all the night he died, before you gave him the injection?"

"No."

"He wasn't? How long had you had the white powder drug in your house?"

"I don't remember."

"Was it brought there for the purpose of killing a dog that you wanted to get rid of?"

"Not when I actually had it. No."

"Did you tell the authorities in Florida that you brought it there for the purpose of killing a dog?"

"I don't recall what I actually said in reference to when I had the powder."

"All right. (weary acceptance. Here we go again, folks) Did you have a dog?"

"Yes."

"Did you want to get rid of it?"

"Yes. In a way."

"What do you mean, in a way? How do you get rid of a dog 'in a way'?"

"Well, the children liked the dog and I didn't."

"You wanted it killed. Right?"

"Well, not necessarily killed, but—"

"You wanted to get rid of it?"

"Yes."

It is an interesting exercise in self-analysis to realize what curious effect the smallest things have on large decisions, when those small things offend our emotional sensibilities. Regardless of how much or how little one believed Marjorie's story as it had unfolded, there had been a likableness about her. The business of the dog diminished it abruptly. One wondered what kind of a mother, what kind of a woman, would wish to dispose of a dog her children liked merely because she did not like it. Is it not the normal reaction to endure the sloppy or destructive habits of the beloved pet for the sake of the children? She had not said the dog was dangerous. She had not said the dog was ill. She had said she did not like it, and it is quite possible that in the case of perhaps at least one juror that this gratuitous revelation had more sway than all the mobility and craftiness of her inquisitor.

Bailey went immediately from dog to husband. "Had Carl told you to give the injection at 3 A.M.—the deadly poison?"

"I don't remember what time."

"Were you acting under his instructions when you did it?"

"Yes. But I don't remember."

"You don't remember what the instructions were. Is that right?"

"If it were a certain time or not. All I knew, it was that night. That night."

"You *did* call Carl at three in the morning, didn't you?"

"Yes. About that time."

"You said your husband was terribly ill, couldn't breathe and needed a doctor, didn't you?"

"Yes."

"Carl came over about three-thirty, did he not?"

"I would say so."

"At that time you told Carl that you had been awakened by the colonel yelling from his bedroom, didn't you?"

"I don't remember what I said to Carl."

"And Carl examined him, didn't he?"

"Yes."

Under the rapid and intense questioning, she could not remember the colonel saying, "I need a doctor." She said at one point that the colonel was out in the hall. Reminded that she had said in the morning session that he was in bed when Carl arrived, she said that she could not remember how Farber got back into bed, whether she had helped him, or Carl had helped him, or both of them, or whether the colonel had made it on his own. She said, as before, that Carl had given her husband an injection. She said it was possible that Carl had suggested the colonel be taken to a hospital, but she could not remember all that was said. She testified that Carl took care of the colonel and went home and came back later in the day and gave him additional treatment, and tried to help him, at least in the beginning. She agreed that she had told the dentist's receptionist that her husband was sick, and that she had called his office to say he wouldn't be in.

"Did you believe that he was sick when you said that to the receptionist or were you making it up?"

And yet once again with that strange resiliency under stress, she came back with the angry reply which once again had that smell of reality.

"I knew *why* he was sick!"

"Because you made him sick with a drug you can't describe?"

"That's right. . . . All I knew is, he was quite ill as a result."

"You say he wasn't ill at all before that?"

"That's right."

"Wasn't he feeling poorly the night before?"

"He was agitated—but he wasn't ill at that point."

"While Carl was there the second time, did Colonel Farber say anything derogatory about you in Carl's presence?"

"I don't recall that."

"Carl *did* recommend that you go to the hospital, didn't he? That you have the colonel taken to the hospital because he was very sick? Isn't that true?"

"Not at that time."

"You say that he did not recommend that you take the colonel to the hospital?"

"I think he suggested it at one time, but exactly when he sugggested it I do not remember."

"So you will leave it that it might have been at the time I described it?"

"It's possible."

And once again many of those listening with the greatest care were, if they had begun to think her story a fabrication, thrust back into that eerie hinterland of emotional illogic. If she was trying to nail the lover who abandoned her for another woman, why not deny firmly Bailey's allegation that anything had been suggested by Carl about a hospital? And why say that Carl had indeed treated the husband? Only two of them had been there with the man soon to die. If it were to be her word against his, and if she were lying, why diffuse the lie with admissions which did not fit a pattern of murder? On the other hand if these admissions were because she was telling the truth, and the murder had been done, why would the murderer have suggested hospitalization, or, indeed, have given the victim any help at all on either visit?

"And you refused, didn't you?" (to permit hospitalization)

"I didn't refuse. No."

"You swear that you did not?"

"My husband refused."

"Did you encourage him to go to the hospital because of Carl's opinion?"

"No. I didn't."

And Bailey glanced at the clock and had that thrusting look again, the look of moving in for the kill.

"Didn't Carl say to you, 'If you people aren't going to follow my advice I will not help the colonel. I will not treat him. I'll withdraw.' Didn't he say that?"

She looked genuinely baffled. "When would he say that?"

"When he left the house a little after noontime on the 30th day of July 1963, didn't Carl say to you and your husband, 'I'm backing out of this if you won't go to the hospital and you reject my advice'?"

Almost contemptuously she replied, "No! He didn't say anything like that at all."

"He didn't say anything like that?"

"No. He didn't!"

"Mrs. Farber, I want you to consider this very carefully. Are you able to tell us from your memory on your solemn oath that he never said that?"

Keuper objected on the grounds that she had already answered that question. The Court sustained him, and Bailey explained that he had a reason for wanting to be very clear on that point. He tried to ask the same question yet again, and again the objection was sustained.

"Isn't it true, Mrs. Farber, that the reason you called Carmela at night instead of Carl was because Carl wouldn't have anything more to do with your husband's illness?"

"No."

"Do you say that it was never suggested at any time by Carl, 'I'm withdrawing from this case because he should be in a hospital and you won't follow my advice'?"

"You are going to have to repeat that."

"Happily! (said with a savage satisfaction) Do you say that he did not, in the afternoon of the 30th day of July of 1963, at any time tell you, 'Don't call me. I won't have anything more to do with this case because he should be in a hospital and you won't go there'?"

"Carl did not say anything like that."

"Was anything like that ever mentioned on that day?"

"Not at all."

"It never was mentioned by either of you, was it?"

"Not at all. No. Not by Carl."

"Was anything on that entire day, before or after the colonel's death in any conversation with you and Carl, mentioned about his refusing to treat the colonel because the colonel wouldn't go to the hospital?"

"No."

With a piece of paper in his hand, he gave her the pussycat smile. "You swear that?"

"Yes."

He held the paper toward her. "Is that your signature, Mrs. Farber?"

"Yes. That's my signature."

He let her take it and read it, and said, "All right. May I see it please."

She handed it back, and looked at him and looked around at the Court and the jury with an air of complete shock and bewilderment.

"But I have never seen that piece of paper before!" It was a cry of protest, and of a demand to be believed.

"How did your signature get on it?"

"I haven't any idea."

"Do you say it's a forgery?"

336

"I don't know how it got on there. I don't even remember signing any paper."

"Did you sign—"

"It's Carl's handwriting on it."

"Did you sign a paper on the 30th day of July 1963 at one P.M. with the following: 'I hereby release Carl A. Coppolino, M.D., from all responsibility for the case of my husband, William Farber. Dr. Coppolino wishes to be released because Mr. Farber refuses to be hospitalized even though he knows he may have had a coronary. Dr. Coppolino only gave emergency care. Signed, Marjorie C. Farber.' Do you remember that now?"

"No sir." She was not angry. She was pleadingly earnest. "I do not remember signing that. That is my signature, yes. But I do not recall."

"Look at it, study it, and tell the jury how it got on that piece of paper under those words. I would like you to tell me how it got there."

"I don't *know!*"

"You tell the jury."

"I don't *know!*"

"Did you sign it?"

"That's my signature and that's Carl's handwriting, but I do not have any memory of signing this paper."

"I'm sure you didn't have any memory when I asked you about it initially, but I am asking you if Carl didn't insist that you sign that release because you wouldn't take the colonel to the hospital when he was having a heart attack?"

"I have no recall of ever signing this piece of paper; and I am telling the truth."

"*You* are telling the *truth?!?*"

She was firming up again, recovering from her confusion. "I am telling the truth, Mr. Bailey. I have never seen this piece of paper before in my life."

"Is there any question anywhere in your mind about the validity of your signature?"

"I know my signature. I know his writing, but—"

He pressed her to say again and again that it was her signature until Keuper objected on grounds of repetitiousness. Thereupon F. Lee Bailey had the release marked D-4 for identification, and approached the bench at his own request. The side-bar conference, as is true of the previous ones, was out of the range of the court reporter's hearing, and thus does not appear in the transcript.

Court was recessed at four minutes of four on Friday, until Monday morning, the twelfth, at 9:30.

At that point, Bailey had questioned Mrs. Farber for almost two hours and fifty minutes. He had paced himself to finish on a particularly damaging note. He had not finished with her. He would continue on Monday, if for nothing else, to make Keuper's redirect a more difficult task.

Chapter Eighteen

After their stories were filed by phone and telex, the working press and the photographers and the magazine people and the Bailey team assembled as on other nights during the jury selection in the big paneled old bar lounge of the American Hotel, advertised as "The Horsiest Place in New Jersey"—a credo confirmed by the scores of Currier and Ives prints of horses and races on the walls, and the silvered shoes of famous horses of the past. The public came in to get a cat-and-the-queen look at the celebrated.

It had the fiesta flavor of all the games men play for life and death stakes—parties before the bullfight, the socializing near the pits at Indianapolis, even the jokes and dates and songs in the officers' clubs when the bloodiest game of all is in session.

Carl Coppolino was back in his cell at the Hall of Records, Department J (for Jail), on the other side of the street and diagonally not more than a hundred yards away from the drinks and the din and the confusions. He was the shadowy pawn in the courtroom game, and a shadowy presence at the evening's festivities.

The focus of attention was the big round corner table where F. Lee Bailey sat in the corner chair, where custody of the other chairs changed constantly as fragments of the defense team formed and dispersed, as hangers-on, newspaper people, sycophants, and assorted wives and companions thereof took turns pursuing often obscure goals. The blue-tinted glass of the lenses of the Leicas and Nikons and Rolleis were aimed at F. Lee, at Mary, at anybody who happened to have any vague look of being a participant—just in case. Noise, smoke, drinks, movement, distractions—and the pervasive flavor of small conspiracies, whispered consultations, notes written and pocketed. It is, after all, a

338

contest and emotions seem to require that objectivity be a quaint concept, and everyone line up on one team or the other.

Once the jury had been sequestered, Bailey could answer press questions about the trial. He was in good spirits. After years of work, he had gotten his acquittal of Sam Sheppard in November. The Boston Strangler case, scheduled for January, seemed to be shaping up according to his plans and wishes. And in this first trial of Carl Coppolino, he felt that he had a better jury than he had expected to be able to get, he had an appreciative judge, and he had done very well that day in court with Marge Farber. Best of all, since the bail hearing in October, he had become convinced that the testimony of Marge Farber and Milton Helpern was all the State of New Jersey had, and he felt he had to discredit if not impeach them both. He was enjoying the game of thrust and parry with the questions asked him.

Yet a Lee Bailey in the best of spirits, in the flush of confidence, is still not the most comfortable person to be with. He is intensely involved in the here and the now, in all the moments and the revelations of the most casual conversation with such an insistence and intensity that companions begin to feel themselves becoming curiously uneasy and uncertain, as though in the presence of a creature not quite of their species, hence unpredictable and possibly dangerous. The quick charm is based upon empathy and awareness, and can give one the feeling one is being made use of for some purpose, immediate or obscure, yet he seems at the same time to be mocking himself and the one he intends to use.

There were two topics that evening guaranteed to irritate him in spite of all the other reasons for euphoria. One was the writeup about him in the December 9 issue of *Time* magazine, peppered with those snidenesses which are the burrs *Time* feels obligated to shove under the celebrity saddle.

"By his own account, Bailey has an IQ of 170." "Bailey already compares himself to 'Clarence' (meaning Darrow), though his monumental self-assurance might not yet convince William Jennings (meaning Bryan)." "Bailey was cool, quiet, subliminally brutal."

The other taboo topic was any hint or suggestion that Marge had weathered her ordeal in good style. But the working press is no respecter of taboos when the result of inserting the needle might be something usable, such as his plans for the balance of his cross-examination of Mrs. Farber.

Bailey was willing to tabulate, over and over, the points with which he wished to have the press corps believe he had "destroyed" her. He was a strange amalgam of contradictions that evening—accessible, almost too accessible, yet frequently testy—euphoric yet often mocking himself—enthusiastic yet cynically bitter—exhibiting personal warmth and charm, yet playing friends, colleagues, members of the team off against each other, creating suspicion and jealousy—hearty and malicious—confident and apprehensive—eager to explain and just as eager to mislead. . . .

It could be possible that a great many of the contradictions in personality he exhibited during the course of the Freehold trial were due not so much to any basic ambivalence or compulsive complexity, but rather to his being at that time in a special kind of transitional phase, one which had neared its end by the time of the second Coppolino trial the following April in Naples, Florida.

There could be a clue to what was happening to him in an article by Stephen Birmingham in *Holiday* magazine for June 1967. Though Birmingham was writing of an entirely different field, in fact was writing of "The Sudden Fame of Michael Caine," acting bears a certain relationship to criminal law, just as the criminal court does to the arenas of show business.

Birmingham wrote, " 'He also has not learned to take his success gracefully,' says a New York woman who found Caine's behavior and enthusiasms 'excessively vulgar.' And yet she seems to have missed the point. Such is the nature of the world of modern theater and films that the actors and actresses one encounters in it tend to be of two kinds. They are either toe-digging, unformed nobodies or thoroughly congealed, diamond-hard celebrities. The process that sweeps the nobody to international fame is usually so swift—and often so unexpected—that it is hard to catch anyone en route. . . . By the time you realize it is happening, it has happened; the nobody has become Somebody, a bored and famous face that brightens only when another bored and famous face comes into the room. But Michael Caine is, at the moment, still in transition. He has emerged from the cocoon so recently that he ogles the future with the cupidity of a candy addict given the run of Barricini's warehouse. Everything is fresh, vivid and exciting. Nothing has had a chance to pall. Because people are suddenly listening to him, he suddenly has opinions on everything—sex, love and marriage, child-rearing, films, theater, integration in the American South, and his own talent. He has not learned, in other words, to be guarded, or even judicious. Whether he will harden into a practiced celebrity is a question still, but at the moment he is a revel of immodesty."

* * *

At seven-thirty or thereabouts, Marjorie Farber came into the bar lounge from the hotel proper, not through the street entrance, wearing the same outfit she had worn in court, and followed closely by Warren Goodrich and George Chamlin, both of whom looked affably ill-at-ease. She came down along the length of the bar and finally reached a point near the angle of the bar where perhaps she could have glimpsed the round table where each night F. Lee Bailey held personal court. Had she looked at the round table she would have seen Lee Bailey, Mary Coppolino, Joe Afflitto and others of the defense team.

Perhaps she merely came far enough down the length of the narrow room to see that all the tables were occupied except a table for four which they had already passed. At any rate she turned back abruptly, and Mr. Chamlin and Mr. Goodrich followed her back to that table. There she sat, an attorney at her right and one at her left, ordered ginger ale, and with lifted chin and cool eye, she looked about at the section of the lounge, meeting any curious stare.

Warren Goodrich and George Chamlin were far more aware than she that this had been staked out as Bailey country, and thus their brief visit had the flavor of invasion. But as if taking sustenance from their client's poise and control, they soon recovered that assurance which had seemed somewhat tentative as they had walked in with Mrs. Farber.

It was interesting that the assembled press, usually more than eager to clot quickly and thickly around any principal in the case, made no move toward the table. Then a Florida reporter who had spoken with her in Sarasota and whom she knew by name, made a tentative approach. She invited him to take the empty chair. "Didn't I tell you it was really going to be something?" she said.

"You were right. It was really something. It must have been rough up there on the stand."

She nodded, and made a rueful face. "As rough as it can get."

He asked her where she was staying, and she said, "I'm not allowed to tell. But I'll tell you this much. I'm staying with friends, and the boat horns keep waking me up in the night."

"Did you bring your children with you?"

"No. I decided it would be okay to leave them in Florida. They've been wonderful about this—very staunch. You see, when this whole thing first came up I knew I had to level with them. They had to know just what had happened and why I had to do what I was doing. So I sat down and I told them the whole mess, right from the beginning to the end . . . but of course we don't really know the end yet, do we? And I said that anything they wanted to ask me, anything at all, anything they could think of that bothered them, they were to come right to me and ask me, and I would give them a straight answer.

"Well . . . they went glooming around for a time. You can imagine what it was like for them. And they'd come and ask a question and I'd lay it right on the line for them. So . . . after a while . . . well, it got to be all right. At least, as all right for them as it is ever *going* to be. And I will tell you something. If I had any clue that they weren't handling it well enough, then I would have brought them along, and they would be right here with me now in New Jersey."

Other reporters, emboldened by what appeared to be a willing interview, approached the table and were waved off by the attorneys who said, "No comment."

Mary Coppolino came from the area of the round table, which was invisible from where Marge sat, and passed Marge's table on her way to the lady's room. Photographers, realizing that Mary would come back by the same route and there was a chance of catching them in the same picture, stationed themselves. As Mary came down the few steps the strobes winked bright, and the photograph was on the front page of Saturday's New York *Daily News*, and in newspapers across the country. Both women wear a half-smile. Four of the principal players were in that long room that evening. Marge, Mary, Bailey, and Frank Schaub. But there was no place to stand to get all of them in the same picture.

Marge had two ginger ales and left with her attorneys. An intense and overinvolved young girl reporter from a New Jersey paper said, "How could she have the *nerve* to show her face here after today?"

"She *had* to," somebody said, "because her name was Cullen, and she's seen bad times and good, and nothing in God's world could ever make her run and hide."

And Bailey said, before he left, "I took one hell of a chance with that release. All I could do was hope she'd forgotten it, and if she hadn't, and if she'd figured out just what to say about it, I could have been walking into it."

And so the party fragmented. It was bad dramatics but inevitable procedure to break up the cross-examination, to suspend it for the two empty days. Reporters, except those from the most distant places, went back to home base. The investigators went out on assignments. F. Lee Bailey went to Helpern's office in

New York, and then flew up to Boston to spend the weekend with Wicki and the kids, and to fly Wicki back Sunday night.

Mary Coppolino went to New York. She did the things that tourists do. But she moved in a little cluster of reporters and photographers. She went to a night spot in the Village and laughed loudly, out of her Alabama heritage, at a Negro stand-up comedian when one of his integration jokes was about a white man moving into a Negro neighborhood, and how they went over and burned a watermelon in his front yard. And she got her hair done at her hotel in New York.

Carl spent a quiet weekend.

The few media people who stayed in Freehold had the inevitable, unending, unresolved bull sessions. They filed side-bar stories. Compulsive curiosity is, as has been said too often, an occupational disease of the journalist. The shades of opinion were extreme.

One veteran of the courts and the newspapers said with ponderous authority, "After Marge's testimony, Lee could rest his case. I never saw such a shambles. She was totally discredited. Keuper has no case left at all. Carl saw the colonel twice and gave him good medical treatment."

At the other end of the spectrum was a lean skeptic from Ohio, who the previous month had watched Bailey win the second Sheppard case. "Now wait a minute! You sound like you're standing there holding those imaginary pails in your hands, friend. She's a bright woman. Right? She's shrewd. Now would a bright woman tell such clumsy lies if she was trying to fix his wagon? Sure, she's bad on the stand. But you have to understand why she's bad. Didn't you ever hear of denial, I mean in the psychological sense. It's where the conscious mind refuses to accept a situation because it hurts too much, so it buries it. She's got partial denial. There's still a lot she really can't remember. The shock of Carm dying was what got her to dredge up *this* much.

"She's ruining herself by telling the truth because the truth has all these holes in it. Use your head. What if the old boy died just the way Bailey wants the jury to believe. Would a shrewd woman like Marge forget that release? Suppose there's an outside chance she *did* forget it. She's hard to rattle. Most of the time she's real cool up there. What would she do? Look at it and hand it back and say, 'Oh, I remember that now. That was in case somebody found out Carl had treated him instead of Carm, and they'd want to know why Carm had signed the death thing. We did that after Bill was dead.' "

And somebody else said, "Wait a minute. She was a good hypnotic subject. Right? So couldn't he have hypnotized her and made her write her name in the middle of a blank piece of paper and gave her a post-hypnotic suggestion to forget she ever did it? Then he could have written that release business on later, over her signature, and dated it and put the time on it, and tucked it away, just in case she ever decided to blow the whistle. That would fit with the way she acted, saying it was her signature, but she'd never seen that piece of paper before."

There was expressed that weekend almost every shade of belief and disbelief.

But it was up to the jury, of course. It always is.

For diversion that weekend, the jurors were taken by the bailiffs, at county expense, to see a movie called *The Liquidators*.

Chapter Nineteen

F. Lee Bailey resumed his cross-examination of Marjorie Farber at 9:30 Monday morning with an initial side-step into the murkiness of the Svengali-Trilby relationship. The defendant sat staring intently at his accuser throughout her entire testimony. Not once did she look toward him, look slightly downward and a little to her right, to meet that dark stare at that twelve foot range.

The thirty minutes of cross-examination by Bailey was just as intense as it had been the previous Friday. The questioning of the witness fills forty pages of the official transcript but most of the interrogation was a rehash of her initial appearance.

Bailey's tactic was simple. Plow the most fertile ground, deeper and deeper. Underscore the areas of absurdities and incredibility, of contradiction and confusion; develop the variations and discrepancies, real or imaginary, that might put the lie to her story in the mind of a juror.

In gentle, almost casual opening questions, Bailey had Marjorie repeat her earlier testimony of coming under Carl's hypnotic influence during sessions designed to stop her smoking habit. She told also that there were occasions where she came out of a hypnotic trance and could not remember all that had happened.

"Did he cure you from smoking?"

"Yes."

"I noticed when you left the courthouse Friday you were smoking."

"I started to smoke again in 1964."

"What month?"

"I think it was in the spring or summer, something like that."

"You told us that you emerged from his power of control in October of 1964. Had you started prior to that?"

"Yes."

Bailey had set the tone for his cross-examination. Sifting through her earlier testimony, which he had studied until nearly midnight Sunday, he began to attack it with sardonic incredulity, broad burlesque, subtle parody, any device appropriate to each line of questioning.

Many of the areas themselves were identical to those covered Friday. But two days had passed. Jurors cannot take notes. It is probable Bailey would have been on safe ground had he assumed there had been considerable weekend discussion between some of the jurors, despite the Court's admonishment that they were not to speak of the evidence and testimony until they were instructed, after the charge, to begin their deliberations. But jurors in complex cases will almost inevitably rationalize on the basis of not quite hearing exactly what was said, and asking another juror what *he* thought was said. Discussion is then inevitable. Insofar as the enforcement of the rules applicable to the sequestered jury in New Jersey, one reporter thought to check out if they were indeed being insulated from media coverage of the trial.

He had only to check the empty bus standing in the parking lot behind the American Hotel during the lunch recess. This was the bus which transported the fourteen jurors and the bailiffs between the Hitching Post Motel where they were housed, the American Hotel where they were fed, and the courthouse, where they sat and listened. On a trial day he saw and identified on the floor of the bus, under the seats, two well-crumpled copies of the most recent issue of the New York *Daily News*.

Bailey, by asking questions in a slightly different form, hoped to more deeply imprint upon the collective memory of the jury those portions of the Friday testimony he thought the jury least likely to believe, as if asking them to learn that ability the Queen had explaind to Alice in Wonderland, about believing several impossible things before breakfast.

Marjorie during this rehash often pointed out that she had answered the same question before, but as Keuper's objections were few and he did not persist with them, F. Lee Bailey was able to stage a rerun of what he intended would be best remembered.

"Why did you call the one doctor who you say had announced a purpose to kill him? Was that to help your husband?"

"At that time, yes. That is what I said Friday. I called Carl to please come help my husband."

"You had forgotten the fact that the poison that you say you had just tried to inject was furnished by Carl Coppolino. Is that right?"

"I would have to agree to that, yes."

"As he handed you these materials, did he tell you, 'This is for the purpose of killing your husband'? Were those his words?"

"I don't recall exactly what he said. He gave me the drug and the syringe and I knew what I was supposed to do."

In a series of brief questions, Bailey had Marjorie repeat the details of the drug delivery to Carl's home by Dr. Edmund Webb, whom she met at the time. She told of preparing the potion in a bathroom glass, filling a syringe with the dissolved powder and plunging the needle into Bill's leg. She couldn't recall details such as the time it took the powder to dissolve, whether the fluid was cloudy or clear, how deep the needle punctured.

At this point, Bailey allowed Marge Farber to introduce a new bit of bizarre testimony into the proceedings. It was a line of questioning that developed slowly and by design, since he was totally familiar with her statement to Frank Schaub, into black humor with Marge Farber the butt of the grisly joke.

"Did he suggest any other methods of killing your husband besides the use of a chemical?"

"No, but he did say, he suggested that I first wrap a towel around a baseball bat and knock my husband unconscious before I used the drug."

"Hit him in the head with a baseball bat?"

"That's exactly what he said."

"Did you *have* a baseball bat?"

"Oh yes. Several of them."

"Did you follow that instruction?"

"No I did not."

"I take it then, you were not under his control to the extent of using the baseball bat. Is that right?"

346

"I couldn't do it."

"Well, you have told us that your acts were under compulsion and instruction from the defendant."

"That's right."

"And that's the only reason you used this so-called needle, true?"

Bailey, with his air of astonished disbelief, his amused glances at the jury to underline the improbability of this aging suburban playmate with her closet full of baseball bats, was making the most of it, but went one half step over the line with the word "so-called."

This stung her, and as on the other occasions when she was angry and indignant, she showed that surprising ability to surge back and turn what was becoming a fantasy into the abrupt flavor of reality, borrowed perhaps from the unquestioned reality of her indignation.

"It *was* a needle! It was not a *so-called* needle! It was a *needle!*"

"A syringe," Bailey said, to parry the anger by correction. (objection sustained)

"But despite the fact that you could not disobey Doctor Coppolino, you say that you, of your own free will, rejected the notion of using a baseball bat?"

Though Mr. Keuper's immediate objection was sustained, "baseball bat" had been said five times. The jury was staring at the dark-haired woman on the stand. Though the detail and the vividness of imagination differs from person to person, it is fair to say that it would be unlikely that any juror could have failed to have some mental picture of an imaginary and incredible scene wherein the colonel's lady swung a baseball bat against the skull of the middle-aged war hero.

Bailey was, of course, exploiting another area of emotional logic, of underlining what he might well believe to be beyond the capacity of the jury to believe. In this instance he was playing a grotesque image against the almost inevitable realization by at least some of the jurors that it would be quite an unlikely form of anesthesia for a professional practitioner to suggest. And, by using the information in the statement she had made to Frank Schaub to lead her into bringing up the baseball bat suggestion, it could have well sounded to some of the jurors like a gratuitous and rather unlikely attempt to make a spur-of-the-moment accusation which would make the young doctor sound more violent and murderous than even the rest of her testimony implied.

347

Conversely, were one to assume that it was fabrication, then it seems to be almost too crude and unlikely to be part of the fabric of an over-all accusation of murder. Thus speculation always dwindles off into such elusive areas of value judgment, that one is at last in the position of the gullible customer at the carnival, trying to guess which walnut shell covers the pea, never realizing that it may no longer be under any of them, but has been wedged into the fleshy crease at the base of the thumb of the manipulator.

Bailey exploited a new area of emotional illogic by eliciting testimony that Marge had loaned Carl $5000 when Carl and Carmela had moved to Florida, to help them build their new home, that Carl had paid interest on the loan and finally repaid it in full. She called it a "businesslike" transaction. His expression and tone said to the jury, "Think *that* one over." It had, for Bailey, a useful incongruity, one calculated to puzzle a juror. It was as if Cleopatra had staked Mark Antony to a home study course. Was this logical behavior for co-murderers, for the hypnotist and his vassal?

In his cross-examination, Bailey then asked her if it was correct that Carl had been retired, or temporarily retired, from the active practice of anesthesiology because of a heart condition.

"So I have been told," said Marge cautiously.

"He was unable to drive, so you would drive him. Is that right? . . . When you two went out together, who did the driving?"

"Generally we went in my car and I drove my car because it happened to be a floor shift car and he didn't know how to drive it."

Five months after the trial in New Jersey, in Theo Wilson's *Daily News* feature on Marge, she wrote:

> But when she and Carl became lovers in February, 1963, Marge said, she believed he had a serious heart disease . . . It was because of Carl's disabling sickness that Marge drove him everywhere he wanted to go—"and he never spent a dime for the gasoline, either," Marge recalled. Marge, asked if she thought Carl had a heart condition, replied, "No . . . not with the active sex life he had. Oh, he used to pop pills in his mouth . . . I don't know what they were, if they were nitroglycerine or saccharine."

Returning to the day of Bill Farber's death, Bailey's volley of more than four dozen questions brought Marge to the point where she described the bedroom scene between Carl and her husband, saying "the general climate was of anger."

348

As he led up to this point Bailey established that the colonel, after receiving an injection that left him groggy and slurred his speech, was resting on the single twin bed, the pillow beneath his head, Carl looking down at him. Marge also testified her husband, "about five, eight and a half, five nine" and weighing "about 155, 160" was a fair match for Carl physically. She also said she had been in and out of the room where the two men were arguing.

"Were they raising their voices?"

"That's the only reason I could have heard them."

Marge's answer was too saucy. It had, perhaps, spilled out as the result of agitation caused by Bailey's persistent plowing of old ground, his general attitude of shifting from low comedy to wicked sarcasm to mocking disbelief.

"Now, when you walked back into the room, did you then see Carl with a pillow?"

"When I walked back into the room that's when I heard Carl say, 'You ungrateful bastard. I saved your life.' "

"Mrs. Farber, did you hear my question? When you walked back into the room did you see Carl with the pillow?"

"No."

"You did not?" (remember that, ladies and gentleman of the jury)

"No, but he was . . ."

Bailey cut her off in the middle of her response and, with his next series of questions, led Marge to recite again the "ungrateful bastard" line only to remind her and the courtroom audience, with disgust edging his voice, she had spoken the line several times. His reason was clear, although unstated. For a woman who had professed under oath she didn't like to use that kind of language she had shown little hesitation in spicing her testimony with the phrase, which through its repetition had taken on the monotonous flavor of the stock James Cagney impersonators: "I'm gonna give it to you, like you gave it to my brother."

Defensively, irritably, Marge replied to Bailey's reminder she had used the line frequently, "I know, but you asked me."

"Mrs. Farber, my question was—"

"I'm sorry."

"—how long—"

"Listen to the question," Judge Simmill admonished.

"How long were you standing there?"

"Be responsive," the judge cautioned.

"I don't know." Bailey turned with a shrug. (ah hah, she doesn't know)

"Was it more than an hour?"

"No."

"Was it less than half an hour?"

"I don't know."

Keuper came to the assistance of his witness with an objection to the Court that Marge had said she didn't know and that should be the end of the questioning. Judge Simmill agreed but not before he ruled that Bailey "has a right to try to limit her lack of knowledge."

Marge explained she left the room when Carl pressed the soiled pillowcase in her hands and went into the laundry room. During this portion of the interrogation, Marge was twice admonished by the Court to be responsive. Just answer the question, don't elaborate on something that is not asked. Don't volunteer.

F. Lee Bailey, after examination of Marge at the Sarasota preliminary hearing, during the first day of testimony in Freehold and again this morning, was probably well aware of the picture she gave the jury as he hounded her with a recitation of testimony she had given time and time again. He knew which of the details were sketchy in her mind and he played upon those. He knew how far he could go before the Cullen-Irish would lash out and she would pick up the points she had lost by her inexplicable and, to some, inexcusable lapses of memory.

Bailey knew also that by limiting her responses and, on occasion, patiently pleading with her not to volunteer that which was not asked, she would nevertheless try to explain her actions for she was apparently aware of the game Bailey was playing. But, in trying to tell it true and in ignoring the rules of the game—don't volunteer, keep it straight and simple—she was placed at the added disadvantage of dueling with the Court. Judge Simmill, as any judge will do, reminded the witness to be responsive, often echoing the words of her interrogator, although his admonishment was as much for Marge's protection as it was to fulfill his obligation to the law.

The prestige of a judge is such that there is perhaps an undue weight put on his participation in the examination of a witness by the jurors listening to the case. If the judge is forced to admonish the witness often, regardless of the reasons for such admonishment, it is safe to assume that the jurors are apt to believe that perhaps the witness is unresponsive because of purposeful evasiveness. Perhaps there is something to hide and it is being hidden.

Thus Bailey, throughout his lengthy cross-examination of Marge Farber and his deliberate concentration upon the fuzziest portions of that testimony, was increasingly portraying the state's eyewitness as a person of odd and perhaps deliberate blind spots.

The role of the judge in the fencing match between Marge and Lee Bailey was inadvertently underscored at one point by the zeal of prosecutor Vincent Keuper.

Marge was telling how Carl had taken the pillow from beneath the head of her unconscious husband.

"Well, he pulled the pillow out from under my husband's head and while he was doing that he said, 'He's a hard one to kill.' "

"Wait a minute. As he pulled the pillow out from under his head—"

"If Your Honor please, I think the witness should be permitted to answer the question," objected Keuper.

"The question is: 'What did you see him do with the pillow?' " the judge repeated.

"And she started to tell us," Keuper replied.

"And she did tell us," the judge said. "She said, 'He pulled it out from under her husband's head.' "

Keuper should have left it at that, but he insisted, "But she didn't finish."

"And he put it over my husband—"

"Wait a minute," Judge Simmill said, turning toward Marge. "Everybody can't talk at once." Marge apologized and Judge Simmill turned toward Keuper.

"Mr. Prosecutor, she wasn't asked what he said or what was said, so that when she started to say what was said she was being unresponsive."

"Mr. Bailey said, 'What did he do with the pillow,' " Keuper argued.

"That was the question and she started to say what the conversation was, but she was not asked that," the judge said. He was becoming impatient with the suddenly persistent prosecutor.

"With all due respect to you, I submit that the witness said this: 'He pulled it out from under his head.' Then she started to say what he did with the pillow and Mr. Bailey interrupted."

"Well, with all due respect to you, I say she started to say what was said. I don't propose to quibble, Mr. Prosecutor." The tone of his voice made it clear he meant exactly what he said and Keuper surrendered with a meek, "All right."

Bailey, who was an amused bystander throughout the exchange between the judge and the prosecutor, resumed his questioning after shooting a discreet, over-the-shoulder look at Teri Plaut, seated before the rail with a suitcase by her feet.

"He pulled it out from underneath my husband's head and put it over my husband's face and neck and he leaned down on it, he just leaned down on it full force. Then he removed the pillow and he opened my husband's eye and he said, 'He's dead.' "

Again, as when she was taken through the scene by Keuper during his direct examination, Marjorie Farber got shaky. Her voice became uneven and her eyes filled with tears. She recovered swiftly, seeming to shake it off, with a lift of chin and narrowing of eyes as if she felt it a kind of humiliation to let Bailey make her show that weakness.

Bailey questioned her about her estimate of how long Carl pressed the pillow down, and while doing so he snapped the fingers of a back-stretched hand at Teri Plaut, who took a bed pillow from the suitcase and handed it to Lee Bailey when he came quickly to get it.

Heading back toward the witness, Bailey asked, "What did you do all this time?"

"I just stood there." There was an aftertone of shame and despair in her voice.

He swung the pillow up and held it close to her face.

"Mrs. Farber, is that the kind of pillow that was used? Would you examine it?" He brandished it at her. Though his voice was stern and as theatrical as his gesture and prop, there seemed to be a little flavor of fun and of mockery in the staged performance, as though he were amused by his own charade, effective though he hoped it might be.

Marge remained totally composed at first, ignoring the outthrust pillow, looking directly into Bailey's face, and saying that it had been "just a normal pillow."

One can suspect that F. Lee Bailey was intent upon geometrically compounding the elements of the grotesque and the absurd by introducing a prop so homely, so familiar to everyone. Yet it is quite possible that it had a flavor he did not anticipate. In our well-ordered culture, all of us are more likely to die in bed than elsewhere, and most of us have seen a deathbed. Sheets and pillows have a symbolic weight, and perhaps it is inevitable in that context that white is becoming the "fashionable" mode for funerals and mourning. On some elemental level the presence of the pillow seemed to make the murder tale more rather than less believable. Also, Lee Bailey had moved into one of the areas where Marjorie Farber seemed to have good recall, which violated his strategy of pounding at her areas of misty vagueness.

It is possible that he began to realize that he was not achieving the anticipated effect, not on Marge, not on the jurors. There

352

was for a few moments a hesitancy about him, as if he debated the advisability of suddenly dropping the entire pillow charade, or wished he could. But he had to go on with it.

He had her come down from the stand to the table she had used before for her demonstration, sans pillow, under direct examination by Keuper. Most people are disadvantaged by public performance, their actions constricted, artificial, unconvincing. But there is that minority, of which Marge is one, who seem "at home in the body," the emotional integrated with the physical, an acceptance of the reality of their own substance, so that it is an unawareness and hence a kind of grace.

". . . Now when the pillow was placed over his face what part of him couldn't you see?"

"I couldn't see his chest and his neck and his head. This area. The top area." She was demonstrating for the Court and her words, her actions, seemed abrupt and distressed.

"So that was all covered?"

"Yes."

"Was the pillow across him horizontally or vertically, if you know." The "if you know" had the same sound of incredulity one would use when asking a draft dodger to tell again how he had bombed Hanoi.

"Across."

"Across like this?"

"Yes."

"Is that correct?"

"Yes."

"Now you say you saw the heel of the defendant's hand on your husband?"

"Both hands were just pushed down . . . just pushed down. I don't know exactly." She was weeping. The courtroom was hushed, fixed on the witness.

"Mrs. Farber." Bailey's voice was metallic, "Was the defendant still standing by the head of the bed?"

"Yes, he was."

"So that he was crossways to your husband, more or less?"

"As I said, the bed was on wheels. There was no headboard. He stood and he just moved up around this way and put the pillow end down."

"Was he standing behind the head of the bed when he did it?"

"Yes. It was possible to do that."

Bailey moved to the chalkboard positioned on its easel between the witness stand and the jury box, back far enough for all jurors to see it, for Marge to see it from the witness box by turning so that her back was toward the judge's bench.

He chalked a vertical oblong to represent a single bed, placed an "O" where a sleeper's head would be, drew an encircled X above the bed, centered, near the head of the sleeper, and turned toward Marge, tapping the symbol with the chalk.

"This was the position of Carl Coppolino at the time he placed the pillow over your husband's head?"

"He was right in back of him."

"Right here?" Bailey asked, pointing to the symbol X.

"Yes."

"Carl is in back of the *head* of the bed, so that your husband's face and body are down this way?" His left hand, holding the chalk, waved up and down over the blackboard.

"Yes."

"So that, Carl *reached* over from behind him and put the pillow over his face?" Bailey demonstrated the action with exaggerated difficulty, straining in his efforts at the precise moment he pronounced the word *reach*.

"He didn't have to *reach* over anything," she said, also accentuating the key, trigger word. "There was no headboard, any more than there is a headboard right now." She realized, as did Bailey, the significance of the absent headboard.

Bailey, after one more question that Carl's arms *came over* the *head* of the bed and *down*, thus giving the impression that if a headboard did exist or if one did not, the homicidal act would still be a difficult one, turned abruptly to getting into the record the details of the drawing on the blackboard and the actions of the witness.

The defense attorney then continued to press upon the listening jurors the importance he placed upon Marge's testimony regarding the pillow, the bed, the victim and the alleged murderer. At one point he attempted to dramatize the scene again by using the exhibit table, a book and the pillow as the bed, the head and the murder weapon respectively.

Late that night at the hotel there were bull sessions among the press people, arguing whether Bailey had hurt or helped himself with what had become known as "the pillow trick."

All such estimates are, of course, based upon guessing the effect on the jury, and it takes a special kind of mental discipline to make value judgments based *only* upon what has actually been offered in the way of testimony, and not letting outside knowledge load the dice.

354

The consensus was that unless he could tie it into the defense medical testimony very explicitly, maybe the pillow trick had given him a small net loss. A reporter who had been at the bail hearing told those who had not been there about how, during Bailey's detailed examination of Dr. Gilman, Gilman had stated that the dented cricoid *could* have been caused by pressure through a pillow.

"So now Bailey uses his demonstration to show that it couldn't have, and later we'll probably get defense experts saying it couldn't have."

Another reporter said, "I guess that because it was just one pillow and nothing else, that's why it seemed sort of a fake. I guess they used to go in for that kind of thing in a bigger way years ago, like long ago the defense attorney who brought a whole taxicab into the courtroom out in California."

During the idle discussion it was generally decided among the press that it would have been far more interesting to have seen all the necessary props brought into the courtroom, including a Hollywood bed without a headboard, a dummy to represent Colonel Farber, and a man of Coppolino's approximate height and weight to roll the bed away from the wall, take the pillow out from under the head and place it over the head and chest and lean on it as had been described.

There was argument as to whether such a detailed re-enactment would have made Marge's description look more or less plausible, but there was no group unity of opinion. The only byproduct was that kind of black humor exemplified by the reporter who kept reminding the others that the anesthesiologist always stands at the head of the operating table.

In the big trials the little groups of reporters always play the game of explaining to each other just how the defense or the state should have proceeded. It is a game solidly based upon ignorance of the law. Only an attorney knows what the Court might be likely to permit. Only a skilled courtroom warrior can predict which seemingly clever tricks might have a most unfortunate result.

The other preoccupation was, of course, the game called Did He or Didn't He. It is an obsessive pastime. In the Coppolino trials at Freehold and later at Naples, Florida, a very few maintained throughout the trial their vociferous membership in the He Didn't group. A few others unvaryingly insisted from beginning to end that He Did. The others went along from day to day in their personal and subjective evaluations of the evidence, building up a structure of guilt until some contradiction would topple

355

it, then building up a structure of innocence until it in turn was toppled by some piece of testimony which did not seem to fit. The adversaries, however, were engaged in quite a different game, one without subjective evaluations. It was the game of evidence. The state was presenting the structure of He Did. But the defense was saying, You are not proving beyond a reasonable doubt that He Did.

And this, of course, is the fascination of such contests as Mossler, Sheppard or Coppolino as opposed to the public torment of such sick, saddening animals as Richard Speck, Albert the Strangler, and Jack Ruby.

When F. Lee Bailey again attempted the demonstration with the table, the pillow, a book to represent the head, he was stopped after Keuper objected that the matter had been gone into time and time again. But the objection was sustained only after Bailey told the court the demonstration was critical as against "other evidence" and he wanted to make the point absolutely clear because there was a lack of clarity—not necessarily in the testimony heard so far—but "from prior hearings in the case."

As he was nearing the end of his cross-examination, Bailey demonstrated the depth and the care taken in the preparation of the defense case by suddenly making effective use of Marjorie Farber's failure to guard her words and her actions during the period which began with her early conversations with law-enforcement officials and ended with the indictment of Carl Coppolino.

When the Carl Coppolino case broke in the nation's newspapers, reporters from Florida, New York City, and the Eastern Seaboard found themselves on the threshold of another of those infrequent celebrity murder cases that promise reams of titillating copy. There was at the time of Coppolino's first arraignment a virtual invasion of Sarasota County and a competitive scramble for interviews with the principals in the case. Marge Farber was the most cooperative interviewee.

Directing her attention to a Florida newspaperman who published one of the earliest interviews with Marge Farber after the indictment of Carl Coppolino, Bailey asked, "Do you remember saying to him, 'I was shocked to find out he was murdered?' Did you make that statement?"

"I was shocked to find out he was strangled."

"Did you make that statement?"

"I don't know whether I said it to him or not, but I know this is my own reaction." She seemed ill at ease and eager to explain

356

the statement for she knew the impression Bailey was trying to give to the jury.

What followed was damaging and, with Bailey's inherent sense of the dramatic, the perfect coda for a cross-examination that had been designed to picture Marge Farber as a vindictive, scheming woman who had concocted a lurid tale to prove, as Bailey had charged in his opening statement, that hell hath no fury . . .

Directing her attention to another newspaperman, Bailey asked, "Did you in the course of that (telephone) conversation say . . . 'Wouldn't it be funny if somebody dreamed this whole thing up?' Did you say that?"

"Yes, because I was—"

"That is all. Your witness."

"Let the witness finish the answer," Keuper protested.

"I didn't ask her why she said it," Bailey snapped, ending his cross-examination. Keuper never asked for an explanation either.

Vincent Keuper began his redirect examination of his witness, Mrs. Farber, at a few minutes after ten. His task was to attempt to restore her to that presumed relationship with the jury which she had enjoyed at the termination of his direct examination, and before F. Lee Bailey had spent a total of three hours and twenty minutes savaging her.

This process is called, by the profession, "rehabilitation."

Few terms used in the law have the special charm of this one, which carries with it the flavor of picking someone up out of the gutter, brushing them off, buying them coffee, and finding them a job and a place to live.

The rules of proper procedure say that on redirect Vincent Keuper was required to remain within those areas covered on cross-examination. However, the Court cannot intervene and enforce this rule. The Court must await an objection from the other side, then make his ruling as to whether the redirect has indeed entered a new area, or whether it is pursuing a line of interrogation which was begun during cross-examination.

One can assume that it was good tactics for the defense to lay back and permit Keuper to go in any direction he wished to, so long as it did not seem damaging to the defense case. The objection need not be lodged when the line of questioning is first begun. Having been permitted to proceed for several questions does not bestow the right to continue that line should valid objection be raised.

One must constantly remember that the state cannot appeal an acquittal, and would have no reason to appeal a verdict of guilty. The defense, on the other hand, is interested in the constant accumulation throughout the trial of every possible error so that in the event of a conviction the appellate court's chance of ruling it a mistrial will be enhanced. The more questions Keuper asked Marjorie, the greater the chance of there occurring a question—or an answer—so prejudicial to the defendant the judge might believe that its damaging effect could not be overcome by admonishing the jury to ignore it. And if he did not so rule, the appellate court, basing their judgment on the official transcript, might decide that the trial judge *should* have so ruled.

Also, Keuper might open up a new area which would give Bailey a chance to score heavily on recross. Bailey listened with a total attention, refraining from halting Keuper in many peripheral areas where it would seem that objections would have been sustained.

Keuper had a lot of ground to regain, not the least of which was the as yet unanswered question as to why she had not gone to the authorities a year before she did, gone to them when in October 1964 she, as Bailey had put it, had "popped out of the trance."

In harsh, impatient questioning that sounded almost contemptuous of the woman before him, Vincent Keuper opened his redirect by capitalizing on an impetuous question posed by F. Lee Bailey the Friday before.

"Mrs. Farber, you were asked the other day, Friday as a matter of fact, by Mr. Bailey about certain threats the defendant made to you. Did he make any threats to you after July 30, 1963?"

"Yes, he did."

"What were those threats?"

"Well, he told me that if I ever did anything about reporting my husband's death that, first, nobody would believe me; and secondly that, and even more important to me, was that he would have me declared insane and institutionalized."

Although Marjorie remembered Carl had threatened her on more than one occasion, her failure to recall a specific time or place did not diminish the impact of her statement. It had, to many in the courtroom, the cold, spine-tingling, hair-raising ring of truth.

Looking at Carl Anthony Coppolino that day, facing slightly toward the right of the witness box and staring with hooded eyes at Marjorie Farber, her accusation was not beyond comprehension.

His skin as gray as the walls of his cell in the Monmouth

County Jail, his hawkish nose accentuated by his loss of weight and the delicate elegance of his spare frame were reminiscent of Hollywood type-casting in Grade B adaptations of Dracula. As one reporter observed sourly, his appearance and composure was one which promised a conviction on purely aesthetic grounds if nothing else.

Satisfied with the apparent reasoning behind Marjorie's reluctance to speak out any earlier on the death of her husband, Keuper then turned to a more delicate area of questioning that was designed to show what triggered her to come forward as the accuser, the nemesis of Carl Coppolino.

Marjorie Farber certainly realized that the destruction of her onetime lover could not be selective. The affected area—Ground Zero—would include, to some degree, herself and her children, and all those related to the Farbers and the Coppolinos by blood or marriage.

It would take a person of considerable confidence and much complexity to have assumed the role Marjorie Farber was now playing. Motivation can never be artistically simplified, nor can one's actions ever be entirely comprehended. In any chain of dramatic events, only the first step—like that of launching a boat into a torrent—is an act of free will. Once afloat we become the victim of all those secondary decisions which must be made hastily and precisely to avoid capsizing.

One must assume that Vincent Keuper keyed his redirect to Marjorie's motivation in taking the stand against Carl Coppolino and, in so doing, exposing herself to incrimination in a murder, and to an oversimplification of those impulses. Complexities and nuances of the motivating factors would be wasted. We demand simple answers—black and white—and this was the answer Vincent Keuper was trying to give to the jurors listening to Marge Farber.

After establishing that Bill Farber had never had a heart condition and that Carmela Coppolino had never attended him prior to July 30, 1963, Vincent Keuper turned to the reason Marge Farber was on the stand.

"Mr. Bailey asked you a question about your visit to Doctor Karow in Sarasota, and in which he told you he didn't want the conversation, he wanted your purpose."

"My purpose—"

"Wait a minute. Will you let me finish the question, Mrs. Farber?"

"I'm sorry."

"He wanted the purpose of your visit. What was the purpose of your visit to Doctor Karow?"

"The purpose was that I had heard conflicting reports about the fact that an autopsy had been—"

"I object."

"If Your Honor please, the door was opened."

"You can't open the door and then shut out anything that may blow in," the judge told Bailey, who said he had no objection to the testimony but that the conflicting reports from an undisclosed source was hearsay. The Court agreed, advising her that she could tell that there were conflicting reports but not to go into it in detail.

Marge Farber's testimony then took the form of a narrative which, on occasion, was interrupted by objections from Bailey and admonishments from the Court, but nevertheless moved inexorably toward at least a partial explanation of her motives for assuming the role of Coppolino's accuser.

"The conflicting reports came from Carl and Carl's mother, and then I had gone to Mr. Shannon because of this and I asked him point-blank as a friend of Carmela's if he would please clarify this particular question in my mind. Was there an autopsy performed on Carm? And there wasn't. He showed me the certificate, the box marked NO was checked so that is when I went to Doctor Karow and told her my story based on some suspicions."

F. Lee Bailey, listening to her narrative, had good cause to remember, and possibly to regret, asking Marge on Friday, just before the mid-afternoon recess, what her purpose was in going to Dr. Karow.

"What was your purpose" is a "why" question. It goes to motive. Bailey had opened up the death of Carmela, and, as the judge had ruled, he had no way of stopping what was now blowing in.

Marjorie recounted the happenings on the eve of Carmela's death in Florida in 1965:

"Carl had called me up and was very angry—this was the 27th of August—and he called me about six-thirty. I had seen him around five. He said, 'I have a black cloud hanging over my head' and I didn't know what he was talking about. He said, 'I don't appreciate you spying on me, your Gestapo methods,' and I said, 'What on earth is the matter with you?' and he said, 'Because Carm is all upset,' apparently because I told her I had met some gal named Mary.''

Her speech was conversational and her normally husky voice

had a nasal ring when she pronounced the word *gal*. The phrase itself—"I had met some gal named Mary"—had a flippancy and an almost hostile impertinence.

"I met her at St. Armand's Circle with Carl. He was sitting in her car . . . the same day, the 27th of August . . ." and Keuper established quickly that this meeting had occurred prior to the call from Carl. She repeated the conversation with Carl a second time and added, "I was completely amazed that he would come up and say such a thing."

She was admonished by the Court not to say how she felt and then continued to testify that Carl had hung up on her, angry, and she didn't talk to him again until the following morning when she called the Coppolino home around 9 or 9:30.

"I called the house and Carl answered the telephone and I asked him—I asked for Carm and then I realized—I said to him 'You sound funny, what is the matter?' and he said, 'Carm's dead,' and I said, 'What did you do to her?' . . . He didn't say anything. And then I begged him if I could come out there and when I found out that—what he told me about Carm's death, and because I was completely shocked. (objection, sustained) Well I asked him on the telephone if I could please come out to be of some assistance, in what capacity I didn't know, and he didn't want me to come out at first, but finally he said all right, I could come out. And I told my daughters that—(objection, sustained) —Then I went out there and he wasn't in his house—he was across the street, and I went across the street and I saw him there, and I just looked at him, and I said, 'I don't know what to say' because of Carm; and there was general conversation about someone had to pick out something for her to wear, and I offered to do that. And so, I went back to their house and I picked out some things, and I picked out a pink suit, and—"

Marjorie Farber was introducing testimony that was, in the strictest sense, hardly germane to the prosecution of Carl Coppolino for the murder of Colonel Bill Farber but, up to this point, there had been little objection from the defense table. One must assume that Bailey, recognizing Keuper's motives in opening this line of questioning, was also taking a calculated risk that still another interpretation could be placed upon Marge's explanation of why she had turned on the man who had been her lover. Bailey was apparently gambling that Marjorie, in her reference to Mary and her obvious chagrin at being shunned by Carl in his "hour of need" would trap herself into assuming the role of the scorned woman hell bent for revenge.

It is perhaps worthy of note that Marjorie Farber's testimony in New Jersey was not—out of necessity—a total disclosure of the events of August 28, 1965. In the 1967 interview with Theo Wilson of the New York *Daily News* Marge hinted, either consciously or unconsciously, at still another interpretation of her willingness to go to the Coppolino home the day Carmela died:

> *Marge said that before Carm died, when she (Marge) used to tell Carl she couldn't live anymore with the knowledge of her husband's death, "he would tell me nobody would believe me if I said he killed Bill. He would tell me he would have me committed."*
> *For the first time, Marge revealed that on the day of Carm's death, while Carl was at a neighbor's across the street after the body had been removed, she went through the Coppolino house "like a dose of salts, looking for a needle." She didn't find one.*

Marge, with Keuper's prompting, continued her testimony about what had happened the day of Carmela's death:

"Then he came back to the house. I remember there was a phone call and his end of the conversation was, 'They have already started the arterial work,' and I asked him what that meant and he said, 'They have not performed an autopsy.' (objection, overruled) Well, I asked him where the children were and he told me at Mary's and I didn't know Mary's last name at that time . . . And then I called Mary, I did find—I went through the personal telephone listings and found a name, Mary Gibson.''

Throughout her testimony Keuper posed very brief, direct, swiftly paced questions, repeatedly seeking direct conversations between Marge and Carl and, at the same time, channeling her answers so that there would be less interruption by defense objections on the grounds she was being unresponsive.

"Did you have a conversation with the defendant that evening?" (The evening of Carmela's death, August 28, 1965.)

"Yes, I did.''

"Telephone or in person.''

"In person.''

"Where?''

"Out near his house. I was driving out that way and quite by accident I came up in back of him in my car and I honked at him and I stopped him and I told him where I had been, that I just had seen Carmela, and that she looked lovely and so he said, "Yes, she was sure sad,' but he didn't go to see her. I—'' (objection, sustained) "Well, he said that—I told him she looked lovely and he said he was sure she did and then he said, he

362

looked at me and he said, 'Things could have been different,' and I, I don't know what he was referring to—'' (objection, sustained).

Marge then told, over the objection of Bailey, that Carl had made an appointment with her the Saturday night following Carmela's death. He came to her apartment.

''He told me it was not true that he was going to marry Mary Gibson. I said, 'Well, I haven't thought about it one way or the other whether he was.' Then he said to me, 'I had even considered marrying you,' and I said, 'Thanks a lot.' (The 'thanks a lot' phrase was given the same reading as a cab driver acknowledging a nickel tip.) And then he started to ask me if I would like to be his housekeeper and I said (with lofty disdain), 'No, I have my own life to live.' I said, 'What about your friend, Mary?' He said, 'Oh, she's too busy with her social life.' Then he said, 'Well, maybe I'll marry her, maybe I won't. You know how I am. Might last a year.' I said, 'Do you think that you are being fair to her. Does she love you?' He said, 'Yes, she does love me.' I said, 'Do you love her?' He said, 'I don't know whether I do or not.' ''

As the testimony began to take on the flavor of imitation soap opera, Bailey wearily told the Court, ''Your Honor, I am going to ask at this point that all of this be stricken. It is wholly irrelevant.''

''Mr. Keuper, where are we going? Aren't we wandering far afield?'' Judge Simmill's questions reflected genuine puzzlement. There was a brief discussion between Keuper, Bailey, and the Court as to how far the prosecutor could probe into the death of Carmela Coppolino—especially with regard to relevancy to the death of Bill Farber—and the Court finally sustained Bailey's objection that the marital matters of Carl and Mary were immaterial.

''Was there anything further said by the defendant to you about the death of Carmela after that? (objection, overruled) Or what he intended to do?''

''He told me he was going to get married.''

''When did he tell you that?''

''Ten days after Carmela died he told me that he had gotten a marriage license. Then he got married within, I don't know, well, October 7th, to the best of my knowledge, is the wedding day and that was my whole motivation for—''

''You are giving us again your mental processes. Please don't do it,'' the Court interrupted. Vincent Keuper did not seek a completion of that answer, as the judge had intervened. But it is a subject for valid conjecture to wonder if Keuper knew how peculiarly unfortunate an impression her truncated sentence left, and if there was any acceptable question which would have given her a chance to clear it up, because surely she could not have meant to imply that Carl's wedding was her motivation for going to Karow and the authorities.

For the intent observer, any specific line of questioning seldom ends where in his judgment it achieves the strongest effect. Almost always they go on too long, or stop short of the objective. But these have to be individual value judgments, and presumably the trial attorneys will cut the cloth to match their measurement of the jury. It was impossible to detect whether or not Keuper had sufficiently clarified Marjorie's attitude and motivation.

In the Theo Wilson interview, following the Florida trial of Dr. Coppolino, Marge said, in a *Daily News* story published May 14, 1967, "I feel more guilty about Carm than anyone else . . . She'd still be alive if I had had the courage to speak up earlier." In a second interview, published the following day, Wilson writes, "When she finally went to the authorities, she said, it was not because she was consumed with jealousy over Carl's quick marriage to another woman, divorcee Mary Gibson," and later, in the same article, "I was not a woman scorned. I was a scornful woman."

The final questions asked by Keuper were, again, designed to counteract Bailey's dramatic termination of the cross-examination which halted Marge in mid-sentence and in shock from learning her husband had been strangled. Why was she shocked?

"Well, when I read the autopsy in the paper and it referred to his cracked—cricoid?—I thought my husband had died of suffocation." It was simple, direct, and understandable.

The recross-examination by Bailey consisted of four quick questions.

"Now, you say Carl threatened you by saying he'd have you committed as an insane person?"

"Yes."

"Did that frighten you, that you might actually be committed as insane?"

"He said . . ."

"Did it frighten you?"

"Of course."

F. Lee Bailey stood in silence for long moments, staring at the witness. She, in turn, gave that characteristic lift of the chin and stared back at him. It is fair to assume that either he had achieved the effect he wanted and was by his silence underlining it, or he was swiftly appraising other possible ways of terminating it.

"All right," he said. "That's all."

He turned on his heel and, as he returned to his seat at the defense table he smiled wryly and wearily at the jurors.

Chapter Twenty

Marjorie Farber's testimony ended shortly before 10:30 that morning. Although she had been subjected to an exhausting cross-examination, she walked from the courtroom with a deliberate and confident stride. She looked neither to the left or right. Then, finding herself in the semi-privacy of the Monmouth County courthouse corridor, she faltered and began to inhale an ammonia capsule one of her attorneys suddenly waved beneath her nose. She began to cry, and said afterward she was glad she had not given "them" the satisfaction of seeing her break down like that in court.

Presumably Marjorie Farber was beginning to show the effects of her ordeal of Friday and this morning. It was hardly the collapse, as some would prefer to believe, of a woman who suddenly realized her appearance had been for nothing—that her story had not been believed, or had been discredited by the defense attorney's cross-examination—for she was to say months later: "We heard the news about the verdict. I cannot tell you the terrible despair . . . the shock. I thought, they didn't believe me; I have gone through all this and what did it prove?

"It was like hearing that President Kennedy had been shot. You heard it, but you didn't believe it. Vicky (her daughter) asked me, 'Should I drive?' I was in shock. That was the worst, the very worst day of all."

Composing herself, Marge Farber left the courthouse that morning and walked down the front steps with her attorneys. She was greeted by a group of photographers who had set up an all-day vigil just beneath the statue of "Liberty Triumphant."

Two memorable pictures appeared in the afternoon editions and the following morning. One was a two-column shot of Marjorie looking directly into the camera and biting her tongue. Both were the work of a New York *Daily News* photographer.

With skill, timing and, undoubtedly a degree of luck, *News*man Danny Ferrell's second picture captured Marjorie Farber at the base of a bust of Abraham Lincoln. The Lincoln bust was cropped from the picture but to the left of a smiling Marge Farber and a smiling Warren Goodrich was the inscription "With Malice Toward None, With Charity For All."

Inside the courtroom, newspapermen rechecked and compared notes on Marge's testimony. Vincent Keuper then summoned his next witness. There was a short wait during which the prosecutor entered into evidence a 1963 New Jersey Bell Telephone Directory, showing a listing in the yellow pages for Dr. Carl A. Coppolino, M.D., "Practice Limited to Treatment by Hypnosis."

We must assume that Keuper's introduction of the telephone directory was, in his mind, necessary to the state's case and also a physical piece of evidence available to the jurors when they deliberated.

Invalided out of his profession for several months at the time the advertisement was placed, Carl Coppolino was, in early 1963, idle but interested in the practice of medical hypnosis. He had practiced medical hypnosis for several years, both as hypnotherapy and as an adjunct to the more common aspects of anesthesiology. Then he had a heart condition and could not work. Carmela had become Assistant Head of Professional Services at Hoffman-LaRoche at a salary of $15,000 a year. Carl's disability insurance policies brought in $600 a month, so there can be no doubt that, between the two of them, they lived more than adequately, maintaining the house with Dorothy Jeffress, the live-in maid.

But, after the years of active practice, he was restless. He began working on a text entitled *Practice of Hypnosis in Anesthesiology* which would be published by Grune and Stratton, Inc., in 1965. And, additionally, he arranged for the listing in the New Jersey directory.

Presumably Keuper reasoned if one were so sufficiently confident and competent to advertise a specialty in hypnosis, there is no reason to question Marge Farber's claim she went to Carl for hypnotherapy to enable her to stop smoking or that it was successful enough to allow her to stop for a year and a half. Secondly, there is little reason to doubt that Carl should have felt any reluctance about helping a neighbor nor any reason to suppose she did not make a reasonably good hypnotic subject. Accepting this, it might be more possible to believe the Svengali-Trilby relationship which Marjorie Farber claimed had existed.

366

Keuper's second witness was Dorothy Jeffress, the Negro live-in maid who had testified at the bail hearing wearing the same green patterned dress she had worn for that appearance.

The questioning of Dorothy Jeffress was brisk and with a ring of familiarity heightened by Keuper's reference to his witness as "Dorothy." Bailey in his turn would make a point of calling her "Mrs. Jeffress."

In thirty-four questions that elicited economical answers of "Yes, I did" or "No, I did not" and "I could" and "I was," Dorothy testified Carmela was at work the day of Farber's death and did not return until 6:00 P.M. She said that Carl left the house about 10:30 or 11:00 A.M. and returned to the house with Mrs. Farber between 2:30 and 3:00 that afternoon. She said they were together for approximately forty-five minutes in the dinette area of the Coppolino home. She also testified that the couple could have been outside, for a time, in the back yard of the home.

Continuing her testimony under the gentle questioning of Keuper—a tactic unlike that which the prosecutor had used with Marge Farger—Dorothy said Mrs. Farber left the Coppolino home "about four-thirty, something to five" and Carmela arrived as usual at six o'clock that evening. Thirty minutes later, the telephone rang. Dorothy answered. It was Mrs. Farber.

"And did you call Doctor Carmela Coppolino to the phone?"

"Yes, I did. Yes."

"And did she talk on the phone in your presence?"

"Yes, yes."

"Then after she finished the telephone conversation, what did she do?"

"Mrs. Coppolino left the house."

"What time was that?"

"Between six-forty and six forty-five."

"Then she returned later?"

"Yes, she did."

"And you were still there?"

"Yes, I was."

"Do you recall what time she returned?"

"About seven-fifteen."

Keuper's questions and Dorothy Jeffress' answers fell into a rhythmic pattern which seemed to blur the significance of her testimony. Each new question came so quickly upon the heels of the preceding answer there seemed not enough time for the spectator to comprehend, much less appraise, the substance of her responses.

"When next after that day did you see Doctor Coppolino, Carl Coppolino, and Mrs. Farber together?"

"The next morning."

"Where?"

"In the dinette area in the kitchen."

"Dorothy, I show you this exhibit marked D-4 for identification and ask you to examine it. Did you ever read that exhibit before?" It was the medical release Marge allegedly signed at 1 P.M. the day of Bill Farber's death, July 30.

"No."

"What did you see, if anything, Doctor Carl Coppolino and Mrs. Farber doing on the *morning following* July 30th? That would be *July 31st.*"

"Well, Doctor Coppolino was at the kitchen table writing and Mrs. Farber was there also. Whatever he wrote, Mrs. Farber signed."

Despite its pertinence, the answer had far less impact than when at the conclusion of Friday's court day Marjorie Farber, shocked and surprised, swore she had never seen the medical release nor had she any recollection of having signed such a statement. Bailey had led dramatically toward his climactic disclosure; Keuper, by his gentleness and his familiarity with the witness, had somehow minimized the impact of her answer.

In the handling of the introduction of the medical release, as stage-managed by Mr. Bailey, and in the attempt to de-fuse this piece of telling evidence, as underplayed by Mr. Keuper, the superior showmanship of F. Lee Bailey was very noticeable. "Showmanship" used in the courtroom context has a questionable semantic flavor, yet one would be hard put to find a more effective tool for underlining those elements the defense is most anxious to have the jury remember. In a trial where much evidence is introduced, only the points most dramatic or most often repeated will be those most prominently lodged in the collective memory of the jurors, and most likely to be discussed during the jurors' deliberations.

Also it is a considerable asset to be able to word questions entertainingly, in a crisp and often amusing style, because what entertains the jurors will keep their attention in closer focus than will the interrogations by persons less articulate, less able to vary the range and tone of voice. Entertainment equals attention, and attention equals memory. Much testimony in even the most dramatic murder trial can be just as dull as the attorneys permit it to be.

Bailey's cross-examination of Dorothy Jeffress was also direct and brisk, but in his manner there was a flavor of remoteness, almost of boredom, of a man going through a necessary routine, but without much interest in the outcome. It had the effect of imparting the impression that he believed her testimony to be of little value to either the state or the defense.

"*Mrs.* Jeffress, when was the first time after July 30th, 1963, that you were questioned about this incident?"

After two hasty and unresponsive replies, she said, "Three years."

"At the time of the incident did you make any *notes* about it?"

"At the time? No I did not."

"Did you keep any *diary* of what happened?"

"No. In my head, that's all."

"You *kept it in your head.* And you remember the sequence of the events of that day pretty clearly?"

"Yes I do."

"When did you first remember that the time she stayed was forty-five minutes to an hour, Dorothy?" (He had stated, in the form of a question, that Marjorie had stayed 30–45 minutes on July 30 and Dorothy had corrected him.)

"I don't recall remembering exactly whether it was forty-five minutes to an hour, but at the present time I was working and I had to be finished at a certain hour to do other things."

"Well now, you have appeared in this court before on a hearing, haven't you, back in October?"

"Yes."

"And you were asked by *me* precisely that same question: How long they were in the house?"

She said she remembered the question being asked and answering "thirty minutes to forty-five minutes, a half hour to forty-five minutes" and at no time testifying Marge had stayed an hour. This was, she told Bailey, the first time she had ever answered "an hour."

Actually, Bailey was engaging in a common trial practice, though with a dual purpose. He was concentrating on a minor discrepancy, thus assigning it major importance while simultaneously diverting attention from what was of more apparent importance in her testimony, i.e. signing of the medical release.

"Have you had some conversation with anyone between the time you testified here in October and today about this case?"

"Yes, I have."

"Did you talk with some representative of the prosecution?"

"I talked to Prosecutor Keuper."

"*Okay*. And you *now* say it was *forty-five minutes to an hour?*"

"Well, forty-five minutes. I said forty-five minutes there."

"You want to leave it as it *was, just* forty-five minutes, *period?*"

"No. I'll just have it as I have it."

After but a moment of hesitation Bailey decided to drop the matter and go on to another point. His instinct appeared to be sound. He had indulged in some strategic quibbling over a minor point, thus firmly fixing that point in the collective memory of the jury.

One might also imagine the jury, exposed to such emphasis on an apparently minor element, beginning to wonder if perhaps they had missed something. As a result they listen more carefully. The veiled hints of Bailey regarding Dorothy's "changed" testimony could then cause the jury to weigh, consciously or unconsciously, subsequent prosecution testimony more skeptically, especially if a witness seemed overly certain, unyielding and, more particularly, familiar with the prosecutor.

Dorothy went on to testify that Carl and Marge, to her knowledge, never left the dinette but volunteered also that she did not always have a clear view of the back yard. She said the couple was drinking.

"What were they drinking?"

"In my eyesight, I saw a bottle of gin."

"*In your eyesight*, you saw a bottle of gin."

"Yes, I did."

"What was there about the bottle that told you it was gin?"

"The label."

"The label said gin?"

"Yes."

"What kind of gin was it?"

"Gordon's." (Laughter in the courtroom.)

"You saw them both drinking?"

"I saw one drinking. I did not see them both drinking."

"Did you keep them under pretty close watch all the time they were there?"

"No, I didn't."

The phrasing and implication of this question has a psychological basis of considerable value, one can assume, when questioning anyone who while at work has had a chance to observe the actions of others. It contains the concealed accusation that the witness might be a snoop, a classification we are all anxious to

370

avoid. In fact it would often seem that those who are most curious and observant will soonest deny it.

"Were you continuing with your housework?"

"Yes, I was."

Then, after a few questions about how long the door to the dinette area might have been closed, Bailey asked, "You didn't make it your business to keep an eye on what Doctor Coppolino was doing in his own home, did you?"

"Never! No, I did not!"

And thus through forcing her by the implications of his questions to affirm her own image of herself as the diligent servant, minding her own business, Bailey further diffused her testimony, and cast an additional cloud on the plausibility of her exactitude in recollection of long-past events.

It is quite possible that when Mr. Bailey turned her back to Mr. Keuper for redirect, he assumed that Keuper would try to nail down the exact sequence of her observation of Coppolino preparing, and Mrs. Farber signing documents, by bringing out, through questions, that the interposition of the death of the man who lived just up the road had sharpened her memory of those few days, and eliciting her denial that there was any possibility she had seen Mrs. Farber signing anything on the afternoon of the day of death. In appraising the line Bailey had taken in cross-examination, it would appear that he had established the groundwork for a potentially destructive recross had Keuper pursued this line in redirect.

But Vincent Keuper had no more questions. The witness was excused. She seemed, for the moment, both surprised and relieved, as she walked forever out of this public contest.

As laymen we have all been victimized by those myths and conventions of fictional drama, wherein the stage attorneys ask all those questions which have become obligatory because they have occurred to us, the audience, and have been made to seem necessary through the dramatist's art. The fictional attorney pleases and excites us by asking those questions. But in the grinding business of the real arena, the areas of tactical and strategic revelation are muted by equivalent areas of strategic and tactical concealment. The chore of each adversary is to take his witness through only such testimony as will contribute to his case, whether it be prosecution or defense, and to block and weaken the attempts of his adversary to diminish the jury-effect of that testimony. Thus there will always be areas avoided by both sides in the direct and cross-examination of any witness, because the minor advantages they may detect are outweighed by the potential vulnerability of the witness under recross or redirect.

The total revelation, customary in conventional drama, is missing, and so when a witness is excused the attentive observer is left burning with curiosity about how she might have answered the questions which he—in his ignorance of the rules of evidence—thinks imperative.

After all, this young woman had lived in the Coppolino household from January of 1963 to December of 1964, just four months before Carl and Carmela moved to Florida. Now she walked off stage, without ever letting us know what reason they had given for letting her go, without telling us if they seemed to be a loving couple, happily married. If they were good to work for. If Doctor Carmela seemed to enjoy her work. If Carmela's mood changed when Doctor Carl went on trips with Mrs. Farber. If Carmela was friendly toward Marge Farber. If the Farber children came to the Coppolino home. How much time each day Doctor Carl worked on the manuscripts of his eventually published books. Who their other friends were. How often they entertained.

Not acceptable testimony, certainly, depending far too much on subjective appraisals, but acceptable in the human sense, as here was someone who had shared the home for twenty-three of the final thirty-one months of the life of Carmela Musetto Coppolino, M.D.

This is the basis for the let-down when the witnesses leave the stand. We yearn for all the revelations of the troubled heart, and all we get are a few hints and clues, as if we were to be given a few hundred pieces of a thousand-piece jigsaw puzzle, and are compelled to lay them out on the table in what we think is the probable pattern, and must then assume what might have gone into all the broad empty areas. As with all jigsaw puzzles, the background areas are the most difficult. Too many of the pieces look exactly alike.

At ten minutes of eleven Dr. Carmelo Musetto was called by the state. He walked slowly to the witness stand, no doubt thinking of the cross-examination by Bailey which would follow Mr. Keuper's direct examination, and remembering the strain and awkwardness of the time he had spent on the stand under interrogation by Bailey at the preliminary hearing in Sarasota. His walk was that of a man in bad health, avoiding all unnecessary exertion. Carmelo—retired general practitioner of medicine—who had named his first-born Carmela—who had married a boy christened Carmelo Anthony Coppolino who became known as Carl.

As had been true of Marjorie Farber, this was his fifth appearance under oath. Both had testified at the preliminary hearing in Sarasota and, prior to that, before one grand jury in New Jersey, and two grand juries in Sarasota. And both witnesses had the reasonable anticipation of appearing at another trial in Florida, provided Carl Coppolino was not found guilty as charged by this New Jersey jury.

Once Keuper had swiftly established the relationship of the witness to the defendant ("His deceased wife was my daughter. He was my son-in-law.") he went directly to Musetto's recall of a conversation he'd had with Carmela and Carl on an August weekend in 1963 immediately after the death of Colonel Farber.

"During the summer of 1963, subsequent to July 30th, did you have a discussion with your daughter in the presence of the defendant relative to the death of William E. Farber?"

"I did."

"When did that conversation take place?"

"It was a weekend in August of 1963."

"Who was present?"

"My deceased daughter, Doctor Carmela Coppolino, Doctor Carl Coppolino, and myself."

"Where did the conversation take place?"

"It took place on the lawn in front of the house at 35 Wallace Road, Middletown Township."

"There was a discussion about William E. Farber?"

"The discussion was about William E. Farber."

"Will you tell the Court and jury what the conversation was?"

"The weather had been hot that summer—" (Objection. Sustained by the Court who told Musetto to relate only what was said by whom and to whom.)

"Do you understand the question, Doctor?"

"I do understand the question, *sir*, and I'm trying to limit myself as to what was said without bringing in what was objected to, *sir*."

"All right, sir," said Judge Simmill.

"May I say what I said first? How it came about, *sir?*"

"Doctor Coppolino was there. You may tell us what was said either by you or by anybody else," advised the judge.

"Thank you, *sir*. I was discussing the hot weather myself, in their presence, and how this weather is at times detrimental to men at a certain age, forty, fifty, sixty, who work behind a desk all week and then on weekends become gardeners and how at times it can be detrimental to them as shoveling of snow is detrimental in the wintertime and my daughter Carmela said, 'Well, there's an example up the street,' pointing to Colonel Farber's house. 'That man died of a coronary and, apparently, it was work he did over the weekend as a gardener that brought on this attack and he died of a coronary' and I said, 'Well, that's unfortunate.' I said, 'Who treated him?' And Doctor Carl Coppolino said, 'I treated him.' I said to Carl, 'You did what? What did you do for him?' And Carl said, 'Yes, I treated him.' I said, 'Then what procedure did you follow, what did you do?' And I must make my point clear in treatment. We doctors, when we say treatment—''

He was reminded by the judge to confine his remarks to the conversation in the front yard and, after apologizing to the Court and the prosecutor, the doctor continued, telling the jury how Carl told him a cardiologist had not been called and that Carl had said he made no attempt to hospitalize Colonel Farber.

Dr. Musetto said he admonished his daughter and his son-in-law, reminding Carl he had a heart condition for which he was drawing disability insurance that could be cut off should the firm learn he had treated a case. He reminded Carl his treatment of Colonel Farber ''went out with high button shoes'' and that he was subject to a suit because he had not followed ''the procedure.''

''Well, he said, 'I'm qualified. I'm able to take care of it.' I said, 'Then you signed the death certificate?' And Carmela, *my deceased daughter*, said, 'I signed the death certificate.' I said, *'You what?'* At this time, ladies and gentlemen (turning to the jury box) I was reprimanding both of these young people. (objection, sustained) *'You* signed the death certificate?' 'Yes.' 'Why did you?' 'I did it to protect Carl.' 'Did you see Mr. Farber alive?' She says, 'No.' 'When did you see Mr. Farber?' *'After* he was dead.'

''I said, 'Did you report this to the medical examiner or coroner?' Whatever it is in this county. She said, 'No.' 'How long was he ill? Was it within twenty-four hours?'

''Again, 'Carmela, did you see this man alive?' 'No, I did not.' 'Well, how could you make the diagnosis?' *'Carl* told me the diagnosis and *Carl* told me what to put down on the death certificate.' So I said, *'My God*, Carmela. I have *never*—I didn't bring you up that way as your father.' ''

The emphasis that Dr. Musetto placed upon Carl and Carmela failing to report the death of Colonel William E. Farber to the proper county authority foreshadowed subsequent testimony the prosecution would introduce through the appearance of Julius A. Toren, Monmouth County's County Physician in 1963, and Robert F. Worden, the funeral director in charge of arrangements for the burial of Colonel Farber.

An article appeared in the April 10, 1967, issue of *JAMA (Journal of the American Medical Association)* entitled "Medical Science in Crime Detection," based upon a study done by the Committee on Medicolegal Problems.

The report discusses the effectiveness of medical participation in the administration of justice, the need of the American community for an adequate system of medical science to aid in the detection of crimes which could go undetected because of inadequate medicolegal investigative procedures.

"The scope of statutory authorization for investigations is related directly to the adequacy of medical participation in crime detection," the article states. "Restrictive laws are undesirable. If investigation is limited solely to those cases in which there exists, prior to investigation, a reasonable basis to believe that death was caused by a criminal act, many homicides are apt to escape detection. In some cases, no basis for belief that a crime has been committed will be found unless an investigation is made. Suspicious circumstances or the mere absence of evidence that death resulted from natural causes may be sufficient to warrant a medicolegal investigation."

This portion of the Musetto testimony established a situation which did not seem to yield to any emotionally logical interpretation, and so it became another of those areas debated heatedly and without solution by the newsmen that evening at the American Hotel after all stories had been filed.

The problem, of course, was to determine in some reasonable way how Carmela had justified signing the death certificate, stating thereon that she *had* attended the dying man and treated him during times when she was probably at her job in Nutley, an hour's drive north.

All conceivable theories of guilt and innocence were tested against the actions taken by the defendant and by his wife, in attempts by people well versed in motivation and deviousness, to make the pieces fit.

"Okay, so her old daddy says she did it to protect Carl's total disability insurance. Now is an insurance company going to put the knock on him for answering an emergency? He was licensed to practice, right? And he was in the yellow pages, practice limited to hypnosis, right? And when Bailey cross-examined

Marge she said Carl said that Bill Farber should go to a hospital. And so we've got a release in evidence that Carl had Marge sign when he wouldn't go to a hospital. So what the hell was Carmela protecting? He had the release. So why should she stick her neck out and falsify a death certificate and then not file it with the County Physician and take a big risk of getting into such a mess she'd maybe lose a very good job. She just doesn't sound like that much of a damned fool. And with a release, why would Carl want her to stick her neck out?''

"Now wait a minute! Try this way. Carl gives up on the colonel. He's said the hell with it. So when Marge finds out Bill Farber is dead, she knows she isn't going to get anywhere with Carl. So she waits until she's sure her good friend Carm is home from work and calls her over. She lays the whole thing in Carm's lap. If she calls in another doctor to sign the death certificate, there's going to be an investigation by the County Physician. Marge is loaded with guilt knowing she should have followed Carl's advice about the hospital. She just didn't think Bill was that sick. Okay, so Carm sees that Marge was negligent, and she also sees that Carl didn't handle it very well. She sees that there are going to be a lot of questions about why didn't Carl phone a cardiologist right off. After all, with his own heart problem, he knew a few in the area. Let's say Carm was no dummy. Any woman that goes through medical school and takes her turn cutting up cadavers isn't going to be any naïve little Italian housewife when it comes to her husband kiting off to Miami with anybody who looks like Marge Farber. And suppose the investigation would get around to the neighborhood gossip about Carl and Marge? It could get to be a very messy thing, with a lot of people getting a lot of wrong ideas about maybe Bill didn't die of a coronary. Carm sees that they both acted like damned fools, so she risks taking them off the hook by filling out the death certificate, and signing it. And how do we know she didn't even *know* it had to go to the County Physician's office. After all, it was going to be in the paper, and she did file it later on with the Bureau of Vital Statistics. She worked in a lab. Maybe she just didn't know the procedure.''

Then someone else would say, "All right, now turn that one inside out and take a look at it. Let's say Marge told the truth about it being murder. So they go back to Carl's house that afternoon, leaving him dead with the sign on the door, and they gradually realize they are up the creek because if Carl signs the certificate they can run into a lot of gossip and an investigation. So they work out a way to con Carmela into doing it, because I'd

376

guess people would be a lot more willing to take her word than Carl's, under the circumstances. So Marge signs a release and they get their stories straight on what happened, and when Carm goes over, Marge gives her the same line you just described and she buys it, thinking it was a coronary occlusion, and wanting to save her husband and her friend from scandal, maybe for the sake of the kids involved."

That concept is discussed, and holes are picked in it, and then someone inevitably suggests that when Carmela went to the Farber house, Marge told her that Carl in a fit of rage had smothered Bill Farber. And unless she comes to the rescue, eight more lives are going to be ruined.

"But wouldn't Carl have told Marge to make certain her daughters were out of the house and then gone over with Carm to help convince her?"

"How about the maid—Dorothy Jeffress? Maybe Carl wanted everything to look normal."

"So what's normal about him *not* going along with Carm?"

"Because he had a release and he'd washed his hands of it."

"And if that is the way it was, what about the Jeffress testimony that she never heard Carm and Carl ever mention the death of the colonel?"

"Musetto testified Carl said he didn't recommend hospitalization."

Every theory ran directly into an emotional improbability, until at last a sour and elderly reporter from Philadelphia said, "I can tell you one thing you can absolutely depend on, gentlemen." After eager questions he savored the dramatic pause and then said, "We are never going to hear Carmela's side of the story."

"Don't bother," said another cynic. "She was hypnotized and wouldn't remember a thing."

Having established that Carl had presumably told his father-in-law that he had not suggested hospitalization for the colonel, Vincent Keuper took a two-year leap forward in time, which brought F. Lee Bailey quickly to his feet.

At this point during the examination of Dr. Musetto, Bailey appeared to genuinely irritate Judge Simmill for the first time during the trial.

Keuper asked Dr. Musetto when he first learned of the death of his daughter, Carmela, and from whom.

"I object, there is no relevancy," Bailey said.

"Mr. Prosecutor, *are* we getting off the track?"

"I don't think so, sir."

"You represent to the Court that this will be connected?"

"I am going to represent to the Court that Mr. Bailey opened this door last Friday afternoon. He talked about the death of Carmela Coppolino and this is related to it."

"If the Court please," Bailey interrupted. "If Mr. Keuper wants to try that case, too, let's bring all of the evidence and try them both, but I see no relevancy to the death of Colonel Farber with anything that happened to Carmela Coppolino."

"Is this in any way connected with the testimony given by Mrs. Farber in connection with Carmela?" Simmill asked Keuper.

"Yes it is. There was some reference made to an autopsy of Carmela."

"I object to that, Your Honor!" Bailey yelled, face reddening. "If Your Honor please—"

"We are going to have a mistrial here!" Bailey announced loudly, interrupting Keuper a second time.

"We are *not* going to have a mistrial unless *I* grant it," Judge Simmill snapped.

"I understand that," Bailey replied, voice lower, and suddenly much milder.

"Don't interrupt Mr. Keuper when he is speaking," the judge continued, as one might rebuke an unmannerly child.

"I apologize."

Judge Simmill, frowning at Bailey, added, "I think it is just common courtesy." Bailey apologized a second time.

Keuper was resuming his questioning of Dr. Musetto about the autopsy when the witness, sagging heavily in the chair, asked for a glass of water and popped what appeared to be nitroglycerin tablets into his mouth. Keuper suggested a recess, immediately granted.

Chapter Twenty-one

It would be pointless to conjecture as to whether Bailey was as indignant and angry as he had appeared to be. The most likely answer is that in the courtroom—as in the confrontations of the old-time gunfighters of Western legend—genuine anger is a disease which only afflicts the amateur. It might have had some effect on a weaker judge, but Elvin Simmill, in his sixty-second year, was a man of tough and flexible mind with a history of but four reversals during his eighteen years on the bench. It is possible that his irritation with Bailey was because Bailey presumed that his imitation of anger and outrage *could* have any effect upon a judge of Simmill's experience and stature.

Bailey, with a clear memory of Musetto's testimony at the preliminary hearing in Florida, was willing to take a considerable courtroom risk to roadblock this area of direct examination.

Keuper had won his point. Just before the recess when Musetto felt unwell, and the wrangling had been terminated, Judge Simmill had ruled that Keuper could question Musetto about the area of the autopsy on Carmela which Bailey had brought up in his cross-examination of Marjorie Farber. He showed every intention of pursuing this matter.

During the recess, in quiet corridor conversations, reporters from the north queried the reporters from Florida about where Keuper was going and why Bailey had objected so violently. Florida reporters, familiar with the preliminary hearing testimony, said that Bailey had opened a door which might let in some testimony that would be inferentially damaging to his client.

Yet when court was reconvened at 11:27, Keuper relinquished his witness to the defense for cross-examination with no further questions. His tactical reasoning for that decision was at that time, and still remains, quite obscure. It is remotely possible that Keuper was so confident of securing a verdict of guilty that he did not wish to create any possible basis for a successful appeal.

Bailey, by the tone of his objections during direct testimony, had indicated what his approach to Dr. Carmelo Musetto would be.

The Musetto testimony was damaging to his client, but even more damaging was the awareness of the jury, their inescapable awareness that here was the father of Carl's dead wife. Every juror knew that Carl was under indictment in Florida for the murder of the dead daughter. And thus the very presence of Musetto as a witness for the state in the case of the alleged murder of Colonel Farber would lead each juror to assume that Musetto also believed that Carl had murdered Carmela.

Bailey's only possible approach was to destroy this witness in the eyes of the jury. The task was formidable. This was a portly, ailing, retired, bereaved physician. Anything less than destruction would create sympathy for the old man.

Had he been a likable old man, Bailey's task would have been impossible.

Our culture places an undue emphasis on the agreeable

personality, on winning ways, on personal charm. Dr. Musetto had spent his active professional life in Boonton, New Jersey, a place which, until the most very recent highway constructions, was too far from the megalopolis to be a bedroom community. It is a small city built upon small steep hills beside a pleasant river. A relatively large percentage of the population is of Italian derivation. Dr. Musetto, over the years, had developed a large and profitable general practice, approaching a six-figure income. He had standing and respect in the community. One can readily imagine him entertaining guests at a reserved table at the Pudding Stone Inn high on the hill overlooking Parsippany Reservoir, that lovely lake which covers the small city drowned when it was built, imagine him ordering expansively and well, and receiving special service and attention from the staff.

One can believe him to have been a good doctor, gentle and reassuring with his patients, making those doctor-jokes which ease the anxieties of the sick. He was a lover of classical music, and played the violin in an amateur string quartet which often performed in public.

His first wife had died of complications attending the birth of her second child, in 1935, a week after the boy was born. She had been a few days past her thirty-first birthday. The infant Andrew had lived but a month and a day. Carmela was twenty-two months old when her mother died. Dr. Musetto married again, a woman four years older than his first wife had been, and by her he had one child, Angela, Carmela's half sister. His second wife took her own life in 1963 at age sixty-two, after years of mental disorders.

The Musetto family plot is in a small Catholic cemetery high on a grassy hill—a quiet place with a long view of the hills, the lake, the river. The names of the dead are carved into the side of the monument which faces the view: LILLIAN EBE MUSETTO. ANDREW. VIOLA R. MUSETTO. And, at the left, under the static vividness of the bouquet of bright plastic blooms and vivid plastic leaves, is carved into the gray marble CARMELA COPPOLINO, M.D. MAR. 30, 1933. AUG. 28, 1965. The M.D. under such circumstances curiously transcends any pretension or vulgarity and pinches the heart.

It was this man, thirty years his elder, that F. Lee Bailey had to destroy in the presence and opinion of the jury. The doctor's vulnerability was twofold. First he had the armor of many skills and assurances. This meant that he had the self-awareness of financial success, the skills and memberships of a respected profession, the self-confidence of his awareness of cultural matters,

380

the awareness of having led a full emotional life, the strength that results from having survived a dangerous heart attack. . . . in fact the armor of having achieved security financially, professionally, emotionally and intellectually.

Secondly, so many years had passed he had perhaps forgotten what it was like to face contempt, a calculated insolence, derision, scorn, disbelief. He was emotionally adjusted to respect. And, in his mannered way, with heavy sighs, with a dragging and patronizing emphasis on the word "sir," and in the frequency with which he larded his responses with that word, he had been registering a little contempt of his own, as if to say that it was unseemly for a doctor to have to conform to the curious little antics and idiocies of these prancing lawyer fellows. He had been overly dramatic when the situation allowed it, as when he had related the conversation about the colonel's death which he'd had with Carl and his daughter. When reprimanded by the Court he had been so overly humble that it became more condescension than humility.

It is certainly neither crime nor misdemeanor to have a public personality which is less than likable. But it put a telling weapon within reach of Lee Bailey. We are all too willing to attribute all manner of faults and flaws, and all kinds of unworthy motives to those persons whom we find unattractive. It was Bailey's obligation to his client to use Musetto as a weapon against Musetto. With enough goading the man might become even less palatable.

Bailey began by asking, "Doctor Musetto, you gave some testimony down in Sarasota, Florida, about the same matters, didn't you?"

"I did."

"You at that time *attempted* [a subtle emphasis] to describe the same conversation that you have just related to us about Colonel Farber's death and so forth."

"As best as I could remember at that time."

"Has your memory increased since that time?"

"Yes *sir*."

"You have remembered some things that you then had forgotten?"

"I have given this a lot of thought and consideration, Mr. Bailey."

"I think the question was this: Have you remembered some things you forgot in September?"

"No. No. I have not remembered things that I had forgotten in September."

"Your memory in September was as good as it is today? Is that right?"

"No, *sir*. I disagree with you."

Bailey then—reading from a transcript of Musetto's testimony at the Florida hearing, began taking the doctor through his previous questions and responses, similar to those given Keuper on direct, and then said, "When you testified about this in Florida, you didn't say anything about Carl claiming that he did not try to put him in the hospital, did you?"

"I remember now."

"You remember *now?*" [polite incredulity]

"I remember better now. If you will allow me to explain to you. You won't. . . . You are not allowing me and you are not giving this court a correct interpretation."

Judge Simmill sustained Bailey's motion that Musetto's comments be stricken.

Next Bailey asked for the specific date when Musetto had suddenly remembered this additional part of the 1963 conversation. He could not remember. Then Bailey pressed him to remember when he had first told anyone of this new recollection, and Musetto said that it was first told in an interview with Mr. Keuper.

"I at that time told him that, in the course of thinking about these things over a period of weeks, I recalled certain things now—I had recalled certain things up to this date that I had—that I did not at that time."

"Do you know, Doctor, that Mrs. Farber testified that Carl *did* try to put him in the hospital? Did you know that?"

"I haven't been here." [I haven't been here in court where I could hear these things, if they happened as you say.]

"Is this the *first* time you have learned that?" [amazement]

"I was reading something about it in the papers over the weekend. How much stock I can take in what is in the newspaper, I don't know, *sir*."

"You needn't believe what you read in the newspapers."

Here it is possible that Lee Bailey experimented to see what would happen if he made a small overture. Perhaps he hoped that Musetto would interpret it as a sign of weakness and switch from a defensive posture to an offensive one. If so, he was not disappointed.

"Thank you, *sir! Thank* you!" said Musetto, in a dramatic and effusive irony that perhaps only he appreciated.

Bailey moved on to get confirmation that Musetto had reprimanded his daughter for signing the death certificate, then asked,

382

"And that was the extent of your testimony down in Florida, wasn't it, the conversation that I have just described to you?"

This form of question might be called the Carrot and Donkey question. The proper answer is, of course, "Yes." But it is phrased in such a way that it seems to the witness that here is an opportunity to add to the testimony, to say that there was more that should now go on the record.

It then becomes—and became—a semantic quibbling, with Bailey insisting on a simple affirmative or negative to the question asked, and Musetto trying, over the objections of the defense, and even the prosecution, to say that there was more, there was more that he had remembered which should be included.

There can be some danger, however, in trying to edge a witness too close to the brink.

"Did you recall this additional testimony when you were on the witness stand in Florida? Just yes or no."

"What additional material, *sir?*"

"The material you have testified to here today that wasn't testified to in Florida."

"Did I recall it then?"

"Yes."

"If I had recalled it then, I would have testified to it." This had a simple emotional logic, an unexpectedly persuasive directness, requiring of Bailey an effort to negate the effect it could have had upon the jurors.

"Then your answer is no?"

"The answer is no. I didn't at that time."

"Sometime between September and today you have recalled additional facts, you *say?*" The subtle weight on the final word was certain to offend a man of Musetto's pride.

"Yes! And I also have recalled certain—"

"Please!" said Bailey with a tactical use of impatience and irritation. "You have answered the question *now*." The stress he gave to "now" gave it the same approximate semantic weight as if he had substituted "at long last."

"Where is your residence, Doctor Musetto?" asked Bailey in a sudden switch to a new area.

"My— Which residence? Permanent or temporary?"

"You have *more* than *one* residence?"

"Oh yes. Yes." [Indifference. "Doesn't everyone?"]

"Tell us about the one you have in Florida."

Keuper, knowing well where Bailey was headed, having read the preliminary hearing transcript, interposed strenuous objection on the grounds of materiality, but the question was permitted.

Musetto gave his Bowsprit Lane address and, under interrogation, stated that he had purchased the house from "Doctor Carl and his present wife, Mrs. Mary."

Again Keuper objected and was overruled.

"And," asked Bailey, "the mortgagee is Carl Coppolino?"

"That is correct."

"Have you had a little dispute with Carl about that mortgage, Doctor?"

"I have." Musetto, as aware as was Keuper of where Bailey was headed, seemed agitated.

"As a matter of fact, did you write Carl a little letter about it?"

Musetto said indignantly, "It is the same letter you brought down below. [Brought up at the preliminary hearing in Florida.] Shall we read it all today? Or just part of it, like you refused to read it the last time?" Musetto stared at Bailey triumphantly, like someone who by careful planning has suddenly and surprisingly bested a deadly opponent.

Judge Simmill said, "Will you please just answer the question and don't ask him questions."

"I am sorry, sir."

"Is that your signature?" Bailey held the second sheet of the two page letter toward Musetto, pointing to the bottom of the page.

"That is my signature. Yes."

"You would like the entire letter read, instead of an excerpt? Is that right?"

"If you please, sir, and I would like to have the pleasure of explaining why I wrote that letter."

"All right," said Bailey with a bland cheeriness.

"If the Court will allow me to," said Musetto.

Simmill said, "The Court will allow you to answer such questions as counsel may put to you, sir."

"Thank you, sir," said the doctor.

Bailey said, "On March 16, 1966, on a letterhead 'Carmelo A. Musetto, M.D., Boonton, New Jersey,' did you state—"

"That is not the whole letter, sir. Why don't you read it all?" Musetto asked this with an air of triumph.

"All right. 'M.D., F.I.C.S., F.I.A.P., A.A.G.P.' "

"All right! What else is on the top of the letter? Diplomate of the—"

"Diplomate of the International Board of Proctology."

"That's right! Let's read it all!"

"442 Birch Street."

"Four what?"

"412 Birch Street. Is that right?"

At that point Dr. Carmelo Musetto, believing perhaps that he had Lee Bailey in confusion and had successfully outwitted him, took off his dark glasses and held them out at arm's length toward Bailey and said, "You need my glasses. 412 Birch Street."

Judge Simmill said irritably, "Wait a minute, Doctor. If you are to prescribe glasses for this man, he will ask you."

Musetto put his glasses back on. "Okay. Fine."

The judge said, "We don't need your help."

Musetto shrugged, saying, "But he is—"

Judge Simmill leaned and glowered Musetto into sudden sobriety, saying, "And don't argue with me, either! Please sit there and answer the questions and be responsive, and don't try to help anybody, either medically or otherwise."

After a moment of silence Bailey said, "Boonton, New Jersey? 97005?"

"Right, *sir*."

"Deerfield 4-4600?"

"Right, *sir*."

Bailey then read the typed name and address of Carl, complete with zip code, an ironic concession to Musetto's demand that the letter be read in its entirety. Keuper objected to the letter being used without being put in evidence. Bailey had it marked D-5 for identification and backed away from Musetto and with great clarity proceeded to read the entire letter:

Dear Carl,

Since my arrival in Florida it has been brought to my attention that it is customary and proper for the Seller of a property to pay for:

1. State Documentary Stamps on Deed. (This was $96 for 591 Bowsprit Lane.)
2. Federal Documentary Stamps on Deed ($35.20 for 591 Bowsprit Lane), and
3. Recording note and mortgage ($3.00)

I paid to the firm of Kirk, Pinkerton, Sparrow, Trawick & McClelland this total amount of $134.20, at the request of Mr. Johnson S. Savary who was handling Mr. McClelland's work during the latter's absence. Knowing that you, the Seller, would not want the situation to be otherwise, I am certain that you will want to reimburse the $134.20 to me upon presentation of these facts to you.

We bought the home at 591 Bowsprit Lane, Longboat Key, Sarasota, Florida, sight unseen. This was a direct transaction with you, with no real estate brokerage involvement. We have been in the house a little over six weeks. On close examination of the condition it was left in, and taking into consideration what we have had to do and what still needs to be done, it is my honest opinion that $32,000 was much too high a price for you to ask, especially from me—one who never hesitated for a moment to help you either financially or otherwise, no matter what, when you were in dire need of it. You and I knowing these facts to be so, it is needless for me to detail them. Furthermore they are too numerous and voluminous to do so.

Being aware of your fairness, honesty and integrity in these matters, I know without a shadow of a doubt that once these facts have been brought to your attention, you will immediately consult your attorney and lower the amount of the mortgage to a realistic value. The amount of the mortgage to be lowered shall be left to your sense of fairness, honesty and integrity which I have always considered to be beyond reproach.

Very truly yours,

DAD
Carmelo A. Musetto, M.D.
(father of your deceased wife
who misses her very much)

F. Lee Bailey, smiling at Carmelo Musetto in a bright, bitter, and knowing manner, let the silence grow after he had finished the reading. In full view of the rapt jury he studied the elderly doctor as an entomologist might study a new specimen.

"That was your letter?"

"That was my letter."

"By writing this letter you attempted to procure a reduction of the mortgage?"

"For a reason."

"You did attempt it?"

"Yes, sir."

"And it hasn't been reduced, has it?"

"It has not been reduced."

"You feel that Carl has been unfair to you?"

"Yes. I do."

And Lee Bailey gave the jury a wistful smile, and shrugged and walked away, saying wearily, "Okay, Doctor."

Vincent Keuper took Musetto on redirect, but only to ask if Carl was the present mortgagee. Musetto said that though he had heard differently, he had no proof but that Carl and Mary Coppolino were still holding the mortgage.

Incredible as it may seem, it had taken F. Lee Bailey only twelve minutes in concentrated cross-examination to devalue most of the usefulness Musetto had to the state's case.

Keuper next called elderly Dr. Julius A. Toren, retired, who had been the Monmouth County Physician from 1947 through 1965, and established that he had not received a report of the death of William E. Farber on July 30, 1963, nor subsequent thereto.

In brief cross-examination Bailey elicited testimony to the effect that Dr. Toren had not received from the funeral director, Robert F. Worden, any report of anything suspicious about the body of the deceased, a report which Worden would have filed had he noted anything of a dubious nature while preparing the body for burial.

After Dr. Toren was excused, Keuper attempted to offer in evidence the death certificate, signed supposedly at the direction of Carl Coppolino by Carmela even though she did not attend the deceased, under the "theory of consciousness of guilt."

Bailey objected to the basis for offering the death certificate in evidence, and when he objected that the prosecutor was "practically testifying" in proposing this theory, Judge Simmill ordered the jury removed and heard arguments from Keuper and Bailey.

Simmill ruled that the death certificate could be marked in evidence as exhibit S-12, but that the jury would have to draw their own conclusions as to guilt, and when the jury was brought back in he ordered them to disregard the statement made by the prosecutor prior to their removal.

It was nearly noon when state witness number five, Robert F. Worden, calling himself "a practitioner of mortuary science" was sworn, and testified that he had gone to the Farber home on July 30, removed the body, prepared it for burial and arranged for the burial. He next identified state exhibit 13 as a picture taken of the body at the time of the autopsy in New York, when Worden had identified the body to Dr. Milton Helpern.

Bailey hastily asked to be heard at the bench.

Whenever such side-bar conversations are taken down by a court reporter and appear in the transcript, there is almost always a flavor of intimacy and informality about it that is quite at odds with what the layman, anticipating a whispering of esoteric legalities, might expect.

KEUPER: I don't want the jury to see this exhibit, if that's Mr. Bailey's objection, and I am merely using it for the purpose of identification of Colonel Farber as the person upon whom the autopsy was performed.

BAILEY: Have you seen the picture?

SIMMILL: No. I caught a glimpse of it. A horrible thing, isn't it?

BAILEY: I intend to have it marked in connection with Dr. Helpern's testimony. I was going to suggest that it be put in an envelope and marked as an exhibit. It's kind of a gory thing to face. That's all. I don't have any legal objection to it, but I don't want them sickened by the thing, either.

SIMMILL: I don't think it's gory. It's just plain gruesome.

BAILEY: Yes!

KEUPER: I'm not trying to inflame the jury. It's solely for the purpose of identifying this as Colonel Farber's body, and that the autopsy—

BAILEY: We're going to admit that.

KEUPER: All right, then.

BAILEY: Just have it marked for identification in case I want to use it cross-examining.

KEUPER: Yes.

SIMMILL: All right.

(End of side-bar conference)

Bailey's cross-examination of Mr. Worden established that the mortician had been in business some twenty-four years at the time of Bill Farber's death and that he had found the colonel lying on his back in the bed on the lower floor of the house. According to Worden, some rigor mortis had set in and there was discoloration of the lower extremities from being dead a little while.

"Did you have an opportunity to observe this body after all the clothing had been removed?" (Bailey had established the body was embalmed the evening of July 30 and that Worden was present during part of this process.)

"Yes, sir."

"Did you get a good look at the face and neck area?"

"I believe I did, yes, sir."

"Did you recognize anything at all unusual about it?"

"No sir, outside of being dead a little while, yes sir." (Bailey had already brought out that when a body lies in one position after death the fluid will settle to the lower part and cause a discoloration reddish or purplish which is called lividity.)

"There was no bruising of any kind around the throat, was there?"

"I did not notice anything."

Worden then told Bailey he was accustomed to looking out for anything suspicious so that it could be reported to the county physician if need be, and habitually made at least a cursory inspection of a body to determine whether an autopsy should be made. This inspection was done on the body of Bill Farber.

He went on to testify that when he picked up the body at the Farber home Marjorie, Carl and Carmela were present.

"Nobody asked you not to perform an autopsy or prevent one from being performed, did they?" Keuper objected with the reminder that Worden was not qualified to perform an autopsy. That was the duty of the county physician.

Bailey rephrased the question, asking. "*Nobody* asked you *not* to cause an autopsy to be performed; *nobody* said anything to you to *prevent* that from happening, did they?"

"No, sir."

Bailey ended his cross-examination with that response and Keuper had no further questions.

The logician can make an interesting analysis of Bailey's final question to the "practitioner of mortuary science."

By inference, F. Lee Bailey was suggesting to the jury that had there been a good reason why Marjorie would have been alarmed at the prospect of an autopsy, it would have been normal human behavior to make some sort of statement or plea to Mr. Worden to prevent any possibility of an autopsy. Thus, if she did not make such a plea or request, no one had anything to fear from an autopsy.

It is a syllogism so fragile it crumbles under any weight of examination. One need only try to devise any possible wording for such a request which would not immediately and automatically make Worden think in terms of hanky-panky.

To make the crudest sort of analogy, how would the owner of a small business he has just burned to the ground suggest to the fire marshal that no one look for traces of candle wax and kerosene in the ashes?

Yet, in the busy give and take of the witness parade, there is no time for analysis of what appears on the surface to be eminently logical and plausible. Bailey has a stunning capacity to create these structures on the spur of the moment, and to set them up much more quickly and frequently than adversaries of less flexible mind and nimble wit can knock them down. His is the art of creating areas of reasonable doubt. One can imagine him as a designer of stage sets swiftly erecting the false-front structures of a cinema cattle town, with the prosecutor lumbering along behind him, trying to kick them down as quickly as they are erected. Yet when they reach the end of the main street, an impressive number are still standing, each individually vulnerable, but, as there was not the time nor the inventive capacity to destroy them at the time they were erected, enough remain standing, so tacked together that each false front conceals the flimsiness of the braces in the rear which hold them upright, thus presenting the look of dimensional permanence and solid construction. This, plus the talent of the good actor or good teacher to make such constructions memorable is, regardless of outcome, well styled to give any public prosecutor a long, hard, uphill run. These minor inventions would not of themselves be totally persuasive, one might imagine, but when they are superimposed upon a pre-planned structure of defense, and serve to reinforce that structure, they become formidable.

To leap at once into the invention of the moment is, of course, a variety of risk-taking. If all factors are not known, or all the known factors not carefully weighed—a process impossible to achieve during spontaneous invention, there is always the chance of abrupt and damaging rebuttal. Yet by pursuing this natural expression of his flexible talent, Bailey often entices the adversary into the same sort of risk-taking and, because the talent for it is almost never equal to his, the adversary creates opportunities rather than problems for Bailey. Risk-taking must be rooted in a fertility of the creative mind, and braced by that rare talent to view the structure as a whole even while focusing upon one small portion.

Mr. Vincent Keuper's next witness for the state was Dr. Edmund Webb, the English-born anesthesiologist who had served with Carl Coppolino on the staff of Brooklyn Methodist Hospital under Dr. George Wallace, the director of the department of anesthesiology, and who had been chief resident in anesthesiology the year before Carl was given that position.

Here, in his own area, Edmund Webb seemed to have a more barbered elegance, a more unhurried and impenetrable aplomb than at the Sarasota hearing the previous September. Under Keuper's questioning he stated that in addition to still being connected with Brooklyn Methodist, he was associate director of medical research at the Squibb laboratories.

Yes, he had known Carl since 1958, had visited him several times at his home in Middletown Township, and had delivered something to Carl at his request, but could not pin down the precise date. In the early part of the year.

"I have taken presents for the children, too," Webb added gratuitously, startling Keuper.

"I beg your pardon?"

Looking somewhat uncomfortable, Webb said, "I have taken many gifts for the children."

He thus established in testimony that relationship with Carl which he had signaled when taking the witness chair after being sworn, by a little nod, smile, and grimace of sympathy at their mutual involvement in this matter which he had directed at Carl seated at the defense table ten feet away.

Keuper could not have helped knowing the relationship between the two young doctors was friendly, but one can assume he had not anticipated Webb's underlining that fact so quickly and unmistakably.

Irritably, Keuper said in a stonger voice. "I'm not talking about the children, Doctor. I'm talking about something that Doctor Coppolino requested."

Offhandedly, and further diffusing the point Keuper was anxious to make, Webb said, "Yes, I'm sure I have taken several things to him."

"At his request?"

"Yes."

"Did he ever *request* any succinylcholine chloride?"

Having made those gentle evasions which were an obligation of friendship, Webb answered that Carl had made his request sometime between March and the middle of May of 1963, and that the substance had been delivered by hand to Carl at his home in Middletown within that same time span. Webb described the function of the drug in anesthesiology and stated that as far as he knew there was no way of detecting its presence after it had been in the body for some time.

Keuper next elicited testimony that Webb had seen Carl several times at his Middletown home after the July 30 death of Colonel Farber, and that on one occasion they had discussed that death.

"I don't remember the details of it," said Webb. "I do remember that I did ask who signed the death certificate and Carmela said that she did. There was nothing of any particular detail that I recall of the conversation."

"At the time that Doctor Carl, the defendant, Carl Coppolino, asked you to bring him some succinylcholine chloride did he tell you what he wanted to use it for?"

"Yes. He said he wanted to kill a cat."

"Did you have any further discussion about its use with him when you delivered it?"

"Yes I did. When I delivered it Carmela saw the package on the table and she said, 'What's that for?' and Carl said, 'That's to kill the Farbers' dog,' to which I said, 'I thought it was going to be a cat.' There was some further discussion. I don't recall what it was. I think it was to the effect that the dog was old or something like that."

Many observers speculated about the significance of Dr. Webb's answer as to the expressed use of the drug he delivered to Dr. Carl Coppolino. One must assume that Keuper was using this purported conversation to plug a number of loopholes, real or imagined, that Bailey could conceivably develop during the presentation of the defense.

Also, we must approach the matter within the same framework in which Vincent Keuper pursued the matter. The basic premise, as it had been throughout the state's case, was that Colonel William E. Farber was murdered by Dr. Carl Coppolino after (1) the injection of the muscle-relaxing drug failed to do the job or (2) the drugged victim had been rendered helpless by the smaller, less muscular defendant.

Thus, at this point in the state's case, we have in testimony the alleged murder of Colonel William E. Farber by the accused, Dr. Carl Coppolino, while the widow of the deceased man looks on, an eyewitness. We have testimony that the death was not reported to the proper authorities and that its cause was other than that certified by the physician signing the death certificate. The prosecutor, with Webb's testimony had presented premeditation and method—however abortive—and, by implication, a conscious effort by the defendant to conceal his act.

Keuper's brief examination ended right there, at five minutes past noon. Those in the press section who had attended the preliminary hearing in Florida three months previously were, with the naïve expertise of the informed layman, ready at that point to deride Keuper for not having asked what seemed to be a particularly obvious question, especially in view of Keuper's having studied the transcript of the Sarasota hearing.

Why had he not asked: "Was that the only time you have ever delivered or sent succinylcholine chloride to Carl Coppolino at his request?"

It is plausible to assume that Keuper did not ask it because he could predict exactly what would have happened. Bailey would have given Webb time to say "No," and then made an objection to that line of questioning and would have asked to approach the bench.

There he would have pointed out that Keuper was seeking to establish, by inference, the doctrine of similar fact by establishing through Webb that there had been but two deliveries of the drug, and the defendant was under indictment for two murders, and that the delivery in each case had occurred between two and five months prior to the death. He would have pointed out that there had been no testimony, no door opened as regards any possible cause of death of Carmela. As the defendant was on trial only for the murder of Colonel Farber, such additional testimony, basically coincidental in nature, could only serve to prejudice the jury against the defendant.

The objection would have been upheld. The jury would have been left with the choice of believing that Webb could have supplied Carl with the drug twice, or ten times, or forty times. And, in view of the prior publicity given the two indictments, were there a conviction, the asking of that particular question could have been sufficient grounds for the appellate court to order a new trial.

In F. Lee Bailey's cross-examination he covered so much of the area he had covered with this same witness in Florida in September, that only the significant departures are recounted.

Bailey's seventeenth question was:

"Have you ever made any test to see how much succinylcholine it takes to cause apnea (cessation of breathing) for a given period of time?"

"That depends on the size of the person. Now, a large person will require more to acquire apnea. Often the duration of apnea is not dependent on the dose of the drug at all, but generally speaking, a large dose will produce a long period of apnea."

"Now, are there different concentrations of the drug for use in intravenous injections on the one hand and intramuscular injections on the other?"

"Yes, there are."

"Are the intravenous injections the faster acting of the two?"

"Yes."

"In other words, if one wished to instantly cause the muscles to relax the intravenous injection would be better suited to accomplish that purpose?"

"Yes."

"How long, assuming an intramuscular injection of a small amount, one or two cc of succinylcholine chloride, would the body be immobilized?"

"It would probably start to take effect within four to five minutes."

"All right. So that following an injection one could get up and walk around?"

"Oh, yes."

"How about an intravenous injection, how soon would one be immobilized?"

"Well, that would probably be a minute and a half to two minutes."

"But there would be at least sixty seconds even with an intravenous injection where the person injected would be able to move around?"

"I think so, yes."

"How many cc's minimum would you say in order to be toxic?" (intramuscularly)

"Rather than cc I would talk grams, weight, measure. You would need something like possibly thirty grams."

"Wouldn't that take an extremely large syringe?"

"Oh it would take a tremendous syringe."

"And if there is to be a one-shot injection to immobilize a patient for, let's say, a five-minute period of time, assuming a man about five eight and a half, 155 pounds in good health, what would you say would be the appropriate dosage?"

"Sixty to eighty milligrams."

"And how many cc's would that be?"

"Well, that would be three to four cc's of concentration, which is usually provided, twenty milligrams per cc."

"And would the amount that you have described necessarily cause death? Would it immobilize the patient?"

"It would immobilize the patient, but I don't think it would prevent the respiratory muscles from acting long enough to cause death."

"In other words, it would wear off soon enough so that the patient would come to?"

"Yes."

Bailey stepped over in front of the bench and borrowed from Judge Simmill the same pencil he had used on Friday in his cross-examination of Marjorie Farber to get her impression of the size of the syringe.

"I ask you to consider a hypodermic syringe with a barrel containing fluid an inch and a half long and the diameter of that pencil. Can you tell me if you have any calculation as to how much fluid that may hold in cc's?"

"Two and a half, three cc's."

"Could that amount of succinylcholine in any form be fatal, in your opinion, if injected?"

"Yes."

It was obvious that F. Lee Bailey had been so confident of a negative answer that he was taken aback. It threw him out of the swift glib ping-pong pattern he had established, and which he was following toward a series of responses useful to the defense.

"It could?! It . . . would take the full injection?"

"Yes. I find that a thousand milligrams can be dissolved in three cc's. It's a very saturated solution, but it could be dissolved in that amount."

This was perhaps the only obvious time during the New Jersey trial when Bailey was unable to bring his considerable warehouse of general knowledge to bear upon an unexpected problem. It is even possible that he lost the chance to retrieve the situation merely by being unfamiliar with the term "saturated solution." No matter how diligently the trial attorney bones up on some highly technical and specialized field, there is always the chance that one word or one phrase from the expert witness will lie outside that necessarily narrow area of his preparation of his case.

He could have recovered completely with one question: "Doctor, I ask you to assume that a person takes the vial of Anectin of the size and strength you delivered to Doctor Coppolino, and that person dumps the crystaline powder into some water in an ordinary bathroom tumbler which might be half full, a third full, or even a quarter full of water, and after it has dissolved, that person draws off a sufficient quantity of that solution to fill a syringe holding three cc's by volume. Could that solution be fatal if injected?"

"No. There would be too much dilution."

But in his momentary confusion at an unanticipated reply, the chance was lost, and the effect of the answer remained.

The forty-ninth question put to Webb on cross was, "Can you describe the kind of container that you gave Carl? By the way, that was not your own product Sucostrin?" (The Squibb brand name for succinylcholine chloride in aqueous solution.)

"It was not."

"Was it a product called Anectin?"

Webb affirmed that it was, and went on to say:

"That's a succinylcholine powder . . . It's a plastic container which is intended to be added to 500 or 1000 cc infusion fluid. The plastic container is about 15 cc's in size. One may either add fluid to the solution to dissolve it and then empty it into the infusion bottle or it is provided with a funnel-like cap which you can squeeze the powder directly into the infusion. In any case, it's intended as a multidose administration, meaning it's meant for more than one patient."

395

"Do you have some recollection of the size of the container that you delivered to Doctor Coppolino in the early part of 1963?"

"It was one such plastic bottle containing a thousand milligrams of the powder."

"What kind of cap did it have on it; how would you go about extracting the powder?"

"I'm not sure at that time that the cap provided on that plastic was the same as is provided now. I think it was, but I'm not sure."

"Must it be broken off in some way?"

"Yes. First of all, there's a seal, a plastic seal which you must break and then you must unscrew the funnel and then it leaves a diaphragm through which you can push a needle. Now if you press the bottle this diaphragm will pop out enabling the powder to be poured out too."

"So the unscrewing of the top alone, I take it, would not enable you to pour the powder?"

"No, you would have to squeeze with some force to get the powder out."

"Is there any delicacy involved in mixing this solution or would just any amount of water do?"

"As long as there is more than two and a half to three cc's I think you would find that 1000 milligrams would go entirely into solution."

"And the concentration would depend on the amount of water, I take it?"

"Yes." Here those in the courtroom who were aware of Bailey's uncharacteristic faltering when Webb had testified that the size syringe as described by Marjorie Farber *could* contain a fatal dose, thought that he had worked his way back to that problem area, and would this time bring out testimony to the effect that mixing it in a water glass, particularly when using part of the powder one time and part another, could not conceivably result in a toxic intramuscular injection.

Then by asking if any qualified anesthesiologist would also be aware of how much was required to produce an apnea fatal if no aid was given the patient, he might well reinforce in the jury's mind the defense concept that Mrs. Farber had invented the whole injection and deadly poison tale.

But again he did not take that opportunity possibly because he was intent on establishing the implausibility of her story through contrasting her description of the container given her with Webb's description of the container he had supplied Coppolino.

However, one can plausibly assume that he was pursuing one of the less valuable aspects, from the defense point of view, of Webb's testimony. Even had the descriptions of the container been much less intricate, and hence easier for the jurors to comprehend, and had he been able to show that the container Marjorie Farber described was totally unlike that which Webb described, all his effort could have been quite easily nullified by the following questions which Keuper could have asked on redirect:

"Doctor, in view of the seal and the funnel and the screw top and the diaphragm you have described, it would present certain difficulties for the lay person to get at the powder, would it not?"

"Yes."

"Is the trade name of the powder prominently and permanently inscribed on the container?"

"Yes sir."

"If a person familiar with the container were to transfer the powder to another, unmarked container, would such a transfer affect the potency of the drug?"

"No sir."

In retrospect it is remarkable that with a witness so obviously friendly to the accused, Bailey seemed to elicit testimony which seemed to confirm rather than refute Mrs. Farber's testimony.

Webb's testimony about how long an injected person might remain ambulatory—three to five minutes—fit Marjorie's account of the way her husband ran into the bathroom.

And so Bailey then developed the unlikelihood of diarrhea, establishing that succinylcholine does not relax the so-called "smooth" muscles, and that the walls of the intestinal tract are made up of smooth muscles, "So that you would not expect an injection of succinylcholine to cause, for instance, diarrhea?"

"No."

It was precisely the answer Bailey was seeking, and thus one can wonder why he continued with a further question which put him back where he had started.

"So the sphincter muscles are not affected. Is that correct?"

"Well, the sphincter muscles aren't entirely smooth muscles."

"What about the muscles of the GI tract?"

"They would not contract."

"So that ordinarily when you use this drug in the course of

your operations the patient, I take it, would not in the normal case have diarrhea or a movement?''

"It's possible the rectum may empty because of the relaxation of the sphincter muscles, but the bowel would not press itself out.''

There were those in the courtroom who, losing track of Bailey's logical development of the defense case, and being unprepared to accept the fact that even for an F. Lee Bailey a cross-examination can turn around and bite, even suspected that Bailey was trying to make the jury believe that Marjorie had possibly filched the drug from the good neighbor Carl and done in the colonel.

Such a strategy, in the face of Lee Bailey's announced intent of proving there had been no murder at all, would have been idiotic. Reasonable doubt must be based upon an edifice of consistent logic, not upon creating mutually exclusive doubts in the hope of confusing the issues at hand.

Bailey dropped that whole line of cross-examination and went at once to the final point he wished to make—that succinylcholine is not a narcotic, is not registered and accounted for in hospitals, that when a doctor draws some from the drug supply room, no record is kept of its removal, and that at the time he brought the Anectin to Middletown, Carl was a licensed physician in the State of New Jersey.

Keuper might have been well advised to have left matters alone, after Bailey's uninterrupted series of seventy-four questions. But Keuper got up on redirect for a brief exchange, and did quite nicely.

"An overdose would be fatal?"

"An overdose—I don't quite know how to answer that. The intended dose is one which causes muscular relaxation. In the course of its proper usage it would not be. But if you do not have a respiratory apparatus available, then even a normal dose may be fatal.''

"A normal dose may be fatal?"

"Yes. It would take respiratory assistance."

Keuper thanked him and sat down. F. Lee Bailey had no questions on recross. The witness was dismissed. Thus Keuper won a gamble that it is possible he was not aware of, the gamble that while he was asking his two questions to drive home points previously made, Carl Coppolino could have shown Bailey in a few whispered words the way to extricate himself from the dilemma of the "saturated solution" dose. And Keuper's redirect questions would have given him ample opportunity on recross.

The half-day session was then adjourned until two in the

afternoon. The jury was taken down to the bus which took them each day of the trial from the Hitching Post Motel to the courthouse and back, and, at mealtime, down the hill to the center of town and around to the municipal parking lot behind the American Hotel, from there, escorted by county personnel, to a private dining room off the rear corridor.

One can readily imagine that though they had been ordered by Judge Simmill not to discuss the developing testimony among themselves, many must have communicated to each other a certain awe at the breakneck pace and sheer volume of information. In one morning they had heard Marjorie again, then Dorothy Jeffress, Dr. Musetto, Dr. Toren, Mr. Worden and Dr. Webb. They might well have felt their circuits were overloaded.

Chapter Twenty-two

As wire-service and afternoon-edition reporters hurried to the available telephones (two on the third floor near the courtroom, a large number in the improvised press room in the basement, and more outside a rear entrance on two mobile trailer racks) the deputies took Carl Coppolino down a long corridor to the waiting elevator.

The corridor was lined with curious spectators. One guard held Dr. Coppolino by the arm and hurried him along in the wake of the guard in the lead. The spectators gawked and whispered. Carl and the guards got into the elevator. Carl smiled invitingly at the clustered curious, pressed the button and said, "Going down?"

As the doors closed he was still the only one in the elevator who was smiling.

Though in accord with New Jersey law, Carl had to be handcuffed during his many trips between the jail and the courthouse, due care was taken to make certain that no juror ever saw him manacled. Mr. Bailey, aware of the jury-effect during the first Sheppard trial when Dr. Sam had been brought into court in handcuffs in full view of the jurors, had requested that the Court make certain the same thing did not happen in this case.

On that Monday, Lee Bailey spent a working recess in the law library at the courthouse. Mary Coppolino, Joseph Afflitto, Teri

Plaut, Andy Tuney and two newsmen stayed with him, and the group had hamburgers and coffee brought up from a downtown restaurant. Bailey stood lounging against a corner wall of the room, frowning with close concentration as Teri and Andy read requested excerpts from the official transcript of the preliminary hearing and the bail hearing, portions of the testimony of Dr. Helpern and Dr. C. Malcolm B. Gilman.

A local attorney came in to research a question of law, stopped suddenly on seeing the group, apologized and said he would come back later. "I'm not a spy or anything like that." Bailey introduced himself, shook the man's hand and told him to go ahead with his research, and the lawyer went into the end of the room where the rows of bookshelves obscured him from view.

As Bailey continued his review and appraisal of prior testimony, Mary sat on one of the oak tables, her legs crossed, and chatted with the newsman researching an article about her which finally appeared in 1967 after the Florida trial. It was published in *Good Housekeeping* and was titled, "Will I Ever Know the Whole Truth?"

As time to return to the courtroom neared, Bailey told Teri Plaut to get hold of a local high school boy named Jack Silverman who had written to Mr. Bailey saying that he was writing a term paper on his choice of career, that he wanted to be a trial lawyer, and wondered if Bailey would have time to talk to him during the trial. Lee Bailey asked Teri to tell the boy he would see him right after the conclusion of the trial day.

Though the popular theory is that F. Lee Bailey has an unexcelled appetite for personal publicity, he made certain that there was no coverage of this human interest story. However, on the following Thursday, the weekly *Freehold Transcript* had a little story about it based on an interview with the boy, wherein he related that based entirely upon his new and reflected glory, one of his high school teachers had asked for a genuine Jack Silverman autograph.

On that Monday either the spectator section was not cleared as on other days, or a score of spectators had found some way of sneaking past the watchful bailiffs. A rather small, middle-aged and determined-looking lady sat with a small picnic hamper on her lap. She lunched there in the courtroom upon a foil-wrapped wedge of imported cheese, crackers, a small tin of paté, and a small bottle of imported white wine. As she lunched she looked about from time to time with a certain hauteur, perhaps thinking it quite inconceivable that any crude creature in a position of minor authority would make so bold as to ask her to go out into the corridor and stand in line with the peasants.

The court was called to order at exactly two o'clock, and Dr. Milton Helpern, Chief Medical Examiner of the City of New York, state witness number seven, was sworn and took the stand.

His face was thinner than at the Florida hearing three months earlier, and he was noticeably more pale. He had been in the hospital for a short stay just prior to the selection of the jury.

Newspaper accounts of his illness ranged from "Coronary Fells Key Figure in Coppolino Case" all the way down to a statement by Mrs. Helpern that the doctor had become overtired and had gone in to rest up.

There was a dramatic tension perceptible in the courtroom as Keuper began direct examination, in anticipation of the confrontation of Milton Helpern and F. Lee Bailey.

For the second time during the state's case, Bailey would have to work a convincing destruction involving a doctor of medicine, another portly man thirty years his senior. In the case of Helpern, however, the destruction would have to be of the expert testimony the man would present, rather than, as in the case of Musetto, an attack upon the subjective substance of the man— his emotional bias.

As with Musetto, Helpern had his first confrontation with F. Lee Bailey at the Sarasota hearing in September, and had been at first startled and then angered by such a direct attack upon his methods and motives, that he could not have avoided thinking it a gratuitous impertinence.

Helpern was thus forewarned that his appearance at this trial would be a brand new experience compared with all the other capital cases at which he had testified in recent years, where, habitually, he had been treated by both sides with that scrupulous respect reserved for all elder statesmen in any exacting field. It would be questionable to assume he was reluctant to face this ordeal. It could even be that he welcomed it. No man becomes a household word in any field—be it a Robert Frost in poetry, or a Senator Dirksen in politics—without being proud, tough-minded, pugnacious, and determined. At sixty-four, Milton Helpern was a vital and competitive old man, veteran of many arenas, who was not going to trot out of the ring just because some new matador waved a cape in his face.

His manner and composure were at odds with his subjective picture of toughness. He was white-haired, avuncular, a man of kindly appearance seating himself and peering over his granny glasses at his interrogator. He had a curiously sweet smile, a gently professorial manner. It was easier to imagine him as a guest professor in seventeenth-century literature, plodding about a New England campus, making dusty little jokes to his classes, forgetting his appointments, but able to exercise that teacherly gift of stimulating the minds and imaginations of the young.

Bailey's avowed chore was made more difficult by the publication in the magazine section of the Sunday *New York Times* on December 4, just eight days before Helpern took the stand, of a feature article on the doctor entitled "Not Whodunit, But Whatdidit?" The long article revealed not the kindly professor, but the driving, competent Chief Medical Examiner of the City of New York, in command of a six-story building containing five floors of laboratories, sixty in all, and a basement containing 128 refrigerated compartments and thirteen autopsy tables, each with a built-in dictating machine.

It showed him in his office, with his forty-one framed diplomas on the wall. It said, ". . . the building is the best medical detection laboratory in the country, and the boss is one of the best medical detectives in the world."

It quoted a former New York Chief of Homicide who had become Assistant District Attorney in charge of the Supreme Court Bureau as saying, ". . . because of Helpern we were alerted to the homicide. He has that thing, you know, that intuitiveness . . . He can *smell* a homicide."

It quoted Dr. Howard Reid Craig, director of the New York Academy of Medicine, as saying, "He is smart, he is tough, he is incredibly dedicated and he is—strange, isn't it, in this business—a very sweet man."

And one of the line drawing illustrations for the article featured a translation of the Latin inscription in the lobby of the Medical Examiner's Building: "Let Conversation Cease, Let Laughter Flee; This Is the Place Where Death Delights to Help the Living."

There had been additional press publicity involving Dr. Helpern and the Coppolino trial again on Sunday, December 11, the day before he took the stand. This time it had been an Associated Press wire story, the result of diligence and imagination on the part of Arthur Everett, the AP veteran reporter covering the trial. It had a large percentage pick-up across the nation.

Everett wrote:

"Sixteen years ago, in the icy cold of a cruel New England winter, a young doctor was on trial for his life in a large, airy,

New Hampshire courtroom. About his head raged a sensational 'battle of the pathologists.'

"Dr. Herman N. Sander was accused of killing a Manchester, N.H., cancer patient by injecting air into her veins. At the time his act was deemed a 'mercy killing,' although he testified that euthanasia played no part in his decision.

"To a degree, his fate depended upon two pathologists—medical detectives who delved into the cause of death.

"For the state, there was a man who is now one of the old lions of his profession, Dr. Milton Helpern, then and now Chief Medical Examiner for New York City.

"On the defense side was Dr. Richard Ford, then 35, only 10 years out of Harvard Medical School, lean, 6 feet 3 and boyish in appearance. He was and is with the Office of the Medical Examiner of Boston's Suffolk County.

"Next week, in another age, another courtroom, and with another young doctor's life at stake, Ford and Helpern are scheduled to meet again in fascinating medical deadlock. Once more it is Helpern for the state, Ford for the defense. . . ."

"In the New Hampshire case, the medical puzzle was whether the victim, a cancer patient, was clinically dead when her doctor admittedly injected air into her veins. Sander said he did so to relieve her family of a useless and prolonged financial burden. The jury found him innocent and at least some of the credit was given to Dr. Ford."

Vincent Keuper began to ask Dr. Helpern those questions about his background, training and experience which would qualify him as an expert witness in the field of pathology.

Helpern spoke in a casual, informal, pleasantly modulated voice . . . an articulate man, structuring his sentences well, choosing the apt phrase.

Because both the New Jersey and the Florida trial of Dr. Coppolino involved expert medical testimony and, in fact, both cases were determined by the degree to which the jury believed the medical testimony, it is useful at this point to take a closer look at the actual process of qualifying the expert witness, of asking him questions about himself in front of the jury in what is called the *voir dire*.

In Courtroom Medicine Volume Three, *Death*, by Houts, published in 1966 by Mathew Bender & Co., Inc., and designed as a guide and manual for the courtroom attorney, there is a detailed analysis of this aspect of the use of the expert witness.

Marshall Houts says, in part, "Any death action that reaches the courtroom will turn ultimately on the 'battle of the experts'.

This means that before the attorney can be successful he must 'sell' his expert witness to the jury.

"Incredible though it may seem, even experienced trial attorneys slough off the *voir dire* as being little more than routine doggerel. They seem to forget that it is a vitally important facet of their proof on both the cause and manner of death. If the jury does not 'buy' the integrity and professional competence of the witness, it may decide to ignore his testimony completely. If this happens, the attorney's case in all probability goes out the courtroom window."

Houts says that the *voir dire* helps the jury decide how much weight to give the testimony of the particular doctor on the stand, and as his model example of exactly how it should be handled, he takes the *voir dire* of Dr. Milton Helpern from an actual trial transcript in a murder case where the problem at issue was whether a cerebral aneurysm had ruptured spontaneously, or as the result of a blow.

The scope and pattern of this model *voir dire* can be illustrated by merely listing the attorney's questions as he asked them of Dr. Helpern:

1. Your name is Doctor Milton Helpern?
2. Are you a duly licensed physician and surgeon?
3. In what state?
4. How long have you been licensed to practice your profession?
5. Are you presently engaged in the practice of your profession?
6. Where did you receive your medical training?
7. Will you please tell us just what are the duties of the Medical Examiner for the City of New York?
8. Is the function of the Medical Examiner similar to that of a coroner in some states?
9. Does your work include the performance of autopsies?
10. During your experience in the Medical Examiner's Office in the City of New York, how many autopsies have you performed?
11. Will you please continue with your experience in the Medical Examiner's office?
12. Are you on the staff, or are you affiliated in any way with any universities or academic institutions?
13. Do you specialize in any particular branch or field of medicine?
14. Would you tell us just exactly what pathology involves?
15. Are you a member of any specialized medical or scientific groups or associations?
16. Will you please tell us what the American Board of Pathology is?
17. What is the object of this Board?
18. What are the special requirements before certification as a diplomate by the American Board of Pathology is granted?

19. Must the applicant take special examinations given by this Board before his certification as a specialist in pathology?
20. Now you have mentioned, I believe, forensic pathology. Will you tell us what this means?
21. I take it then that this certification as a diplomate by the American Board of Pathology is over and above your license to practice medicine?
22. Am I correct in assuming that this certification by the American Board of Pathology is on a national basis?
23. Are you the author of any textbook or any scientific papers in the field of pathology?
24. During the course of your experience in the past thirty years in the office of the Medical Examiner of the City of New York, have you had occasion to observe many cases in which the cause of death was a subarachnoid hemorrhage due to a ruptured aneurysm of the cerebral arteries?

Houts says that this model *voir dire* "presents the doctor in the most favorable light. It permits him to put his best foot forward. Staying within the bounds of good taste and modesty, the jury learns the doctor's professional skills and accomplishments.

"It captures the interest of the jury and makes them think: *Here is a man who has received the best possible training. He has practiced forensic pathology in various parts of the world. He must be widely recognized as an authority on the subject since he has written extensively on it; and his book is used at a number of medical schools. I want to listen to what this man has to say about this subarachnoid hemorrhage or ruptured aneurysm or whatever it is he is going to talk about.*

I like the way this doctor looks and talks. He seems to be confident of what he says; but he isn't cocky or know-it-all. Those last two witnesses were awfully dull. I had a terrible time keeping my mind from wandering. This fellow looks like a welcome relief. I'm going to square around here in my chair and listen to what he has to say.

Houts next gives another example:

1. Now, Doctor, your name is Michael P. Connor?
2. And you practice medicine here in this state?
3. Now will you just tell us a little something about your qualifications, please, Doctor?

"This," says Houts, "is horrible courtroom technique for it places the doctor squarely on the horns of a dilemma."

He then gives a probable monologue the doctor would have to

405

relate about himself and goes on to say, "Regardless of how modest and self-effacing the poor doctor may attempt to be, his position is a difficult one. That same juror who was so impressed with the doctor's personality and professional qualifications when the *voir dire* was handled in a dignified question and answer format, may now think: *Well, this guy is sure pleased with himself. Seems to think he's the greatest bone man that has ever come down the pike. I don't know. He may be all right; but I've always been a little leery about people who think they know everything there is to know about a subject. I'm going to take what he has to say with a grain of salt. Kind of pompous: probably had everything handed to him on a silver platter.*

Houts points out that, "When confronted with an opening *voir dire* situation of this nature, many doctors react quite naturally by relating only the barest minimum of information about their background and professional accomplishments. They are inclined to omit offices they have occupied in medical associations, books and articles they have published, honors that have been accorded them.

"About all the jury learns is that the doctor is licensed to practice medicine, he has received the routine medical training, he is a specialist of some kind. In other words, he is just one of a thousand men who is permitted to take the client's money for rendering some service in the case."

Houts underlines the final essential stratagem which can be covered in the *voir dire*. The expert witness, "should be chosen on the basis of his knowledge of and experience with the exact pathological entity involved in the cause and manner of death. This should be emphasized to the jury as part of the *voir dire*. The attorney misses an extremely valuable tool of proof if he fails to show the jury the detailed experience of the witness as it is honed down to this particular set of facts (the medical problem in the case at issue)."

The short questions and long answers in qualification of Dr. Helpern take up over five pages of the official transcript.

Then, with the autopsy report in hand, which Helpern said he could get along fairly well without, but might need to refer to for specific measurements dictated as he had personally performed the autopsy, on Saturday morning, July 16, five months prior to the trial, he proceeded to describe the autopsy:

"The body at that time was in what is known as a sealer, a zippered bag, and had been placed there after it had been removed from the grave in which it was interred. It had been identified as a body being brought in, and it had been brought in

406

in this tarpaulin, a zippered tarpaulin, and an outer casing, a metal casing. . . . The remains of the deceased were removed from this zippered bag and placed on the autopsy table.

"It was lying in a prone position in the bag when I saw it—that is, face down—and I placed it on the table in a face-up position. As a result of its lying in the bag some earth covered the surface of the body which incidentally was clothed in a military dress uniform. And then I carefully rinsed away all of the earth and dirt from the surface of the body and made my observations as I went along.

"The deceased was dressed in a military officer's uniform. The cloth was fairly well preserved considering the post-mortem interval of three years. The fabric in places had sort of rotted away, but on the whole it was very easily recognizable, and I had it photographed after it was washed. I had a photograph taken by our own police department in New York to indicate the state of this body.

"I then described the body as it was found in the uniform. It was completely dressed including shoes, socks, trousers, military blouse and tunic, shirt, tie, and underthings. The cloth, of course, was considerably rotted by the fact that the body was lying in a moist environment. And, nevertheless, certain significant observations could be made of the clothing as the clothing was removed.

"When I removed the blouse, that is, the military coat, there was a decoration over the left upper pocket in the usual place. And then I noted that the shirt, that is, the top shirt, was quite rotted away. The fabric had sort of disappeared from the collar, and yet the collar buttons were very neatly placed, and the celluloids which are used to stiffen the collar were there intact and undisturbed. They were lying there in the usual position. So that, aside from the fact that the cloth was rotted, there was nothing to indicate that anything more had happened than the rotting of the fabric due to the long submersion."

Here Keuper took advantage of Helpern's gesturing toward his own throat to have the doctor emphasize through repetition the observed fact of the undisturbed collar buttons and celluloid collar stays resting in the throat of the deceased.

"The tie was also in its regular place, and the tie I thought was of a nylon fabric. I removed all of the clothing including the shoes and the socks. The soles of the feet, that is the skin of the outer layer of the skin of the soles of the feet were softened and were stuck to the fabric so that when the socks were removed, the skin, the outer layer of the skin also came away with it.

"That in essence is the description of the clothing. All of the articles were there and except for the rotting there was nothing to indicate any localized disturbance of these bits of clothing, of these coverings.

"After removing the clothing I then examined the body very carefully and described it externally. My external observations of the skin and the descriptions indicates that the surface of the skin had been considerably altered by the long period of time that had elapsed and by the post-mortem changes. In other words the skin wasn't intact as far as the outer coverings themselves. . . . I was especially looking for puncture wounds, but the condition of the body did not warrant any valid observations as to the presence or absence of any punctures. And I could not determine whether such punctures were present.

"I also observed the subcutaneous fat, the fat under the skin, had been converted into a substance which we pathologists call adiposere, and that is a waxy or lardaceous substance. It has somewhat the consistency of lard except that it may be a little heavier. This was very lardaceous.

". . . I spent a good deal of time going over the extremities, the trunk, both upper and lower extremities looking for a possible evidence of a puncture site—that is, a needle puncture site—which I could not find.

"I then incised, cut through, the fat which was quite firm and not at all liquefied, and this was due to the fact that the body had been embalmed prior to burial. There was evidence of this. And this embalming had to some extent preserved this body to permit me to make such observations.

"Now the fat under the skin was quite firm and I cut through this in many, many places and made many many slices and spent a long time trying to see whether I might find a needle track in the fat, but I wasn't successful."

He sat at his ease, the amiable uncle, directing his narrative at the jury. This was not a flat, dreary, unemotional technical report. The old man was genuinely, unmistakably involved in his work, and so intensely interested that he described and discussed it in the manner one might expect of the single-minded golf-bore who takes you verbally around the course with him, describing every stroke, every club used, every putt and recovery shot. The 20,000 autopsies he had personally performed had so totally insulated him from the almost universal squeamishness of mankind concerning the dead, and especially the long dead, that had he happened to notice the woman in the spectator sections sitting

408

huddled and gray, swallowing hard, her palms pressed tightly against her ears, he would have been bewildered.

"There were a few areas in which there were some dark streaks, but when these were studied under the microscope they were found to be streaks that had been made by the insect larvae that had invaded the body after death. There are tiny insects that do invade the body even though it is embalmed and produce peculiar tracks, and these were very evident in the microscopic examination. But I wasn't able to determine more than that.

". . . After looking at the extremities, I then opened the body and examined the body cavities and the organs in a systematic fashion. In the body I found nothing unusual except the post-mortem change incident to the long post-mortem period.

"I examined all the organs of the abdomen. I examined all the organs of the chest. There was evidence I was more aware of when I got in the body than I was aware of on the surface of the body, that this man had had a gall bladder operation. There was some scar tissue replacing the gall bladder and on the liver. The organs of the abdomen were in relatively normal condition except for the post-mortem change. They were in the normal position and they did not show any evidence of disease.

"I found all the organs, the liver, the spleen, the pancreas, the adrenals, the kidneys, the aorta, the bladder, the prostate. And I might say that the angenitalia did not permit valid observation due to the maceration and decomposition incident to the long interval.

"I then examined the head—in fact, the head was really examined first, but subsequently opened, that is, the skull cap was removed. I might say in describing the face that the soft tissues were rotted away exposing the bones of the face. The top of the skull showed no soft tissue at all, and the soft tissues on the side of the face were also converted into adiposere, which is a brittle-like substance and can be very easily broken during the process of removal.

"The eyes were no longer there, but the eye caps which the embalmer had placed in the eye sockets over the eyeballs—which is part of the process of the preparing of the body for burial—these eyecaps were still in place and undisturbed. The teeth showed slight loosening due to changes—at least I attributed it to that. There was no indication of any injury that I could recognize in the teeth or on the face or in the skull. The ears were quite soft and had lost a lot of soft tissue.

"I removed the brain and it was quite soft, and had shrunken due to dehydration. The brain had really sort of dried out and laid in the back portion of the head, and it was a very soft consistency. But careful sectioning did not disclose any evidence of disease in this brain, only the post-mortem change.''

When Dr. Helpern then began to testify about the neck, Mr. Keuper reminded him that he had not described the condition of the heart when he had covered the internal organs.

"Thank you. The lungs were very much collapsed and what we call autolyzed, that is, decomposed, due to the post-mortem changes. The heart itself was in surprisingly good condition as far as preservation goes. It weighed 300 grams on the scale. It was normal in size. It was obviously badly decomposed, but it was normal in configuration, the shape of it was normal, and the size of it was normal, and the valves of the heart, the lining of the heart, and the muscle of the heart all appeared normal. And then I very carefully examined the coronary arteries.

"The coronary arteries are the arteries that nourish the heart. They are the first branch that comes off the aorta, which is the large blood vessel coming out of the left side of the heart, and they have large openings. These relatively large openings are called ostia or ostium in the singular. The ostium of each coronary artery appeared normal. The aorta around this area appeared normal.

"Then I made serial sections, that is, cross-sections through the main coronary arteries—that is, the left coronary artery and the right coronary artery. The left coronary artery is a little bit to the side. The right coronary artery presents itself in front, and I sectioned this at intervals of about one eighth of an inch with a sharp scalpel, going crosswise like you would cut across a pipe to see where it was blocked . . . To see whether the channel which carries the blood to the heart muscle was blocked.

". . . The coronary arteries are perhaps the most important arteries in the body as far as our immediate survival is concerned. These coronary arteries carry the blood to the heart muscle. If the heart muscle doesn't get an adequate blood supply then of course there will be a disturbance in function. Sometimes the coronary arteries are blocked abruptly, suddenly, acutely—and sometimes they are blocked gradually.

". . . I was looking for the evidence of sclerosis of the coronary arteries. In other words, the blocking of the coronary arteries is usually a result of, or a complication of a disease we call arteriosclerosis. As one gets older the arteries become less resilient. They become thicker. And the degree of thickening constitutes the severity of this disease.

"Now I examined these coronary arteries at intervals of one

eighth of an inch—that is, I made sections, first through the right one and found very little evidence of this disease of arteriosclerosis, and no significant narrowing of the channel, so that the artery was entirely capable of carrying an adequate amount of blood to the heart muscle. There was no anatomical evidence of disease in these arteries.

"I then sectioned the left coronary artery and that artery, right after its commencement branches into one branch which runs down in the front of the heart in the grooves between the left and right ventricles—the heart having two sides, each side having an auricle and a ventricle—the left coronary artery divides into a left anterior descending branch, as it is known technically. This artery is a very important one, as are the others too, and in sectioning this left anterior descending branch, I found a light to moderate amount of coronary arteriosclerosis. But in evaluating this very carefully and thoroughly at the time of the autopsy, and examining all of the sections, the amount of narrowing of these arteries, the amount of thickening of the wall that might produce a narrowing, never produced more than 25 percent off the normal.

"In other words, at no place was the artery less than 75 percent good, as far as carrying blood. And, in most cases it [the sclerosis] was much less than that—that is, it carried more than 75 percent.

"So I would say in evaluating this from long experience with studying these hearts, that the degree of arteriosclerosis in this heart in the left coronary artery had produced no more than 25 percent diminution of lessening of the channel. . . . At least 75 percent of the channel remained.

"I also sectioned another branch of the left coronary artery, which is the circumflex branch. This showed minimal athero-or arteriosclerotic change. . . . We can say that it was practically absent in that vessel.

"I also very carefully examined the arteries for the presence of a thrombus or a thrombosis. . . . The term coronary thrombosis means the clotting of the blood in a coronary artery during a person's life. There was no evidence at all of any coronary thrombosis in this man. The arteries were quite empty and collapsed. In other words the lumen was something that you had to more or less interpret, because after the post-mortem period had set in there was no blood to speak of in these arteries and the arteries had collapsed. But there was no thrombus. There was no significant narrowing of any of the coronary arteries induced by disease.

"The heart muscle appeared quite normal. There was no

411

indication that this man had ever suffered an acute attack of myocardial infarction. . . . (or) any myocardial infarction either recently or in the past. There were no scars in the heart muscle, and I would say that for a man of the age of the deceased, which I understand was fifty-two, that this was a normal heart and I so interpreted it as that. There was minimal atherosclerosis in the aorta throughout its entire length.

"The next thing I did is dissect the tissues of the neck. The skin of the surface of the neck was quite macerated and in no longer a normal condition, but it was there. The soft tissues were there. I dissected these up and then I very carefully removed the organs. I could recognize the thyroid. The muscles were very much autolyzed. The thin strap muscles of the neck were autolyzed. Then I carefully removed what remained of the tongue. The tip of the tongue had rotted away, but the base of the tongue was still present. I excised that with the throat organs and very carefully examined that without cutting it and without prying it open.

"It was immediately evident, or very soon evident, that one of the components of the larynx, known as the voice-box, which is the structure in the neck which includes the Adam's apple or the thyroid cartilage, and then below the Adam's apple there is a ringlike structure in front which expands into a firm structure in back. And then there are other smaller components which are not pertinent to our discussion at the present time.

"I noticed that the cartilages were ossified—that is, they had become bony as they do in a middle-aged person. They no longer have the normal elasticity of the cartilage of a young adult or of a child. Both the thyroid cartilage—the Adam's apple—and the cricoid cartilage were ossified.

"Then, on carefully fingering the cricoid cartilage, which is the ringlike formation of the cartilage below the thyroid I immediately became aware of abnormal mobility. In other words, instead of being firm in my hand as it is in ordinary conditions, and I have handled thousands and thousands of these larynxes, this larynx had a very peculiar feel. It was immediately evident, or soon evident, that on gentle palpation that it was broken in two places. It was broken on the left side and also broken on the right side.

". . . A segment of this bony structure, originally a gristly structure, was loose. And the impression you got in feeling it was very much like feeling . . . an old ping-pong ball that has been dented and then you hit it to sort of bring (spring) out the dent. The dented portion never feels quite right. That is just the way

412

this thing felt. Subsequently I took this cartilage which was evidently broken in two places and then soaked it in some formalin to loosen up the layer that covers this bone. Originally it was called perichondrium, but now we call it periosteum because the structure was bony instead of gristly.

"I stripped this layer off and then very clearly could demonstrate the fractures of this structure. So there was a double fracture of the cricoid cartilage which only can occur if there is a localized force pressing against that area and a force of . . . a considerable amount of force. In other words, merely touching it with the hand doesn't do it. You really have to press in very hard to break that ossified cartilage, the cricoid ring in front, and it's a fairly commonly observed injury. We see it not infrequently and it was present in this case."

A photograph of the larynx was introduced. After it was marked in evidence and had been examined by Bailey, Dr. Helpern at Keuper's invitation, went to the rail of the jury box and, moving from one end to the other, showed the photograph to the jurors, describing and explaining it to them. A small ruler had been placed under it at the time it was photographed to show the size.

When Helpern returned to the witness stand, Keuper by question and answer brought out that the photograph showed only the fracture on one side. Dr. Helpern announced that he had brought the actual specimen along. An assistant of Helpern's, seated inside the rail on the state side, took a glass jar to Helpern. The larynx, about the size of a child's clenched fist, and of the mottled yellow-white color of very old ivory, was visible in the jar, immersed in a colorless perservative.

Helpern requested a towel, removed the jar lid, fished the larynx out and, after putting the jar on the exhibit table, dried the specimen and his fingers and, after examining the specimen said, "This is the larynx including the thyroid cartilage and the cricoid cartilage and the portion of the trachea which I removed at the time of the autopsy which I performed on the body of the deceased in this case, the body identified as William E. Farber."

His preceding testimony, regardless of its clinical content had been, after all, merely a voice, words, a picture—forms of communication. This was a rather horrid reality. The conventions and entertainments of our society, and the perfumed and unctuous ceremonies of death and burial insulate us from reality. There is no doubt but that many in both the press and spectator section, unwilling or unable to achieve this comprehension of reality, thought at first that it was perhaps some clever plastic

413

model designed to demonstrate the fractures Helpern had described. Realization came slowly, much like the double-take which is a staple of comedy skits, and when it came, there were separate little grunts, sighs, murmurs of dismay. It violated one of the more primitive taboos of the culture to bring such an internal and personal bit of the long dead into this public place. Through this voice-box had come the rhymes and songs of childhood, the recitations in school, the words and sounds of love, the words and sounds of anger, commands, explanations, laughter and sobs, argument and agreement, truth and lie . . . all those life-sounds a man must make from the newborn squalling to the ultimate rattle.

Certainly never in even the most outrageous and grotesque images and imaginings which flicker through the mind of every man, could Bill Farber have ever devised this particular image, of Dr. Milton Helpern getting down from the stand and trudging over to the jury rail, and in kindly, patient, professorial manner—yet with hair ruffled enough to look somewhat like the kindly old wine-maker fondling an oversized cork—showing and explaining this ossified throat-box to fourteen people, saying: "This is the fracture which I just demonstrated in the photograph. If I put my thumbnail very gently I can separate it even more than it shows in the photograph and then on the other side is another fracture, which is more palpable and not as cleanly shown as this one, but it's there, and if you put your hand on that—if anybody wants to feel this, which I'm sure nobody wants to do—you can feel this other fracture and this segment just goes right in."

No one showed any inclination to touch the artifact.

"It has an abnormal consistency which you recognize if you know about these things. See the other fracture right on this side and this one here? In other words, there's a double fracture of the cricoid cartilage." At one point during the demonstration to the jury, Lee Bailey had moved over, apparently to lean in and see exactly what Helpern was doing. But as Vincent Keuper could not be at all certain that Bailey wanted only to look, and perhaps wary of how, with his sharp wit, Bailey could destroy the mood established by the presentation of the specimen, Keuper moved over and interposed his big frame and totally blocked Bailey out of the scene. As Bailey could not very well trot around to the other side of Helpern without looking absurd, he ambled back to the defense table.

Returning to the witness stand, Helpern said, "Now I also have the hyoid bone here, which is the bone at the base of the tongue, which I haven't discussed because I do not find anything abnormal with it. I separated it from this structure, but it is part of the whole structure known as the larynx. The hyoid bone is usually included in any consideration of this structure, but the injury is found in the cricoid cartilage in front.''

The final step was for the state to secure from its expert witness his opinion as to the cause of death. As he was about to give it, Mr. Bailey objected, stating his reason to the Court:

"Because, in the first place we have nothing so far but an injury to the cricoid cartilage and some discussion of the arteries. Now the doctor has given no indication that he knows whether the injury was ante-mortem or post-mortem. He has not indicated whether he was given a history, and no indication whatsoever that he knows how this body was dug up, or whether a spade was stuck through the neck, and I think this is critical to the foundation before he can reasonably give an opinion as to whether this had anything to do with the cause of death.''

Keuper withdrew his question and rephrased it, saying, "Doctor, assume that this defendant, and I am pointing out the defendant here, Carl Coppolino, did on the 30th day of July 1963, lean his full weight down on the head, face and chest of the body of William Farber with a pillow. Assuming those facts do you have an opinion within reasonable medical certainty as to whether or not that act on the part of this defendant could have caused the condition which you observed when you autopsied his body?''

After more wrangling, during which F. Lee Bailey made certain that the history of pressure with the pillow was included in the opinion as to cause of death, Dr. Helpern testified that that act on the part of the defendant could have caused the condition which resulted in death.

It was then three o'clock. Of the hour Helpern had spent under direct examination, at least forty minutes had been extended monologue.

When Keuper finished, Judge Simmill announced a short recess.

Only those who'd had enough for one day left their seats in the spectator section. Out in the hallway those members of the news media who did not have to file stories exchanged theories and opinions.

The consensus was that Helpern, thus far, had been hugely plausible and persuasive, a veritable grandfather-image to the jurors. But, of course, Bailey had not had his chance as yet to chop away at that image. Several of the reporters were derisive of the whole routine of the larynx being presented in the jar of formalin, and having to be taken out and dried off before exhibition.

415

It turned out that those few had been privileged to see another larynx, source unknown, which was being carried around by one of the experts who would testify for the defense.

The hollow cylindrical object could be slipped onto a ring finger for display, like some bulky and monstrous talisman dating back to the dinner parties of the Borgias.

Chapter Twenty-three

Bailey's cross-examination of Dr. Milton Helpern was intended to achieve in the minds of the jurors a greater willingness to accept what would quite obviously be flatly contradictory opinions from the defense medical experts to be called later.

F. Lee Bailey knew well that, all by himself, he could not create in the minds of the jurors a sufficient reasonable doubt as to whether a homicide could have been committed. Helpern was too skilled, too imposing, too experienced a witness to be toppled in cross-examination. All Bailey could hope to do in cross-examination would be to chip a few little cracks in the façade, and chip them in exactly those places where his medical experts saw the best chance of refutation, and make those cracks as memorable as possible in the juror's minds.

Then, when his own experts would take the stand, on direct examination he would, he hoped, drive the wedges of their experience, education, plausibility, squarely into those cracks and enlarge them to the necessary stature of a reasonable doubt.

He knew that the direction of his questions would clue Helpern as to the areas of his testimony the defense experts thought contestable, and that Helpern would seek to strengthen those areas during the cross-examination, if Bailey was not agile enough to stop him.

One area, the "collapsed coffin theory," had already been telegraphed during the empaneling of the jury. And, forewarned, Helpern had put a special emphasis, with an assist from Keuper, on the precise and undisturbed positioning of shirt buttons, collar stays and the necktie, as well as the eye cups. He had also throughout his testimony reiterated the lack of any damage to the body or the clothing other than the damage of the long postmortem period and the dampness of the grave site.

Bailey, in a chatty, politely interested manner, began with an attempt to cast doubt on Milton Helpern's account of his own activities during the qualifying process. He remarked that 20,000 autopsies came to about one a day for sixty years, after asking Helpern if he ever took a day off. When he asked if Helpern had done all 20,000 personally, or if he had supervised some of them, Helpern rose to the challenge and said that if he wished to include the ones he had supervised, the figure could be tripled.

"Sixty thousand?!"

"Sixty thousand. That's right."

"When you supervise them you are standing right there all the time or are you going in and out?"

"I'm doing some very essential part of them . . . Not like a foreman."

"Not like a foreman? . . . How does a foreman supervise an autopsy?"

". . . Not like a foreman. When I say supervise, I'm taking an active part in it."

"Oh. You enter some phase of the autopsy."

"That's right."

Bailey fashioned, in view of the jury, a small grimace which seemed styled to imply that if Dr. Helpern personally took a hand in examining these thousands upon thousands of corpses, just how much personal time, care and attention could he have given to the body of the colonel?

Bailey switched abruptly to the statement by Marjorie Farber, establishing that Helpern had read it through before performing the autopsy.

"Of course, the history is an essential part of the diagnosis of cause of death in every case, isn't it?"

"Not in every case. In many cases, yes."

"Well in this case it certainly is?"

"In this case it is and it isn't."

"You say it is and it isn't? It is essential, but it's not essential?"

"In other words, you can determine from the larynx alone that you are dealing with a violent death."

Establishing that because of the statement, Helpern would not have expected to find evidence of strangulation in what was apparently a case of smothering, Bailey asked about the residual evidences of asphyxiation. Helpern responded that such evidences are very very difficult to evaluate and that one would never find any in a body dead three years.

Pursuing the question of finding evidences of smothering in a fresh body, Bailey at last cornered Helpern into giving the

417

answer he was looking for: "If you do a fresh autopsy in a smothering case and if you are alert to this finding, you can find them (pin-point, or petechial hemorrhages) in the whites of the eyes, way back. You may or may not be able to find them in the face and you may or may not find them in the larynx."

These two professionals were fencing carefully. When Mr. Bailey made any slight error in terminology, Dr. Helpern would correct him with a patronizing gentleness. Helpern was alert to expand any answer into further support for his findings, and Bailey was alert and abrupt in stopping him. When he sensed the answer which Bailey was seeking, Helpern gave answers which made Bailey reword questions until finally the form of the question was so precise it was no longer possible to give a partial answer.

Asked if he could determine a smothering by residual evidence if he examined it immediately, Helpern responded, "I would say if you had a body that was given to you as a smothering case, if you recognized that or were advised about that as a possibility and you had the opportunity of examining this body at the place where it was found, then you might be able to see certain subtle signs that would confirm your impression or suspicions and so on. On the other hand, if a body that has been smothered is placed in a certain position, then even though you examine the body fresh it may be very very difficult and in many cases impossible to determine this from the autopsy."

Asked if in the many, many autopsies he had conducted he had come up with opinions of smothering, Helpern said he had and went on to say, "I would say that this is the most difficult area of autopsy work, to determine, to establish the cause of death by autopsy of a smothering case because in a smothering case there may not be any other associated injury to give you a clue and it's a type of death, a type of violent death in which the scene can be altered so that the findings are not necessarily conclusive of this mechanism."

Then, after securing Helpern's agreement to the concept that there is no way of telling at the time of the smothering of a victim whether or not there is going to be residual evidence left for a pathologist to find, Bailey posed a key question: "But if one were to begin to smother another human being, having in mind the fact that an autopsy would follow immediately and perhaps evidence of the smothering, there is no way to know whether in the course of that smothering changes are taking place which will enable the pathologist to show that a smothering has taken place?"

The implication of the question was, of course, that certainly Carl Coppolino, M.D., would know that smothering might or might not leave evidence of the cause of death, and would not know whether or not an autopsy would follow immediately, and thus would not have been likely to take a risk so foolish.

"Well, he may find changes in a smothering, but unfortunately, the changes which you find in a smothering, unless the process of smothering had produced associated injuries, there is no way in which you could definitely say from the findings that this was a smothering. He can develop a suspicion of smothering, you see. And in the cases that we have been successful at arriving at a cause of death we were fortunate in getting to the scene on time before these subtle signs had disappeared. You know an autopsy is not an automatic procedure."

Helpern had managed to make a complete inversion of Bailey's logic, and had established the inference that because smothering *was* so difficult to detect and because the signs were so subtle and disappeared quickly, and because autopsy is considerably less than inevitable, smothering might indeed be a shrewd murder method for anyone familiar with medical facts to select.

"I know, Doctor, and before we get into a lecture, I think you have answered the questions." Bailey revealed a certain irritability at ending up in a thicket. He backed off and went at it another way. First he established that, of course, Helpern had not been at the scene of death, and that all the information he had about it was second hand, and that a layman would be most unlikely to detect anything which might make him feel that a person had been smothered.

Then he asked what symptoms or evidences Helpern might expect to find in a fresh autopsy, consistent with smothering.

"I would say that if I had the opportunity to examine a case in which smothering had occurred, I would find hemorrhages in the eyeballs. I would find hemorrhages, perhaps in the folds of the eyelids, that is, the conjunctivae. I might even find hemorrhages in the skin of the face, very fine hemorrhages in the skin of the face. These are quite variable. You might find some in some person with delicate skin. You might find the skin slightly rubbed and shiny, but aside from that, there wouldn't be very much."

"How about when you peel the skin back, do you find anything inside the head with reference to petechial hemorrhages?"

"In smothering cases when you reflect the scalp there may be hemorrhages in the tissues inside the scalp. In other words, you

419

see these small hemorrhages, but this would just be another finding. It all adds up to a suspicion.''

The pattern continued. Would they be found in ordinary natural death? In some cases of sudden death, they might occur in the process of dying. Wouldn't you become suspicious of smothering? Yes, if I found no other cause. Would you need to remove the eye to find the hemorrhages? No, you just fold back the lid. Wouldn't it be something a mortician might notice while inserting the plastic caps over the eyes before burial? He might or might not. Is there any explanation why these appear in some smothering cases and not in others? Hard to say—interruption of ingress of air, congestion, and also struggling would make the hemorrhages more likely to appear.

They had fenced before, in another state, about the details of a different death, but in the far more informal arena of a hearing, where no jurors are present, and more latitude is customary. In the bull ring, the animal will often return to a particular area of the ring where he feels safer. This is his *querencia,* and in that area he is more dangerous and more unpredictable. The symptoms and evidences of death formed Helpern's *querencia,* forcing Bailey to advance with caution. He had neither expected nor wanted to hear that struggling is one of the factors which create hemorrhages, after Marjorie's testimony that her husband had been unconscious when the pillow was placed over his face.

Bailey had worked his way back to his key question in that particular sequence, and tried it again, wording it more specifically: ''. . . It certainly would be fair to say that a doctor who undertook to smother anybody would certainly run the risk that he might leave evidence in the form of hemorrhages that could cause investigation. He would not know in advance whether or not they would occur. Is that true?''

''It depends on the doctor, and I would say that the method of killing by smothering is one of the most difficult to detect.''

''You have told us that, sir, several times.''

''That's all I'm trying to say. You asked me the question.''

''I understand. But I put it to you again, assuming that a doctor knew that small hemorrhages are often the result of smothering, there is no way to tell by looking at a given individual whether or not that will occur in this individual if smothering is accomplished.''

''Again, that would depend on where the doctor is operating. There are some parts of the country where you can smother people with impunity and no one looks. There are other places where the bodies are scrutinized carefully and more routinely and

I would say the hazard of discovery after smothering varies greatly in different parts of the country."

"Assuming that an autopsy might follow, the hazard would be there, wouldn't it?"

"Yes . . . Not just an autopsy, but an understanding autopsy. That's what I'm trying to say."

"One that would be competent by your standards, Doctor?"

"That's right."

"The hazard *would* be there?"

"That's right."

F. Lee Bailey then established that in thirty-five years Dr. Helpern had testified in Massachusetts, New Hampshire, New Jersey, Florida, Ohio, and Canada, presumably to underline how Helpern made his standards of competence widely available. He then dropped his line of questioning, but as with all important and intricate cross-examinations Bailey conducts, it is impossible at the time a particular line is abandoned to guess whether he will return to it later, perhaps from a position strengthened by intervening testimony. Only when he has achieved a major and effective victory, as in Marge Farber's testimony about the medical release, can one be reasonably certain he will leave that area alone.

He turned abruptly to a line of questioning designed to foreshadow defense testimony about exhumation damage to the body.

He asked about the decomposition of the outer layers of the skin.

Helpern said, "The layer that you normally find on the outside had disappeared and sort of separated from the deeper layers. And the skin was quite soft and portions of it had disappeared. For example, the soft tissues from the hands had almost completely disappeared. The soft tissues from the top of the head had almost completely disappeared."

"And some had been rubbed away?"

"No. There was no indication that anything was mechanically rubbed away. I think that things can fall away. In other words, the top of the head can be completely skeletonized by a process of maceration. In a *sense* it's a rubbing away. You see this in bodies which are submerged, and I would say that this body had been subjected to considerable moisture."

"You opened the tarpaulin in which it was carried and you found that the scalp had separated, had it not, in the course of being carried?"

"No. When I examined the body I found the scalp was no longer present."

"Wasn't it found in the tarpaulin?"

"No."

"It was not?" (mildly incredulous)

Helpern in a tone of weary and exasperated impatience said, "No, no. The scalp was *absent,* Mr. Bailey."

Bailey established then that the only information given Helpern about the exhumation was by Robert Worden, the funeral director who had brought the body to Helpern and who had identified it, and who had said that the sides of the coffin and the outer box had collapsed. Helpern had the name of Clark Foster, the funeral director who had actually gone to Arlington and disinterred the body, in his notes, but had no recollection of meeting the man or speaking to him.

Bailey's next attack was focused on the autopsy report itself, as by dropping the collapsed coffin line just when he did, along with the mysterious Clark Foster, he mystified the jury and whetted their appetite for things to come.

Establishing that Helpern had dictated the autopsy report as he was performing it, Bailey asked, "Is that the form in which we presently find it, or has it been modified?" Here again is demonstrated the invaluable leverage that precision in the use of the language bestows on the trial attorney. All noted criminal lawyers, past and present, have had in common the habit of omnivorous reading (without which no man can ever develop a taste for the structure of the language), an appreciation of the nuances of meaning of words, a towering vocabulary, and the gift of selecting from it that word or phrase which has precisely the desired effect. "Has it been changed?" "Has it been altered?" "Has it been corrected?" No other word has the exact impact as "modified," with its semantic value of having subtly altered something to achieve a different goal than was originally implicit in the material.

But any pathologist with experience on the witness stand knows this veiled slur is inevitable and prepares for it. Helpern responded by saying it had been edited, but that both the original transcript and the stenographic notes themselves were available, implying that if Bailey had any intention of following this line, the original could be produced for comparison.

Next Bailey asked to know when the opinion as to the cause of death had been "appended" to the autopsy report. When Helpern began speaking of awaiting chemical and microscopic reports, Bailey stopped him, reminding him the question had asked for a time when the medical opinion had been prepared.

Helpern's best recollection was that he had signed the final report sometime in October. Bailey then brought up Dr. C. Malcolm B. Gilman, the Monmouth County Physician, and Helpern testified that Gilman was present throughout the autopsy, which was finished at 8 P.M., on July 16, and when the autopsy was finished Helpern had told Gilman then and there that because of the finding of the double fracture of the cricoid cartilage, he was of the opinion that it was a homicidal death, but that the final opinion and report awaited the receipt of all other information.

"Now a fracture of the cricoid cartilage may be ante-mortem and it may be post-mortem, may it not?"

"As a general proposition?"

"No. It may be one and it may be the other? I'm not asking for odds."

"We're not asking about this case?"

"We are going to take this case in a minute. *Can* the cricoid cartilage be fractured after death occurs?"

"Of course it can!"

"After the time you discovered this cartilage, and prior to the time you formed an opinion, did you make any effort to get any of the details of the exhumation? Just yes or no."

"Yes. I had details of the exhumation at that time."

"You learned from the people who did the digging and lifted the body up how this was accomplished?"

"Yes."

"What did they tell you?"

"I was told they had difficulty getting the body out. The grave was rather wet, and that when they took the outer boards of the outer box in which the coffin was contained, that these boards were collapsed. But I was also told that the top of the coffin was intact. And, not only that, but that the inner lining of the coffin was intact. And that there was no soil on the body when it was first observed."

"When you got the body it was covered with soil, wasn't it?"

"It was mixed with soil, yes."

"And the uniform had been soaked in muddy water?"

"It was soaked and there was considerable soil on it, and I had to wash it away."

"What did you learn beyond the facts that I have just recited about the elevation of the body from the grave?"

"I was told that the body was lifted out of the grave and then placed in the tarpaulin. . . . And also that the inside of the casket did not contain any soil."

"Who told you this?"

"Dr. Gilman."

"So you relied on this information in forming your opinion?"

"Yes."

"You never questioned any of the gravediggers?"

"I did not."

"So far as you know when the grave was redug, they came upon the top of the casket, found the sides crushed in and somehow lifted the body out?"

"No. The body was in the casket. The cover of the casket was intact. That the casket had collapsed on the sides, but that when the casket was opened, I was told that there was no indication of any soil having gotten into the box, or that any soil had contaminated this body or gotten onto the surface of it prior to its removal from the casket."

"Was the body lifted out of the casket, or what remained of it?"

"I don't know how they got the body out of the casket. I wasn't there and I don't know."

"Do you have any idea as to whether the top of the casket that you say was remaining was removed, and the body lifted out separately, or whether the whole unit came out at once?"

"I don't know."

"Do you know how the body got from the grave into the tarpaulin?"

"No. Except that I assume it was placed there."

"I assume that before arriving at an opinion in this case, you were anxious to determine whether or not any external force was applied in the exhumation of the body to this area of the neck. Was that important?"

"Certainly. Certainly."

"You endeavored to get all the facts."

"I received the information about the exhumation from Dr. Gilman, yes."

"If a spade had been driven into the neck, that of course would affect your opinion, wouldn't it?"

Bailey was moving about, changing position and stance, and there was a subtly "merry" flavor about him that bespoke of satisfaction at the way this line was progressing. The jurors could not have failed to note this change in manner, nor could they have failed to become increasingly curious about just how the gravediggers *had* gotten that body up out of the hole.

But the blithe and savage irony of the spade comment stung Helpern.

"I think if a spade had been driven into the neck, Mr. Bailey, I would have observed it even if it hadn't been told to me."

424

"You would have observed the spade or the symptoms?" asked Bailey, perhaps a little too quick to correct a grammatical flaw.

With heavy emphases, and obvious irritation, Helpern said, "I would have observed the effect of it, and there was *nothing at all* in my findings to suggest in *any way* that the surface of the body had been in *any way* disturbed. As I indicated in my description of the clothing when I described the shirt, had *anything* like what you said taken place, I would hardly expect to find the celluloids in place. I would hardly expect to find the shirt buttons in place. I would hardly expect to find the tie in place. And there was *nothing at all* to indicate an injury incident to the exhumation of the body. And I might say that I am *familiar* with post-mortem injuries."

An immediate distraction was essential, and Bailey said, "Yes, I am sure you are." He clasped himself by the back of the head and yanked his head down, pressing his chin against his chest. "Doctor, can the damage that you have found to this area of the larynx be caused by the head bending down like this with some force?"

"No."

"It cannot be done this way?"

"No, no." (impatiently)

"Must it result from direct pressure?"

"(In) my experience with these cases, it must result from direct pressure right over the cricoid cartilage."

Holding his knuckles against his throat, Bailey said, "So that the pressure in this case would have to have been applied right in this area in order to cause that damage?"

"In that area and also over the cricoid in order to break it in two places."

"This is the requirement?"

"That's right."

"The pressure would have to be applied directly?"

"That's right."

"And a bending forward of the neck, however great the force, wouldn't cause that particular kind of damage, you say?"

"In my experience, no." There was a sudden wariness in Helpern's response. Bailey had sought and received the same answer in so many similar ways that it had begun to be evident it was an answer Bailey wanted the jury to remember, an answer he found valuable to the defense. Helpern, as well as many others in the courtroom must have realized that without transition

425

Bailey had somehow shifted from graveside damage to the murder itself as Marjorie had testified to it.

If the suspicion existed, Bailey confirmed it by asking, "Doctor, let's talk instead about smothering someone, about strangulation. Will you describe to the jury the parts of the body that cover the cricoid cartilage?"

Through interrogation Bailey established that the cartilage is covered with perichondrium, that connective tissue which is found on every cartilaginous structure.

When two highly intelligent men are in conflict, and in addition have taken a noticeable dislike to each other, the baiting can sometimes become markedly childish, as in this exchange.

"Doctor, on top of the pericardium, what did you find?"

"On top of what?" (imitation of confusion)

"Pericardium."

"Pericardium?!" (Has this young man lost his mind?)

"Pericardium. What did you find on top of that?" (Impatience. Stop stalling)

"The pericardium is the sac which encloses the heart."

"I am sorry. Maybe I used the wrong term." (irritation with self, and with the doctor for picking him up on the error)

"Peri*chon*drium," said Helpern.

"Good!" (Congratulations. You've had your fun. Maybe we can get on with it now)

"I'm sorry." (What am I supposed to do if you confuse me by trying to use big words you don't understand?)

"What did you find on top of that?" (impatience)

"The perichondrium?" (One last jab. You're quite sure that's what you mean?)

"Yes!" (exasperation)

"There are some loose connective tissues there. There is a membrane, a connected tissue membrane between the cricoid and the thyroid, so that the cricoid can move on the thyroid. When a person talks the whole thing is not rigid. There is a certain amount of motion between the joints of the thyroid. And, on top of the perichondrium you find connective tissue, and then you find muscles. You find the cricoid-thyroid muscle, which is found anteriorly and posteriorly."

"Now what is it that we find covering the cricoid? The skin?"

"I'm sorry." (I don't quite understand the question)

"What is it that we find when we look in the area of the cricoid?"

"You see the skin!"

"What does that consist of?"

"Skin?"

"Yes."

"Skin has an outer layer of epidermis with a few hairs coming out of it, and a few oil glands coming out of it, and sweat glands, and then it has a deeper layer of dermis, or true skin, and that is made up of connective tissue with blood vessels."

"Where do the blood vessels run? Under the skin and over the cricoid cartilage?"

"They don't run under the skin and over the cricoid. The cricoid is considerably removed from the skin. When you look at the cricoid, or in the area where the cricoid is, you see the skin, but the cricoid is quite deep to the skin."

"I understand that, but between the skin and the cricoid are there any blood vessels of some kind?"

"There are muscles on the cricoid cartilage, and there are blood vessels all over this area."

Having previously gone over the process of the ossifying of cartilage into bone in the middle years, brittle yet strong, Bailey asked, "When blood vessels under the skin are subjected to severe pressure they may rupture, may they not?"

"They may."

Establishing that in cases of strangulation bluish marks will be found on the throat, Bailey then asked if Helpern had made an effort to learn the immediate post-mortem appearance of the cadaver on the day of death.

Helpern said he had been told there was no suspicion of any bruising of the skin, but was not surprised as in many cases no bruising of the skin occurs.

Bailey reminded him that he had said it would take considerable direct pressure to fracture the cricoid, through the skin, and would not this cause ruptures of the blood vessels? There might be deep ruptures, yes. Might they show on the surface, as bruises? Yes, sometimes we see it on the outside too.

Helpern said that he had not specifically asked if bruises were present, but had merely assumed that if they *had* been there, he would have been informed of it. Bailey told him his assumption was correct, then asked if Helpern had brought with him the numerous slides of the cross-sections of the coronary arteries. He had. But in previous conversations with Bailey, Helpern had gotten the impression he would not be asked to project them, and so had not brought a projector. When Judge Simmill said with some irritation that certainly a slide projector was not unique, and couldn't one be found somewhere in Monmouth County so that they could finish with Dr. Helpern's testimony, he was told that it had to be a special projector able to project the microscopic and actual bits of tissue fixed and waxed on laboratory glass slides. The judge then suggested they go on as far as possible, and leave the slides for Tuesday morning.

Bailey continued for eighty more questions. His first line of approach was to have Helpern explain how he visualized the actual smothering.

"I think this is a general situation of a pillow being applied over the nose and mouth. But in those descriptions the pressing force sometimes strays, and the pressure can be applied not through the pillow but through the edges of the pillowcase. There are a lot of possibilities . . . I was told that this man was smothered with the use of a pillow. Now that doesn't limit my evaluation to the pressure necessarily coming through the thickest part of the pillow."

Establishing that Helpern did not know where the assailant was standing with respect to the victim "in memory of this so-called witness," Bailey asked if it was of any importance for Helpern to know.

"No. I would say that the general statement about the attempt to smother with a pillow, even if the neck hadn't been mentioned as a specific item, would be sufficient for me with my experience to say that whatever force was used went further and produced this injury. Now, this injury was not essential to having a person die by smothering."

"No question about it."

"But it happened, and it is a very important indicator of what happened."

"You believe that it happened based on the fact that you found it and heard a history, right?"

"Well, I believe it happened because I believe that this injury is the main part of the cause of death, with or without smothering, because of its almost characteristic location. This is a common injury in persons who are strangled. . . . When a person is strangled, you can't possibly analyze each pressure and so on. This is a violent pressure and things happen very fast, and I would not be able to say the particular pressure produced the injury, except that one of the pressures on the neck broke the cricoid cartilage, and that this cricoid cartilage doesn't break merely by touching. You have to really push in on it to break it."

Pressed and harried by Bailey, Helpern stated in several different ways that he could give no opinions on the smothering on the pillow, and the varieties of pressures. "My opinion is based on the finding of this double cricoid fracture. That is my indicator."

Pushed further he said, "I would say that in all the bodies I have examined, and I have examined many exhumed bodies—I have examined many bodies that have been buried under building collapses—I have never seen this type of injury as an isolated injury."

"You have never seen this type of injury as an isolated injury?"

"That's right."

And here began a direction of interrogation which was most difficult to interpret in the light of what Bailey was trying to accomplish. Perhaps had he been able to elicit the answers he sought the pattern would be easier to understand.

Also, he began to use more and more the art of artifice of the hypothetical question. The hypothetical question is commonplace in its simpler forms in the interrogation of expert witnesses on cross-examination. For example, "Assume you found no water in the lungs, Doctor; would you still say with reasonable medical certainty that this was a death by drowning?" In the use of such a question is implicit the possibility that a defense expert, destined to appear later, can come up with some other explanation of the presence of water in the lungs.

However, the use of the intricate hypothetical, that which demands more than one basic simultaneous assumption, is a rarity because there are few attorneys who, in the give and take of cross-examination, have a sufficiently disciplined and orderly mind to keep such complex hypotheticals from degenerating into nonsense. Multiple assumptions used simultaneously are in the province of symbolic logic. The obvious danger, of course, is that in the process of entangling the expert in the maze of hypotheses, the average juror, who must be assumed to have less intellectual discipline than either the interrogator or the expert, will become so lost in the thickets he will become overly sympathetic to the bedeviled expert.

First Bailey asked Helpern to assume that the only evidence that could be given was of pressure applied with the heel of the hand through the thick part of a pillow. He demonstrated by placing hand over hand, locking his elbows and leaning on the corner of the defense table. "Isn't it fair to say that there is no way through that pillow to concentrate pressure sufficient to break that cartilage?"

Helpern said it would be easier without the pillow, but that it

429

could be done, that the skin would be protected but the deeper structures wouldn't be.

When Bailey asked him if there were any such cases in his experience, Helpern said that there had been cases where in an attempt to smother, the cricoid had been fractured, and added, "When a violence such as this occurs, it is the sort of thing that is not capable of a subjective analysis by the person doing it or by somebody necessarily watching it, unless one is a trained observer."

"You are doing quite a bit of interpreting about the history given and whether or not the witness is to be trusted. Isn't that true?"

Keuper objected to the question and was overruled.

Helpern said, "You don't have to be concerned about the witness. This injury speaks for itself."

This brought the usual significant little stir and rustle from the two score closely packed members of the press section, and the busy scribbling to retrieve the exact words before they faded from memory. It is the sort of simplistic distillation of much testimony which makes for clarity in the leads of the news stories.

Yet rather than hasten past what seemed to be a damaging pronouncement, Bailey said, "You say that this injury by itself is proof of homicide? All by itself?"

"Yes."

"No question about it?"

"Yes, in this case."

Oddly, there seemed to be an air of guarded satisfaction about Lee Bailey as he went to the exhibit table and selected the cricoid, state exhibit 15 and took it over in front of the witness stand.

"I show you a cricoid cartilage which you have removed from the body exhumed after three years interment. Is there any way from this cartilage alone and nothing else, no other reference, to determine when that injury occurred?"

It then began to be possible to see the first faint outline of what Bailey was accomplishing, and why he had so solidly underscored that pronouncement by Helpern that the injury to the cricoid spoke for itself. Helpern had jettisoned all the Farber testimony insofar as the reasonable medical certainty of the cause of death was concerned.

Helpern's answer to Bailey's question at that point was not responsive. He related the care with which he had removed the larynx and how he had not made the mistake some people make,

430

of prying one open before careful external examination, and then being unable to say whether it was already broken, or was broken in the process of prying it open. He affirmed that he was certain he had not broken this one.

Bailey brought him back into the pattern: "Doctor, what about the time from the moment of death until it was delivered to you? Do you know whether or not someone else might have done something that would break it?"

Helpern again reiterated there was no evidence from the examination of the body in its clothing of any injury to the neck, and again brought up the undisplaced celluloids and neat position of the collar buttons. He stated he was quite certain that the fracture did not happen during exhumation.

"Even if it was dropped smack down on the cartilage?"

Dr. Helpern said it could not happen, and spoke again of examining the bodies of people crushed by the collapse of buildings, and said "You do not get an injury like that as an isolated injury."

Bailey then moved to a hypothetical question almost outrageous in its simplicity. He asked Helpern to assume that no pressure had ever been applied to the cricoid during the life of the deceased, and asked him if that would affect his opinion.

In asking this, Bailey discovered that Dr. Helpern either would not or could not cope with such an assumption. Possibly Helpern, professionally attuned to objective findings, did not truly comprehend the question. Perhaps he understood it, but thought there would be some kind of trap which Bailey would spring were he to give the obvious, and yet to him, improbable and meaningless answer.

For question after question, Bailey asked the doctor to assume no pressure had been applied, and Helpern persisted in giving answers involving the findings of the application of pressure.

At last, when they were at complete deadlock, Judge Simmill said, "Pardon me." He leaned toward Dr. Helpern. "If there was no pressure on the cricoid cartilage then it wouldn't have fractured. Is that right?"

"It wouldn't have fractured," said Helpern. "That's right."

The judge said, "Is that what you want, Mr. Bailey?"

"Yes."

"Ask them like I do, and you get it quicker," said the judge.

Bailey, with grin and nod, turned back to the witness. "No question about that?"

"That's right."

So, within moments, Bailey moved back toward the same

hypothetical again, but from a different angle, and again Helpern refused to accept it. Mr. Keuper objected on the basis that there were no grounds for such an assumption in the case, and was sustained. Moments later as Bailey was trying to elicit from Helpern some indication that the injury could have happened in some other way, Keuper again objected, but on the grounds that the questions were repetitious. Bailey protested that he was seeking clarification from the witness, but the objection was sustained.

Bailey's final question was, "Now tell us the various stories you were told about the death."

Keuper objected. The judge called both attorneys to the side bar. The conversation was inaudible to the court reporter. When it was finished, a recess was taken until the next morning.

Back at the hotel, those news media people who were attending their first major trial were unanimous, almost, in explaining at long length just exactly why Carl Coppolino's case was absolutely hopeless, and just how it had happened. Keuper was the big avenging angel of justice. Helpern had been the rock upon which all defense hopes had smashed. Poor Lee had done a lot of adroit scrambling and scurrying, and he was really a very entertaining guy to listen to and all that, but anyone looking at the faces of those jurors could tell in a minute that Coppolino was cooked. Bailey hadn't *really* been able to break Marge. She kept bounding back. And old man Helpern hadn't yielded an inch. Why, toward the end there, Bailey's questions weren't making any sense, even! He was getting desperate because he knew he'd blown it. Anybody could see looking at Coppolino that he knew it too, the way he just sat there, face like a gray mask, unmoving. It sure was obvious now why Vince had never lost a capital case.

But the cadre of seasoned professionals in the press corps had seen this phenomenon too many times to risk any hasty appraisals.

Regardless of how strong or how weak the state's case might be, this is always the low point for the defense, as the state is completing its presentation.

In baseball terms, call it State versus Visitors. State and Visitors both have a chance to come to bat in the first inning. Then State takes a long, seven inning, uninterrupted turn at the plate, and scores all the runs possible. In the State portion of the eighth inning, with the score 13 to 0, it is all too easy to assume the game won. But the Visitors have seven full innings coming up, and by the time the adversaries are ready to split up their turns at bat in the ninth, it can well have changed to a 13 to 20 ball game.

Additionally the neophyte trial-watcher makes the mistake of dumping all the testimony he has heard into the same pot with all that he has read about the case, all that he has heard from other reporters, from attorneys, from lawmen, forgetting that in the jury selection the defense made an attempt to select, as nearly as possible, fourteen people whose *only* source of information on which to base a judgment would be what they heard in court.

There is another factor which can most easily be explained through the use of analogy. In cross-examination the defense attorney will lean heavily upon points which make little or no sense to jury, press, or spectators. It is too easy to assume that the defense is floundering during its cross-examination. Imagine instead that in his lengthy cross of Marjorie and of Helpern, Bailey was carefully aligning and adjusting and focusing some of the dramatic stage lighting for his own presentation. His stage as yet was empty. But he had created bright areas at apparently random places, and the reasons would not become clear until his own witnesses came on stage to stand in precisely those places he had spotlighted. Then would come meaning and revelation. Then it would be time to say in chorus, like so many Nipponese: "Ah, so!"

Yet, during the latter part of the Helpern cross, Bailey had seemed a little below his prior standard of acuteness.

A visiting attorney, standing at the bar at the American Hotel that evening, gave a possible answer. "Very nice bit of foot dragging," he told some newsmen. "Very very cute."

Asked what he meant, he explained that with a witness as formidable as Milton Helpern, it is dangerous to permit the state to so arrange the tempo that all direct and cross takes place on the same day. It leaves too strong an impression. It is too unified. Also, it does not give the defense a chance to confer with its own experts about the testimony given while the examination is still going on.

Somebody said, "But it was just an accident that Helpern's people didn't bring that projector along. If it hadn't been for that, Simmill would have had them finish with Helpern today."

"Don't kid yourself. If they'd had a projector, Bailey would have raised so many questions about every single slide, he would have been about half through the set when it was time to recess. Bailey broke up the tempo. He's softened the effect on the jury of the great Doctor Helpern by splitting his testimony into two hunks, with a night's sleep in between. Bailey was dragging his feet because he wasn't absolutely certain Helpern was the state's last witness, and he wanted to keep it going until recess time, so they wouldn't have a chance of shoving in a supporting medical witness. Bailey has other areas he wants to develop with Helpern. You can count on that. But he didn't want to get into them today, not without checking with his own witnesses. Finally he got too repetitious and Simmill broke it up, but apparently it turned out that Helpern is the state's last witness, so he was home free. Understand, all this is guesswork on my part. I think it was well worth a try, and I think he got away with it.''

Somebody asked him how he thought Helpern had done.

The attorney shrugged. ''Who knows? The whole case is the medical testimony. Was the guy killed, or was it a natural death? If the jury ends up believing he was killed, they'll go along with the Farber testimony. If they end up thinking there wasn't any murder, they'll decide she's a liar. Ask me how Helpern did after the verdict is in, fellows.''

''What do *you* think, sir?''

''I think it's about time for a nightcap.''

Chapter Twenty-four

Because of a conference in chambers between Lee Bailey, Vincent Keuper, and Judge Simmill, the opening of the session was twenty minutes delayed on Tuesday morning.

Dr. Helpern's assistants had set up the screen on its tripod stand so that it was between the prosecution and the defense table, directly facing the jury. The projector was in front of the jury rail, a heavy, cone-nosed projector of the type necessary to project the actual fragments of human tissue fixed and dried between the two glass plates of standard laboratory slides.

In that position neither the judge nor the press section could see what appeared on the screen. One spectator who had a good view of it said that the slides looked to him like aerial views of the Amazon River Basin, or some kind of contemporary art.

If it is true that Lee Bailey contrived to break Helpern's testimony into two separate portions in order to dilute the impact of his opinions on the jurors, certainly there was an additional advantage in being able to review all that Helpern had said on Monday and isolate the vulnerable areas and plan how to focus the balance of the cross-examination upon them.

The consensus of opinion around the American Hotel was that the state would finish its presentation by noon. In fact Teri Plaut, Bailey's gumshoe girl had stated firmly that the defense team expected to come to bat after the lunch break, or possibly before.

Seated inside the rail, and far to the right near the jury box where they would have a good view of the screen were the defense medical experts.

Bailey had Helpern take the witness stand before showing the slides. Helpern looked rested and amiable. He toyed with a collapsible metal pointer while answering Bailey's questions about the slides the jury was about to see.

Through question and answer it was explained that Helpern had removed the coronary arteries from the body and had cross-sectioned them at one eighth inch intervals in order to determine the extent of coronary artery disease visible in the artery, and observe any narrowing of the artery due to the disease.

Helpern described to the jury the three layers in the wall of the coronary artery, like a three layer wall of a garden hose which encloses the lumen, or the channel through which the blood flows. "On cross-section it appears as a circle," said Helpern, "and if the artery is distended, then it will be circular. If the artery is collapsed it will be a slitlike structure."

Atherosclerosis, he explained, is a disease of the arteries whereby they lose their natural resiliency and become sclerotic, no longer elastic. Degenerative changes take place in the artery, especially in the middle layer, and as a consequence lime deposits form in the artery upon the innermost layer of the arterial wall. He repeated his testimony of the previous day, saying that the examination of the colonel's coronary arteries revealed a maximum narrowing of not more than twenty-five percent.

Because of the three-year interval from the time of death to the autopsy, the arteries, Helpern said, had collapsed. They were empty and the weight of surrounding tissues had flattened them. There was no embalming fluid left in the arteries, but the tissues of the arteries had been preserved by the embalming fluid they had originally contained.

Bailey next had Helpern explain just how the slides were prepared. At considerable length Helpern described the process. The chunks or blocks of arterial tissue an eighth of an inch long are trimmed, then placed in formalin for additional preservation. Later an alcohol treatment is used, along with another solvent, to draw all the water out of the tissue and dissolve out the fat at the same time. Then gradually the dehydrated tissue is suffused with another fluid which mixes readily with paraffin wax. The blocks are placed in melted wax, and the wax enters the tissues. Then they are chilled and when the wax has hardened, the excess is trimmed off and the block is placed on a slicing machine called a microtome, and sectioned into slices one five thousandths of an inch thick. [In theory about 120 slices could be prepared from a block an eighth of an inch thick.]

The thin slices are floated onto glass slices, warmed so they will stick to the slide. The paraffin is dissolved out with a special chemical. Then, to make the detail visible, two dyes are used, hematoxylin and eosin. The first stains the nucleus of the tissue cell blue, and the eosin stains the other portions of the tissue red. After staining the moisture is removed and the tissue again dehydrated. The paraffin solvent is again placed on it, and the slide cover put over it, stuck in place by a drop of balsam. Then the slide is ready to be viewed through a microscope, or a microscopic projector, as had been set up.

Dr. Helpern's explanation was perhaps thrice as lengthy as the description given above. In later discussion of the testimony between newsmen interested in the tactical advantage of guiding Helpern into this lengthy description, it was the general consensus that the process itself, all that dehydration and removing fat, soaking in other fluids, adding wax, slicing, dehydrating again, and adding more fluid, all these processes seemed to turn the specimens from the dead tissue of a human being to a kind of scientific abstraction, a laborious process ending up with a little scrap of something or other that had to be dyed pink and blue so you could see it at all even at extreme magnification. The lay mind might well respond with skepticism rather than with respect for the scientific approach.

When Bailey asked how many sections he had brought along, mounted and ready to be projected on the screen, Helpern talked about so many sections from this arterial branch, and so many from that, and did not give a total number of slides, but added, "I didn't make serial sections of the entire coronary tree, but I included all the sections which had the most advanced lesions I could find in this case, to demonstrate the extent of the disease." He explained that by lesions he meant the presence of arteriosclerosis.

As an example of how difficult it is to isolate potentially significant questions in cross-examination until any trial is completely over and the verdict is in, there were two portions of this cross-examination which make an informative contrast. At the end of that portion of it, just before Helpern left the stand to show the slides, Bailey, with a certain display of irritability, tried to get Helpern to say that one blockage in an artery would cause death, and Helpern finally replied that a blockage is not necessary, that a significant lesion of one artery could cause death, or a general distribution of a great many. At the time a spectator might easily consider Helpern's reply perhaps the most potentially significant one of the first portion of the morning cross-examination. But later testimony in the case would show that the most significant exchange occurred ten minutes earlier when Helpern was explaining the circulation of the blood and Bailey led him off into testimony about what the mortician does to preserve the tissues, draining the blood out of the system and replacing it with embalming fluid, the essential element of which is formalin.

"What does formalin do?" Bailey asked.

"Formalin coagulates tissue and preserves it. It is a preservative of the tissue."

"If the tissue during life has been torn or ruptured in some way so that hemorrhage occurs in the tissue, the formalin would preserve that too, would it not?"

"Yes, it would."

Lee Bailey went on to questions about the flattening of the coronary arteries, concealing any sign of the satisfaction he must have felt at inserting a question and answer which would be so useful to him later.

Dr. Milton Helpern put on a seemingly interminable slide show. He pointed and he lectured and he explained, slide after slide. It seemed almost as if he had decided that if Mr. Bailey asked to see slides, he would see the whole collection. His manner was professorial, kindly, and infinitely eager to present every detail.

When he began, Carl Coppolino moved his chair—walked it on its casters to where he could see the screen. It is not known whether he lost interest after the first slide, or realized it put him in awkward relationship to the jury, or was advised by his counsel to get back to the defense table. He went back, and for the rest of the show he sat there just beyond the screen, visible to the jury in profile, staring toward the bench.

Dr. Helpern at first positioned himself to the jury's left of the projector, to that side of the projector farthest from the bench. But there, without his realizing it, he was blocking the view of the screen of the juror on the end of the front row, the end nearest the spectators, George Phillips, the Ukrainian engineer. As Helpern began speaking, Phillips stood up, bent out over the rail, reached one arm as far as he could, and took Dr. Helpern by the upper arm and firmly and slowly moved Helpern out of his way. Helpern turned and stared at him in total astonishment. Phillips sat quickly back in his chair, arms folded, and gave Helpern a single abrupt continental nod. Helpern repositioned himself as Phillips had so directly suggested, and picked up the thread of his explanation. Phillips looked at about five slides with total attention, and then slumped into a position of greater comfort and, arms still folded, seemed almost to be dozing. He did not give the impression of shirking the juror's duty. He managed to look as if he had made his own analysis and appraisal of that portion of the evidence, and had no need of having it repeated over and over in order to comprehend it.

It is sufficient to quote only the discourse on the first slide: [Farber 7/16/66 L.A.D. 1-1—meaning, in addition to name of deceased and date of autopsy, that it was section one of block one taken from the *l*eft *a*nterior *d*escending coronary branch.]

"This is the left anterior descending branch and where the coronary sclerosis in this person happened to be most severe. I might say that the process in the right coronary and in the left circumflex branch were practically absent. This shows a vessel, an artery which is collapsed and here you have a thickening of the inner lining. This is the atheromatous plaque and normally the intima, or the lining, is this thick, and I am pointing right here, and it has been deposited, as it frequently does, to form this mass of connective tissue. This is all in the artery wall. This is part of the intima. It's extrinsically placed. That is, it's not concentric, but excentric and it lies on one side of the intima, and there you have it, and I would say this lesion here is a lesion which is readily recognizable grossly and also through the microscope. It is an entirely quiescent lesion. There is no evidence of any hemorrhage in it. There is no evidence of any activity in this lesion, and the lumen, in my opinion, is quite adequate in this artery. It's somewhat flattened, but if you blew this out, if the arteries had been injected and blown out to show them as circles, then this would come out to about here, you see, and the opening would come to about here."

Lee Bailey came closer and stared at it, and asked if the plaque, or deposit, did not seem to be a brighter shade of red. Helpern said it was, that it took a redder tinge from the stain than did the artery itself.

"And can you tell us about this apparent slice, this here?" Lee Bailey asked, pointing at the screen.

"This here is an artifact produced in the cutting of the section," Helpern explained. "In other words, when it's flattened out—

these are very delicate, they're five thousandths of an inch thick and you not infrequently get this type of folding, and it's purely an artifact that any pathologist would recognize.''

Here are the difficulties Helpern faced with a lay jury. Imagine taking an old pipe of some soft metal with, at various distances along its length, old encrusted deposits that, at no point, constrict the fluid-carrying capacity of the pipe to less than 75 percent of the original volume of fluid which could pass through it. Then you hammer it to varying degrees of flatness, put some curves in it, and then saw it into thin wafers but without changing the position of the pipe so as to compensate for the bends as it goes through the saw. The expert can easily interpret what he sees. The lay person has to make the effort of imagining each wafer back in its original round state. Because of the bends, some of the wafers will be open at top or bottom, and of strange and unusual shape. Next imagine the pipe metal itself and the deposit on the interior as being tinted two quite similar shades of red. Lee Bailey kept pointing out the strange shapes and relationship.

"Are you saying, Doctor, that this section in here came from the missing part of the wall?''

"No! No! No!'' (exasperation and indignation)

"It came from somewhere else?'' (exaggerated innocent mystification)

"No! It's part of the—what's above there. You see what I mean? In other words, this happens to be a slice. When the thing is cut out horizontally the artery is distorted and the lining sort of dipped down and it appears now as a separate structure occupying what looks like the channel, but you must believe me when I tell you that the lumen here did not contain anything, and that this represents the curious way in which these arteries curve and the way in which this was sectioned, and you can very easily demonstrate that from the rest of the block.''

"Is that section a piece of chaff that somehow got on the side? Is that it?''

"No! It's not *chaff!* It's part of the artery wall!''

"It just broke away from the inside?''

"No, no, it didn't break away from the inside! It's *part* of the inside! It appears to be separate because it was dipping down when the section was cut out. In other words, in handling this slide the technician, instead of keeping it crosswise, the tissue rotated.''

And on and on, with Dr. Helpern trying to demonstrate why the arteries were sufficient, and Mr. Bailey with a bland guile making the presentation as confusing as possible. During the confusions, Bailey managed to elicit Helpern's opinion that a good job of embalming had been done on Colonel Farber's body.

On one slide which Helpern was willing to admit that the stricture looked like more than 25 percent of the original inner diameter, Bailey jumped on Helpern's use of the word "moderate."

"When I said moderate I was considering the worst sections I could find. That is, the most extensive disease I could find. And I added that up to moderate. . . . In other words, this man was fifty-two years of age and it would be very surprising if his coronaries looked like a person of twenty-two or twenty-five. This is quite a common finding in persons in that age group."

"You say that everyone who is fifty-two has that much disease present?"

"I would say that most people of fifty-two have more than that, some people have less than that, and that this is about average."

As Dr. Helpern continued with the slides, Lee Bailey for a time interrupted with questions about the more confusing ones, forcing the pathologist into explanations which seemed to contribute to the confusion rather than lessen it. And then Bailey wandered away from his vantage point near the screen and the jury, toward the judge's end of the small courtroom.

When Helpern finished his uninterrupted explanation in detail of L.A.D. 5-3 and called for the next one to be projected by his assistant, Bailey said wonderingly, "How *many* of those do you have?"

"I have quite a few, Mr. Bailey."

"All right."

"I thought I'd show them all."

"Do you have any estimate of how many there are?"

"We're about . . . half through," said Dr. Helpern. Bailey strolled back and asked a few questions about the next series of slides, shrugged and walked back and sat on the corner of the defense table, head cocked, arms folded, expression quizzical and ironic. Dr. Helpern had begun on the coronary arteries on the right side of the heart.

"Doctor," said Bailey, "would you say that the right side is less diseased than the left side?"

"I would say that the atherosclerosis was more marked in the left coronary artery."

"Then there is no apparent purpose in running through all of these because you have already told us that the principal disease existed in the slides already demonstrated. Is that correct?"

"Well, I only have about four more, and I might just as well run through the whole."

"Would you *like* to show them?" The flavor of the question was gentle, patronizing, tolerant.

"As long as I am showing them. I am bringing everything here, and I don't want to be seemingly holding back on anything."

"Oh no. No, I'm *sure* you wouldn't."

As Helpern began a detailed explanation and appraisal of slide R.C.-2, F. Lee Bailey moved casually around and stepped up into the witness stand and sat in the witness chair. He yawned, and slumped and laced his fingers across his middle, just below the gold gleam of the watch chain across his tailored vest. He closed his eyes and yawned hugely. It was a most daring impertinence, a piece of showmanship carefully staged to look utterly natural, and one must realize that it could not have been pre-planned, but had to be an invention of the moment. Obviously the jury was very aware of it. Judge Simmill slowly straightened and looked at F. Lee Bailey and looked at the jury. Even to a jurist of Elvin Simmill's confidence and control and aplomb, this act by Bailey was an affront to the dignity of the Court. An objection by the state would have given Judge Simmill a chance to express an obvious irritation with Bailey's tactic. Perhaps Mr. Keuper was on the verge of objecting. Perhaps Judge Simmill was just about to find outlet for the emotion he was expressing by a growing frown. But at what might well have been the final second, Mr. Bailey got up and went back to the defense table, rested a haunch once more on the corner of it, and masked another great yawn with his fist. The room was semi-darkened by the adjustment of the metal blinds to make the images on the screen brighter by contrast. There had been a great many slides. Dr. Helpern had talked for a long time, and had said the same words many times. Two jurors seemed to be asleep. Yawns are infectious. Three or four jurors caught the disease and yawned. And suddenly there was no new slide. The assistant turned the projection bulb off. The cooling fan whirred.

"Is that the end, Doctor?" Bailey asked with an air of hopefulness.

"Yes, thank you. Both are the coronary arteries. If you desire sections of the other tissues they are all there." He motioned toward the slide box on the projection stand. "I have 107 slides in all of the tissues that I sectioned, but I think you wanted to see the coronaries."

"We won't terrify the jury with 107 of anything," Bailey said, and asked Dr. Helpern if he would once again take the stand. But the judge ordered the mid-morning recess at that time.

Chapter Twenty-five

During the first part of the morning session, Mary Coppolino had been absent from her usual place in one of the chairs just inside the rail in front of the press section. She had come in at about ten-thirty, during the slide presentation, accompanied by Carl's mother, Anna Fiore Coppolino, Mrs. Lettore "Leo" Coppolino, making her first appearance at the trial of her son.

[As far as is known, neither Leo Coppolino, the father of the accused, nor Helen Ann Coppolino, the only other child of the Coppolino marriage, a nurse eight years younger than Carl, ever appeared in any of the several courtrooms to observe the proceedings.]

Anna Coppolino certainly did not match the type-casting image of the Sicilian mother. She was a small tidy woman with brown curly hair, and rather pale skin. She wore glasses with pale plastic frames, a sensible cloth coat with a fur collar, pearl button earrings. Had one no opportunity to hear her speak, she might more reasonably have been type-cast as the middle-aged wife of a small town Methodist minister somewhere in the Midwest, yet with the black dress, pearl necklace, pale mink collar on the dark coat, little hat with a short semi-veil, she looked a bit too urban and stylish for that particular background.

She had arrived alone by bus from Brooklyn that morning and had been met by Mary and some newspeople at the wretchedly depressing Freehold bus station, and brought to the courtroom.

At the recess, she and Mary had gone to the defense table where Anna Coppolino had given Carl's necktie a little straightening pat, and had brushed at one shoulder and lapel, then cradled his narrow cheeks between her small hands and gave him a quick fleeting kiss. Carl seemed to accept these public attentions rather stiffly and awkwardly, and indeed his mother seemed constrained in expressing them.

When she spoke there was only a slight accent revealing her

foreign origin, conditioned by that other distinctive accent of Queens and Brooklyn. She was a small woman and she did not seem the least bit flustered or ill at ease. She looked about her with a calm curiosity. When Mary introduced her to friends among the press, Anna Coppolino looked appraisingly through the lenses which enlarged and distorted her brown eyes slightly, made certain she caught the name and occupation, and was entirely gracious in acknowledging the introduction. There was about her an impression of strength and resolve and, in some odd way, command.

When the trial resumed, with Helpern on the stand, Bailey went back to emphasize a statement which had seemed trivial at the time Helpern first made it.

"Prior to the time you began to exhibit these slides, I believe you told us that when tissue is ripped or torn or damaged, that hemorrhage may ensue in the tissue, and this will be preserved by the formalin?"

"Yes. The fixation will fix the hemorrhage, yes."

"Would you agree, Doctor, with the general statement that autopsies do not automatically provide the correct answer in homicide cases, contrary to the general impression?"

"That's correct."

"Would you also agree that: The misinterpretation of many forensic autopsies has and will continue to result in serious miscarriages of justice?"

Helpern with a small and mischievous smile said, "I'll go along with that, yes."

"You wrote it, didn't you, Doctor?"

"That's right. That is why I am going along with it."

"Would you say, Doctor, that as a general principle care must be exercised during the transportation of the body that it isn't mutilated, and nothing is done to interfere with the anatomical lesions which are present on the surface? Rough handling of the dead body may produce confusing post-mortem injuries?"

"That's right."

"Would you also agree that in all cases studied by a medical examiner or coroner, a knowledge of the circumstances preceding and sometimes following the death is of paramount importance in the subsequent evaluation of the post-mortem findings? The forensic pathologist cannot separate himself from such an investigation?"

"That's right."

"Is it correct to say that in smothering, the autopsy may reveal evidence of asphyxiation and the suspicion of homicide, arising from the investigation of the dead body at the scene and the surrounding circumstances?''

"That is correct.''

"Did you in the *New York State Journal of Medicine* in an article by you entitled 'Medical Legal Investigation, May 15, 1965,' use a case history to discuss the problem of determining which of more than one possible cause was responsible for death, and state on page 1266 of that issue: 'This is only one of the many examples in which the cause of death cannot be established by post-mortem and autopsy examination alone'?''

"That is correct.''

Bailey next quoted from one of the standard texts in the field of forensic pathology and legal medicine, a text authored by Gonzales, Vance, Helpern, and Umberger. "On the other hand, in cases of smothering, carbon dioxide asphyxiation, drowning, and some cases of ligature strangulation in which the diagnostic signs are not always obvious, it may be difficult to identify in the exhumed body as their characteristic appearance may be obscured by the embalming process'?''

"That is correct, and I said that yesterday.''

"And you continue to say that any evidence of smothering is no longer available, if it ever was?''

"That is correct. . . . The body was in such condition that no opinion could be given as to whether or not this person had been smothered. And I said: If the body had only been smothered and there were no other injuries, then I would not have been able to detect such an occurrence.''

"You have in that bottle which has been marked as an exhibit something besides the larynx, and I think you said that was the hyoid bone?''

"That's right.''

"And, in some cases of strangulation, these are found to be fractured, are they not?''

[In *Death* by Houts, 1966, Chatper 5, pp. 54 and 55, in explaining autopsy procedure, Houts writes, "In cases in which manual strangulation is suspected, however, it may be necessary to remove the respiratory passages and their associated structures in one piece. This is done by elongating the lateral incisions on each side of the neck and dissecting the organs away from the skin on the front and sides and from the spine in back. When dissection is properly performed, all the neck structures, the thyroid, larynx, pharynx, trachea, hyoid bone, and even the tongue can be removed en masse, while keeping the various structures in their normal relationships. In manual strangulation there often may be no external evidence of extreme pressure; but swelling and hemorrhage will be evident within the neck structures. Most often, since the pressure of strangulation is uneven, there will be a resultant fracture of the hyoid bone.]

Bailey, in an another abrupt switch of direction, asked Helpern to describe the inside of the larynx, as regards tissue and other material.

After he did so, Bailey said, "Now, if you were to exert pressure on my cricoid cartilage right now and push in hard enough to break it, what would you expect to happen to the tissue inside?"

"I thought you were going to ask what I would expect to happen to me." That, of course, is one of the quicksand areas Bailey presents to any man of intelligence and wit during cross-examination. There is always the temptation to try to parry with Bailey's own weapons, quickness and quips, and an agile irony.

"Well, I can promise you *I* wouldn't defend you."

"I'm sorry, Mr. Bailey." (sorry you would not be available)

"Did you understand my question?" A sudden and aggressive harshness completely changed the mood.

Bailey wanted to know what would happen if his cartilage were broken while he was still alive, what would happen to the tissue inside the larynx. "It would hemorrhage, wouldn't it?"

"There would be some bleeding, and this bleeding would be minimal. In other words, when the cricoid cartilage is broken in the way which you just indicated, the muscles which are on the cricoid cartilage, that is the crico-thyroid muscle, would be bruised. And even though it may not be evident on the outside, when you started dissecting you would find evidence of hemorrhage under the mucous membrane, and as a result of the associated asphyxia phenomena, depending upon how long it took you to expire with that procedure, there would be more or less punctate hemorrhages, or petechial, which you talked about yesterday, in the lining."

"A dead body doesn't bleed, does it?"

"I would say you can bruise the tissues after death and produce hemorrhage, but generally speaking, if the heart stops it isn't the type of bleeding we think about in a live person."

"Now, in attempting to determine for yourself whether or not the injury with which we are concerned, to this larynx occurred before or after the death of Colonel Farber, did you examine the tissue for hemorrhage?"

"I examined the tissue for that very carefully, but the state of the tissue precluded any observation of hemorrhage. In other words, whatever hemorrhage was there was no longer discernible in the tissue as I saw it. In other words, the evidence of the type of hemorrhage you see in a fractured cricoid cartilage which is inflicted during life was no longer evident. The fact that I couldn't find it after three years of death would not permit me to conclude it wasn't there, and I found no evidence of it after three years of death."

"And you don't have any evidence that there was hemorrhage which has disappeared?"

"I don't have any evidence. All the evidence I have is the double fracture of the cricoid."

"Now the fracture which you showed us yesterday of this cartilage you agree could have been caused after death when this body was exhumed just by cracking the way you could do it during life. Isn't that true?"

"I suppose if a funeral director got a notion to do that, he could fracture the cricoid cartilage."

"Without hypothecating the methods, it *could* have happened post-mortem?"

"Well, that's a possibility. Yes."

"Now if it did happen post-mortem, especially after the embalming, there wouldn't be any hemorrhage in the lining of the larynx, would there?"

"If it happened post-mortem I would say that one would not see any petechial hemorrhages. You might still see some bleeding around the fracture site, that is, where the break occurred and the tissues were actually torn. There is blood in those tissues and the vessels and it can bleed out, that is, it can be forced out, but you would not get the associated petechial hemorrhages if someone had done that."

Again Bailey nailed down the fact of no observable hemorrhage. "It's not there, is it?"

"All I can say is that the condition of this tissue, of this structure is such that I cannot give you any valid opinion as to whether it was there or not."

"But," said Bailey persistently and aggressively, "if there never *was* any hemorrhage there, Doctor, if it's established that there never was any hemorrhage in that lining at all, that would be an indication that this is a post-mortem injury, would it not?"

"If there were no hemorrhages at all in the tissue that would suggest that, provided the observation could be validly made. In other words, if you . . ."

"I think you have answered the question."

"If you examined the tissue immediately after death . . ."

Well, I have to explain this, because I examined this larynx three years after this man died.''

"Exactly."

"And there was certain brownish discoloration which I didn't want to allude to, that could very well have resulted from a chemical change in blood, but I left that out because I could not form a valid opinion about it.''

"So you still can't form one, can you?''

"I didn't form one. I already told you that.''

"Why do you allude to it now, Doctor, if you say you didn't want to?''

"Because you're bringing up the subject, Mr. Bailey,'' said Helpern in an aggrieved and irritable tone, "about the absence of hemorrhage in a post-mortem fracture. I'm trying to say . . .''

When Bailey interrupted, Mr. Keuper asked that the witness be allowed to finish his answer.

Lee Bailey said, "I don't think I'm forced to take a lecture with every answer, Your Honor. I'm trying to get an answer.''

"I agree with you,'' said Judge Simmill, "but when you ask him *why*, then you must take the reasons.''

Bailey tried to repair his tactical mistake by asking if he could withdraw the question. Keuper pointed out that the doctor had started to answer and should be permitted to finish his answer. The Court so ruled. Bailey with shrug and sigh said, "All right, Doctor. Finish your answer.''

"All I'm saying is that if I examine a post-mortem fracture immediately after it's inflicted, then I can evaluate the absence of hemorrhage in those tissues, but after three years I cannot make a valid observation or arrive at a valid conclusion as to the presence or the absence of hemorrhage. In other words, I cannot say that there wasn't any hemorrhage there.''

"You can't say there was, and you can't say there wasn't, can you?''

"I can't say. I already said that. If I can't say there wasn't any, then the same thing applies, and I can't say there was.''

Bailey then put a hypothetical question to him, asking him to assume there never was any hemorrhage in this case.

"If I were asked to assume that there was never any hemorrhage in this case and that all I found was the fractures of the cricoid, then I would say that I would be willing to say that this is not an ante-mortem injury.''

"So if the jury should find that there never was any hemorrhage present in the lining of this larynx, then assuming that fact you would have to say it was post-mortem?''

Keuper objected and was sustained. Bailey said to the judge, "May I approach the bench and make an offer of proof?"

"No," said Judge Simmill. "You may not!"

"Hmm?" said Bailey, a sound duly recorded by the court stenographer and typed into the official transcript.

"No. You may not. He has already told you that if there was no hemorrhage, assuming that, then he could not say that the fracture of the cricoid was ante-mortem."

"All right," said Lee Bailey and looked slightly disconcerted at the unexpected resistance on the part of Judge Simmill.

He then quoted to Helpern a portion of the autopsy report which said that the muscles of the larynx were extensively autolyzed and did not show any recognizable hemorrhage. Helpern admitted authorship. Next he quoted from the book Helpern had helped author. "Hemorrhages occuring around the fractures and in the laryngeal and adjacent structures are an important indication that the damage was inflicted during life." Helpern had written it and agreed with it. Bailey read him another selected quote from the same work. "It is important to determine reliable criteria which will establish that the injuries of the neck are ante-mortem, thus if grouped abrasions are present on the skin of the neck and hemorrhages are found in the submucosa and intrinsic muscle of the larynx, it is correct to conclude that the trauma was inflicted during life."

When Helpern announced that, too, was correct, Bailey moved closer to him, and closer to the point of this final portion of his cross-examination.

"Doctor, I think you said at the outset of your testimony today and again a few minutes ago that if hemorrhage occurs in the tissue during life, embalming will preserve the hemorrhages."

"For a certain time, yes."

"And how long a time would you say the preservation would be there?"

"Depending upon the condition of the body. I have seen hemorrhage demonstrable after a year of the post-mortem period . . . and I don't want to quibble one month more or less."

"Is that the limit in your judgment?"

"It's not the limit, but after three years the subtle hemorrhages that you would get—or the fine hemorrhages that you would get in a case of manual strangulation—will no longer be demonstrable."

"What happens to them?"

"They disappear."

"Tell us how."

448

"If you had a big hemorrhage there, I mean a hemorrhage of any size, you would find it. I mean you would find some evidence of it, but I have seen even fairly large hemorrhages disappear after that time."

"How can you tell they have disappeared unless you have seen them earlier?"

"What I would say is that large hemorrhages are demonstrable after a variable period of time, but the type of hemorrhage you see in a manual strangulation after three years, the fact that I didn't find them would not mean that they were not there."

"But it might mean that they were never there?"

"I said I cannot form any opinion about the presence or absence of the hemorrhage. If I found them, I would say they were there. But if I didn't find them I wouldn't say they weren't there."

The spectator unaware of the rhythms of the adversary ceremony might easily have assumed at this point that F. Lee Bailey was floundering. His questions, linked in series, all seemed to end up back at the same impasse. It might seem as if through repetition he was trying, without success, to move Milton Helpern one half step backward, thus creating a small and rather obscure point for the defense. It is well to remember that when the court had recessed the day before, Bailey's case was at its lowest point, as it is safe to assume that the jury reaction was by and large the same as the reaction of the press and public.

Compared with all the weight of the state's case, Bailey seemed to be trying to put out a barn fire with a water pistol as he persisted in digging away at the business of hemorrhages. But it is never the obligation of the defense to create a counterweight of testimony of greater mass, weight and momentum than that the state has presented. Nor is it even imperative for the defense to create an area of reasonable doubt which would bring the whole structure toppling down. The structure can still stand, but the doubt must be inserted into it, dovetailed into it if you will, so that reasonable doubt translates to reasonable alternative. Bailey could not, himself, furnish the reasonable alternative. The advocate in court is not under oath. He does not testify. He can only clear the way for the testimony he intends to present.

For the pro-football addict, here is a suitable analogy. In his cross of Helpern, Bailey was running downfield patterns, with head and body feints, cutbacks, hooks, crossovers. He was learning how he could, when it was time for the ball to be thrown to him, get past Helpern with it. The football spectator seldom watches the subtle contest of preparation. But he watches the eventual pass play and sees the receiver break into the clear and make the catch. To continue the analogy, the defense does not have to outscore the state in order to win. It needs only to make one substantial, obvious and memorable gain.

So Bailey asked Helpern if he knew of any case where a manual strangulation hemorrhage had remained detectable after three years of preservation in formalin, in the lining of the larynx. Helpern said he did not, and added that he had not broken open the larynx because prying it open creates artifacts, and also because the lining, or mucosa was in such a deteriorated condition he could not reasonably expect to find petechial hemorrhages after three years. Bailey then asked him if the hemorrhages on the outside of the larynx couldn't be other than petechial, or pin-point hemorrhages, and couldn't he expect to see those from the outside. Helpern replied that the soft tissues outside the larynx had been too far decomposed for any valid observation of such a hemorrhage.

Bailey next moved to the specifics of what a hemorrhage would look like in soft tissue, saying "if you were to choke me now," as his lead, and clamping his own hands on his throat. This talent for selecting the personal and the vivid and the semi-grotesque image—that of kindly old doctor choking dynamic young attorney—is what rivets jury attention because it is entertaining. And the juror entertained by the small charades will remember the area being discussed at the time.

Helpern replied that the fixation of the blood in bruised tissues by formalin turns the red hemoglobin to gray, and had the tissues of the throat been there, which they hadn't, the recognition of the blood in the tissues would be possible.

It is possible to trip while running pass patterns, and Bailey's next questions, about whether or not a person could live after a fracture of the cricoid cartilage was an approach which, it is possible, he could have regretted making. Helpern said that in some rare cases death did not result. He said he had seen accident cases where the injuries were more extensive.

"And they still lived?"

"I would say that it's a very serious injury and they can recover, but what seems to be the point that doesn't get across is that *this* injury of the larynx is of an isolated type. It's a double fracture of the cricoid. And this injury is almost characteristic of strangulation, that is, compression of the neck by the hands or by the forearm and so on. And the finding of that injury I have never found as an isolated occurrence in any case but a strangulation."

Bailey very swiftly shifted to another area, asking Helpern about how morticians generally move bodies around while preparing them for burial. Keuper objected that Helpern was not qualified in this area, but Helpern indicated enough familiarity with the process to be permitted to answer the questions, testifying that prior to embalming the funeral director keeps the head propped up on a block to prevent blood from draining into the face and suffusing it with a blue tint, that any such discolorations are frequently massaged out during the preparation of the body, and then after the body is laid out it is treated with a cosmetic.

"Isn't it common practice to tie the hands together across the chest when they move the body around, so they won't flop?"

Keuper objected, but Bailey assured the Court he would connect it up with something relevant. Helpern answered that the hands could be at the chest or at the sides and that sometimes they might be tied, but generally speaking, they're not tied. Bailey then approached the question of how a body is actually moved about, customarily by two people.

"Assuming that one is at the back of the head and one grabs the feet as the body is taken from the embalming table to the cart and then to the casket and moved around in the casket to be positioned, isn't it common to grab the body right by the neck and move it by the neck?"

As Lee Bailey had begun his question, he had moved around the defense table to stand behind his client. As he said, "grab the body right by the neck" he put his hands on Coppolino's slender neck. As he said "move it by the neck" he pulled Coppolino back and lifted him slightly.

It would be interesting to know who was the most startled, the witness, the judge, the jury, or the accused. There was an audible gasp and some thought a rather sour and speculative look on the face of Judge Simmill. Again, shock equals entertainment equals jury attention equals jury memory. It is, of course, precisely the same technique every gifted classroom teacher uses instinctively.

Keuper made his third objection to this line of questioning, this time with the indignation of a man personally offended by a lapse of taste, affronted by this attack upon the traditional mystery of the handling of the dead. Helpern was permitted to answer, and there was irritability with a hint of scorn in his tone.

"I would say not in the way in which you just indicated. The body is usually picked up by the shoulders. The body has already been, or it hasn't been, embalmed. It's not picked up by the neck. No one squeezes the neck." Helpern tried to expand his answer over Bailey's interruption, and Keuper asked that Helpern be permitted to finish his answer, but the Court ruled that he already had.

Bailey switched suddenly to another area, asking Helpern in what percentage of cases he ordinarily could not determine the cause of death.

Helpern switched just as abruptly as Bailey, to gentle smile, self-deprecatory shrug. "Well, the older I get, the percentage gets larger."

"How high is it today?"

"When I first started out I thought I knew the cause of death of every person. But I would say that there are approximately five percent or more, somewhere between five and seven percent of cases where we cannot determine the cause of death either because we don't have the history or because a chemical portioning has taken place and the chemist can no longer discern the presence of the poison and the effects are not demonstrable in the tissues. And then there are some diseases that do cause death particularly in young people where the anatomical evidences are not clear and certainly we have a whole large group of cases of infants who die unexpectedly and under very tragic circumstances."

"One last question, Doctor. I take it from what you have written, as I read it this morning, that of some importance in diagnosing the cause of death in a case such as this would be the observations of any attending physician who was present during the last hours of life?"

"I would say the observations of a reliable physician might prove helpful in a particular case. It's important to know how a person died, if you can get that information. The more information you have about a case the better you are able to determine this, but there are many causes of death which become evident at the post-mortem examination and more or less contradict any prior impression. . . . We see many cases of death certified as coronary thrombosis, and in a fair number of these cases we find that the cause of death wasn't coronary artery disease, even though a substantial amount of coronary artery disease is found."

"In many cases of doubtful cause of death or non-apparent cause of death an attending physician is apt to put down coronary occlusion or heart attack of some kind?"

In the manual on courtroom medicine titled *Death*, Marshall Houts has this to say about those cases where the cause of death is not determined:

"Conscientious pathologists of skill, experience and integrity say that there are a number of deaths in which the exact cause of death simply cannot be determined with complete certainty. Obviously, it is not possible to know the precise number of cases that fall within this category. It is not a situation that lends itself to statistical evaluation since, nearly always, *some* cause of death is 'selected' for the death certificate.

"Up until shortly after World War II, some pathologists estimated they could not find a clear-cut cause of death in perhaps 5 percent of the cases they autopsied. I am told that now the more accurate figure may be 2 percent."

"It's sort of a wastebasket diagnosis," Dr. Helpern replied, "and I will accept every case as such. And sometimes we can't verify it, but the verification of these cases leaves many cases where *that* cause of death is proved wrong. This is one of the difficulties. But there are situations where a person has two causes of death, two possible causes. And you cannot tell unless you have reliable observation as to how the man died, as to which one did it. Take a man with an old brain injury which might cause convulsions, cause him to die, and the same man might have very severe coronary disease. Now which do I select as the cause of death? . . . If I can get a reliable history that the man died with convulsions . . . I would attribute his death to the old brain injury. If the man suddenly clutched his chest and died . . . I would call this a death from coronary artery disease."

"Is it fair to say, Doctor, that apart from this larynx, just assuming you found no difference, that you would be unable to give us the cause of death at this time apart from that?"

"If I didn't have the larynx in this case, I would have to say I didn't know what this man died of."

Bailey thanked him and walked away. Keuper stood tall, and excused Dr. Helpern and, at two minutes past noon, told the Court that the state rested its case against Carl Coppolino.

Judge Simmill announced a five-minute recess.

Quite obviously the word used in Mr. Bailey's final question was "injury," not "difference."

Over 5000 pages of official transcript formed a substantial percentage of the reference material for this book. It was all taken down by official court reporters on stenotype machines and transcribed from those strange groups of letters which the machine imprints on the long white tapes, letter groups meaningless to anyone not trained in stenotype operation and, quite often, meaningless in part even to any other stenotype operator.

It is a highly skilled occupation. It requires not only long training and practice, but also a special quality of mind somewhat akin to a talent for languages. Some who try to learn how to use the machine, no matter how great their motivation, never quite manage to "break through." This means that they never reach the point where the fingers press the keys to form the letter-group symbols for the sounds the ears hear without the operator being actually aware of his own finger movements. It is like what Yogi Berra said about hitting, that you can't think and hit too when you're up there at the plate.

By and large the transcripts reflect with a reasonable accuracy what happened in the courtroom, but they reflect, in percentage error or lack of it, the intricacy, speed and audibility of the testimony and argument, the cumulative weariness of the steno-type operator, as well as those errors in transcription from tape to typewriter due to carelessness, misinterpretation of the symbols, or indifference to the sense of the question or answer transcribed.

Estimates of the percentage of cases where an official transcript must be prepared, as against the total number of cases where the obligatory tapes are filed away, runs between one half percent and three quarters of one percent. A more careful investigation indicates that one tenth of one percent might be closer to the reality, even in these days of appeals. Civil as well as criminal cases are included in this appraisal, of course. Thus for every thousand hours of courtroom stenotyping, perhaps one hour will eventually be converted to official transcript form.

Just as in the taking of shorthand notes, the longer a person works as a court reporter, the more individual his arbitrary codes and symbols become, and the less likelihood there is of anyone else being able to prepare a suitable transcript from his or her stenotapes should accident or death intervene.

Without trying to cast aspersions on a specialist occupation, it is quite obvious that the hallowed institution of the court reporter with stenotype machine is technologically obsolete, clumsy, inaccurate, expensive, and unnecessary, and could easily be phased out without damage to the purse or employment of those court reporters now functioning.

The tape recorder has come of age, in reliability, sensitivity, compactness and flexibility of operation. With the proper placement of microphones, the court reporter would be far more useful and effective to the business of the court were he seated at a table operating the tape recorder, wearing an ear plug monitor as assurance that the proceedings were being properly recorded, and keeping a simple time log matched to the standard indexing device on the tape recorder so as to provide a reliable record of who is speaking at all times.

When the Court orders a question read back, it would be far

simpler and quicker to use tape reverse and have the reporter locate the question through the ear plug speaker, then switch to a small p.a. system to play back the question in the identical manner and voice and with the identical emphasis with which it was originally asked.

The double-locking devices on modern tape recorders make inadvertent erasure of the tape as unlikely as an inadvertent bonfire starting among the stenotapes.

The master tape would be in the custody of the Court, of course, but in the case of a long and involved trial, modern highspeed tape duplication methods could make it possible for the judge, at his discretion, to supply tape copies to both the plaintiff and the defendant during the course of the trial. And in checking matters of law and argument, a similar tape copy, with index and time log, might be of considerable assistance to the trial judge when his personal notes prove inadequate to his needs.

Additionally one might suspect that quite often in cases of appeal and review, the appellate court might find useful, for example, the actual tone and emphasis and flavor of a judge's charge to the jury in addition to having the unemotional printed word for study.

But, perhaps even more important, tape duplicates could be parceled out for stenographic transcription so that, in the case of appeal from a criminal conviction, a transcript could be prepared within a week or two rather than the several months which now often elapses, due mainly to the bottleneck of interpretation of the stenotapes. They would certainly be more accurate and more inclusive of all testimony. And one might hope that they would be cheaper. Today the man of small means who wants to appeal to a higher court after a trial that lasted, let us say, three days, must pay perhaps a thousand dollars for an official transcript of his trial at the rate, customary in most places, of about one dollar a page.

As the rates are based on the number of pages, one finds some extraordinarily large type faces used in transcription. With giant type, wide margins, double spacing, large indents, quadruple spacing between question and answer, an average number of words of between eighty and a hundred and twenty per legal-size page is not unusual. And the number of pages can be artificially inflated by binding the transcript in as many separate folders as conscience will permit, thus making it possible to include a detailed index of the entire proceedings in each folder, as well as new title pages, all, of course, at a dollar a page.

In all practicality, it is vain to expect the judicial system to adopt a technology so admirably suited to its needs. One need only see for how many years the use of the stenotype machine was resisted as if it were some sort of frivolous gadget, unsuited to the dusty dignity of tradition. And now that advance is in turn as obsolete and cumbersome as the windup phonograph. In a few places tape is now being used as a back-up system, and there are instances of tape being used all by itself when stenotype operators of sufficient skill have, for some reason, been unavailable to the court. But with miles to go, progress is measurable in inches.

Chapter Twenty-six

The first witness for the defense was Dr. Joseph W. Spelman, Chief Medical Examiner for the City of Philadelphia.

Dr. Spelman gave an impression of dry, humorless, fussy precision. He was in his late forties, and could have passed as a CPA, or a loan officer in a small bank. F. Lee Bailey, at the suggestion of Dr. Ford, a friend of Dr. Spelman, had phoned Spelman in Philadelphia late Monday night and asked him to be in court the following morning. And so Dr. Spelman had sat inside the rail and watched the slide demonstration and listened to the Helpern testimony.

In the qualifying *voir dire,* Spelman presented substantial credentials: Yale Medical School, internship in pathology at the University Hospital and New Haven Hospital, two years chief of the laboratory at an Army General Hospital, a Rockefeller fellowship in the Department of Legal Medicine at Harvard, and prior to his eleven years stint as Chief Medical Examiner in Philadelphia, he had held the same post for the State of Vermont, at the same time also teaching at the University of Vermont as an associate professor of pathology, teaching, primarily, courses in cardiovascular disease, particularly coronary artery disease. He stated that he was presently Visiting Professor of Forensic Pathology at the University of Pennsylvania, Temple University and Jefferson Medical College.

Bailey had removed the larynx from the jar previously and dried it off. The exhibit number, S-15, was on the jar. He handed the larynx to Dr. Spelman and asked him to look at it.

456

Spelman took it and, with pursed lips and small frown, turned it this way and that, rather like an archaeologist appraising the possible importance of a new find out at the dig. He handed it back and, under questioning, testified that he had examined it earlier that same morning, and had consulted with Dr. Richard Ford about it. He had noticed the fracture in the cricoid area during his prior examination.

"From your examination of that larynx alone, do you have an opinion as to whether or not that fracture occurred prior to or subsequent to the death of the person whose larynx that was?"

"I do have an opinion."

"What is that opinion?"

"In my opinion that fracture is undoubtedly post-mortem."

It was very blunt, very positive, and it came along astonishingly soon, just minutes after Spelman had been given the oath.

When Bailey asked for the basis for his opinion, Spelman said, "In my experience with a considerable number of strangulations and fractures of the larynx, hemorrhage has been an invariable accompaniment of such a fracture. It involves not only the larynx but also the muscular structures about the larynx. Many of the muscles have been removed, I notice. But there is no vestige of a remaining hemorrhage there. I have seen hemorrhages in exhumed bodies for many years after burial. And I believe that if any hemorrhage which had occurred during life had been prsent, that that would still be visible in this specimen."

Spelman did not recall seeing a strangulation case which had been buried as long as three years, but he remembered seeing hemorrhages in other areas which were readily visible in excess of three years. In discussing hemorrhages he made the point that, as they had seen in the microscopic slides in the morning, blood cells were still present in the coronary arteries, but, "I do not see blood cells or collections of blood cells present in this larynx."

Bailey then asked him for his opinions about the condition of the coronary arteries, as shown in the Helpern slides. He said he saw what he considered to be severe arteriosclerosis. Asked his opinion if the condition was severe enough to be a possible cause of death, Dr. Spelman said loudly and firmly, "The degree of atherosclerosis that I saw is a competent cause of death in and by itself."

Baily turned Dr. Spelman over to Keuper for cross-examination. Keuper, as with his other examinations during the state's case, stood erect at the corner of the state table where he sat alone. This placed him near the end of the jury box furthest from the witness.

In his hard and uncompromising tone Keuper asked if the absence of hemorrhage was the reason for his opinion the injury was post-mortem. When Spelman said it was, Keuper asked, "Would you expect to find hemorrhage present, or evidence of a hemorrhage present, after three years interment?"

"I believe I have answered that," Spelman said. It was not the kind of answer one expects from an experienced professional witness. Nor did Spelman's attitude, one of muted antagonism, seem customary in such proceedings.

"I am asking the questions now, Doctor," Keuper said in a voice that left no doubt as to who would control and direct the examination. "Do you know of any other case of a fractured cricoid cartilage of a peron who had been buried for a period of three years and you found evidence of hemorrhage present?"

Spelman said he had not seen such a case himself. Keuper asked him if his testimony was based solely upon his brief examination of the larynx. When Spelman began to explain that his opinion was based also on the testimony of Dr. Helpern who found no hemorrhage, and in addition, not only on his own experience but on his training, Keuper interrupted him, saying, "I'm not asking you about your experience. I am asking you about your examination today."

Quite obviously Dr. Spelman was becoming annoyed. An angry witness is not a good witness. Bailey objected on grounds he probably knew were aside from the point, merely to give the witness time to settle down.

"How long did your examination take this morning?"

"Five minutes!" Spelman snapped.

"Was it a microscopic examination?"

"No!"

At that point Lee Bailey turned almost completely around in his chair and put his forearm along the back of it, and rested his chin on his forearm, and looked directly and steadily at Vincent Keuper, and smiled and smiled and smiled his knowing pussycat smile. Keuper could not look at the witness without, at the same time, seeing Lee Bailey's face. He could have solved the problem by approaching the witness.

He started to ask the next question, stopped, and in a voice that went up the scale and cracked in indignation and distress, he said, "Mr. Bailey! Please will you let me look at the witness and talk to the witness?"

Of course, Bailey was not actually blocking Keuper's view of the witness in any way. With wide, mock, innocent astonishment, Bailey said, "Go ahead and look at him!" He shrugged and turned around again. The mission was accomplished. Dr. Spelman had composed himself.

Keuper then pursued the matter of Spelman testifying he had seen evidence of the presence of hemorrhage in a body buried longer than three years. Under examination, Spelman finally narrowed it down to one case in Vermont of a person with a fractured nose where there was definite hemorrhage into the soft tissue about the nose after having been buried for five years.

Until the next few questions, few in the courtroom had thought the Keuper arsenal contained a talent for effective ridicule.

Keuper boggled at him in brute amazement and said, "You found evidence of a fracture of the nose?"

"That is correct!" Spelman was sounding waspish again.

"And you found evidence of a presence of hemorrhage?" *Do you mean to say that if somebody busts your nose, you bleed? How about that?*

Keuper studied him for a long moment. "How many other cases, Doctor?" he asked gently.

"I believe it is the only one."

"The only one," Keuper said wonderingly. He shrugged. "That is all, Doctor." He sat down.

Bailey had to come back on redirect to effect some rehabilitation of his witness after the apparently effective savaging by Keuper. He began by asking about the effect of embalming fluid on hemorrhages. When Keuper objected to it as improper redirect, Bailey rephrased it in a way which caused the Court to permit it, over Keuper's renewed objection. Bailey led Spelman into delivering a semi-lecture on formalin, autolysis, enzymes and hemoglobin, a process that could comfort Spelman and at the same time restore the doctor-image in the collective mind of the jury. As his final question Bailey asked him if there was anything else about the larynx which Spelman felt might bear on the determination of when the injury occurred.

"There is no evidence of separation of the tissue such as would be caused by active bleeding into the tissue. So, even if the hemorrhage has faded, the tissue would remain separated by the hemorrhage, if there is any sizable extent of hemorrhage. Admittedly the mucosa or mucous membrane is gone. That is no longer available to see if there were hemorrhages there. But there should be still visible stains where the hemorrhage had been on the inner surface of that larynx, and these are not present now."

Keuper's only question on recross was if Spelman's opinion would have been different "if you had examined that exhibit immediately upon its removal from the body of Colonel Farber on July 20th, 1966?"

"Let me say this. I would like to have seen . . ."

"May I have an answer to my question, Doctor?"

The court reporter read the question back. Spelman said, "I see nothing that would lead me to believe my opinion would be different."

Trials in fiction are always excessively tidy. There are no dangling bits, no residual questions. The parts fit together without chink or flaw. But reality is all a tangle of loose ends, matters left unresolved and unanswered.

What would Dr. Spelman have liked to have seen?

Why did Vincent Keuper stop him from telling what he would have liked to have seen?

Dapper Dr. Edmund Leslie Webb, who had appeared the day before as a state witness, was Bailey's next defense witness. As became apparent, Bailey's only use of him was to have him bring along an apparent duplicate of the container of Anectin which he had delivered by hand to Carl Coppolino in 1963, Anectin being the trade name used by the Burroughs Wellcome pharmaceutical firm for succinylcholine in powdered form. Webb testified that it was a duplicate of the container of one thousand milligrams he had given Carl, and explained how the plastic container was sealed and how it was used. Bailey's obvious point was to show the jury how different the container was in both size and style of opening than the container previously described by Mrs. Farber as the one she had handled and opened and used. It was designed, Webb testified, to be used to add the drug to the fluid in an infusion bottle, the kind of bottle that is hung from a high place and, by gravity, drips medication into the vein of the patient. One stripped off a yellow seal, then removed a cap thus exposed, which in turn revealed a sterile nose which would be inserted into the infusion bottle. Then when the flexible plastic bottle was squeezed, a plastic seal inside the neck of the bottle would be broken by the pressure and the powder would squirt through an inner tube into the infusion bottle.

Webb said that though the package was not intended for use with a hypodermic for injection, it could be used that way. One would have to remove the outer yellow seal, unscrew the plastic tube inside thus exposing the diaphragm, then break the diaphragm by squeezing the bottle, or merely push a needle through the diaphragm and add a fluid to the powder inside, then draw the powder in solution back up through the needle into the

460

syringe. Webb testified that the container he had brought was substantially the same as the one he had given Coppolino, that about that time there had been some change in the inner diaphragm, but nothing significant.

Keuper, on cross-examination, moved at once to try to impeach the testimony of the witness, establishing first that Webb had been a friend of Carl Coppolino for many years, was still a friend, and would very probably want to help Carl in any way he could.

It turned into a curious wrangle. It seems that Keuper was carrying a container of Anectin in his pocket. When he took it out it looked identical to the one Bailey had used during direct. Keuper seemed hugely indignant, as full of earnest wrath as one of the early prophets. "Do you recall my visit to you in Brooklyn on December 2nd of this year?"

"Yes, I do."

"And do you recall my asking you for a sample of the succinylcholine chloride?"

"Yes, I do."

"And do you recall giving me this?" Keuper held it in front of the witness' nose.

"It is a very similar one, yes. I'll say it probably is the one I gave you."

"Do you recall the conversation about this container?"

"I do not. We *had* one."

In tones of thunderous scorn Keuper said, "You don't recall telling me that it was not in the same kind of container? The succinylcholine chloride that you delivered to Doctor Coppolino was not the same kind of a container as this exhibit?!" Webb said he didn't mean to give Keuper the impression it was a different container. "Can you describe the container that you gave to Doctor Coppolino in 1963?"

"Yes. It was one identical except for a change in the diaphragm to the sort that you have now. These have been in use since 1956 or '59. Other than the change in the diaphragm it would be, to all intents and purposes, the same."

"BUT YOU DIDN'T TELL ME THAT IN BROOKLYN, DID YOU?"

Bailey objected on the basis of not having any assurance there would be evidence presented of earlier contradictory statements, and was overruled. Keuper asked when Webb had found out about the change in the container. Webb said he had found out about the slight modification of the diaphragm the previous afternoon. It was brought out that Keuper had Dr. Gilman and someone else with him when he had talked to Webb in Brooklyn.

Bailey on redirect picked Webb up and brushed him off and, after having Webb testify that his courtroom testimony was substantially identical to what he had told Keuper when Keuper had visited him earlier the same month, handed him back to the tall prosecutor.

Keuper went after him again and after digging away at the conversation he'd had with Webb eleven days earlier, Webb said at first, "I probably said to you on December 2nd, 'This is one of the ampules or vials we are using now.' As far as I recall they were precisely the same in 1963."

Bailey came back on redirect, and investigated the actual change in the container, a change in the shape of the interior diaphragm from a shape, prior to about 1963, like, according to Webb, "a bowler hat"—which caused Simmill to say, "We call them a derby hat"—to a flat diaphragm. Webb testified that the change of the diaphragm did not change the procedure for use, either with infusion bottle or hypodermic, and the witness was then excused.

As it was nearly one o'clock, Bailey's next witness was sworn and qualified as an expert, and court was recessed for the lunch hour. And, as at the time of other noon and evening recesses, press people and spectators crowded toward the rear door of the courtroom which remained closed, locked and guarded until the jury could be taken out and started on their way down under bailiff supervision to the waiting jury bus.

Under these circumstances, knowing that the wait was inevitable and there was no place to go until the door swung open, it was curiously irritating to be shoved and buffeted by a minority segment of the newspeople who, conditioned no doubt by too many old movies about scoops and reporters, felt they had to claw and pry their way to some fancied vantage point by the guarded door. With the phone truck below and the newsroom phones in the basement, there were more than enough to go around. The difference between standing where you were and bulling your way to the door was, at the very most, seven seconds, a time differential that could be more than made up by galloping down the stairs, if the urgency was real rather than imaginary. In that little jammed area, as in all other situations that arose during the trial, the pros played it cool and the minor leaguers panted and scrambled.

During the noon break, there was a considerable confusion about exactly what had happened about the vial of Anectine.

462

Keuper's angry accusation that Webb had told him the powder given Coppolino had been in a different container had gotten all entangled and confused with the "bowler hat" change Webb had only learned about on December 12.

Obviously, the plastic vials entered as exhibits did not lend themselves to the description by Marjorie Farber, either as regards size or method of opening. But, as one of the senior reporters from Philadelphia said, "So what? Assume Carl *did* give her the powder. If it was in something that made it awkward to get at, he'd put it in something else. And if he didn't give it to her, and if Bill Farber really died of a coronary and she made the whole bit up to fix Carl's wagon, she could say he *did* put it into something else. And in any case, what real difference would it make if Webb *did* tell Keuper it was in a different container. I see it this way. Bailey was blowing smoke, so Keuper did a little showboating to take it off the direction Bailey had aimed it, and plant the idea that there's a lot of choices about what that powder could have been in. The big thing so far today was Spelman saying that the degree of arteriosclerosis he saw was a competent cause of death."

Of all the appraisals and analyses and insights volunteered during the first mid-day break after the Bailey team had come to bat, perhaps the most apt and inclusive comment was made by Mrs. Anna Coppolino, mother of the accused.

Talking to a reporter she said wonderingly, "It isn't much like Perry Mason at all. It isn't even like the movies."

Chapter Twenty-seven

Dr. Richard Ford, a man in his fifties, was the third witness for the defense. He was a man of unusual appearance and manner. He was tall and spare and bony, facial bones sharp against sallow skin. His gray hair was cropped to a half inch length that covered his long skull like a cap. He wore glasses with dark, heavy, plastic frames.

He sat in the witness stand with an unusual absence of any random movements at all. He stared unwaveringly, unblinkingly, and with a total lack of expression at F. Lee Bailey.

When he answered each question, he spoke in a loud, flat,

slow, carefully articulated voice. It was a harsh, spaced tone, with no inflection, no emotion. It was the voice one might reasonably expect the computers of the future to use once they have been programed for audible response. It was, in fact, very like the traditional motion picture voice of the alien life forms on remote planets far more advanced than ours.

I have returned with earthling specimens for our laboratories. They call themselves man.

Dr. Ford's manner on the stand was in marked contrast to his speech and personality away from the courtroom. One can conjecture about the advantage of this highly stylized manner of presentation which is, in fact, used by many experts who are called on to testify often. As with the almost mechanical methods of the professional poker player, it divorces all personality from the facts at hand. Personality involves an intrusion of the emotions, and emotions provide the leverage whereby, in cross-examination, a man can be rattled and tricked. As the style of this kind of courtroom demeanor does not change in any respect regardless of whether under direct or cross-examination, the opinions as projected with such a harsh and hollow finality, take on an impressive and ponderous weight and become that much more difficult to soften or diffuse. A minimum space is left for any attempt to qualify words that fall like stones.

He was the Senior Medical Examiner of Suffolk County, Massachusetts, which includes the city of Boston, and had held that post for sixteen years, after a four year stint as associate medical examiner.

Harvard Medical School—1940. Interned in pathology at Peter Bent Brigham Hospital, and in surgery at Boston City Hospital. In World War II was the commanding officer of a combat surgical hospital in the Pacific Theatre. Then four and a half years at the Harvard Medical School as a research fellow in "forensic medicine for legal medicine, if you prefer, in pathology." In '49 made acting head of department of legal medicine at Harvard Medical School. Became associate clinical professor in 1952, and head of the department. Resigned a year and a half ago. Was also a lecturer in legal medicine at Tufts, Boston University, and Yale Medical schools. Had given expert testimony in court in six New England states, in Georgia and "once in Persia."

"Welcome to New Jersey," said Lee Bailey, and continued the *voir dire*. Ford had done completely, or assisted in, or supervised, between seven and eight thousand autopsies. For fifteen years he was in charge of a seminar for state police

464

investigators from all over the country and from foreign countries. He said he had been contacted about the death of Colonel Farber about a month previously.

Bailey's first question was to ask Ford what materials he had been furnished, and he said he had a copy of Helpern's autopsy report, Marjorie Farber's statement under interrogation in Florida, and some sworn testimony by Dr. A. Malcolm B. Gilman, the County Physician of Monmouth County. But Keuper objected when Bailey asked Ford if the testimony of Mrs. Farber about the pillow and the alleged relative positions of the victim and defendant had been explained to him, objecting on the basis of wanting to know who had explained it, if it was an authentic explanation, and whether it was taken from the official trial record.

Bailey had explained it to Ford, and asked Ford to state his understanding of it so that the jury could determine if it accurately reflected previous testimony.

In his computerized, outer-space voice, and with an admirable economy of words, Ford said, "You described to me the person of Colonel Farber lying on a bed without a headboard, and an alleged attack upon him as he lay on that bed, consisting of a man taking a pillow crosswise and placing it across his face and neck, and then leaning on it with the heels of his hands, one upon the other."

Ford then testified that on the previous Friday in the New York City hospital room where Dr. Helpern was a patient, with about eight people present, Dr. Ford had examined the larynx—after Helpern had it washed in running water—the intact hyoid bone, and a large number of miscroscopic slides of the coronary arteries, and also of lung and kidney and windpipe and skin tissue. He had listened to Helpern's morning testimony, and had read a transcript of the testimony given by Dr. Milton Helpern the previous day. He had examined Helpern's slides through a microscope. Then Bailey had Ford give a short lecture on arteriosclerosis, and how fatty crystals, crystalline estercholesterol, build up on the inner walls of the coronary arteries and restrict the flow of blood, and then can cause death in several spontaneous ways, or under the stress of physical exertion or emotional excitement.

Bailey asked him what he had learned about Farber's heart from reading that section of the autopsy dealing with it. Ford said Helpern had stated that he could see no areas of scarring, but that the state of the muscle was poor. Helpern had reported the heart as being partly decomposed. Bailey next asked him if a decomposition of part of the heart would affect the validity of the examination, and Ford said that it would, because, "You just might not be able to see the damage that existed."

"What damage would you find in a heart if the heart had been instrumental in causing death, or a defect of the heart?"

"You might find accumulation of cells due to inflammation of damaged muscle from lack of blood supply. You might find actual dissolution of muscle. And you might find scars, old or fresh."

Ford said these evidences would be visible in any visual examination of the heart after its removal, and certainly microscopically.

Bailey had led up very methodically to his key testimony from Dr. Ford, and was ready to ask, "Do you have an opinion as to the severity or extent of the coronary disease of Colonel Farber at the time of his death?"

"I do."

"What is that opinion?"

"That is was severe."

"Now, absent from any other apparent cause of death, do you have an opinion as to whether or not the examination of those arteries as you saw them is sufficient to support an opinion as to the cause of death?"

"Yes."

"And what is that opinion?"

"That there was sufficient atherosclerosis in Colonel Farber's coronary arteries to account for his death."

Bailey returned then to some of Ford's previous testimony from his lecture on heart failure, and asked him to elaborate on what severe exercise might do. Keuper objected that there was no testimony as to Colonel Farber engaging in exercise of any kind. Bailey was permitted to continue on the basis of his assurance that he would connect it up.

At that point it could be reasonably assumed that Vincent Keuper felt some alarm about the status of the state's case. He knew that it was not enough for the defense to merely propose, backed by the opinion of experts, that Colonel Farber had died of a heart attack. There had to be other supporting evidence to elevate the defense theory to the status of reasonable doubt.

Keuper was a carpenter who had showed the jury a set of blueprints and a pile of materials and argued that the blueprints plus the materials would equal a houseboat. Bailey was now taking the same blueprints and materials and showing that the end result might quite reasonably be a boathouse.

466

Ford said, ". . . a man may indulge in an unusual procedure such as pushing a car that is stuck in the snow, or running for public transportation. He may complete his exercise, go sit down and thereupon show signs of difficulty in catching his breath, in being pale, perhaps sweating, and he may survive this or he may die. This is what is commonly referred to as acute coronary insufficiency. If it is sufficiently prolonged, then the actual functioning of the heart is interfered with. Instead of the heart pumping as a unit each time it squirts blood both to the lungs and to the body, it will start to quiver. The muscle bundles will quiver and they will not function as a unit and not function as a pump. This is called fibrillation and is the usual cause of death with narrowed arteries."

"Assume that someone dies while the heart is fibrillating rather than pumping. Is there any pathological evidence left to the examiner when he opens the heart and examines it after death, to indicate that fibrillation took place?"

"Not so far as fibrillation itself is concerned. Usually there are signs of the disease process."

"In the heart itself or in the artery?"

"In the artery, and sometimes in the heart itself."

"From the arteries that you have seen would death by ventricular fibrillation in this case be consistent with the condition you have observed with Colonel Farber?"

"Yes."

Bailey moved directly to the next cornerstone of the state medical testimony. "From your examination of the larynx in question did you observe fractures in the cricoid cartilage?"

"I did."

"And do you have an opinion on whether or not these are consistent with strangulation, from your experience?"

"The mere presence of a fracture in the absence of hemorrhage is merely an indication of some impact, some force applied to that particular cartilage rather discretely (discretely used in the medical sense of indicating something within a small area) is inadequate to establish a cause of death as due to strangulation."

Bailey next elicited Ford's opinion as to whether the fracture had occurred before death.

"In view of the state of preservation of that larynx, it wasn't damaged in life. There is no hemorrhage. There is adequate tissue there, and I have found through the years that in no case of pressure on the larynx, or the windpipe below it, in no case where there is pressure applied can you say that death occurred unless you find some hemorrhage to indicate the force of that

467

pressure. . . . Hemorrhage is the release of blood from blood vessels into tissue spaces. The blood is deposited there. You can't wash it off, in contrast to an injury occurring after death either by a knife or a break where any oozing of blood can be washed off. . . . In view of the state of preservation of that specimen of the larynx, any hemorrhage occurring in life should be visible now in that specimen."

After some questions which retraced roughly the same area in order to nail it down more solidly in the group memory of the jury, Bailey asked Ford for his opinion on whether force exerted through a pillow by means of the heels of the hands could cause the double fracture of the cricoid cartilage.

"It is unlikely," said Ford.

Bailey then asked Dr. Ford the question he had asked Dr. Helpern, about how dead bodies are moved about. Keuper objected and Judge Simmill said, "Sustained. We are interested in this body." It might be possible the judge was not entirely satisfied with the extent to which Bailey had succeeded in "connecting up" the cross-examination of Dr. Helpern about this matter. Bailey asked to approach the bench to make an offer of proof, and was given permission.

At the side bar, with Mr. Keuper standing just behind Lee Bailey and leaning forward to hear, Lee Bailey and Judge Simmill conducted their discussion in that practiced voice level which threatens to, but never quite does reach the ear of any juror.

"Your Honor, if the witness were permitted to answer he would say that the common ordinary method of moving a dead body from table to cart and so forth consists of one man grasping the body by the neck with the fingers under the back of the neck and the thumbs over the larynx, and another man picking up the feet of the body, and this is the common ordinary way in which such bodies are moved."

"The funeral director who handled this body was here," the judge said. "He was available yesterday. He was on the stand and he was sworn." Meaning, of course, why didn't you take the chance when you had it?"

"We have interviewed him," Bailey explained, "and we couldn't pin down who actually delivered the damn thing. He is pretty vague. I don't think anyone can say which person picked him up and moved him to the cart and what position he was in."

The judge said, "That is probably so, but I don't think the ordinary way in which dead bodies are handled is evidential. The question is: What happened to this particular body?" Keuper's objection was sustained and Bailey's objection to the ruling

468

noted. Bailey turned Ford over to Keuper for cross-examination without further questioning.

Keuper began with a hypothetical, asking Ford to assume the colonel had died of a coronary thrombosis, and asking what the symptoms would be. Ford said he would expect to find a thrombus in the coronary, and Keuper said that his question concerned symptoms prior to death.

Ford testified that he would expect a fall in blood pressure. Asked to assume the blood pressure had not been taken, Ford said he could determine an approximate blood pressure by taking the pulse with his fingers. And, in the absence of either of those two tests, he said he could infer the blood pressure was low from such signs as pallor, sweating and difficulty in breathing.

"What is the indicated treatment, Doctor, for one suffering from a coronary thrombosis assuming that you had arrived at that diagnosis?"

"Immediate bed rest, perhaps morphine for pain. Immediate steps to get an electrocardiogram."

"If you were not a cardiologist or one specializing or practicing cardiology, what would you do?"

"I would call for a cardiologist."

"Anything else, Doctor?"

"I'd hospitalize them."

"Anything else?"

With his first glint of hard humor, Ford said, "Turn the case over to someone else. I'm a pathologist."

It was difficult to comprehend what Keuper was reaching for with his series of questions, and, when he switched suddenly to the larynx, it was impossible to tell whether he had gotten what he had sought, or had given up the search. Possibly his only purpose in the first half of his cross was to use a defense witness to show that Dr. Coppolino had not acted in a professionally responsible manner, if Farber had been having a heart attack, and, by further inference, if Farber had really been having a heart attack, it was more probable that Coppolino would have acted as Ford had indicated a non-cardiologist should act. It seemed so remote from the matters covered in direct examination, one wonders if an objection as to it being improper cross would have been sustained. However it would be highly unlikely for Bailey to so interrupt what appeared to be a most unproductive line of cross-examination.

Reconfirming where and when Dr. Ford had examined the larynx, Keuper asked, "At that time did you examine that to determine whether or not there was any evidence of a hemor-

469

rhage?" Ford said he had, and found none. "Do you know whether or not a hemorrhage had been removed, or the evidence of hemorrhage had been removed?"

"I asked Dr. Helpern about it and he said there was none."

With a certain asperity, Keuper repeated, "I said, did you find any evidence that it had been removed?"

After a certain immobile hesitation, Dr. Ford replied in a way that made him seem more than ever like a computer rendering a verdict on data retrieval. A computer might have said, "Input data incomplete." Ford boomed, "I think that question incapable of being answered."

As such dicta is the prerogative of the Court, Judge Simmill said acidly, "Doctor, just answer the question, and don't form any opinion as to incapabilities."

Keuper repeated, "Did you find any evidence that a hemorrhage had been removed, from your examination of the exhibit?"

"No."

"Had *anything* been removed from the cartilage?" At this point one reporter was victimized by the black and savage wit of the man sitting next to him, who leaned close and whispered a possible answer to Keuper's question: "Yes. All the rest of the colonel." The unfortunate victim made strangling sounds which he hoped would go unnoticed. Black humor is an inevitable ingredient in all the blood sports—war, bullfighting, auto racing, and murder trials. And no doubt the Romans had some real thigh-slappers about the Christians and the lions.

Ford answered yes, something had been removed. "The overlying soft tissue."

"Isn't that where you would ordinarily find the hemorrhage?"

"Partly."

And that was the point at which Vincent Keuper ended his cross-examination, on a seemingly unresolved note. This blurred the emotional logic of the situation as it seemed to leave only that untenable alternative that Dr. Helpern, in whose custody the larynx had been from the day of autopsy until it became an exhibit in the trial, had for some curious reason, or out of some incomprehensible mental lapse or uncharacteristic professional ineptitude, removed the very thing that he had testified would be supportive proof of his contention of manual strangulation.

On redirect Bailey, over Keuper's objection, was permitted to ask what other places besides the overlying tissues hemorrhage would be found. "More especially in the lining underneath," Ford replied.

F. Lee Bailey then had Ford reconfirm the coronary symptoms

of pallor, sweating, difficulty in breathing and low blood pressure typical of a coronary, then asked if Ford would expect to find anything irregular about the heartbeat.

"I would expect to find it rapid, thready, not easy to feel each separate beat, and perhaps the beat is suppressed, so that instead of an even rhythm it would be irregular."

"Is vomiting consistent with suffering a coronary?"

"Frequently."

"How about diarrhea?"

"Can be."

Bailey then had him reiterate that he might administer morphine as an emergency measure, had him identify Demarol as a morphine substitute, and say once more that he would recommend hospitalization.

On recross, Vincent Keuper asked what Ford would do if the heart attack victim refused to go to the hospital.

"I would get a witness to the fact that I had recommended it."

And again Keuper had Ford state that he would call in a cardiologist, and Dr. Ford was excused.

The direction and the focus of Vincent Keuper's cross-examination of Dr. Richard Ford points up one necessary ingredient in both the prosecution and the defense in those criminal trials where expert witnesses give crucial testimony in areas of professional discipline which of necessity lie well outside the expertise of any attorney, no matter how diligently he may have done his homework. It should be entirely evident that a medical expert's testimony can be attacked only when the cross-examiner knows in what areas of the direct examination the responses were not in line with opinions held by most other members of the profession. It is only through searching cross-examination of such areas of vulnerability, with full knowledge of what he is attempting, that a courtroom attorney can, by causing the expert to add qualification after qualification to statements made too baldly under direct examination, enfeeble the weight of the expert's testimony in the jury mind.

To lift an example from Bailey's direct examination of Dr. Ford. Ford said, "This is called fibrillation and is the usual cause of death with narrowed arteries."

For the sake of this example it is not necessary to know whether the statement is true or false. It is certainly quite obvious that prior to the trial Vincent Keuper would have thoroughly prepared himself on the question of coronary artery disease, knowing that Mr. Bailey was going to attempt to establish an area of reasonable doubt as to the cause of death of Colonel Farber.

Yet a man in the profession of law certainly cannot become thoroughly knowledgeable in the profession of medicine through his research in a specific area of medicine. There was no recess between Bailey's direct examination and Keuper's cross. Keuper, as throughout the trial, had sat alone.

He could have had no possible access to the material of the direct examination prior to hearing it, either to the questions Bailey would ask, or the responses Ford would give.

And thus, for any statement made by Dr. Ford, Keuper could not determine out of his own knowledge whether that opinion so stated was a majority opinion held by the medical profession, or whether it was an opinion held by a very few, of which Dr. Ford might be one. This factor of general acceptance by the profession would seem to be part of the background necessary to a productive cross-examination, a background available only through the immediate advice of a cardiologist, someone who could have, with the Court's permission, sat beside Mr. Keuper and, prior to the cross-examination, indicated where Dr. Ford had been in medical areas open to argumentation.

In following his procedure, Mr. Keuper was merely following a practice long accepted in courtroom law. The practice is based upon the theory that because expert testimony is presented in front of a jury of laymen, the courtroom attorney need not attack that testimony on an expert level, but need only ask the "common sense" questions a juror might ask. He can then leave refutation to his own expert witnesses. The flaw would seem to be that this approach can leave questionable or vulnerable testimony by an opposition expert largely intact.

Were a key witness to give testimony in Chinese, any attorney in an adversary proceeding would expect to have the services of a translator at his elbow. The expertise of the expert has become, with the scientific revolution, very nearly a foreign language to all of us.

Anna Coppolino, mother of the accused, was Bailey's next witness. She sat stiff and erect on the stand, her eyes shifting swiftly from Carl to Lee Bailey to the jurors and back again as she answered the questions in a thin but reasonably audible voice.

After establishing that Carl's parents had frequently visited their son in Middletown, and that she had learned of Colonel Farber's death on the day he died while speaking to Carmela

472

over the telephone, Bailey asked her about the Sunday before the colonel died. She said she was visiting her son that day.

"My son, my husband and myself, we were sitting in front of the door in the shade and the rest of the family had gone to the beach because it was a very very hot day."

She said she had met Colonel Farber previously, that she could see the Farber house from where they were sitting, and she saw the colonel that day.

"He was mowing his lawn for a long long time."

"How long would you say he was working at mowing the lawn?"

"Well, the family had gone to the beach and we were sitting there, oh, between two and three hours reading the papers, my husband and I, but before that Mrs. Farber had drove along in her car."

Judge Simmill leaned toward her and corrected her gently. "Mrs. Coppolino, the question is: How long did you see Colonel Farber mowing the lawn on that Sunday?"

"Oh, about two or three hours and it was a very hot day."

"You said the temperature was high?"

"Very hot," said Anna Coppolino with a little nod.

"Was he working at this consistently or just intermittently?"

"Consistently," she said, and tried to tell what her husband had said about it, but Keuper's sustained objection halted the hearsay.

There had been a confirmation of the yard work in Marjorie Farber's statement to Frank Schaub given a year earlier in Florida:

Well, Sunday was a very very hot day and Bill was working out in the yard and Carl's family were visiting him. His mother and father and sister. And Carl didn't want to be with his family and, well, he and I went to the movies. It was so hot he had to go someplace where it was air-conditioned. There were all these excuses and reasons. He could always get away with it because his family, you know, he was the lord and master in everything. So that may sound sarcastic but that's the way it was. And, well, that was on Sunday, and I was supposed to do this thing that night. He had even suggested I knock Bill out with a baseball bat, and wrap a towel around it. Good God!

The movie house where Marjorie Farber claims they went that hot Sunday afternoon was showing Frank Sinatra in *Come Blow Your Horn*.

Lee Bailey then abruptly shifted to Florida, saying, "Mrs. Coppolino, at some point you were in Florida after the death of your daughter-in-law?"

She said she was, and had arrived in Florida the day after Carmela was buried in New Jersey. She said she stayed at her son's house and that Marjorie Farber had come to that house and they had talked together two or three days after the burial.

"What did Mrs. Farber say with respect to Carl and herself?"

Keuper objected valiantly and vainly, but Bailey said he would not lead the witness into general conversation, and the judge directed the witness to report just the conversation.

"The conversation was about that she wanted to marry my son. Of course she wanted to bring up the children just like my daughter-in-law would have liked." This comment about the children was said with evident venom.

She said Mrs. Farber had mentioned this on several occasions. Bailey asked her to testify about the next one she recalled.

"We were sitting outside by the pool, her and I, and she had a little dog there and I told her she was crazy, that she was old enough to be his mother. And I also said, 'Ten years from now you'd be his grandmother.' . . . She said that she knew and loved the children very much and she knew that she would bring them up just like my daughter-in-law would have liked."

When Bailey turned her over to Vincent Keuper, and every attorney in the room knew that Keuper's most probable course of action would have been to rise, say, "No questions, Your Honor," and sit himself down again. It is the traditional response to motherhood on the stand when the state avows its intention to seek the death penalty. The jury is aware, certainly, of mother love. When the prosecutor refuses to ask the mother any questions, a little sigh, a shrug, a sad and understanding smile will readily underline for the jury his awareness that it is futile and disastrous to attack motherhood, the flag, Stephen Foster or apple pie.

Yet perhaps Vincent Keuper felt himself compelled to try to counter the tangible emotional impact of that little woman up there, so visibly scornful of the older woman in her son's life. In fact, in spite of all the testimony of more potential consequence during that day, the New York *Daily News* lead read: "Doctor Carl Coppolino's small, dark-haired mother came from her Brooklyn home today to testify for her son in his fight to avoid the electric chair, and to give the lie to his chief accuser, Mrs. Marjorie Farber, his onetime mistress."

Keuper arose to his old testament height and said in gruffness and accusation, "Mrs. Coppolino, as a matter of fact didn't you say to Mrs. Farber that, 'I thought you were going to marry Carl'?''

She stared at him in apparent startled astonishment. "Oh never!"

"You never said that?" Incredulity. Later, during the evening, in an informal strategy appraisal a local courtroom attorney was to insist that this particular question and answer was a guarantee that Keuper had a rebuttal witness up his sleeve who would testify to the willingness of Carl's people to have him marry Marjorie. Otherwise, he said, the question made no sense.

Next he asked her if she was sitting there all the time and watching Farber mow his lawn for three hours.

"We were reading the paper and Colonel Farber was right up on the hill. You couldn't miss him." She said it was between one and four in the afternoon.

"Do you know he went to work the next day, Monday?"

"I don't know." Her tone and her small shrug indicated a total indifference as to whether or not the colonel went to work.

"And worked all day?"

"I don't know."

"You don't know that?"

"No," she said, frowning at him. (Why should I?)

Bailey then called a Dr. Leo Wollman, an obstetrician and gynecologist, with a related specialty of psychotherapy through hypnotherapy. He was a fleshy and swarthy-skinned man, and had he been available for bit-part casting on serial television, he would have found himself playing such roles as a cab driver, jazz musician, or operator of a small night club. Reality does a notoriously poor job of type-casting. He was in his fifties, and had received his medical education in Britain, graduating from Edinburgh, with internship and residency in Cumberland Hospital and Leeds General. He said he delivered about eighty babies a year, using hypnotherapy as a pain ameliorator in eighty to ninety percent of his cases.

In that part of the *voir dire* most related to the impact of his testimony, Dr. Wollman said, "I am the president of the New York Society of Clinical and Experimental Hypnosis, and the past president of the Metropolitan New York Society of Clinical Hypnosis. I am the editor of the newsletter of the American Society of Clinical Hypnosis, and consulting editor of the newsletter of the Society for Clinical and Experimental Hypnosis. I am the editor of the news bulletin of the Institute for Comprehensive Medicine, a member of fifty-eight scientific organizations, and

475

have published twenty-nine papers relating to this field." He named the physicians from whom he had received instruction in medical hypnosis, and said that he had lectured on the subject at the University of Pittsburgh, Columbia and Brooklyn College.

It is pertinent to remember that in conducting his direct examination of Dr. Wollman, F. Lee Bailey had the special advantage of having previously attended seminars and taken instruction in hypnosis, and was a reasonably skilled lay hypnotist, with a grasp of the several theories of the mechanics and psychology of the phenomenon.

Bailey led Wollman into a question and answer explanation of hypnosis, what it is and what it does.

Here are those selected quotes from his testimony which seem to best serve Lee Bailey's obvious objective in putting the doctor on the stand, to make Marjorie Farber's testimony about her hypnotic state appear to run contrary to medical fact.

"Hypnosis is an exaggerated awareness of what's going on. It's the opposite of sleep and it's always accompanied by a complete physical relaxation of the body."

"The hypnotherapist tries to get the attention of the patient directed on something . . . We usually have the attention directed on some part of the body. We call this an ideomotor or ideosensory method. The idea of the position of a hand or the idea of an alteration in the sensation of the hand as being lighter is what we direct their attention toward and when we have their attention completely directed on this one objective it's usually easy to give them a suggestion which they will follow."

If the hypnotist wishes the subject to do something, "He suggests this in the form of an idea and usually states when this idea is to take place."

In order for the subject to respond, "The motivation must be strong, otherwise it will be ineffective."

Possible to hypnotize someone against their will: "Definitely not."

"About 95 percent of the people can be hypnotized in one degree or another. Some are better than others. . . . We usually regard three stages, light, moderate and heavy. I would say only about five percent," can reach the heavy or deep stage, as against 80 percent able to reach the moderate stage.

Determination of whether or not a patient is hypnotized: "This is very difficult because there is a thing called role-playing which sometimes makes the determination of the depth of the hypnosis extremely difficult. There are some people who are role-players who want to do what the hypnotist suggests because they don't

476

want to embarrass him, and by playing the role they sometimes go into a hypnotic state.''

"The trance could be spontaneously terminated or it could be brought to an end by a cutoff signal which the hypnotist always—at least the ones who are thoughtful—would provide for the patient or subject. He will say, 'When I count to five you will gradually become more and more awakened, aroused, refreshed.' This gives the patient or subject at least five seconds or more to acquaint themselves with the gradual change toward a full awareness.''

"I have found in my experience that it is impossible to have a subject do something or perform an act which they feel they are morally unable to do. I find it difficult to accept the idea that people have done such things as we sometimes read about or hear about.''

Bailey asked him if he had ever been able to cause a person to do, or start to do, something which would normally be against their desires or moral responsibilities.

"Yes. I have found that occasionally. In an experimental situation in a teaching group we ask the subject to touch something that we say is sharp, but they do it and then we find out after they are aroused what their reasoning was. And usually they have said, 'I didn't think that you would have me do anything that would hurt me and therefore I had no compunction about touching it. I thought it looked sharp, but it wasn't.' In other words, there is some thread of reality even through the hypnotic state which doesn't allow them to accept this as an act that would hurt them.''

As it was then three o'clock, the mid-afternoon recess was called. For those who must file stories, major trials are never in comfortable balance for the reporter, because, just as in the daily total of all national and international news, there is inevitably too little or too much. The break in the morning after the slides of the heart tissues created the problem of finding something to phone in, some trivia to expand to newsworthy size. The mid-afternoon break created the reverse problem of trying to winnow too much down to manageable size.

And this, of course, is the reason why hard news coverage of any continuing situation, such as a murder trial, will always be out of balance with reality. The apparatus of all the media is geared to using established personnel to fill established space, in column inches or air time. And that time and space must be filled with material which has the flavor of importance and tension the public expects of news coverage. Imagine, for example,

477

a day where absolutely nothing of any importance or excitement happened anywhere in the nation or the world. Because the apparatus exists, just as much time and space would be used to report the events of the day as would be used on a day of myriad disasters and catastrophes. And nothingness would be reported with the same vibrant presentation as are significant events.

It is a sort of Parkinson's Law of news coverage that because the supply of news will always be more than or less than the space available for it, news media will always be inadvertently guilty of exaggeration or suppression. And when each trial day is given a roughly equivalent weight and space, the faithful reader will end up with a warped comprehension of the relative significance of the testimony given and hence, after most trials, a feeling of shock and disbelief at the final verdict, a feeling seldom shared by those at ringside.

Chapter Twenty-eight

Bailey resumed his direct examination of Dr. Wollman by establishing that Wollman had read a portion of the Farber testimony in transcript, all of her testimony as given on Friday, December 9.

Wollman testified that a subject in a trance state could have their eyes open, that speech would be slowed, sometimes slurred, and response a little delayed, that they would walk in a lethargic way with movements much slower than ordinary.

Then Bailey asked what would happen to a person under hypnosis if they were given a suggestion repugnant to them.

"I have found two things to take place. In some people they respond immediately by crying and waking up out of the trance. Others are reluctant to do anything and just stay in a stupor without moving."

"Now is there such a thing as a continuing trance that lasts over a period of weeks or months?"

"No, there isn't."

"Have you ever heard of such a case?"

"I have read about it, but only in pulp magazines."

Bailey regressed to a series of semi-qualifying questions styled to affirm the respectability of hypnosis as a recognized medical

478

treatment, approved by the American Medical Association and the American Psychiatric Association, used to relieve pain, allay fears, and as an anesthetic process, then asked, "Did you learn in the testimony of Mrs. Farber that on some occasions she felt that she was compelled to do the bidding of the defendant, and on some occasions she acted on her own?"

"Yes. I read that."

"Do you find that to be consistent with any known state of hypnosis?"

"In my opinion she wasn't hypnotized."

Bailey relinquished the witness. Keuper came to his feet and stood in his customary place beside the state table and asked Dr. Wollman his procedure with a new patient.

Wollman said that first he would determine whether the person had a satisfactory reason for wanting hypnotherapy, and would then take a complete history and, if he thought it necessary, make a physical examination. He would then explain hypnosis to the patient so that there would be no misunderstanding.

When Keuper asked him if he conducted any test to determine if the patient was sufficiently suggestible, Wollman answered, "I find that is completely unnecessary, because if the person isn't highly enough motivated, they wouldn't have come to me in the first place, and the suggestibility tests are really wasteful in terms of time. We can, in making a suggestibility test, go a little further and hypnotize the patient as a continuation of the test."

Asked if it was necessary for the patient to be unaware he was being hypnotized in order to determine how good a subject he might be, Wollman said it was not necessary. Keuper had him describe his induction process, then asked if he was familiar with the induction process involving holding imaginary buckets with imaginary weight being added to one. Wollman said he was, but that it was a suggestibility test. He remembered that portion of the Farber testimony dealing with the buckets and the balloons, and said that was a suggestibility test. He said that the induction process as given in her testimony, about sitting in a chair and putting her fingers on the table was one accepted technique of induction.

Keuper next asked about the phenomenon of post-hypnotic suggestion. Wollman said some people would respond to a post-hypnotic suggestion given them while in a trance state and others wouldn't.

Vincent Keuper wanted an expression of opinion from Dr. Wollman on whether a post-hypnotic suggestion could be given

479

along with another suggestion to forget that it had been given once the trance was ended. He chose an assumption that Dr. Leo Wollman obviously and actively resented.

"Let's assume I can place you in a hypnotic trance, and I say to you, Doctor: 'Five minutes after I arouse you from this trance, I am going to snap my fingers, and when I do you are going to start to dance, but you are going to forget that I made the suggestion to you.' Now after that person is aroused and five minutes occur . . . and I snap my fingers and the person dances, they won't recall that I told them, will they?"

"*Before* I answer that correctly, I can only say that I don't believe the patient will dance after five minutes if you snap your fingers, because no medical person would subject any patient to that sort of nonsense. He would never have another patient." It is obvious that with no desire to be unresponsive, Dr. Wollman felt an ethical obligation to draw a firm and resolute line between medical practice and show business.

"I am not asking you whether a medical person would or not. I am talking about a hypnotist."

"I am not a lay hypnotist. I use it for medical purposes, and I have never done this type of work that might embarrass my patients."

Once he had upheld the dignity of his profession, Wollman was willing to give Keuper an answer. "If, as you say, all this has occurred, it doesn't necessarily mean to me that the patient was hypnotized. It merely means to me that they do not want to embarrass the hypnotist. Or else they have within them the ham that wants to entertain, and this is a perfect excuse, because: 'I have been through a hypnotic state. I got a post-hypnotic suggestion, and I did it not because I wanted to but because he made me do it.' I don't say that's so."

Keuper first had Wollman admit that he had seen vaudevillians do it, then charged Wollman with knowing that it could be done, but Wollman said emphatically that it couldn't be done.

So with an admixture of anger and bafflement, Keuper said, "How do you explain it is done and then you said it can't be done?"

"Because it isn't done as a post-hypnotic suggestion. It is done because the person wants to do it, and no other reason!"

Keuper stared at him. "If I am in a hypnotic trance and I do some silly thing after I am aroused, I *want* to do it?"

"Yes sir. For no other reason."

"If I am at a party and I stand on my head in front of the people present, I do that because I *want* to do it?"

"It could be that you are a frustrated Yogi. Yes, you do it because you want to do it, not because you were hypnotized into doing it. That is my statement."

Keuper retraced his steps and seemed relieved that Dr. Wollman did, after all, believe in post-hypnotic suggestion, but only insofar as the subject had the motivation to follow the suggestion. He testified further that post-hypnotic suggestion was self-limiting, in that it tended to fade with time.

He admitted that the suggestion could be reinforced by placing the patient in the trance state again. Keuper then asked him if a formal induction process was necessary to hypnotize the patient.

"Not even the first time. No sir."

"Sometimes by the snap of the fingers, or look of the eye, or tone of the voice, you can hypnotize the person?"

"If the person is expecting to be hypnotized anything can set them off."

"By the holding of the hands, or nodding of the head, they can be hypnotized?"

"Anything. Anything."

Keuper then turned the doctor back for redirect examination by Lee Bailey.

The obstacle Keuper faced in his cross-examination was not because of any lack of knowledge on the part of the doctor, or any desire on his part to blur the outlines of his specialty. The problem was one of communication. Because the doctor was dealing in what had been thought a black and deadly art just a few decades previously, his whole approach professionally had been to so simplify and explain and rationalize the process as to reassure the patients he had treated during his thirteen years of hypnotherapy. The greatest assurance one can give a patient is to tell him that hypnosis can never induce him to do anything he does not *want* to do. It makes everything safe and clean and tidy and rational. Yet is the range of human needs and desires that simple? Is any man aware of his wants? One wonders how Dr. Leo Wollman would have answered the final question in this imaginary exchange:

"Doctor, you have told us that a patient will follow a post-hypnotic suggestion only when motivated to follow it. Is that true?"

"Yes, it is."

"And so if the suggestion is in accord with our desires, we will obey?"

"That is right."

"Is it not an accepted concept in psychiatric work, Doctor, that we are able to conceal our own needs and desires from our conscious minds and bury them deeply in our subconscious when those needs and desires run contrary to what we consciously believe to be an accepted ethical and moral posture?"

"That is a simplification, of course, but in general it is true."

"When you told us that a person would follow a post-hypnotic suggestion only if he wanted to perform the act suggested, did you mean to limit that obedience only to those wants and needs and desires which exist in the conscious mind?"

"Not necessarily, but. . . ."

"You have answered the question. Assume, Doctor, once again, that I am at a party and I am hypnotized by a lay hypnotist who gives me the post-hypnotic suggestion to stand on my head when he snaps his fingers. You suggested that I might do so if I were a frustrated Yogi. Now assume that though I have had this desire to make a public fool of myself, I have buried it so deeply in my subconscious mind that as I go about my daily work I am totally unaware of this deep motivation. But because it is there and has been there all along, I do stand on my head. Now, based on these assumptions, Doctor, once I had obeyed the suggestion and stood on my head, and then gotten back to my feet and realized what I had done, and saw the people laughing at me, would I be aware of the fact, in a sudden surge of self-awareness, that I had always wanted to make a fool of myself?"

"No, but you see you would be able to blame the hypnotist."

"Would I believe, Doctor, that he had made me do something against my will, and would I have the conviction that he had tricked me and trapped me, and exerted a control over me which I had not been able to resist?"

Lee Bailey asked on redirect, "Is it possible for the hypnotist to cause the subject to forget what transpired in the course of the trance?"

"The patient may be told to have amnesia or forgetfulness for a certain period. This does not necessarily have to take place. When it does take place it is only because the memory is painful and the patient chooses to forget it."

"Does it last indefinitely?"

"No. That's an impossibility. . . . It will return."

Bailey then referred to Dr. Wollman's testimony that a mere nod could put the patient in a trance, and asked if the desire of the patient to be hypnotized had to be present each time.

"Yes, because this is in reality autohypnosis," Wollman replied saying that autohypnosis was self-hypnosis where one allows the conditions already experienced to take place again.

"Doctor, having in mind your entire background and experience in the science of hypnosis and the facts which you have read in the testimony of Marjorie Farber as of Friday, December 9th, I ask you whether or not you have an opinion as to whether it is possible for Mrs. Farber to have acted in a homicidal or hostile fashion against her husband as a result of hypnotic compulsion?"

The doctor had an opinion. "I do not think this is possible," he said.

So Mr. Keuper on recross, stood up and asked, "Doctor, do you have an opinion as to whether or not a person could be hypnotized to the extent that they would endeavor, try to do it and reach a certain point, and then stop? Rebel?"

And he had an opinion on that, too. Affirmative. He thought it could be done.

And that brought Mr. Bailey back at once on a re-direct which he probably had not anticipated.

"Doctor, if a suggestion were given to a subject under hypnosis instructing the subject to perform some hostile act, such as to kill a loved one, how far do you think the person might progress, assuming that they were under hypnotic trance to start with, before the suggestion would be rejected and the action would stop?"

"Based on my experience, I would say as soon as a suggestion were voiced the patient would become hostile, angry, come out of the trance or run away."

Thus Mr. Keuper had to come back at once on re-recross and ask how Wollman reconciled the two contradictory answers.

Wollman said, "It's the intensity of the suggestion that you didn't specify. You didn't say anything about kill." He then used the hostile act of throwing water in a person's face as an example. He said they might pick up the water, but then drink it. "Then it is your opinion that if someone were told to take a needle and the needle contained a drug and put it into the leg of her husband, that they couldn't go just so far and then stop without doing it?"

"If it were couched in such a way that they were told this was a joke, and this was not serious and it wouldn't do anyone any harm they might go up to the point of introducing the needle to the skin, but it's unlikely that they could go farther."

Keuper drove home the point that if they believed what they were told, they would then do it, and sat down.

Mr. Bailey took the witness on re-reredirect for one final question before he was excused. "Well, Doctor, if the person were told that the needle contained a deadly poison would they go so far as to stick it in the skin?"

"No. Because they wouldn't believe it."

Lee Bailey's final defense witness of the day was Dr. James A. Brussel of New York City, Assistant Commissioner of Department of Mental Hygiene in New York State, and a psychiatrist, a criminologist, neurologist, and apparently competent to give opinions on hypnosis. He was a man of about sixty, of slender build, with a pronounced New York City accent, and a totally self-confident manner.

His qualification statement, given in a kind of machine-gun condensation is worth repeating just as he gave it:

"B.A. in Science, University of Pennsylvania, M.D., medical school, two-year rotating internship including six months of pathology, five-year residency in psychiatry and neurology. I am certified in both specialties. In World War II, was Chief of Neuro-Psychiatric Center in the Korean conflict, with Department of Mental Hygiene starting as a resident to my current post of Assistant Commissioner, teaching, lecturing and post-graduate courses, consultant and member of various societies, author of books and articles in those fields. . . . I have been consulted by the New York police, the Boston police, chiefly in an attempt to construct and build the appearance, the habits of unknown guilty persons. If I have to mention it, I identified the Mad Bomber ten years ago to the New York City police before he was apprehended, down to the point of notifying the police that when they found him he would be wearing a doublebreasted suit and it would be buttoned. Which is what happened."

And, inevitably, he had been retained by the Commonwealth of Massachusetts at one time in connection with the case of the Boston Strangler, one of Lee Bailey's pending cases at that time.

Asked about hypnosis he said that he could tell what it is, but that how it works has never been expressed in a way satisfying to the entire medical profession. He said he had used hypnotism to relieve symptoms on a temporary basis prior to treatment of the patient by psychotherapy. When Bailey queried him about any study he had made of hypnosis as it relates to criminology, he got a staggering compound answer that would have reminded any sports recorder of Casey Stengel.

"Yes, when I was doing casualty work in the North Korean conflict, when I worked with the FBI and the counter-CID, these men were very anxious to . . . I was doing research for Burroughs Wellcome in making a person talk under the influence of amphetamine. They wanted to know why I couldn't hypnotize a suspect that would be one of our own men of having talked to an enemy agent in Juarez, across the river, what he said, what he had done, and it is very basic, Mr. Bailey, no one can be hypnotized into doing anything that has the remotest suggestion of pain. Now I don't mean hurt, emotion, pain or pleasure to the unconscious implying that he is endangering himself, placing himself in a position that is against his or her security or that violates a principle that has sunk into the unconscious that he or she acquired in early training was right or wrong, something like that.''

He took a deep breath and looked expectantly at Mr. Bailey who hesitated and then said, ''From that, Doctor, can you tell us whether or not a person could be compelled to commit a criminal act that he or she did not want to commit through the use of hypnosis?''

''If he or she did not want to commit it without hypnosis and the unconscious was also against it, no amount of hypnosis would induce this.''

Establishing that Dr. Brussel had read the same testimony given by Mrs. Farber as had Dr. Wollman, Bailey asked his opinion if she could have been compelled to act as she did by hypnosis.

''Only if she wanted to do it,'' said Dr. Brussel, and said she could not be made to do it against her will.

Asked about whether a person could remember what happened during trance state, Brussel said that a person under light or moderate trance would recall. ''I personally feel not all will remember under a so-called deep hypnotic trance, no.''

''There would be forgetting?''

''Well, we resent the word forgetting. But it wouldn't be recalled. Let me put it that way. Settle for that.''

Under questioning Brussel testified that a person in a deep trance state would conduct themselves so abnormally it would be noticeable to others around them. Bailey reminded him of Mrs. Farber's testimony that she could remember some of the details surrounding ''the alleged transaction'' but not others, and asked him if this was consistent with a deep trance state.

''No.''

Bailey asked him about Mrs. Farber's testimony that at times she felt under a compulsion to commit acts, and at another closely related period she would have free will, and asked the doctor if this was consistent with conduct in a hypnotic trance.

485

He was reluctant to give a yes or no answer, but said yes and was permitted to expand on his affirmative answer.

"If she wanted to do what she says she was under compulsion to do, she would do it. If she did not want to do it, no amount of hypnotic compulsion—to use a very bad term—will induce her to do it."

Keuper on cross-examination went directly to whether or not a person in a hypnotic trance can be given a hypnotic suggestion. He came up against the same answer as Wollman had given him. Yes, if they want to do it.

But this time he expanded his question further and said, "If a person wanted to do something and wouldn't do it on their own, could it be suggested to them in a hypnotic trance to do it?"

"The answer to that, Mr. Keuper, has to be possibly, because you are suggesting that there is a conflict between the conscious and unconscious mind, and that must be individualized. I have to give you possible in that answer, and I want to give you as fair and articulate an answer as I can, I must say possibly. To push a little further, I would doubt that it would be done because there is real doubt in the individual's mind as an element of guilt, and this the unconscious will not tolerate no matter what school of psychiatry a psychiatrist adheres to."

After a great many false moves and false starts and areas where communication kept breaking down, Keuper finally phrased his follow-up question in a way that was satisfactory to him, and an acceptable question to the expert.

"A subject receives a suggestion while in a hypnotic trance from a medical hypnotist to do something that he had no thought in mind of doing before he went under the trance, but was willing to do it, and it was suggested to him. Would he do it?"

"Yes."

Next, using as an example the curing of the smoking habit through post-hypnotic suggestion, Vincent Keuper tried to pin down Dr. Brussel on how long such a suggestion would be effective. Brussel, as Keuper kept rewording and relaunching his question, kept answering that it depended on the individual and the degree of desire. Keuper wanted to know if when the effect of the suggestion faded could the hypnotist reinforce it with a mere snap of the fingers, or whatever other small signal had triggered the post-hypnotic suggestion after the first hypnotic trance. When he could get no specific answer, the exchange degenerated into an irritated wrangle, with Keuper saying, "Doctor, I am not a hypnotist. I am asking you a question. You are the expert."

"I have news for you, Mr. Keuper. Psychiatry does not have the answer to everything. All I can tell you honestly, if you were responsive to a hypnotic suggestion and it works for an hour, or for a lifetime, there is no hypnotist who can tell you how long you are reacting to yourself, or that when you were started on it by hypnosis, you then found what you were doing was really to your liking, and you abandoned the habit. I am being as honest as I can."

Vincent Keuper wound it up with a final question that seemed to come full circle back to the first portion of his cross-examination of the previous witness, Dr. Wollman.

"The only time hypnotism will work is if a person wants to do the things that they are asking the hypnotist to help them do?"

"Yes."

And that was all for that witness, and all for that last full day of testimony in the matter of Monmouth County Court Law Division Criminal Indictment No. 391-65, The State of New Jersey versus Carl Coppolino.

The direction and import of the expert testimony on hypnosis was strangely paradoxical. F. Lee Bailey's intent was clear. If her behavior had been inconsistent with hypnotic trance or suggestion, then Marjorie Farber had lied about the hypnosis, and having lied about that, had also lied about the cause of death and the circumstances of death, willingly endangering herself to nail her ex-lover, motivated by the merciless venom of the woman scorned.

Yet Vincent Keuper had done a very subtle and skillful job of changing the direction and meaning of the expert testimony on hypnosis. By seeming to phrase his question out of an innocent ignorance of the whole field, by giving the impression of having acquired all opinion of hypnosis from stage entertainers, as no doubt most of the jury had, he was able to hammer endlessly and relentlessly at the professional opinion that the hypnotized person will obey suggestions to perform only those acts they want to perform. He seemed to be, quite indirectly, showing why he, during his direct examination of Mrs. Farber, his key witness, had remained so harsh, so aloof, so totally unsympathetic.

The jury would remember the reiterated suggestion, "That man has got to go." So Keuper was leaving it up to the jurors to make that next bridging step and say, in effect, Coppolino *is* a medical hypnotist, having listed himself in the yellow pages as such, and his mistress *did* want her husband dead, and so she readily accepted the suggestion and now holds herself blameless, first on the grounds that she was a very good subject, and secondly because she could not quite bring herself to go through with it.

In effect he had turned the testimony of Bailey's experts into a direction useful to the prosecution, through the inference that she would not appear to be in any trance state, and would have free will because the suggestion matched her need.

There was a third physician in the courtroom who, had he not been the defendant in the case, could very probably have been qualified as an expert in medical hypnosis. In 1963, the year the affair began and the colonel died, Carl Coppolino had begun work on the medical text titled *Practice of Hypnosis in Anesthesiology* which was later to be published by Grune & Stratton, Inc., priced at $6.50. The dedication in the front of the text was "To Carmela Anne—Wife—Companion—Critic."

The following passages have been taken directly from that text.

. . . *Some laymen have offered as an objection to hypnotism, the statement that the morals of one undergoing hypnotism are at stake. This is not true, since any suggestion or command contrary to the moral code of the subject immediately brings him out of the trance. Of course, the moral strength or weakness must be taken into consideration, with the reaction being the same, just as if one were awake.*

. . . *When the physical examination is proposed the patient often resents or even refuses. Tact and patience is required and an explanation given which will reveal that such an examination is for the protection of the patient. When this is done in an assuring kindly manner it results in a wholly amiable surrendered patient and successful therapy. The physician should avoid abruptness in questioning which may cause resentment and he should exhibit an air that is assuring instead of fear arousing. Once the patient has been induced to surrender his body and himself, such symbolic surrender permits the surrender of will, under passive hypnosis.*

. . . *Guilt complexes often cause the patient to seek hypnosis. The psychological fact that there is appeasement for the guilt-troubled person in being hurt, leads to this since they erroneously imagine that hypnosis is an unpleasant experience. They expect humiliation and discomfort from it and they feel that they will be compelled to combat against their own will. Their conscience is relieved by such self-punishment.*

. . . *The most even tempered and kindliest doctor must, if using hypnosis, give commands. They must be such that the* strongest-willed patient will be brought to submission. It can easily become a habit, and too often the authoritative method will totally fail, where the passive would have been extremely successful and easy.

. . . A moral or honorable person cannot be rendered immoral or unkind or dishonest by means of hypnosis. If he reveals any of these regrettable traits under hypnosis, he would reveal them without it, because it is his nature. The hypnotherapist is a professional person, cultured, intelligent and one of integrity and dignity. He would not stoop to such unfair acts as some believe, even if it were possible.

. . . The patient who is naturally impulsive is more likely to enter the hypnotic state easily and completely than is one who wants a logical answer to everything before accepting it.

. . . Rational acts usually follow impulse. This impulsive characteristic in us all is of great value to the hypnotherapist, for it is only when the patient ceases to "think the situation through" and no longer feels the need of doing his own thinking, that the hypnotist has free rein. He then is able to secure obedience of his every command. There is no resistance on the part of the patient because he has reached the state of blind faith where he no longer cares to reason or resist.

. . . If one were dealing with strictly normal persons at all times, there would be less obligatory learning. The hypnotherapist, just as any professional person, must handle all types, among them psychotics and just plain "nuts". The trained therapist recognizes the psychotic usually by his changing moods. . . . He is a direct and most disturbing menace to the untrained therapist and hypnotizing him is as unpredictable as any other dealings with him.

. . . Although the doctor's first consideration is for his patient, there are cases where his own well-being should be protected too. There can always be false charges against the hypnotist, of wrong-doing of various kinds while the patient is under hypnotism. For this reason, a nurse, other person, or tape recorder should be a part of the session, whether the patient is a child or adult, either male or female. Especially is this necessary if the patient is a disturbed or unstable person.

. . . Doctor Harold Rosen, who is Associate Professor of Psychiatry at Johns Hopkins University, urges that physicians using hypnosis should examine the patient for mental conditions before attempting that form of treatment, because many doctors have become involved in the most unpleasant difficulties caused by rendering the same approach and treatment to those both

489

mentally unbalanced and those normal. It just does not work out. In other words, an abnormal person can develop a psychosis from the knowledge that he was hypnotized, or he can be fearful, because of his mental unbalance, that something wrong is going to be forced upon him when under hypnosis, and carry that belief with him when he emerges from trance, simply because he had it in his mind before and it has never left. . . .

The courtroom emptied, after the jury had been escorted out of range. The newspeople scattered to file stories and then reassembled at the bar at the American Hotel under all the old prints and pictures of dead horses, and the silvered racing shoes they had worn while winning. Bailey and Keuper went into the judge's chambers to discuss the legal problems relating to the Florida indictment.

Carl Coppolino was taken out, cuffed, loaded into the van and taken down to the jail where, later in the evening, Lee Bailey would visit him and confer with him, presumably about whether or not Carl would take the stand in his own defense.

It was obvious that the drama was entering its final stages. As a racetrack oriented reporter put it, "We're coming around the clubhouse turn into the stretch."

The average of all estimates was at least one more full day of testimony, which would include Keuper's rebuttal witnesses, which were assumed to include a cardiologist and maybe an expert on hypnosis, and maybe a witness to the conversation Keuper had with Dr. Webb back on December 2.

It was obvious, because Bailey had been telegraphing it all along, that he would have to put on somebody to substantiate "the collapsed coffin" theory.

But would he put Coppolino himself on?

If they are any indoor sportsmen more futile than a batch of newspeople sitting around trying to appraise the possible maneuvers of the defense and the prosecution in a dramatic murder trial, it has not yet come to mind. But the guessing is compulsory, even to those old hands who should know better.

A rough rule of thumb is that if the defense has a comfortable lead going into the final stages of its case, don't risk putting the defendant on. Risk, it should be said, is not related in this sense to guilt or innocence. It relates only to the impression the accused will make on the stand, not only during direct, but during cross, and so it also relates to the ability of the prosecutor to savage the accused effectively.

Whether or not the defense has a comfortable lead is something locked away in the collective jury brain. And the simple act of taking a seat in the jury box has the inevitable effect of turning even the most mobile and expressive countenance into something like one of those stone heads on Easter Island.

Divining the jury opinion is possible only in the indirect way of taking one's own reaction to the sum of all the testimony thus far and trying to judge how it affected those fourteen strangers.

The consensus was that F. Lee Bailey had come back a long, long way from his sorry position as of the recess on Monday night, and if he maintained momentum he just might gain a tiny lead—measured in reasonable doubt—if the anticipated gravedigger testimony was effective. But a tiny lead was not enough, not with the possibility of rebuttal witnesses of unknown effectiveness.

The opinion was expressed that Carl would make a bad witness. But someone else said that he could not see how anything could be any worse than the impression he made on the jury by just sitting there, pawing officiously through the files and papers of his attorneys, writing notes, whispering advice to whoever sat near him, acting more like a self-appointed consultant than the accused.

"Listen. Hold it a minute. A buck says Bailey knew right from the start of this thing he'd have to put him on. With the prison complexion and the hooded eyes, he looks just shifty enough and spooky enough to fit the jury's idea of how somebody should look if they were capable of doing what Marge claims he did. So if the reasonable doubt isn't big enough, they'd be inclined to fry him on account of that impression. And another thing. Bailey led every single juror to believe that the Doc might not take the stand, and they are sitting there just aching to hear his explanation of all this, and you can believe it, and they will all love their old buddy, Lee Bailey, if he gives them that treat."

Mary Coppolino left her new mother-in-law at the motel at the edge of town and came in for a drink, thus activating the strobes and flash bulbs. Later, with some of the defense team, she went next door for pizza.

It was on the evening of that day that, by joint effort and contribution, a song was composed, one of the underground songs which appear spontaneously at all notorious murder trials. It is another exercise in dark and grisly humor. Often, as for example in the case of the Mossler trial, the end product is unprintable. But this one achieved its impact and contrast through being in the form of a gentle and nostalgic ballad, but one with a last line which could prickle the hair on the back of the neck.

This one was a parody of "Smile the While," and was sung softly, slowly, and well out of the earshot of any of the actors on the court stage. It was titled "The Colonel's Lament."

> *Smile the while*
> *You slice my heart in two.*
> *When the trial*
> *Rolls by I'll say adieu.*
> > *Put me back into my grave,*
> > *With all those parts, you'd like to save.*
> *This has been*
> *A funny time for me.*
> *Waxed and sliced*
> *For everyone to see.*
> *Farewell, Carl*
> *And Majorieeeeeee. . . .*
> *Til we meet againnnnn.*

To those who properly assess this as a cheap and witless vulgarity, and an affront to the dignity of a proceeding where a man was being tried for his life, let it be pointed out that man's capacity for irony, outrage and sacrilege has always been his most effective armor against emotional involvement.

Chapter Twenty-nine

The first part of the Wednesday morning session began with the seventh witness for the defense, one Leo Clark Foster, the funeral director and embalmer who, back in July, had been engaged by the Worden Funeral Home to go to Arlington National Cemetery and exhume the body of Colonel Farber and transport it to New York City for autopsy.

Leo Clark Foster was a youngish man of indeterminate age, with a vague and listless face, a vague and listless manner, and an air of apprehensive humility. Aside from a certain tonsorial elegance of temple and sideburns, he was sufficiently standard and average and unremarkable in appearance to make one quite certain ore had seen him a dozen times before, somewhere, perhaps standing on a street corner waiting for something or somebody.

492

Bailey sped him through the establishing questions. Yes, he had driven alone down to Washington in a 1966 Chrysler station wagon, taking with him just a disaster pouch which, he explained, was a rubber pouch used for cases such as drownings and fires. "I have this with me at all times anyway," he said.

He met a Mr. Hysong in Washington at the Hysong Funeral Home at ten-thirty and Mr. Hysong went with him out to the cemetery, where they went to Colonel Farber's grave.

"Can you tell us whether or not that grave is located in proximity to any well known landmark within the cemetery?"

"It's just below the Unknown Soldier's grave, yes sir."

They found the gravediggers there, and Mr. Hysong's son, but the grave had not been touched as yet. He did not know the names of the gravediggers. The gravediggers had started to open the grave sometime after lunch, after twelve-thirty. Leo Clark Foster had not returned to the site until about three-thirty in the afternoon, by which time the grave had been dug, and the lid had been taken off the outer box exposing the casket.

There was water in the grave, he said, and water in the box. "Everything was wet." The outer box was made of wood and the casket was made of wood. When he looked down into the hole, he could see the top of the casket.

"The men were moving this lid and the casket top. The whole top of the casket was being moved and the men were taking this out in pieces."

The men continued to work as he watched the entire lid being removed in pieces. Once the lid had been removed he could see the lower extremities of the body, the rest of it being covered by the casket lining which is ordinarily glued to the inside of the lid. Nobody would touch this, he said, and so he went down into the grave and removed this lining, exposing the body.

He saw then that the pressure of the moist earth had pushed in the sides of the outer box which in turn had pushed the sides of the casket in against the arms of the body, so constricting it that it was impossible to lift the body out of the casket, or lift out casket and all. Under the pressure the sides of the casket had become concave, wedging the arms and shoulders tightly. At Bailey's invitation, Foster stepped over to the blackboard and drew a crude sketch of the box, casket and body to illustrate the problem.

As it was then late in the afternoon they did no more work that day. Because of the many tourists visiting the nearby Tomb of the Unknown Soldier, they took another outer box and put it on top of the grave and covered it with boards, and left to return the next morning. By the time Foster arrived at mid-morning, the problem of extrication had been partially solved by digging a second grave directly beside the opened grave, and about six inches deeper. As there was no wall of earth between the two holes, it was in essence an enlargement of the original grave.

The disaster pouch was placed in the bottom of the second grave, after the side of the casket had been pulled away and lifted out.

"Then the gravediggers were instructed to pull Colonel Farber from this, from the left to the right so he could be put in the disaster pouch. The men wouldn't handle him. I was standing on top of the grave watching this. They took what we call two vault hooks. They are L-shaped hooks. I guess the ends of them are about eight, ten inches long, and one was placed across his right shoulder, and the other was placed around—between his hip and his knee, and they started pulling him."

"What was the purpose of the hooks? Was he to be slid across into the disaster pouch?"

"That's right . . . When they pulled, because of the—he was in the casket. The bottom of the casket had, of course, bedding in it, and when he was pulled, he turned over from his left to his right and landed on his face . . . Right in the disaster pouch. . . . The disaster pouch was zipped up. There were ropes put on the top. Two handles. One across him and the middle two handles, and one across the foot handles, and he was raised to the top of the grave. Then he was taken from the top of the grave, after we took the ropes off. He was taken from there and placed under a tent . . . by six men on the handles of the disaster pouch. And . . . he was placed down again and put into this Ziegler case which we transport bodies in. . . . A Ziegler case is a metal container about 75 inches long by 20 wide, made of light steel, and the top is put on and screwed down all the way around. Mr. Hysong had brought that with him."

"When the body was set in the case, was it fairly tight on the sides, or was it loose enabling it to move around?"

"I am sorry?"

"Was the case wide enough so that there was room on either shoulder or room on the sides of the pouch?"

"He just set in it."

"How about the ends? Was the pouch as long as the interior of the case?"

"Yes. Just about. Uh huh."

"I take it that when the disaster pouch was zipped up, the body was face down in the pouch?"

"That's right."

"Having flipped over?"

"That's right. Nobody would touch him."

"Did it remain face down the rest of the time you had it?"

The Ziegler case was placed in the back of the station wagon and Foster then drove the body to New York to Bellevue Morgue.

"Do you remember who took delivery of this case?"

"Colonel Helpern was right there. He must have."

"Doctor Helpern?"

"I'm sorry. Doctor Helpern."

He had then departed, leaving the case and pouch. In his final answer on direct he said that he had not received any special instructions on the handling of the body.

Before beginning his cross-examination Vincent Keuper had a typewritten sheet marked exhibit S-17 for identification, and then took it over to the witness. Only when he had a physical object, such as the photographs of Marjorie Farber's home, or the disputed Anectin container, or a document, did he question at close range. From the rigidity of his back and the tone of his voice, had he questioned from back at his usual place by the state table, Foster would have felt considerably more comfortable.

"Mr. Foster, I show you an exhibit marked S-17 for identification, and ask you to take a look at it."

"Yes sir."

"PUT IT IN YOUR HAND AND TAKE A-HOLD OF IT!"

"Y-Yes sir."

"Does that contain your signature?"

"It does."

"Did you prepare that statement?"

"I did."

"Did you type it yourself?"

"No sir."

"Somebody typed it for you?"

"That's right."

"Did you read it after it was typed?"

"Yes."

"And is everything in there true?"

"No. I told you . . ."

"The question is: Is everything in there true? Yes or no!"

"No."

"What isn't true about this statement?"

"The part that I was there when the box was opened, that the outer box was taken up, the lid of it."

"You were not there then?"

"No sir."

"When for the first time did you tell anyone that Colonel Farber fell on his face while being removed from the coffin or casket to the disaster pouch?"

"When was it?"

"When for the first time did you tell anyone that he fell on his face?"

"I am sorry. I don't know. I told Doctor Helpern when I went to New York. He knew it."

"When you prepared this statement you said nothing about Colonel Farber falling on his face, did you?"

"Yes, I did!"

"Point it out."

Foster read from the report:

"When the men were pulling the remains to the disaster pouch there was approximately an eight-inch drop from the disaster pouch, causing the remains to turn over from left to right, stomach side down."

"You recall your testimony here this morning when you were questioned by Mr. Bailey, that you said he fell on his face while being removed from the casket to the disaster pouch?"

"I said face down."

"You said face down?"

"I said from—he came out of the casket and turned over from his back to his front, face down."

Keuper asked that the exact wording be located and read back by the court reporter, Mrs. Wardell. After a search she found the place and read, "When he was pulled he turned over from his left to his right and landed on his face."

"My choice of language is wrong," Keuper said acidly. "I said, 'Fell on his face.' Did he land on his face? Is that what you meant?"

"I meant he turned over from his back, face down."

"Not a question of landing on his face or falling on his face?"

"No."

Keuper then took him back to his previous testimony of seeing the intact lid of the casket when he arrived.

"Was that removed in your presence?"

"Yes."

"While it was being removed were you careful?"

"Yes. The men were instructed so."

"Being careful that nothing fell on Colonel Farber's face or body?"

"That's right."

"*Did* anything fall on Colonel Farber's face or body while the top of the casket was being removed?"

"No."

Keuper had him describe the lining that rested on the upper part of the body. It was very light, and was the usual satin material with which caskets are lined.

"While you were present did any part of the casket fall upon the head, neck or upper part of Colonel Farber's body?"

"No sir."

"While the body was being removed from the casket to the disaster pouch was the upper part of his body disturbed at all?"

"Only when it turned over."

"You say just turned over. Was that from the process of removing it from the casket to the pouch?"

"Yes."

"Did anybody touch the upper part of the body at all then?"

"Nobody touched him at all. No sir."

As Vincent Keuper resumed his seat, face stern, Lee Bailey was understandably eager to make an attempt to salvage and rehabilitate his witness. Foster looked saddened and miserable.

Bailey directed his questions to the problem of the broken casket lid. Foster said it was intact when he got there, that one of the gravediggers had to break it to get it out, and he could not remember if he saw the actual breaking of the lid. But he saw it coming out in pieces.

"Do you know what they broke it with? Shovels or something?"

"I would say shovels. There was nothing else there."

Bailey made a muscular gesture as of someone driving a spade into the ground. "Shovels jammed down right into the top of the casket?"

"No."

"How did they do it? Did you watch it being done? Just your best recollection."

"I'm trying to think," Foster said, and one can imagine a certain amount of difficulty in trying to say something that would save him from the wrath of both Bailey and Keuper.

"All right. Take a minute."

"Shovels were used, but I know they weren't jammed."

"Did you watch them being used?"

"No sir."

"You didn't? Then how do you *know* they weren't jammed?"

"I don't know," said Foster miserably.

But Keuper got up when Bailey finished, and made Foster read aloud a paragraph from his report. "We broke through the lid of the casket being careful that nothing fell on Colonel Farber's face.''

"So you were present when the lid of the casket was broken open, right?"

"Yes."

"And while it was broken open nothing fell on Colonel Farber's face?"

"That's right."

But here came Bailey again as soon as Keuper was done.

"Didn't you say just a moment ago, sir, that you didn't see the casket being broken?" Now Bailey seemed angry with him too.

Keuper objected that Bailey was trying to impeach his own witness, and was overruled. Bailey said, "I'm not trying to impeach him!"

"Let's not quibble," said Judge Simmill. "I have ruled in your favor."

"I understand, Your Honor."

"Don't paint the lily," said the judge obscurely.

"Mr. Foster," said Bailey, "give us your best recollection. Did you actually see with your own eyes the process, the means by which the coffin lid was broken up?"

"No."

"So that you don't know what may or may not have fallen on the colonel's face from your own knowledge, do you?"

"I was right there and the men were taking these pieces out with shovels."

"Now prior to the time you saw pieces coming out did you hear any noise consistent with the shattering of wood?"

"No."

"Then you don't know how they were broken?"

"The casket is glued and I would think because of the water that the sections of the casket would possibly come apart. That is why there wasn't a lot of noise with shovels digging into wood."

"Were they big pieces or little pieces?"

"Different sizes."

"What was the littlest piece you saw?"

Foster indicated with his hands a piece about six or eight inches long, and he said the biggest piece he saw was two feet long.

And then Foster was once again confronted by Keuper who, after apologizing for belaboring the point, asked him how they were getting the pieces out of the grave. He said they were just putting the shovels under the casket pieces and throwing them out.

"At any time did any of those shovels touch the body of Colonel Farber?"

"Not that I could see. No."

To Foster's quite obvious dismay, Bailey came charging back at him, and the back of Mr. Bailey's neck was red. "I thought you said you didn't see the casket top being broken up, sir!"

Keuper objected to Bailey savaging his own witness, but the judge said he would permit it, then pointed out to Bailey that he had made a statement rather than asked a question.

"Mr. Foster, let me put it this way? From the moment you first looked in and saw the casket top intact until the moment that it was completely broken up and removed with the shovels, were your eyes off the grave at any time?"

"Yes."

"All right. How much of the time during that interval?"

"Very little, but they were."

Bailey turned away and yet again Keuper came to his feet. It was possible to think of Leo Clark Foster in the terms of the old joke about the sparrow who inadvertently flew into a badminton game. He had taken the stand with an evident humble desire to please both attorneys, and had managed somehow to bring both of them down upon him.

Keuper went back to the report Foster had written and had typed, and established that it had been written because Keuper's office had phoned him and asked him for a report, and no attempt had been made to influence what went into it, other than Keuper's request that he write out exactly what happened. Foster said his wife had typed it, and he had written out what had happened, and that information was right in that exhibit, yes sir.

"Now, has anyone spoken to you since you prepared this exhibit or had it prepared and signed by you?"

"Yes sir."

"Who?"

"Mr. Bailey's office."

Thereupon, Lee Bailey asked to see the document. And with two brief questions to the witness established that Foster had supplied Bailey's office with a duplicate of the statement. Bailey produced his copy, and asked that it be introduced in evidence. And so S-17, as marked for identification, became defense exhibit 8, entered in evidence, Bailey through implication informing the jurors that as he had the statement all along, he did not feel that bringing Foster to the stand as a defense witness was inconsistent with the statement originally given the state.

And Leo Clark Foster was excused. It can be assumed he was glad to leave the courtroom.

Here again, in the testimony of a witness there appeared one of those odd little incongruities which, for a time, do not yield to logical appraisal. As the statement for Keuper's office was written subsequent to Helpern's autopsy report of the finding of the double fracture of the cricoid, it is understandable that the report should contain reference to the care used to keep anything from falling onto the body. But, as was widely reported in the papers, and according to testimony given at the bail hearing in October, the autopsy was ordered on the colonel without any thought of finding the damage to the larynx. Yet apparently Mr. Foster, in delivering the body to "Colonel" Helpern, mentioned that the corpse had landed on its face.

After reflection the reason becomes apparent. Mr. Foster knew that at the autopsy they were going to open the metal case, lift the disaster bag onto the autopsy table, unzip it and find the body face down. This was a startling departure from accepted procedure. Bodies belong face up. Doubtless it had bothered him now and again on the drive from Washington to New York to be aware of the body there in back of him in the Chrysler station wagon, riding face down. So the comment to Helpern would have been in the nature of an apology to explain that it was not a question of carelessness or indifference, but of a mishap which could not be conveniently corrected at the grave site.

Additionally, while the "fell on his face" dispute was being pursued so energetically by Mr. Keuper, there seemed one point so obvious that in later discussion no one could understand why Keuper had not made it. The answer, perhaps is that it is far easier to think of such matters sitting back behind the rail than when standing in the arena of the court. The imaginary exchange might have gone like this:

"Mr. Foster, you have told us that there was water in the grave and water in the outside box. I believe you said 'Everything was wet.' Is that true?"

"Yes, sir."

"You have testified that the adjoining grave, or enlargement of the grave was dug to a depth of six or eight inches below the Farber grave. Is that correct?"

"Yes sir."

"Did the water in the grave run off into the lower level of the enlarged portion?"

"Yes sir."

"Did it all soak into the soil, or did some remain?"

"Some remained, sir."

"How deep would you say that standing water was?"

"It was more like just soft mud, sir, from the fresh digging."

"And the disaster pouch was then spread over this soft watery mud?"

"Yes sir."

"Were there any coffin fragments or any other kind of hard material in the bottom of that hole where the opened disaster pouch was spread?"

"No sir. The side of the coffin had been taken out of the grave."

"Were there any hard portions of the disaster pouch, such as handles or reinforcements under the upper portion of the body where the body was rolled into the pouch?"

"No sir."

"You testified that after the casket lid had been removed in pieces, you went down into the grave yourself and you removed the casket lining from the upper portion of the body. Is that correct?"

"Yes sir."

"When you uncovered the upper part of the body, I ask you if you noticed the neck area?"

"I don't know what you mean?"

"I have reference to the condition of the clothing around the chest and neck area. Was it possible to observe it?"

"Yes sir. He was in uniform."

"Describe the throat area of the uniform."

"He had a necktie. But the shirt . . . well, it was gone."

"But the necktie was there?"

"Yes sir."

"Properly tied with the knot in the proper location?"

"Yes sir."

"But of course you had no opportunity to observe, did you, whether or not this was disturbed when he rolled over into the mud?"

"No sir."

"Once the disaster pouch was zipped up, you never in fact saw the body again, did you?"

"No sir."

"Did you happen to notice anything else about the head and

neck area of the body which might be something that a professional embalmer and funeral director might notice? I am not making reference to the state of preservation of the body."

"Well . . . the eye caps were still in place, sir."

"No more questions."

There was, of course, throughout the trial, a fastidious effort to keep from shocking and horrifying the jurors with any realistic description or photograph of the true condition of the body.

From Volume Three of *Courtroom Medicine*, by Marshall Houts, titled *Death:* "The exhumation and autopsy of a body that has been buried for weeks or months is not a pleasant task. The pungent, permeating odor of decaying flesh can upset castiron stomachs and turn the strongest of us into weaklings.

"One pathologist thinks that the odor clings to the hairs inside his nostrils and remains for days so that everything he eats for a period after an exhumation smells and tastes like putrid flesh. The odor is so foul and lasting that this man burns all the clothing he wears during an exhumation, including cheap tennis shoes especially purchased for the occasion, in an incinerator just as soon as he is finished.

"For this reason many pathologists simply refuse to take exhumation cases. Those who do expect to be paid well for their rather unpleasant experience, even though the actual work may require only three or four hours.

"A competent, experienced, *forensic* pathologist will charge a minimum of from $300 to $500 for his services at an exhumation.

"The attorney should be prepared to pay a comparable amount to the licensed mortician and the cemetery officials for preparing the body for the pathologist, and for its reburial. Their services include taking the body out of the ground, arranging a suitable location for the autopsy, and reburial.

"Since the body smells so badly, most funeral directors do not want to have the autopsy performed in their funeral parlors. The normal routine is to set up a tent at a location in the cemetery and bring electricity and water to it.

"In evaluating the desirability of an exhumation and autopsy, the attorney should keep in mind that he is thinking in terms of an expenditure of between $600 and $1000 at a minimum.

"Chapter 4 discusses the selection of the expert in death action cases. All that is said there should be multiplied many times in geometric progression when it comes to choosing the proper man for an exhumation autopsy.

"He should be not only a pathologist but also a *forensic*

pathologist, and then a *forensic* pathologist experienced in exhumations. An exhumation autopsy is no place for the amateur and the uninitiated. There are too many built-in traps and hurdles.

"Not only must the autopsy surgeon recognize the artifacts caused by embalming, he must also differentiate those conditions due to decay, putrefaction and mummification from ante-mortem conditions. The task is not easy even for the most skilled and experienced 'prosecutor' as the man in charge of an autopsy is sometimes called.

"The inexperienced examiner not only may make erroneous positive findings. He may also completely overlook something of critical importance that the experienced eye would have seen.

"Dr. Richard O. Myers, Northridge, California, who has probably done as many exhumation autopsies as any man in the country, tells me that his experience has been that an exhumation is an 'all or nothing' type of investigation. By that he means that he either finds nothing of any real significance as it relates to the cause or manner of death; or he finds conclusive proof. There are very few gray and speculative areas developed at an exhumation."

After Foster was excused, Bailey explained to the Court that even though a subpoena had been served on Mr. Shannon of the Shannon Funeral Home to come up and testify for the defense, Mr. Shannon was alleging hardship because of sickness of both he and his wife and had hired counsel in Florida to prevent enforcement of the subpoena. "The question is either to wait and litigate the matter down there or to do without Mr. Shannon and I feel we can do without Mr. Shannon. I don't want the jury to feel that we represented he would be here knowing he wouldn't. We have tried."

"You may proceed," said Judge Simmill.

"I call Doctor Coppolino," said Lee Bailey. There was a sudden shifting and murmuring and a sudden feeling of increased tension in the courtroom. Carl Coppolino got up from the defense table, was sworn, and took the stand. He wore a dark blue-green suit of a shiny and somewhat iridescent weave. He seemed composed, earnest, confident and under control.

With the very first establishing question, Carl Coppolino half-turned in the chair to face the jury. Lee Bailey for the first time in the trial stood well back, near the defense table, and stayed there in one place throughout the direct examination. He seemed to be making an obvious effort to leave the entire scene to Carl Coppolino. There was little inflection in his voice, and he kept the form of his questions as simple and direct as possible. For the first and last time during the trial, F. Lee Bailey became almost invisible. The contact was between Carl and the jurors, as though the jury, collectively, was asking the questions, and he answered the jury rather than his counsel.

His voice was rather thin and boyish, in a medium pitch. His accent was that of Queens and Brooklyn, of the public schools and Fordham University and the state-supported medical school, the accent of the New York born and bred professional man. He sat at times with one hand braced against the arm of the chair, elbow akimbo, gesturing with easy Mediterranean elegance with the other hand, his face often quite expressive. The whole projection of personality was that of an earnest professionalism, seeking belief, but not to the extent of being overly ingratiating in order to achieve it.

After establishing that he was professionally licensed in New Jersey to practice anesthesiology, and had been licensed since 1958, Bailey asked, "When did you first meet Mrs. Farber?"

"August or September of 1962."

"Where did that meeting take place?"

"In Middletown. . . . I was walking up the road with my wife, Carmela."

Bailey established the Wallace Road house numbers, the distance and relationship of the two houses, and that Coppolino had also met William Farber, then asked, "Now, do you recall an instance where you had a discussion with Mrs. Farber about her desire to stop smoking?"

"Yes."

"What did she say with respect to smoking?"

"Well, she felt that she ought to stop smoking because she was suffering from quite a lot of respiratory difficulties."

"Did she recount any of these difficulties to you?"

"Yes. In fact she had returned recently from Fort Monmouth Hospital for a checkup to see what these respiratory difficulties were."

"When did this discussion take place, to the best of your recollection."

"In January of 1963."

"Did you discuss with her the ways in which she might stop smoking?"

"No. Not at that time."

"Did you later have a discussion on the subject?"

"Yes."

"How frequently would you see Mrs. Farber between August (1962) and January (1963)?"

"I believe I saw her on two separate occasions."

"Doctor, in August 1962 were you working?"

"Yes."

"As an anesthesiologist?"

"Correct."

"At some subsequent time did you cease to work on a full time basis?"

"Yes."

"When was that?"

"About the middle of December, 1962."

"What was that occasioned by?"

"That was brought on by coronary artery disease. I had an acute attack."

"Now, in early February, tell us the discussion you had with Mrs. Farber about smoking."

"Well, in early February 1963 in her home I had a discussion with her about smoking. Actually the subject was brought up by Mrs. Farber. She wanted to know if I could help her in any way. She seemed to have tried many different remedies that most people use to stop smoking, from chewing mints . . ."

Vincent Keuper stood up and said, "May we have the answer limited to the conversation?"

"Yes," said the judge. "Tell us what she said."

"She would like to know if hypnosis would be of any value to her in stopping smoking."

"What did you tell her?"

"I said before I could answer that question I would have to ask her several questions to evaluate her as a potential subject for hypnosis."

"Did you ask her those questions?"

"I did."

"In the course of the answers did you obtain some of her history?"

"Quite a bit of it."

"After that did you use hypnosis in an effort to help her stop smoking?"

"Not at the time, but subsequent."

"When was the first time you attempted to use hypnosis to help her in her desire to stop smoking?"

"I believe it was the following day."

"And where did it take place?"

"In her home."

"Who was present?"

"Just Mrs. Farber and myself."

"Did you put her under hypnosis at that time?"

"Yes."

"Did you give her any suggestions while she was under hypnosis?"

"Yes."

"What suggestions did you give her?"

"Well, to the best of my recollection I gave her suggestions referable to the fact that when a desire would come upon her for a cigarette, she would ignore it and substitute perhaps something else, or if that didn't work and it didn't suit her, and she didn't accept that suggestion, that if she did in fact light a cigarette and start to inhale it would become so distasteful for her that she would immediately put it out. And if she continued to do this and realized it was distasteful to her, she would eventually stop smoking."

"Was this the only time you hypnotized Mrs. Farber in an effort to assist her in her desire to stop smoking?"

"No."

"How many other times were there?"

"There was one other time."

"How long after the first occasion did this take place?"

"At least six or seven months later."

"I draw your attention to the early morning hours of the 30th of July, 1963, and ask you where you were at that time?"

"I was at home sleeping."

"Did something happen?"

"The telephone rang."

"Did you answer it?"

"Yes."

"Who was on the telephone?"

"Mrs. Farber."

It is interesting to note that even the most professional of witnesses will often answer the direct question and also the implications of the question. Did something happen? Mrs. Farber telephoned. Carl Coppolino answered in the simplest possible form. The telephone rang. As quite obviously Bailey had not taken him through this whole dialogue, bit by bit, it is a tribute to Coppolino's poise and self-control that he could keep constantly in mind Bailey's probable instruction to him to just answer each question in turn, with responsive answers, but without embellishment or volunteered information. Also, remember, Coppolino sat and listened to a great deal of testimony, and one can assume that he had considerable interest in paying attention.

506

"What did she tell you, if anything?"

"In an agitated voice she told me that her husband, Bill, was ill, and could I rush right over."

"What did you do?"

"Before I could ask her anything, she hung up. So, I placed the phone back on the receiver, got up, got dressed, and went downstairs and got into my car and drove up the road to her house."

"When you got to the house did you meet her at some point?"

"No, not outside the house."

"Where did you first see Mrs. Farber?"

"I entered the house through the front door and she was at the landing there, and I spoke with her there."

"What did she tell you?"

"She told me that her husband was calling out for help, and that she rushed down from her bedroom to his, and that she found him in bed, pale, sweating, gasping for air, and that he requested her to call for a doctor. 'I need a doctor.' "

"Did you go somewhere after you had this initial bit of information?"

"Yes. We went down the several steps to the lower floor toward his bedroom, but he wasn't there."

"Doctor, this house has been described as a split level. Can you tell us how the levels were split?"

"Most of the living quarters were on the upper level. As you come into the front door you can go either up the steps to the kitchen, or you can go down the steps to the lower part of the house."

"So that the front door is located halfway between the levels?"

"Correct."

"When you went in, you were halfway between the levels. By the way, did you go up or down?"

"Down."

"Where did you go in the lower level?"

"Right in the foyer or the hallway, because there are several exits out of that hallway."

"After you received the information about the colonel's condition, where did you go?"

"I saw the colonel right away. He was in the bathroom."

"How far is the bathroom from the front door?"

"I would say approximately thirty feet."

"Now, how was he positioned in the bathroom when you first saw him?"

"He was sitting on top of the seat of the toilet."

"Was the lid down?"

"Yes."

"And how was he dressed?"

"In his pajamas."

"Will you describe for the jury the observations you made about his apparent condition when you first encountered him?"

"He was obviously pale. He was perspiring profusely. He was holding his head, and we did have some conversation in the bathroom."

"What was said?"

"He said that he felt very weak, and he could hardly move and he could hardly breathe."

"What did you do for him, if anything?"

"Mrs. Farber was right next to me, and I told her, I said, 'Marge, let's get him back to bed first of all.' "

"Did you get him back to bed?"

"Yes. She took one side of him under his arm, and I took the other side under his arm, and between both of us we helped him from the bathroom back to his bed."

"What did you do when you got him back to bed?"

"I first made sure that he sat, and then I gently lowered the upper part of his body while Mrs. Farber took his legs and swung them so that he wouldn't have any exertion in getting into bed."

"What kind of a bed was it, Doctor?"

"Twin bed."

"He still had his pajamas on at this point?"

"Oh yes."

"When you got him into bed, what did you do?"

"The first thing I did was feel his pulse."

"Will you describe what you felt about the pulse at that time?"

"Yes. It was quite rapid, and I calculated it was anywhere between 80 to 120 beats variable. One point might be 80, another point might be 120, and it was quite irregular."

"What would a regular pulse have been for a man that age?"

"Since he had been sleeping and had been in a quiet position, I would expect the pulse to be around 70 to 80, certainly not more than that."

"What else did you observe initially about this man once you got him in bed?"

"He was very pale, perspiring, still gasping for air, and holding his chest. And I questioned him."

508

"What did he tell you?"

"He told me that several minutes before, and that was the best he could tell me—I tried to ask him whether it was fifteen minutes or half an hour, and he said it was several minutes before—he woke up suddenly, couldn't breathe, felt a pressure on his chest. He had difficulty in breathing. And finally, when he could breathe, called for Marge. And I arrived on the scene."

"After your initial examination, did you do something?"

"I left immediately."

"Where did you go?"

"I went back to my car and I went back home."

"Why did you do that?"

"To get my medical bag."

"Where was that located?"

"Upstairs in the bedroom."

"Why did you keep it in the bedroom?"

"We actually had two medical bags. Carmela and I each had our own medical bag, and we kept them in the bedroom because of the children. We didn't want them poking around in the bags. They were full of drugs and instruments and whatnot, for safekeeping."

"Drugs you keep in the bag as a matter of course?"

"Yes."

"Why hadn't you brought it with you?"

"Actually I was in such a hurry to get there I forgot to take it with me."

"When you went home and got the bag what did you do?"

"When I went home and got the bag I rushed right back downstairs, back in the car up to Mrs. Farber's."

"What did you do?"

"I went into the Colonel's bedroom. He was still in bed. His condition had not changed at all. There was only a few minutes time that had elapsed from the time I left until the time I arrived, and I proceeded to open my medical bag, took out my blood pressure cup and took his blood pressure. I again checked his pulse."

"Do you recall what the blood pressure was the first time you took it on the morning of July 30th?"

"Yes. One hundred over seventy."

"And what would you expect it to be normally?"

"A man of his age, I would expect it to be at least one forty, probably over eighty or ninety."

"Tell us what else you did."

"Well, naturally, when you take a blood pressure with a blood

509

pressure cup you use a stethoscope. And using the stethoscope I listened to his heart and the sounds were muffled. They weren't coming in clearly. And also, even though I knew his pulse was irregular from feeling it with my hand, I could hear his heart beats and they also corresponded with my first initial impression that he had an irregular pulse. Again, as I said before, he was perspiring and still complaining of a pressure."

"Complaining of what?"

"Oppression, pressure of his pain, in his chest."

"All right. Go ahead."

"So I began treatment."

"All right. How did you treat him? First of all, at this point had you made any diagnosis, tentative or otherwise?"

"Yes. From what he had told me and from my clinical observations I made a tentative diagnosis that the man obviously had suffered some sort of coronary episode. Whether it was an acute coronary insufficiency, whether a coronary spasm, or whether he'd gone fully into an acute myocardial infarction, I didn't know."

"Stop here. Tell the jury what a coronary insufficiency is."

"A coronary insufficiency is a situation or an episode where the coronary arteries go into spasm for some reason—could be emotional tension—could be exercise. Actually it occurs when you sneeze or cough it goes into spasm. And when it goes into spasm the blood supply is blocked off temporarily so blood can't get to the muscles, the muscle that's feeding from this artery, the muscle of the heart that's feeding this artery. So what happens is you get a decreased blood supply to the heart and you get decreased oxygen. When you get decreased oxygen, you immediately get chest pains or you get a sensation of oppression. The progress usually occurs that first you get a sense of oppression. It becomes worse if the vessel continues to remain closed for a period of time. Now by a period of time I mean a minute, two minutes, three minutes. The pressure will increase to develop the pain and then, since you have cut off part of the blood supply to the heart the heart rate becomes irregular. Accompanying this there will be other signs. The patient will begin to sweat, will not be able to catch his breath, gasp, and other things could happen."

"Now, Doctor, would you explain a myocardial infarction?"

"A myocardial infarction is the follow-up of this acute coronary insufficiency. When you have a myocardial infarction this means that the vessel that clamped down never reopened. So that the tissue that this vessel was feeding dies. Infarction means dead

510

tissue. So the tissue of the heart dies and the myocardial infarction just means dead tissue of the heart because of the clamping off of this vessel. Now there are several reasons why the vessel could clamp off. One is from arteriosclerosis. Another reason is that it can go into spasm because of external stimuli.''

In describing coronary insufficiency, Dr. Carl Coppolino was in fact describing the disease and the symptoms for which he had been receiving full disability payments from his health insurance policies. In describing both insufficiency and infarction his manner, precision and control of his material seemed typical of the approved manner of answering questions in the oral part of an examination for a medical degree, when a board of examiners will sit and listen to the applicant expound on those areas of knowledge he presumably has studied.

Lee Bailey asked, ''What are the symptoms that you observed that you found to be consistent with these conditions, coronary insufficiency, myocardial infarction that caused your diagnosis?''

''The fact that he woke up first of all from a sleep with pain or oppression—number one. Number two—that he started to perspire profusely and gasp for air to such a point that he finally struggled out of bed to get to the bathroom, because, associated with this, he felt nauseous or nauseated, although he didn't vomit when he was in the bathroom. When I arrived on the scene and we escorted him back to bed, as I said before, he had an irregular pulse and he had heart sounds that were muffled and he had a low blood pressure. All of these were the history to me. My diagnosis was what I gave. It was either an acute coronary insufficiency or the beginning of a myocardial infarction.''

''When you got back and took the colonel's blood pressure and so forth, did he do anything irregular?''

''No. Not at that time. I began treatment.''

''What treatment did you give him?''

''Well, he was apprehensive first of all because of his suffering and this oppression. I gave him Demarol.''

''What is Demarol?''

''Demarol is a synthetic narcotic. It comes from the morphine family. I gave him 50 milligrams of Demarol, I.M.''

''What is I.M.?''

''Intramuscular.''

''What does Demarol accomplish?''

''Demarol accomplishes two purposes. One is to immediately relieve the pain that he was having or the oppression and the second purpose is to quiet him down, relieve his apprehension. But its primary use is as an analgesic, to remove the pain.''

"Did you give him any other drug?"

"Yes."

"What?"

"Well, I was very concerned with his irregular pulse and I felt that he had what we call premature ventricular contractions. His heart would go bump-bup. There would be a pause. And then bump-bup-bup, and then another bump-bup, and this is consistent with irregular pulse or premature ventricular contractions. There is a specific drug for this treatment. It is called Pronestyl. It's a procaine amide. I gave him this drug intravenously."

"This accomplished what?"

"Well, this decreased the irritability of the heart. The heart becomes irritable because there is less blood supply to it than normal and the procaine amide, or Pronestyl decreases the irritability of the heart and by its action changes the rate from an irregular rate to a regular rate, which is what we want to have. In addition I gave him some Nembutal, 50 milligrams I.M., or intramuscular."

"What is Nembutal?"

"Nembutal is a barbiturate, and the sole purpose again is to induce a sense of relaxation, drowsiness or sleepiness."

"Is this standard treatment for a person suffering coronary difficulty?"

"Yes, at home. Unless you . . ."

"I mean on a first aid basis?"

"Yes. That's right."

"What happened after you administered these drugs?"

"Well, I didn't administer drugs one right after the other. It took about a half-hour interval while I was doing this, checking him all the time. The blood pressure cup was still on his arm all the time. I checked his blood pressure again. It still was 100 over 70, but his pulse now was regular. His appearance had not changed markedly. He still was quite pale and was still perspiring but he began to speak more freely. In other words, he was not complaining of pain nor was he complaining of gasping for air. He had no difficulty in breathing so he conversed with me in almost normal tones and we had a conversation."

"What was said?"

"Well, the first thing he wanted to know was was he going to die, which I avoided answering. And I was administering to him but he kept persisting. 'Now, Carl, tell me,' he says, 'am I seriously ill? Am I going to die?' I said, 'No, Bill,' I say, 'you're not going to die.' I said. I said, 'But you're ill,' and I said, I told him at that time, I said, 'I feel that you need better care than what I'm giving you at this particular time and I suggest that we immediately call for an ambulance, the Red Bank Volunteer Service, and take you to Fort Monmouth.' "

"Was Mrs. Farber present at this time?"

"All the time."

"What did Colonel Farber say in response to your recommendation?"

"He didn't answer me right away."

"Did Mrs. Farber say anything?"

"She said, 'No,' immediately, but he didn't answer me right away because when she said, 'No,' he went into quite a long harangue with Mrs. Farber that was not complimentary to her."

"They had an argument?"

"They did."

"Without going into the details of that, did you continue to stay and look after the colonel for a period of time?"

"Immediately I cut the argument off quite short because this was no place and no time, I told both of them. And I told Bill, I said, 'Listen, you have to go to the hospital,' and he says, 'No, I'm not going to the hospital. I don't want to go to the hospital.' "

"So he refused? Himself?"

"Yes."

"All right. Go ahead."

"Well, about three or four minutes later, no more than that, all of a sudden he began to vomit and vomit profusely. Most of the vomit was on the right side of him and his head was on a pillow and he began to struggle with the vomitus in his mouth. He almost started to aspirate his own vomitus."

"When you say aspirate, what do you mean?"

"That means to breathe in the vomitus material so that he was choking and sputtering. So I immediately wiped out his nose and his mouth and put him in the classical anesthesiologist's position, which is the head up, the chin up in position to open up his airway, tilt him over to the side, drain out the vomitus to clean out as much as I could, to see if I can induce him to cough some of it up, which I was not able to do, but I got most of it up. His color turned a bit dusky and I think that possibly, though I'm not sure, some of the material got onto his vocal chords so that his vocal chords immediately closed off and he didn't get any air for a while, so his color changed a bit. As I was cleaning out the vomitus and getting him controlled I again administered a drug. Sparine. I gave him 50 milligrams of Sparine intramuscular. Sparine has a dual purpose. It's a tranquilizer and it's also an anti-emetic. In other words it prevents vomiting and nausea. Bill, of course, prior to his vomiting was quite agitated because of the argument that he was having with Mrs. Farber."

"Yes?"

"That is the reason why I used Sparine as a tranquilizer and also as an anti-emetic."

"These drugs, by the way, you had in your medical bag."

"Oh yes."

"You carry this as a matter of course?"

"Oh yes." (Of course, of course. Doesn't everyone?)

"What happened after you cleaned up the vomitus and got him resting again?"

"I again insisted that he go to the hospital."

"And what was said?"

"Because now we have another indication that possibly, or in my opinion, with the nausea and vomiting, to me this was another clinical sign that this man was having a cardiac problem."

"Is vomiting consistent with a cardiac problem?"

"Nausea, vomiting is."

"I didn't ask you this before. Did you see any diarrhea that night?"

"None whatsoever."

"In the bathroom or anywhere else?"

"No."

"Go ahead."

"I again asked him to go to the hospital. Both Mrs. Farber and the colonel refused almost simultaneously. At this point he seemed to be comfortable. So I went into the den, which is going now from his bedroom across the foyer that I had been into, where the bathroom and the entrance to the bedroom is, onto the other side into the den or the playroom, and I sat down with Mrs. Farber because I wanted to find out from her why she refused to send Bill to the hospital. 'He has all the privileges of Fort Monmouth. He is a retired colonel. It wouldn't cost him a penny to go there.' Well, her explanation was the fact that first of all, Bill didn't want to go. That was number one. She had to respect his wishes and I told her that in his condition, since he was a sick man, his wishes didn't really count to the extent they would as somebody who was well, that it was her responsibility to assume. And then I asked her would she please let me call an ambulance and send him to the hospital. She refused."

"Now, at some point did you leave the Farber residence after that first session of treatment?"

"Right at this point I left the Farber residence."

"Do you remember about what time in the morning it was?"

"It was about six in the morning."

"Now, do you have an opinion as to whether or not the colonel's condition when you left had altered at all from when you arrived?"

"To me he seemed to be improved, better, but certainly not well."

"Did the improvement take place after the vomiting?"

"Yes."

"So you went back to your home?"

"I went back to my home."

"Did you come back to the Farber residence at some time later on?"

"Oh yes. I went back."

"What time about?"

"About ten, ten-thirty in the morning."

"What was your purpose in going back?"

"Well, I told Mrs. Farber before I left that I would look back on Bill in a couple of hours."

"When you went back at ten, what did you find?"

"Well, when I arrived there about ten or ten-thirty, I entered the house through the garage, and as I was going through the garage, through the door into the area where Bill's bedroom was, I could hear voices."

"Anything unusual about the voice?"

"Yes. They were angry voices."

"Did you recognize the voices?"

"Oh yes. It was Bill and Marge."

"What were they doing?"

"They were arguing."

"Go ahead. What did you do?"

"I had my medical bag with me. I went into the room and again I pleaded with both of them to stop this, first of all. It wasn't good for Bill. And second of all, they could find another time to do this. And I took a look at Bill and he seemed much better. He seemed to have improved. His color seemed to be a little better. He had stopped his perspiring, but his pulse was still irregular. I examined him. I took my blood pressure cup out again and put it on his arm. His blood pressure at this time was about 120 over 70 which in my opinion still was a little low but it was much better than it was a few hours earlier. But, his pulse was still irregular. When I asked him the general question, 'How do you feel?' his answer was, 'Lousy.' And, I again told them that I still felt that he had a coronary or coronary condition, that

515

he needed better medical attention, and I again asked him if he would please go to the hospital."

"Doctor, how long did you stay in the Farber residence on this occasion when you arrived about ten or ten-thirty in the morning?"

"Oh, about two hours."

"Prior to the time that you left, had you said anything to either of the Farbers with respect to your continued assistance as a physician?"

"I certainly did!" (forthright professional indignation)

"What did you tell them?"

"I told Bill and I told Marge, who was there all the time with me, that I could no longer render any aid whatever to Colonel Farber, because both of them refused to get what I considered proper medical attention for this patient, and that, under the conditions, I was going to withdraw from the case, and that I wanted Mrs. Farber to sign a release removing me from any responsibility for this case whatsoever. And I told Bill Farber the same thing."

"When you left the Farber home where did you go?"

"When I left the house, Mrs. Farber came with me. We went home to my house."

"Was Dorothy Jeffress working that day?"

"Yes."

"Was she a live-in maid at that time?"

"Yes."

"When you and Mrs. Farber arrived at your home, where did you go?"

"When we arrived at my home, Mrs. Farber stayed downstairs in the kitchen-dinette area, and I went upstairs in the den to get my notes."

"Did you bring some notes downstairs?"

"Oh yes."

"And where did you and Mrs. Farber go then?"

"We were in the dinette area."

"Did you go out into the back yard at anytime on that day?"

"I never left the house."

"While you were in the dinette did you write something out?"

"Well, I continued the notes that I had started at nine o'clock that morning."

"Before you finished the notes, did you write something out?"

"Oh yes. I wrote out the release that I just had finished as to Mrs. Farber and Colonel Farber."

516

"And did you see the release that was shown to Mrs. Farber and Dorothy Jeffress while this case was being tried?"

"Yes."

"Is that the same release?"

"That is the same release."

"Was her signature on it?"

"Yes. She signed it right there."

"Did she put up any fight about signing?"

"No."

"Did somebody, by the way, have a drink of gin?"

"Yes."

"Who did?"

"I did."

"How long did you and Mrs. Farber stay around your house on this occasion?"

"Let's see. I would say about an hour, an hour and a half."

"What time would you say that Mrs. Farber left?"

"Between two and three that day."

"Did you leave the house at any time after you had returned with her and written out the release?"

"I left that evening."

"Prior to the time that Carmela came home from work did you leave the house at any time?"

"No."

"Did you ever see Bill Farber again alive?"

"No."

"What time did Carmela come home from work?"

"Carmela got home about a quarter to six, six o'clock."

"Where did she work?"

"Hoffmann-LaRoche in Nutley, New Jersey."

"What kind of work did she do?"

"She was assistant medical director of professional services at Hoffmann-LaRoche."

"What is Hoffmann-LaRoche?"

"It is a pharmaceutical company."

"We have had the name of Del Torto come into this case with respect to some letter. Do you know Mr. Del Torto?"

"Very well."

"Where did he work?"

"Hoffmann-LaRoche also. In fact, he used to be a next door neighbor of ours."

"Did he and Carmela ride together (to work)?"

"Often."

"When Carmela got home, did you have any conversation with her?"

"I did."

"Had you had prior to this time any conversation with her about the difficulty at the Farbers'?"

"When I arrived at six o'clock in the morning and went upstairs, Carmela was up and I had conversation with her at that time."

"And, after you had a conversation with Carmela, did the telephone ring?"

"Now you are talking about when she came home from work?"

"In the evening, yes. I'm sorry."

"Yes, we were sitting down and having dinner and the phone rang."

"About what time was it?"

"About six-thirty."

"Who answered the phone?"

"Dorothy Jeffress."

"And, after she answered the phone, to whom did she give the instrument?"

"She called from the kitchen and she said, 'Mrs. C., it is for you.' "

"Did Carmela go to the phone?"

"Yes."

"Did you hear her conversation?"

"The only thing I heard was Carmela said, 'I'll be right up.' "

Bailey tried to ask for the conversation then between Carl and Carmela, but the hearsay objection by Keuper restricted him to merely asking if a conversation had taken place, and, after it was concluded, what Carmela had done.

"She went upstairs, got her medical bag, went downstairs, got into her car and went up to the Farbers'."

"And what was the next thing you heard from either Carmela or from the Farber reisdence?"

"I didn't hear from the Farber residence directly. I called them."

"What did you learn?"

"When I called them, I got Carmela on the phone, and she told me that Bill was dead."

"Not what she told you."

"Oh."

"As a result of the conversation you had with her, where did you go, if anywhere?"

"I went up to the Farber residence."

"When you got there, what did you find?"

"I entered the Farber residence through the front door, and I went into the kitchen, and in the kitchen were Mrs. Farber and Carmela, and I had a conversation with both parties."

"After that conversation did you go somewhere else in the house?"

"I certainly did."

"Where did you go?"

"I went right downstairs into Bill's bedroom."

"What did you find?"

"I found Bill in bed on his back, and he was dead."

"Did you notice anything about him that would help you with the time of death, from your first observation?"

"Well, quick off—as a quick idea, I wrote down that he possibly had been dead maybe anywhere from three to five hours."

"Why did you make this—"

"Because he was blue and he had lividity."

"What causes a body to turn blue after death?"

"Settling of the blood."

"Where was the lividity?"

"Mostly in the lower part of his body and the lower part— when I say lower part I mean right along—"

"You mean the back part?"

"That's right. Since he was lying flat on his back with his head up like this, he had the lower part of his body bluish and some bluish tinge to his face."

"Did you notice the presence or absence of rigor?"

"I can't really remember, Mr. Bailey."

"At some time later did somebody else come to the house?"

"Yes."

"Who?"

"Mr. Worden."

"The same one who testified in this case? Robert Worden?"

"Yes."

"Did you talk to him at all?"

"Oh yes."

"How long after your arrival did he appear?"

"Oh, I would say about fifteen minutes."

"How long were you there? Were you present when the body was removed?"

"I was present, but I didn't see the body removed."

"Some people came with equipment and took it out?"

"Mr. Worden came with two assistants."

"They had a vehicle with them?"

"They had a vehicle with them, and while I was upstairs speaking with Mr. Worden—." Here for the first time Carl deviated from the rigid discipline of responsive answers, and Keuper immediately objected, and was upheld, and the witness said, "I am sorry."

"The body was taken out and you didn't see it?"

"I didn't see a body removed."

"What was the total time you spent in the Farber house that night?"

"After the body was removed?"

"Yes."

"A good hour, because several things occurred."

"Did Carmela stay the hour?"

"I believe Carmela went home and came back."

"But when you left eventually was she with you?"

"Oh yes."

"Did you attend the funeral?"

"No."

"Who signed the death certificate, if you know?"

"Carmela."

Bailey got the certificate from among the exhibits and had Carl identify the signature on it as Carmela's.

"Now, were you present when this was filled out?"

"Yes."

"When was it done?"

"That evening."

"Now I notice that it says here above the signature: 'I attended the deceased from three-thirty A.M. to six A.M. Last saw him alive at one-thirty P.M. above date. Death occurred approximately four P.M. on the date above from the best of my knowledge from the cause as stated.' Did Carmela attend from three-thirty to six?"

"No."

"Did Carmela attend at one-thirty?"

"No."

"Where did she get the information to put in there?"

"From Mrs. Farber and from myself."

"Prior to the time that she put her signature on this death certificate, had you given her whatever history and diagnosis you had in the case?"

520

"I told her when I got home at six A.M. in the morning. That was part of the conversation we had."

It was then ten-fifty. Carl Coppolino had been on the stand under direct examination for just about forty minutes.

"Your witness," said Mr. Bailey to Mr. Keuper, and the judge called a fifteen minute recess.

Here then was highlighted once again that subjective and personal problem of appraising the words and the actions of others in light of emotional logic. The jury is Everyman, saying, "Would I do that? Is that how I would respond? How do all these things fit my lifelong habits of self-protective belief and disbelief? Where lies that little ring of truth, and where has the ring of truth been a calculated artifice? Do I accept the murky, warped, dramatic world of Marjorie Farber, sometimes consistent, sometimes inconsistent, sometimes remembered, sometimes clouded, all a continuing shift of motivations, a flavor of a bored and restless suburban mischief that led from the triteness of the affair into the horrid scene of the smothering? Or do I relate more readily to the tidy and more consistent and somewhat pompous exposition by young Doctor Coppolino, who was at least human enough to forget to take his medical bag with him on an emergency call? I am a juror. All that medical stuff! One says normal deposits on the arteries, and two say enough to kill him. One says ante-mortem fractures and two say post-mortem. All the time, looking at him sitting right there looking right at me, a dozen feet away from me, can I see him in a terrible rage like she said, with his eyes bulging, holding a pillow over Bill Farber's face and telling her he was a hard one to kill? Doesn't it come down to that? If he *did* do it, or if he *didn't* do it, maybe it would be the same story that he would tell. So I have to figure out, using my own common sense, who is lying. So his wife died and he married somebody else, not her. And so if he is supposed to be tried for killing his wife, maybe all that means is that she is making such an attempt to fix his wagon, she got him indicted for that too. Maybe she is hanging around his neck like that bird in the poem about the Ancient Mariner. Marge Albatross. So maybe he did it. Maybe. But right up to this minute, I'm not completely convinced he did, and maybe that is what they mean by reasonable doubt. Once Mr. Keuper gets a chance at him, it could all change again. Or maybe there'll be more witnesses. They told us not to make up our minds until both sides are through. I *never* heard such an idiotic piece of instruction in my *life*. How in the world do they expect me to sit here and listen to all this and keep myself from making up my mind? I've made it up twenty times, sometimes one way, sometimes the other way. If we went in there right now to deliberate, I'd say let him go. But there's more to come."

In the corridor those newspeople who did not have to scurry off to file stood looking dazed and thoughtful. They leaned against the plaster walls and sighed. Attention so concentrated can be totally exhausting. And even then, of course, attention is always flawed. The human brain is not styled for perfect in-put. Experts in semantics tell us that any trigger word or phrase which excites some inner memory or conflict or hang-up in the mind of the listener will create an internal random noise which for a greater or longer period short-circuits any comprehension of the words which follow the trigger word or phrase.

To take an invented but plausible example, suppose a reporter had promised his wife that he would airmail his paycheck for deposit to his bank to cover a rent check she had already written against the account. And when Carl Coppolino in his testimony about calling for an ambulance said, "the Red Bank Volunteer Service," the word *Bank* could trigger the awareness that he had completely forgotten his promise and had not airmailed the check. So he sits there, hand poised over his notes, receptivity blocked while he figures out just how he'd best handle the oversight. When he tunes in again on the testimony, Carl is talking about trying to cut an argument short, and he has to figure out from the following testimony what argument they are talking about.

That is why, no matter how severe the discipline of trained attention, the official transcript of any trial will contain things the reporter never heard, and cannot imagine how he missed. The discipline of keeping the subjective mind under control is, even though imperfect, vastly exhausting.

The consensus was that Coppolino had been very very good, thus far. But testimony comes in two flavors, depending on who asks the questions.

There was no way to guess how Keuper might do with his cross-examination, because there was no way to tell what Keuper might have held back pending the possibility of Carl's testimony.

Suppose, for example, a prosecutor might have a particularly damaging piece of evidence in a capital case. Suppose it flatly refutes testimony he can reasonably expect the defense to present. There is no rule which requires him to present that as a part of the state's case during the state's turn. He can save it, knowing that it will fit into his cross-examination of the accused, if the accused is placed on the stand, or into rebuttal, in either case.

To clarify by example: It so happened that when Mrs. Farber was shown the release she had signed, and which she could not remember signing, she noticed that the body of the release, in Carl's handwriting, was in ink of a different color than her signature. Of itself this would not be of any particular significance, as each could have used a different pen. But suppose that through some chemical dating process, Keuper could produce in rebuttal an expert to testify that the signature pre-dated the body of the release by weeks or months. Assume also that Keuper could produce as a rebuttal witness a medical hypnotist who would attest to the feasibility of a hypnotist with a subject who could achieve a deep trance level, inducing a subject to write their name on a piece of blank paper and giving them the post-hynotic suggestion to forget they had done so. Assume further that Keuper could produce in rebuttal a handwriting expert who would point out that though the signature was indeed the signature of Marjorie Farber, it showed the typical characteristic changes that one can expect when a person signs their name while under hypnosis.

It could then be reasonable to expect Keuper to devote a significant portion of his cross-examination to the actual details and mechanics of the preparation and the signing of the release.

All this, of course, is presented here not to imply that any such events occurred, but merely to indicate why it would be foolish to attempt to appraise the weight of the testimony of the accused based only on the direct examination.

Perhaps the only comment by anyone which had some validity during that mid-morning break was when a wire service reporter said, "For people who lived practically across the street from each other, they certainly didn't care much for walking."

Chapter Thirty

Carl Coppolino squared around in the witness stand to face Vincent Keuper, and to answer Keuper's questions directly.

Keuper began with the autumn of 1962, with the times and places where Carl had been with Marjorie. First was on the street in front of the Farber home. The next time was about a month later at a party at the Coppolino home. The third time was at a Christmas or New Year's party, attended by many people.

He had seen her alone, he said, at her house in February, for the first time, as the result of a telephone call, but he could not remember who had called whom. On that occasion he had discussed hypnosis with her.

Keuper held up a copy of Coppolino's book titled *Practice of Hypnosis in Anesthesiology* and had him identify it, and verify that it had been published in 1965. Keuper wanted to know if the book had been in the process of being prepared for publication when Carl Coppolino had visited Mrs. Farber's home in February of 1963.

"No."

"When was the idea for the book conceived?"

"The idea of the book was conceived while I was in practice in Methodist Hospital in Brooklyn in 1961, and in 1960."

Establishing that he was not actively engaged in the practice of medicine in 1963, Keuper then asked about the listing in the yellow pages in the 1963 New Jersey Bell Telephone Directory, saying "Practice Limited to Treatment by Hypnosis," and Coppolino said he had arranged for that insertion.

"Were you engaged at that time in the practice of hypnosis?"

"No."

"Did you engage in the practice of hypnosis in February 1963?"

"As a medical specialty?" Keuper had the question read back and Dr. Coppolino said in response, "I used hypnosis in 1963, yes."

"Am I using the wrong term when I say engaged in the practice?"

"Yes, because hypnosis is a medical specialty and I wasn't in medical practice."

"If you were in active practice, and in your practice you used hypnosis, would I be correct when I say you practiced hypnosis?"

"Mr. Keuper, I never used hypnosis in active practice, *as* hypnosis. In my medical practice as an anesthesiologist, I used it as an adjunct."

"But you don't call that practicing hypnosis as an adjunct to your practice of medicine, regardless of your specialty?"

"Not as you refer to the listing in the telephone book."

"My term should be— Did you use hypnosis?"

"Correct." In February of '63? "Yes." More than once? "Yes." Upon someone other than Mrs. Farber? "No." Just Mrs. Farber? "Just Mrs. Farber." On February 4th, 1963, the first time? "In February but I don't know the date." On your first visit to her? "No." On the second visit? "Yes." Do you recall when the second visit was? "The next day." February 5th? "The date I don't know."

"If the first visit was on the 4th, the next day was the 5th. Isn't that so?"

"I didn't say the visit was on the 4th."

"I am suggesting to you that your first visit was on the 4th."

"If you say the first visit was the 4th, then the 5th was the first session."

This kind of uninspired quibbling, though it sounds more like a playground argument than a conflict between adults, does serve a purpose, much like the jabs at long range in the first round of a prizefight. The courtroom lawyer is on his home ground. Though it seems a childish ploy, it is an effective weapon when used on a nervous, apprehensive and not particularly logical nor articulate defendant. Jabbed off balance by this ancient and honorable device, the defendant is opened up for more telling damage in future rounds. Coppolino was not angered or intimidated by the device, and certainly not confused. His manner was one of patience in correcting the illogic of his questioner—patience, and a rather patronizing tolerance.

Keuper asked him to describe the induction procedure used on Mrs. Farber. "I had Mrs. Farber sitting in a comfortable chair with armrests. It was an upholstered chair, and I asked her to place her head back—it was sort of a high chair so that she could comfortably put her head back—and relax to the best of her ability. And the first thing she did immediately is what I am doing now." He sat erect and crossed his legs, arms on the arms of the witness chair. "She had her legs crossed. This I told her to uncross. This is a natural phenomena with patients. And to keep her both feet on the floor and to keep her hands in her lap and to try to relax as much as possible. Then I told her to pick a spot in the room, something that she liked that she could look at, and concentrate her attention. And she chose a figurine which was on a coffee table nearby the chair. And so I asked her to concentrate all her attention on the figurine. And while she was concentrating her attention on the figurine, I started to speak to her."

"And you placed her under hypnosis?"

"During the course of speaking with her and as she was following my suggestions, she eventually went into a hypnotic trance."

Keuper then had Coppolino describe the testing procedure he

had used on Marjorie Farber the day before he hypnotized her. He described the business of the pails and the balloons much as Mrs. Farber had remembered them. Keuper then asked for the post-hypnotic suggestion about smoking which had been given her under hypnosis, and had Coppolino affirm that there had been no order to her to forget the suggestion had been made, and thus she could remember the suggestion when she came out of the trance, and she did stop smoking.

Under questioning, Carl said that he had seen her the following day, "When I was sitting outside in front of my garage on the lounge chair and she drove up in her car and pulled into the driveway."

They had talked, he said, and she had been there for about an hour. "Did she at that time place her hand on your hand while you were sitting out in the driveway?"

"I don't recall that."

"Did you place your hand on her hand?"

"I don't recall that either."

"Do you recall the conversation, or what you were talking about that day?"

"General conversation was about Fort Monmouth because, if I recall correctly, she just came back from shopping at the commissary and I didn't know what a commissary was."

He did not believe he had seen her again that day, but did see her, he thought, the following day again at her house, which, by Keuper's reckoning, would have been the seventh of February. The subject of hypnosis, he said, was brought up, "Only insofar as I asked her had she still not smoked and she said, 'Yes, I haven't had a desire for a cigarette yet.' "

"When did you first become intimate with her, Doctor?"

"That didn't occur until we went to Florida. . . . In April of 1963."

"During the month of February or March of 1963 you were not intimate with Mrs. Farber?"

"No."

"You understand my use of the word intimate, don't you?" This with a contemptuous old testament thunder.

"Quite well," said Dr. Coppolino.

"How did this Florida trip come about?"

"That came about as a joint venture, so to speak. Both Mrs. Farber had her idea of why she wanted to leave and go to Florida, and I had mine."

"What were her ideas? Did she express them to you?"

"Oh yes. Quite profusely."

526

"You tell us what her ideas were, and tell us what your ideas were about this trip to Florida."

"Her ideas were that she wanted to get away from Colonel Farber. They were having quite a bit of marital problems, so much so that it was always quite a tense situation, and they couldn't even have their meals together. The atmosphere in the house was terrible. Victoria and Elizabeth who were their two younger children often would escape downstairs into the TV room and have their dinner down there to avoid the unpleasant scenes that were going on upstairs. Bill was very agitated with Marge. Marge was very agitated with Bill. Both were seeking a divorce action, each for their own separate reasons. And it got to the point where I think everybody was on everybody else's nerves in their house, and she was looking for a change of scene. At this particular time, which was again March or April of 1963, I had been almost exclusively confined to my house because of the cold weather, and because of my coronary condition. Cold weather would exacerbate it. I would feel ill and have to take more nitroglycerin. Time was hanging heavy on my hands and I wanted a change of scenery. Carmela had just gone back to Hoffmann-LaRoche. [after the birth of Lisa Marie in December] . . . She returned to Hoffmann-LaRoche in February 1963, and she could not accompany me on any trip that I would like to take because she couldn't get the time off. But I could not travel by myself because of my past history. I had to have somebody with me. So that is why I say, when I said it was a joint venture, each one had their own idea of why they wanted to take a trip."

"Was this trip discussed with your wife Carmela and also with Colonel Farber before you finally decided to go together?"

"Extensively."

"And they both agreed that the two of you could go off by yourselves?"

"Correct."

"How did you get to Florida?"

Carl testifed that they had flown down, stayed at the Cadillac Motel on North Miami Beach in separate rooms, had stayed about seven to ten days, and during that time had sexual relations.

In comparing Marge Farber's testimony about the trip to Miami and Carl Coppolino's testimony, the way spectators, press and jury inevitably do, it was somewhat like looking at the same scene through two quite different lenses. But through either lens—the hot, misted, wavy lens of the Marjorie view, a merging and confusion of raw color, or the cold, sharp, historical, black-and-white lens of the Coppolino vision—the incongruous

527

soap-opera relationship was the same: the vital, pungent, saucy colonel's lady and the semi-invalid young anesthesiologist, eighteen years her junior, flying off together with the permission of the sedate colonel and the diligent and orderly young Dr. Carmela to that renowned fun-spot in the last month of the sun season. Though Carl's earnest and tidy explanation came closer to creating a suspension of disbelief than had Marjorie's, to any married person in the courtroom who tried to relate such a junket, and such a permissiveness to his or her own situation, the inevitable subjective reaction was, "Oh *come* now!"

With the trip affirmed by the testimony of both witnesses, one needed, as has been said before, to have practiced what the Queen advised Alice, to believe several impossible things before breakfast. No matter how one turned it, shaped it, fitted it, it would not quite go past the barrier of common emotional logic.

"Where was this love plan evolved?"

"There wasn't any love plan."

"No love plan?"

"No."

"You never wrote out any directions as to what Mrs. Farber should do when she returned home?"

"No."

"You never told her that she should occupy a separate bedroom from her husband?"

"No. I didn't care what Mrs. Farber did at her house."

"After you returned from Florida, did you again resume your intimate relations with Mrs. Farber?"

"Not right away."

"How long after?"

"Well, I don't know. Approximately a month."

"You were married at the time, weren't you?"

"Oh yes."

"Your wife was going to work every day?"

"Yes."

"And you were incapacitated because of a heart condition?"

"Correct."

"When for the first time did you discuss with Mrs. Farber that Colonel Farber had to go or had to die?"

"I never discussed it."

"You never did that? Did you ever discuss with Mrs. Farber different ways or means or methods of killing a person?"

"Absolutely not!"

"Did you ever suggest to Mrs. Farber succinylcholine chloride?"

"No."

"A drug that could be used and an overdose would kill and leave no trace in the system?"

"I discussed that drug with Mrs. Farber. Yes."

"Did you ever tell her that the drug could be used and an overdose would kill and cause instant death, and there would be no trace of it left in the system?"

"No. I didn't discuss the drug in that fashion."

Keuper asked him to relate the conversation about the drug.

"Well, Mrs. Farber had a dog named Wolf. Wolf was a collie. This was actually the children's dog. During the early years that they had had it, the dog was hit by a car and it was never quite the same after that. In fact, the dog began to become vicious and have fights with other animals on the street, particularly one dog, a German shepherd that lived next door to me at the Grutzners, called Baron. And these two animals had a fight one day and Wolf really sliced up Baron quite badly, and Marge was upset about this. And she felt that she would like to have Wolf disposed of, but the children loved the dog so much, she couldn't see calling the ASPCA, or giving the dog away because there would be some turmoil in the house, and there was enough turmoil already. So she asked me if I knew any way that we could dispose of this dog." After Keuper had interrupted to place emphasis on his use of the word "we," Carl continued. "I said I didn't have anything, I said. And I said to her, 'I presume you are referring to some sort of needle or drug or agent' and she said yes, and I said No, I didn't have any. I said, 'But if you wish to dispose of the dog, I will try to make arrangements to procure a drug that I think could do the purpose.'"

"And what drug did you have in mind?"

Coppolino testified that he had succinylcholine in mind, that he was familiar with it having administered it while practicing anesthesiology at Methodist Hospital and Riverview, and though he did not know how much an overdose would be, he knew it would kill.

"And at the time wasn't it thought that it would leave no trace in the body?"

"At that time that piece of information I had not available to me."

"Did you *ever* learn that, Doctor?"

"Well, when we read the medical literature about a specialty we learn many things about different drugs."

"Did you ever learn that this drug could not be detected in the system after death?"

"All I learned is that the drug broke down into products that were normal body products, period."

"So if it broke down into normal body products, it could be taken as a normal body product, couldn't it? Isn't this true?"

"It depends on when you take the specimen."

"When you discussed this drug with Mrs. Farber was there any conclusion arrived at, any decision made as to whether or not you should get it for her?"

Dr. Coppolino said that she had thought it a good idea, and so he had called Dr. Webb and asked him to bring some. Keuper asked him if he had not told Webb he wanted to use it to kill a cat. Carl said he hadn't. Keuper asked him if he had listened to the Webb testimony and Coppolino said he believed that Webb stated that the drug was to be used to kill the Farber dog. In four terse answers—No—No—Never did—Never—Carl denied ever giving the drug to Mrs. Farber, instructing her how to use it, giving her a syringe and instructing her in its use.

"What was the purpose of obtaining it if you didn't give it to her?"

"The purpose of obtaining it was for what I already said. However when the drug arrived and we had it, she changed her mind. She didn't want the dog disposed of because Elizabeth heard about the situation that possibly Wolf would 'leave.' How Wolf was going to leave, Elizabeth didn't know, and the children got upset and so the idea was just dropped."

Keuper then asked him if he had kept the drug. Carl Coppolino said he had. Keuper showed him the vial obtained from Webb December 2 and asked if it had been in a container such as that or similar. Similar, Carl said. Asked if he had removed any of it, Carl said he had never opened the container. He did not recall precisely when Webb had delivered it to him, and under repetitive questions again denied delivering it or a disposable hypodermic needle to Marge Farber. He said he believed he'd had the conversation about the drug with Mrs. Farber in June of 1963.

"At any time during June of 1963, did either you or Mrs. Farber suggest that Colonel Farber should die?"

"No."

Keuper stood for a silent moment staring at the accused. In an elaborately sarcastic tone, Keuper said, "That's ridiculous, isn't it?"

"Yes," said the accused calmly with a little affirmative nod.

Keuper then took him over that part of the direct examination dealing with being called to the Farber home, forgetting the medical bag, going back for it, finding the colonel in the condition previously described.

"At any time did Mrs. Farber tell you that she had attempted to inject Colonel Farber?"

"No."

"Did you at any time tell Mrs. Farber that she should take a baseball bat and wrap a towel around it and strike Colonel Farber before she administered this drug to him?"

"No."

After spending a moment going back over where Carl testified he had found the colonel, and how he had helped him into bed, Keuper went off into the question of the visibility of the Farber home from the Coppolino home. He showed Carl the photographs already introduced in evidence, reaffirming the distances and geographical relationships between the two houses. His reason for so doing were not clarified, as he went immediately to the treatment Carl had given the colonel, according to his testimony in the direct examination—Demarol, Pronestyl, Nembutal, Sparine. He went over the time sequence of the visits, and back over Carl's testimony about recommending hospitalization many times.

"Doctor, at any time did you call the First Aid?"

"No."

"At any time did you call in a cardiologist?"

"No."

"You knew cardiologists in Red Bank, didn't you?"

"Yes, very well." He knew Doctors Kelly and Sheehan, who were treating him for his heart ailment.

"But when Colonel Farber refused to go to the hospital you just threw your hands up. That's it?"

"No, I didn't. I spoke to the responsible person. Mrs. Farber."

"Was Mrs. Farber the responsible person?"

"She was the responsible person because her husband, the patient, was ill and he didn't have the full responsibility of making that decision."

"So you thought you had discharged your obligation, Doctor, when you told the responsible person, Mrs. Farber, that he should go to a hospital?"

"I didn't discharge my responsibility. I told them that he should go to the hospital. They refused. I was powerless to do anything."

After quibbling about the semantics of the phrase "discharge of responsibility" and some confusion resulting from Keuper asking about one call on the patient and Coppolino answering

531

about an earlier one, Carl related, "I told them, 'You have to get yourself another doctor. I refuse to assume any responsibility.' "

"And that's when you left?"

"That is correct."

"And at that time his condition indicated that he should go to a hospital, didn't it?"

"It certainly did."

"And you walked out of the house, didn't you, *Doctor?*"

"I could do nothing else."

"I said you walked out and you left the house, didn't you, *Doctor?*"

"With Mrs. Farber."

"And you went back to your house, didn't you, *Doctor?*"

"I did."

"And you wrote out a release, didn't you, *Doctor.*"

"I did."

Keuper showed him the release, dated 1:00 P.M. July 30, 1963, and read it to him. "I hereby release Carl A. Coppolino, M.D. from all responsibility for the care of my husband William Farber. Dr. Coppolino wishes to be released because Colonel Farber refuses to be hospitalized even though he knows he may have had a coronary. Dr. Coppolino only gave emergency care." Keuper asked, "Before Marjorie C. Farber signed this exhibit did you let her read it?"

"Certainly!" Carl said and explained that she also read the rest of his notes on the case. Asked if he had explained to her what it meant, Carl said, "I certainly did, and I also explained to Bill before we left that if he needed any further medical attention he would have to get another doctor. That was the whole reason for that."

"Knowing his condition you didn't return again that afternoon, did you, *Doctor?*"

"I did not. I had withdrawn from the case."

"And you didn't call any other doctor to attend him, did you, *Doctor?*"

"No."

"When for the first time did you tell your wife Carmela that you had attended Colonel Farber?"

Coppolino testified, as in the direct, that he had told Carmela at six in the morning when he had returned from the Farber home. And so, as Keuper pointed out in question form, Carmela had gone to work knowing that Farber had been ill during the night.

"And was it because you had refused to have anything further to do with Colonel Farber that Mrs. Farber called Carmela that evening?"

"I don't know why Mrs. Farber called Carmela that evening."

Keuper showed him the death certificate. Each time he had a physical piece of evidence he stood, toweringly, in front of the seated witness. Affirming that Carmela had signed it, Keuper said, "And she made false statements in this death certificate, didn't she?"

"I don't know what you mean by false."

Keuper said with exasperation, "Well, look at it, Doctor! Read it!"

Keuper pointed out each false statement in the certificate, making Carl testify that they were not true. This was the point in the cross-examination where Carl was the least effective, seeming to make an effort to conceal agitation. And it was at this point that Keuper gave the most convincing impression that he was moving steadily and implacably toward some revelation which would work great damage to the defense case.

"Now, Doctor, why didn't you sign this death certificate?"

"I had withdrawn from this case."

"And that is your only answer?"

"That is right."

"Even though you saw Colonel Farber's dead body when you went back that evening?"

"Yes. I saw Colonel Farber's dead body."

"And that's all your wife saw—was Colonel Farber's dead body when she went there that evening. Is that true?"

"And she never was in attendance on this case, was she?"

"She never saw him alive." [on the day of his death]

"And all the things here that Carmela has said, you did."

"Yes."

"I believe you testified that you did not attend the colonel's funeral?" Carl said that was correct. And with this question it was evident that Vincent Keuper had departed from the question of the signing of the death certificate. In the annotation of chess games, the standard method of comment on an unexpected move by either opponent is to put an exclamation point or a question mark directly after the description of the move. Thus QB-KKt5(?). Then in the footnotes after the complete annotation will appear a comment regarding each move especially marked. A particularly brilliant move may receive (!!) as an award. A particularly disastrous one might merit (??).

The chess game however is all on top of the board, with no factor of chance whatsoever. The courtroom conflict is murky, the strategies indistinct. Entirely aside from any conjecture as to the guilt or innocence of Dr. Carl Coppolino, a comment on this portion of Mr. Keuper's strategy in cross-examination is in order. There was one area of emotional illogic in the story of the release and death certificate as Coppolino had related it. Perhaps, had he been questioned about it, he could have given a suitable explanation for the discrepancy. Keuper had led so carefully up to it, that it is possible he wanted the obvious questions to occur to the jurors—as they did to the newspeople—and let them draw their own conclusions, rather than give the accused any chance to explain away the emotional logic.

He led up to a visible flaw, yet stopped at the last moment and turned away. Again it becomes one of the dangling bits never resolved. The illogic, which Dr. Coppolino was never given a chance to explain, can best be illustrated by inventing a series of questions which might have followed the question, "And all the things in there that Carmela said, you did?" Here no attempt is made to give the answers the defendant might have made.

Your wife held a responsible and well-paid position with Hoffmann-LaRoche, is that true?

In order to perform her duties, it was necessary that she have a license to practice medicine in the State of New Jersey, is that not so?

Are not pharmaceutical houses, by nature of their business, particularly anxious that the highest ethical standards and practices be maintained by their employees of professional status?

Would it not have been a simple matter to prove that your wife was at work on the premises of Hoffmann-LaRoche at the very time when, according to this death certificate, she was attending the deceased?

Is not falsification of a death certificate, knowingly and deliberately, a serious offense within the profession of medicine, with possible loss of her license to practice?

If she had lost her license in New Jersey, is it not probable that her employment at Hoffmann-LaRoche would have been terminated?

Is it not true that after completing this death certificate no attempt was made to file a copy of it with the Office of the County Physician, as is customary and required?

Regardless of whether the failure to file with the County Physician was by innocent oversight or attempt to conceal falsification, is it not reasonable to assume that such failure to

534

file might well have directed special attention to the certification of death had it been discovered?

With a signed release in your possession, and having washed your hands of the case, you were evidently not obligated to sign the death certificate. Is that true?

As she did not attend the deceased during his illness, your wife was not legally entitled to sign the death certificate. Is that true?

If neither you nor your wife had signed the death certificate, certifying that one or the other of you had attended the deceased during his illness, would not certification of the cause of death have been the obligation of the County Physician, and hence based upon an autopsy of the body to determine the cause of death?

You have testified that your refusal to sign the death certificate was based solely upon the fact that you had withdrawn from the case, and so you then had no concern that your total disability policy might be questioned merely because you had given first aid to a sick neighbor in the middle of the night?

Now then, Doctor, as the release in your possession placed you in the clear, can you explain to this jury what special circumstances there were surrounding this sudden death which induced your wife Carmela to take such a dangerous risk to her professional reputation and her important position at Hoffmann-LaRoche?

Did you give your wife any reason to believe that if an autopsy were performed on the body, you and Mrs. Farber might find yourselves in serious trouble, and that the lives of eight living persons—you and your wife and Mrs. Farber and the five children of the two marriages, to say nothing of her parents and yours, might be ruined?

There is nothing in the testimony of the trial to indicate that Dr. Coppolino could not have given a plausible and acceptable response to this line of inquiry. All that is evident is that Vincent Keuper led up to it and then, before trying to nail it down, abandoned it. One possible conclusion is that Mr. Keuper was aware that plausible responses would be forthcoming, and thus preferred to make his point by innuendo. Or it may merely be that when one sits in the stands, it is easy to second-guess the quarterback and score at will from anyplace on the playing field. Often such hindsights are long delayed.

For example, four months later, during the Naples, Florida, trial of Dr. Coppolino, two reporters who had been at the New

Jersey trial were discussing the possibility of Carl being placed on the stand to testify in his own behalf. The cross-examination of Carl Coppolino by Vincent Keuper was discussed, and suddenly one reporter asked the other if the Demarol which Carl had testified that he had given the colonel by intramuscular injection could have also been a practical way to put a pet dog to sleep, inasmuch as it was supposed to be a laboratory version of morphine.

Were such a question to be brought up in an examination of possible guilt or innocence, it would be unfair, as the accused might well have a very rational reason to why it could not be used.

By the same token it is also unfair to say that the question did not occur to Mr. Keuper during his cross-examination of Coppolino. There is no way of knowing but that it did occur to him, and he had excellent reason for not asking it. Hindsight can too often detect oversight where none existed.

Keuper had moved on to the events of the day following the death. Carl said that Marge Farber may have been in his home, but he did not recall her being in the dinette. He denied writing out anything in the dinette in the presence of Mrs. Farber and Dorothy Jeffress the day following the death. "That never occurred."

He said that he was with Marjorie Farber that day. "We went all over. To Fort Monmouth to have Colonel Farber's will processed. We went to Worden's Funeral Home to pick out things. We were busy."

Under questioning Carl said he could remember the big things about that day, such as the funeral home, but not the other things, such as whether or not he had been with Marge in the dinette of his home. He stated that he saw her regularly after the colonel's death.

"Did you continue your intimate relations with her?"

"After a period of time."

"How long did those relations last?"

"On and off for about a year."

"When those relations were severed, you were still living in New Jersey?"

"Yes."

"So that when you moved to Florida that was at an end?"

"Oh, for a long time."

"And both of you knew it was at an end?"

"Oh yes."

"When did you move to Florida?"

536

"April 1965."

"When did Mrs. Farber move to Florida?"

"August 1965."

"When did Carmela die?"

"August 28th, 1965."

"1965?"

"Yes."

"Do you recall seeing Mrs. Farber the afternoon before Carmela's death?"

"Yes."

"Do you recall who was with you at the time you saw her or she saw you?"

"Yes."

"Who?"

"Mary."

"The present Mrs. Coppolino."

"Correct."

"The two of you together?"

"That's right."

"You were seen by Mrs. Farber?"

"Yes."

"Do you know whether or not Mrs. Farber told Carmela that she had seen you and Mary together?"

"Oh yes. She told Carmela."

"Did Carmela tell you that you had been seen with Mary?"

"Well, Carmela already knew I was with Mary."

"I said: Did she tell you that someone had told her?"

"She told me that Marge called her up and told her that: 'I saw Carl with Mary Gibson in the car.' "

"As a result of Carmela telling you that, you called Mrs. Farber on the phone, didn't you?"

"I called Mrs. Farber on the phone."

"What did you say when you called her?"

"First of all, I asked her why did she bother to call Carmela to tell her I was with Mary when she knew all along that Carmela knew that I was playing bridge with Mary, and also that she knew that Mary had been over at our house for lunch."

"During the course of your telephone conversation with Mrs. Farber that night—this is the night preceding Carmela's death— did you tell her that there was a dark cloud over your head?"

"No."

"Did you tell her that you didn't like her Gestapo tactics, her spying on you?"

"I told her I didn't like her spying on me, yes."

"What else did you say, Doctor?"

"I told her that Carmela knew Mary and that it was no surprise for her to find out that I was with Mary."

"Did Carmela also know that you were intimate with Mrs. Farber?"

With brows arched high, Coppolino said, "Not to *my* knowledge, no." He gave additional emphasis to "my" by tapping himself over the heart with the clenched fist of his right hand.

"Did she know you had been out on many occasions with Mrs. Farber?"

"Oh yes."

"Never objected to that?"

"Never."

"Never objected to your being out with Mary?"

"Never." And a sustained objection cut short that direction of query.

Keuper asked when Carl had next spoken to Marge, and he testified that Marge had phoned the house and he had told her that Carmela was dead.

"Do you recall Mrs. Farber saying to you, 'What did you do to her?' "

Bailey's objection was overruled, and Carl said, "Mrs. Farber never made that statment."

"Was Carmela's death discussed with Mrs. Farber on that occasion?" Bailey objected but the question was permitted. Carl said yes. Bailey then asked that that line of questioning be permitted for only a limited purpose.

The judge explained, "We are not, of course, trying the death of Carmela at all. There is no injection into this case whatsoever. This is merely for the purpose of attempting to attack the witness's credibility, and it isn't considered for any other purpose."

When Keuper next asked Carl if he had gone to see the body of his wife after she was laid out at the Shannon Funeral Home in Florida, Carl said he had not and Lee Bailey made firm objection. Keuper informed the Court that there was testimony by Mrs. Farber in the record on that point. Lee Bailey said it was volunteered information, unresponsive, and believed it had been stricken, Keuper said it had not.

"If you are going to make a point of it," said Judge Simmill, "we will look at the record. Is there going to be a point made of it?"

538

"I will drop it," said Keuper, having, of course, made his point.

Exploring Carl's contacts with Marge subsequent to Carmela's death, it was testified that Carl had talked to Marge by phone about a week after the death, and later in person close to three weeks later, about the middle of September.

"And the subject of the conversation was that you had obtained a marriage license to marry Mary Gibson?"

"No."

"Did you obtain the marriage license to marry Mary Gibson?"

"Much later."

"When?"

"September 24th."

"How long after Carmela's death?"

"A little less than a month."

Keuper stood for a few silent moments staring at the accused. Carl stared back at him. "No further questions, *Doctor*," Keuper said and sat down abruptly. The cross-examination had lasted but fifty minutes. So much more had been anticipated, it was an abrupt let-down of almost shocking impact on the press and spectators. A complex trial piles up great stacks of questions one hopes that the accused will answer, and so one hopes he will be put on the stand so that there will be a chance to see what the response will be, to see if there are logical explanations to what seems illogical, to see if contradictions in the testimony of others can be solved by the accused.

The cross-examination seemed to consist of a few random directions of inquiry, none carried to resolution, plus quite an amount of repetition of the testimony given on direct examination. It seemed brief and oblique.

Lee Bailey stood up and conducted a brief redirect. He showed Dr. Coppolino four handwritten sheets of paper which he identified as his notes which he had made at nine o'clock on the morning of July 30th after treating Colonel Farber, and the additional notes he had made after he had received the release from Mrs. Farber early in the afternoon on that same day.

He testified that those notes had been in his possession in early July of 1966, at which time he had turned them over to an attorney in Tampa, Florida, named James McEwen. He said that when he had given them to McEwen they were stapled together, with the release on the bottom, and had been stapled that way ever since July 30, 1963.

"As a physician, Doctor, practicing in the State of New

Jersey, is there any requirement you know of for keeping records of the attendance of a patient?"

"I keep records on all patients."

"Did you do any private work outside of the hospital?"

"No."

"As a matter of habit in the hospital, did you keep notes of observations when treating a patient?"

"Oh yes."

Bailey established that the notes had been given to McEwen before the indictment was returned in from the New Jersey case.

Keuper had some questions to ask before the papers were marked in evidence. He leafed through the sheets, having Carl restate which portion had been written at which time.

He read the last paragraph, "I made Mrs. Farber sign the release, and told Bill to get another physician."

"Correct."

"You signed it Carl A. Coppolino?"

"Yes."

"That is an accepted practice and procedure for physicians to record a complete history of everything said by the patient, and anybody present at the time of the treatment?"

"Especially if they think another attending doctor would be called in and would want the information."

"You have gone into great detail and put in your report for your own records things said by the patient and things said by those who were present?"

"Yes."

"Even the fact that you obtained a release from Mrs. Farber?"

"Yes."

Keuper then said he had no objection to the papers being marked in evidence. There were no further questions by Mr. Bailey or by Mr. Keuper. The witness was excused. It was twelve past noon.

After Mr. Bailey had straightened out some of the matters concerning the other exhibits, and had the Musetto letter and the Louise Dennis letter marked in evidence, he said, "The defense rests."

Both attorneys were standing. The Court asked, "Is there any rebuttal?"

And in the press section, in an innocence of expectation, notebooks were turned to a fresh page.

"No rebuttal," said Mr. Keuper.

And so, except for final arguments and then the jury verdict, it was over. All the evidence was in.

540

At first the court was recessed until two in the afternoon, but when Judge Simmill discovered that the defense had requests for material to be included in the charge to the jury, but had not yet prepared such paragraphs, though in New Jersey they are supposed to be handed up at the close of the testimony, the recess was extended until the following morning.

There was an air of bafflement and confusion among the press. The end seemed to have come all too abruptly.

Jack Cole, a commentator from Channel 3 in Philadelphia had been covering the trial. At twelve-thirty he tracked Keuper to the prosecutor's office and later reported the following conversation with Mr. Keuper, after Cole had asked him what he thought the verdict might be.

"I'm in pretty good shape," Mr. Keuper said. "You want to know why?"

"Yes."

"Because he never denied he put the plastic bag over his head."

"What?"

"Because he never denied that business about the plastic bag and strangling him. There's testimony in the record about that and he's never denied it."

Jack Cole, who has a law degree, knew precisely what Keuper meant and what the implications were. But when he told other newspeople about it, they were inclined to believe Keuper had been putting Cole on. But the courtroom lawyers at the bar at the American Hotel explained that Vincent Keuper was indeed quite serious in his belief that it gave him an advantage in the closing argument.

It was in truth an ancient weapon of prosecutors back in those less sophisticated days, not really very many years ago, when thunderous rhetoric could be more persuasive than an exercise of logib. The way to counteract this prosecution device in those cases where the accused took the stand was for the defense counsel to make certain he asked the defendant if he had indeed committed the crime in question, in painful detail. [Did you pick up the gun? Did you aim it at the deceased? Did you then pull the trigger? Did you fire the shot that killed the deceased?]

Lee Bailey had not covered this conventional gambit in his direct examination, and one might suspect that it was not through oversight. And so it gave Vincent Keuper a chance to proclaim that on the stand both in direct and cross-examination, the accused had never denied killing Colonel Farber. It was hoped that the jury would skip over the awkward little matter of a person being unable to answer a question they had not been asked, and leap immediately to the personalized conclusion that had they been an innocent accused and had a chance to get on the stand, they would have certainly let the world know they hadn't killed anybody, loudly and clearly.

As in most of the other inexact sciences, criminal prosecution is an area wherein the device sometimes achieves an inflated importance while the reality is forgotten.

Directly after lunch F. Lee Bailey repaired with Joseph Afflitto and Joseph Mattice to one of the old residential suites adjoining the hotel where one of the people covering the trial had installed, on the kitchen table, the same kind of typewriter Bailey most often used, an IBM Selectric with carbon ribbon and Courier type face.

There he sat, and with the occasional suggestion from his associates, he neatly and rapidly and expertly typed the suggested paragraphs for inclusion in the judge's charge, provided the judge approved them.

It was quite evidently a new side of the many-sided Lee Bailey, one which up to that point his associates had not been aware of.

There was the rapid clacking, the infrequent pause to select a word, once in a while a minor correction. The crisp end product was entirely in order for presentation to the Court.

"You know," said Joe Afflitto musingly, "it certainly would be one big fat advantage of any lawyer to be able to do that himself when he has to."

Chapter Thirty-one

F. Lee Bailey began his summation to the jury at nine-thirty. As the court reporter did not transcribe this portion of the trial, and as a substantial portion of Lee Bailey's summation was extemporaneous, the only source is the news coverage as taken from the reporters' notes.

He began in a low key, quiet, conversational, moving casually about in front of the jury rail, addressing himself to the individual jurors in a random selection which, by the time he had finished must have meant he had, in effect, spoken at least thrice to each one of them, and by his directness of gaze and mobility of expression, reaffirming that highly personal communication he had established with each of them during the *voir dire*.

He explained that the jury should realize that when he was finished the state would have the right to speak to them, and thus held the power of rebuttal. He said that perhaps some of them might have been disturbed by his sarcastic handling of Marge Farber, the state's key witness.

Then he began to be more emphatic. "This case is not a case at all! In the same words she used to the reporter from Florida, this was 'something dreamed up.' "

". . . There is of course the honorable science of hypnosis. The only evidence regarding the so-called magical powers of the black art came from the defense. Without it, you would have had no explanation at all of the science of suggestion . . ."

". . . The state would have you believe that the practitioners of this recognized medical science are forever ready, at their whim, to turn their victims to homicide. I ask you to use your collective memory, the combined power of the memory of twelve people to dtermine if there was any expert testimony which could possibly be interpreted to permit such a take-over . . ."

". . . Marjorie Farber speaks of mystic powers and strange compulsions, of a black cloud, of exotic electricity, not that simple chemistry that draws woman to man. She calls it a black power . . ."

Lee Bailey next had the control—and the impudence—to risk a bawdy pun.

"Marjorie Farber's troubles began with her tale . . . (hesitation) . . . of woe." The timing was elegant. The hesitation was sustained long enough to convey his meaning to the more sophisticated jurors, but did not last long enough to clue those others who could have been offended by ribaldry.

Then in a truly savage and biting sarcasm, and raising his voice to oratorical pitch to heighten the effect, he declaimed, ". . . she would have the world believe that out of her slumber comes the robot, the automaton, guided and directed by that master of the black art, her controller! Her convenience of slipping in and out of hypnosis exceeded only by the convenience of her forgetful memory!"

He then recounted the circumstances of the alleged murder, at one point taking the container of Anectine out of his pocket. He said after the trial that he had also been carrying a dental floss container around for several days, thinking there might be some

543

chance of using it in effective comparison, but had decided against it.

". . . Of the medications administred to Colonel Farber, any of those drugs given in quantities beyond the tolerance of the human body would be fatal. Yet she has him resorting to the pillow, which was jolly, but why didn't Carl Coppolino use some available undetectable method on this ailing man? . . ."

". . . We saw the remarkable convenience of her memory when suddenly, right on the stand, she 'remembered' something about an autopsy for the very first time . . ."

"Would it not be more plausible if, after the ghastly deed, this grim reaper should have escaped into the hills with his bounty, the fruits of this driving love? But instead we have him driving around from the military base to the funeral home, helping with the homely neighborly details of death."

". . . The Widow Farber, enriched by fifty thousand dollars in insurance, followed Doctor Coppolino to Florida, and like a swarm of locusts, descending on the defendant after the death of his wife, and when she finds she cannot have him, her reprisals begin apace in an old and classic story: If I can't have you . . ."

He put heavy emphasis on the Louise Dennis letter wherein Mrs. Farber complained about Carl's treatment of her, and underlined her attempted persecution of Dr. Coppolino.

". . . This woman who goes for all or nothing, her story is not persuasive. It is an agony of contradiction. Carl Coppolino does not forget like Marge Farber does. She called him up and asked him what would happen if they dug up Bill. Only an innocent man would have said, as he did, 'What do I care?' Once she had gone to the police with her preposterous story, from then on, Marge had only to ride with the waves, having set in motion against the accused that lop-sided power, that behemoth, the State of New Jersey . . ."

". . . You have seen how she was trapped into denying her own signature. The prosecution was good enough to put on a witness who had seen her sign the release. It need not concern us too much that the obliging witness had the time wrong . . ."

". . . If Dorothy Jeffress had not appeared for the State, she would have appeared for the defense . . ."

". . . Then into the picture sails Doctor Helpern, a take-over sort of guy, a man given to ungenerous and dangerous opinions. 'You don't have to be concerned about the witness,' he told us. 'The injury speaks for itself.' This Grand Opinion, when challenged, crumbles down and is meaningless. Doctor Helpern was geographically boxed by expert witnesses . . ."

544

". . . The body of Colonel Farber has been disgraced by this exhumation. What kind of a woman would unfold this grisly story to the daily tabloids and put her children through the ordeal? Yet a woman with two teen-age daughters spilled this mess . . ."

"And maybe she spilled the beans when on the stand she told us of 'the other me.' We have no evidence that Marge snuffed him out." He lowered his voice to almost a whisper and said, "I wonder if she just let him die. I wonder if she just let him die . . . out of *spite!*"

". . . but there is the problem of the colonel's body . . . dug up in a cursory fashion. They had problems. He had been there years in a wooden box. I don't know and I don't care if the cricoid was fractured there at the exhumation, or if it was fractured earlier. We know that it was fractured after death . . . We're stuck with whatever story they throw at us, and that included the time of death . . ."

". . . Doctor Musetto is a man entitled to some sorrow, I suppose. But he had no compunction about putting his daughter's memory on the line for a couple of thousand dollars . . ."

". . . We have heard Prosecutor Keuper ask an expert in medical hypnosis if the prosecutor could be made to stand upon his head." And here was Bailey, the phrase-maker at his ironic best as he said, "The intricacy of that spectacle would be heartwarming, but I doubt that it could be done . . ."

". . . If hypnosis were what Marge Farber would have us believe it is, you would now be feeling a compulsion in favor of the defendant . . ."

"As to Marge's re-enactment of the deadly drama, it becomes quite obvious that one cannot get the heels of the hands on the cricoid from the position she described. I doubt that your human experience would enable you to comprehend the malice of a Marjorie Farber. She comes on like Sarah Bernhardt, crying, but unschooled in the art of drama . . ."

". . . As a trial draws to a close, the counsel for the defense will always ask himself, 'Have I done enough?' In times past there were giants of the bar who could sway juries with oratory. But the juries of today are too educated to allow preposterous theories to be rammed down their throat . . ."

"Yes, I put the defendant on the stand, perhaps unnecessarily." He struck a commanding pose and, frowning, said in oratorical style, "You might hear something like this: The defendant never denied his guilt!" He shrugged and in the voice of reason said, "The defendant can speak only like any other person who took that stand. And when he hasn't had an opportunity to answer a question, it is because the prosecution did not wish to hear the answer . . ."

He clamped his hands on the rail and leaned toward the jury, and gave a grinding weight to his closing words: "There is *nothing* to connect the defendant with a homicide, indeed if there ever *was* one!"

Bailey's summation had lasted fifty-five minutes.

Vincent Keuper began his summation immediately. He planted himself in front of the jury and moved very little during his shorter summation. At times he made conventional and pre-planned oratorical gestures. He seemed to address himself to an abstraction called The Jury, as opposed to Lee Bailey's wandering, turning, abrupt style of seeming to address first one juror, then another.

". . . When I prepared this case I made a determination to ask for the maximum penalty. After listening to all the evidence I am *convinced* that Coppolino should die! In twelve years as your prosecutor I have never been as certain of guilt. The defense has supplied me with so much testimony I will take more time than usual."

"I hold no brief for Mrs. Farber. Mrs. Farber is not on trial here today, or in the whole case. I hold no brief for her and will make no attempt to defend her. To me her acts are disgusting, deplorable and disgraceful. I would go so far as to say both of them conspired to kill Colonel Farber . . ."

"I brought no expert on hypnosis. I knew the defense would. But before this trial began I had acquired more knowledge of hypnosis than I may have seemed to possess during the trial. I agree that suggestion is the catalyst required. I agree that you cannot hypnotize anyone to perform an act unless he or she wants to do that act. If the desire to murder is lying dormant in my mind and I am given the proper suggestion, then I will kill . . ."

". . . In this case we had a willing suspect. She hated her husband. She wanted to kill her husband. Coppolino told her to. She reached the brink and prepared the solution, and rebelled, although she wanted to and had been told to. She could go just so far. She couldn't do it. And that's the end of the importance of hypnosis in this case . . ."

". . . This man is a clever man at suggestion. During the course of the interrogation of jurors, Mr. Bailey asked if the jurors would hold it against the defendant if he failed to take the stand, and, on the stand, to admit or deny he committed murder.

He took the stand, and was never asked, nor testified nor denied killing Colonel Farber. That is damaging testimony because it is absent testimony . . ..''

". . . The accused is a man with a talent to treat and help people. He is called in. He administered a number of drugs, and observed the patient. And then he walked away and took the only person in attendance with him. He left the man to die . . . *or left him dead!* When they left, Colonel Farber was dead, and they went to the Coppolino home and wrote out his death warrant . . .''

"What doctor would walk out on a patient and not try to provide some help? Do you just walk out and leave him to die? Would you call the doctors at Fort Monmouth and tell them? No, Coppolino does not do that. Nothing was done by this man because he had to go home and start preparing his defense against murder . . . Because that is the start of the defense. At that time Doctor Coppolino did not trust Mrs. Farber. He did not know at what time she would blow the whistle. He got her to sign the release and thought 'Ah! Now I'm home free!' but in doing so he signed his own death warrant . . .''

He spoke of Bailey's numerous promises to connect things up, and of Bailey's promise to produce Mr. Shannon. There was a heavy-handed sarcasm in his voice.

"Doctor Milton Helpern, an eminent physician and pathologist, was *not* called as a professional witness to answer hypothetical questions. Doctor Helpern is the one who performed the autopsy, who took the body apart. His was the testimony of a man who examined and demonstrated and explained. He showed you heart channels seventy-five percent open, normal for a man of the colonel's age. He wanted to show you every part of the evidence. The other pathologists had the same opportunity to use the same slides and the same projector to show you just how they thought the arteries were blocked. Why didn't they do so?''

"We had other experts who examined the larynx for five minutes and gave their 'expert' testimony. One of them based his testimony on a single nosebleed. The nose is so full of blood vessels it will bleed if you blow it too hard. You heard Helpern say that he found a brownish stain on the larynx, but he would not identify it as blood because he could not be *absolutely* sure . . .''

"But we are trying Carl Coppolino, not expert witnesses. Marjorie Farber testified that after the death of her husband, she talked to the defendant on the night preceding his wife's death.

Coppolino complained to her about her Gestapo tactics. That following morning Carmela died.''

F. Lee Bailey jumped up swiftly and with what appeared to be anger, made loud objection and moved that Keuper's last comment be stricken from the record. Judge Simmill overruled the objection and asked both attorneys to approach the bench. A whispered conference went on for possibly two minutes, then both men resumed their places as before and Keuper continued.

''. . . And shortly thereafter, Mrs. Farber and Coppolino talked again, and a few days subsequent to that he procured a license to marry another woman. He procured it less than thirty days after the death of his wife . . .''

''Not only was Carl Coppolino successful in suggesting things for Mrs. Farber to do, but also for his wife to do. She lied for him. She supplied false information. And why was it that Coppolino did not sign the certificate? Why did he say? 'I gave up the case. I walked out on it.' Of the two of them, Coppolino and his wife, he was the only one who knew anything about it. He arranged for Marjorie Farber to call Carmela. Both Mrs. Farber and Coppolino thought the colonel had been smothered. It wasn't until the autopsy that strangulation was determined as the actual cause of death . . .''

''I accepted the responsibility of asking for the death penalty. Now that responsibility shifts to you, to share with eleven others. That state has proved Carl Coppolino willfully, feloniously and with malice aforethought killed and murdered Colonel William E. Farber. Under *no* circumstances shall you permit him to walk out of this courtroom a free man.''

It was then ten minutes before eleven. Keuper's summation had lasted twenty-five minutes. Judge Simmill called a recess and said that the court would reconvene at quarter after eleven.

During the recess the standard diversion of guessing which side was in the lead was suddenly far less academic. The returns were in. Except for the judge's charge, the jury had everything they were ever going to have, as a basis for their vote.

The disparity between the various corridor opinions was startling and astonishing, ranging from acquittal in fifteen minutes, to guilty in ten minutes, to a hung jury in three days.

''Here in Monmouth County,'' said an area reporter, ''the good old rule of thumb is they stay out for one hour for each day of trial. So they'll be out four hours, and then they'll come in with first degree, because Vince isn't likely to win thirty-three in a row and lose this one.''

If one circulated and picked up a wide spectrum of opinion, a certain pattern began to appear. Among attorneys, and among newspeople with a legal background, and among newspeople who had attended a great many murder trials, they thought Bailey was very probably home free. You can never be certain, they said. Some mulehead could hang the jury up. But it looked like not proven, with a verdict by evening sometime.

At eleven-fifteen court reconvened and Judge Elvin Simmill gave his charge to the jury. He spoke with a persuasive directness and ease that would have seemed almost informal were it not for the careful structuring of his sentences, and a few elegant and ornamental turns of phrase a man of his intellect would inevitably add to any prepared material, even if it were only a letter to a friend.

Much of such a charge to any jury in a capital case is required by law. Certain things must be said. However, it seems a pity that in this country, as opposed to the procedure in Great Britain, the trial judge is not permitted to make comment upon the specific evidence and testimony presented, weighing, appraising and evaluating it in the light of the law. In England, after a complex case, the judge's charge to the jury may last many hours, and serves as a review of all pertinent matters introduced during the course of the trial.

For example, when a Dr. Adams was tried in England for the murder of an elderly patient, a Mrs. Morell, the judge's charge lasted the better part of two days. Here is a portion of it, to show in what detail the testimony is discussed in capital cases in England:

"The Attorney-General has laid stress on the statements the doctor made to Superintendent Hannam, and some of them are difficult to justify on the evidence as we know it now: that she was in 'terrible agony' at the end, for example. We know very clearly now that she was not. Prhaps that was a lapse of memory and quite understandable. But, again, you might have liked to have heard his own explanation about it. You might have liked to have heard, too, his own explanation about 'easing the passing,' a phrase which might be used quite innocently, but, on the other hand, a phrase which might perhaps go further. However, you must take into account not isolated phrases but the trend of his statements on the whole, and it seems to me that the statements as a whole do show from the beginning to the end that it had never crossed his mind that he was faced, or might be faced, with the charge of murdering Mrs. Morell."

And, in discussing the matter of case record notebooks kept by the nurses, the judge dealt with a seeming oversight on the part of defense counsel: "Mr. Lawrence has not anticipated the point and he did not deal with it in his final address to you; but if he had he might perhaps have asked a rhetorical question too. 'What does the prosecution say these books prove—innocence or guilt? If guilt, why did the doctor preserve them? If they prove innocence, then surely it does not matter where they came from or who has been keeping them.' "

Obviously this additional leeway on the part of the trial judge imposes greater responsibility. He is, in a sense, intruding into the process of jury deliberation, yet must take care to do so with maximum fairness to both prosecution and defense. The role of the English judge, in the words of Charles Dickens, is that of "turning the suit of clothes now inside out, now outside in."

In this book something of the same stature as the English charge to the jury has been attempted, to take evidence and testimony and examine it from opposite directions, from the presumption of guilt and the presumption of innocence, using both the facts as presented, and the emotional logic of the actions of the parties concerned as guides to these conflicting assumptions. But the purpose is not that of establishing either alternative, but merely to show how an adversary proceeding is but the process of presenting evidence in such a manner that a jury will decide which assumption is most plausible. When matters of evidence can be interpreted in only one way, the result must be either a dismissal of charges, or a confession of guilt, and there will be no trial.

Judge Simmill told the jurors that their recollections of the evidence and testimony in the courtroom would take precedence over the summations as given by both sides, and over the judge's charge to them. They would pay no heed to any mannerisms by the judge which they might have thought significant, no heed to what objections he sustained and overruled, no heed to prior news media coverage, no heed to the Florida indictment against the defendant.

He told them that their first task in their deliberations would be to decide if there had been a murder, or if the death of the colonel had been by natural causes. Murder is the killing of a reasonable person by an act of violence. Should they decide murder had been done, they should then proceed to decide whether the defendant had committed it, and acquit him if they believed it had not been proven beyond a reasonable doubt, and convict him if it had been proven beyond such doubt.

"Reasonable doubt is not mere possible or imaginary doubt,

but that state of mind which exists after all the facts of the case are considered, an abiding conviction of the moral certainty of the charge. The law does not require proof of an absolute certainty, merely proof to the extent that the actions of the defendant are inconsistent with any other rational theory."

He defined the legal differences between first and second degree murder, telling them that in the case of any doubt as to between the degree, in case of conviction, they were to find the defendant guilty in the lesser degree.

He reminded them of the "cloak of innocence" to be enjoyed by the defendant until a verdict was returned. He mentioned the testimony of Marjorie Farber only to say that they were to weigh her testimony in the light of her credibility, and later along pointed out that they were entitled to believe a portion of the testimony of any witness, and were not bound by any stipulation to either believe all, or nothing at all.

He spoke of premeditation, pointing out that there was no limit of the time required by which design must precede murder, but that merely it must precede it by some unit of time. "It matters not how brief it is."

He spoke of the testimony of the expert witnesses, saying that the jurors were to give due consideration to the demeanor and the consistency of all expert witnesses in determining to what degree they would find their testimony credible. Expert witnesses, he said, "Are to provide aid, not domination; to enlighten but not to control."

"The judge is the judge of the law; the jury is the judge of the facts."

Using one of the paragraphs submitted by the defense, he reminded the jury that when the defendant took the stand, "he was not permitted to volunteer anything, but required only to answer the questions put to him by the defense and the state."

He closed by asserting once again that they were to review the facts in order to arrive in their decision, and were charged to avoid making any decision based upon "passion, bias, prejudice or sympathy with either the defendant or the deceased."

The charge to the jury took thirty minutes. At quarter to noon the bailiff put the fourteen names in the wire cage and spun it and took out the first name, the name of the juror who, by lot, would be the foreman. The first name was George Phillips, the Ukrainian mining engineer employed by Anaconda who had said, "I step off the line myself sometime." F. Lee Bailey had said during the jury selection, momentarily forgetting the New Jersey numbers game, "There's my foreman!"

The other eleven names were drawn. Philibert, Ellis, Treger, Lingenfelter, Snyder, Jerram, Salisbury, Samsel, Schwartz, Pleshko and Loosch.

The destiny of the anesthesiologist was to be determined by a young ice-cream manufacturer, a Methodist clergyman, a junior executive with Western Electric, a registered nurse, a lineman for a utility company, an accountant, a mining engineer, a television engineer, a retired plant manager, a highway engineer, a housewife and a plant foreman.

By the luck of the draw the two left over, who would be the alternates and be sequestered until the verdict was returned, in the event one of the twelve would become ill, were Mrs. Marjorie McFadden, the working wife, a clerk-stenographer at the Army base, and Mrs. Marian DePagnier, the machine operator who had been the only one selected by Lee Bailey with no *voir dire*.

The jury had become a single organism, and suddenly and shockingly there was an amputation and the two women stood apart, side by side, their expressions strained and troubled, their eyes moist.

One tried later to describe how she had felt as name after name was called, with each name increasing her chance of becoming an alternate. "I don't know *how* I felt. I didn't want to have to decide such a thing, but I wanted to know just how everyone felt. After all, you spend all this time and . . . you're a part of it and then you're not. You don't have a vote. I felt sort of . . . a wonderful relaxation and relief, and at the same time I felt left out of everything, and sort of foolish and irritated. We'd kidded about it, you know. Everybody said they *wanted* to be an alternate, but . . . maybe nobody really did. It's sort of like . . . having to leave before the movie is over because you have to take the sitter home."

At 11:53 the jury retired to begin deliberation. They took all the documents entered in evidence into the jury room with them. The door was closed. The bailiff stood outside the door. The jury did not take another piece of evidence into the jury room. It rested on the floor just outside the door, afloat in a glass jar—the larynx of Colonel William Farber, AUS Ret.

The spectators stayed in their seats. Carl Coppolino was not returned to the jail, but was taken down to a small detention cell on the ground floor of the courthouse. The defense team and a good portion of the press drove down the hill to the American Hotel. The newspeople who left the courthouse area kept careful tabs on the whereabouts of F. Lee Bailey, knowing that once the jury knocked on the door and announced they had reached a verdict, they would be held in the jury room until the attorneys and the defendant took their places in the courtroom.

Twenty-three dollars were collected from reporters for a pool on the jury. It is bad form and not acceptable to wager on the verdict. But it is acceptable practice to make up a pool on how long the jury will be out, regardless of verdict. The elapsed time was from when the jury retired, at 11:53, to when the foreman would announce that a verdict had been reached.

Twenty-two of the wagers covered the time span from forty-five minutes to eight hours and thirty-seven minutes. One off-beat bet was placed for forty-two hours. It is intriguing to note that with the off-beat bet left out of the tabulation, the average of the remaining twenty-two guesses came to four hours and thirty-one minutes. The jury remained out for four hours and thirty-four minutes.

The winner—who guessed 4:33—was Ed Linn, the journalist then involved in doing a biography of F. Lee Bailey.

After lunch when one might reasonably assume that the defense team would have adjourned to the bar lounge for refreshment where they could await the call from the courthouse in comfortable surroundings, F. Lee Bailey instead gathered up the group—Mary, Teri Plaut, Joe Afflitto, Andy Tuney, Ed Linn—and went back up to the courthouse, saying, "It isn't going to help Carl's morale any to know we're waiting it out in a bar. He's up there, and that's where we should be."

And so on that gray damp December Thursday, everyone went back up the hill to the courthouse. The newspeople drifted about. For a time F. Lee Bailey paced slowly and rather theatrically up and down the corridor outside the courtroom, hands locked behind his back, leather heels striking the tiled floor heavily and audibly, as he discouraged anyone who tried to fall in step with him to ask questions.

The spectators occupied all available seats, waiting in a buzzing and deadly patience. The majority of them expected a guilty verdict, and they knew that when it came they would be able to watch the accused, and watch his wife, and watch his mother, and thus witness at close range a memorable anguish. Happy endings, so compulsory in escapist entertainment, are far less intriguing in life. People gather in the street and stare up at a sick human on a high and naked ledge, and chant, "Jump! Jump!"

There was a young mother with two small children out in the corridor, with no chance of getting a seat. The small children were tired, bored and they whined constantly. She was heard to tell them, "But we can't go home until grandma comes out of that room, honey. We have to wait for your grandma." And grandma was going to wait for the verdict.

The press people went up and down the stairs from press room to corridor to snack bar. Tension was a very tangible thing, expressed in smiles too quick and broad, jokes too sick, laughter too abrupt.

The television networks had arrived. Three big vans, importantly labeled, and crammed with electronic gear had taken up position widely spaced around the perimeter of the courthouse grounds. NBC, ABC, CBS. The network research people infiltrated the groups of newspaper people who had been with the trial since the beginning. This is called instant research, a suitable preparation for instant news, for something totally safe, totally shallow, that will take up thirty seconds of air time on network news and be forgotten as soon as it is said.

One evidence of how inadequately the television news programs prepare themselves for this kind of news is their willingness to move in, with lights and camera, when a principal in one of these trial dramas is being interviewed by the press. As the TV-men do not know what questions should be asked, and the newspaper people do, they let the newspaper people ask the questions, and in that sense they hitchhike on the interview and, more often than not, are on the air before the newspapers containing the interview hit the streets.

As the pictures and the sound are both going onto the film strip, it becomes a curious kind of plagiarism. Today one does not see anywhere near as much of this on network time as was possible a year or so ago. The reason is that the hard-nosed newspaper people, realizing that they were being unfairly used by another media in competition with theirs, came up with a curiously effective defense.

They merely began to salt their questions here and there with a few earthy expressions, of Anglo-Saxon derivation, unsuitable for television broadcast. "Mr. Bailey, is Dr. Sheppard ———ed off at the treatment he got in the papers this time?" "What the ——— does Dr. Sam plan to do now that it's all over?" "Is he going to sue the Cleveland papers, or doesn't he give a ———?"

The roars of indignation from the television crew have been ample proof of the effectiveness of the device. Of late the television people have to conduct their own interviews, and find out in advance what questions to ask.

*   *   *

554

Bailey paced. Mary Coppolino sat alone in the courtroom inside the rail. A little before four o'clock Bailey got word that the bailiff on guard outside the jury room had heard the jurors laughing. He had that information verified and then he seemed to relax. "We're in," he said. "They'll be out soon now. They're staying in there just long enough to dignify the verdict."

At nearly four-thirty the Court was ready for the verdict. The jurors had announced at four-thirty that they had reached a verdict. There must have been, for the first time, over eighty spectators and press combined. The bailiff at the rear door had relaxed the rules, stipulating only that people had to be sitting down. So each two chairs held more than two people. Carl Coppolino was brought in, accompanied by the warden and four uniformed guards. There were then seven uniformed guards in the courtroom.

As soon as Judge Simmill had taken his seat at the bench and the court had been called to order, the judge said very firmly, "There will be *no* demonstration in this courtroom when the verdict is delivered."

He asked that the jury be brought in. Everyone watched intently as they filed into the box, to see if any of them looked at Carl Coppolino. There is the totally unfounded belief that when a jury brings in a guilty verdict, no juror will look at the defendant. To those assembled it appeared that not one of them looked toward Coppolino, but later Coppolino was to say that to his enormous relief the Reverend Snyder gave him a quick glance, and a fleeting half-smile.

The jurors names were called off. Asked for the verdict, Foreman George Phillips, standing, said, "We, the jury, find the defendant Carl Coppolino not guilty."

There was a strange sound from the spectator section, a sound unlike the sounds we are accustomed to hear from audiences. This was a single animal sound, half-grunt and half-sigh, impossible to identify by putting the tag of a single emotion upon it. Shock, regret, dismay, release of tension, all those and something more—something far more primitive.

Anna Coppolino turned abruptly in her chair inside the court railing and began weeping on the shoulder of Mrs. Teri Plaut. Mary, her eyes filling with tears, stared at the back of her husband's head as he stood facing the bench.

The strange and murmurous sound stopped when Judge Simmill said sharply, "All right! there will be no demonstration!" He thanked the jury and dismissed them, saying, "I strongly suggest to you that if somebody tries to talk to you, merely tell them that you do not care to discuss the matter." (of what had gone on in the jury room)

This seemed to amuse some of the jurors, who smiled as they filed out, perhaps wryly aware of the intensity of the pending inquisition from wives and husbands and friends.

Lee Bailey was on his feet immediately to ask that his client be released, as the $15,000 bail set by the State of Florida on the second indictment had already been posted.

Judge Simmill replied that he had no authority to release Coppolino, as the Governor of New Jersey had agreed to turn Coppolino over to the Florida authorities immediately after the disposition of the New Jersey case, and that this agreement had been made with the Governor of Florida in conjunction with the rendition warrant. Judge Simmill gave the impression that he agreed with Bailey that the procedure did not make much sense under the circumstances, but he had no authority to order the release of the acquitted man. At Bailey's request that Carl Coppolino be sent back to Florida quickly, Sheriff Paul Kernan informed the bench that he had deputized Chief of Detectives John Gawler to fly to Florida the next day with Coppolino under his custody.

Judge Simmill adjourned the court. Anna Coppolino was the first person to reach Carl. Carl was suddenly hunched by spasmodic sobbing and, weeping, his face mottled red and white, as he reached out to her he said in a choking voice, "Momma, I didn't do it."

Next, still crying, he held Mary in his arms, and to her he said, "I never did anything."

Then they took him out to the familiar van in the dusk, past clamoring, excited teenagers, and took him down to his cell in the Monmouth County Jail, where on this final night there would be no "suicide guard" posted just outside the bars, watching him continuously.

Night comes quickly in mid-December. Near the big television network vans, the camera lights made glaring islands of white in the darkness, and the directors and newscasters snared everyone they felt might contribute anything of the slightest interest, running off hundreds and hundreds of feet of film of which only a very small fraction would ever be telecast.

At the front of the courthouse, far from the television trucks, Vincent Keuper came out into the night, a tall man in a dark overcoat and dark brown felt hat, briefcase in hand. He came down the wide stone steps completely alone, walked to his car and got in and, still alone, drove off toward home.

556

By six o'clock the paneled bar lounge at the American Hotel was crammed full of people. Every chair at every table was occupied. The bar was lined four and five deep, with six bartenders working at top speed. Every other inch of space was full of people standing in tight conversational groups, leaning toward each other and roaring at each other, nose to nose, in order to be heard over the din. The air, heavy with body heat, was sour blue with cigarette smoke. Flash bulbs and strobe lights winked almost constantly. These were local lawyers, press, radio, television, magazines, defense team, sightseers, courthouse personnel, and even two of the jurors, bellied up to the bar, cheerfully answering any and all questions. People leaned against people, grinning, sweating, shouting, drinking—all in the release of tension. The crowd around Lee Bailey was the thickest and most insistent, thrusting menus, paper napkins, even dollar bills toward him, demanding his autograph. He signed amiably enough. In face and posture he looked jaded, let-down, as if too many resources had been spent too quickly.

As he reached for a slip of paper to sign another autograph he noticed that it was being handed him by one of his wife's two aunts who had come over from New York City for the end of the trial.

"Come *on!*" Lee Bailey said. "You can get this anytime."

"It's for a friend," she explained. "And I didn't want to forget to get it."

Lee Bailey was too harassed to notice that there was already some writing on the slip of paper. He learned later in the evening what the other writing said. "I promise to buy my wife, Wicki, a mink coat for Christmas 1966." And he did.

There seemed to be a great many pictures being taken of people kissing people in the heat of celebration.

The switchboard at the hotel was jammed with incoming long-distance calls from all over the country, calls of congratulation as the news media spread the word of another Bailey victory.

Lee Bailey gave two more pieces of newsworthy information to the press. He announced that the Florida case was so weak he doubted that the state would ever take it to trial. He announced that Carl Coppolino was entering suit against Marjorie Farber for one million dollars for malicious persecution.

There was little if any rehashing of the case. It seemed almost as if all the sideline analyses that had gone on during the trial had given everyone enough of the second-guessing game.

The press had wormed the story of the deliberations out of

557

several of the jurors. As is usually the case, there were conflicts, and the newspaper people pooled their information and decided which story seemed most authentic and plausible and filed that one, so as to avoid contradicting one another.

Most probably there had been five ballots, on whether the colonel had died of heart disease or had been strangled. The first was 8 voting that it was a natural death, 3 voting for strangulation and guilt, 1 undecided. And then it went 9 to 3, 10 to 2, 10 to 2, 12 to 0.

The Bailey group, with all those of the news media and related pursuits who were deemed acceptable guests at the more private celebration upstairs ("the ones in the white hats") began to untangle themselves from unlikely acquaintanceships and eerie conversations in the bar and go on up to where the chilled champagne was being opened. It is fair to say that quite a number wished the next day that they had stopped off in the hotel dining room between the festivities in the bar and the upstairs party.

The upstairs arena consisted of several rather small, low-ceilinged rooms that opened into what had been for a time a small club, and was used for private parties. The ceilings were very low. The lights were dim. Smoke hung in layers. A grinning Joe Afflitto sat with Wicki Bailey on one knee and Teri Plaut on the other, while the women gave him a cold champagne shampoo, the traditional rite of the pennant winner. Most of the conversations were so simultaneous that no one heard much of what anyone else was saying. Many glasses were raised to "good old Carl over there in the pokey, the genial host who couldn't make it to his own celebration party."

Later along, boxes of giant pizzas were brought in, ordered from the restaurant down the street. And there was some singing, and at last, champagne gone, the party and the people began to fade. Couples sat on the stairs, mumbling to each other. The trial was over, and the victory had been celebrated.

The next day after almost everyone was gone, one of the accredited reporters was checking out. He asked the pleasant woman at the desk if it had all been what she had expected.

She frowned and said, "No. I didn't really know what to expect but I thought all these newspaper and television people and so on would be very difficult to please. I thought they would be, you know, sort of picky."

She smiled. A few moments earlier she had hugged and kissed

one of the departing girl reporters, and they had promised to write each other.

"But you know," she said, "I expected they'd get terribly drunk, like in the movies. But they didn't at all. And they were so wonderful to wait on, and so nice to all of us." Just as when she had said goodby to the girl reporter, her eyes misted slightly. "I'd say they were just about the nicest bunch of people who ever stayed here." She hesitated, bit her lip and then said, "Except maybe for the telephone company."

At about that same time Carl Coppolino and Mary were aboard a southbound commercial jet heading for Tampa, Florida, flying at 29,000 feet, at 585 miles per hour ground speed. Aboard in the party were John Gawler—the detective guarding him, a reporter and a photographer from the New York *Daily News,* a reporter from the New York *Post,* a reporter from a Florida paper.

Dr. Carl Coppolino was ebullient, exuberant, his face grinningly expressive of triumph, his gestures expansive. He had a highball in his hand. He spoke of how he had felt the hate in the courtroom. He said the low point was Dr. Helpern's testimony, and he said that after Helpern was through, he had said to Lee Bailey that if the charge stood up, it would be because of Helpern's testimony.

He spoke of how all the time that Marjorie Farber was on the stand he had never taken his eyes off her, but that she had not looked at him at any time. He spoke of his plans of doing a syndicated column on medicine and public health. He stated to one of the reporters that he might like to employ him as a press agent. He said that they would win the suit against Marge Farber and pick her clean. He said "I want to go to trial in Florida. I shall insist on a trial. Do you realize they have me under indictment? They could just let it lie if I don't insist on action, and then, months or years later, some smart young district attorney could come along and take me to court! I have to get this thing off my back, one way or another."

He said, "That man Keuper couldn't think of enough names to call me in his summation. I thought he was running out and I wanted to make a list of some more for him." He laughed. Winners laugh a lot. He was, after too much silence, caught up in compulsive talking.

He leaned over and kissed his wife, then turned to the reporters and said, "When I first met this girl she used to kiss with her

559

eyes wide open, looking over my shoulder. I used to say to her, 'What the hell are you looking at?' '' And he laughed again.

"It was my decision to take the stand," he said. "I wanted to take the stand after what that woman said about me. I wanted to speak for myself."

"I'll have to get a public relations man," he said. "You know as well as I do that every damned TV show and radio program is going to be after me. Hey, how is Sam Sheppard? Still with Arianne?"

Once they had deplaned at Tampa International, and John Gawler had officially turned Coppolino over to Sheriff Ross Boyer who had then released him verbally from further custody, before Carl drove off with Mary in a borrowed Cadillac to stay incognito at a luxurious motel in the Tampa area, he gave a brief interview before the camera and microphone of a Tampa television station. He said, "I am going to insist on a trial. I hope they have the guts to go through with it."

They had. And they did.

Afterword

After a successful motion for a change of venue by the defense team headed by F. Lee Bailey, the trial of Carl Coppolino for the murder of his wife, Carmela, began on April 3, 1967, in the Collier County Court House in Naples, Florida.

Jury selection was completed on Monday, April 10, with Circuit Judge Lynn Silvertooth presiding and with State's Attorney Frank Schaub directing the prosecution.

On April 28, after fifty-eight hours of court proceedings and three-and-a-half hours of jury deliberation, Carl Coppolino was found guilty of murder in the second degree and was then and there sentenced by Judge Silvertooth to the Florida State Prison at Raiford for the rest of his natural life.

The prosecution had asked for a verdict of guilty of murder in the first degree. Under Florida law, as explained in Judge Silvertooth's charge to the jury, a jury can bring back a verdict stating a lesser degree of guilt.

Fifteen metropolitan newspapers sent reporters to Naples to

cover the trial. The wire services and area television channels were also represented.

F. Lee Bailey's motions to set aside the verdict or grant a new trial were denied. He appealed the verdict to the Court of Appeals of the State of Florida for the Second District and the appeal was denied.

For about one year, beginning in 1974, after Coppolino was transferred to a minimum-security facility at Avon Park, near Tampa, he was permitted to leave the prison with his wife on furloughs of up to thirty-six hours. But this program was terminated for all inmates guilty of serious crimes after abuses by other prisoners.

In October of 1979, the Florida State Probation and Parole Commission released Coppolino on lifetime parole, stating that the decision to release was based upon the prisoner's excellent record.

However, it is reasonable to assume that his release was in part due to efforts of his second wife, Mary Gibson Coppolino, who in 1977 embarked upon a spirited campaign to have her husband released.

She focused public attention upon the testimony given in the Naples trial by Dr. Milton Helpern, the medical examiner from New York City who had autopsied Carmela Coppolino, and his associate, Dr. Joseph Umberger, who had conducted scientific tests of the body tissue in an attempt to verify the presence of the substance that the State claimed had been injected into the buttock of the deceased by the accused. Helpern and Umberger testified that their tests showed that a lethal amount of the paralytic—succinlycholine chloride—had been injected.

In 1977 Mary Coppolino said that two toxicologists, Richard Coumbis and Franco Fiorese, had been suspended by Dr. Helpern at the time of the trial because of their willingness to contradict him on the matter of the proof of the existence of succynlcholine and were now willing to so testify. Milton Helpern and Joseph Umberger had since died of natural causes.

When interviewed, the toxicologists said that they had acquainted F. Lee Bailey with their doubts but that he declined to call either of them to the stand.

Mary Coppolino's campaign won political support from Florida Representative Arnett E. Giardeau, Chairman of the Florida House of Representatives Committee on Corrections, Probation and Parole. In a prepared statement, Giardeau said that Helpern and Umberger "had intentionally fabricated the facts in their perjurious testimony against Dr. Coppolino which resulted in his conviction."

In a UPI news story on June 6, 1979, Dr. Milton Helpern's widow, Beatrice Helpern, was reported as saying that she welcomed scientific questioning, as did her husband, especially when the guilt or innocence of a person is at stake. "I am not disputing what they say about Umberger's testing," she said. "But Coppolino wasn't convicted on that test alone and to say the evidence was 'fabricated' is to smear two men who are not alive to answer that outrageous charge."

After his release Coppolino wrote a book titled *The Crime That Never Was*, published by Justice Press, Inc., in 1980, and toured the country promoting the sales of the book.

Carl Coppolino served twelve-and-a-half years. Corrections officials state that in Florida the average "life" sentence lasts about eight years.